The Collection

Also by Cathy Glass

Damaged
Hidden
Cut
The Saddest Girl in the World
Happy Kids
The Girl in the Mirror
I Miss Mummy
Mummy Told Me Not to Tell
My Dad's a Policeman (a Quick Reads novel)
Run, Mummy, Run
The Night the Angels Came
Happy Adults
A Baby's Cry
Happy Mealtimes for Kids
Another Forgotten Child
Please Don't Take My Baby
Will You Love Me?
About Writing and How to Publish
Daddy's Little Princess
The Child Bride
Saving Danny
Girl Alone
The Silent Cry
Can I Let You Go?
Nobody's Son

CATHY GLASS

The Collection

HarperElement
An imprint of HarperCollins*Publishers*
1 London Bridge Street
London SE1 9GF

www.harpercollins.co.uk

Damaged first published by HarperElement 2007
The Saddest Girl in the World first published by HarperElement 2009
The Silent Cry first published by HarperElement 2016
This collected edition published 2017

1 3 5 7 9 10 8 6 4 2

A catalogue record of this book is available from the British Library

ISBN 978-0-00-825231-1

Printed and bound in Great Britain by Clays Ltd, St Ives plc

MIX
Paper from
responsible sources
FSC™ C007454

FSC™ is a non-profit international organisation established to promote the responsible management of the world's forests. Products carrying the FSC label are independently certified to assure consumers that they come from forests that are managed to meet the social, economic and ecological needs of present and future generations, and other controlled sources.

Find out more about HarperCollins and the environment at
www.harpercollins.co.uk/green

CONTENTS

Damaged 1

The Saddest Girl in the World 345

The Silent Cry 677

Damaged

Chapter One

Emotional Blackmail

The phone rang. It was Jill, my link worker from the fostering agency.

'Cathy, it's not two carers, but five,' she said. 'Five, since coming into care four months ago.'

'Good heavens.' I was astonished. 'And she's only eight? That must have taken some doing. What's she been up to?'

'I'm not sure yet. But Social Services want a pre-placement meeting, to be certain she doesn't have another move. Are you still interested?'

'I don't know enough not to be. When?'

'Tomorrow at ten.'

'All right, see you there. What's her name?'

'Jodie. Thanks, Cathy. If you can't do it, no one can.'

I warmed to the flattery; it was nice to be appreciated after all this time. Jill and I had been working together now for four years and had established a good relationship. As a link worker for Homefinders Fostering Agency, Jill was the bridge between the foster carers and social workers dealing with a particular case. She coordinated the needs of the Social Services with the foster carers, and provided support and help as it was needed. An inexperienced foster carer often needed a lot of back-up and explanations of the system from their link worker. As Jill and I had been working together for some time, and I was an experienced foster carer, we were used to each other and got on well. If Jill thought I was up to the task, then I was sure she meant it.

But a pre-placement meeting? It had to be bad. Usually the children just arrived, with a brief introduction if they'd come from another carer, or with only the clothes they stood in if they'd come from home. I'd had plenty of experience of both, but none at all of a pre-placement meeting. Usually there was a meeting between everyone involved in the case as soon as the child had been placed in foster care, but I'd never been to one held beforehand.

It was my first inkling of how unusual this case was.

The following morning, we went about our normal, quiet routine of everyone getting up and dressed and having breakfast, and then the children made their way off to school. I had two children of my own, Adrian who was seventeen, and Paula, the youngest at thirteen. Lucy, who had joined the family as a foster placement two years ago, was fifteen and now a permanent member of our family, just like a daughter to me and a sister to Adrian and Paula. She was a success story: she had come to me hurt and angry and had, over time, learned to trust again, and eventually settled down to a normal existence where she had only the usual teenage angst to fret about, instead of the turmoil she had known as a child. I was proud of her, and she was testament to my belief that love, kindness, attention and firm boundaries are the basis of what any child needs to flourish.

As I saw the children off to school that morning, I felt a twinge of apprehension. The child I was going to learn about today would most certainly need all those things in abundance, and if I took her on I would have to be prepared to say goodbye to my relatively peaceful, steady routine for a while, until she learned to trust me and settled down, just as Lucy had. But that was the point of fostering – it wasn't easy by any means, but the rewards were so enormous. Besides, I had fostered almost continuously for over twenty years now and wasn't sure I could really remember what life before it had been like.

Once the children had left, I went upstairs and quickly changed from my joggers into a pair of smart navy trousers and a jumper, and headed for the Social Services offices. I'd been going there for years now, and the journey there was as familiar as the one to my own house. I also knew the drab grey décor, fluorescent lighting and air of busy activity and only-just-contained chaos very well indeed.

'Cathy, hello.'

As I entered the reception area, Jill came forward to

meet me. She'd been waiting for my arrival, and walked up to me with a welcoming smile.

'Hi, Jill. How are you?'

'Oh, fine, thanks. You're looking well.'

'Yes – life is good at the moment. The children are doing well, completely wrapped up in their lives and in their schools. Time for another challenge, I suppose.' I smiled at her.

'We'd better get along to this meeting. I think they're ready for us.' Jill led me along the corridor to the meeting room. As we entered the room, it was obvious at once that this was a big case: there were already about a dozen people sitting round the enormous oblong mahogany table. What did it mean? From what Jill had told me, I could tell that this was not a run-of-the-mill fostering situation – not many children get through five carers in four months – but then, no child was ever run-of-the-mill. They were always unique and their troubles distinctly their own. Removing a child from its parents was never going to be a humdrum, everyday event; it was always traumatic, emotional and difficult.

Nevertheless, something told me that this was far more complex than anything I'd yet encountered. I felt another stab of apprehension, like I had when Jill first told me about the case the day before, but I was also interested. What could this child be like, to warrant so much involvement from so many people?

Jill and I took the two vacant chairs at the far end, and I felt every eye was on me, assessing my suitability.

The chairman was Dave Mumby, the Social Services team leader, and he began the round of introductions. On his left was Sally, the 'guardian ad litem': she was appointed by the courts to represent Jodie's interests. The lady next to her introduced herself as Nicola, Jodie's home tutor.

Home tutor? Why isn't the child in school? I wondered.

Next was Gary, Jodie's current social worker. He explained that he was about to leave the case, and hand Jodie over to Eileen, who was sitting next to him. I looked at Eileen carefully – if I was going to take Jodie, then Eileen and I would have to work closely together. At first glance she was nondescript: a woman in her forties with an unruffled and calm air about her. So far, so good.

I wasn't surprised that I was already witnessing a change of social worker. It happened all the time – it was the nature of the job that people had to move on – but it was unfortunate for the children and families involved, who were always having to learn new faces, build trust and forge fresh relationships with endless strangers. Although I knew it was something that couldn't be altered and was just part of the system, with all its flaws, nonetheless I felt for Jodie. Changing social worker would mean yet more disruption for her, and I wondered how many social workers she'd been through already.

Next, Deirdre introduced herself. She was the agency link worker for Jodie's current foster carers. Then it was my turn, and the eyes of everyone around the table turned to me.

I looked around the table, meeting the various gazes. 'I'm Cathy Glass,' I said, as clearly and confidently as I could. 'I'm a foster carer from Homefinders Fostering Agency.' There wasn't much more I could add at this stage, when I knew so little about what was going on, so I passed on to Jill.

After Jill came someone from the accounts department, followed by a member of the local authority's placement team. As they spoke, I looked over at Gary, Jodie's current social worker. He was young, and could only have been in his mid-twenties. How successful had he been at forging a relationship with Jodie? I wondered. Perhaps Eileen, as a woman, would fare better at empathizing with the little girl, so the change of social worker might be for the better in this case. I hoped so.

Once the introductions were complete, Dave thanked us for coming, and gave a brief outline of what had been happening, or to use the correct terminology: the case history to date. I warmed to Dave immediately. He was gently spoken but forthright, and looked directly at me as he spoke. I made a mental note of the salient points: Jodie had been on the 'at-risk' register since birth, which meant that Social Services had been monitoring the family for eight years. Although there had been suspicions of emotional and physical abuse by Jodie's parents, no steps had been taken to remove her or her younger brother Ben and sister Chelsea. Then, four months ago, Jodie had started a house fire by setting light to her pet dog – I shivered at this, struck by the peculiar cruelty of such an act – and that had been the catalyst for Social Services to take her and her siblings into care. Ben and Chelsea had both been placed with foster carers and were doing well. But Jodie exhibited 'very challenging behaviour'. I heard Dave deliver this euphemism and raised my eyebrows. All foster carers knew what that really stood for. It meant 'completely out of control'.

'I think it would be useful,' said Dave, looking at me, 'for you to hear from her social worker now. Gary's been on the case for two years. Feel free to ask any questions.'

Despite his youth, Gary was confident and methodical as he gave me an overview of Jodie and her family.

'I'm afraid that the general picture isn't good, as you'd expect. There's severe disruption inside the family. Jodie's mother is an intravenous drug user and her father is an alcoholic. In recent years, Jodie's suffered a number of injuries while at home, including burns, scalds, cuts, bruises and a broken finger. All of these were recorded at hospital, and although it was suspected that some of the injuries were non-accidental, it was impossible to prove that this was the case.'

Gary went on with his tale of neglect and misery while I concentrated on absorbing the facts. It was an appalling case history but I'd heard similar stories many times before. Nevertheless, it never ceased to amaze and horrify me that people could treat their children with such cruelty and indifference, and I was already feeling for this poor little girl. How could any child grow and be normal in such circumstances, and with such parents as her role models?

Gary continued, 'Jodie's no longer in school because of the recent moves, which is why she's been assigned a home tutor. She has learning difficulties and a statement of special needs.'

That was straightforward enough – I was used to looking after children with developmental delays and learning difficulties. I suspected that Gary was giving me the censored version of Jodie's case history. In all my years of fostering, I'd never heard of a child going through five carers in four months. When he paused and looked at me, I seized my opportunity.

'It would be helpful if you could tell me the make-up of the families of the previous carers,' I said, hoping to discover clues to explain why Jodie had gone through so many, so fast. 'How many children did they have, and were they older or younger? Had the carers had experience with this type of child before?'

Gary coughed and looked a little shifty. 'The previous placement breakdowns were purely circumstantial,' he said. 'One of the couples were first-time carers and Jodie should never have been placed with them – that was an error on our part and it's no surprise that it didn't work out.'

That was fair enough, but as he went through the other placements, he sounded unconvincing to my ears: the others had all been experienced professionals, and yet one couple had lasted only three days. Gary's explanation that circumstances were to blame was clearly a damage limitation exercise for Jodie's sake, so that I didn't get frightened off.

Deirdre, who was the link worker representing Jodie's present foster carers, felt obliged to speak up in their defence. After all, if Jodie was as harmless as Gary was making out, it didn't exactly reflect very well on their ability to cope.

'Jodie has delayed development,' she said. 'In most respects, she acts like a three- or four-year-old rather than an eight-year-old. She throws terrible tantrums and is consistently aggressive and uncooperative. Her behaviour is violent, abusive and destructive. Even though she's only been with Hilary and Dave a short time, she's already broken a number of objects, including a solid wooden door.'

I raised my eyebrows. Quite a feat for an eight-year-old.

But Deirdre wasn't finished yet, and she went on with her litany of Jodie's faults and shortcomings. Jodie's carers had described her as 'cold, calculating, manipulative, very rude and totally unlikeable'. Harsh words to pin on a little girl.

Surely, I thought, someone could say something nice about her, even if it was only that she liked her food. Children in care tend to eat ravenously, because in the past many of them haven't known when the next meal would arrive. But no, not so much as 'she does like her chocolate'. It appeared that Jodie did not have a single endearing feature. Instead, there was just a list of transgressions, with a footnote that her present carers had found her physically frightening: Jodie was a big girl, and she had threatened them.

I looked at Jill and we exchanged glances. Threatened them? I thought to myself. But she's only eight years old! How dangerous can she be? I began to feel as though I was on Jodie's side. What must it be like, having everyone dislike you so vehemently? No wonder she wasn't able to settle anywhere.

The next person to speak was Sally, the guardian ad litem, who briefly outlined the legal position: Jodie had been taken into the care of Social Services under what is known as an Interim Care Order; that meant she'd been removed from home against the parents' wishes and was now in the temporary care of the local authority. Proceedings to decide Jodie's future were now beginning; if the court judged that she was better off at home, and all the fears for her safety there were put to rest, then she would be returned to her parents' care. If not, and the court still considered that she would be in danger if returned home, her care order would become a Full Care Order, and Jodie would be permanently removed from her parents, to long-term fostering, adoption, or – the least likely option – some kind of residential care home. This whole process is lengthy and complicated, and while it is supposed to take as little time as possible, it usually takes at least a year, sometimes longer, before the court comes to a final decision.

When Sally had finished, she was followed by the home tutor, Nicola, who explained that she'd been teaching Jodie for a month, using material that was working towards Key Stage One, which is designed for pre-school children. This might sound shocking but, in my experience, it was not unusual. I had, in the past, cared for children who couldn't read or write long after their peers had mastered the three Rs. A difficult background and home life often seems to produce children who are unable to learn as quickly as those from a stable family.

Next, the finance representative confirmed that funding would be available to continue the tutoring until a school had been found. I glanced at the clock on the wall: nearly an hour had passed. Everyone had had their say, and Dave was looking hopefully at Jill.

'If Cathy doesn't take her,' he said, 'our only option will be a residential unit.'

This smacked of emotional blackmail, and Jill rose to my defence. 'We'll need to consider what's been said. I'll discuss it with Cathy and let you know tomorrow.'

'We need to know today,' said Deirdre bluntly. 'She has to be moved by midday tomorrow. They're adamant.'

There was silence around the table. We were all thinking the same thing: were these foster carers as unprofessional as they sounded? Or had Jodie somehow driven them to this level of desperation?

'Even so,' said Jill firmly, 'we'll need time to discuss it. While I haven't heard anything that would make me advise Cathy against it – she's very experienced – the decision must be hers.' She looked sideways at me.

I felt everyone's eyes on me, and a desperate desire to hear that I would be willing to take this little girl on. So far, I had heard from Gary that she was an innocent victim whose extraordinary record of getting through carers was nothing to do with her, and from Deirdre that she was a little devil incarnate, whose size, strength and sheer nastiness were completely out of proportion to her age. The truth, I felt, must lie somewhere in between. Even taking a balanced view, however, I could see that Jodie was a handful, to say the least.

I was unsure. Was I ready to take on a child with behavioural problems at this level? Could I – and more importantly, could my family – take on the kind of disruption it would surely involve? I couldn't help quailing a little at the thought of embracing the sort of challenge I was sure this child would pose. But on the other hand, my formula of love, kindness and attention mixed with firmness had not let me down yet, and when all was said and done, Jodie was only a child; a little girl who had been given a terrible start in life and who deserved the chance to begin again and have a little of the happiness every child needed. Could I really let her face the alternative? Now that I'd heard her story, could I really walk away?

I knew at that moment that I couldn't. I had to give her that chance. As soon as I'd walked into that room, I'd known in my heart that I would take Jodie. I wouldn't be able to turn my back on her.

'She's too young to go into a residential unit,' I said, meeting Dave's look. 'I'll take her and give it my best shot.'

'Are you sure?' asked Jill, concerned.

I nodded, and there was an audible sigh of relief, particularly from the accounts lady. It costs upwards of £3,000 a week to keep a child in a residential unit, so getting me to take her for £250 a week was a good piece of business.

'That's wonderful, Cathy,' said Dave, beaming. 'Thank you. We all think very highly of you, as you know, and we're delighted that you're willing to take this one on.'

There was a murmur of agreement and a general feeling of a burden being lifted. The meeting was over. For now, the problem of Jodie was solved. Everyone stood up, gathered their things and prepared to get back to work, move on to other cases and think about other situations.

But for me, a few words and a snap decision had changed my life. For me, the problem of Jodie was only just beginning.

Chapter Two

The Road to Jodie

I had started fostering twenty years before, before I had even had my own children. One day I was flicking through the paper when I saw one of those adverts – you might have seen them yourself. There was a black-and-white, fuzzy photograph of a child and a question along the lines of: Could you give little Bobby a home? For some reason it caught my eye, and once I'd seen it I couldn't stop thinking about it. I don't consider myself a sentimental person, but for some reason I couldn't get the picture out of my mind. I talked about it with my husband; we knew we wanted a family of our own at some point, and I was looking forward to that, but in the meantime I knew that I could give a good home to a child who needed it. I'd always felt a bond with children and had once had ambitions to teach.

'We've got the room,' I said, 'and I know I would love working with children. Why don't we at least find out a little bit more about it?'

So I picked up the phone, replied to the advertisement and before long we found ourselves on an induction course that introduced us to the world of foster care. Then, after we'd satisfied all the requirements and done the requisite training, we took in our first foster child, a troubled teenager in need of a stable home for a while. That was it. I was hooked.

Fostering, I discovered, is by no means easy. If a carer goes into it expecting to take in a little Orphan Annie, or an Anne of Green Gables, then he or she is in for a nasty shock. The sweet, mop-headed child who has had a little bad luck and only needs a bit of love and affection to thrive and blossom and spread happiness in the world doesn't exist. Foster children don't come into your home wide-eyed and smiling. They tend to be withdrawn because of what has happened to them and will often be distant, angry and hard to reach, which is hardly surprising. In worse cases, they can be verbally or even physically aggressive and violent. The only constant factor is that each one is different, and that they need attention and kindness to get through their unhappiness. It is never an easy ride.

The first year of fostering was by no means easy for me – and come to think of it, no year since has been what I would call 'easy' – but by the end of it I knew I wanted to continue. A foster carer will generally know almost at once if it is something they want to carry on doing or not, and certainly will by the end of that first year. I'd found something I had a talent for, and that was extremely rewarding and I wanted to carry on, even while I had my own children. I found that the difference

I made to my foster children's lives, even if it was a small one, stayed with me. It was not that I was the most selfless being since Mother Teresa, or that I was particularly saintly – I believe that we do these things for our own ends, and mine was the satisfaction I got from the whole process of making things better for children who needed help.

While my children were small I fostered teenagers, as it's usually recommended that you take in children who are at a different stage to your own. As Adrian and Paula grew up, I began to take in younger ones, which meant that I never had to deal with the kind of serious drug problems that are endemic among a lot of teenagers these days – for which I am most grateful. My two grew up knowing nothing other than having foster children living with us, so it was something they accepted completely. Of course, when they were little, they were sometimes frustrated at having to share me with other children. Foster children, by definition, need a lot of time and attention and sometimes that felt never-ending to my two. After a day of pouring my energies into fostering, with its meetings and training, I would then have paperwork to see to, and that took its toll on the amount of time I had left over for my own family. But no matter how much they resented missing out on some of my time, they never took it out on the foster children who shared our home. Somehow, they seemed to understand that these children had come from difficult backgrounds, and that they had had a rough start. In their own way, my children were sympathetic and did their best to make life a bit easier for whichever troubled child was living with us. It's something I've noticed in other children besides my own – there is often a lot more understanding and empathy there than we would expect.

Adrian and Paula have certainly had to put up with a lot over the years – particularly when my husband and I divorced – but they have never complained about all the troubled youngsters coming and going in their home. Over the years, we've experienced all types of children, most of whom have exhibited 'challenging behaviour'. The majority of children who come to me have suffered from neglect of one sort or another, and funnily enough that is something I find relatively easy to understand. When parents have addictions to drink or drugs, or suffer from mental problems, they are obviously in no fit state to care for their children properly and look after their needs in a way they might be able to if they could overcome their problems. This kind of parenting is not purposefully cruel in the way that actual physical and sexual abuse is cruel – it is a sad side-effect of a different problem. The ideal outcome is that a child will be returned to its parents once the factors that caused the neglect, such as addiction, have been remedied.

A child who has suffered from neglect will have had a miserable time and can arrive in my house in a very troubled state. They can be full of brashness and bravado, which is usually a disguise for a complete lack of self-esteem. They can often be out-and-out naughty, as a result of having no boundaries or parental guidance at home, and as a way of seeking attention. Their anger and resentment can stem from the unpredictable nature of life at home, where nothing was ever certain – would Mum be too drunk to function today? Would Dad be spaced out or violent? – and where the borders between who was the adult and who was the child, and who was caring for whom, were often blurred. They may try to destroy things, or steal, or be manipulative and self-seeking. And, to be honest, when you know what some of them have had to put up with in their short lives, who can blame them?

The way that I've found is usually best with children from this kind of background is fairly simple: I provide stability and a positive environment in which good behaviour is rewarded with praise. Most children desire approval and want to be liked, and most are able to unlearn negative behaviour patterns and accept different ones when they realize how much better and easier life is with the new order. For many of them, a regular routine provides a blessed relief to the chaos and unpredictability of life at home, and they soon respond to a calm, positive environment where they know certain things will happen at certain times. Something as simple as knowing for sure when and where the next meal is coming from can provide an anchor for troubled children who've only ever known uncertainty and disappointment. Routine is safe; it is possible to get things right inside a routine – and getting things right is lovely when it means being praised, approved of and rewarded.

Of course, simple as it may sound, it is [illegible]
straightforward. And sometimes children [illegible]
who've suffered much more severe levels of [illegible]
who need much more professional help to get [illegible]
their experiences. Many have learning difficult[illegible] and special needs. Some are removed from home too late, when they're teenagers and have suffered so much that they are never able to get over what has happened; they're not able to respond to a positive environment in the way a younger child might, and their futures look a lot bleaker.

Nevertheless, almost all my fostering experiences have been good ones, and the child has left our home in a better place than when they arrived.

As I drove home from the meeting at Social Services that day having agreed to take on Jodie, I knew that this child might be more of a handful than most, and wondered how best to tell the children about our new addition. They wouldn't be best pleased. We'd had children before with 'challenging behaviour', so they knew what was in store. I thought of Lucy, who'd been with us for nearly two years, and was very well settled. I hoped Jodie's disturbed outbursts wouldn't set her back. Adrian, at seventeen, kept pretty much to himself, unless there was a crisis, or he couldn't find his shirt in the morning. It was Paula I was most worried about. She was a sensitive, nervous child, and even though Jodie was five years younger than her, there was a risk she could be intimidated. Emotionally damaged children can wreak havoc in a family, even a well-integrated one. My children had always reacted well to the other children who had joined our family, even though we'd had a few rocky times, and I had no reason to think that this time would be any different.

I suspected the children wouldn't be surprised by my news. It had been a few weeks since our last foster child had left, so it was time for a new challenge. I usually took a break of a couple of weeks between placements, to refresh myself mentally and physically, and give everyone time to regroup. I also needed to recover from the sadness of saying goodbye to someone I'd become close to; even when a child leaves on a high note, having made excellent progress and perhaps returning home to parents who are now able to provide a loving and caring environment, there is still a period when I mourn their going. It's a mini-bereavement and something I have never got used to even though, a week or two later, I'd be revved up and ready to go again.

I decided to raise the subject of Jodie over dinner, which was where most of our discussions took place. Although I consider myself liberal, I do insist that the family eat together in the evenings and at weekends, as it's the only part of the day when we're all together.

For dinner that night I served shepherd's pie, which was the children's favourite. As they tucked in, I adjusted my voice to a light and relaxed tone.

'You remember I mentioned I was going to a pre-placement meeting today?' I said, aware they probably wouldn't remember, because no one had been listening when I'd said it. 'They told me all about a little girl who needs a home. Well, I've agreed to take her. She's called Jodie and she's eight.'

I glanced round the table for a reaction, but there was barely a flicker. They were busy eating. Even so, I knew they were listening.

'I'm afraid she's had a rough start and a lot of moves, so she's very unsettled. She's had a terrible home life and she's already had some foster carers. Now they're thinking of sending her to a residential unit if they can't find someone to take her in, and you can imagine how horrible that would be for her. You know – a children's home,' I added, labouring the point.

Lucy and Paula looked up, and I smiled bravely.

'Like me,' said Lucy innocently. She had moved around a lot before she finally settled down with us, so she knew all about the disruption of moving.

'No. Your moves were because of your relatives not being able to look after you. It had nothing to do with your behaviour.' I paused, wondering if the discreet message had been picked up. It had.

'What's she done?' Adrian growled, in his newly developed masculine voice.

'Well, she has tantrums, and breaks things when she's upset. But she's still young, and I'm sure if we all pull together we'll be able to turn her around.'

'Is she seeing her mum?' asked Paula, her eyes wide, imagining what for her would be the worst-case scenario: a child not seeing her mother.

'Yes, and her dad. It will be supervised contact twice a week at the Social Services.'

'When is she coming?' asked Lucy.

'Tomorrow morning.'

They all glanced at me and then at each other. Tomorrow there would be a new member of the family and, from the sounds of it, not an easy one either. I knew it must be unsettling.

'Don't worry,' I reassured them. 'I'm sure she'll be fine.' I realized I'd better be quick, as once dinner was over they'd vanish to their rooms, so I cut straight to the chase and reminded them of the 'safer caring' rules that were always in place when a new foster child arrived. 'Now, remember, there are a lot of unknowns here, so you need to be careful for your own protection. If she wants you to play, it's down here, not upstairs, and Adrian, don't go into her room, even if she asks you to open a window. If there's anything like that, call me or one of the girls. And remember, no physical-contact games like piggy back until we know more. And, obviously, don't let her in your room, OK?'

'Yes, Mum,' he groaned, looking even more uncomfortably adolescent. He'd heard it all before, of course. There are standard codes of practice that apply in the homes of all foster carers, and my lot were well aware of how to behave. But Adrian could sometimes be too trusting for his own good.

'And obviously, all of you,' I said, addressing the three of them, 'let me know if she confides anything about her past that gives you cause for concern. She'll probably forge a relationship with you before she does with me.'

They all nodded. I decided that that was enough. They'd got the general picture, and they were pretty clued up. The children of foster carers tend to grow up quickly, as a result of the issues and challenges they're exposed to. But not as quickly as the fostered children themselves, whose childhoods have often been sacrificed on the pyre of daily survival.

After dinner, as expected, the children disappeared to their rooms and the peace of another quiet evening descended on the house. It had gone off as well as I could have expected and I felt pleased with their maturity and acceptance of the situation.

'So far so good,' I thought, as I loaded the dishwasher. Then I settled down myself to watch the television with no idea when I'd next have the opportunity.

Chapter Three

The Arrival

It was a wet and cold spring day in April. Rain hammered on the windows as I prepared for Jodie's arrival. She was due at midday, but I was sure she'd be early. I stood in what was to be her new bedroom, and tried to see it through the eyes of a child. Was it appealing and welcoming? I had pinned brightly coloured posters of animals to the walls, and bought a new duvet cover with a large print of a teddy bear on it. I'd also propped a few soft toys on the bed, although I was sure that Jodie, having been in care for a while, was likely to have already accumulated some possessions. The room looked bright and cheerful, the kind of place that an eight-year-old girl would like as her bedroom. All it needed now was its new resident.

I took a final look around, then came out and closed the door, satisfied I'd done my best. Continuing along the landing, I closed all the bedroom doors. When it came to showing her around, it would be important to make sure she understood privacy, and this would be easier if the ground rules had been established right from the start.

Downstairs, I filled the kettle and busied myself in the kitchen. It was going to be a hectic day, and even after all these years of fostering I was still nervous. The arrival of a new child is a big event for a foster family, perhaps as much as for the child herself. I hoped Jill would arrive early, so that the two of us could have a quiet chat and offer moral support before the big arrival.

Just before 11.30, the doorbell rang. I opened the door to find Gary, soaking wet from his walk from the station. I ushered him in, offered him a towel and coffee, and left him mopping his brow in the lounge while I returned to the kitchen. Before the kettle had a chance to boil, the bell rang again. I went to the door, hoping to see Jill on the doorstep. No such luck. It was the link worker from yesterday, Deirdre, along with another woman, who was smiling bravely.

'This is Ann, my colleague,' said Deirdre, dispensing with small talk. 'And this is Jodie.'

I looked down, but Jodie was hiding behind Ann, and all I could see was a pair of stout legs in bright red trousers.

'Hi, Jodie,' I said brightly. 'I'm Cathy. It's very nice to meet you. Come on in.'

She must have been clinging to Ann's coat, and decided she wasn't going anywhere, as Ann was suddenly pulled backwards, nearly losing her balance.

'Don't be silly,' snapped Deirdre, and made a grab behind her colleague. Jodie was quicker and, I suspected, stronger, for Ann took another lurch, this time sideways.

Thankfully, our old cat decided to put in a well-timed appearance, sauntering lazily down the hall. I took my cue.

'Look who's come to see you, Jodie!' I cried, the excitement in my voice out of all proportion to our fat and lethargic moggy. 'It's Toscha. She's come to say hello!'

It worked – she couldn't resist a peep. A pair of grey-blue eyes, set in a broad forehead, peered out from around Ann's waist. Jodie had straw-blonde hair, set in pigtails, and it was obvious from her outfit alone that her previous carers had lost control. Under her coat she was wearing a luminous green T-shirt, red dungarees and wellies. No sensible adult would have dressed her like this. Clearly, Jodie was used to having her own way.

With her interest piqued, she decided to take a closer look at the cat, and gave Ann another shove, sending them both stumbling over the doorstep and into the hall. Deirdre followed, and the cat sensibly nipped out. I quickly closed the door.

'It's gone!' Jodie yelled, her face pinched with anger.

'Don't worry, she'll be back soon. Let's get you out of your wet coat.' And before the loss of the cat could escalate into a scene, I undid her zip, and tried to divert her attention. 'Gary's in the lounge waiting for you.'

She stared at me for a moment, looking as though she'd really like to hit me, but the mention of Gary, a familiar name in an unfamiliar setting, drew her in. She wrenched her arms free of the coat, and stomped heavily down the hall before disappearing into the lounge. 'I want that cat,' she growled at Gary.

The two women exchanged a look which translated as, 'Heaven help this woman. How soon can we leave?'

I offered them coffee and showed them through to the lounge. Jodie had found the box of Lego and was now sitting cross-legged in the middle of the floor, making a clumsy effort to force two pieces together.

Returning to the kitchen, I took down four mugs, and started to spoon in some instant coffee. I heard heavy footsteps, then Jodie appeared in the doorway. She was an odd-looking child, not immediately endearing, but I thought this was largely because of the aggressive way she held her face and body, as though continually on guard.

'What's in 'ere?' she demanded, pulling open a kitchen drawer.

'Cutlery,' I said needlessly, as the resulting clatter had announced itself.

'What?' she demanded, glaring at me.

'Cutlery. You know: knives, forks and spoons. We'll eat with those later when we have dinner. You'll have to tell me what you like.'

Leaving that drawer, she moved on to the next, and the next, intent on opening them all. I let her look around. I wasn't concerned about her inquisitiveness, that was natural; what worried me more was the anger in all her movements. I'd never seen it so pronounced before.

With all the drawers opened, and the kettle boiled, I took out a plate and a packet of biscuits.

'I want one,' she demanded, lunging for the packet.

I gently stopped her. 'In a moment. First I'd like you to help me close these drawers, otherwise we'll bump into them, won't we?'

She looked at me with a challenging and defiant stare. Had no one ever stopped her from doing anything, or was she deliberately testing me? There was a few seconds' pause, a stand-off, while she considered my request. I noticed how overweight she was. It was clear she'd either been comfort eating, or had been given food to keep her quiet; probably both.

'Come on,' I said encouragingly, and started to close the drawers. She watched, then with both hands slammed the nearest drawer with all her strength.

'Gently, like this.' I demonstrated, but she didn't offer any more assistance, and I didn't force the issue. She'd only just arrived, and she had at least compromised by closing one.

'Now the biscuits,' I said, arranging them on the plate. 'I'd like your help. I'm sure you're good at helping, aren't you?'

Again she fixed me with her challenging, almost derisory stare, but there was a hint of intrigue, a spark of interest in the small responsibility I was about to bestow on her.

'Jodie, I'd like you to carry this into the lounge and offer everyone a biscuit, then take one for yourself, all right?'

I placed the plate squarely in her chubby, outstretched hands, and wondered what the chances were of it arriving intact. The digestives pitched to the left as she turned, and she transferred the plate to her left hand, clamping the right on top of the biscuits, which was at least safe, if not hygienic.

I followed with the tray of drinks, pleased that she'd done as I'd asked. I handed out the mugs of coffee as the doorbell rang, signalling our last arrival. Jodie jumped up and made a dash for the door. I quickly followed; it's not good practice for a child to be answering the door, even if guests are expected. I explained this to Jodie, then we opened it together.

Jill stood on the doorstep. She was smiling encouragingly, and looked down at the sullen-faced child staring defiantly up at her.

'Hi,' said Jill brightly. 'You must be Jodie.'

'I wanted to do it,' protested Jodie, before stomping back down the hall to rejoin the others.

'Is everything all right?' Jill asked as she came in.

'OK so far. No major disasters yet, anyway.' I took Jill's coat, and she went through to the lounge. I fetched another coffee, and the paperwork began. There's a lot of form filling when a child is placed with new carers, and a lot of coffee. Gary was writing furiously.

'I've only just completed the last move,' he said cheerfully. 'Not to mention the three-day one before that. Is it Cathy with a C?'

I confirmed that it was, then gave him my postcode

and my doctor's name and address. Jodie, who'd been reasonably content watching him, and had obviously been party to the process many times before, decided it was time to explore again. She hauled herself up, and disappeared into the kitchen. I couldn't allow her to be in there alone; quite apart from the risk of her raiding the cupboards, there were any number of implements which could have been harmful in the wrong hands. I called her, but she didn't respond. I walked in and found her trying to yank open the cupboard under the sink, which was protected by a child lock, as it contained the various cleaning products.

'Come on, Jodie, leave that for now. Let's go into the lounge,' I said. 'I'll show you around later. We'll have plenty of time once they've gone.'

'I want a drink,' she demanded, pulling harder on the cupboard door.

'OK, but it's not in there.'

I opened the correct cupboard, where I kept a range of squashes. She peered in at the row of brightly coloured bottles.

'Orange, lemon, blackcurrant or apple?' I offered.

'Coke,' she demanded.

'I'm sorry, we don't have Coke. It's very bad for your teeth.' Not to mention hyperactivity, I thought to myself. 'How about apple? Paula, my youngest daughter, likes apple. You'll meet her later.'

'That one.' She tried to clamber on to the work surface to retrieve the bottle.

I took down the bottle of blackcurrant and poured the drink, then carried it through and placed it on the coffee table. I drew up the child-sized wicker chair, which is usually a favourite.

'This is just the right size for you,' I said. 'Your very own seat.'

Jodie ignored me, grabbed her glass, and plonked herself in the place I had vacated on the sofa next to Jill. I sat next to Gary, while Jill pacified Jodie with a game on her mobile phone. I watched her for a few moments. So this was the child who was going to be living with us. It was hard to make much of her so early on; most children displayed difficult behaviour in their first few days in a new home. Nevertheless, there was an unusual air about her that I couldn't quite understand: it was anger, of course, and stubbornness, mixed with something else that I wasn't sure I had seen before. Only time would tell, I thought. I observed Jodie's uncoordinated movements and the way her tongue lolled over her bottom lip. I noted almost guiltily how it gave her a dull, vacant air, and reminded myself that she was classified as having only 'mild' learning difficulties, rather than 'severe'.

A quarter of an hour later, all the placement forms had been completed. I signed them and Gary gave me my copies. Deirdre and Ann immediately stood to leave.

'We'll unpack the car,' said Ann. 'There's rather a lot.'

Leaving Jodie with Gary and Jill, I quickly put on my shoes and coat, and we got gradually drenched as we went back and forth to the car. 'Rather a lot' turned out to be an understatement. I'd never seen so many bags and holdalls for a child in care. We stacked them the length of the hall, then the two women said a quick goodbye to Jodie. She ignored them, obviously feeling the rejection. Gary stayed for another ten minutes, chatting with Jodie about me and my home, then he too made a move to leave.

'I want to come,' she grinned, sidling up to him. 'Take me with you. I want to go in your car.'

'I don't have a car,' said Gary gently. 'And you're staying with Cathy. Remember we talked about it? This is your lovely new home now.' He picked up his briefcase and got halfway to the door, then Jodie opened her mouth wide and screamed. It was truly ear piercing. I rushed over and put my arms around her, and nodded to Gary to go. He slipped out, and I held her until the noise subsided. There were no tears, but her previously pale cheeks were now flushed bright red.

The last person left was Jill. She came out into the hall and got her coat.

'Will you be all right, Cathy?' she asked, as she prepared to venture out into the rain. 'I'll phone about five.' She knew that the sooner Jodie and I were left alone, the sooner she'd settle.

'We'll be fine, won't we, Jodie?' I said. 'I'll show you around and then we'll unpack.'

I was half expecting another scream, but she just stared at me, blank and uncomprehending. My heart went out to her; she must have felt so lost in what was her sixth home in four months. I held her hand as we saw Jill out.

Now it was just the two of us. I'd been in this situation many times before, welcoming a confused and hurt little person into my home, waiting patiently as they acclimatized to a new and strange environment, but this felt different somehow. There was something in the blankness in Jodie's eyes that was chilling. I hadn't seen it before, in a child or an adult. I shook myself mentally. Come on, I cajoled. She's a little girl and you've got twenty years' experience of looking after children. How hard can it be?

I led her back into the living room and, right on cue, Toscha reappeared. I showed Jodie the correct way to stroke her, but she lost interest as soon as I'd begun.

'I'm hungry. I want a biscuit.' She made a dash for the kitchen.

I followed and was about to explain that too many biscuits aren't good, when I noticed a pungent smell. 'Jodie, do you want the toilet?' I asked casually.

She shook her head.

'Do you want to do a poo?'

'No!' She grinned, and before I realized what she was doing, her hand was in her pants, and she smeared faeces across her face.

'Jodie!' I grabbed her wrist, horrified.

She cowered instantly, protecting her face. 'You going to hit me?'

'No, Jodie. Of course not. I'd never do that. You're going to have a bath, and next time tell me when you want the toilet. You're a big girl now.'

Slowly, I led my new charge up the stairs and she followed, clumsy, lumbering and her face smeared with excrement.

What had I let myself in for?

Chapter Four

A New Little Sister

Foster carers aren't saints. We're just ordinary parents with space in our homes and hearts for one more. But as I turned on the shower, and helped Jodie out of her clothes and her soiled underwear, I wondered if my heart was truly big enough. I put her under the shower of hot water and began to sponge her down. My stomach lurched as the heat intensified the smell, and I closed my mouth and tried to breathe through my nose. I cleaned her face and hands, then between the folds of pale skin around her middle. Jodie was pear-shaped, which is unusual for a child, and she had hips like a middle-aged woman. She was docile, though, lifting her arms in the air and making no effort to help. She seemed to enjoy being treated like a baby. I consoled myself that at least the rest of the family weren't home to witness the new arrival's house-warming trick.

I couldn't help feeling puzzled by it – she hadn't been distressed by her accident at all, and it was unlikely that someone of her age had no bowel control and wasn't aware of when they were about to do a poo. So had it been deliberate? Surely not. It was probably anxiety.

I helped her out of the bath and wrapped a towel round her. 'Dry yourself, Jodie, while I put these in the wash.' I scooped up the soiled clothes and carried them downstairs to the washing machine. I added a few drops of disinfectant to the soap, and turned the dial to 80 degrees. The sound of Jodie talking to herself floated down from the bathroom and I could hear her muttering isolated words and phrases which didn't string together, and didn't make any sense.

Returning down the hall, I took the largest suitcase and heaved it upstairs. 'You OK, Jodie?' I called, as I crossed the landing.

Silence, then, 'Yeah,' before she lapsed into gobbledegook once again.

In her bedroom, I unzipped the case, and picked out joggers, a jumper and underwear, and carried them through to the bathroom. She was standing as I'd left her, wrapped in the towel but still dripping wet.

'Come on,' I encouraged, 'dry yourself. You're a big girl now.'

She shook her head sulkily, and I started patting her dry. She was like a seven-stone infant, and very cumbersome, and I was sure some of this was due to the rolls of fat.

'Don't want those,' she said, spying the clothes I'd brought in.

'OK, when you're dry we'll find some others. You've got lots to choose from. Now come on before you get cold.'

She pulled out of the towel and darted naked along the landing to her room, where she began rummaging through the clothes. She held up a pair of pink shorts and a T-shirt. I tried to explain that they weren't suitable for the chilly weather, but I might as well have been talking Russian for all the response I got.

'How about these jeans?' I said, holding them up. 'And this blue top is nice and warm. Now find yourself some underwear and get dressed, come on, quickly.'

She held up a pair of knickers and struggled into them, then continued picking over the clothes. She was chattering continuously, but when I tried to join in the conversation she would stare at me blankly, before continuing with her search, and the next unintelligible monologue. Finally, she settled on a pair of black trousers and a grey jumper, and stood waiting for me to dress her. Just to hurry things along, I gave in to this demand, then began clearing up the heaps of discarded clothes, folding and hanging them in the drawers and wardrobe. Jodie had said nothing about her bedroom, and when I asked if she liked it, she responded with a blank, dismissive stare. She picked up a soft toy, and hurled it at the door. 'Not mine! Don't want it!' Her face screwed up in anger.

'OK, but don't throw it. I'm sure you've got lots of your own. I'll put these away and find some of yours. You'd prefer that, wouldn't you?' I gathered up the other toys and moved towards the door.

'Where you going?' she demanded, her scowl intensifying.

'To put these away and bring up some of your own toys.' I smiled and left, aware another scene had been narrowly averted.

I dropped the unwanted toys on to my bed, then went downstairs and opened some of the holdalls. They were filled with clothes, a ridiculous amount; she couldn't possibly have worn them all if she'd changed three times a day for a fortnight. The next bag I opened was crammed full of small plastic toys: dolls, animals and gifts from McDonald's. It was like a school fête tombola. I lugged the bag upstairs.

'Have a look at these,' I said brightly, 'while I sort out the rest of your clothes. There's a toy box under the bed, you can put them in there.'

Her face softened, and we worked side by side for a few minutes, although I sensed the peace was tenuous. I wasn't wrong. Five minutes later she threw a plastic crocodile into the box, then ran out of the room, and into Adrian's bedroom next door.

I followed. 'Jodie, would you like to look around now? We can unpack later.' She was pressing the buttons on Adrian's mobile, which he'd left recharging by his bed.

I went over and gently took it from her. 'We won't touch that, it's not ours. This is Adrian's room.' She looked at me doubtfully. 'He's my son. He's at school. You'll meet him later.'

She dropped the phone on the floor, then took a flying leap on to the bed, where she started clumsily bouncing up and down. I reached for her hand. 'Come on, I'll show you the other rooms, then fix you some lunch.'

The mention of lunch sealed it, and with another leap she was beside me, floorboards juddering, and then she dashed out, along the landing and into the next bedroom.

'This is Lucy's room,' I said, catching up. 'She's fifteen. She's been with us for two years and you'll meet her later too.'

She rushed out of Lucy's room and round to Paula's, where she spotted Paula's rag-doll pyjama case propped on the bed.

'Mine. Mine!' she cried, snatching it to her chest. 'I want it.'

'It's Paula's,' I said gently. 'It's special, she got it for her birthday.'

'Mine,' she growled. 'I want it. Get me one or I'll kick you.'

I frowned and gently prised it from her arms. Was that how she'd accumulated all those toys: buy it or I'll kick you? I repositioned the doll on the pillow, then took her hand and led her out. I opened the door to my room just enough for her to see in. 'This is where I sleep, but of course it's private. All our bedrooms are private, and we don't go into each other's unless we're asked.'

She grinned, with a strange grimace that gave her an unpleasant, malevolent air. She stared at the double bed. 'Have you got a man?'

I shook my head. 'No, I'm divorced. I have a big bed all to myself.'

She threw me a pitying look, and I decided she'd seen enough of my bedroom, and closed the door. On the landing I took the opportunity to reinforce our privacy rule. 'Jodie, we all have our own bedrooms and they have our special things in them. No one will come into yours, and you mustn't go into anyone else's without being asked. Do you understand?'

She nodded vigorously, but I suspected her acquiescence was more to speed lunch along rather than a genuine commitment. 'I'm hungry! I want crisps and chocolate.' She lumbered down the stairs, bumping into the banister. I caught up with her in the kitchen, as she flung open the drawers and cupboards.

'OK, wait a minute, I'll find you something.' I took down a multipack of variety crisps and let her choose one. She wrenched open the packet of smoky bacon, and started cramming fistfuls into her mouth. 'What would you like in your sandwich? Ham? Cheese? Peanut butter? Or Marmite?'

'Marmite and chocolate spread.'

I laughed. 'Not in the same sandwich, surely?'

But she just stared at me, uncomprehendingly. 'I want a drink.'

'Can I have a drink, please?' I corrected, deciding it wouldn't do any harm to introduce some manners. I made one Marmite sandwich and one chocolate spread, then took down a glass and added some orange squash.

'Me do it,' she said, grabbing the glass from my hand.

'All right, but gently. Don't grab, it's not polite.' I showed her how to turn on the tap, then waited while she filled the glass. 'Do you like to help, Jodie? Did you used to help at home? At your other carers'?'

She plonked the glass down on the work surface, then adopted the pose of an overburdened housewife, with her hands on her hips, her chin jutting out, and an expression of resolute grumpiness. 'Cooking! Cleaning! And you bleeding kids at me feet all day. Don't know why I 'ad you. You're a pain in the arse!'

I could see she was role-playing, probably repeating what she'd heard her mother say, but I suspected there was also some truth behind it. As the eldest of three, she was likely to have had some part in bringing up her brother and sister while her parents were too drunk or drugged to care. It reminded me why we were going through this experience, and the flash of insight Jodie had given me into her past helped me to gather my energy and face the volatile moods and constant demands that I knew were coming.

The afternoon passed, I'm not certain how. We didn't unpack, as all my time was taken up with trying to keep Jodie's attention for longer than two minutes. I showed her cupboards full of games, which we explored a number of times, trying to find something that would engage her. She liked jigsaws, but the only ones she had any hope of completing consisted of a handful of pieces, and were designed for two-year-olds. I had seen developmental delays before in children I'd fostered, and was used to dealing with learning difficulties. Nevertheless, I was beginning to suspect that Jodie was closer to the 'moderate' spectrum than the 'mild' that Gary had described.

We sat together on the carpet, but she hardly seemed to be aware of my presence. Instead, she muttered meaningless asides to people called Paul, Mike and Sean: 'See this bit. In there. It's a horse. I told you! I know. Where?'

They weren't the names of anyone in the immediate family that I knew of, so I assumed Jodie was playing with her imaginary friends. This kind of behaviour isn't unusual in children, even in eight-year-olds, but I'd never seen a child distracted to quite this extent.

'Who are these people?' I asked eventually.

She looked at me blankly.

'Paul, Mike and Sean? Are they your imaginary friends? Pretend ones, that only you can see?'

I was met with another uncomprehending gaze, then she looked menacingly over my left shoulder. 'Mike, if you don't watch what you're doing I'll kick you to death.'

When Paula and Lucy arrived home at 3.30, I was trying to manoeuvre Barbie into her sports car beside Ken. I heard the door close, followed by Lucy's reaction as she saw the bags I hadn't had time to move. 'Christ. How many have we got staying?'

'Only one,' I answered.

To prove it, Jodie jumped up and dashed down the hall. 'Who are you?' she demanded, hands on hips, assuming the grumpy housewife pose again.

The girls said nothing, but I knew what they were thinking. With her odd features and aggressive posture, she wasn't exactly the little foster sister they'd been hoping for.

'This is Jodie,' I said positively. 'She arrived at lunchtime. Jodie, this is Lucy and Paula.'

She stuck out her chin, in a take-me-on-if-you-dare attitude.

'Hello,' said Lucy, with effort.

'Hi,' Paula added weakly.

Jodie was blocking their path, so I gently placed a hand on her shoulder to ease her out of the way. She pulled against me. 'Get out!' she suddenly exploded at the girls. 'This is my home. You go!'

I was shocked. How could she believe this when I'd told her about the girls and shown her their rooms? They laughed, which was understandable, but not advisable. Before I could stop her, Jodie rushed at Paula, kicking her hard on the shin. She jumped back and yelped.

'Jodie! Whatever are you doing?' I shouted, as I turned her round to face me. 'That's naughty. You mustn't kick. This is their home as much as it is yours. We all live together. Do you understand?'

She grinned.

'Are you OK?' I asked Paula. She'd experienced aggression from foster siblings before – we all had – but never so immediate and pronounced.

She nodded, and I eased Jodie back as the girls went up the stairs. They always spent time unwinding in their rooms when they got home from school, while I prepared dinner. I took Jodie through to the kitchen, and reinforced again how we all lived as one family. I asked her if she'd like to help, but she folded her arms and leant against the worktop, muttering comments, most of which were impossible to follow. 'They're not mine,' she grumbled.

'The potatoes?' I responded. 'No, I'm peeling them for dinner for us all.'

'Who?'

'Who are these for? For all of us.'

'In the car?'

'No. You came here in the car. We're in the kitchen now.'

'Where?' she asked, lifting the lid on the pan I'd just set to boil.

'Be careful, Jodie,' I said. 'That's very hot.'

'I was walking,' she said, and so it went on, with Jodie mumbling disjointed phrases, as though she had a basket of words and pulled them out at random.

She helped lay the table, and I showed her which would be her place. We always sat in the same places, as the children preferred it, and it made life easier.

'Paula! Lucy! Dinner,' I called. Adrian was playing rugby that evening, so his dinner was waiting for him in the oven. The girls came down and we all took our places. Once she was seated Jodie suddenly became angry that she couldn't sit in Lucy's place.

'Lucy always sits there, Jodie,' I explained. 'It's her place. And that's your place.'

She glared at Lucy, then viciously elbowed her in the ribs.

'Jodie, no! That hurts. Don't do it. Good girl.' I knew I should ask her to apologize, but it was our first meal together so I let it slide. She was still staring at Lucy, who shifted uncomfortably away. 'Come on, Jodie, eat your meal,' I encouraged. 'You told me you like roast chicken.'

The front door opened and Adrian came in, still muddy from playing rugby. He was over six feet tall, and stooped as he entered the kitchen. I hoped Jodie wouldn't find him intimidating, but reassured myself that he had a gentle manner, and children usually warmed to him.

'Adrian, this is Jodie,' I said.

'Hi Jodie,' he smiled, taking his plate from the oven and sitting opposite her. She transferred her glare from Lucy to him, and then wriggled down in her chair, and started kicking him under the table.

'Jodie. Stop that,' I said firmly. 'No kicking or elbowing. It's not nice.'

She scowled at me, then finally picked up her knife and fork and started eating. I watched her out of the corner of my eye. She could barely grip the knife and fork, and her movements were so uncoordinated that her mouth had to be inches from the plate to have any chance of getting the food in.

'Would you like a spoon?' I asked after a while. 'If I cut it up first, it might be easier.'

'My gloves,' she said. 'It's hot.' Then, for no apparent reason, she jumped up, ran round the table three times, then plonked herself down, and started eating with her fingers. I motioned to the rest of the family to say nothing, and the meal passed in an unnatural, tense silence.

I was relieved when dinner was over, and I suggested to Jodie that she might like to help me load the dishwasher. As she came into the kitchen, she spotted Toscha sitting contentedly by the boiler.

'Why's it looking at me?' she demanded, as though the cat had some malicious intent.

'She's not looking at you, sweet. Cats often sit and stare into space. She's found the warmest spot.'

Jodie lurched towards the cat with large, aggressive strides, and I sensed another kick was about to be delivered. I quickly intercepted her. 'Come on, Toscha's old, we'll leave her there to sleep.'

I decided the dishwasher could wait until Jodie was in bed, and took her into the lounge. I tried to amuse her with more games and puzzles, while Adrian, Lucy and Paula did their homework upstairs. By seven, I was exhausted. She needed one-to-one attention to keep her involved in anything, and the meaningless chatter that never stopped was starting to get on my nerves.

'Let's go up and finish your unpacking before bedtime,' I suggested.

She stood up. 'I want the park.'

'Not today, it's too late. But we'll go tomorrow if it's nice.'

She turned her back and started talking to David, another imaginary friend. I caught the odd words – 'you see … in there! …' – but nothing that related to the park or the games we'd played, and I consoled myself that her imaginary world would fade in time as she started to feel safe with us. It took a mixture of coercion and repetition to persuade her upstairs, where we unpacked another bag, then changed and washed her ready for a story at eight. She found a book she'd brought with her: *The Three Little Pigs*. I read it to her twice, then coaxed her into bed and said goodnight. As I left, I went to turn off the light.

'No!' she screamed in panic. 'Not dark. I'm scared of the dark. You stop it!'

'All right, sweet. Don't worry.' I turned it on again, then dimmed it to low, but she still wasn't happy. She would only stay in bed if it was left on full.

'Would you like your door open or closed?' I asked, as I ask all the children on their first night. How they sleep is very important in helping them to feel secure and settled.

'Closed,' she said. 'Shut tight.'

I said goodnight again, blew her a kiss, then closed the door and came out. I paused on the landing and listened. The floorboards creaked as she got out of bed, and checked the door was firmly secured, before returning to bed.

At nine Adrian, Paula and Lucy came down to make a snack, and we sat together in the lounge. I had the television on, but I wasn't watching it. I was mulling over the day's events.

'Well, what do you think?' I asked, smiling at Lucy as she handed me a cup of tea.

'She's weird,' said Lucy, sitting down next to me.

'I don't like her,' said Paula, then looked at me sheepishly, expecting to be told off.

'And what about you, Adrian? What's your first impression?'

'She reminds me of that doll Chucky in the horror film. You know, the one that's possessed by the devil.'

'Adrian!' I admonished, but I felt a cold shudder of recognition. With her broad forehead, staring blue-grey eyes, lack of empathy, and her detachment from the real world, she could easily have been possessed. I caught myself; whatever was I thinking? She was just a child who had been through some miserable times and needed our help – there was nothing more sinister to it than that. I had taken this challenge on and now I owed it to Jodie to see it through for as long as she needed me. Part of her problems no doubt stemmed from people falling at the first hurdle when it came to dealing with her, and passing her on for someone else to deal with. I couldn't do that to her again.

I tried to look relaxed. 'I'm sure she'll improve with time.'

Chapter Five

Self-Harm

Perhaps I was haunted by the lingering image of the possessed doll, for suddenly I was awake, with my eyes open and my senses alert. I turned and looked at the alarm clock: it was nearly 2.15 a.m. I listened. The house was silent. Yet something told me all was not well; a sixth sense from years of looking after children.

I eased my feet from the duvet and felt for my slippers. The house was cold, as the central heating had switched off for the night. I fumbled to get my arms into my dressing gown, tied it loosely, and opened the bedroom door. Suddenly, I gasped in shock. Jodie was standing outside the door, her face covered in blood.

'What is it? What have you done?' I frantically searched her face and neck for the source of the blood. 'Where are you hurt? Tell me! Come on, quickly!' I couldn't find anything, but the blood was fresh.

In a trance-like state, she slowly raised her hands and showed me her palms. They were smeared with blood, but I still couldn't find any sign of a cut. I pulled up her pyjama sleeves, and then I saw it. She had a cut on her left forearm, about an inch long, which was lightly seeping blood. I steered her into the bathroom, and took her to the sink. I turned on the tap and ran the cut under cold water. She didn't even flinch and I wondered if she might be sleepwalking.

'Jodie?' I said loudly. 'Jodie! Can you hear me?'

She grinned at her reflection in the mirror, and I knew that she was awake.

'What happened? How did you do this?'

She met my gaze in the mirror, but said nothing.

I washed the wound thoroughly and examined it. It wasn't deep, and wouldn't need stitches, so there shouldn't have been nearly this much blood. It seemed that she had smeared the blood deliberately, for maximum effect. But how? And why? No one had mentioned anything about Jodie self-harming, but I doubted this was the first time she'd done it. I looked closer, and saw there were other fine, pink scar lines running up both arms. How recent they were was difficult to tell.

'Stay here, Jodie,' I said. 'I'm going downstairs to fetch a bandage.'

She grinned again. That strange, mirthless smile seemed to hold meanings I couldn't fathom, and it gave me the shivers. I covered her arm with a clean towel, then went down into the kitchen, where I opened the first-aid box and took out a large plaster. My mind was reeling. She wasn't even distressed, which made it all the more worrying. Just as before, with her soiling herself, there was that cool calmness and detachment that was so strange in such a young child. It was as though she didn't feel the pain, or perhaps wasn't even aware of what she'd done. She couldn't have cried out when she'd cut herself, as I would have heard her – years of fostering had made me a light sleeper. I suddenly had an awful image of Jodie sitting silently in her room, squeezing the cut, then wiping the blood on her face.

Upstairs again, I found her looking in the mirror, grimacing, but not from pain. She appeared to be trying to make herself as ugly as possible, screwing up her face, and baring her teeth in a lopsided grin. I peeled the backing from the plaster, sealed the cut, then wet the flannel and wiped her face and neck clean. I washed my hands in hot soapy water, remembering too late that I was supposed to wear gloves when dealing with wounds, to prevent cross-infection. In the panic of the emergency, I'd forgotten.

When she was clean and dry again, I felt a sense of normality returning. 'All right, Jodie,' I said encouragingly. 'Let's get you back into bed.' She still didn't speak.

I led her round the landing as Lucy appeared at her door. 'You OK, Cathy?' she asked, her eyes only half-open.

'Yes, don't worry. I'll explain tomorrow.'

She nodded and shuffled back to bed.

In Jodie's room I found her duvet in a heap on the floor. There was no blood on it, but on top was a small fruit knife I'd never seen before. I picked it up. 'Where did you get this?' I tried to keep the accusation out of my voice.

She finally spoke. 'Hilary and Dave's.' Her previous carers.

'Do they know you've taken it?'

She shook her head mischievously, as though being caught out in a game. I could hardly tell her off. I was more annoyed with the carers for giving her access to it, but I did understand. I had learned only from experience that leaving a child for fifteen seconds in the vicinity of the kitchen could produce untold dangers. I'd once fostered a teenager who had self-harmed, but I'd never known a child of Jodie's age doing it. If a child has been physically abused at home, they can have very little respect for their bodies and are often careless about hurting themselves. Deliberate self-harm is relatively rare and is usually the preserve of teenagers. I'd never heard of an eight-year-old purposefully slashing herself with a knife. It was very worrying.

'Have you taken anything else?' I asked gently.

She shook her head, but I checked the room anyway, then remade the bed.

'Come on, in you get. We'll talk about this in the morning.'

She shook her head angrily. 'Park,' she demanded. 'I want to go to the park. You said.'

'It's the middle of the night, Jodie. We'll go tomorrow. No one goes to the park when it's dark. All the gates are locked.'

'Open them!'

'I can't. I haven't got the keys.' I realized the absurdity

of this conversation. 'Jodie, get into bed and go to sleep before you wake the whole house.'

'No. Don't want to.' She made towards the door.

I caught her lightly round the waist and gently drew her to me. 'Come on, good girl, into bed and I'll tell you a story. We'll go to the park in the morning. When it's light.'

She struggled for a moment, then flopped against me. I eased her into bed, and drew the duvet up to her chin. I looked at her little head on the pillow, blonde hair falling over her face. I perched on the bed and stroked her fore-head until her features relaxed. 'Jodie, you must be hurt-ing very badly inside to cut yourself. Is there anything you want to tell me?'

But her eyes were already heavy with sleep. 'Story,' she mumbled. 'Free 'ickle pigs.'

'All right.' I continued to stroke her forehead, and began the story which I knew by heart. Her eyes closed and her breathing deepened. I kissed her cheek, then quietly came out and closed the door.

At five o'clock I was woken by a loud crash. I threw on my slippers and dressing gown, and staggered to her door, disoriented from lack of sleep. I gave a quick knock and entered. 'Jodie! Whatever are you doing?'

She was up and dressed, with a football in her hand, and the contents of the shelves strewn across the floor.

'Put that away,' I said crossly. 'You don't play ball in here.'

'I do.' She clutched it protectively to her chest.

I went to take the ball from her, but she gripped it tighter. I was annoyed with myself, as I should have known it would only make her more defensive. I changed tack. 'OK, Jodie. You put it down and get back into bed. If you can't go to sleep, sit quietly and look at a book. I'll tell you when it's time to get up.'

I didn't wait for a reply, but came out and closed the door. Without a full-scale confrontation, I hoped she might do as I'd asked. I waited and listened. The room fell silent, so I returned to bed, and propped myself on the pillows. Five minutes passed, then I heard her door open, and then another. I ran along the landing in my nightdress and saw Adrian's door open. I rushed in and found her trying to climb into bed with him.

'Jodie! Come away,' I cried. 'Not in there.'

I eased her off. She was a big girl, and a dead weight without cooperation. Adrian groaned and turned over. I put my hands under her arms, and manhandled her out on to the landing. She plonked herself down on the floor, folded her arms, and set her face into a scowl. I took a deep breath, and knelt down beside her.

'Jodie, you can't stay here, pet. Come into your bedroom and we'll put the television on. Everyone else is asleep.'

She thought about this for a moment, then threw herself on to all fours and started crawling towards her room, her hands and feet thumping on the floorboards. I followed her in, relieved that I'd had even this much cooperation. She sat on her bedroom floor, cross-legged, staring expectantly at the blank screen. I switched the TV on, and flicked through the channels. It was too early even for children's programmes, but the football seemed to capture her interest.

'Keep the volume down,' I whispered, 'then you won't wake the others.'

I wrapped the duvet around her shoulders, then returned to my room for my dressing gown and slippers. I went downstairs and turned the central heating on. It wasn't worth going back to bed. I wouldn't be able to sleep now – my thoughts were going nineteen to the dozen and my head was buzzing with everything that had happened.

I made a cup of coffee, and took it into the lounge. Jodie's room was directly above, and all was quiet. I sat on the sofa, resting my head back, and took a sip. Suddenly, the calm was shattered by a man's voice, booming loud with distortion. I gasped – the racket was bound to wake the whole house. I rushed upstairs to her room, and instinctively turned off the TV.

'It's mine,' she shrieked, and lunged at me with her hands raised into claws. 'I want it. Get out! Get out of my fucking bedroom!'

I took her by the shoulders, and held her at arm's length. 'Jodie, calm down and listen to me. I told you to keep the volume low. Everyone is asleep and you'll wake them up with this noise. When you're calmer, we'll put it on again. Do you understand?'

She made eye contact. 'I want the TV.'

'I know, but shouting and swearing won't get it.'

I was too tired to give her a lengthy lecture. 'Now sit down and I'll switch it on, but keep the volume low.'

She resumed her cross-legged position on the floor, and I turned the TV on. I tucked the remote into my pocket, and returned to the lounge. I sat and yawned, as the sun rose on a crisp spring morning. Our first night together was over.

Chapter Six

A Very Troubled Child

'You mustn't thump, kick, bite or push,' I said, for the third time that morning. 'Not Lucy, Paula, me or anyone. It hurts. It's bad. Do you understand?'

She said nothing. It was nearly 11.30 on Saturday, the day after Jodie had arrived, and the girls had come downstairs after their weekend lie-in. Lucy was greeted with a kick from Jodie.

'I don't want to have to tell you again, Jodie. Do I make myself clear?'

She pulled a face and stomped off down the hall.

'Sorry, Lucy,' I said. Lucy shrugged. We all knew there was not much to be done about Jodie's vicious behaviour except to keep reinforcing that it was bad and that she mustn't do it.

A moment later Jodie reappeared, her fists clenched and flaying the air. 'It's them! I'll kick you to death! Get out! I hate you all!'

Her eyes blazed as she tried to kick Paula this time, who deftly stepped out of the way. I went towards her, and avoided the kick aimed at me. 'Jodie,' I said evenly, 'Jodie. Calm down and come here.'

She screamed, then dropped to her knees and started thumping her face and head viciously. She badly wanted to hurt herself. As Jodie pounded her head with her fists, I knelt down behind her and took hold of her arms, crossing them in front of her body. She was still screaming, and her legs were thrashing, but with her arms enfolded she couldn't harm herself or me. I held her close, so that her back was resting against my chest. The screaming and thrashing reached a peak, and then eventually subsided. I waited patiently until she was calm, then slowly relaxed my hold.

'OK?' I asked gently, before I finally let go.

She nodded, and I turned her round to face me. We were both still on the floor. Her cheeks were red and blotchy, and she looked surprised, probably because I'd managed her anger, rather than fleeing for safety into another room. A moment later I helped her up, then took her into the kitchen, where I sponged her face and gave her a drink. She was calm now, calmer than I'd seen her since she first arrived. I hoped she'd got something out of her system.

Paula reappeared in the kitchen. 'Jodie, would you like to do a jigsaw puzzle with me?' she asked casually.

'That's a lovely idea,' I said, amazed at Paula's resilience and generosity. She understood that Jodie's violent behaviour wasn't directed at her personally; Jodie wanted to strike out at the whole world because she was hurting so much, and whoever was standing in her way would bear the brunt of her pain. Paula could sense this, and was prepared to forget and offer friendship and time. I was very proud of her.

'Shall we go to the cupboard and choose one?' Paula asked.

We found a jigsaw and went through to the lounge, where Paula and Jodie settled down to assemble the puzzle. I left them to it and returned to the kitchen to prepare lunch. I could hear Paula suggesting where the pieces should go, and Jodie replying, 'That's it, my girl. You can do it.' She was like a little old woman, but at least she was relating to Paula in a positive way.

With her short attention span, it didn't take long for Jodie to become bored, so Paula laid out some paper on the kitchen table, and tried to help her paint, while I made a cup of tea. Jodie could barely grip the paintbrush, and couldn't grasp the concept of painting a picture 'of' something.

'What's that you're painting, Jodie?' Paula asked.

'Dark.'

'Is it a sheep, or a horse? That looks a bit like a big horse.'

Jodie didn't respond, intent on her clumsy project.

'Maybe you could paint the sky with this nice blue?'

'No. Black,' Jodie said.

Despite Paula's encouragement, Jodie continued to paint nothing but large, dark splodges, with no interest in the other colours, and no apparent desire for the paintings to represent anything. I'd seen this before; children who have been abused and are hurting sometimes only use very dark colours. It's as if their senses have shut down and they don't notice anything about the world around them, so they don't see colours and shapes in the same way normal children do.

We ate lunch in relative calm, although it felt more like dinner to me, having been up for so long. The peace lasted into the afternoon, and I thought now would be a good time to take the photograph of Jodie that was required for the Social Services' records. I fetched my camera, and explained to Jodie why I was taking it.

'Is it all right to take your picture, sweet?' I asked. It was important to give Jodie as much control as possible, to increase her feeling of stability and security.

She shrugged, which I decided to take as consent. Paula moved to one side, so I had just Jodie in the picture. I looked through the lens, and framed her head and shoulders against the wall, centring her in the viewfinder.

'You can smile, Jodie,' I said. She was looking very stern.

I saw her mouth pucker to a sheepish grin, then an arm came up, and she disappeared from view. 'Very funny, Jodie. Come on, stand still.' I was still looking through the lens. Then her other arm came up, and with it her jumper.

I lowered the camera. 'Jodie, what are you doing?'

'Taking off my clothes.'

'Why?' asked Paula, and quickly pulled Jodie's top back into place.

She didn't answer. She was staring at me, but not scowling, so I quickly took the photograph and closed the camera. 'Jodie, we don't normally take our clothes off for a photograph,' I said. 'Why did you do that?'

She took a piece of the jigsaw and tried to place it. 'Want to,' she said, lowering her voice. 'Want to. My clothes.'

'I know, sweet, but why take them off for a photograph? I didn't ask you to.'

She turned to Paula. 'You helping, girl, or not?'

I smiled at Paula, and nodded for her to continue. I went over to my filing cabinet under the stairs and unlocked it. I wasn't going to jump to conclusions about Jodie's behaviour, but I had to make a note of it in the log. I took out the desk diary that the fostering agency had supplied and settled down to write everything that had happened so far. The 'log' is a daily record of a child's progress, and is something that all foster carers keep. It is used to update the social workers and to monitor the child's progress, and it's sometimes used as evidence during care proceedings in court. I was assiduous about keeping it up to date because I knew only too well how one incident could blend into another and how disturbed nights could all seem the same after a while. Detail was important: only with careful notes could a pattern of behaviour start to emerge. I made a note of exactly what had happened: the self-harming in the night and the strange detachment; the lashing out at other people and violent tantrums marked by Jodie's desire to hurt herself;

and this strange and unsettling response to having her photograph taken. Why had she started to take her clothes off?

I was resolute that I would not rush into any hasty judgements. I needed to accept Jodie exactly as she was for the time being and then see what came from the pattern of her behaviour. I was uneasy, though, and also found it cathartic to be able to put it down on paper.

With the other two out for the day, Paula and I took it in turns to entertain Jodie throughout the afternoon, but despite this, and for no apparent reason, she threw another full-scale tantrum. I allowed her to continue for a few minutes, hoping it would run its course. When it didn't, and the high-pitched screaming became intolerable, I enfolded her in my arms as I had before, until she had calmed down. Later, I made another note of Jodie's erratic behaviour in the log. I was doing a lot of writing.

Our first weekend with Jodie was an exhausting and disturbing experience. Although none of us said anything, it was obvious that we were all thinking the same thing. But it was early days and we all knew from experience that children can settle down after an initial bout of odd behaviour.

'She's a very troubled child,' I said to Jill when she phoned the following Monday to see how things were going. I told her about the self-harming and the violent and aggressive tantrums.

'Yes, that is bad,' said Jill. 'It's very disturbed behaviour, particularly in such a young child. Do you think you can cope with her?'

'I'm determined to try,' I said. 'She's hardly been here five minutes. I want to give her as much of a chance as possible. Besides, we knew she was not going to be easy from the start so we can't be surprised if she's a handful at first. I'm keeping detailed notes of everything that happens, though.'

'Good. We'll just have to monitor it and see how it goes. You're definitely the best person she could possibly be with, so as long as you're happy, I know she's in safe hands.'

I listened out for Jodie – she was occupied watching a Tiny Tots video – and then went through my log for Jill, trying to think of something positive to say. 'She eats well. Actually, she gorges. I'm having to limit her intake. She nearly made herself sick yesterday. Apart from a healthy appetite, she doesn't have much else going for her at present, I'm afraid.'

'Do you think she can be contained within a family, Cathy? If she can't, the borough will have to start looking for a therapeutic unit, and they're few and far between. I have every faith in your judgement.'

I appreciated the compliment, but it was small comfort. I was already exhausted. I was worried about whether or not I'd be able to see this through and the prospect of failing before I'd even begun did nothing for my stamina. 'She's got contact with her parents tomorrow and her tutor's coming for a couple of hours next week. Perhaps a familiar face might help settle her. She's been seeing her tutor since September.'

'OK, Cathy, we'll see how it goes. I'll update Eileen. What are you going to do with her today?'

'Retail therapy. Courtesy of Tesco's.'

Jill laughed. 'I'll give it a wide berth.'

Jodie apparently loved food shopping, unlike the rest of my family who could think of nothing worse than a trip to the supermarket. She was in her element, pushing the trolley up and down, telling me what we should or shouldn't buy. In fact, she was so enthusiastic I had to limit her exuberance, and return some items to the shelves.

This wasn't unusual; children in care often seem to feel that all their problems can be solved by a bottomless purse. Children I'd looked after often had a desperate need for material goods. In the homes they had come from money was often short, and when there was any it was frequently spent on drink, drugs or cigarettes. When I started buying my foster children little treats, they would often find it very exciting and pleasurable: treats were something they had very little experience of. But I always had to be careful about managing their expectations, as they could very quickly become demanding and assume they'd be given anything they wanted. Jodie was a different case, though; from the looks of her luggage and her weight, treats had never been in short supply –

which meant that she was used to getting anything she fancied. I hoped it wasn't going to be too much of a struggle restricting her to a sensible limit, but experience was already teaching me to expect a battle.

'Three packets of cereal is plenty,' I said. 'Choose one you'd like and we'll put the others back.'

She wanted them all, of course, and every packet of biscuits, and every dessert in the freezer cabinet, so I was spending as much time taking things out of the trolley as I was putting them in, but at least she was occupied and content.

It took nearly two hours to complete the weekly shop, and as we finally reached the check-out Jodie spotted the display of sweets, tantalizingly placed at the side of the aisle. I started unloading the trolley on to the belt, and told her to choose a bar of chocolate as a treat, because she'd been such a good girl and helped.

'One,' I repeated, as the bags of sweets started raining into the trolley. But I could see her previous cooperation was waning fast. 'Take the chocolate bonbons, you like those.'

'Want them all!' she shouted, and then sat on the floor defiantly.

The woman queuing behind us was clearly unimpressed by my parenting skills, and shot me one of those looks. I unloaded the last of the shopping, including the bonbons, onto the conveyor, and put the other sweets back on the rack. I watched Jodie out of the corner of my eye. Her anger was mounting, as she crossed her legs, folded her arms and set her face in a sneer. She kicked the trolley so that it jarred against my side. I clenched my teeth, pretending that it hadn't hurt. I pulled the trolley through the aisle and positioned it at the end, ready to receive the bags of shopping.

'Are you going to help me pack?' I said, trying to distract her. 'You were a big help earlier and I could do with your help now.'

She refused to make eye contact, and I began to wonder how I was going to remove her from the aisle, but I was determined that she wouldn't get what she wanted by making a scene in public.

'Don't want those sweets,' she suddenly yelled. 'Don't like them.'

I looked at her. 'Don't shout, please. I've said you can choose one, but hurry up. We've nearly finished.'

People were now openly staring. Petulantly, Jodie hauled herself to her feet, picked up a family-sized bag of boiled sweets and threw them at the cashier.

'Jodie!' I turned to the cashier, who was busy exchanging meaningful glances with the woman behind us. 'I'm so sorry.' I paid, apologized again, and we left.

Outside, I ignored Jodie's screams for the sweets and pushed the trolley fast towards the car. I unlocked the doors and strapped her under her belt. 'Stay there while I load the bags into the boot. I'm cross, Jodie. That was very naughty.'

I watched her through the rear window. Her jaw was clenched as she muttered to herself and thumped the seat beside her. I knew how she felt; I was in the mood for thumping the seat myself. It had been a draining experience already and all I could do was prepare myself for more hurricanes and hysteria. Giving in to tantrums wouldn't help her or me in the long term.

I took the trolley back, then got into the front seat.

'Give me the sweets,' she growled. 'Want them now.'

'When you've calmed down and apologized, Jodie. I'm not having that behaviour in public.'

'Give me them, or I'll poo on your back seat,' she threatened.

'I beg your pardon? You most certainly will not!' So, I thought, she was prepared to soil herself if I didn't give her exactly what she wanted. Is that what had happened on the first day? Was this her trying to exert her will, rather than anxiety or poor bowel control? And much as I didn't want her to make a mess on the back seat, I wasn't prepared to give in to this kind of blackmail.

'Jodie, if you mess on the back seat deliberately you won't get any sweets all day. You can't just make a fuss and get everything you want. I'm sure you didn't at your previous carers.'

'Did. Everything. I made them.'

I started the car and pulled towards the exit. I didn't doubt that what she was saying was true. Given Jodie's appalling behaviour, it was no wonder her previous carers had given in to her demands, just to keep her quiet. Presumably, this was how she'd acquired the piles of clothes and toys that she'd arrived with. I glanced in the rear-view mirror. She stuck out her tongue, then started kicking the back of my seat.

'Jodie, I know it's a hard lesson, pet, but being naughty won't get you what you want. Just the opposite, in fact.'

'I had everything I wanted at home,' she said, suddenly more coherent.

'Really,' I replied, unimpressed.

'I made them, or I'd tell.'

I hesitated. 'Tell what, Jodie?'

There was a long silence. 'Nothing. Can I have my sweets now, Cathy? I'm sorry. I won't do it again.'

'OK, just as soon as we get home.'

As we pulled into the driveway, the sour smell coming from the back seat made me realize that she had made good on her threat. It would be another unwelcome date with the shower for us as soon as we got through the front door.

Chapter Seven

Contact

'Did the previous carers say anything about defecation as a means of control?' I asked Eileen, Jodie's social worker, when she phoned the next day. It was the first time we had spoken since I'd met her at the pre-placement meeting, and I was glad to hear from her. A good social worker can make all the difference on the case, and I was hoping that Eileen and I would have a supportive working relationship. 'She threatens to make a mess if she doesn't get what she wants, and she's done it twice. The first time I put it down to anxiety but the last time was in the car when I wouldn't buy her all the sweets she wanted. She threatened to soil all over the back seat and then she did it.'

Eileen paused and I was sure that the answer would be yes, although it would probably be qualified. Jodie's modus operandi was too polished to have started when she came to me; she'd clearly been using defecation as a form of blackmail for a little while.

'There might be something in the file. Why? Is it going to be a problem?'

The idea that a child threatening to poo herself when she didn't get her own way and then carrying out her threat *not* being a problem almost made me want to laugh. I could hear in Eileen's voice the worry that I might be about to hand Jodie back, and the implication that, if so, I was overreacting a bit. Constant soiling might not seem like a big issue to her, but then she wasn't the one who had to clean it up.

'If I'm going to be able to meet this child's needs,' I replied, 'it's important that I'm given all the relevant information. Could you check and get back to me, please?'

'I'll have a look in the file,' she said, but I doubted she would. If she hadn't familiarized herself with the case already, there was little compunction to do so now Jodie had been placed with me. I knew from long experience how these things worked.

Eileen changed the subject. 'Contact has been confirmed for tomorrow,' she said, using the social-work term meaning a meeting between a child and its natural parents. 'The escort will collect her at six, if that's OK.'

'That's fine. But why is it so late?'

'Jodie's father can't make it from work any earlier and he's most insistent on seeing her. He hasn't missed one yet.'

I heard Eileen's inference. Clearly she felt that this showed a commitment on his part, which suggested a strong attachment between father and daughter. If all went well over the next few months, and Jodie's parents could get their lives in order, there was a good chance

Jodie would go back to them. Generally, the Social Services try to rehabilitate families wherever possible. The final decision would be made by a judge, at a care hearing in the family court.

'Was there anything else?' Eileen asked, clearly hoping there wasn't.

'Her behaviour is as stated.' I'd told her everything that had happened, just as I had Jill, but Eileen didn't seem to have much in the way of response to any of the reports of self-harm, violent tantrums or anything else. I could feel my heart sinking as I realized that it was unlikely Jodie was going to get the kind of support I'd hoped for from her. 'Let's hope we can make a difference,' I finished.

The next morning, I was woken by Jodie stamping down the stairs at 5 a.m. I was getting used to the disturbed nights – she was calling out for me a couple of times a night and seemed to be suffering from nightmares – and the invariable early starts. I'd had a feeling this would be a pattern with Jodie: in general, the more disturbed children are, the more troubled their nights are and the earlier they rise in the morning. Sometimes that can be because foster children have been used to the responsibility of looking after younger siblings and have quite often had to get their parents up in the morning and make the family breakfast. In other cases, it is because they are on constant alert and consequently unable to sleep much at a time because their survival mechanism is always switched on. So it was no surprise that Jodie was up and about at dawn.

I leapt out of the bed and hurriedly followed; the last thing I wanted was Jodie left alone in the kitchen. I managed to persuade her to go back to bed, but each time I thought I'd settled her, she'd be off again minutes later. By the third time I was fully awake, and there was no point going back to bed. I sat in the living room, trying to read, with one ear alert to what Jodie was up to.

A couple of hours later I heard Paula get up, followed shortly after by Lucy and then Adrian.

I had started preparing breakfast, when I suddenly heard Jodie shouting. Rushing upstairs, I found Paula standing in the bathroom doorway wearing only a towel, while Jodie sat on the landing, glaring at her menacingly.

'Whatever's going on?' I asked.

'I'm trying to get past, but she keeps kicking me,' replied Paula, obviously frustrated and vulnerable.

At this, Jodie started screaming and banging the floor with her fists and feet. I waited for her to calm down, then went over and gently lifted her to her feet and guided her towards the stairs.

'Come on, Jodie, why don't you help me make you some breakfast? You must be hungry by now.'

She resisted at first, but eventually followed me downstairs, presumably feeling that she'd won this battle, and Paula was allowed to continue getting ready in peace.

Downstairs, Jodie agreed to lay the table, while I boiled the kettle and set out four cups. She'd already been extremely trying this morning, but as I watched her lay the table I was reminded of how difficult her life was. Even in performing this simple task, Jodie's limitations were obvious. She couldn't grip the cutlery, because her motor skills were so poor; instead, she clamped the pile to her chest. Predictably enough, on her way to the table she dropped one of the spoons. She grunted in frustration, then dropped the rest of the cutlery on the table, making a loud clang. She picked up the stray spoon from the floor, licked it on both sides, then wiped it on her sleeve, and proceeded to set the places.

It was no surprise that she was so clumsy. Poor motor skills and bad coordination are all part of developmental delay. I was no expert on the matter, but I knew that a lack of stimulation of an infant's brain could have a severe impact on its growth and development. Even being given a rattle to hold helps a baby learn about how the world works and teaches the muscles and brain to respond, so that it can master its environment. Later on, reading books and playing with jigsaws and puzzles help the brain continue to grow and learn. While I didn't want to leap to conclusions about what had happened to Jodie in the past, I couldn't help wondering if neglect and a lack of stimulation had contributed to her acute malcoordination and clumsiness. It certainly wouldn't be the first time I'd seen it, though never this pronounced.

'Well done, Jodie,' I said, with exaggerated enthusiasm. 'You've been a big help'.

She barely responded to my praise, and that too was unusual. It was odd to meet a child who didn't enjoy approval. She seemed very shut off and far away, and nothing I said seemed to reach her. I'd been expecting something of the sort but the extent of it was beginning to puzzle and worry me.

I poured Jodie some Rice Krispies, and finished making the tea. Paula and Lucy came down together and sat at the table. Jodie's mood switched immediately, as it seemed to when the other children came into the room. I could see her becoming tense, and her eyes narrowing with anger. She looked up at Paula with an unpleasant grimace, then started poking her in the ribs.

'Stop that, Jodie!' I said, but she persisted. Paula tried to fend her off, and then lost her temper, and poked her back. Jodie started screaming, making the most of the minor assault.

'Paula, you mustn't do that!' I said, angry with her for losing control. 'Now, the pair of you behave!'

'Sorry, Mum,' said Paula.

'And apologize to Jodie, please,' I said, feeling slightly guilty. I knew Paula would feel this was unfair, with good cause, but it was in all of our interests to make it clear to Jodie that you didn't poke, and you apologized after doing something wrong.

'Sorry, Jodie,' Paula muttered, without looking up. Jodie was still clutching her side melodramatically, so I decided there was little chance of coaxing an apology out of her, and left it at that.

'Thank you, Paula. That was the adult thing to do.'

The children left for school, and Jodie helped me to clear the table and load the dishwasher, thankfully without any mishaps. Then we sat down in the living room and I tried to interest her in some games. I decided now might be a good time to broach the subject of her contact. She would be seeing her parents twice a week for an hour at a contact centre, with a social worker present all the time. Meetings with natural parents are generally arranged some time in advance, but my policy was to remind the children only on the day, as mention of it could often unsettle them. In my experience, children tended to play up just before contact so I made the time available for this emotional upheaval as short as possible for all our sakes.

'Jodie,' I said brightly, 'you'll have your bath later this afternoon, because you're going to see your parents tonight.'

She looked at me blankly. Had she understood? She carried on playing, mashing stickle bricks together. After a moment, she asked, 'Am I going in a van?'

'No, the escort will pick you up here in a car, just like when you were at your previous carers. They'll take you to meet your parents, and then bring you back here.'

'Not going in a van. Hate them. Blimmin' vans,' she replied, becoming more animated.

'That's right, Jodie, the escort will pick you up in a car. I know your dad's looking forward to seeing you. That will be nice, won't it?' Apparently, however, I'd lost her attention, and she returned to her playing, with a puzzled expression on her face. It was hard to tell what she made of the prospect of seeing her mother and father again.

Jodie was difficult for the rest of the day, as I'd expected. She had two more tantrums before lunch, and caused me a minor panic when she knocked a picture off the wall, smashing the glass, then tried to pick it up. In the afternoon, I kept her occupied with a singalong video in the lounge, while I prepared dinner. At four o'clock Adrian came in warily, and was relieved not to be greeted with a kick from Jodie. He joined me in the kitchen, and told me about his day. It felt like a long time since we'd had the chance to have a chat in peace without screaming, tantrums or violent fits, even though Jodie had been with us less than a week. It was lovely to have a few moments with my son and I knew how important it was to snatch any opportunity to spend time with my own family in the often demanding first weeks of a new placement.

Adrian went to take his bag up to his room, and I was pleased to hear him go into the lounge first, to say hello to Jodie. However, my moment of pleasure was short-lived, as I suddenly heard him shout, 'Oh God! Mum, come in here!'

I rushed into the hallway, as Adrian marched upstairs. In the lounge, I found Jodie sitting on the sofa with her legs in the air and one hand in her knickers, masturbating.

'Jodie, stop that!' I said firmly.

'Why?' she barked.

'If you want to do that, you go to your room and do it. It's private. Is that clear? Now, either go upstairs or sit properly please, good girl.'

She glared at me for a few seconds, and I prepared myself for another tantrum, but eventually she pulled her skirt down and sat up straight.

I was puzzled and disturbed by this new incidence, of this time highly sexualized behaviour. I knew that it was not unusual for very young children to masturbate, even if it wasn't generally talked about; but by the time a child was eight years old he or she usually had a sense that this was not something to be done in public, even when the child had learning difficulties. Was Jodie intending to be observed? Given that we were always in and out of the lounge, she must have known she'd be seen. Was she trying to shock us, or was it something entirely unconscious? An act of self-comfort, or a physical habit as harmless as sucking her thumb? I didn't know the answer, but anything that came within the framework of sexualized behaviour had to be noted down. I made a mental note to log it in the diary, and raise it with Eileen the next time we spoke.

When the girls arrived home from school they were both greeted with a vicious thump, and I wearily told Jodie off. She had another full-scale tantrum, and I again had to restrain her. Eventually, she calmed down, and I finished making the evening meal, which was spaghetti bolognaise. We sat down to eat, and I cut up Jodie's spaghetti for her.

'Want burger,' she demanded, pulling a face.

'We'll have a burger another night. I've done this for now.'

She picked up her plate and hurled it against the wall. It hit the wall with a crack and the plate fell in pieces to the ground. There was a vivid splash of dark bolognese mixed with strings of spaghetti on the wall. It began sliding downwards, before dropping on to the floor. We all looked at it in silence for a moment and then I felt the children gaze at me in shock.

Anger and frustration rushed through me. I had put up with Jodie's bad behaviour all day and was worn out with it and her. Now she had thrown a perfectly good meal away, caused a terrible mess and upset us all, for no good reason that I could see.

'Go to your room!' I snapped. 'I've had quite enough of this for one day!'

She struggled down from her seat, and as she left the table, punched Lucy in the back of the head, hard, with a closed fist. She stormed out of the room, slamming the door with such force that a piece of plaster fell from the ceiling. Lucy didn't say anything, but I could see the tears welling in her eyes. I hugged her.

'I'm sorry,' I said, mortified that I could have caused my children such pain. 'I think I've made a mistake. I shouldn't have accepted her. This is too difficult for all of us. I'll speak to the social worker first thing in the morning.'

At a little after six the doorbell rang, and a dishevelled young man introduced himself as Jodie's escort for contact. Jodie bounded down the stairs and left in a cheerful mood, waving goodbye as she walked up the garden path. Was she completely unrepentant, I wondered? Was she even aware of how bad her behaviour had been, or the sad atmosphere which now pervaded the house?

It was the first moment of real peace in almost a week. The children were upstairs doing their homework. I sat in the living room with the television on, although I wasn't paying attention. Instead my mind was in turmoil. Life with Jodie was not only far from easy, it was well-nigh impossible, and for the first time I was beginning to feel as though I might not be able to reach her. Jodie was the most disturbed, demanding child I'd ever come across; she was so cold and unresponsive, with no desire to be liked. It was not possible to find a way to mediate with her because she had no interest in meeting me halfway. It seemed as if she didn't want to change but was content to remain in her far-off state, shut into her own world, expressing herself through tantrums and violence. In my experience, human relationships are all about give and take and mutual needs for affection and approval being met. If one party has absolutely no need of anything the other party has to offer, then where can the compromise come? That's how it was with Jodie. I had never known a child so shut off, or so unseeking of warmth and affection. It seemed that the task I had set myself of caring for Jodie and somehow breaking through the huge barrier of emotional coldness around her had magnified itself a hundred times. I was in a no-win situation. I couldn't have Jodie stay, because it was unfair on my children; her behaviour was just too disruptive. I couldn't bear to see their home life and their security undermined and destroyed when they had just as much need of love and stability as Jodie, even if it was less pronounced.

On the other hand, I knew what sending Jodie back now would mean. Not only would it be yet another rejection, and another black mark against her name, turning her into an object of fascinated horror – 'Six carers in four months! Just think how awful she must be!' – but it would also condemn her to a children's home. I knew that a children's home was not the right environment for Jodie, and also that it would probably mean that her last chance of living in a normal family was gone for good. If I didn't keep her, then no one else would take her in. And what was the point of being a foster carer if you couldn't help the most troubled children?

As I sat and worried, I heard three pairs of feet coming down the stairs. Lucy and Paula entered and sat either side of me, while Adrian disappeared to make us a cup of tea. I was touched; the children had come to comfort me about my failure. Adrian returned with a tray of drinks. 'There you go, Mum,' he said.

'Thanks, love.'

Adrian looked at the girls, then cleared his throat. 'Mum, we've been thinking,' he said, and paused.

'Oh yes?' I replied, expecting another request to extend their coming-in time.

'Yes. We want Jodie to stay, for a while at least. We think we should wait, and see how it goes.'

I couldn't say anything for a moment while I absorbed this, taken aback by their generosity. Life had been pretty miserable for the last week, and home, far from being a refuge of safety and contentment, had become a place where vicious kicks, punches and sudden attacks, along with spine-curdling yelling, high-pitched screaming and disturbed nights, were just par for the course. Were my children really prepared to put up with this indefinitely, when I had offered to hand Jodie back and restore calm and quiet to our home? Yet again, I was stunned by their extraordinary kindness and maturity when it came to the children we fostered. I looked over to Lucy and Paula. 'Are you sure?' I asked anxiously. I didn't want them to regret this. 'Is this really what you want? She'll probably get worse rather than better in the short term.'

'We all want her to stay,' said Lucy firmly. 'We know she'll get better. And if not we can always kick her out next time!' She grinned mischievously.

I felt a surge of relief, as well as immense admiration for my children. I know I'm biased, and I'm sure other parents feel the same about their kids, but at moments like these I couldn't help but swell with pride.

It was after eight by the time Jodie returned from seeing her parents, and she was in high spirits. So were we. We'd had almost three hours' respite, and we had a new sense of purpose. Jodie proudly showed us the dolls and sweets her father had given her. She also pointedly told me twice he had bought her burger and chips. I smiled. I was used to being played off against the parents of my foster children. No doubt the parents got the same kind of thing themselves. Apart from her boasting, Jodie had nothing else to say about her contact with her parents.

It was well past her bedtime, so with my usual mixture of coercion and repetition I took her up to the bathroom, then saw her into bed. She didn't want the new dolls, but instead chose a large panda she had brought with her, and snuggled into it. I read her a short story, then said goodnight. I left the light on, came out and closed the door. I was feeling optimistic. Now Jodie had seen her parents, she might start to settle, with the two halves of her life running side by side. I sat in the lounge, and picked up the book I'd been trying to read for a fortnight. It was a comic satire, and it made me laugh out loud. At 9.30 Paula called from the landing that she was ready for me to tuck her in; it was a ritual she wasn't too old for, as long as her friends didn't find out.

As I went in, I noticed her rag-doll pyjama case wasn't on the bed. 'Where's Betsy?' I asked.

She looked at me, with her eyes large and imploring. 'Don't be upset, Mum, but I think there's been an accident.'

'What sort of accident?'

She nodded at the wardrobe. I went over and slid the door open. Lying at the bottom was Betsy, with her head ripped off, and stuffing falling out of her neck.

'This isn't an accident, is it, pet?' I picked up the dismembered parts. 'Why didn't you tell me sooner?'

'I didn't want more upset, Mum. It's only a toy. Really. It doesn't matter.'

I sat on the bed, reminded once again of how much the family had to put up with. 'I'm sorry, love. I watched her like a hawk today. The only time I didn't was when I was in the loo. I'll try and find another one, but in future you must tell me. I know you feel sorry for her but if there's any chance of us helping her, she's going to have to learn. OK?'

She agreed, and we had a big hug, then I left her reading and continued my night-time rounds. I knocked on Lucy's door, and waited for her shout of 'Come in!' She was in her pyjamas, propped on the pillows.

I sensed immediately that something was wrong. 'Not you as well?' I said.

She opened her bedside cabinet, and took out her makeup box. I looked at the congealed mess of black mascara, blue eye shadow and beige foundation.

'It's my fault,' she said quickly. 'I shouldn't have left it on the bed.'

'Of course you should! You have every right to leave your things out in your room. I'll speak to her first thing in the morning.' I repeated what I'd told Paula – that I'd replace it, but she had to tell me immediately if it happened again, so that I could deal with it at the time. It seemed that Jodie hadn't taken my explanation about privacy very much to heart.

She took my hand and gave it a squeeze. 'Cathy, was I this naughty when I first arrived? I don't remember.'

'No. You had your moments but I wouldn't have expected any different. You'd had a lot of moves but you soon settled. What we're seeing in Jodie is severely disturbed behaviour.'

She looked away. 'I know I shouldn't say this, but sometimes she gives me the creeps. When she stares at me, it's so cold I think she could kill me.'

'It's OK. I understand. She hasn't had much love and I'm hoping we can change that. Now off to sleep. You've got your science exam tomorrow, haven't you?'

She grinned sheepishly. 'I will, and thanks for looking after me. I do love you, you know that, don't you?'

It was the first time she'd said it, and ironically it had taken the hatred of a disturbed child to cement our relationship. 'I love you too, sweet. You're a good girl. Jodie couldn't have a better example.'

Chapter Eight

Julie

Jodie had been living with us a little over a week when her eighth birthday arrived. I'd got so used to thinking of her as eight already because that's how the Social Services had always referred to her, but in fact she was on the tail end of seven years old when she arrived. Jodie celebrated her birthday with her parents at the next contact session and spent her actual birthday with us.

When she got back from her birthday celebration with her parents, Jodie was loaded down with more bags of big, cheap, glittery toys of the kind that would last five minutes, and hold her interest for half that time. But if the amount was anything to go by, Jodie was certainly used to getting plenty of what she wanted. Even so, just as with the new things she had brought back from her previous contact sessions, the novelties and toys didn't hold much charm for her. It seemed she liked getting them, but after a moment or two they had no worth or meaning.

I asked Jodie what she would like to do for her birthday and she announced that she would like to go bowling, which surprised me. Bowling didn't seem to be something that a child with such bad coordination would enjoy much, but it was her birthday and if that was what she wanted, then that was what we would do. Bowling it was. As Jodie wasn't at school, there were no friends to ask along, so it was Jodie, Paula, Lucy, Adrian and me.

First, we opened her presents at home. I'd put a lot of thought into what to get her. I could tell she liked dolls' things, and she seemed to treasure her life-size doll, Julie, so I bought her a doll's car seat, just like the real thing, and a doll's high chair. She unwrapped her presents without the excitement I would usually have expected in a child, examined them and then pushed them to one side without any further comment. I felt vaguely hurt, and rather mystified. It wasn't that she didn't like them – it was just as though nothing had any value for her, and I couldn't understand why. But I quickly put the anticlimax of the gifts behind us, and we all left for bowling.

As I'd suspected, Jodie couldn't bowl to save her life, but she seemed to have a good time anyway, although she did her usual stomping about, hands on hips, ordering everyone around. But there were no tantrums, either in the bowling alley or later in McDonald's, which was where she wanted to go for dinner. But then, as it was her birthday, we were all obediently doing what she wanted and she rewarded us by not throwing a screaming fit or landing a punch or two. We all went home, satisfied that Jodie's birthday had gone as well as it possibly could.

One morning, after Jodie had been with us for a fortnight and the day after a contact session with her parents, I left her playing in her room until everyone had gone to school. She wasn't happy about this, but I needed to establish some sort of working routine, and a peaceful breakfast would be a good start. Once the others had left for school, I went up and told Jodie she could get dressed, and asked her what she wanted for breakfast.

'Nothing. Hate you,' she snarled and poked out her tongue. 'Bugger off.'

'That's a pity,' I said, ignoring the swear word, 'because I like you, and I'm looking forward to our day together.'

She stared at me as though I'd finally lost it. 'Why? Why do you like me?'

'Because underneath that angry Jodie is a kind and happy Jodie waiting to come out. Now get dressed and come down for breakfast.'

And she did. Without arguing. I gave her lots of praise and mentally awarded us both a gold star.

The tutor was coming to give Jodie her lessons but she wasn't due until 1.30, so in the morning we went shopping to replace Paula's pyjama case and Lucy's makeup. In the car, I explained to Jodie where we were going and why. She didn't comment, and I wasn't looking for a confession, so I restated our rules regarding other people's bedrooms and property and left it at that. I found what I was looking for in the department store, then took the escalator to the top floor, and headed for the café. We both had a piece of apple cake, and sat by the window, looking down on the street below. We could have been any normal mother and daughter on a day out, and I wondered, not for the first time, what had happened to knock Jodie's life so far off course. She seemed much more deeply damaged than Gary had led me to expect in the case history he'd given at the pre-placement meeting. Whenever I wondered what had happened to her, I put a mental stop on myself. Not only was it unprofessional to make assumptions but I knew that it was far too early to see any patterns in her behaviour. As it was, Jodie kept me so busy that it was impossible to stand back and see the bigger picture. At least I would get a couple of hours to catch up on paperwork while she was with her tutor that afternoon.

We finished our drinks, then had a look around the shops on the first floor. I could see Jodie was flagging, so we decided to call it a day, and walked over to the lifts. I showed Jodie how to push the button, and explained to her how the lift worked. By the time it arrived, there were a number of people waiting, but we were the first in line. We walked in, and stood at the back. Jodie held my hand, but as the doors started to close she pulled my arm and started shouting, 'No! Make it stop! Don't want to!'

I quickly leaned in between two women and pushed the button to reopen the doors, apologizing as I led Jodie out.

I bent down and put my hands on her shoulders. 'What's the matter, Jodie? There's nothing to be scared of.'

'Don't want to,' she moaned. 'I'm not going in there!'

'That's OK, we don't have to if you don't want to. We'll just take the escalator instead.'

We walked over to the escalator, and Jodie gripped my hand as we descended. 'I'll take my dad in there,' she said, her face crumpling.

'What, in the lift?'

She nodded. 'I'll scare him. See how he likes it. I'll show him.'

'Why do you want to scare him, Jodie?'

But she just shrugged. She had closed down again, and the door that had briefly opened on her past had slammed shut.

Jodie recovered quickly from her fright, and by the time we returned home I was feeling positive again. I praised her over and over, telling her what a nice time I'd had, and how much I had enjoyed her company. She said she was hungry, so I left her playing with Julie, her life-size doll, and went into the kitchen. She wanted peanut butter in her sandwich, and I spread it thinly. I was determined to do something about her weight. I set the plate on the breakfast bar and poured a glass of squash, then started towards the lounge to tell her it was ready.

Something made me hesitate before going in. Perhaps it was the quiet. I couldn't hear the usual babble that accompanied everything Jodie did. I looked round the half-open door, and froze. She was still playing with Julie, but had pulled the doll's dress up, and was licking between its naked legs. She was making low, grunting noises as if from pleasure, and seemed totally oblivious to my presence. I walked in and Jodie looked up.

'That looks a strange game, Jodie,' I said evenly. 'What are you doing?' I knew that showing any alarm or surprise was not the way to go, and telling her off would be counter-productive. Besides, I needed to know if she understood what she was doing.

She glanced down between the doll's legs, then up again at me. There was no embarrassment. 'Kissing,' she said, with a grin. 'She likes kissing, she does.'

'Isn't it an odd place to kiss her? We usually kiss each other on the cheek.'

She looked surprised. 'But you haven't got a man. Mans kiss here' – she pointed to Julie's naked crotch – 'and girls here.' She jabbed her forefinger at her cheek.

I went over and sat on the floor beside her. I needed to stay calm, so that Jodie would too, and to keep her talking for as long as I could. I had to find out what she'd seen, deal with it, and inform the social worker. She wouldn't be the first child to have watched an adult video, or slept in the parents' bedroom with no partition – I hoped that this was all it was, Jodie acting out something she had seen when she wasn't supposed to. I would log it down in my notebook, though, in case any other kind of picture emerged. I tried to remain professional: calm but direct.

'Jodie, can you tell me how you know men kiss there?'

She shrugged. 'Just know. Girls like it and men do it. Mummies, daddies and girls.'

'And were you pretending Julie was a mummy or a girl?'

'Don't know. A lady.'

'OK, so if Julie was the lady, who were you pretending to be?'

'The man!' She frowned, impatient at my slowness.

'Any man? Or were you thinking of one?'

She hesitated, screwing up her brow. 'Don't know. A daddy. A big big daddy.'

I couldn't read anything into this. All men were daddies to her, as they are to many young children. I needed to steer her round to describing what she had seen, and where, but before I could get any further she suddenly jumped up and started kicking the doll viciously.

'It's her fault!' she shouted, her eyes blazing. 'It's her fault! I told her no! Now look what you've done! I told you to keep your big mouth shut!'

I flinched as the doll's plastic head clattered against the radiator. She was shouting at Julie as if repeating something that she'd heard. I took her arm, picked up the doll, and led the three of us to the sofa. 'Come on, sweet, calm down. There's no point in hurting Julie.'

She cradled the doll in her lap, and stroked her head, whispering words of comfort, trying to make her better. 'Don't worry,' she said. 'You're safe with me. Sshh. Sshh. It was wrong of the man, wasn't it?'

'Yes,' I said, not sure if she was talking to the doll or me. 'What the man did seemed very wrong.' I paused. 'Jodie, sometimes we see things that we don't understand. It looks like people are hurting each other and it can make us very unhappy. Did you see a man kissing a woman there?' I pointed to the doll's legs. 'What we call our private parts?'

'Yes.'

'Where did you see this? On television?'

'In the bedroom and the car,' she replied clearly.

'The car? I don't understand. Was there a television in the car?'

She shook her head.

'But you saw this in a bedroom and a car?'

She nodded.

'Whose car was it?'

'The man's. It was a big van.'

I paused. 'Was it a film, Jodie, or was it real?'

She screwed up her eyes, as though blotting out the image. Her reply was barely audible. 'Real. He was there. The girl and the daddy.'

'And who was the girl? Do you know her name?'

She crushed the doll's face into her chest. 'Jodie. Me. Jodie's bedroom. Daddy's car.'

'Your daddy?'

'Yes.'

Chapter Nine

Disclosure

We sat quietly for some time. I had my arm around Jodie, and she had hers around Julie. My heart was thumping and my mouth was dry. This was the very worst confirmation of my suspicions. The little pieces of evidence had all been pointing this way but I had forced myself not to jump to conclusions and I'd been hoping against hope that what I feared would not be the case. I knew that Jodie had now given me the key to all her suffering, hurt, self-loathing and despair.

I had to continue asking her questions and make the most of this moment when she was willing to talk, but I was holding back. I didn't want to hear the answers, didn't want to know the extent of what had happened to this poor child – but my professional, practical side told me that what she said now would be crucial in determining her future, not only in terms of whether she would return to her parents, but also with a view to a possible prosecution. As part of my foster-care training, I'd attended sessions on aspects of sexual abuse. I had learned that the first disclosure is vital, as children rarely lie, and what they said should be recorded verbatim so that it could be used in court. It was important that I handled it properly. My training had told me that I must not lead her, but had to question her in such a way that would let her tell me in her own words what had happened. Unfortunately, I had not been told much more than this and I had certainly never been in a situation like this before. But I had learned how to deal gently with children who revealed experiences of violence and neglect, and I knew that I would have to draw on that now and hope that it was the right way to help Jodie open up.

I looked down at the doll. She had used it to represent herself, and it was no coincidence that she'd given it a name similar to her own. Children sometimes use role play to dramatize things that they can't express verbally about themselves.

'Jodie,' I said, quietly. 'You've been very brave telling me this. I know how difficult it is. Now I want you to try and tell me everything you remember so that I can help you. OK?'

She nodded.

'Good girl.' I paused and took a breath. I needed to be careful. I couldn't lead her otherwise it would invalidate any evidence which might later be used in court. 'When I came into the room just now you were pretending Julie was you and you were your daddy.' The term stuck in my throat. 'If we do that again do you think you can show me what happened? I know it's difficult, pet.'

She nodded again and I gave her a hug, then took the doll from her arms and lay her on the sofa between us. I put on her pants, and covered them with the dress. If this was to be any use, she needed to show me step by step what had happened, as it would have to stand up under cross-examination.

'OK. So Julie is now Jodie. Where is she? In the car, bedroom, kitchen, garden? You tell me.'

'Not the garden, silly,' she grinned. 'The bedroom.'

'Right, so whose bedroom is it?'

'Mine. Jodie's bedroom. At home.'

'And what is Jodie wearing?'

'Her pyjamas.'

'So we'll pretend these are her pyjamas.' I pointed to the doll's pants. 'Is Jodie in bed or hasn't she got in yet?'

'In bed,' she stated categorically.

'And is the light on or off?'

'Off.'

'Now tell me, is Jodie asleep or awake?'

'Sleep.' She screwed up her eyes to demonstrate.

'OK, good girl. So Jodie is asleep in her bed. Now what happens?'

We both looked at the doll. She thought for a moment, then stood and went over to the door. 'I'm coming in,' she growled, broadening her shoulders and stamping across the floor, in her interpretation of an adult male.

'You're coming into Jodie's bedroom? Who are you?'

'The daddy. My daddy. I'm in Jodie's bedroom now.'

She stomped up to the doll, then hesitated and looked at me.

'Do you want me to move?' I asked.

'Over there.' She pointed to the far corner of the room, by the door.

I walked into the corner and stood as unobtrusively as I could. I was trying to make sure I remembered every detail, as I would need to write it all down later, as accurately as possible. I watched as she leaned over the doll, lifted up its dress, then roughly pulled down the pants and took them off. There was no self-consciousness, as she parted the doll's legs, and nuzzled her head deep between the open thighs. She made low grunting noises as she had before, then flattened herself on top of the doll, her head overlapping, face down into the sofa. Her bottom began rising and falling in a rhythmic jerk, and she breathed louder and louder. Her head came up and she let out a long groan before lying completely still. It was an accurate portrayal of sexual intercourse. I felt sick to the pit of my stomach.

The room was quiet. I looked at the raped doll, and tried to hide my revulsion and desperate pity for this poor little girl. No eight-year-old should be able to do this, or know of such things, or have suffered them. I could hardly bear the thought of what she had been through, and was filled with terrible rage towards the animal who'd done this to his own daughter. My eyes stung with tears of anger and sadness, but I blinked them back.

I took a deep breath. This wasn't a time for my emotions. I needed to be calm and dispassionate for Jodie's sake. She wasn't embarrassed, but climbed off Julie and came over to me. 'Did I do well?' she asked, unfazed.

I smiled weakly. 'You're a brave girl, Jodie.'

But it hadn't taken bravery. Jodie had shown no self-consciousness or hesitation; it was almost as if this had been part of what Jodie regarded as normal life. I took her hand and led her to the sofa, where we sat side by side, both looking at Julie. I was aware that there were some discrepancies I needed to clarify. I gave her hand a little squeeze.

'You did very well, Jodie. There are just a few things I'm not sure about. I want you to try and think back and answer my questions. If you don't know or can't remember, say so. Don't guess or make it up, all right?'

She nodded.

I kept hold of her hand, and turned sideways to look at her. Her expression was completely blank. 'Just now, you were pretending to be your daddy, right?'

She nodded again.

'And the real Jodie was asleep in bed with the lights off?'

Another nod.

'If you were asleep, how do you know he came into the bedroom like you showed me? He might have crept in on tiptoe, or even crawled across the floor. You were asleep with your eyes closed, weren't you?'

She thought for a moment.

'If you don't know, or can't remember, say so,' I reminded her.

'I can,' she said. 'I was sleep sometimes, and sometimes I was awake.'

'I understand. Do you remember what he was wearing?'

'Jeans and top,' she said without hesitation. 'He always wears them.'

'Did he keep them on or did he take anything off?'

'He took the zip off.'

I assumed she meant he undid the zip, but again I needed to clarify. 'Can you show me what you mean?'

She stood, undid the top button of her jeans and pulled down the zip.

'I see. And did he stay like that while he was on top of you?'

'No. More.' She dropped her jeans to her ankles, and was about to pull down her pants.

'OK. Leave them on, just tell me.'

'His pants down with his jeans,' she said.

'Round his ankles?'

'Yes.'

'I understand. Pull your jeans up again, good girl.' I helped her to do up the button, and settled her beside me on the sofa.

'Was Daddy naughty, Cathy?' she asked. Her brow creased as she thought about this.

'Yes he was, Jodie. Very naughty.' I'm not supposed to make value judgements about the parents, but there was no question in my mind that Jodie had to know immediately that this was very wrong and that she was in no way to blame.

'Naughty Daddy,' she said, and thumped her fist hard on her knee. 'He hurt me. I want to hurt him. See how he likes it.'

I put my arm around her, and drew her to me. I wished I had it in my power to draw out her hurt and heal her. 'It's all right, Jodie. You're safe with me now. It won't happen again, I promise.'

'OK, Cathy,' she said, far too easily appeased. I knew that this placid acceptance and lack of emotion meant that we had come nowhere near the heart of her suffering.

'Jodie, you said just now he hurt you. Can you tell me how?' It was a dreadful question, but I knew it was one she would be asked later by the Child Protection Officer, and it was important to get her initial answer on record.

'He made my tummy sore, here.' She pushed her hand between the top of her legs. 'And he wet himself and it tasted horrible.'

'Tasted? Did he put something in your mouth?'

She screwed up her face and made a spitting motion. 'When we was in the car, he weed in my mouth.'

I turned away to hide my reaction. I was burning with anger and humiliation, the humiliation which Jodie should have felt, but didn't. I wasn't about to tell her it wasn't wee. There was no point, and the naïve terminology, using the only point of reference she had, not only made it all the more pitiful, but also underlined its authenticity. I had no doubt she was telling the truth.

I turned to look at her again. 'One last thing, Jodie, I need to know. Did this happen once or lots of times?'

'Lots, Cathy. Naughty Daddy. Cathy, why are you crying?'

I couldn't help myself any longer. I was weeping. 'Because I've heard something sad, sweet.'

'Why is it sad?'

The fact that she didn't understand the horrendous nature of what had happened to her made it even worse. 'Because this is a very bad thing, Jodie, and it should never happen to anybody.'

'Yes. Naughty Daddy,' she said again. 'Can I have my lunch now?'

Chapter Ten

Reporting

I considered cancelling the tutor, but she was probably already on her way. Besides, Jodie was looking forward to seeing her, and I needed the time to phone Jill and tell her what had happened, without being overheard.

My mind was reeling from the disclosures. I couldn't help replaying them over and over in my mind, hearing and seeing the awful truth as portrayed through the words and actions of an innocent eight-year-old girl. It was hard to get the frightful images she'd evoked out of my mind, and as I went about the homely, normal actions of making lunch the horror of what I had just learned overlaid everything I did. It felt as though an awful poison had been released into the atmosphere, and I couldn't shake the sense of dread and revulsion that engulfed me.

Jodie, on the other hand, seemed to have recovered quickly, and devoured her sandwiches, crisps and yoghurt, then asked for more.

'You've had enough,' I said, ignoring the protests that followed.

In the conservatory, I cleared the small table that would act as a desk, and laid out some paper and pencils ready for Nicola's arrival. Jodie followed me round, excited at the prospect of seeing her tutor again. When the doorbell rang she flew to answer it, but then remembered my warning, and waited for me to join her.

'Good girl,' I said, and she gave me a hug.

I'd met Nicola briefly at the pre-placement meeting, and I'd been immediately impressed. Her calm, firm approach was exactly what Jodie needed. Jodie clearly shared my enthusiasm, as she greeted Nicola like a long-lost friend. Nicola seemed pleased to see her too, and she chatted pleasantly to Jodie as she took off her coat and gathered her things together.

We went through to the conservatory, where Jodie clambered into her seat, and started scribbling furiously on the paper I'd laid out. In a good impersonation of Mary Poppins, Nicola delved into her large upholstered bag, and brought out a huge assortment of workbooks, sheets and brightly coloured teaching aids. Jodie was mesmerized.

'We'll get started now,' Nicola said efficiently. 'I usually take a break halfway through. Perhaps we could discuss her progress then?'

'That's fine. I'll bring some drinks and snacks for half time.' I checked she had all she needed, then left them to it, grateful to have been relieved of the responsibility, if only for a couple of hours. Upstairs, I closed my bedroom door so I wouldn't be overheard, then perched on the bed with the phone at my side. I ran through what I was going to say. I hadn't had time to write up my log notes yet, but it was all still clear in my head, and depressingly vivid. I keyed in the numbers, and the secretary answered.

'Jill, please. It's Cathy.'

'I'll put you through.'

A click, then Jill's voice. 'Hello Cathy, is everything all right?'

'No. It's not. Jodie's been sexually abused. I'm sure of it. She couldn't make up this lot.' I quickly ran through the disclosures, explaining how Jodie had used the doll to tell me, and repeating what she'd said almost word for word.

Jill was silent for a second, and then asked, 'How are you, Cathy? No one had any idea.'

No idea? Knowing what I now knew, it was hard to believe that no one could have guessed what was going on – but I had to give the Social Services the benefit of the doubt. Obviously if anyone had suspected what was happening, Jodie would have been removed earlier. But how could they have missed all the signs, and for so long? Perhaps they'd focused on the obvious physical abuse of knocks and burns and broken bones, rather than a deeper and more vicious evil.

Now that I didn't have to control my emotions in front of Jodie, I could feel the shock and upset welling up in me.

My eyes pricked and my vision blurred as hot tears filled them. I felt such an awful mixture of impotent fury and utter sadness on Jodie's behalf. Nevertheless, I couldn't let myself fall to pieces. I had to be strong, for Jodie's sake. I took a deep breath. 'I'm upset, obviously. But at least it's out in the open. And it does explain why she's so disturbed. In fact, it explains a lot of things – it's no wonder she wants to hurt herself and has shut herself off from the world. And, Jill, it sounds like it's been going on for years. She was quite matter-of-fact in the way she described it, as if it was normal.'

There was another pause. I knew Jill was affected by what I had told her. Revelations of sexual abuse are something that anyone in children's social work will encounter, but they never lose their power to shock and horrify, and Jodie's story was particularly appalling. The idea that a small child could have been undergoing this kind of ordeal over a period of years was almost too awful to contemplate.

After a moment's silence, Jill swung into action. 'Right, I'll contact Eileen as soon as we've finished. We'll have to look at contact ASAP. I'll need your notes. Can you write them up while the tutor's there and email me over a copy?'

'I'll do my best.'

'Jodie obviously trusts you, Cathy, more than she's trusted anyone before. She's been in care for four months and said nothing. What I don't understand is where was the mother while all this was going on.'

'I know. From the way Jodie told it, it's hard to imagine that her mother didn't have any idea. But I just don't know. She wasn't mentioned.'

'Would Jodie answer a direct question if you asked?'

'I'm not sure. She told me this, but it was as a result of playing with the doll. I think it was triggered by being in the lift.'

'The lift?'

'Yes. When we went shopping, she was scared in the lift, so much so that I had to stop it and take the escalator. It was like she equated the fear to being scared with her father, and I think that may have been the catalyst for the disclosure. Do you want me to ask about her mother?'

'Yes. But don't push it. It might all come out now she's started, or it might take time. See what you can find out and get as much information as you can – obviously, as gently as possible.' I heard Jill draw her breath in sharply. 'For Christ's sake, she's been on the at-risk register since birth and there's been nothing! Someone's head is on the block for this.'

Jill was angry, understandably, just as I was. Although her role was mainly supervisory, Jill cared deeply for the children we fostered. You couldn't do this kind of work without becoming emotionally involved.

'You know, Jill,' I added, 'she talks a lot of stuff and nonsense with all her imaginary friends. Sometimes it's hard to get a word of sense out her. But I've never seen her so clear and focused as when she was describing this. It was like she was a different person.'

'Thank goodness she's with you. Let me get things moving and speak to you later. If there's anything else call me straight away.'

'OK.'

I replaced the receiver and leaned back, daunted by the responsibility. Now Jodie had opened up, there was no way I could terminate the placement, whatever she threw at me. Without realizing it, Jodie had invested a lot of trust by telling me. I couldn't let her feel that her trust had been misplaced. I stood up and went downstairs. As I passed the lounge I could hear Nicola reading a series of short words, which Jodie was repeating in her childish voice; she sounded like a four-year-old.

I continued along the hall to the front room, took the foster carer's log out of my desk, and started writing up my notes. I wrote quickly, trying to get everything down as accurately as possible, and I'd covered a page and a half when the phone rang. I answered immediately, expecting Jill or Eileen.

'Hello?' I said. There was no reply.

'Hello?' I said again.

Still nothing. Yet the line was open, someone was on the other end. I listened, and thought I heard a rustle as though someone had jolted the receiver. Perhaps it was a child trying to get through, hesitant, wondering if they had the right number. Perhaps it was my friend Pat, who now lived in South Africa, and phoned once a month – there was often a problem with the connection. I tried once more. 'Hello?'

The line went dead. I hung up, then dialled 1471. The automated voice spoke, 'You were called today at 2.20 p.m. We do not have the caller's number.'

I stood for a moment pondering, then returned to my desk. Could it have been Jodie's parents? In theory, they shouldn't have had any of my personal details, but years of fostering had made me naturally suspicious. I finished writing up my notes, then began typing them on to a Word document. A few minutes later I heard Jodie bounding down the hall.

'Cathy! It's break time. Where's me trainers? We're going to the park.'

'The garden,' corrected Nicola, from the back room.

I clicked 'Save' then went into the hall and helped her into her trainers and coat. She rushed through to the conservatory and I opened the door to let her out. Nicola joined me at the French windows, and we stood watching Jodie's uncoordinated efforts to set the swing in motion.

'Poor kid,' Nicola said, then she turned to me. 'Cathy, she said something rather worrying earlier and I think you should know.' I met her gaze. 'It was while we were working on the letter T. One of the words I gave her was T for trousers. I showed her a picture of a pair of trousers, and she got very annoyed and wouldn't look at it. Then she said, "My daddy takes his trousers off. He's naughty, isn't he?"'

'I understand where that's come from,' I said, and I briefly explained the nature of Jodie's allegations, without giving specific details; confidentiality has to be respected, even with the tutor. 'I've alerted her social worker,' I added. 'I take it nothing like that's been said before?'

'Not to me, but there was that episode at Hilary and Dave's. I expect they told you.'

'No.'

'Oh. Well, I'm not sure exactly what happened, but Dave told the social worker that at times Jodie behaved as though she fancied him. She was flirting, and going into his bedroom when Hilary wasn't there. I understand they called an end to the placement when she tried to touch him through his trousers.'

'No, I wasn't told,' I said, my voice tight, 'and I should have been. I've got a son of seventeen. It's very bad social work practice.'

I knew from experience that dealing with Social Services meant coping with an endless series of petty mistakes and failings. The sheer size of the huge machine, and the number of cogs involved, meant that errors were constantly being made. I was used to that, and I could deal with it. I understood that human error happens and that, with so many cases to process, mistakes are made. Nevertheless, I wanted to trust that when something important happened, something that had immediate relevance to a child's state of mind or health, or the vital decisions being made on that child's behalf, then people would take care and be extra sure that things were done correctly.

Looking back, I could see obvious instances of sexualized behaviour before today's revelation: I had seen Jodie with her hands down her knickers, furiously masturbating in public like no normal eight-year-old child would; I'd seen her trying to climb into bed with Adrian and occasionally sidle up to him, try to sit next to him or grin and bat her eyelids at him. Flirting was the word for it, if I'd thought about it properly. The problem was that Jodie took up so much of my time, energy and mental strength that I rarely had the opportunity to stand back and observe her objectively and analyse her behaviour. It was obvious now that she was treating Adrian in a sexual manner because her experiences at the hands of her father had taught her to view all males as sexual beings first and foremost. Everything was beginning to fall into place. Now I realized that this was part of a pattern, and that others had noticed it too.

If there had been evidence before of sexualized behaviour, why hadn't anyone begun to come to the obvious conclusion – that someone was sexually abusing Jodie? And why on earth had I not been told about her behaviour towards her previous carer?

I bit back my anger. None of this was Nicola's fault and I didn't want to dump my frustrations on her.

After fifteen minutes we called Jodie in from the garden. I helped her off with her trainers, then returned to the front room and continued typing from my log, while Nicola and Jodie returned to their session.

Once I'd finished, I emailed the file to Jill. Perfect timing! I'd just turned off the PC, as Jodie marched into the room.

'We're done! Come and see me work!'

I went through and admired the letter and number work, then arranged the next session for Thursday, and Jodie and I saw Nicola out. As soon as she'd gone the phone started ringing, and it didn't stop for the rest of the afternoon. Jill told me the team leader had convened an emergency strategy meeting, with the time and venue to be announced shortly. She would let me know when there was any more information.

Next, Eileen called me. I was glad to hear from her, but I didn't get quite the response I'd been hoping for. Somehow, she didn't seem to be too shocked or horrified by what the child in her charge had suffered.

'I've heard what's happened,' she said in her flat way. 'Has Jodie said any more since?'

'Not much more, but she did make a comment to her tutor today,' I said, and told her what Jodie had said to Nicola. I reminded myself that social workers often have to retain a bit of distance and put up walls between themselves and their cases, in order to protect themselves from getting too involved emotionally and becoming unable to do their job properly. Nevertheless, I couldn't help feeling that Eileen just didn't seem very bothered, or to empathize with Jodie at all.

'Right,' said Eileen with a sigh, as she noted down what I'd said. It almost seemed as though the most depressing aspect of all this for Eileen was the amount of extra work it would involve for her.

I took a deep breath and asked about Jodie's relationship with the previous carer, Dave.

'It'll be on the file if there is anything,' she said, using the same excuse as last time.

I felt like saying, 'Well, read the bloody file then!' but settled instead for a repeat of the more diplomatic, 'I'd be grateful if you could give me any relevant background information. It's even more important now.'

I put the phone down, frustrated. Really, this wasn't something I should have had to tell her. Why hadn't Jodie's social worker familiarized herself with the case by now? She obviously still hadn't read the file – neither had she been to visit Jodie yet. They barely knew each other and good social work practice said that she should be establishing a relationship with the child for whom she was legally responsible. Nor had she offered to come round now, to offer her support to Jodie and demonstrate her concern.

Thank goodness for Jill. She seemed to appreciate the gravity of the situation and phoned again to tell me that the strategy meeting had been convened for later the same morning. Because Jodie wasn't in school, and it was too short notice to find a babysitter, Jill said she would go in my place, and let me know the outcome.

Sally, the guardian ad litem appointed by the court to represent Jodie's interests, phoned next. I'd liked Sally right from the start: she showed exactly the right mix of professionalism and concern that reassured me that the right steps would be taken for Jodie. She called to hear from me in person the details of what had happened to Jodie – and she said how sorry she was, and how dreadful that the abuse had not been discovered before. She had to be objective, of course, but it was clear that Jodie's case had touched her, and I appreciated her showing that. Once again, I repeated the details of Jodie's disclosures. Sally thanked me for all I was doing, and gave me her home telephone number in case anything else should emerge.

Finally, the phone stopped ringing. I put the kettle on, and tried to settle Jodie with play dough, but she was having none of it. She was high on the frenzy of activity, rightly believing that it related to her. Luckily, Paula and Lucy arrived home from school, and they distracted her long enough to allow me to collect my thoughts.

A little while later, the phone rang again. It was Jill.

'Hi, Cathy. I'm just calling to let you know the outcome of the strategy meeting. Contact with both of Jodie's parents has been suspended with immediate effect, until further notice. Can you tell Jodie please?'

'So she's not seeing her mum either?' I asked, surprised.

'No. Until they know more, they're playing safe.'

'All right. I'll explain to her. Goodness knows how she'll take it.'

'As we said earlier, it would be great if you could try and find out where the mother was while the abuse was taking place.'

'I'll try.'

'Between you, me and the gatepost, this looks like one hell of a balls-up by Social Services. All hell's broken loose while they try and find out how this could have happened.'

I hung up and looked at the clock; it was already 5.30, and I hadn't even thought about dinner yet. I wearily went through to the conservatory, where Paula and Lucy were doing a good job helping Jodie model the dough. I decided to deal with the contact first, as I didn't want her to feel in any way responsible for not seeing her parents.

'I need to have a chat,' I said to the girls. 'I'll explain later.' They took my meaning and left. 'Thanks for your help,' I called after them.

'I'll explain later,' Jodie repeated. I heard the girls laugh.

I squatted down beside her and began talking to her about being safe, keeping safe, and how safe she felt with me.

Obligingly she said, 'I wasn't safe with my daddy, was I, Cathy?'

'No you weren't, pet. And because of that, Eileen feels it would be better if you didn't see either of your parents for a while, until it's all sorted out.'

'OK, Cathy,' she said, not in the least perturbed. 'I'll tell her.' Then she stood up, and started a conversation with herself, in which she told Jodie she wasn't seeing Mummy or Daddy because she had to be safe.

That was too easy, I thought. It's not normal. After all, she'd been with them for eight years. I'd dealt with many children who'd been neglected or even abused, and no matter what they'd been through, they always had some emotional connection with their parents. I'd never seen a reaction like this before. I moved on to the second matter of Mum's presence during the abuse. Jodie sat down again, and picked up a lump of multicoloured dough.

'Jodie, you know what you were telling me earlier? Can you remember where your mummy was while your daddy was in your bedroom?'

'It's a cat!' she exclaimed, pulling the dough into an elongated pear shape.

'Is it? That's nice.' I leaned closer. 'Jodie, when your daddy was in your bedroom doing naughty things, where was your mummy?'

She shrugged and curled her tongue over her top lip in concentration.

'Was she in the house, Jodie, or out? Did you tell her what he was doing?'

'I told her,' she said, thumping the dough with the palm of her hand. 'I told her. I said I want a cat. Get me one now.' Then she was off, in search of Toscha. I didn't pursue it. I'd have to wait until she was ready.

Chapter Eleven

Cooking and Cleaning

In the middle of the night I was woken by the most terrifying screams. I didn't have time for my dressing gown and slippers. I hurried out of bed and rushed on to the landing, dizzy from standing too quickly. I flung open Jodie's bedroom door. She was on the floor thrashing from side to side, screaming at the top of her voice, gripped in a paroxysm of fear.

'Jodie!' I shouted, trying to break through her nightmare. 'Jodie, it's Cathy!' But her screams drowned out my cry.

I dropped to my knees and took hold of her hands. Her face was screwed shut, and she was clawing at her eyes, trying to gouge them out. I pinned one arm under my knee, and the other above her head. She was fighting for all she was worth, and her strength was incredible, as though the demons had risen up to do battle against her.

'Jodie! Open your eyes. It's Cathy. You're safe with me.'

Her teeth gnashed and her feet drummed the floor. I held on, and kept talking. 'Jodie! You're safe in your room. It's a nightmare. Nothing can harm you here.'

The screams peaked, then died, and her body went limp. I heard a gush of water, then a stain appeared on her pyjamas. Her eyes flickered open, and her head slowly turned. She looked up at me, fixed and staring, then turned her head and vomited. It was like the end of a seizure.

'All right, Jodie. It's OK. Everything's going to be all right.'

She murmured, and her eyes started to focus. I relaxed my grip, and cradled her against me. The smell of vomit and urine made my stomach heave. 'You're safe, Jodie. Nothing can harm you here. I'll take care of you. Don't worry, pet.' I gently rocked her.

She whimpered, then wrapped her arms tightly around my waist. 'I don't want it in my mouth. Tell him. Tell him it makes me sick, Cathy.'

'It won't happen again, pet. I promise. You're safe.'

'I told her to make him stop. I did. But she wouldn't listen.'

'Who, Jodie? Who did you tell?' She started to cry again. 'It's OK. Don't worry. You can tell me when you're ready. Only when you're ready, pet.'

I held her until she was completely calm, then brought her to her feet, and led her to the bathroom. I cleaned us both, then helped her into a clean pair of pyjamas. She was silent and exhausted. I steered her round the landing and tucked her into bed, then sat on the floor next to her, stroking her hair.

Eventually, she fell asleep. I left the light on as I crept out of her room and gently closed the door. I returned to my bedroom for a clean nightdress, my dressing gown and slippers, then went downstairs. It was 3 a.m. Jodie's screams must have woken the others, but they seemed to have turned over and gone back to sleep.

In the kitchen I filled a bucket with hot water, added some disinfectant and left our nightclothes to soak. There was little point in returning to bed yet. I wouldn't be able to sleep – I was too full of Jodie's suffering, and I half expected her to wake again any minute. I hadn't seen anything like this before in any child I'd looked after, and it had left me stunned and drained. I leaned heavily against the work surface, and watched the clock on the oven tick over another minute. Toscha purred around my legs, uncertain if it was time for breakfast. I poured her a saucer of milk, then made myself a mug of tea.

My thoughts went to the packet of cigarettes on top of the broom cupboard. I'd put them there when I was giving up, six months ago. I had managed to quit by only having one when it was essential, and making them difficult to reach. I dragged the breakfast stool into place and climbed up. I felt a stab of guilt as I opened the packet and slid one out. The matches were in the childproof cupboard under the sink; I had thrown all the lighters away. I unlocked the back door and stepped outside. I'd never smoked in the house.

The night was cold and clear. I couldn't see the moon, but the deep black sky was a blanket of twinkling stars. The cold air was a relief from the heavy atmosphere which now pervaded the house. The match flared in the darkness, as though highlighting my transgression. I held it to the tip and inhaled. I felt that old familiar rush, at once intoxicating and reassuring, then another surge of guilt, but I inhaled again, concentrating on the ritual, allowing myself to think of nothing else. By the time I'd finished, I wasn't sure if I felt better or worse.

Returning inside, I put the matches back in the cupboard, and secreted the cigarettes in a more accessible drawer. It was still quiet upstairs, so I went into the lounge and switched on the television. There was ice hockey on Channel Five. I turned the volume down and gazed absently, while my thoughts travelled faster than the puck. Whatever had that child suffered? I could only begin to guess. And who was this 'her' whom she had told? Her mum? An aunt? A teacher at school? I was amazed that nothing had been picked up before. Jodie had been on the at-risk register since birth, so she should have been visited by social workers every couple of months. I couldn't believe that none of them noticed anything untoward in her relationship with her father, as it sounded like the abuse had been going on for years. Surely her mother must have known – but that was another avenue that I couldn't bear to go down yet. At some point I must have dropped off, for suddenly the ice rink had been transformed into a weather map, and dark rain clouds were covering most of southern England. The clock in the corner of the screen said it was nearly 6.30, and the house was still silent. Perhaps telling me about the abuse had proved cathartic for Jodie; perhaps she'd be less disturbed as a result. I crept upstairs, and took the opportunity for a long, relaxing shower. As the hot water drummed on to my neck and shoulders, I felt the tension dissipate, and prepared myself for a new day.

As I dressed, I felt rejuvenated and ready for action. I hung up the towels, and heard Jodie stir. Within minutes she was off, screaming abuse and trashing her room. I went in and tried to resettle her. When this failed, I told her off, and when that failed, I ended up having to remove the television as a punishment.

Fearful of the damage she might do if left unattended, I allowed her downstairs to breakfast with Lucy and Paula, which turned out to be a massive error of judgement. From the moment she sat down, she tormented the girls by poking and kicking, digging her spoon into their breakfasts, and generally making herself disagreeable. Paula left most of her Weetabix, in a bid to escape, while Lucy finally gave her a tap on the hand and flounced off to finish her toast in her bedroom. By the time Adrian appeared, my nerves were in tatters, and my morning serenity had all but vanished.

'What you staring at?' she demanded as he sat down. Jodie seemed to have a particular fear of being looked at, and was never happy if she felt she was being observed, getting upset with whoever was looking at her. I'd noticed when she arrived that she avoided eye contact and preferred to look at people's chests when they were talking to her. Similarly, she'd never been able to relax, always jumping if someone walked into the room as if she was on constant alert and ready to take flight if she had to. I hadn't really thought about it before, but now, in the light of what she'd told me, everything took on a sinister significance.

Adrian shifted awkwardly and concentrated on his breakfast.

I saw her grin, that ghoulish contortion of her face, then quick as a flash she scooped up a handful of porridge, and hurled it at him.

'Jodie! Stop that!' I cried, and took her bowl away. 'That was naughty. Now I've got to clean his blazer. Look at the mess you've made.'

She sneered. 'That's what you're here for. To clean and cook. Get on with it, bitch.'

Adrian couldn't believe what he'd heard, and neither could I.

'I beg your pardon?' I said. She looked as if she was about to repeat it so I interrupted. 'Don't you dare say that. If you think I've got nothing better to do than clean up after you, you're very much mistaken. You've lost your television today, and if there's any more it'll be for the rest of the week.'

I washed her hands, sponged down Adrian's blazer, then cleared away the breakfast things. I didn't speak to Jodie or make eye contact with her. I wanted her to feel my disapproval. I appreciated that she had suffered a great deal in her life, but the only hope for her future was for her to try and understand how to function in a normal family and in society. She had to learn what behaviour was acceptable and what kind of treatment of others was entirely wrong.

Only when I'd loaded the dishwasher and seen Adrian, Lucy and Paula off to school did I make the peace. 'No more swearing or throwing things around. Do you understand? It's naughty, and you're not a naughty girl.'

'No. I'm sorry, Cathy,' she said, temporarily chastened.

'OK. Would you like me to read you a story now?'

'Yes please, Cathy.'

I gave her a hug, and we went into the lounge, where she picked up half a dozen books and dumped them on my lap. We sat side by side on the sofa, and Jodie asked for another hug. I put my arms around her, and thought now might be a good time to ask her about her mum, as she was subdued and reasonably cooperative.

'Before I start, Jodie, I want to ask you something about last night. You remember you were upset and I came into your room?' She looked at me blankly, which was nothing unusual, so I decided to continue. 'You said you told someone about what Daddy was doing? You said you told her to make him stop.' She was still looking at me, and her brow furrowed in concentration as she tried to remember. 'Jodie, who was it that you told? Can you remember? I know it was a woman because you said "her".'

She pulled slightly away, and took the top book off the pile. 'Free 'ickle pigs. I told the free 'ickle pigs, and they blew my house down.'

I smiled inwardly at this quite witty diversion. 'No, you didn't. Now be sensible. It's important.'

'Can't remember. Can't. Really, I can't, Cathy.'

'OK darling, let's read.'

That afternoon, I phoned Jill, and told her I hadn't had any success. 'She genuinely doesn't seem to remember. I'll have to wait until she's ready.'

'OK. You're doing everything you can, Cathy. This is not unheard of. In some cases, when a child is emotionally traumatized, the brain can shut down to protect the child from the horrendous memories. Once the child feels safe again, they may be able to release a bit more, but only to the extent that the brain feels able to cope with it.'

It sounds like a mechanism I could do with, I thought to myself. I finished my conversation with Jill feeling a little comforted. I could only hope that this was a turning point for Jodie. Now that she'd been able to reveal what had happened to her, perhaps she would begin to get better.

I couldn't have been more wrong.

Chapter Twelve

Monsters

It was weeks before Jodie felt safe enough to reveal any more, and during that time her behaviour, far from improving, deteriorated still further. She became increasingly violent, not only towards me and the other children, but also towards herself. For some reason, she frequently became distressed at the dinner table. In the middle of a meal, she would suddenly start clawing at her face, or tearing at her hair. At other times, she would scratch and pinch her arms, leaving marks and bruises. I would quickly restrain her, of course, wrapping her in my arms until she'd calmed down.

She was also defecating again. After the first couple of instances, she had calmed down and stopped messing herself, but now it started up again and was worse than before. Now she was simply smearing shit all over herself and then, if I didn't get to her quickly enough, over the house. There was no apparent pattern or motive, but she did seem to understand that messing up fabrics would lead to a more severe telling-off than smearing impermeable surfaces (such as the walls or banister) and she appeared to make a point of avoiding getting it on the sofa and curtains. As usual, it was impossible to understand Jodie's motives, or even whether she was really aware of what she was doing.

As a result of her activities, the house constantly smelled of disinfectant. One evening as I prepared for bed, I saw that the skin on my hands had become chapped and red, and my fingertips were puckered from all the detergents. This habit of Jodie's was unpleasant for everyone in the house, to say the least, even though we probably have an unusually heightened tolerance of poor hygiene, having dealt with a number of foster children with similar problems. I don't think I'll ever forget the day I looked round one teenage girl's bedroom, trying to find the source of a persistent nasty smell. When I peered behind her wardrobe, I found a stash of used sanitary towels, dating back to when she had first arrived six months before.

Despite the violence, the insults, the excrement, the lack of sleep and numerous other traumas, the children were remarkably patient with Jodie, as they now knew the reason for her behaviour.

Shortly after the first disclosures, I sat down with them one evening and told them about the abuse, and warned them about some of the additional difficult behaviour we might expect. It was important to tell them because Jodie was as likely to disclose to them as to me, so they needed to be prepared. Besides, they were already hearing things that she had started saying. Just as she had with Nicola, she was beginning to drop casual references about what had happened to her into conversations. I had to tell them what she was talking about.

With Paula being only thirteen, there were certain physical aspects of the abuse that I had to explain to her in detail: when Jodie mentioned her father weeing in her mouth, for example, they had to know she meant oral sex. Not only was this embarrassing for all of us, but I was once again reminded of the potentially negative effect fostering might be having on my children. How healthy was it for Paula to learn about sex in this context? Was there a risk that it might harm her relationships in the future?

The children were, as I'd expected, shocked and horrified. I wished that I hadn't had to bring all this into their worlds as well, and it was awful to see them struck dumb as they absorbed the implications of what I was saying. The fact that Jodie's father had done this to her was clearly a difficult and near impossible concept for them to cope with. They were already used to hearing about the difficult backgrounds of other children I'd fostered – it was often important for their own protection that they knew what had happened – but this was beyond all of that.

'As you know, this is strictly confidential,' I reminded them, and they nodded at me, their faces serious. They'd always understood that anything they learned in the house had to stay there and was not to be repeated to anyone. I trusted them completely.

After we had this chat, the children became even more tolerant of Jodie's behaviour. They tried to spend more time playing with Jodie, and remain sympathetic even when she was screaming at them to 'Get out of my fucking house!', or lunging at them with a kick. Nonetheless, their patience had limits, and when Jodie interrupted one meal by graphically describing how blood had dripped from her finger when her mother had purposely cut it, Lucy lost patience. 'Gross!' she exclaimed, then she picked up her plate, and took her dinner into the living room.

One summer's afternoon, when Jodie had been with us for about four months, Jill came round for one of our regular meetings. Although, being a link worker, she had no statutory obligation to visit us (unlike Jodie's social worker), good practice dictated that she should come round every four to six weeks to see how things were going, offer a bit of support and check my log notes.

As it was a glorious sunny day, we decided to take Jodie to the park. Despite having been up most of the night with nightmares and general distress, as she often was, Jodie was full of energy, and restless to get out into the sunshine. I, on the other hand, was simply worn out.

'So, how's she doing?' asked Jill, as we walked through the park's immaculately tended flower garden. Jodie was marching a few metres ahead, anxious to get to the playground, and apparently oblivious to the dazzling array of colours and scents around her.

'She's getting worse,' I replied. 'She's having more and more of those hysterical screaming fits, for no apparent reason, and once she recovers she seems barely aware of what's happened. That's why Nicola didn't stay for the tutoring this morning; about once a week Jodie's simply unmanageable, so we have to give up and cancel the session.'

'And how's she sleeping?'

'Not wonderfully. She wakes up at five, sometimes earlier. She had been learning to stay in her room and play quietly. But over the last few weeks she's started having dreadful nightmares, which seem to be more like hallucinations. They're completely real to her, and sometimes they seem to continue after she's woken up. It's awful, you wake up to her screaming, and find her writhing on the floor, then she's like that off and on for the rest of the night. It's got to the point where I keep a chair outside her room on the landing, so once I've settled her the first time I just sit there waiting. If I'm lucky I get to doze for a few minutes, until she starts up again!'

'You must be absolutely shattered.'

We arrived at the playground, where Jodie jumped on a swing and started working herself higher and higher.

'Careful, Jodie,' I warned, then stood with Jill on the grass verge, where Jodie could see me watching. She had no sense of danger or instinct to protect herself, and would swing out of control, then fall off, if allowed to.

'How did the hearing test go?' Jill asked. I had taken Jodie for a test the previous week, as there had been occasions when she didn't seem to hear what was going on around her.

'I think it's OK. We're waiting for the doctor's letter but the nurse seemed to think there was nothing wrong with her.'

'So she is shut down?' asked Jill, referring to the way some badly abused children seem to switch off their senses, as a way of protecting themselves. If you can't see, hear or feel anything, it might not be happening. When they shut down in this way, these children become less aware of what's going on around them, and less conscious of things that we usually take for granted, like noticing the pleasant taste of food, or recognizing that the water in the bath is too hot.

'I think so,' I replied. 'There are certainly signs. Hardly anything gives her any pleasure, and she doesn't seem to be sensitive to temperature: even when it was really cold, I had to fight with her every day to stop her wearing just a T-shirt and shorts. There are days when she is on a relatively even keel, I suppose, though I couldn't describe even those as good days. If we manage to get through a day without a full-scale tantrum, we've done extremely well. That's very rare.'

Jill looked at me sympathetically. 'You're working tremendously hard, I know that. You're doing a brilliant job, you really are.'

I smiled weakly. Compliments were nice, but what I really wanted was a good night's sleep. I was constantly exhausted, and although my patience was just about lasting out I felt at the end of my tether.

We started walking back, pleased that the outing had so far passed without incident. The sun was still bright, but I was keen to capitalize on Jodie's good behaviour. If we could get home without any drama, it would allow me to praise and reward her, and we could set a positive precedent for how a day out should go. Jill and I each took one of Jodie's hands, as we ambled back through the park.

'I must admit I'm concerned about the absence of any improvement,' I said, using deliberately vague language so that Jodie wouldn't realize that we were talking about her. 'The disturbances are getting worse, especially at night.'

'And have any of the disclosures dealt with the maternal presence as we discussed?'

'No. She tells me about those events time and time again, but there's hardly any new information coming out. Frankly I'm worried sick, things seem to be getting worse rather than better. Is there no practical advice you can give me?' I tried to keep the edge of desperation from my voice.

'No more than you're already doing,' Jill said sympathetically. 'And to be honest there's a limit to what you should be expected to cope with. It's quite possible that the emotional trauma is so severe that only a therapeutic unit can put it right. I tell you what, I'll have a look and see what's available. I won't do anything, I'll just have a look.'

As we reached the corner of my street, I allowed Jodie to run ahead, while Jill and I walked in silence. I had been hoping for some practical advice, but the level of Jodie's disturbance seemed to be outside Jill's experience too. I was disappointed, but I vowed to press on. I saw Jodie had stopped further up, and was crouching with her back to me, intently focused on something in the gutter. 'Jodie,' I called. 'What are you doing? Come here.'

She turned around, grinning, then held up a dead pigeon, proudly displaying it like a trophy. The bird's head slumped sideways, and its breast had been torn open, so that its bloody insides were exposed. Jodie stared at it, fascinated.

'Jodie! Put that down, right now!' I said firmly. She stared at me, then slowly turned away, poking at the pigeon's bloody flesh, and dropped it back in the gutter.

'Yuck,' Jill said.

I cupped Jodie's elbows in my hands from behind and steered her, arms outstretched, towards the house. Jill got straight in her car without coming in, as she had another meeting to go to. I manoeuvred Jodie in through the front door and straight to the kitchen sink. She looked up at me as I filled the bowl with hot water and soap.

'We had a nice time at the park, didn't we, Cathy?'

Her face was flushed, happier than I'd seen her in weeks. I smiled back. I couldn't be angry; after all she hadn't really done anything wrong. But I was concerned at the ghoulish fascination the dead bird had inspired.

The next morning it was clear early on that something was different. Jodie wasn't screaming at five o'clock, nor six, nor seven. I had time to shower, dress and dry my hair. I made the children's packed lunches, and even drank a cup of coffee in peace. Then I started to worry.

I crept up the stairs, tiptoed to Jodie's door, and listened. There was silence. She wasn't even talking to herself, which she usually did continuously, even in her calmer moments. I knocked and went in. She was lying on top of the duvet, flat on her back, with her eyes wide open, staring at the ceiling. She was so still that for a moment I feared she could be dead.

'Jodie?' I shook her shoulder. 'Jodie?' She gave a small twitch at the corner of her eye. 'Jodie? What's the matter? Are you ill?'

She didn't move. Her arms and legs were held straight, so stiff it was like they were encased in concrete. I knew this wasn't a fit, or at least not like any fit I'd ever seen. I placed my palm on her forehead. It was warm, but not feverish.

'Jodie? Can you hear me?'

I shook her again, this time more robustly. 'Jodie, look at me. Tell me what's wrong. It's Cathy. Jodie? Can you hear me?'

She blinked, then slowly turned to look at me. Her pupils were dilated, and there were large dark rings around her eyes. When she spoke, it was in a flat monotone. 'He came here last night. You said he wouldn't, but he did. I know, I know who it was.'

I knelt down, and held her hand tight. 'No sweet, no one came here. You've remembered something and it seems real.'

'I didn't tell. I didn't tell because she saw. She saw, Cathy. She saw, and didn't stop him.'

'Someone saw Daddy do naughty things to you?'

She nodded.

'Who, sweet? Who was it?'

She stared straight at me, eyes wide with terror, her cheeks deathly pale. I could see the pulse throbbing in her neck.

'Mummy. Mummy saw. I said make him stop but she didn't. She laughed and watched. They all did.'

I turned cold. 'They? There were others there?'

'Uncle John, and Ken, and Aunt Bell. They took pictures when Uncle Mike did it.'

'Uncle Mike?'

Her face was blank, she was looking at me and talking, but it was as though she was in a daze.

'He lay on me, same as Daddy. I didn't want to. It hurt. Daddy held me when it was Uncle Mike's turn. I was shouting and screaming, so Daddy put his thing in my mouth. Aunt Bell said, "That'll shut her up." And they all laughed.' She was shaking with fear.

I tried to hide my horror and concentrate on what I was hearing. I needed to make sure I remembered all the names and details, to get as much evidence as I could while she was talking. I didn't know when or if she would open up again. I stroked her forehead, and whispered words of comfort.

'Jodie, you're safe now. The doors are locked and bolted. We have a very good alarm. No one can get in. What they did was the most dreadful thing any adult can do to a child. They are very wicked people, Jodie.'

She nodded, but without conviction. 'They gave me lots of sweets and toys.' She glanced at the overflowing toy boxes.

'Did they buy all these?' I asked. She nodded again. So that's what they were – not presents, not things designed to bring pleasure; they were bribes, to buy silence and compliance. No wonder they meant nothing to her. 'Jodie, good adults don't buy children presents because they've done bad things to them. Was it to stop you telling?'

'It was our secret. They said if I told, horrible things would happen. I'd be taken to a dark cave and a monster would come and chew off my arms. Will he, Cathy?' Her voice rose fearfully. 'Will he come here and bite my arms off?'

'No, absolutely not. The only monsters are those people, and they won't come anywhere near you, ever again. I promise, Jodie.'

She thought about this, and then a sad smile crossed her lips. 'Aunt Bell was nice. She didn't do things. She only watched.'

I shuddered at this twisted logic. 'That's just as bad, Jodie. She watched you being hurt and didn't help. She should have stopped them. That's what I would have done. Where were they when they were watching?'

'In my bedroom.'

'And the car? You once said something about a car? Who was in the car, Jodie?'

'Mummy and Daddy. Mummy took the pictures of Daddy and me. It's a very big car. We was in the back. It was dark. I don't like the dark. The camera made it light up. Will he be told off, Cathy?'

'I sincerely hope so, sweet. All of them. I'll tell your social worker, and she'll tell the police. The police will want to talk to us, but don't worry, I'll be with you.'

I was still holding her hand and stroking her forehead, reluctant to let go. It was well after seven, and I should have been waking the others for school. 'Is there anything else you want to tell me now? You've been very brave and it's important you tell me if there is.'

She shook her head. I cuddled her for some time, then gently eased her into bed, and tried to focus my mind.

'Cathy?' she said suddenly.

'Yes, sweet?'

'Did your daddy do those things to you?'

'No. Absolutely not,' I said. 'Never in a million years. He's a good, kind man. Most adults are.'

'And Paula and Lucy's daddy?'

'No. Paula's daddy never hurt her. Lucy's daddy hit her, which is why she's here. But he didn't hurt her like that.'

'Was it my fault, Cathy? I didn't want to. Mummy said I was lucky. She said it was because he liked me so much. She said I should belt up and enjoy it. She said I was Daddy's girl.'

'She was wrong, Jodie. Parents cuddle their children to show their love. They don't hurt them. And it wasn't your fault, Jodie. Don't you ever believe that.' I gave her another hug, then she asked for the television, and for the first time since arriving she seemed content to stay in bed while the others got up.

I left her room and stood for a moment on the landing, trying to compose myself. I was ice cold and trembling with rage. I could see Jodie being held down by her father. I could see the others watching. I could hear their laughter. It was little wonder she was in the state she was. I knew now where her anger had come from, and I now shared it. I had not wanted to believe it could be any worse than Jodie's father subjecting her to the vile acts she had described, but now, to my horror, I realized that it was much, much worse than anyone had suspected. She had been the victim of the most awful kind of abuse I could imagine, where not just one of her parents subjected her to the most degrading treatment any child could suffer but where both of them were complicit, and so were other adults. I could feel the nausea churning in me as I realized that it was not only her parents, in their position of precious care and trust, but many others who had conspired to turn Jodie's world into a nightmare of suffering and perversion; they had reversed everything that should be good in a child's life, turning it into something so deeply wicked and evil that I couldn't find the words to describe what I thought of it.

No wonder the poor child had cut off the world around her. No wonder she had no sense of being able to relate to other people, when all she had experienced was cruelty and pain. No wonder she tried to beat herself, maim herself and smeared herself with filth – what else had she ever known?

Somehow I made breakfast, and saw Adrian, Lucy and Paula off to school. As soon as they were gone, I phoned Jill and told her everything.

'It's worse than we thought,' I said. 'Much worse.'

As I reported what Jodie had said, I could sense Jill taking in the scale of what had happened. She breathed in sharply as I told her that Jodie had been abused by a circle of complicit adults, photographed and watched and jeered at.

'Oh my God, Cathy. I can't believe what that child has been through. This should be enough to start a police prosecution,' she said. 'I know it must have been awful to hear all this from her, but you've done a great job.'

I didn't feel like I'd done a good job. I felt as if I'd been party to Jodie's suffering. I felt ashamed to be an adult.

'Do we know how long it's been going on?' she asked.

'I think quite a while. She asked if my father did it to me, and was surprised he didn't. The way she describes it, it sounds like it was the norm, part of everyday life, and it's only now she's realizing it's wrong.' I paused. 'Jill, at what age can a child be raped?'

'Any age. There are cases as young as six months.'

I cringed.

'Cathy, this has all the hallmarks of a paedophile ring. Was she ever shown the photographs?'

'Not as far as I'm aware. She didn't say.'

'OK, write it all down when you have a chance. Eileen's on annual leave...'

'Again?'

'Yes, so I'll speak to Dave Mumby. They'll want a forensic medical and a police memorandum interview. I'll get back to you. How are you coping, Cathy?'

'A damn sight better than Jodie. Bastards!'

Chapter Thirteen

Integration

There's a joke among foster carers that goes like this: How many social workers does it take to change a light bulb? Thirteen. One to find the bulb, and the other twelve to hold a meeting to discuss how best to change it. It's not much of a joke, admittedly, but it does encapsulate how we often feel about the inability of Social Services to take action when it's most needed.

Following Jodie's latest disclosures, Dave Mumby wanted to set up a meeting, but not until Eileen could be present, which wouldn't be until well into the following week, as she was indeed on annual leave. As Jodie's social worker, Eileen had a statutory obligation to visit Jodie in placement every six weeks, and yet the two had still never met. Although Eileen phoned every now and then to get a report on Jodie's progress, I got the impression that it was more to save herself the trouble of having to visit us than any real interest in the case. Perhaps she had a very busy workload – but then, so did all social workers – or maybe she was better than most at not getting too personally involved in a case. Whatever it was, it not only saddened me that Jodie didn't have a social worker to take an interest in her and champion her cause, but it was also highly unprofessional. I wondered if Dave Mumby, her team manager, knew.

Jill reported back to me that the nature of the meeting meant that I wouldn't have to attend, and she would represent us both. In the meantime, she said, Dave had asked if I could focus my attention on finding Jodie a school, as her parents had made a formal complaint about her lack of education. Jodie had left her previous school when she was taken into care, and the speed of her various moves, then her behaviour, had precluded finding her a new one.

I was flabbergasted. Jodie's parents would now know what they were accused of. When a child makes an accusation, the parents are always informed of the nature of the allegation. Moreover, when all contact between Jodie and her parents was abruptly stopped, the reasons would have been given. I was doubly amazed that Dave was acting upon this as a priority, while delaying the meeting.

Jill suggested that I try Harvestbank, which was a local primary school with a good record for taking children with learning and behavioural difficulties. Jodie already had a Statement of Educational Needs, which is a document outlining the child's particular needs, completed after he or she has been assessed by an educational psychologist. Jodie's needs were severe enough that her statement authorized funding to pay for a full-time assistant in whichever school accepted her. This meant, in theory at least, that a school might have an additional incentive to take her, if they were short on funds.

I phoned Harvestbank, and spoke to the deputy head. She was a pleasant lady, who explained very nicely that they had more than their quota of special needs children, and were stretched to the limit. She suggested I try again in six months' time. I thanked her, and hung up.

Opening the Yellow Pages, I highlighted all the primary schools within reasonable travelling distance, and began making the calls. The next four schools gave me the same response: each of them was over their quota, and there was a waiting list. So much for the sweetener of extra funding. I set the phone down, and took a deep breath. I wondered if I should approach the school Adrian and Paula had gone to. It only had a small special needs department, but they knew me and my family, and I had had a good relationship with the staff. I took another deep breath, and dialled the number.

The secretary remembered me, which was nice, and she put me through to the headmaster, Mr Rudman. We exchanged a few pleasantries on the passing of time, and he asked me how Adrian and Paula were doing. I said they were doing well, and buttered him up by telling him what fond memories they had of the school.

'I'm still fostering,' I said, and then explained about Jodie, adding that although she had behavioural problems I had found them manageable. I made light of the rapid succession of foster carers, and said his was the first school that had come to mind; a little white lie, but in aid of a good cause.

'I'll see the statement,' he said, 'although you appreciate I'm not offering a place. It will depend on the level of provision, and whether we can best meet her needs.'

I thanked him effusively, then phoned Jill to arrange for the statement to be faxed over. Buoyed by this, and in dire need of some exercise after nearly an hour on the phone, I rescued Jodie from the congealed heap of paper, glue and paint which had kept her occupied.

'It's a dog!' she exclaimed.

'That's lovely. Now we're going for a walk to the post office.'

I helped her wash her hands, then brushed her hair, and changed her top. By the time we left the house, she looked quite presentable, in a smart yellow T-shirt which I knew was one of her favourites.

There was a pleasant breeze as we walked up the street, but Jodie was anxious, and grabbed my hand as a car drove past.

'Cathy,' she said.

'Yes, Jodie.'

'Is my dad hurting my mum?'

'I hope not, Jodie,' I replied, uncertain quite what she was asking.

'He is,' she responded. 'Poor Mummy.'

We carried on walking, and I watched Jodie as she frowned, apparently still troubled by this idea. Eventually, she looked up at me.

'I don't want him hurting her,' she said, then jutted out her chin, and clenched her fists. 'I'll kill him.'

Again, I wasn't sure what to say. Did she feel guilty about leaving her mother to deal with her father alone? Should I correct her anger, or encourage her to face these issues? It might not have been very professional, but my personal feeling was that she had every right to feel angry, and every reason to want to kill him. I decided to address the possible guilt. 'If he hurts her, Jodie, I think she should leave him, and tell the police. But she's an adult and she can make that decision for herself.'

I hoped she understood what I was trying to say – but then, I wasn't even sure what she was telling me. Was she hinting at domestic violence? Perhaps she had seen her father hitting her mother. Or perhaps she had witnessed them having sex and assumed it must hurt her mother as much as it hurt her.

I changed the subject to something lighter as we reached the high street. We walked past the various shop fronts with their colourful signs and enticing displays, and I remembered how excited I'd felt as a little girl, being taken out shopping by my parents. I could still remember my initial thrill at the strange sights in the fishmonger's window, and the mysterious smells at the shoe-mender's. I looked sadly at Jodie, who was staring straight ahead, alert for danger, and oblivious to the sensory pleasures around her. The world was not a place she could enjoy like any normal child; it lacked excitement and stimulation for her. She had been deadened to everything because of what she had suffered. It was heartbreaking.

I did what I had to do at the post office, and because she had queued patiently by my side I bought Jodie a packet of Smarties as a reward. As we walked back down the high street, I noticed she had gone quiet again.

'What shall we do when we get home, Jodie?' I asked.

She was silent, and I could see her face had set.

'Is something the matter, Jodie?'

'What were they starin' at?' she muttered. 'Don't stare at me.'

'Who, Jodie? In the post office?' I asked. She didn't contradict me, so I continued. 'But no one was staring at you, sweet. They were probably just looking at you because you look so smart in your lovely T-shirt.'

She didn't respond, so I decided to leave it. You could never really persuade Jodie of anything, or have any kind of discussion with her. Caring for Jodie was rather about coping with her needs, and trying to distract her before she could get too upset. We walked a little further, as a middle-aged man in a suit came the other way.

'What's he fuckin' starin' at?' Jodie muttered as he approached. As far as I could see, the man didn't seem to be looking at us at all.

'Jodie, don't be rude.'

As the man got closer, she said it again, louder this time: 'What's he blimmin' starin' at?'

He must have heard this time. I smiled at the man apologetically, and he looked away, embarrassed.

'Jodie, that was rude. You've no reason to worry, no one was staring at you.'

'I'll show 'em,' she muttered. 'No one'll stare at me. I'll kill 'em all!'

Jodie's mood didn't improve once we got home, but for some respite I let her watch *Mary Poppins*, which was her favourite video, while I did some chores. I put on a load of washing, and began emptying the dishwasher, all the while wondering about Jodie's strange behaviour. I had noticed before that she seemed to have a particular anxiety about being stared at; this was one reason why mealtimes had become so unbearable, as she would constantly bark 'What you starin' at?' to anyone looking even vaguely in her direction. I had suspected that this anxiety might have been linked to the abuse, but now, as the extent of it was revealed, her phobia became even more understandable: if there had been a number of people present, watching Jodie, it was no wonder if she had a horror of being looked at.

After about half an hour I'd finished what I needed to do and joined Jodie in the living room, bringing with me a carton of Ribena. She was staring blankly at the screen, while Bert serenaded Mary as they strolled through the magical chalk landscape. After a while, she turned and looked at me, and then came and sat next to me on the sofa.

'You know, you've got really little eyes,' she said.

'Have I?' I said, surprised. If anything, I had always felt my eyes were one of my better features and I was rather proud of them.

'Yeah, really piggy little eyes. Like a little pig. Oink! Oink!' She grinned, as if expecting me to join in the hilarious joke.

'That's not a very nice thing to say, Jodie. Don't be rude. We don't make personal remarks in this house.'

'But you have. Stupid little eyes. That's why you can't even see where you're going. Stupid!'

This was a strange thing to say, and it sounded like something Jodie must have heard before, an insult that had been thrown at her, and that she was now mimicking. Apart from being inaccurate, it had a level of detail and logic which Jodie wouldn't have been able to come up with. Was this something Jodie had been told at home? Before I could pursue this, the phone rang. Oh no, I thought, it will be the school calling to tell me there isn't a place after all. Only a rejection would have come so quickly. I smiled and tried to sound bright. 'Hello,' I answered.

'Hello, is that Margaret Brown of Bowham Close?'

I looked anxiously at Jodie. It was my address but Margaret Brown was the name of Jodie's mother.

'No, it's not. Who's this?'

'Oh, I'm sorry. My mistake. I'm calling from Ear, Nose and Throat at St John's Hospital. About Jodie Brown?'

'Yes. This is Cathy Glass, Jodie's carer.'

'Sorry, I've just found the note on file. The doctor's letter is in the post, together with a prescription for some ear drops. Doctor wants a follow-up appointment for Jodie in a month.'

I made the appointment, noted it in my diary, and hung up. I wasn't happy. I had given specific instructions to the hospital that my details should be kept confidential and, to avoid confusion, should be kept separate from Jodie's parents'. It was clear this hadn't happened. This time they had called me asking for Margaret, but next time they might just as easily call Margaret asking for Cathy Glass. All she would then need to do would be to ask the receptionist to confirm her latest address, and she and her husband would be led straight to my door. Then, Jodie and I would have bigger things to worry about than my piggy little eyes.

Chapter Fourteen

The Park

Eileen returned from her holiday, and Dave was finally able to convene his strategy meeting. Jill attended in my place, and things suddenly started to happen. I was told to make a number of appointments for Jodie. First, she would have to be assessed by a child psychologist, to help the Social Services decide how best to proceed with her case. She would also have to have what's called a 'memorandum interview'. This is a videotaped interview with a police Child Protection Officer, which in this case would be the starting point for a criminal prosecution of Jodie's father and, hopefully, the other abusers too. Jodie would also have to see a police doctor for a forensic medical – an intimate gynaecological examination – to verify her claims.

I immediately started to worry about the forensic medical. It was traumatic enough for an adult to be examined in this way, but for an abused child it could be seen as another assault. I had given Jodie my promise that nothing of that kind would happen to her again, and I was frightened that she would think I'd broken my word and lose her trust in me.

In the meantime, our days had settled into something of a routine. On Mondays, Wednesdays and Fridays, Jodie's tutor would come in the morning, and then in the afternoon we would go out, usually to the park. On Tuesdays and Thursdays we went shopping, although Jodie and I had somewhat differing views about this. Jodie enjoyed shopping more than anything, whereas for me it was perfunctory. Jodie seemed to relish causing a scene in public, aware that there was little I could do in response. These tantrums were designed to bully me into buying her something, but I could never give in, as this would set a precedent by rewarding bad behaviour. However, Jodie had clearly used this technique successfully for years, so I wasn't expecting her to unlearn it any time soon.

The sessions with Nicola were improving, in terms of Jodie's behaviour, but she was making little progress in her education. In my view, this lack of progress was only partly attributable to Jodie's learning difficulties and delayed development and more likely a result of her emotional state. A further problem was that Jodie seemed to have no interest in learning; she could never see the point of any of Nicola's exercises, and it was very difficult to motivate her, as she apparently had no desire to win approval.

My worries increased one afternoon when I did finally receive a call from Mr Rudman's secretary: he was dreadfully sorry, but he didn't feel able to offer Jodie a place.

'Back to the drawing board,' I said to Nicola, and spent the second half of her session on the phone, trying to interest another head teacher, but without success.

'The trouble is,' Nicola said, 'she really needs a special school, but unless her statement can be changed to say this, there's no chance.'

'How long would it take to get it changed?'

'Anything up to a year.'

We agreed that this wasn't an option, so after Nicola left I set out more paper, paint and glue, and spent another hour working through the Yellow Pages. It was demoralizing work, but by the end of it I'd found another head who was willing to look at her statement. The school, Elmacre Primary, was five miles away, through the city traffic, but at least they had a vacancy.

The most enjoyable times I spent with Jodie tended to be our visits to the park. Jodie was less anxious in open spaces, presumably because there were fewer people around. She enjoyed playing on the swings, and I was slowly encouraging her to engage with the world around her, by pointing out pretty flowers and trees, and telling her the names of distinctive birds.

We often bumped into people I knew, and I hoped this kind of friendly contact would be helpful for Jodie. I'd lived in the same area for twenty years, so we would often run into someone I knew on any trip out. I would introduce Jodie, as I do with all the children I foster, but instead of saying 'Hi', or smiling shyly, she'd stick out her chin, screw up her eyes, and cackle like a witch. She had recently developed this cackle, and I wondered if it was a defence mechanism, to stop people getting close. If so, it was certainly effective; only the resolute would try and pursue a conversation. Fortunately, most people knew I fostered, so no one was too offended.

Despite my various schemes to broaden her horizons – which had included the zoo and a local museum – Jodie seemed only to enjoy the park, specifically the park playground. As soon as we reached the gate, she would rush in, and head straight for the swings. She rarely played with other children, or even acknowledged they were there. This was hardly surprising, as she barely interacted with me. Instead, she would swing up and down, muttering or singing to herself, until it was time to leave. She was the same when we tried to play sociable games at home; she preferred to play by herself, in her own little world.

On the few occasions she did initiate contact with other children, it was usually out of curiosity. She would see a smaller child doing something interesting, or wearing something that caught her eye, so she would walk over and stand in front of them, and stare at their chest; she still had a complete aversion to eye contact. Understandably, the other children would find this quite intimidating, although this didn't seem to be Jodie's intention. Nonetheless, it often led to a scene, with the child running to its mother to complain about 'that girl'.

On one occasion, we were in the playground, and a young father came in with his two daughters. There's an area in the playground for very young children, as these two were, so that was where they went to play. For some reason, this piqued Jodie's interest, so she followed them over and stood there watching as they clambered over the castle-shaped climbing frame. I was a few metres away, keeping an eye on her. At one point, one of the girls was coming down the slide, and Jodie went over to watch, and stood a bit too close to the bottom so that she was in the little girl's way. The girls' father marched across, put his hands on Jodie's shoulders and said, 'Come on now, out of the way.'

I thought this was a little over the top, but I came over quickly and apologized to him. 'Sorry about that. Come on Jodie, come and play on the swings.'

We turned and walked away, and as we did the man shouted after us, 'You want to learn to keep your daughter under control.'

This was definitely uncalled for, but I didn't respond, and Jodie and I carried on playing. A few minutes later a smartly dressed, middle-aged lady came into the playground, and headed purposefully towards us.

'Excuse me,' she said to me, 'this is Jodie, isn't it?' She leaned down towards Jodie and smiled. 'Hello, Jodie, it's lovely to see you again.' Jodie looked at her, and carried on swinging lazily. She held out her hand to me. 'Hi, sorry, I'm Fiona. I used to be Jodie's teacher.'

I shook her hand. 'Hello there, I'm Cathy. I'm Jodie's

foster carer.' I usually wouldn't mention that I was a foster carer, for fear of embarrassing the child, but in this case it seemed safe to assume that Jodie's teacher would know she had been taken into care. 'How long did you teach Jodie for?'

'A year,' Fiona replied. She smiled at Jodie. Jodie looked back at her, blankly. Did she even recognize her? I wondered.

'I must say,' Fiona continued, 'it's nice to see Jodie looking so well, and so clean. It looks like you're doing an excellent job.'

'Oh, thank you,' I replied. 'Yes, we're plodding along, aren't we, sweet?'

Jodie nodded her head, not really understanding.

'How long has she been with you?' asked Fiona.

'A few months now. She had a number of carers before me, but it looks like she's settled now.'

'Oh good. I'm sure that's just what she needs. Well, I'll let you get on and enjoy your afternoon. Jodie, it was really lovely to see you, and nice to meet you, Cathy.'

She left, and I stood on the grass verge, watching Jodie play. The father of the young girls started walking towards me, and my anxiety level rose.

'Excuse me,' he said. 'I don't want to bother you. I just wanted to apologize for my tone.'

'Oh, right,' I said, relieved. 'Well, it doesn't matter.'

'I overheard you say you were a foster carer, but I'd just assumed she was your daughter.'

'Not to worry. Sorry we were in the way.'

He smiled apologetically, and walked back to his girls.

As we walked home, I marvelled at the double standards. As a foster parent, you often have to deal with strangers who are quick to blame you for a child's difficult behaviour. If they find out you're fostering, however, they suddenly take a very different view. But why do they feel the need to criticize in the first place? Being a parent of any kind is difficult enough, without having to deal with strangers' condemnation.

A few days later, I received a call from the headmaster of Elmacre: he said he was very sorry, but they couldn't offer Jodie a place. My spirits sank, but he then explained that he had a colleague at a different school who might be able to offer a place. The colleague was Adam West, of Abbey Green School, and he had now been given my details and would shortly be in touch. I thanked him effusively, and with a grin on my face relayed the good news to Jodie.

'Not going,' she replied. 'Hate school. Hate you. Hate everything.' She stuck out her tongue, and stamped down the hall.

Chapter Fifteen

Past and Present

I was woken at around 2 a.m. by screams from Jodie's room. I pulled on my dressing gown, and staggered along the corridor, feeling like I'd only just gone to sleep. I gave the door the usual quick knock, and went straight in. Jodie was lying in bed, holding the duvet over her head, clutching it tightly with her fingers. I sat on the edge of the bed, and Jodie stopped screaming. 'What's the matter, love?' I asked.

'It's the eyes!' she moaned, terrified.

'What eyes, sweet? Come out from under there so I can give you a hug.'

'No! They're everywhere. The eyes in the walls, staring at me.'

I put my hand on the duvet where her feet were, to try and comfort her. 'Jodie, love, I know you're scared, but it's your imagination. There are no eyes here. No one's watching you. Please give me a hug.'

'They're here!' she shouted back. 'I can see them, coming at me! I'm not stupid. Make them stop, Cathy!'

'Jodie, shush,' I said firmly. 'Now come out from under there, and I'll show you. There's nothing there, I promise. I'm here with you, and I wouldn't let anything happen to you, would I? I'm here to protect you, that's my job, isn't that right?'

She fell silent for a second, and then loosened her grip on the duvet. I eased it down, and she clambered up and hugged me.

'Now look, Jodie. You see, there's nothing there.' I walked over to the wall, and rubbed my hand across it. 'See? There's no one here.' I sat back down on the bed. Jodie's cheeks were red, and her forehead was hot and sweaty. She was genuinely scared; whatever these visions were, they were very real to her. What had started as straightforward nightmares had gradually developed into something closer to hallucinations. Increasingly now, when I went in to her room to comfort her, I would find her in a strange state that seemed somewhere between sleeping and waking; sometimes it would seem as if she were awake but still trapped inside her nightmare. I couldn't tell if she was truly aware of what was happening but it seemed that whatever she was seeing was taking on a greater reality.

'Will you read me a story?' she asked.

'Yes, OK, but then you have to go to sleep, all right?'

'All right.'

I read her the story, and put her to bed, but at four o'clock she was screaming again. I went back and resettled her, but an hour later she started up again. There was no chance of getting her back to sleep now, which meant there was no chance of me sleeping, so I went downstairs for a cup of coffee and a much-needed cigarette. I stood on the patio in my dressing gown and slippers. It was still dark and I knew the sun wouldn't be up for another half hour. I smiled to myself, as I wondered how many other mums knew exactly what time the sun came up.

It was a cold autumnal day. Summer had now passed us by and Jodie had been living with us for over six months. It was hard to remember a time before Jodie now, or a life that was lived without this intensity. Jodie and her problems occupied me constantly, and there was little in my life that wasn't filled with looking after her and her needs. Now that the weather had turned cold, it was becoming quite a challenge to persuade Jodie to wear suitable clothes. Later that day, we left the house to go shopping, but as I went to close the door I realized I'd forgotten my own gloves. I left Jodie on the doorstep, while I popped inside to retrieve them. Suddenly the door slammed and Jodie was running up the hall towards me.

'Whatever's the matter?'

'My dad. He's outside!'

'What? Where is he?' I felt a rush of fear. It was far from unlikely that Jodie's parents had been able to track me down, if the usual mistakes and errors had been made.

I had a particular dread of seeing Jodie's father; I wasn't scared for myself – I didn't feel that I was in great danger from him – but I was terrified that Jodie's safe place in my home could be contaminated and threatened if she ever laid eyes on her father while she was here. And what was more, I never wanted to set eyes on him myself. The very thought of him made me feel physically sick. 'Where did you see him, Jodie?'

'In his van. Driving up the street.'

'Go in the living room and stay put.' I walked outside, drawing the door to behind me. I looked out from the doorstep but couldn't see a van. I walked up the path and on to the pavement, peering up and down the street. I knew from what Jodie had said before that her father drove a white van, but I couldn't see any vans at all. I looked up and down but there were definitely no white vans. I looked once more and then, seeing nothing, I went back inside, relieved.

'It's OK, Jodie, there's no van. He's not there. He doesn't know where we live, so I'm sure it wasn't him. It must be someone else's van.' I gave her a hug. 'Shall we go to the shops now, or do you want to wait a bit?'

'I'll come,' she said passively.

I reassured her again and, holding her close, led the way to the car. As we drove into town I watched her in the rear-view mirror, as she anxiously kept watch in every direction, presumably looking for vans.

I parked in the multi-storey and bought a ticket for two hours. As we entered the shopping mall, we were immediately transported into a fairyland of illuminated trees, sparkling foil garlands and a giant Father Christmas booming 'Ho ho ho!' I felt a surge of panic, as I compared the stores' festive preparations with my own. I'd done nothing yet, and as I counted up the weeks I realized we were only six away from Christmas Eve. I picked up a basket, and we made our way round the department store.

Jodie was as ever an enthusiastic if not discerning shopper, and she happily grabbed any gaily packaged parcel that came within reach. While we shopped, I talked to her about Christmas and told her about the little traditions that she could expect with us, like decorating the house and the tree, the family service at our church on Christmas Eve, and the pillowcases we all hang on our doors before going to bed. I told her about the glass of sherry and the mince pie that we leave out for Santa, along with carrots for the reindeer. Jodie listened with mild interest but contributed nothing of her own experiences. She didn't even mention her last Christmas with her parents, which is usually very poignant for children in care. Instead she grasped the material aspect of the festival and started telling me a long list of all the presents she wanted this year, which was, in a nutshell, anything brightly coloured – preferably pink and sparkly.

'What did you get last Christmas?' I asked, interrupting her.

'Shoes,' she said. 'Black ones for school. But they wasn't wrapped.'

'And what did you do on Christmas Day? Did you play games?'

She nodded. 'We went up the pub and played darts. Mum had lots of beer and fell over so we had to go home. They went to sleep, so I put a pizza in the oven and after that they felt better.'

I sighed. What a miserable Christmas – and to think that Jodie had assumed responsibility for her parents like that, particularly with her problems! I'd quickly guessed that she had taken a big portion of running the home on to her seven-year-old shoulders. For all her malcoordination and poor motor skills, she'd told me once how to mix a baby's bottle and she knew how to cook fish fingers in the oven. But if her Christmas was joyless, it was no worse than others I'd heard of from my foster children who'd never known the excitement and pleasure of waking up on Christmas morning to bursting pillowcases and presents under the tree. 'Well, Christmas will be very different this year, Jodie, and I know you're going to enjoy it.'

'Will I, Cathy?' she said, and her face lit up.

'Yes. I promise.' As we carried on shopping, I resolved that she would have the best Christmas I could possibly give her – it would be one way that I could try and restore a piece of her childhood to her. I couldn't wait to see her pleasure on the day itself, even if it was over a month away.

I found presents for my nieces and nephews, then spotted a pair of Winnie the Pooh slippers which would go into Paula's sack. Not wishing to have the surprise ruined, I discreetly placed them at the bottom of the basket, and distracted Jodie while I paid. I did the same with the other stocking fillers, including a Tweenies jigsaw for Jodie, and some fancy hair conditioner that Lucy had mentioned. I would be doing all my shopping with Jodie this year, so it would have to be furtive and piecemeal, but it would be worth it.

When we arrived home, Lucy and Paula had just beaten us in. They were in the hallway, removing their coats and unloading their schoolbags.

'We've been to Christmas,' Jodie shouted excitedly.

'Shopping,' I added. 'I've made a start.'

'Yes, shopping,' Jodie repeated. 'And my daddy was naughty, he took his clothes off and weed on me.'

The girls laughed uncomfortably. Neither of them knew what to say.

'Jodie,' I said, 'we went shopping this afternoon. What your daddy did happened more than a year ago. Don't link the two. It's confusing.'

But she often did this, running past and present together in a continuum of now. Right from the start she had had no conception of time, but her inability to distinguish between past, present and future seemed to be getting worse.

'Do you want to play a game?' asked Paula.

Jodie stared blankly back.

Paula persisted. 'Let's all do a jigsaw together!'

'What about Barbie?' asked Lucy. 'I'd love to play with your Barbie dolls.'

'No!' snapped Jodie. 'My dolls! Cathy, can I watch a video?'

'Wouldn't you rather play with the girls, Jodie?' I asked. 'I'm sure that would be much more fun, and I know the girls would like to hear all about your day at the shops.'

Jodie sighed, exhausted by my unreasonable demands. 'Please, Cathy,' she pleaded. 'I been good?'

I reluctantly agreed, and let her take one of her Early Years videos upstairs. The girls went up to their rooms, and I could see they were a little hurt. Of course, they had no particular desire to play Barbie dolls with Jodie, but no one likes being rejected. Paula and Lucy had been trying to spend more time with Jodie, and to become her friends, but she was impossible to break through to. Most children, no matter how bad their behaviour, do essentially want to be liked, and to feel the approval of those around them. Jodie, on the other hand, simply couldn't have cared less. When the girls wanted to play with her, she wasn't pleased or flattered, and it didn't even occur to her that she might hurt their feelings. She was completely oblivious.

Her relationship with Adrian was even more distant. Because of the nature of the abuse she had suffered, Jodie regarded all males in sexual terms, and would try to flirt with them, or rub provocatively up against them. There was nothing deliberate about this, it was simply the kind of behaviour which had characterized her relationships with men in the past, and it was going to take an awfully long time to reverse this pattern. As a result, Adrian found her very difficult, and tended to just stay out of her way.

As I began peeling the potatoes for dinner, I heard loud thumps coming from upstairs. I was about to climb the stairs, ready to go up and deal with yet another scene, when I realized what the noise was. Jodie's video contained song and dance routines for the children to join in with. Jodie was simply dancing along to her video.

As I returned to the kitchen, I felt immensely sad. Given the choice between playing with my daughters or watching a video on her own, Jodie had had no hesitation in choosing the video. It wasn't even that she didn't like the girls; if she had the option of being alone or of spending time with anyone, Jodie would always choose to be alone. Her history had taught her that the company of others could only bring pain and rejection, and this lesson had isolated her from the world.

My fear was the effect that this awful legacy was likely to have on the rest of her life. Jodie's hostility, defensiveness and delayed development meant that she really had nothing going for her. She wasn't pretty, bright or talented. She wasn't kind, warm or vulnerable. She was still overweight, despite my efforts, although her weight had stabilized. She was rude, unpleasant, aggressive, violent, and she had absolutely no desire to be liked by anyone. It was a mixture that was bound to alienate her and she had no tools to win other people over, nothing at her disposal to make others wish to be around her, or to win her affection.

As far as I could tell, not one person had ever taken an interest in Jodie in her entire life, except those that had wanted to hurt her. Not one person had ever loved her. But as I listened to her clumsy, arrhythmic stomping coming from upstairs, I felt more drawn to her than ever. Surely it wasn't too late for her? She was only eight years old, for goodness' sake. Could her entire life really be mapped out?

I hoped fervently that there was time to heal her broken personality, and I longed to put her back together again so that she could have another chance at the childhood that had been so cruelly taken from her. I was determined to try my very best for this child and if love, attention, kindness and hard work could do anything, I would not stop until she was better.

Chapter Sixteen

The Spider's Web

It was a beautiful, crisp winter morning in early December; the sun was a soft golden ball in a clear sky. Jodie's usually pale cheeks were glowing red from the cold and the exertion of riding her bike. Every so often she stopped to flip back her scarf, part of a set I'd bought: a lilac hat, scarf and gloves with a fluffy trim. Only prolonged coercion had stopped her from wearing them in bed. Finally I'd done something right!

I set a brisk pace as we approached the park gates, and my mind was racing. I was anxious, and for once my worries were not entirely down to Jodie. The previous day we had visited Abbey Green School, and met the headmaster, Adam West. Although the visit had gone well, Mr West had said that he wouldn't be able to offer Jodie a place until funding had been approved, which might take three months. Jodie would have to continue with Nicola, her tutor, in the meantime, but this clearly wasn't meeting her needs. Jodie desperately needed not only education, but also the routine of school, and the company of other children.

I paused by the entrance to the park, and called Jodie back. Strung between two shrubs was a large spider's web, still in the shade, sparkling white with dew.

'Look at this, Jodie! A spider's web. Isn't it beautiful?' I said. 'Like one of those decorations we saw in the shops.'

'Beautiful,' she repeated. 'Really beautiful.'

'And can you hear that rustling in the undergrowth? I bet that's a bird.' We stood very quietly and listened. Moments later we were rewarded, as a large blackbird with a fiery orange beak quickly hopped across the path. Jodie's face beamed.

'Beautiful. Really beautiful,' she said again, and I knew the phrase would be repeated for the rest of the day.

We made four laps of the park, then headed back. I always felt better after a walk, and for Jodie the energy release was essential, otherwise she'd be hyperactive for the rest of the day. She waited at the park gates, and we crossed the road together, then she sprinted ahead to the top of our road. Arriving at the gate, she heaved her bike up the step. To a stranger watching her who didn't know anything of her past, she could have been any normal child arriving home, cheeks flushed from the cold air, looking forward to the warmth of home and the comfort of a hot drink. Just for a moment, I pretended to be that person, so that I could briefly enjoy the pleasure of seeing Jodie as she could be, if all of our efforts paid off.

We took off our coats, and I wheeled her bike through to the conservatory. I heated some milk and made us both a mug of hot chocolate. We sat either side of the kitchen table. I passed Jodie the biscuit tin and she dived in, grinning.

'One,' I said. 'You had a cooked breakfast.' I took a sip of my drink and set it down. She followed suit.

I took a deep breath. Now was the moment that I had to broach the subject that had been on my mind all morning. The innocence of our park trip was about to be sullied with the darkness of the adult world that Jodie had been so brutally exposed to. 'Jodie,' I said.

She met my gaze, the blue-grey eyes blank as usual.

'I need to explain something. Can you listen carefully?'

She nodded.

'When we've finished our drinks, we're going out in the car. Do you remember Eileen?'

She wouldn't remember her, of course, even though Eileen had finally made her first visit. A few weeks before, she had come round to introduce herself. Jodie was unlikely to recall it and I could hardly blame her, as it had been a flying visit, to say the least. After a few uncomfortable minutes, Eileen had made her excuses and gone on her way. She clearly wasn't at ease with Jodie.

Jodie looked blank at my question, so I carried on. 'Eileen's your social worker, you remember? Well, Eileen wants you to have something called a medical, where a doctor will examine you, but there's nothing to worry about. I'll be with you.'

In an ideal world Eileen would have come around herself to explain to Jodie what was going to happen, but I'd given up expecting anything like that.

'Will you, Cathy? That's nice.' She dunked her biscuit, then began licking off the melted chocolate.

'The doctor will have a look at you, to make sure you're OK. Do you remember that you had a medical when you first came into care? It will be like that, but this will be a bit more thorough.'

'Will I have to take me clothes off, Cathy?' she said, more interested in the biscuit than the conversation.

'Yes. But it will be a nice lady doctor. She's used to children, so there's nothing to worry about. She's going to look at your body, particularly where Daddy and Uncle Mike hurt you. You know, what we call our private parts.'

I waited for a reaction: fear, horror or outright refusal, but there was nothing. She finished her drink, wiped the back of her hand across her mouth and stood up, leaving me wondering if she'd fully understood.

'If you think of any questions,' I added, 'tell me and I'll explain.'

Strapped in the back seat, she resumed chattering about anything and everything, including medicals in general. Had I ever had a medical? Had Lucy and Paula? Did they have to take their clothes off and show their private parts? Did Adrian? I stopped that line of questioning, and switched on the radio. A bouncy pop song came on.

'My mum likes this song,' she said. 'She likes the boy singer. We listen to it in the pub.'

'You used to listen to it in the pub,' I corrected her. As usual, Jodie seemed unable to distinguish between then and now but I was trying to point out the difference whenever she muddled them up, in the hope that she would begin to put what was finished behind her. I worried that she was still existing emotionally in the bad place she had come from, and if that was the case she was unlikely to begin her recovery. 'We don't go to the pub now. That was in the past.'

'Why, Cathy? Why can't we go to the pub?'

'I don't think it's the right place to take children. I prefer the park for an outing.'

'My mum thinks it's right, so does my daddy, and my auntie Bell.'

'I dare say.'

'Cathy, is my mummy having a medical and showing her private parts?'

'No. Not as far as I know.'

She paused, as though weighing this up. Then her voice piped up again. 'She should. My daddy does naughty things to her as well.'

I glanced in the mirror. It was a throwaway comment, but loaded with connotations, as many disclosures are. 'How do you know that, Jodie?'

She shrugged. 'Don't know. Just do.'

She had shut down again, and I knew there was no point in pursuing it. I was sure that she meant that she had seen her father and mother having sex and it was no surprise that she couldn't distinguish between that and what happened to her. When she said it was 'naughty', did that mean she was starting to accept that what had happened to her was wrong? Or was she just repeating back what I had said to her? It was so hard to know with Jodie how much she understood and accepted.

The rest of the journey passed with Jodie singing along to songs on the radio, many of them near word perfect. I always found this unreasonably irritating: how could she remember these daft lyrics, but not her ABC?

The medical centre was housed in a purpose-built bungalow and offered a range of paediatric services. I'd been there before with other foster children for general health checks, but never for a forensic medical; I couldn't help feeling very apprehensive because I had a fair idea of what was in store for her. I knew that the police didn't do this very readily with young children who are likely victims of abuse, because it can seem like another form of assault. I had talked it over with Jill earlier and she had reassured me that if Jodie put up any resistance or seemed distressed, the doctors would stop immediately. There was no question of forcing her to go through with it.

It was always a struggle to find a parking space, but I spotted a gap at the kerb, and anxiously tried to parallel park, while a van waited impatiently behind.

'You been here before?' Jodie asked, releasing her seat-belt.

'Yes. For eyesight and hearing tests.'

'Did they look at your private parts?'

'No, sweet. Stay put, and I'll let you out.'

I went round and opened her door. She jumped on to the pavement and I took her hand. I had no idea which department we wanted and the entrance board didn't seem to cover private parts. I approached the receptionist.

'Jodie Brown,' I said. 'We've a forensic medical booked for twelve-thirty.'

She glanced at the appointment list. 'Oh yes. We're waiting for the police doctor. Take a seat over there. She shouldn't be long.'

I steered Jodie to a small recess with four plastic chairs, and a box of well-used toys and books. A door led off, with a sign that read 'Consulting Room One', and a small metal plate marked 'Vacant'. Jodie brought me a pop-up book of Cinderella. I had just opened it and begun to read, when a smartly dressed woman walked over. She was in her late fifties, with bright red lipstick and horn-rimmed glasses.

'Cathy?' she smiled. 'I'm Linda Marshall, the police doctor. And you must be Jodie?'

She wasn't what I was expecting at all, and from the look on Jodie's face I gathered she wasn't what she was expecting either. With her red plaid suit, sheer black stockings and high stilettos, she wouldn't have looked out of place at a department store beauty counter.

'Sorry to keep you waiting,' she said. 'How are you?'

'Fine, thanks,' I answered for us both.

Jodie eyed her suspiciously. 'Are you a doctor?' she barked.

'Yes,' she whispered conspiratorially. 'But children tell me I don't look like one. Shall we go in?'

Jodie immediately dropped my hand and took hold of the doctor's. I followed them into the consulting room. There, a young woman in a white medic's coat was sitting behind a small desk, looking much more like the kind of doctor we had expected. She came round the desk and shook my hand.

'Hello there, I'm Dr Pratchet,' she said. 'I'll be carrying out the examination today, with the help of Dr Marshall here. Do sit down.'

I took the only available chair and looked around. A long reclining couch with leg rests dominated one side of the room. At its foot was a large spot lamp on an adjustable metal stem, which was switched off for the moment. I shuddered, aware of what was in store.

Dr Pratchet returned to her desk, and Linda Marshall perched on the edge of the couch. Jodie went straight for the toy box in the corner, which she upturned, spilling its contents across the floor. I shot her a warning glance.

'I'd like to ask you a few questions first,' Dr Pratchet said. 'You're all right playing there for a few minutes, aren't you, Jodie?'

Jodie grinned at me, holding out a toy she'd found. 'Look, Cathy!'

'Yes, it's a jack-in-a-box, like the one at home. Put it back when you've finished, good girl.'

The doctor opened an A4 folder, and pulled out a bundle of papers. 'Jodie's eight and a half now? And she's been with you since the third of April?'

I could tell that the doctor was well aware of the contents of Jodie's file and knew exactly why we were there. 'Yes, that's right.'

'How is she generally? Eating? Sleeping? Behaviour?'

I gave her a brief summary of Jodie's state: that she ate well but her nights and general behaviour were becoming increasingly difficult.

'And does she understand why she's here?'

'I've explained she's going to have a medical, and you will need to look at her private parts to make sure she's OK.'

She nodded, and I assumed she approved of my explanation. 'Apart from what Jodie's said, have you noticed any other indicators? Soreness, a rash, discharge?'

Foster carers can't afford to be squeamish. 'No, but she does soil herself a lot. It's not deliberate, as it used to be. It's more that she doesn't seem to quite make it to the toilet in time. Or if she does, she's not very good at cleaning herself up. I'm often changing her and washing her so it wouldn't necessarily be obvious.'

'Quite,' Linda Marshall agreed.

Dr Pratchet made a note and then looked up at Jodie. 'OK, we're going to start by measuring and weighing you, Jodie. Do you think you could jump on those scales?'

'Jump' was not the best choice of word, as Jodie took it literally. With a resounding leap, she threw herself on to the platform. The sprung metal plate clanged and shuddered.

'Gently,' I said redundantly.

Linda read out the results and Dr Pratchet noted them down. 'Good girl. Now, can you climb on to this couch for me? It's a bit high; do you need some help?'

Jodie, oblivious to what lay in wait and eager to demonstrate her agility, scrambled up. She sat with her chubby legs dangling over the edge, grinning at me proudly. I watched as Dr Pratchet opened her desk drawer and removed a stethoscope and a wooden spatula. Looping the stethoscope around her neck, she tucked the spatula into her coat pocket. I shuffled my chair back to allow her to pass. I could feel my anxiety level rising fast.

'I'm going to have a look in your mouth first, Jodie,' she said. 'Say aaah.'

Jodie opened her mouth wide. Dr Pratchet placed the spatula on her tongue, and the two women peered in. I could guess what they were looking for. If Jodie had been forced into oral sex, there was a chance she might have contracted a sexually transmitted disease in her mouth, but I hadn't seen any sores or white thrush spots when I'd helped brush her teeth.

'Excellent,' said Dr Pratchet. 'Well done.'

Jodie closed her mouth, and grinned at me. I smiled back reassuringly.

'Now, can I listen to your chest?'

Linda gently lifted up Jodie's jumper, waiting for Jodie to give permission by raising her arms, and Dr Pratchet listened with her stethoscope. I felt reassured: they certainly knew how to put a child at ease. I relaxed a little.

'Excellent,' she said again. 'You're doing very well. Aren't you a big girl?'

Jodie beamed, as though she'd just won a medal, but I was aware we were approaching the next stage of the medical, and I was praying for Jodie's continued cooperation. The doctors wouldn't force her to go through with it, but without this evidence there would be little chance of a prosecution.

'Can you lie down on the couch for me?' asked Linda, patting the bed.

Jodie flopped back in her cumbersome way and cackled loudly.

'We need to have you further this end,' said Linda, and eased her down, so that her legs hung over the edge. Dr Pratchet switched on the lamp.

'Would you like to come and hold her hand?' Linda asked, looking over at me.

I manoeuvred my chair so that I was sitting beside Jodie's head, and held her hand. I was pleased to be doing something. Dr Pratchet passed Linda a blanket, and she covered Jodie's body.

'I'm going to slip off your trousers and pants,' she said, and discreetly removed them under the blanket. 'Good girl. Now let your legs go floppy, and I'll put them in the right position.'

She raised Jodie's knees. It was an ungainly, vulnerable position, but with the blanket covering her she at least retained some dignity.

Linda joined Dr Pratchet at the foot of the couch, and

both women put on rubber gloves and began the examination. I stroked Jodie's forehead and held her hand tight. Her cheeks flushed, and she bit her bottom lip.

'Won't be long,' I said, 'then we can go home.'

The women began discussing what they saw. I recognized the word 'lesion', but none of the other terms were familiar. Their tone was flat and professional, revealing nothing.

'It hurts,' said Jodie. I squeezed her hand, willing them to hurry up.

Dr Pratchet suddenly straightened. 'All done. You've been a very brave girl. You can get dressed now.'

I breathed a sigh of relief and helped Jodie sit up and dress, while the two women shed their gloves into the bin.

'We'll send the report to the social worker,' said Linda. 'You can reassure Jodie she's quite normal.'

This was all we would be told for now. The social worker would eventually pass on to me anything I needed to know. Jill had said that this could take anything from ten days to a month. I thanked them warmly, took Jodie's hand, and we walked out into the winter afternoon sunshine.

'You were very brave,' I told her. 'You won't have to go through that again. It's over now.'

'I wished it was a man,' she said, giving a little hop beside me.

'What? Doing the examination?' I was surprised. Surely a man performing that kind of procedure was the last thing Jodie would want, after what she'd been through. 'Why?'

'Ladies hurt more than men, 'cos they haven't got a willy.'

I stopped and turned to her as the significance of her words sank in. 'What do you mean? What ladies? How do they hurt you?'

Her brow furrowed, as she searched through her limited vocabulary to try and explain. 'My mum and Aunt Bell, they had to use things because they haven't got willies.'

'Use things? What, on your private parts?'

'Yes. Like the doctors. They poked things inside me.'

I froze. Oh please, no. How much more could this child have endured? 'What things, Jodie?'

'Spoons, like the one the doctor put in my mouth. Only it was silver.'

'Are you saying that Mum and Aunt Bell put a metal spoon in your private parts?'

She nodded. 'It was cold. Daddy warmed it in his hands first. He was kind sometimes, wasn't he, Cathy?'

It was too much. I could no longer hide my anger with the people who'd done this to her. 'No, Jodie, he wasn't. He was wicked. They're animals. All of them. I hope they rot in hell!'

Chapter Seventeen

Nosy Cow

I sat at my desk writing, logging in my diary the vile details of Jodie's sexual degradation. I felt sick to my core. The active involvement of Jodie's mother in the abuse was such an appalling inversion of the maternal role and everything we feel mothers should be. We foster carers were supposed to be non-judgemental but there is a cut-off point and, for me, this was it. I could hardly bear to record Jodie's childish conclusion that, because her father had warmed the object used to defile her, this act of kindness made him less culpable.

As soon as Jill received my emailed report, she phoned. 'Jesus,' she said. 'It's a wonder the poor child's functioning at all with all this.'

'She isn't really. And she's functioning less with every new disclosure.' As I said it, I realized the truth. On a day-to-day basis, there were ups and downs, bad days and better days; but if I stood back for a moment and considered it all carefully, I could see that in reality it was a steady decline. Jodie was getting worse. 'I'm out of my depth, Jill.'

Jill could hear the rising panic in my voice. She said soothingly, 'OK, don't worry. You're seeing the psychologist next week, aren't you?'

'Monday.'

'Why don't you ask her for some strategies to help? I know that's not why she's there, but she might be able to offer something. It's worth a try.'

'Thanks, Jill. That's a good idea.' I felt a small vestige of comfort. 'I'll see what she says.'

Jill was right. The psychologist had been appointed by the court to assess Jodie as part of the ongoing care proceedings, and it wasn't her role to advise me, or to offer therapy for Jodie. Still, it was a glimmer of hope – surely she would have some idea of what I might do.

The bureaucratic wheels were grinding slowly on, as Jodie's case worked its way through the system. Jodie had been brought into care under an Interim Care Order, which meant that the court would decide at a later date whether to return her to her family, or to issue a Full Care Order. The psychologist would meet Jodie a number of times before filing her report, as this was a crucial part of the court's decision-making process.

The court had set dates for two 'direction hearings' in January and March, which would be followed by a 'final court hearing' in May. The purpose of the direction hearings was to allow the judge to consider the evidence that had been presented so far, so that he or she could take interim decisions in the child's interests, without having to wait for the final court proceedings to be resolved.

Throughout the process, the guardian ad litem would meet with all the parties and provide the judge with an objective assessment, making recommendations in the best interests of the child. In practice, judges tend to be guided by the guardian ad litem, and usually follow his or her recommendations.

If a Full Care Order was granted at the final hearing, the local authority would become Jodie's de facto guardian, and Social Services would place her either with a long-term foster family, or into a residential care home, or, if she was very lucky, they might find a family to adopt her. However, given Jodie's age, aggression and learning difficulties, this last option was extremely unlikely.

Before the first meeting with the psychologist, Jodie was scheduled for the police memorandum interview. This interview, as well as being part of the care proceedings, would also be used in the police investigation, with a view to prosecuting Jodie's parents and any other abusers. Jodie would be interviewed by specially trained police officers from the Child Protection Unit, and I hoped that she would be as forthcoming with them as she had been with me.

We arrived for our appointment with the Child Protection Officers in good time, which gave Jodie a chance to peer into the police cars parked outside the station. I pressed the buzzer for entry, then gave our names to the PC on reception. He came out from behind the desk and showed us through to a special suite. As we walked in, I felt reassured: the suite was clearly designed to set a child at ease. The room was brightly furnished, with a big red sofa, lots of toys and colourful *Lion King*-themed wallpaper. Two WPCs in civilian clothes stood and introduced themselves.

'Hello, you must be Jodie,' one said brightly. 'My name's Kelly, and this is Harriet.'

Jodie grinned while I shook their hands.

'Coffee?' Harriet asked.

'Yes please.'

'And squash for Jodie?'

'Thank you,' I said.

Harriet left the room while Jodie brought a jigsaw from a toy box and the three of us began assembling it. Harriet returned with the drinks and a packet of biscuits. We sat for a while, as the WPCs tried to engage Jodie's attention, asking her about her hobbies, her favourite television programmes and so on. Jodie, however, remained oblivious to their chat, preferring to sit in the corner exploring the toy boxes. After a while, Kelly got on her hands and knees and tried to join in with Jodie's games, but this too was only partially successful. I didn't think Jodie was being deliberately hostile, it was just that she didn't see the need to interact, even though I had explained the importance of our visit both that morning and the night before.

Explaining to Jodie what was going to happen had been a delicate process. I had tried to make it clear that some nice, kind people would be asking her questions about the things she had told me had happened to her, but there was not much more I could add without being in danger of prejudicing any eventual court case. I couldn't say, 'You must tell the police the naughty things that Daddy did to you,' in case I was in any way putting ideas into Jodie's head. All I could do was ask her to tell the truth. If it came out in the interview that I had put any detail in her head, then it could be used by the opposing barrister in an effort to disprove Jodie's claims.

I hoped that Jodie had understood how important it was to be frank and honest with the officers but, as ever, it was hard to tell what she had absorbed. I crossed my fingers that she was in a compliant mood, as she had been in the medical, and hoped she would enjoy being the centre of attention. Many foster children are like this: before they come into care they've often been neglected and ignored, so when they are given lots of attention and a host of professionals involved in the case is brought into their lives they can sometimes become little stars. On occasions, Jodie could thrive on being at the centre of things, so I hoped that this would work in her favour today.

Another ten minutes passed, then Kelly suggested we make a start. She touched Jodie's arm softly and said, 'We're going to go through to what's called an interview room in a minute. I know Cathy's told you all about it. It's just through there.' She pointed to the door.

Jodie looked up. 'Is Cathy coming?'

'Yes, to begin with, and then she'll come back and wait in here, and we'll have a chat in there. Now, while we have our chat, a very nice man is going to video us, so we can remember everything we talked about later on. Does that sound OK to you?'

Perhaps Jodie had lost interest in the toys for suddenly, very obligingly, and to my great relief, she stood up and took hold of Kelly's hand. 'Come on then,' she said. 'I want to be in the video.'

I followed them out of the door and into the next room, where a young policeman, also in civilian clothes, greeted us.

'Hello, Jodie,' he said. 'I'm John. I work the camera. Do you want to come and have a look?'

The interview room was small and bare, with three plastic chairs, a central light, and a blackout blind over the only window. I was surprised how austere it was; I'd imagined it would be more child-friendly.

John showed Jodie and me where the camera was mounted, and where he would be standing, hidden from view by a screen. 'We're going to make a video of you, and record what you're saying. Is that OK, Jodie?'

I remembered the photo I'd taken of Jodie when she'd first arrived at my home, and how she'd tried to take off her clothes. Would she be upset now at this strange man wanting to video her? She hadn't been bothered when I'd explained it to her earlier, and so far at least she seemed unfazed, as she nodded her assent.

'Can you sit in this chair?' Kelly said, helping her up, while John discreetly moved behind the screen.

'Cathy's going to wait in the room next door now, while you stay with us, all right?' Harriet said.

Jodie wriggled in her chair and gave a little wave, and I left the room. As her carer, I was not allowed to be present during the interview, in case it affected her testimony. Memorandum interviews have to be done under controlled conditions, in order for them to be admissible as evidence in court.

I returned to the bright, cheerful suite, which seemed such a contrast to the small, dark interview room. I sat down, but I found I couldn't relax, so I decided to pop outside for a cigarette. The wind was piercing, and I took shelter in a doorway, furtively puffing while I worried about what was going on in the interview room. What Jodie said now was crucial because without her evidence on tape there would be little chance of a prosecution. At her age and with her learning difficulties, there was no way she could go into a witness box to testify. The adversarial nature of our legal system, even in child abuse cases, would mean that she could be cross-examined by a barrister. There was no way she would be able to cope with that, and what child of less than ten who had been through what she had could? As a result, it was little wonder so few cases came to court, let alone ended with a successful prosecution of the abusers. I smoked only half the cigarette, then stubbed it out, and felt only half-guilty. I pressed the buzzer to re-enter the station, then made my own way to the suite. I paced, then sat, and paced again. Twenty minutes passed, then the door opened and Kelly stuck her head round.

'We're giving it another ten minutes, then we're going to call it a day. We've not had much luck, I'm afraid.'

I nodded, my heart sinking, as Kelly returned to the interview. I wandered over to the window, which looked out over the courtyard at the rear. I watched as a patrol car pulled in, and two uniformed officers climbed out, sharing a joke. As a foster carer, I often have dealings with the police, not only with child protection issues, but also with runaway teenagers, or those who've committed offences. Theirs was a difficult job, and I'd always had the utmost respect for the police, particularly the Youth Offending Team, who have to have the patience of saints.

A sense of depression engulfed me. I could imagine that if Jodie hadn't opened up by now, she was unlikely to. I knew what she was like when she didn't want to talk. There was no forcing the issue – she was as immovable as a mountain. She had just a few short minutes left to tell the police what they needed to hear if there was any hope of punishing the people who had made her suffer so terribly.

While I waited, I wondered, not for the first time, about Jodie's brother and sister. Had they been made to suffer in the way that Jodie had? I hoped not, but it was unlikely that I would ever find out. I was only given information that was strictly relevant to Jodie and all I knew was that her siblings were with other carers now. My hope was that, because they were so much younger than Jodie, they might have escaped what Jodie had gone through.

A short while later I heard Jodie's voice outside the door. It opened and she bounced in. 'We did the video,' she grinned. 'It was really good.' She rushed over to the toy box.

I looked up hopefully at Harriet and Kelly, who shook their heads. Harriet motioned for me to join her, while Kelly helped Jodie into her coat.

'She wouldn't talk, I'm afraid,' said Harriet. 'She kept telling us how she wanted to rip her father's head off, but she wouldn't say why, or give any details. We won't try again while she's so young, but we'll keep the file open for the future. Hopefully one day she will be ready.'

'Thank you,' I said, unable to hide my disappointment. 'I'm sorry she wasn't more cooperative, but it isn't altogether surprising.'

'No. Certainly not, not with everything that's gone on. I dealt with that family years ago. God knows why she was left there so long.'

I was intrigued but the police woman didn't say any more and confidentiality would not allow her to. Clearly the police had been involved with the family at some level but it could have been for anything from parking offences to petty crime or drug dealing. Nevertheless, I had the feeling that Harriet had formed the impression that something had been going on in the house ... but I would never know for sure.

I buttoned up Jodie's coat, and the two WPCs saw us out. As soon as we turned the corner, Jodie's good mood disappeared.

'Cathy, is the monster going to come? Is it going to come and do what they said?' Her questions were breathless and anxious. 'I think that monster's coming. He's under my bed and he wants to chew up my hands while I'm asleep.'

'No, sweetheart, it's not, I promise. Why do you think that?'

'My dad and Uncle Mike said if I ever told anyone, it was going to come.' The anxiety in her voice rose higher until she was ranting. 'It's going to chew my arms and legs off! That's what's going to happen!'

'No, sweet,' I said, trying to pacify her. 'It's not going to come. You did your very best with the police, I know that. You were a good girl and nothing is going to hurt you. You're safe with me, you know that, don't you? There's no monster.'

As I tried to calm her, I realized that it was this fear that had stopped her from talking to the police. Instantly my anger flared at the power the abusers still had over her. She was unwittingly protecting them because the terror they had planted in her was so strong that it overrode everything else.

'You're safe with me, Jodie,' I said, as we headed for home. 'I promise.'

* * *

That night, when I turned on the ten o'clock news, the screen was dominated by a rock star, arrested as part of a worldwide investigation into child pornography on the Internet. The police had seized his computer and found images of children on the hard disk.

I seethed with anger. How did these perverts think the photographs were obtained? For every image downloaded, a child had been abused, and a life and personality destroyed. The end result was children like Jodie, fractured and hurt almost beyond repair. As far as I was concerned, the person buying this filth was just as responsible as the abuser, and I had no sympathy for his fall from grace, or for the claim that he was researching a book.

Our appointment with the psychologist was set for Monday afternoon. Although this was our first meeting with Dr Burrows together, Jodie had seen her once before, while she was with her second carers. For some reason, she seemed reluctant to see her again.

'But Dr Burrows will be able to help you,' I explained. 'Everyone wants to help you, Jodie, but first we have to tell Dr Burrows what we know. You need to say what happened so that people can make it all better.'

'None of her damn business,' she snarled. 'Nosy cow.'

'What isn't her business?' I asked. But she wouldn't be drawn. I suspected her parents had warned her against this kind of thing, and against cooperating, fearing that a psychologist would be a particular threat to their shameful secret.

They needn't have worried. From the moment we arrived, Jodie was hostile and uncommunicative. She wouldn't answer any questions, not even on innocuous subjects like her favourite toys, or what she liked to eat. The only answers she did give were monosyllabic or gibberish.

Dr Burrows was professional and business-like, and clearly knew how to connect with children, but she was making no progress with Jodie. After a while, she gave up trying to ask straightforward questions and tried a different approach. She brought out a pad of paper and some coloured pencils.

'Jodie, would you be able to do some drawings for me? I'd like to see some pictures – how about drawing me a picture of your mum and dad at home?'

This did seem to soften Jodie a little, and she took up a pencil and began to draw in her clumsy, malcoordinated way. We watched as she scrawled out a picture. I'm not a psychologist but I was at a loss to see how her pictures could be of any use. They were childish pin-men drawings, with oversized heads, and no detail. Jodie, however, clearly felt that she had done more than enough, as all further questions from the doctor were met with, 'Don't know. Piss off.'

At last the hour's session drew to a close. It felt as if it had been a bit futile, and I took the opportunity to ask the doctor if she could suggest anything to help me cope with Jodie's needs.

'Her main need is primary care,' she replied. 'I can see you're performing that admirably. She'll respond to continuity and firm boundaries. I'm very pleased she's placed with you. You're doing an excellent job.'

Compliments are all well and good, but what I had actually asked for was advice. I felt exasperated and very isolated. I wasn't trained for this – I was just muddling through in the dark, beset by fatigue, confusion and the sense of being hopelessly out of my depth. The tools and training I had just weren't sufficient for Jodie's needs, I realized now. The doctor was clearly excellent but she didn't seem able to grasp that I couldn't divorce Jodie's primary care from her mental welfare. I dealt every day not just with feeding her, amusing her and keeping her clean, but also with tantrums, violence, nightmares, waking visions, hallucinations and abject terror. Those things couldn't be fitted nicely into a one-hour slot. I lived with them day and night.

As we left, I felt more alone than I had in my life.

Before I knew it, Christmas was only ten days away, but my excitement of a few weeks ago was now hard to muster. It was going to be a low-key affair this year. I'd already bought and wrapped most of the presents, and decorated the house, but my heart wasn't in it. I tried to put on a brave face for the sake of the children, but I'd scaled down the usual arrangements. I was simply too exhausted to cope with a full-scale celebration. My parents were coming for Christmas Day, along with my brother and his family. I usually had a small party for friends and neighbours on Christmas Eve, but it wasn't going to be feasible this year. I explained to them that I had rather a lot going on at the moment, and I'd have them round when things were calmer. I hoped no one was offended.

In quieter moments, when I had time to reflect, I could see that I was becoming too involved in Jodie and her suffering. I was getting sucked into the abyss of her emotional turmoil, and although I was aware of it I couldn't seem to shake it off. She occupied my thoughts continuously. When I tried to read a book, I would find myself turning the page without having followed any of the plot. It was the same with the radio or television. I was constantly preoccupied by Jodie, and my own state of mind was suffering. Her distorted perception was colouring mine. It felt as though the evil that had corrupted Jodie's world was creeping out and corrupting my home as well. There seemed to be a poison in the air, and Jodie was its innocent transmitter. I decided I needed a break to put things back in perspective. I called Jill.

I explained to her that I was becoming physically and mentally exhausted. 'Jill, I'm not kidding, I need a break. Just some time to regroup and get my strength back, and think of something else for a bit. My own children could do with a bit of my time and attention as well. Could you look into arranging respite, please? Any weekend in January will be fine.'

'Of course,' she replied. 'You deserve a holiday. More than that, you need one, if you're going to be able to stay the course. I'll look into it this afternoon. The only problem is, Cathy, I'll have to find carers who are up to it. They'll need to be very experienced, with no younger or similar-aged children. I can think of one couple in Surrey. I'll see if they're free.'

'Thank you. I'd be grateful.' I put the phone down, my spirits lifting just a little.

Chapter Eighteen

Fire

The next day, Jill phoned to arrange her last visit before Christmas. We chatted for a while. Jill asked me if Jodie ever mentioned her brother and sister.

'Occasionally,' I replied, 'in the context of something she's telling me about home.'

'She doesn't ask to see them?'

'No, she doesn't.' And it suddenly occurred to me how unusual this was. The bond between siblings in care is often strengthened by separation, so even if the children aren't seeing their parents, Social Services usually make sure that contact is arranged between the brothers and sisters. 'Are there any plans for them to keep in touch?' I asked.

'Not at present. There were concerns about Jodie's treatment of them. I think they had reason to believe that she could be a bit heavy handed with them, which is why they all went to separate carers.'

I could imagine that. Jodie often lashed out when she was frustrated. 'What about Christmas cards and presents?' I asked.

'We can certainly pass them on, if she wants to send them.'

That afternoon, I asked Jodie if she wanted to go Christmas shopping to buy presents for her brother and sister.

'No,' she said. 'Don't want to.'

'How about sending a card? I'll help you write it if you like.'

'No. Hate them.'

'Why do you hate them, Jodie?'

She thought for a moment. 'Mum liked them more than me. She took them away when Dad came into my bedroom.'

'OK, pet, I think I understand.' I wasn't sure exactly what she was telling me but it was quite possible that the younger ones had been protected in some way from what Jodie went through. No wonder she would resent them. Perhaps she'd even hit out at them because she was jealous of their escape and wanted to punish them. It was conjecture, of course, but I hoped for the other children's sakes that they had been left alone.

Not only was Jodie cut off from her parents, she was also isolated from her siblings. With no grandparents in the picture, and abusers for aunts and uncles, this meant we were the only family she had. I thought of my own children, and the extended family who wouldn't hesitate to step in and look after them if anything happened to me. This wasn't such an issue now, but it had been a real concern in the past. My husband had left when Adrian was Jodie's age, and in darker moments I had welcomed the safety net of knowing that were I to fall under a bus they would be loved and cared for just the same. Jodie, on the other hand, had no one in the world but us.

Instead of shopping, Jodie wanted to do some painting, so I covered the table with paper, and set out the paints, brushes and a pot of water. I tied Jodie's apron around her, and left her for a few minutes to work on her masterpiece. When I came back to check on her, I was impressed. Jodie had produced a number of pictures which actually looked like something.

'Do you like them, Cathy?' Jodie asked proudly.

'I really do. These are excellent, Jodie. Can you describe them for me? Tell me what they are?'

'All right. This one is a house.'

'That's very nice. And those are the windows, aren't they?'

'Yes, windows. This one's a car. And this one's my dog, stupid old dog.'

I jolted to attention. At the pre-placement meeting, I had been told that Jodie had set fire to her dog, and had nearly burned her house down in the process. It was this incident that had finally led to her and her siblings being taken into care. 'I see,' I replied. 'Can you tell me more about the picture?'

'Yes I can. This is our dog, Sam. He's a big brown dog, always woofing.'

'And why did you say he was stupid, Jodie?'

'I don't know,' she replied impatiently.

'There must be a reason why he's stupid. You can tell me.'

'He's all ugly and burnt. He's horrible.'

'Oh dear. How did he get burnt?' I asked, trying to keep my voice light and relaxed. We were still standing side by side, looking at the pictures, and I was anxious not to put pressure on her. Jodie shook her brush in the water, then tested it on the paper. Finding it was still not clean, she dipped and shook it again.

'Jodie, can you tell me how Sam got burnt? I promise I won't be angry.'

'Jodie did it,' she muttered. 'I put all the bog roll on him, then used Mum's lighter. He was jumping and jumping, and woofing, and started running around, and everything was burning.'

'Where were your mum and dad when you did this?'

'They were at Uncle Mike's.'

'Were you on your own?'

'No, Ben and Chessie was there.' Jodie's sister's name was Chelsea, but she had trouble pronouncing it. 'I was looking after them.'

'So what happened next?'

'I picked up Chessie, and took her and Ben in the garden, and the stupid dog came and started rolling in the dirt. It looked all ugly, with its hair hanging off, and it stinks. And it made a lot of noise. I went in the hall and dialled 999, and the firemen came and put it out.'

'That was sensible, calling the firemen. You saved Chelsea and Ben.'

'Yeah,' she said, grabbing a fresh sheet of paper.

'Jodie, can you tell me why you wanted to hurt your dog?'

'Wasn't my dog,' she snapped. 'Daddy's dog. I told you.'

'Oh, right. Can you tell me why you wanted to hurt your daddy's dog?'

Her brow furrowed in concentration. Gradually, her face hardened, and her fist clenched around the brush. 'I hate him. I hate them, and I wanted to burn the house down and get out. It's a horrible house.' She thumped the table. 'And I want my daddy arrested. He's horrible, he sat on my face. They should arrest him, kill him!'

'But why set fire to the dog, Jodie? Why not burn the curtains or the sofa if you wanted to burn the house down and get out?'

'You are silly. I get smacked if I mess up the settee. Can I have a biscuit now, Cathy?'

While I got her a biscuit, I wondered if Jodie had set the dog alight as a way of punishing her father by hurting something he loved. Or perhaps, despite all her learning difficulties and developmental delays, Jodie had worked out a way to get herself out of that house. The frightening thought was that if she hadn't done what she did, she might still be there, undergoing that vile degradation day after day.

* * *

In the days that followed, Jodie became increasingly distant. I renewed my efforts to draw her into the heart of our family, but she remained fiercely resistant, acting as if she needed no one and could manage alone. I'd seen this kind of behaviour before – self-sufficiency is not unusual in abused or neglected children, as they've often had to be resilient in order to survive – but Jodie took it to a new level. Any expression of care or concern from us was met with outright rejection, or sneered ridicule. She wanted no part of the daily support or interaction that made up family life, and erected barriers to emphasize her separateness. One afternoon, Paula and Lucy joined us for a shopping trip, but Jodie refused to walk with us, instead she walked six paces in front or behind, and barely spoke a word. The next day, I took Jodie to the cinema to see *Lilo and Stitch*, and she pointedly sat two seats apart from me. She only rejoined me when the lights went down, as she was scared of the dark. She'd never been to the cinema before and she didn't show much excitement either before or afterwards. It was another sign of how dulled and desensitized she was. She basked in her loneliness, and I was completely at a loss to know how to break through.

My only hope was that Christmas would strengthen our relationship. After all, there's nothing more family oriented than Christmas.

Chapter Nineteen

Special Little Girl

Nicola came to give Jodie her last lesson before Christmas, and the following day the girls' school and Adrian's college both broke up. Suddenly, the five of us were together all day. However, I use the term 'together' loosely, for although we were under the same roof, togetherness was avoided, and not only by Jodie. Adrian, Paula and Lucy spent most of their time in their rooms, and when they did come down they were met with a kick, a punch or a volley of 'What you doing? Get out. It's my house now' and so on. Her attitude to the others had not softened much in her time with us. Illogically, the more attention I gave her, the more jealous she was of the others.

I explained to Jodie over and over again that we all lived together, as a family, but she wasn't open to reason. Even so, although she didn't want the family, it seemed that she did want me. Her possessiveness had been consolidated by the weeks when there had been just the two of us during the day, and I was starting to resent it. She demanded my constant attention, and I saw that she was doing what no other child had done before: undermining the fabric of our family. Normally, I would have dealt with this by trying to put some distance between us, but this was virtually impossible with Jodie, because of the high level of her needs.

Jodie's hostility and aggression had a powerful effect on everyone in the house and created an unpleasant atmosphere. Even when she was up in her room, we could feel it in the house, like a malevolent presence. At dinner, on the occasions when we did all eat together, I would have to carry the conversation, as the children had become inhibited by Jodie's endless snapping and kept quiet. We were even looking at each other less, because if any of us looked in Jodie's direction this was liable to set her off. One glance could quickly lead to a tantrum, and no one wanted to be responsible, however indirectly, for ruining yet another meal.

We were also communicating with each other less, as the nature of Jodie's abuse meant that we were limited to a very narrow range of conversation. We couldn't, for instance, discuss Lucy's new boyfriend, even though he was pretty much the only thing on her mind. In fact, men of all ages had become effectively taboo in our house; we were even wary of discussing pop stars on TV.

With the girls at home, I became acutely aware of the physical distance that Jodie had created between herself and the rest of the family. In the first few months after her arrival, Jodie had needed lots of hugs and comfort, but recently she had cut out almost all physical contact, even when she woke screaming in the night. I was always hugging and kissing the girls, and to a lesser degree Adrian, and this made it immediately apparent how isolated Jodie had become. I tried to remedy this, of course, but when I tried to hug her before she went up to bed, or asked her to sit next to me on the sofa, she would make a joke of being disgusted, and either shake her head or simply run away.

I was always upset when she did this, because it was clear that she was terribly sad and lonely, and I wanted nothing more than to show her the affection and love that my children took for granted. I'm no psychologist, but my guess was that the legacy of abuse had tarnished physical contact in her mind, and made it uncomfortable and frightening. It was an awful catch-22: Jodie needed affection more than anyone I'd ever known, but the means by which affection is communicated would only contribute to her anxiety.

Sally, the guardian ad litem, came to visit and asked to spend some time alone with Jodie. I left the two of them in the lounge, and took the opportunity to spend some time with Lucy and Paula, while Adrian was out with his friends. Jodie had been disruptive and aggressive all morning, and I found Paula sitting despondently on her bed. 'I wish I was back at school,' she admitted. 'I'm dreading Christmas. She'll ruin it.'

'No she won't. We won't let her. And we may find it's

just what she needs to open her heart. I know it's difficult, but she can't keep this up for ever.'

'Can't she? She's done a good job so far. I daren't even bring my friends home because of how she is.'

I was taken aback. My usually sociable daughter was now too embarrassed to bring friends home. I went over and hugged her. 'I'm sorry. I didn't realize. How about you arrange a sleepover when she's away on respite? Videos, midnight feast, the lot?'

She brightened a little. 'OK, Mum. I'm sorry.'

'No need to apologize. I understand.'

I went into Lucy's room, but the second I mentioned Jodie's name she turned on me.

'It's all we ever talk about. Jodie, bloody Jodie. I'm sick to death of her. I wish she'd never come. You won't change her, Cathy, whatever you do. Surely you can see that by now? She's evil. She needs a bloody priest, not a carer.'

I wondered if Sally had noticed the tension in the house, for as she was about to leave she paused in the hall and placed her hand on my arm. 'Cathy, you're doing a really good job, but make sure you and your family don't suffer. These children can play havoc with your emotions. Remember, her damage isn't your responsibility. You can only do so much.'

I found Sally's words comforting. It was nice to hear someone say something positive and to recognize what was going on. I respected Sally – she managed to combine professionalism with an ability to empathize that made me feel she understood.

Later that afternoon, Eileen phoned. 'Hello, Cathy,' she said, in her flat, plodding way. 'We've got a bit of a problem.'

'Oh yes?' I replied, unperturbed. I was used to social workers telling me 'we' had problems. It usually meant that something unpleasant was coming my way.

'When we sent a copy of the doctor's letter to Jodie's parents, someone forgot to blank out your details, so I'm afraid they sent them your name and address.' As usual, she didn't sound very sorry at all. I was furious. I'd been worrying about the Ear, Nose and Throat department being indiscreet, but meanwhile the Social Services had been handing out my details. I thought back to the silent phone call I'd received when Nicola had been with us; could that have been Jodie's parents?

'I see,' I said. 'That's really going to make Jodie feel safe! I can't say I'm surprised, though. When did it happen?'

'I'm not sure exactly. We only found out when Jodie's mother phoned today, demanding contact. She threatened to come to your house if we didn't arrange it. Obviously, we told her that was unacceptable, but I thought you should know.'

'Thanks,' I said tersely. 'And what did she say? Is she still planning on coming round?'

'I don't think so. She only mentioned it once. But don't worry, if she does come round we'll apply for an injunction straight away.'

Yes, I thought, but an injunction's only a piece of paper. I'd had angry parents turning up on my doorstep before, and I knew waving a scrap of paper at them wouldn't have had much of an effect. If a child is on a Voluntary Care Order, or we're working towards rehabilitating the child so that he or she can go back home and the parents are cooperating, then there's no problem in them knowing where the child and I live. Indeed, sometimes contact takes place in my house. But that clearly wasn't the case here, far from it. It was blindingly obvious that the highest level of care should have been taken to protect my details and that hadn't happened.

Eileen was impervious to my frustration, and there wasn't much I could do about the situation now. An injunction was as useful as locking the stable door after the horse had bolted.

'Right,' I said stiffly. 'Thanks for letting me know.' And ended the call.

I was angry, of course, but, as I'd said to Eileen, I wasn't terribly surprised. While the care proceedings are in progress, there are a huge number of documents flying around, between the parents, solicitors, social workers, the guardian ad litem and others. The present system relies on someone in the office at Social Services remembering to blank out the confidential details from every document, so it's inevitable that there will be mistakes. In my experience, about 50 per cent of parents are given my address at some point, which in my view is unacceptable.

As a result, when there is a breach of confidentiality, we as a family have to take special precautions. My children always look through the spyhole before answering the door, and if it's someone they don't recognize, they don't open it; instead, they fetch me. Foster children don't answer the door at all. On top of this, we have an expensive alarm system, a Chubb lock, and I always look up and down the road before leaving the house. After a while it becomes second nature, and we have all learned that we simply have to accept the risks. Thank goodness that, apart from some nasty verbal confrontations, none of us has been placed in real danger.

My patience with Eileen, however, was stretched to the limit a few days later. For reasons known only to themselves, Social Services decided to call a meeting to discuss Jodie's mother's threat to come round, and they wanted Jill and me to attend. We marvelled that they had the time, so close to Christmas. And what were we going to discuss in any case? No one could take back the information now that it had been released; taking out an injunction forbidding Jodie's parents to come near my property would have been pointless; the only other option was to move Jodie to new carers, which was clearly in no one's interests – especially not Jodie's. And who would take her anyway, with her complex needs, and at such short notice?

The meeting went as I had expected. We discussed all the possible options, before deciding on the sensible course: namely, to do nothing. I was relieved to get out of there and was just shaking my head at the monumental waste of time we had all been through when Eileen caught up with me in the corridor.

'Cathy, just before you go, can I give you this? It's a Christmas present for Jodie. Her father asked me to pass it on to her.'

I stared at her, astonished, as she held out a well-used Tesco carrier bag.

'I'm not sure it's really appropriate, Eileen,' I said, with forced diplomacy and reminding myself of my professionalism. 'Contact has been suspended, and present-giving is usually classified as contact, particularly in a case like this. Jodie feels very hostile towards her parents at the moment, understandably.'

'Oh, right,' she replied, mulling this over. 'Do you want me to give it back then?' As she said this, she pulled the unwrapped present out of the bag, presumably to show me how harmless it was, and that I was being over-cautious. It was a bright pink, long-sleeved T-shirt, with 'Daddy's Little Girl' printed on the front in big sparkly letters. Eileen looked at it, then held it up. 'So you don't think Jodie would like it?' she said.

I was almost lost for words as I looked at her holding up a T-shirt that was just about the most bitterly ironic thing I'd ever seen.

'Eileen,' I said, slowly and deliberately, 'Jodie has been sexually abused by her father, probably for most of her life. I don't think a T-shirt calling her daddy's little girl is very appropriate, do you? If I gave her this, Jodie would be terrified by the sight of it.'

The penny dropped. 'Oh, yes. Right, I take your point. We'll give it back then. Have a lovely Christmas!'

By the time I reached my car, I was still shaking my head in astonishment.

Chapter Twenty

Christmas

I was determined to make sure Jodie enjoyed Christmas, and started to feel part of the family. I knew from sad experience that foster children have often missed out on Christmas in the past. In fact, because they're at home for at least two whole days, and their parents tend to drink more, it can be the worst time of year for many children.

I remembered my previous placement, Callum, a sweet-natured ten-year-old. Callum had lived with his mother, who was a non-functioning alcoholic. That meant that she was incapable of leading a normal life, she was too locked into the prison of her alcohol dependency. The Christmas before Callum came to me, his father had sent him a cheque, which his mother had subsequently taken and spent on drink. On Christmas Day, she'd woken up after midday with a hangover, and then tried to make Christmas dinner. She hadn't done any shopping, so she'd peeled the breadcrumbs off some chicken nuggets, and tried to pass it off to Callum as roast turkey.

Despite her drink problem, Callum's mother hadn't been violent or abusive towards him, but her alcoholism had been such that Callum had had to look after her, rather than vice versa. For the previous three years, he hadn't had a single Christmas or birthday present. The Christmas he spent with us, I bought him a skateboard, helmet and kneepads, and when he opened them he ran out of the room, because he didn't want us to see him cry.

On Christmas morning, Jodie was up before six as usual, but she seemed to regard it as just another day. The previous night, we had all hung pillowcases on our doors, and these were now full of presents. I led Jodie downstairs and showed her that the glass of sherry, mince pie and carrots had all disappeared, which meant that Father Christmas had come to visit in the night.

'That's nice, Cathy,' she replied, as if humouring me. Throughout the morning, even as we opened up the presents under the tree, Jodie remained fairly flat, but she did seem to have some understanding of the importance of the day. She behaved well and generally joined in with the family. As I watched her, I hoped that, even though she wasn't showing much enthusiasm, the goodwill of the day was having some impact, and that she would remember it fondly in the future.

In the afternoon my parents arrived, along with my brother Tom, his wife Chloe and their six-year-old, Ewan. Suddenly the house was full of noise and excitement, and

I realized how cut off we had all become from our normal lives. For one thing, I hadn't had any adult company for more than a week. Jodie had met all of my family before, when they had come round to visit me in the usual run of things, and they always included the children I fostered, treating them like members of the family. Nonetheless she seemed a little startled when they all arrived at once, and she remained inhibited for most of the day.

After I'd made a round of drinks, we all gathered together in the lounge, ready to exchange presents. My family had brought some for us, and we had kept theirs under the tree, ready and waiting. We were all excited, but I could see that this was another ritual which was new to Jodie. As the presents were handed out, she stared at the others, taking cues on how to behave. She watched Ewan as he opened a present, and then she followed suit. She looked at it blankly, and I had to coax her to show excitement.

'That's lovely, Jodie, isn't it? You can play with that this afternoon. Will you say thank you?'

She did as she was told, but without any of the excitement and shining eyes that Christmas usually brought to children. Throughout the day, she didn't seem ungrateful for what she was given, and she did seem to like some of her gifts, but it was sad to see her having to mimic the enthusiasm and happiness that came naturally to the others.

After dinner we sat around and played games, as we slowly recovered from the meal. The girls worked hard to include Jodie, but she grew irritable, perhaps worn out by the excitement of the day. She went through the motions of playing the various games, but didn't seem to derive any pleasure from them. When she didn't win she became angry, and slammed her fist on the arm of the sofa. When she did win she was flat; she couldn't take any pleasure from it, and couldn't celebrate gregariously with the others. When we cheered for her, she joined in, but it seemed hollow.

Some time later she seemed to become frustrated and started holding her nose. I ignored it at first, suspecting that she was simply seeking attention, but when she persisted I eventually asked what was wrong.

'My nose hurts,' she said, her voice muffled by her hand.

'Oh dear,' I replied. 'Can I take a look?' She removed her hand, but squirmed away when I tried to touch her face. 'I can't see anything wrong. Is there anything I can do?'

'It hurts!' she moaned.

'Why does it hurt, Jodie? Have you done something to it?'

'It hurts.' She was getting louder, and did seem to be in pain.

'OK, well, come with me, and we'll put a cold flannel on it.' I took her into the bathroom and put the wet flannel to her face. 'Can you tell me what you did, Jodie, to make it hurt?'

'It was him. He whacked me in the face.'

'Who, Jodie?'

'Daddy! He thumped me,' she wailed, sounding like she was about to cry.

I had been sitting next to her in the living room, so I knew that nothing had actually happened. However, even though the pain seemed to be imagined, in the sense that she obviously hadn't been injured today, it was totally real to her. It sounded like she was remembering being hurt in the past, and was transposing the memory on to the present. We stood in the bathroom for a while, until she'd calmed down, then we went back to the lounge to rejoin the others.

At eight o'clock we stood on the doorstep and waved as my parents and my brother's family drove off home. I closed the front door. I was relieved that Christmas was over, even though it had gone as well as I could have hoped. Jodie had been somewhat overawed by the occasion and the large gathering, but she had behaved reasonably, and I hoped that some of the warmth of the season had got through to her. While it hadn't proved a breakthrough, and hadn't touched Jodie emotionally in the way that Callum had been touched, I hoped that Christmas would now mean something good to Jodie, and that she'd had a small taste of what other children enjoyed every year.

Chapter Twenty-One

A New Year

As the New Year approached, my spirits rose. A new year offers a new start, and anything seems possible on the first of January. Giving up smoking, however, was not on my list of resolutions, and I was now sneaking outside upwards of seven times a day, deluding myself that I would quit again when things were calmer. But when on earth would that be?

Despite my hopes, Jodie showed no improvement as the New Year passed. Her behaviour continued to be difficult and hostile, and her nights were increasingly disturbed by nightmares and hallucinations. She was having more incidences of remembered pain now, and these became linked to disclosures; Jodie would complain that her arm hurt, and this would lead to the memory of her mother hitting her with an ashtray, or her father scalding her with hot water. In all of these cases Jodie's pain seemed to be completely genuine, despite my attempts to explain to her that the injuries she was describing had happened months, sometimes years, ago.

Although I didn't think she was fabricating the remembered pain, I was becoming increasingly aware that she was lying in other situations. Often, she was so convincing that I found myself questioning what I'd seen, and doubting the evidence of my own eyes. If I caught her red-handed in the middle of some misdemeanour, she would so emphatically deny that it was happening that I had to stop and reassess what I was looking at. She had sometimes told lies when she first arrived, but I had assumed that she had been reverting to past experience, telling lies to avoid punishment, so it had been somewhat understandable. Now, however, she must have known that she didn't have to worry, that there was never any risk of her being physically or emotionally punished. Why, then, did she feel it necessary to deny her actions so vehemently?

She also started making false accusations, making up stories about the other children, even when I was in the room and had obviously seen that nothing had happened. She would claim Lucy or Paula had kicked, pinched or bitten her, which was clearly ludicrous. If anything, they were scared of her, quite understandably. When I pointed out to her that I had been in the room the whole time, and had seen that no one had gone near her, she flared up.

'She did. She did! Why don't you ever believe me?'

She was so passionate and convincing, I was often tempted to reconsider, and had to remind myself of what I'd seen.

At other times I caught her deliberately hurting herself. It wasn't like the time she had cut herself so chillingly. Now it seemed more as though it was done in anger, in a fit of fury or passion, when she would thump herself, pinch herself, thud her head against something or pull her hair. Then she blamed it on one of her imaginary friends. Some friend, I thought. I would have to patiently tell her that actually she was the one who was doing it, as no one else had touched her. This self-harming was one of the most disturbing aspects of Jodie's behaviour, and the pinches, scratches and thumps she inflicted sometimes produced marks, which she then used to convince herself even further that someone had been attacking her.

Even more worryingly, a week into the New Year the different voices she sometimes used began to suddenly take on identities of their own. Adrian's mobile phone went missing, and after a lengthy search I eventually found it in Jodie's toy box, which was on a shelf in the conservatory. Jodie hadn't stolen anything before, but she did have problems respecting other people's property, and I had been trying to teach her that we couldn't just help ourselves to what we wanted, that we had to ask the owner first.

'It wasn't me, honestly,' she repeated, looking me straight in the eyes and speaking in a babyish voice. 'It really wasn't. I'm not big enough to reach.'

Adrian and I both looked at the shelf, on which Jodie had just placed the toy box with ease.

'Of course you are,' said Adrian. 'It's just above your waist.'

'No,' she insisted, heightening her baby voice. 'It was her.' She pointed to the space beside her. 'It was Jodie.'

'You're Jodie,' I said wearily.

'No. I'm Amy. I'm only two, and I can't reach.' She rubbed her eyes, and pouted like a toddler. I told her again that she mustn't take Adrian's mobile, and left it at that.

A day later, the separation of her personality took on another, more sinister form. She was up at 5.30 in the morning, so I went in to settle her. She was sitting on the bed playing with her music box, and clapping loudly.

'Quietly, Jodie,' I said. 'Find something to do that's quiet if you've had enough sleep.'

She spun round to face me. Her features were hard and distorted. 'No,' she shouted, in a gruff masculine voice. 'Get out or I'll rip you to pieces. Get out! Bitch!'

I instinctively took a step back. 'Jodie! Don't use that word. Now calm down. Find something to do quietly. I mean it. Now.'

She stood and brought herself to her full height. She advanced towards me, with her hands clawed, baring her teeth. 'I'm not Jodie,' she growled. 'I'm Reg. Get out or I'll fucking kill you.'

I wasn't going to tackle her in that mood. I closed the door and waited on the landing. My heart was racing. I heard her pacing the floor, cursing my name, along with the rest of the family's. 'Wankers. Evil wankers. I'll rip their heads off.' She growled again, and then it went quiet. I opened the door and looked in. Jodie was in bed looking calmly at a book. Apparently, the old Jodie had returned.

As a foster carer, I'd seen some pretty extreme behaviour in children and to a certain extent I was used to it – but not this extreme. This was new. Jodie's imaginary friends seemed to be taking her over.

'Who's Reg?' I asked later that morning, as we emptied the dishwasher together. Jodie looked up at me uncomprehendingly. 'Do you know someone called Reg? I thought you mentioned his name when I came into your room first thing this morning?'

She shook her head, and carried on sorting the cutlery. 'There's someone on Mum's telly called Reg, but he's horrible. I don't talk to him.'

'And there's no one else you know called Reg?'

'No.'

And I believed her. Reg, like Amy, seemed to have taken on a life of his own, without Jodie's knowledge or consent.

When I told Jill about this, she was very surprised. 'This is highly unusual. If I'm right, then it sounds like D.I.D. – Dissociative Identity Disorder.'

D.I.D. is a rare and complex response to stress, she explained, where the personality splits into a number of different identities, in order to cope. Often, one identity has no idea what the others are doing.

'That sounds exactly what she's doing,' I said. 'It's very unnerving. Why is she doing it with us? It hasn't happened before. Why would it start happening now, when she's more secure than she's ever been?'

'Perhaps it's because it's only now that she feels safe

enough to remember the abuse. I suspect that before, she wasn't even able to accept and process what was happening to her. She blotted it out in order to survive. You said that she was very calm and accepting at first – remember how she passively began to take her clothes off when you wanted to photograph her? There was no fight in her, because she needed to keep going. However, now that she's removed from the abuse, she can start recalling it and piecing together what happened.'

I told her about the remembered pain, and how real it seemed to Jodie.

'That makes sense as well,' said Jill. 'She couldn't afford to feel the pain at the time, so she's feeling it now. She's receiving an onslaught of information, physical and mental. Because she's remembering all these awful things, her brain's on overload, and can't cope. By splitting her awareness, at least part of the self can be kept safe. So far you've seen baby Amy and an angry adult male. Does she have an adult female side as well?'

'Now I come to think of it, yes. I thought she was just imitating her mother, but now I'm not so sure. She tries to chastise Lucy and Paula as an angry housewife.'

'Does she refer to her by name?'

'Not that I've heard, no.'

'It's the classic form. Baby, adult female, and adult male. We've all got these components in our personalities, but when we're mentally healthy they're all rolled into one.' Jill paused. 'To be honest, I'm really worried.' I was now feeling extremely concerned myself. Jodie, it seemed, was reacting to the terrible things that had happened to her. I had no idea what to expect or if I would be able to cope with the fall-out of her extraordinary emotional trauma.

Jill asked, 'Have you told Eileen?'

'No. She's been out of the office recently.'

'I'll try and get through to her. And make the psychologist aware of this. If I'm right, this is a severe personality disorder.'

'Jill?' I asked tentatively, as something occurred to me. 'When she's in one of these states, can she do things that she wouldn't normally do? I mean, this Reg seems like a very angry character, and she seems to be quite strong when she's being him.'

'If she was any bigger I'd be getting her out of there. Adults with D.I.D. can assume superhuman strength and do things they wouldn't normally. But presumably you could restrain her if necessary, even when she's Reg?'

I paused. 'I think so.'

'And you want to continue?'

'Yes.' The further along this road I went, the more impossible it seemed to turn back. 'Now I know what it is, it doesn't seem quite so intimidating.'

'Good. It's really quite interesting, you know.'

Interesting for Jill, maybe, with her ability to assess the situation at one remove. For me … well, interesting wasn't quite the word.

That afternoon, I sat Adrian, Paula and Lucy down, and explained what Jill had said. They stared at me, open-mouthed.

'Jodie's got several personalities who possess her at different times?' said Adrian, trying to get it straight in his mind. 'And she has no idea that she's doing it?'

I nodded. It sounded crazy.

'Bonkers,' said Lucy. 'Stark raving bonkers. She's totally off her trolley.'

Paula laughed. 'I think I'll be the Queen of Sheba, and you can all wait on me and bring me gifts.'

I smiled. 'It's not an act, though, darling. She doesn't choose this. It just happens – it's her mind's way of dealing with what she's been through.'

'Will she be getting therapy?' Adrian asked, aware that she had seen a psychologist.

They all looked at me for an answer.

'Not until the assessments are complete, which won't be until nearer the final court hearing. Jill says this condition can pass of its own accord, and in the meantime the best advice is to ignore it. There's no point in challenging her because, as we've seen, she can't remember what the other characters have said or done.'

So we tried to ignore it and carry on, in the hope that it would pass, but now it escalated. Three or four times a day baby Amy, angry Reg or the nameless female matriarch suddenly took over and obliterated Jodie. It was often a very sudden change, usually lasting ten to fifteen minutes. Not only would Jodie's voice change, but each personality had its own type of body language. When she was in character as Reg, she would draw herself up to her full height, shoulders back, chest out, making herself big and masculine. As Amy, she cowered and her face was babyish and pouting. Her angry housewife stood aggressively, with short, angry movements and an unpleasant grimace. The change would occur in an instant, and revert just as suddenly when Jodie returned.

When baby Amy appeared at dinner, Paula couldn't resist cutting up her food and feeding her. 'I've never had a baby sister,' she grinned, as she wiped Jodie's chin. Conversely, when angry Reg took over, we all ran for cover. And knowing what the problem was did help, even though anyone watching would probably have thought we were the ones who were stark raving bonkers.

I informed both Eileen and the psychologist of this new and disturbing facet of Jodie's mental health, but heard nothing from either of them. I could understand it in the psychologist's case – it wasn't her role to offer me advice or therapy tips – but I was disappointed that Eileen still wasn't able to offer any support or even show much interest, although by now I didn't expect anything different. It was just another small piece of Jodie's tragedy that she had been assigned a social worker who was, to say the least, ineffectual.

Jill remained highly supportive – and the best we could do was just to hope that things would somehow get better.

The spring term began, and to my utter relief the secretary at Abbey Green School finally phoned to confirm that funding had been approved, and Jodie could start the following Monday. She suggested we visit the school on the Friday afternoon, so that Jodie could spend some time with her class, and get to know her support teacher. I wondered whether to tell her about the D.I.D. Should I try to warn her about Jodie's erratic and bizarre behaviour? Would the school even have heard of D.I.D.? I decided not to mention it. They had Jodie's Statement of Educational Needs, and if anything untoward happened I was sure they'd call me. Besides, I wanted Jodie to start with a clean slate.

Now that Jodie had a school place, there was no further need for a home tutor. Nicola phoned to wish Jodie luck and say goodbye, and Jodie spoke sensibly to her for a good twenty minutes. After she hung up she came over to me solemnly.

'Nicola is a good adult, isn't she, Cathy?'

'Yes, sweet, she is. Most adults are, as you'll discover.'

Jodie nodded thoughtfully. I felt a spark of hope. Perhaps she was taking tiny, slow but definite steps towards being able to regain her trust in adults.

Later that day, Jodie's social worker Eileen paid us a visit, her second in almost ten months. Predictably enough, it went much like the first and was not a success. Jodie was hostile from the start, and Eileen had great difficulty relating to her. It is usual to leave the social worker and child together, so that they can talk privately, but each time I tried to busy myself away from the lounge, one of them would immediately call me back in. Jodie would want another drink, or a jigsaw, or the television turned on, or Eileen would want to ask something trivial. For some reason Eileen seemed to want me there; I suspected she was anxious, or possibly even afraid of Jodie. After going back and forth a number of times, I decided I might as well join them, so I sat down with Jodie, and tried to get her to calm down and speak more quietly. A quarter of an hour later Eileen picked up her briefcase and, with a tight-lipped smile, left. She had done her duty.

'Good riddance,' said Jodie, and slammed the door behind her.

I didn't disagree.

Chapter Twenty-Two

The Fox and the Owl

It was mid-January. After a brief lull, the weather had turned bitterly cold, and we had three full days of snow. Jodie relished the excitement, and on the few occasions when I couldn't immediately take her out into the snow, she would gaze out of the window, transfixed.

The children's moods had lifted too. Now that they were back at school they seemed to have found a new burst of empathy for Jodie. Paula, in particular, appeared to have benefited from venting her frustrations before Christmas. We hadn't actually arranged the sleepover yet, but she had had a number of friends round, and had made a point of encouraging Jodie to join in as part of the group, bless her.

One such afternoon Paula's friend Olivia came for lunch, and they decided to go for a walk in the snow. My street is on the rim of a large valley, and the views are quite spectacular. Jodie pouted when she realized they were leaving, so Paula asked if Jodie and I would like to join them. Jodie was thrilled, so the four of us wrapped ourselves in coats, scarves and boots, and headed out.

As we walked up towards the high street, Paula and I each took one of Jodie's hands, as the pavement was icy. However, despite our best efforts Jodie kept slipping over, each time falling on her bottom. The third time it happened, she remained sitting on the pavement. She crossed her arms, rolled her eyes, and sighed theatrically, 'Here we go again!'

Paula and I grinned at each other in delight. Jodie's usual response to this kind of adversity would have been a bitter tirade: 'Who put that bloody ice there? Why are they doing that to me? It's your fault! Hate you!' and so on. Instead, she'd seen the funny side, and actively made an effort to try to make us laugh. It might not sound like much, but for us it felt like progress, and we joined in gratefully.

Jodie's first day of school was approaching, so I took her shopping for her new school uniform. We bought two navy skirts, two jumpers with the school logo printed on them, and three white short-sleeved shirts. Jodie had behaved well in the shop, enjoying the attention, but she became angry when I opted for knee-length socks rather than tights. She wanted to have tights like Lucy and Paula wore, but I knew she'd have difficulty putting them on again after P.E. In the end, I came up with a sensible compromise, and bought Jodie a pair of white, lacy tights that she could wear at weekends.

As we arrived home, Jill phoned and told me apologetically that the couple she had been considering for respite wouldn't be able to do it. Reason left unstated.

'Great,' I said tetchily. 'I'm promised regular breaks because of the high level of Jodie's needs, but because of that high level of needs it's impossible to find a carer.'

'I'm sorry, Cathy. I'll keep looking.'

'Yes, please do. Outside the agency if necessary.' What I meant by this was that Jill should approach a different fostering agency for a carer. This wasn't ideal, as standards varied, and the carers could be some distance away, but it was only one weekend and I needed a break.

On the Friday of that week we had arranged a visit to Jodie's new school. The visit wasn't till the afternoon, but Jodie was up early, as usual, and she immediately got dressed in her new uniform. I didn't think this was a good idea, but I was anxious to avoid any unnecessary confrontation, so I let her keep it on, and tucked an apron round her while she ate. Despite my efforts, by the time she'd had her breakfast and lunch her uniform contained a good helping of both. I sponged off the stains as best I could, and we arrived at the school gates looking reasonably smart for the afternoon session.

Abbey Green hadn't been my first choice, but as we arrived I was immediately impressed. The small, carpeted reception area was bright and welcoming, and the smiling receptionist greeted us warmly.

'Hello there, Jodie. It's very nice to meet you,' she said, and then phoned through to the Head, who appeared with courteous promptness.

'Adam West,' he said, shaking my hand. 'Hi, Jodie. Very pleased you can join us.'

He could only have been in his mid-thirties, but his friendly, informal manner quickly put me at ease. 'I thought we'd start with a tour of the school, then you can spend some time with Jodie's class, if that sounds all right?'

'Fine,' I said, then turned to Jodie. 'That sounds good, doesn't it?' She hid behind me, clinging to my skirt, all her bravado evaporated.

He led the way through the double doors and along a short corridor. 'There are six classrooms leading off the main hall,' he explained, 'which doubles as a canteen and gym.' As we went in, I could smell the residue of boiled greens and gravy, one constant factor shared by thousands of schools all over the country. The walls of the hall, like those of the corridors, were lined with examples of the children's work, and Mr West proudly described the various projects that had inspired this work. There were paintings, drawings, essays, poems and computer printouts, all based on a handful of themes, such as faraway lands, water, animals and designing a house. He was so enthusiastic and child-centred in his approach that I thought to myself: if this school can't cater for Jodie's needs, then no one can.

We arrived at Jodie's classroom, and the Head knocked before we went in. A sea of faces looked up curiously, before returning to their work.

'Caroline Smith,' he said, leading us to the class teacher. 'This is Cathy Glass, and this is Jodie.' We shook hands. 'The lady over there is Mrs Rice, the classroom assistant. She'll be helping Jodie.'

I glanced over to the table and smiled. Mrs Rice was a homely woman in her early fifties, wearing a floral patterned dress. She gave us a little wave. Jodie's confidence had increased during the tour, and she started wandering between the tables, peering over the children's shoulders. One boy shifted uncomfortably.

'Jodie, come here,' I called. But she ignored me.

'Don't worry,' said Mrs Smith. 'They're just finishing a piece of creative writing from our literacy hour. She can look.'

Mr West took his leave. 'If you have any questions, I'll be in my office at the end of the day.'

I thanked him, then spent some minutes with Mrs Smith, as she explained how the tables were grouped. She suggested I have a look around, so I did, feeling intrusively conspicuous. I felt like a giant as I walked among the miniature tables and chairs. The blue group was obviously the brightest; their writing was neat and detailed, with few grammatical mistakes. Mrs Rice's table, the orange group, was a different matter. These children were struggling to produce a handful of legible lines, and their work was full of corrections. Nonetheless, even the weakest of these was well above Jodie's standard. Jodie could barely write her own name.

'Would you like to join your table now?' Mrs Smith called to Jodie, from across the room. 'The spare chair beside Mrs Rice is your place.' Her request was gentle but firm. Jodie, who apparently wasn't quite ready, sized her up. I could see Jodie had one of her take-me-on-if-you-dare expressions, and my heart was in my mouth. Not now, Jodie, I thought, please let's not have a refusal and a tantrum on your first visit.

Now the other children were looking too; presumably they were used to responding immediately to any request from their teacher. Jodie stared at Mrs Smith, but then, to my relief, she lowered her gaze and plodded heavily over, flopping in her chair with a dramatic sigh.

Mrs Rice gave Jodie a pencil and paper. I crept round the edge of the room and perched myself on a stool by the window. The classroom overlooked the playground, and an older class was in the middle of a P.E. lesson. The room was quiet save for the occasional scraping of a chair and the hushed voice of Mrs Rice giving assistance to her group. I noticed that there were more boys than girls, and wondered whether, with their friendships already established, the girls would allow Jodie in. The poor girl needed to make friends just as much as she needed the education, and children can be very forgiving if they feel it's justified.

The children finished their essays, and Mrs Smith asked who would like to read one out. Half a dozen hands shot up, including Jodie's. A boy called James was chosen first, and he'd written about the night-time adventures of a fox called Lance. The story had a clear structure, and used lots of adjectives, and when he was finished the other pupils gave him a big round of applause. Next came Susie, whose story cleverly centred around the observations of a wise owl, from his vantage point high up in the trees. I gathered, from the content of the essays, that they'd been told to write about nocturnal animals. Susie was given her round of applause, and the teacher said they had time for one more. Jodie's hand flew up again, waving for all she was worth.

Mrs Smith exchanged a glance with Mrs Rice. 'Come on then, Jodie. Let's hear yours.'

I cringed with embarrassment; I could see she'd only produced a handful of scribbles. 'Class, this is Jodie,' said the teacher. 'She'll be joining us from Monday.'

Jodie stood up, and proudly held the paper at eye level, as she'd seen the others do. She pretended to read loudly and confidently, but her story was simply a string of unrelated words, punctuated by the occasional 'owl' and 'fox', with nothing intelligible in between.

'I saw the fox, to see, and I say don't, and the fox was him, and he … No. And then the owl. Where he was … He got far, and Mr Owl. Watch it. I told you, over there. So the fox went and in the night, you see, I said! Then they went. Then the fox was at night and the owl, but he was not, and I said. So I go to fox, and the owl …'

Fortunately Jodie was oblivious to the nonsense she was producing. I looked at the blank stares of the other children, and prayed they wouldn't laugh. After a couple of minutes, with no end in sight, the teacher thanked Jodie and told her to sit down. There was no applause, but neither was there any sniggering, and for that I was truly grateful. Jodie didn't appear to notice anything amiss at all – in fact, she was full of high spirits and rather triumphant.

The last hour was given over to self-chosen activities, during which the children worked on any aspect they liked of the topics covered during the week. I walked round the classroom once more. Some of the children were on the computers, adeptly cutting and pasting, while others were devising crosswords, stories, or producing pictures to complement their writing. Jodie was drawing a series of large boxes, and colouring them orange, blue, green, red and yellow. She explained to me that these were the class's different groups. I praised her, impressed that she'd picked up this much, then I wrote the names of the colours beneath them for her. Five minutes before the bell, the children packed away their things, and sat on the carpet in front of the teacher. They chanted, 'Good afternoon, Mrs Smith!' and the teacher wished them a happy weekend. As they collected their bags and coats and filed out, the teacher asked Jodie how she'd enjoyed her first afternoon.

'Brilliant,' she said. 'I want to come every day. For ever and ever!'

Chapter Twenty-Three

Granddad

One of the remarkable things about Jodie that I had noticed right from the start was that she had absolutely no conception of time. She would discuss events from years ago as if they were happening right now. Equally, if we had something planned for a few weeks' time, she would expect it to happen immediately. The day after the school visit she wanted to go again, and no matter how many times I explained to her that schools didn't open on Saturdays, she couldn't understand. Instead, she was convinced it was my fault.

'It's Saturday,' I explained, for the fifth time. 'No one goes to school on Saturdays. Be a good girl and take off your uniform, and we'll hang it up ready for Monday.'

'No! Don't want to! Shut up! It's mine and I'm going!' She sat cross-legged on the floor, with her arms folded, angry and defiant.

I crouched down. 'I know it's yours, sweet, and so are all these other lovely clothes. How about you wear your new lacy tights, as we're going to see Grandma and Granddad later.' I took the tights out of the drawer, and placed them with a skirt and jumper on the bed. 'It's up to you, but they'll look very smart with your denim skirt.'

I left the room, came downstairs and made breakfast. Half an hour later Jodie appeared in the clothes I'd laid out.

'Well done, Jodie. That's a wise choice.'

Every situation had to be handled with infinite care, if there was to be any chance of cooperation. I couldn't simply say, 'Put on your shoes, it's time to go.' Jodie would have to believe that it was her decision, and that she was in control. I knew where this had come from. When Jodie was being abused she had had no control over anything, so now she needed to be constantly in charge, just to feel safe. Unfortunately for me, the result of this was that even the simplest request would be met with a stubborn refusal, unless she could be persuaded that she herself had made the decision. I had to use diplomacy and coercion if I wanted anything done, and it could be very draining.

A visit to Grandma and Granddad's was just what we all needed, to smooth away some of the tensions within the family, and boost our morale. Jodie thought the world of my parents, as did Adrian, Lucy, Paula and all the other children we had looked after. Mum and Dad were in their early seventies, and they were the archetypal grandparents, with endless patience, and all the time in the world to indulge their grandchildren.

As we arrived, Jodie was on good form, and greeted my parents warmly. We all went into the living room, when Jodie caught sight of my parents' dog, Cosmo, a rather sad, passive, old rescue greyhound. Jodie suddenly screamed, then rushed across the room and started whacking him with her fists. The poor dog yelped, but Jodie was on top of him and he couldn't move. Dad and I rushed over and pulled her off, and I asked her what on earth she was doing.

'It looked at me!' she shouted, still glaring at the frightened dog. She had never shown any fondness for animals but she had a particular aversion to dogs. Perhaps it was because of her father's dog, or that, in the pecking order she was used to, the dog was the one she could kick and hurt without any fear of reprisal. She certainly never had any empathy for anything more vulnerable than she was.

'But it didn't mean any harm,' I said firmly, as my dad stroked the poor animal, then let him out into the garden. 'Now behave yourself. We said we were going to have a good day, didn't we?'

Jodie nodded sullenly.

'I tell you what,' my father said. 'Why don't you help me feed the fish? They haven't been fed yet, because they were waiting for you to arrive. We can all do it together, if you like. How does that sound?'

Jodie liked that idea, so she took Paula's hand, and the two of them followed my father into the garden while Cosmo watched from a safe distance. Adrian and Lucy, who considered themselves too mature for this kind of entertainment, sat in the living room, listening to their mp3 players, which had so far kept them mute since Christmas.

I joined Mum in the kitchen, and helped her prepare lunch, as we caught up on the latest news. As usual, I was soon doing most of the talking, and it was mainly about Jodie. I found it very cathartic to discuss abnormal behaviour in the context of my mother's very normal existence, and it helped that my mother was a good listener.

'Anyway,' I said at last, 'hopefully we'll turn a corner soon. So tell me, what have you two been up to?'

She recounted the various hobbies and interests which filled their very active retirement. Eventually the girls and my father streamed in through the kitchen door, while Jodie loudly enthused about the Golden Orbs which had come to the surface to feed. Mum and I served lunch, and I seated Jodie between the two of us. Her plate was piled high with chicken, roast potatoes, three vegetables and gravy.

'I wish I lived here,' she said, gazing adoringly at Grandma. Mum believes everyone needs 'feeding up', even when it's obvious they really ought to be on a diet.

As the meal progressed, I noticed Jodie taking more than a passing interest in my father, who was seated opposite her. She watched him intently, as he peered down through his spectacles at his plate, then over them to retrieve his drink or to talk to one of us. I assumed she was wondering about the way he used his spectacles, which were only for close focusing. Mum offered us second helpings, and I limited Jodie's. She sulked at this, resenting the fact that my father had filled his plate, but he needed it: age had thinned him down, rather than piling on the pounds.

'Granddad?' she asked suddenly, setting down her cutlery.

He looked up over his glasses. 'Yes, dear?'

'Are you Cathy's daddy?'

'That's right. She's my daughter.'

She thought for a moment, clearly trying to work something out. 'So, you're their granddaddy?' She pointed at Adrian and Paula. I smiled at Lucy, hoping she wouldn't be offended at Jodie's faux pas.

'Yes, that's right,' Dad replied. 'Well done.'

She glowed at the praise, and I was impressed that she'd finally made the connection, which she'd struggled with since she first met my parents. 'So if you're their granddad,' she said, still watching him, 'did you do naughty things with your willy to them when they was little, like my granddaddy did to me?'

Everyone fell silent. My father stopped eating and looked at me.

'Jodie! Of course not!' I said sharply. 'I've told you before, normal families don't do those things. Granddad is a good man. Now finish your dinner, we'll talk about this later.'

Jodie, blissfully ignorant of the shocking impact of what she'd said, picked up her knife and fork, and carried on eating contentedly.

My parents were shocked; I could see it on their faces. Jodie had asked her question with such ease, as if it were a perfectly natural assumption. We quickly changed the subject, and talked loudly of other things, but meanwhile I was thinking about what she'd said. Her grandfather? I wasn't even aware she had grandparents; there was no reference to them in the records. I wondered if she was confusing Dad and Granddad, or if there really was a grandfather involved? Did this mean there was yet another abuser present in Jodie's life? Was there anyone who hadn't had a part in destroying her? I glanced at my father, who was still subdued after Jodie's bombshell, and wondered again at the great divide between healthy and abusive families. Could her perception ever be changed? Perhaps one day she'd be able to accept that what happened to her was abnormal and wrong, and that most families functioned very differently. But at times it seemed a forlorn hope.

I kept a close eye on Jodie for the rest of the afternoon, and Mum helped her with some colouring and cutting out. We were never able to leave my parents without a final cup of tea and slice of homemade cake, and we didn't say our goodbyes until just after six. There was an accident on the motorway, so it was well past Jodie's bedtime by the time we finally arrived home. I decided to leave asking her about her granddad until the following day, but as I tucked her into bed and dimmed the lights she suddenly asked, 'Why didn't Granddaddy do naughty things to Adrian and Paula? Doesn't he love them?'

I looked at her in the half-light. She was snuggled deep beneath her duvet, with only her blonde hair visible, falling in strands across the pillow. How could I begin to unravel the confusion between normal affection and the warped gratification that she had known?

'It's a different kind of love, Jodie. Completely different from the one between two grown-ups. And what was done to you wasn't love of any kind. It was cruel, and very, very wrong. You'll understand more when you're older.'

I wanted to leave it at that, to go downstairs and make a cup of coffee, then maybe sit in the lounge and read the paper. But if I didn't follow this up now, Jodie might have forgotten it in the morning, sucking the awful memory back into the black abyss of denial.

With a now familiar surge of anxiety at what I was about to hear, I turned up the light a little, and sat on the chair beside her bed. Her eyes peered over the duvet, and I stroked her forehead.

'Jodie, pet, did your granddad hurt you in the same way your daddy and uncle did?'

She shook her head. 'No, Cathy. They was nicer.'

'They? How many granddads did you have?'

'Granddad Wilson and Granddad Price.'

'So there were two then. And how were they nicer, Jodie?'

She thought for a moment, as the lines on her forehead creased, and I hoped she was about to tell me that they'd taken her to the zoo, or bought her an Easter egg, the kind of things normal grandparents do.

'They lay on top of me, but they didn't hurt. They just peed in the bed. It was because they loved me, Cathy.' She said it so matter-of-factly, she might as well have been recounting a trip to the zoo.

'No it wasn't. It was wrong, Jodie. Adults don't show love like that. What they did was cruel. It's got nothing to do with love.' But I could see how ejaculation without penetration might have seemed kinder to her, when compared with the other abuse.

'Were Mummy and Daddy in the room when this happened?' I asked.

'Sometimes.' She nodded. 'And Uncle Mike, and someone I didn't know.'

I held her hand and stroked her forehead. 'Is there anything else? Can you remember any more?'

She shook her head. 'Can I have a story now, Cathy? *Topsy and Tim's New Shoes*?'

She wasn't upset, and I found that I wasn't either. I was becoming as desensitized as her. I read her the Topsy and Tim story, then said goodnight and went downstairs. I made a note of the conversation in my log, then stepped outside for a cigarette. As I stood there in the freezing night air, I wondered if there was a course I could take in basic psychotherapy. I decided not. If I made an amateur attempt to help Jodie, it would probably do more harm than good. All I could do was continue along the same lines as I had been, using a common-sense approach which restated normality, but did little or nothing for the profound psychological damage that had already been done. Not for the first time since Jodie's arrival, I felt completely inadequate.

On Sunday morning Jodie was buzzing with energy, and I had to deal with a barrage of questions about school. Would she have homework? Was there playtime? Did the teacher have a husband? A daddy? Would it rain? Adopting my usual policy of trying to burn off some of her nervous energy, I took her out on her bike.

'It's so cold,' I remarked, pulling up my collar. 'I think it could snow again.'

'What's snow?' she asked, as we climbed the hill. I tried to remind her as best I could, telling how much she had loved it earlier in the month when it had snowed over three days, but Jodie suddenly decided that she wanted snow immediately, and became angry when I couldn't or, according to her, wouldn't produce it. A full-scale tantrum ensued, and she lay prostrate on the pavement, banging her fists and demanding snow for a good fifteen minutes. It would have been comical if I hadn't been so cold. When we got back to the house, I sat her in front of a video until dinner was ready. She was just as hyperactive after dinner, and had another tantrum when I wouldn't go out to buy her some ice cream. I managed to persuade her to take a bath, and this calmed her down enough for bed at seven. Tomorrow would be her first day at school for more than a year, and I was praying that it would be a good one.

Chapter Twenty-Four

Friends

Jodie was up and down all night, but in the morning she was bright and excited, whereas I was just exhausted. She changed into her school uniform, and we only had one small hiccup when she demanded to wear her lacy tights, but I eventually managed to dissuade her.

We arrived at school early, so we sat in the car for a while, listening to the radio. Although Jodie was excited, I could tell she was also a little nervous, and I was nervous too, on her behalf.

I held Jodie's hand as we walked up to the school gates. I gave it a squeeze, and we entered the school building. Mrs Rice came and met us in reception. Because of Jodie's learning difficulties, it had been arranged that I would hand her over to Mrs Rice every morning, and she would hand her back at the end of the day. I gave Jodie a hug, and watched anxiously as Mrs Rice led her down the corridor.

As soon as I arrived home, the phone rang. It was Jill; she'd received the notes I'd emailed on Sunday about Jodie's granddads, and she'd already spoken to Eileen.

They had checked the records, and confirmed that there were definitely no grandparents on the scene; it was done with such speed that I wondered if Eileen's manager had spoken to her. Jodie's maternal grandmother was alive, but had fallen out with her daughter years ago, and there was no contact between them. Jodie had never known her grandfathers on either side. There was a pause, as Jill waited for me to come to the obvious conclusion.

'They're in the same category as the so-called uncles, paedophiles in the guise of family members?' I said. Jodie had previously described some of her other abusers as uncles and aunts, but it appeared that these were not actual relatives; rather, they were friends of Jodie's parents, who had been described as family members as an easy way of introducing strangers into the home environment.

'We think so. It looks as though Jodie's parents must have been part of a network. The police are running a check now for registered offenders,' Jill replied. 'If the names Wilson or Price come up on their list for the area they'll take them in for questioning. But I have to be honest, Cathy, I'm not optimistic. If these people haven't been convicted before, they won't be on the list. There's another thing too. Eileen's had the results of the forensic medical back.'

'Yes?'

Jill lowered her voice. 'It confirms that Jodie's been penetrated, but without DNA, or third-party evidence, there's not enough for a criminal prosecution. She has been abused, but to get a conviction you need to prove who was responsible.'

'Who on earth do you think must have been responsible? Isn't it clear that Jodie's telling the truth? The forensic result just confirms everything she's been saying.' I sighed. 'So what now?'

'We keep going, and hope something comes up. Eileen's realized that Jodie's due for an LAC review – it's actually overdue. Is it all right if we have it at your house? She's suggested Thursday afternoon at two o'clock.'

'Yes, that's fine.'

'Eileen wants Jodie to be there. I know ... an afternoon off school when she's just started, and I know she won't be able to contribute anything. But Eileen's suddenly one for the rule book, and she is within her rights to insist.'

I felt the mixture of anger and frustration that so often seemed to dog me when dealing with Eileen. 'OK, I'll pick her up from school at lunchtime,' I said, and, after a quick goodbye, hung up.

LAC stands for Looked After Children, which is the official term for children in care. A LAC review is a regular meeting, required under the Children's Act, and attended by all those involved in the child's case. The purpose of the meeting is to report on the child's progress and decide on any actions which need to be taken. Jodie's parents wouldn't be present, of course, because contact had been suspended, but the guardian ad litem, the child's social worker, her team leader, the headmaster, Jill, Jodie and myself would all be there. However, since Jodie was still functioning at the level of a four-year-old, her presence was likely to offer little more than disruption.

With Jodie at school, I vowed to make the most of my first free day in months. I sat on the sofa and started to plan my day. Three hours later I woke up, and as I came to I chided myself for the time I'd wasted. It was now 12.45, and I had less than two hours before I'd have to make the return journey to school. I rushed to the supermarket, but by the time I got home I realized I'd have to give up my fantasy of reading in peace for an hour. Still, I comforted myself, I must have needed the sleep. I was getting so little at night, and that was broken every few hours by Jodie's night-time torments. No wonder I couldn't keep my eyes open the minute I had the opportunity to relax.

I arrived back at the school and waited by the gates, exchanging smiles with a few of the other mothers. Had they heard about Jodie already, I wondered? How would the other children have described her? Mrs Rice appeared, with Jodie jumping up and down beside her, and told me Jodie had had a good day. This was confirmed in the car, as Jodie wouldn't stop talking all the way home. She told me over and over again about all the children in her class, most of whom were now her new best friends – and she wanted all of them to come round for tea, just like Paula's friends did.

Adrian, Lucy and Paula were already in when we got home, so Jodie had a new audience for her excitable monologue, and they listened with patience. It continued throughout dinner to the extent that I had to remind her to eat, which was definitely a first. She settled easily that night, as she was physically and emotionally exhausted, and I did much the same.

Just after midnight I was woken by the sound of Jodie sobbing on the landing. I pulled on my dressing gown, hurried out of my room and found her lying on the carpet outside Paula's bedroom. Her face was crimson, and she could hardly breathe for crying. I put my arm around her, and led her back to her room. I sat beside her on the bed and cuddled her until she was able to speak.

'Cathy,' she said, through sobs, 'when I was at my school I had a friend, but then she wouldn't be my friend any more.' I passed her a tissue, and waited while she blew her nose.

'Don't upset yourself, pet. You'll make lots of new friends now.'

'But she was my best, best friend. And she came to my house. But then she wasn't allowed, because of what I said.'

My sleep-fuddled brain started to focus. 'What did you say? I'm sure it wasn't that bad. Friends fall out all the time, Jodie, even best ones.'

She shook her head. 'I told her. About Mummy and Daddy and Uncle Mike. And she told her mummy and daddy, and they said she couldn't come and play.

Her mummy said it was a bad house. But I'm not bad, am I, Cathy?'

I held her closer to me. 'No, sweet, of course you're not bad. She meant what was happening to you was bad. It was never your fault. You mustn't think that.' As I comforted her, my mind was whirring. She had told someone. Other adults had been made aware of the abuse. Could this be the third-party evidence that was needed to secure a prosecution? I was fully awake now.

'You did right to tell, Jodie. Her mummy and daddy should have told the police instead of stopping her from playing. What was her name? Can you remember? It's important.'

She sniffed. 'Louise Smith. She lived next door. I won't tell my new friends, will I, Cathy?'

'No, there's no need. You can tell me anything you want, and you know that I'll do something about it.'

She sniffed and managed a smile.

'Good girl. You did the right thing. Now I want you to try and get some sleep. We don't want you tired for tomorrow.'

I tucked her in, and stroked her forehead until her eyes closed. I was tense and focused. Jodie had had the courage to tell someone, but that courage had not only gone unrewarded but, in her eyes, it had led to further punishment, as she had been prevented from seeing her friend. I could imagine why Louise's parents had kept quiet: they hadn't wanted to get involved, and they'd wanted to protect their own child. However, by keeping quiet they'd left an innocent victim open to further abuse. All they needed to have done was to make an anonymous phone call to the NSPCC, the Social Services or the police, and that would have been enough to start an enquiry. Whenever this kind of allegation is made, the police or Social Services have to look into it.

I went back to bed, but I couldn't settle. In the end I gave up, and went downstairs and made myself some hot chocolate. I stood in the kitchen, warming my hands on the hot mug. There were wider implications to what Jodie had said. Living next door, the Smiths must have seen the comings and goings. They probably knew who these so-called aunts, uncles and granddads were, by face, if not by name. If the police interviewed the Smiths now, with the allegations out in the open, surely they'd have to tell the truth? I knew the council estate where Jodie had grown up well; I'd looked after kids from there before. It was a tight-knit, closely bound community, where everyone seemed to be in and out of each other's houses. How many other residents had known what was going on, but remained silent, fearful of the potential consequences? How did they sleep at night?

Chapter Twenty-Five

Denial

'But they must know something!' I insisted to Jill, when she phoned a few days later. 'They were in and out of each other's houses all the time. The girls were best friends.'

'Yes, but the Smiths claim they still are friends. They say they're astonished by the allegations, and have even offered to give a character reference for Jodie's parents. I'm sorry, Cathy, but I don't think we're going to get anything useful out of them.'

I went quiet. I could feel the walls of conspiratorial silence that had imprisoned Jodie closing in again, and it was frightening. 'So why did they stop their daughter from going to play, if her parents were so bloody respectable?'

'Well, they say they never did. Look, Cathy, I don't doubt what you're saying, or what Jodie's said. But Eileen's actually spoken to them, and it seems there's no chance of them talking, and the police are of the same mind. If these so-called granddads were registered offenders it would be different, but they're not. The fact is, all we've got is the word of a confused eight-year-old with learning difficulties, who won't even speak to the police. It's not enough to bring a case.'

'She's not that confused,' I snapped. 'Not when it comes to this; she's clear and focused.' I took a breath; there was no point shouting at Jill. 'I'm sorry, I'm just frustrated. It looks like they're going to go scot-free, while Jodie has to bear all the consequences of being brave enough to tell the truth.'

'I know it's frustrating, but Jodie doesn't need to know there won't be a prosecution. At least it's good for her that she's been able to disclose, but we'll have to accept that's as far as it's likely to go at present. The police have said they'll keep the file open, in case anything new comes up.'

'I'm going to have to distance myself,' I said wearily. 'I'm becoming too involved.'

'You wouldn't be such a good carer if you weren't, Cathy. And I'm still working on that respite. I haven't forgotten.'

I felt like going round to the Smiths' myself, and begging them if necessary to come forward. I stood on the patio smoking, working out what I would say. If I looked into their eyes, could I shame them into admitting what they knew? If I told them about Jodie's nightmares, about how her life had been destroyed, could I change their minds? I inhaled deeply, but as I stubbed out the cigarette I realized I couldn't do it. It would have been a completely inappropriate, unprofessional thing for a foster carer to do, and I would probably have lost my job, and therefore lost Jodie. Besides which, I doubted it could have done any good. If they'd resisted the best efforts of the police and Social Services, they weren't likely to be swayed by me. I went inside and closed the kitchen door. Yet again I felt Jodie's frustration.

I took some comfort from the fact that Jodie was finally in school, and hoped that the routine of it would give her something else to occupy her mind. But this routine was doomed to be interrupted by constant reminders of her past. Thursday arrived, and I had to pick her up from school at lunchtime, so that she could attend the LAC review.

By three o'clock there were six of us in my lounge, sitting with coffee and digestives. Astonishingly, Eileen had turned up a whole hour late, with no explanation beyond a half-hearted, 'Sorry, I was held up.' She proceeded to distribute copies of her agenda, and the meeting finally began.

Jodie was suddenly the centre of attention for reasons she didn't understand, so naturally enough she played to the audience. With hands on hips, she strutted up and down, shouting instructions, and telling everyone off for talking every time they spoke. She said she was 'playing at schools'. Jill and I exchanged knowing glances; we'd had a feeling this might happen.

Despite Jodie's disruptions, Eileen persisted in working through her agenda, and raised her voice above Jodie's when necessary. It quickly turned into a circus. Adam West gave his report, which was minimal, since Jodie had only been in school for three and a half days. Then, as he had another meeting to go to, he made his apologies and left. Jodie wasn't happy at this. Why should he get to go back to school and have fun, if she couldn't? She was on the point of a full-scale tantrum, which I averted by replenishing the biscuits, and reassuring her she could go tomorrow.

Because of Jodie's behaviour I was constantly in and out of my chair, and as a result I could barely contribute to the discussion. I was also uncomfortable, as I felt that talking about Jodie while she was there was demeaning for her, and likely to reinforce the very issues and behaviour that we were trying to move on from.

'Would you like to contribute anything, Jodie?' Eileen eventually asked. 'This meeting is after all about you.'

'Contribute means to say something,' I explained, as Jodie gawped blankly.

'No!' she shouted. 'And I've told you before to stop talking, or you'll miss your playtime.' I was pleased the headmaster had left, and was no longer here to see this Dickensian portrayal of his award-winning school.

An hour and a half later we were finally finished, having fulfilled the statutory obligation, but accomplished next to nothing. I would have liked us to address Jodie's desperate need for therapy, but this didn't seem to be an option until the childcare proceedings had been resolved. The team leader and the guardian left first, then Eileen made a move to follow.

'It was nice meeting you again, Jodie,' she said, tucking her notes into her briefcase.

'Was it?' she said. 'Why?'

Eileen forced a smile. 'Because you're a lovely little girl.'

The condescension and insincerity was evident even to Jodie. There was a moment's pause as her features changed into a set that I knew well, while Eileen remained blissfully ignorant of what was coming.

'No, I'm not!' Jodie boomed, in her deep masculine voice. 'I'm Reg, and I'm angry. Have you locked up that fucking father yet?' And before I could stop her, she kicked Eileen on the shin.

I quickly enfolded and restrained her, as Eileen rubbed her leg.

'I'll see you out,' said Jill, leading her down the hall.

'That was very naughty,' I said to Jodie. 'You don't kick, whoever you are.'

But as quickly as Reg had appeared, he vanished, and by the time Jill returned Jodie was sitting happily on the floor, engrossed in her Lego.

'So that's Reg,' said Jill grimly. 'I know you told me about this, but nothing prepares you for seeing it in action. It's so chilling. I've seen it before years ago, but my goodness – only the severest kind of trauma could provoke this in such a young child.'

'This is the first time she's turned into Reg in front of strangers,' I said.

'Well, I'm pleased I've had the opportunity to witness this first hand.'

'Yes, I expect Eileen was as well,' I replied dryly.

We both smiled.

Now that Reg had been released in front of others, he had no hesitation in making another appearance, this time with a different audience. I had just returned from taking Jodie to school when the secretary phoned. 'Hello, Cathy, we have a problem. Jodie's not hurt, but the Head has asked if you could come straight away.'

My coat was still on, so I retrieved my keys from the hall table and headed back, my mind racing. What could she have done now? When I arrived, the secretary showed me straight through to the Head's office. He was seated sombrely behind his desk, and I sensed that the distance between us was deliberate, to emphasize the seriousness of the conversation we were about to have.

'Thank you for coming so promptly,' he said, briefly standing and waving to the seat opposite. 'I'll come straight to the point. We've had rather an unfortunate incident this morning, which resulted in Jodie slapping another child's face.' One incident of slapping wouldn't necessitate my being summoned before the Head; we both knew that. 'I'll be perfectly frank, Mrs Glass. It wasn't so much the slapping that upset the child, and the rest of the class, but the behaviour that accompanied it.'

I raised my eyebrows questioningly.

'Jodie was completely out of control over something

really quite minor. She was kicking and shouting vile abuse, then blamed it on someone called Reg. We don't have anyone with that name in the class, but she was adamant. It took two members of staff to calm her down. Now, obviously I haven't known Jodie for very long, but her reaction was very disturbing, and seemed quite out of character.'

Out of character indeed. I decided I had no alternative but to come clean. I told him about Jodie's D.I.D., and what we'd witnessed at home, then reassured him that there was a psychologist involved. I omitted to mention that the psychologist was only conducting assessment, rather than therapy. I also touched on her two other characters, and he nodded in recognition.

'Mrs Rice mentioned that Jodie sometimes talks in a babyish voice. We had put it down to nerves – you know how children can regress if they're anxious – but you're saying it's part of the same problem?'

'It could be, yes.'

'And presumably her social worker's aware?'

'She is.' Even more so after yesterday, I thought.

'And you say it could disappear of its own accord?'

'That's what I've been told, yes.'

'Normally we'd exclude a child for the rest of the day after an incident of this nature, but there seems little point if she doesn't even know what she's done. I'll keep her here and monitor it.'

I thanked him, and asked him to pass on my apologies to the other child, and the staff. 'I'll speak to Jodie later,' I said, feeling duty bound to offer something. 'I'm sorry you've had to deal with this in school.'

I came out of the office, aware that I'd had a narrow escape. It was clear that Mr West wouldn't tolerate Reg's behaviour indefinitely. I spoke to Jodie about it that evening, but it was a waste of time. Sometimes she appeared to remember nothing at all, and sometimes she appeared to know what I was talking about when she blamed it on Reg or Amy. We could both begin to lose our sanity if we went on too long trying to work out what was happening. As far as she was concerned, I was accusing her of something which she herself hadn't done, and I didn't pursue it for fear of undermining the trust that she'd placed in me. Yet again, this was another incident which demonstrated that Jodie desperately needed therapy to start as soon as possible. It simply wasn't good enough to wait until the end of the court proceedings. I decided to pressure as much as I could for treatment to begin.

'She does need to be in therapy,' the psychologist agreed, when I took Jodie for her next appointment at the clinic the following week. 'How long is it until the final court hearing?'

'It's set for May.'

That was almost four months away. She sighed and rolled her eyes. 'And have you noticed any improvement, generally?'

I looked at Jodie, walking in circles in the middle of the room, muttering to herself. 'She hasn't defecated for some time. And on a good day I have some level of cooperation, although she's plagued by flashbacks even then. Yesterday she was convinced she could see her dad's face on the curtains in the lounge.'

'She was hallucinating?'

'Yes, but it was completely real to her. She said I must have let him in without telling her, and she was hysterical. At night she wakes up screaming, and when I go in she's convinced there are people in the room who want to hurt her. I can see her eyes focusing on them, even though she's staring at blank space. It can take hours to reassure her. She seems to be actually reliving the pain she felt at the time.' I shuddered. 'My family find it very upsetting.'

'They would. With post-traumatic shock the abuse is constantly being revisited. Are you having regular breaks?'

I smiled stoically. 'I'm still waiting. There's a problem in identifying suitable carers, because of the level of Jodie's needs.'

She made a note in her pad, then looked at her watch.

'Cathy, there's one more test I'd like to do with Jodie. Would it be all right if you waited outside? It's just a game,' she reassured Jodie, who clung to my arm, wanting to come with me.

I sat on one of the chairs in the corridor, and Dr Burrows closed the door. It may have only been a game, but Jodie was in no mood to play; I could hear her shouting at the doctor to shut up and go away. Dr Burrows' even tone persisted for ten minutes, then the door opened and Jodie rushed out.

'Blimmin' doctors,' she cursed. 'Why don't they mind their own fucking business?' She had reached the exit by the time I caught up with her.

Over the following weeks Jodie continued to enjoy school, although there was no noticeable improvement in her behaviour or condition. In fact, rather than the school having an effect on Jodie, it seemed instead that Jodie was affecting the school. One afternoon when I arrived to collect Jodie I noticed that Mrs Rice's eyes were red and puffy. 'Are you OK?' I asked, hoping this wasn't too intrusive.

'Yes, I'm fine,' she laughed, still sniffling. 'I just got a bit emotional.'

'Oh, I hope it's not anything that Jodie's ...'

'No no no. Well, not exactly,' she interrupted. 'Actually, could I have a quick word?'

Mrs Rice obviously didn't want to talk in front of Jodie, so I sent her off to run around the playground for a few minutes, while Mrs Rice and I walked over to a quiet spot.

'Some of the children had their hearing tests today, and Jodie started talking in class about some kind of medical she'd had. We were pleased that she had something to contribute, obviously, but then suddenly she started saying these awful things about … She said she preferred it when a man did it, and it became clear she was talking about … well … you know.'

'Oh, I am sorry. She doesn't know the difference between what's appropriate and what's not.'

'No, it was fine. I interrupted her before the other kids twigged, but she seemed to want to talk about it, so I spoke to her at playtime, just the two of us. Anyway, I just wanted to make sure you were aware of the details. The only new aspect seemed to be that she mentioned an aunt being involved, as well as her mother, but she didn't give a name for the aunt. That was all.'

'OK, thank you for letting me know. She has told me about the aunt before. I'm really sorry you've had to deal with all this.'

'Oh, don't worry, I'm sure it won't be the last time!' She smiled. I patted her on the arm, and Jodie and I headed home.

On the Friday the school held a fête for Comic Relief. The sun was out, so the stalls were set up in the playground, rather than in the hall as had been expected. The children wore red, the teachers wore wigs and silly costumes, and even some of the parents were wearing red plastic noses. There were stalls with sweets and cakes, games and tombolas, and a set of stocks where the braver teachers allowed themselves to be pelted with wet sponges. It was great fun, and Jodie revelled in it. I stood watching her, as she hared around the playground, being chased by three of her classmates. They were all soaking wet, and their faces were flushed with the excitement. Jodie's pigtails swung in the air as she dodged and ran from her new friends, laughing wildly. It was probably one of the happiest moments of her life.

Chapter Twenty-Six

Links in the Chain

The school handovers were not just designed to ensure Jodie's safety; they also allowed the teaching assistant and me to keep each other fully updated with Jodie's progress. Each morning I gave Mrs Rice a brief summary of how Jodie had been the night before: how she'd slept, what her mood was like, any problems to look out for and so on. In the afternoon Mrs Rice would do the same for me, which was useful, especially when Jodie was upset or angry at school.

As Jodie settled into her class she seemed to get on reasonably well with the other children, largely because most of them were bright enough to stay on polite terms with her while keeping their distance. However, there was one other pupil in the orange group who had behavioural problems, a boy called Robert, and he was Mrs Rice's other main charge. She sat between Jodie and Robert in class, and spent most of her day working with the pair of them on a one-to-two basis, keeping their work loosely related to what was going on in the broader lesson. This kind of teaching is known as 'differentiating work'.

One afternoon, as Jodie trudged unhappily down the steps, Mrs Rice explained to me what had happened. The class had been drawing with pastels, and Robert and Jodie had both reached for the red pastel at the same time. Robert got there first, so Jodie sat back in a huff. She glared at her picture, glared at Robert, then got up out of her chair, walked behind Mrs Rice and grabbed the pastel out of Robert's hand. Robert started crying, and Mrs Rice naturally told Jodie off and made her hand it back. Jodie was furious, and shouted that it was Robert's fault, and called him 'four eyes'. This upset Robert even more, as he'd only recently started wearing glasses, and Jodie was eventually persuaded to apologize. When the lesson finished, the children went out for playtime. In the playground Jodie spent some minutes standing in silence, while staring at Robert. Then she walked over and punched him, and the pair of them had to be separated.

On the way home she was still furious, thumping and kicking the back of the passenger seat. 'He's bullying me, Cathy! I hate him, I hate him!' Jodie often had tantrums in the car, as she knew there was little I could do to stop her.

'Jodie, calm down and sit still. I won't tell you again.'

'No! Shut up!'

'Jodie, there'll be no television tonight, I'm warning you. You haven't had the best of days. Enough!'

She pouted in silence and I tried to explain the rationale behind her being told off. 'You grabbed the red pastel from Robert, then called him a very hurtful name. That's why Mrs Rice was annoyed.'

'Yes, but I needed it. Why won't anyone believe me?'

Over the following weeks, Jodie's complaints about Robert became a regular feature of our drives home, and often our evenings too. Jodie was adamant that Robert was bullying her, no matter how many times it was explained to her that she in fact was bullying him. I did feel sorry for Robert. He was a quiet, anxious boy, with more than enough problems of his own, and Jodie brought out the absolute worst in him.

Jodie's relationship with Robert was just one of numerous problems at the school, and I quickly came to dread the sound of the secretary's voice, as it usually meant we were in trouble. However, the next worry I was faced with regarding school was unrelated to Jodie's behaviour. One evening at dinner she was telling me about her classmate Freya, and my attention had wandered. Jodie's stories tended to ramble, and rarely had a point or resolution. However, when Jodie mentioned Freya had visited her at her old house I quickly paid attention.

'Did you say Freya came to your house when you lived at home?'

'Yeah.'

'The house you grew up in, with your mummy and daddy?'

'Yes,' she sighed.

'And she's in your class now?'

'Yeah.'

'So were you and Freya friends from your last school?'

'No, she didn't go to my school.'

'So how did you know her?'

'Because she came round, and we played Barbie.'

'So did your mummy and daddy know hers?'

'Yeah, from the pub.'

'I see. And do they still see each other, do you know?'

'S'ppose so.'

Oh shit, I thought.

The next day at school I went in to see the Head. If Freya's parents were still friendly with Jodie's parents, it was almost certain the news of which school Jodie now attended would filter back. This raised the possibility that her parents might come to the school and confront us, or even try to snatch her. Jodie would be terrified at the sight of her father in what she thought was a safe place, let alone if he approached her. The school run is fraught with anxiety when you're fostering, as you're an exposed target. Parents do occasionally try to grab their children at the school gates, and the advice we're given is that we have to let the child go, and call the police.

The Head suggested that Jodie and I should use the staff entrance from now on, and he gave me the security code. Although this was a sensible precaution, it meant that in yet another small way Jodie had been made different from her classmates, and her past was once again hampering her future.

The following Sunday, Jodie, Paula and I went for a walk in the park. We were walking up the hill through the centre of the park, when an elderly lady coming towards us slipped and fell. It was dreadful to witness; her wrists failed to break her fall, and she cracked her nose on the tarmac. Paula and I ran up to her, and I gave her first aid, while Paula phoned for an ambulance on her mobile. I used a wad of clean tissues from my bag to stem the bleeding, all the while talking to her, making sure she didn't go into shock. Her name was Maureen and she was clearly badly shaken; her frail body was trembling. Her face was grazed, her nose appeared to be broken and one of her wrists had swollen up. We waited until the paramedics arrived, and explained to them what had happened. The ambulance took her off to hospital, and we returned home. Throughout all of this, Jodie had stood by quietly watching.

That evening at dinner it was still on our minds.

'I hope that poor woman's all right,' Paula said. 'I could have cried.'

'What do you want to cry for?' Jodie asked.

'That poor lady, who fell over in the park.'

'Why? She didn't hurt you.'

'No, I know that,' Paula said patiently. 'But she was badly hurt and she was old. When you see something like that it makes you sad, doesn't it?'

Jodie stared back at her, clearly not understanding the emotion she was trying to describe.

I decided to try and help. 'We don't like to see other people get hurt, Jodie, because we know how bad it feels ourselves. If you'd fallen over, you'd be hurt, wouldn't you?'

Jodie thought for a second. 'Yes. That poor lady.' She then repeated the phrase throughout the rest of the evening. I was glad to hear her making the right noises, but it sounded hollow and I wasn't actually convinced she felt it. It wasn't that Jodie was being wilfully callous, she just didn't seem to have any sense of empathy. I wondered if this was why she could be so cruel to animals, and so rude and violent to other people. In all the time she'd been with us, I'd never once seen her cry out of sadness; her tears had only ever come from rage and frustration. However, although she hadn't yet learned to empathize, she had learned that people expected her to sound sympathetic, so she would mimic the reactions of others, to appear normal and fit in. Looking back, she'd done the same thing at Christmas, when she'd copied the others' reactions when opening her presents. Likewise, when I pointed out a beautiful sunset, she might repeat the phrase, 'What a beautiful sunset!', but again it sounded hollow, as though she couldn't actually see or appreciate its beauty.

* * *

Some weeks later I arrived at the school to collect Jodie at the end of the day. As she came down the corridor, I saw she was being escorted by the Head, rather than Mrs Rice. I took a deep breath and braced myself. What had she done now? We exchanged hellos, then he took me to one side, out of Jodie's earshot.

'Don't worry,' he said, 'she hasn't done anything. I just wanted a quick word. Mrs Rice has decided to take some time off, so we have a new teaching assistant starting tomorrow.'

'Oh, I see,' I said, taken aback. 'It's rather sudden. She didn't mention it. I hope she's OK.'

He nodded. 'I think she just needs to take some time out. You know what it's like working with children, and TAs tend to be on the front line. Like you foster carers.'

I nodded in agreement.

'Sometimes you just need a break, don't you?'

'Yes, I know the feeling.' I smiled weakly, wondering if I would ever get the break I'd been promised at the beginning of the year.

As I left, I felt sad for Mrs Rice. I'd seen her upset often enough to realize that Jodie was partly responsible for wearing her out. She wasn't used to hearing about the awful things that Jodie had been through, and she'd never dealt with a child this difficult and disturbed before. Jodie was constantly on edge, and alert for danger: fight or flight. If she heard the slightest noise, she'd spin round, ready for action. When you spend long enough in the company of a child like Jodie, you can soon find yourself on a heightened state of alert, and it becomes very difficult to switch off and relax.

I certainly felt myself becoming increasingly overwhelmed by Jodie's life, and all the pain, fear and distress she had suffered.

Chapter Twenty-Seven

Silence

The poet T.S. Eliot wrote that April is the cruellest month, and it seemed that this year he was exactly right. As April approached, the gloomy days and permanently grey skies gave no hint of anything different, in the past or the future. The winter seemed endless, as the temperature plummeted. It was hard to believe that Jodie had been with us for almost a whole year, but the anniversary of her arrival was near.

I drew up my collar, and loitered outside the travel agent's window. I fantasized about the cut-price offers to the Caribbean. How I'd have loved to put us all on a plane and head for an island in the sun. But it was impossible. Although my purse might just have coped with it, I knew Jodie wouldn't. On top of all her other problems, she had become so fearful of adults that even a visit to our local newsagent, with whom she previously used to chat, would now produce a panic attack. A packed flight would have been intolerable for her, and I doubted the airline would charter a plane just for us.

I moved away from the tempting window display, and turned towards the supermarket. My mobile phone rang; it was the school secretary.

'I'm sorry, Cathy,' she said. 'Jodie's inconsolable. She's convinced her father has come to take her. Can you come straight away?'

I turned and headed back to the car.

Fortunately the roads were quiet, so twenty minutes later I was walking down the path towards reception. A high-pitched scream erupted from inside, and I knew it was Jodie. I pressed the security buzzer, and the secretary showed me through to the medical room. Jodie was clinging to the radiator, her eyes wide and staring, her body rigid with fear.

'Don't make me go with him! Please, Cathy, please,' she begged.

The new assistant, Miss Walker, who got on well enough with Jodie, knelt beside her, talking softly, trying to reassure her, but I could see Jodie was way past that.

I moved towards her, but she backed away. 'No one's taking you away, Jodie,' I said firmly. 'He's not here, I promise, and you know I don't lie.'

She opened her mouth, about to scream, but I didn't give her a chance.

'No, Jodie. I mean it. Stop it. There's no one here. Now calm down, let go of the radiator, then we can have a cuddle.'

The young assistant eyed me suspiciously. Jodie looked from one to the other, then at the door. She started to relax her grip. 'Good girl. That's better.' She finally let go.

I went over and took her in my arms, as Miss Walker quietly slipped out.

'He was here,' she sobbed. 'At my old school. He came to collect me, then we went in his car.'

The rest was muffled by her sobs, but I knew how it would go. The past had once again transposed itself on to the present, with flashbacks that felt as real now as when the abuse had happened.

'It's all right, pet, I promise you. It won't happen again. There, there. It's OK.'

Once she was calm I led her to the car, and we drove home. It was eleven in the morning, but she wanted to go straight to bed. She said she was tired, and her bed was nice and safe. I took her upstairs and helped her out of her uniform. I tucked her in, and she fell asleep straight away. I came back every half hour to check on her, but she didn't stir. At two o'clock in the afternoon I decided to go in and wake her, as I knew if she slept too long she'd be up all night.

She had changed position, and was now lying flat on her back. Her eyes were open and she was staring at the ceiling.

'Feeling better?' I asked, but she gave no acknowledgement. I opened the curtains, took her jeans and jumper from the wardrobe, and laid them on the bed. 'Put these on, pet, and I'll make you a snack, then we could take your bike to the park for a bit. You'd like that.'

Usually she was adept at telling me exactly what she did or didn't like, but this time she made no sound or movement. I looked closely at her, then I perched on the bed and eased the duvet from under her chin. 'Jodie, are you all right, sweet?'

Her eyes were focused on some distant point above her head. I tried chivvying her along. 'Come on. Get dressed while I make you a sandwich, then we'll go out.' She remained staring, giving no clue that she'd even heard me.

I decided it was probably best to leave her, in the hope that she'd think about the park, and rally round. A quarter of an hour later, when she still hadn't appeared, I went up to check on her again. She was exactly as I'd left her: flat on her back and staring into space. I sat on the bed and started talking, reassuring her that I understood how difficult it was, but that eventually everything would be sorted out; she had her whole life ahead of her. Still she said nothing, and remained immobile. I tried firmness, then coercion, then bribery, then finally I tried to physically lift her from the pillow, but none of it worked. She flopped back like a rag doll, and I was really starting to worry. I hovered in the doorway, then, leaving the door wide open, went to the phone in my bedroom. I called Jill and told her about the day's events.

'It could be part of the post-traumatic shock,' she said. 'The flashback she had at school could have caused her brain to shut down for protection.'

'So she'll come out of it?'

'She should be recovered by the morning. I suggest you let her sleep it off. If you need help during the night call the emergency social worker, but I doubt it'll be necessary.'

I returned to Jodie's room and tried once more to rouse her. When this failed, I reluctantly closed the curtains and came out, leaving the door ajar. A little later the children arrived home, and I explained what had happened. They came with me as I checked on her every half hour, but there was no change, and an eerie hush descended on the house, as music and televisions were kept low. By the time I went to bed her eyes were closed and she seemed to be sleeping. I left her light dimmed and her door open, and went to my room.

At four in the morning I was woken by a small voice outside my bedroom door. 'Cathy, Amy's wet the bed.'

I leapt up and hugged her. 'No problem.' At least some part of Jodie was back. I changed her sheets and pyjamas, as she continued chattering in her baby voice. 'Amy's good girl. She tells Cathy. Amy wants potty.' I didn't mind; anything was better than that dreadful comatose silence. I tucked her in, then left her snuggled up with a teddy, contentedly sucking her thumb.

In the morning I was surprised to find Amy was still in occupation, and she remained so throughout breakfast.

'Stop babbling in that silly voice,' Lucy eventually snapped; she was never at her best first thing in the morning.

I shot her a warning glance. 'I'm sure she'll be gone by the time we get to school,' I said. But an hour later, as I kissed Jodie goodbye and passed her over to Miss Walker, she toddled off still in character as Amy, with the tottering gait of an infant just learning to walk.

As I drove home I got stuck in traffic, so I phoned Jill from the car and updated her. She asked me to email my log notes over as soon as possible, so she could forward them to Eileen, the guardian ad litem and Dr Burrows. It was after midday by the time I'd finished typing, and I was about to make some lunch when the phone rang. Please let it not be the school again, I thought. I hadn't even started the housework yet, and I still had to do the supermarket run.

It was the school. 'Hi, Cathy,' the secretary said, and I braced myself for the bad news. 'Mr West asked me to call to let you know Jodie's been fine today.'

'Thank you,' I sighed with relief. 'Thank you very much.'

Jodie's good behaviour continued through the evening, but it turned out to be a false dawn. The next morning she was sobbing uncontrollably and despite my best efforts I couldn't get her to tell me why. As I sat on her bed, watching her weep, I again felt completely ineffectual as a carer, and tried to remind myself that this was no ordinary childhood trauma.

By 9.00 a.m. she was no better, so I phoned the school and told them she wouldn't be coming in for the morning, but that if there was an improvement I'd bring her for the afternoon. There wasn't. Nor the following day. By the end of the week Jodie had been in school for a total of one and a half days, and she was deteriorating before my eyes. When she wasn't crying she was staring into space, removed and distant from anything I could say or do. She was hardly eating, and my previous policy of restricting sweet and fatty foods went out of the window.

'What about a chocolate biscuit?' I asked, trying to get a spark of interest out of her. 'Or there's ice-cream in the freezer?'

But nothing could tempt her, and she was surviving on the odd mouthful of sandwich and occasional handful of crisps.

It was extremely distressing. I'd never seen any child like this before and I was at a complete loss to know how to deal with it, or how to help Jodie. I phoned the only person I could think of who could give me support and advice at a time like this. Jill agreed to come round at once.

'This can't go on,' she said when she saw Jodie's state, which alternated between the heart-rending crying and total blankness. 'She needs help. Now.'

She phoned Eileen, but was told she was on annual leave once again, and the new team manager, Gail, was in a meeting. Jill left a stern message, requiring a call back as soon as she was free.

'Jill?' I asked. 'Is it possible for a child this young to have a nervous breakdown?'

'There are cases, yes, but it's very rare.'

We looked at each other, both thinking the same thing. The extent of Jodie's abuse was rare – so why shouldn't she be suffering a nervous breakdown? If there was any child who was a prime candidate for a complete mental collapse, it was her.

Jill tried talking to Jodie, who'd spent all morning propped on the sofa staring silently into space. It was a slightly different approach to mine. Jill didn't ask her any questions. Instead, she just recounted stories of various children she knew, hoping these would prompt a reaction. However, the end result was the same: a blank stare, which eventually gave way to silent tears. I did the only thing I could: I held her tightly, and reassured her it was going to be OK. Jill had nothing else to offer, so she left, saying she'd phone regularly, and promised to alert Dr Burrows.

The doctor phoned within the hour and asked to see Jodie first thing Monday morning. She said she'd cancelled an appointment to fit her in, and although I was grateful I wasn't even sure I'd be able to get Jodie out of the house. I asked if she could make it a home visit.

'I'm afraid not,' she replied apologetically. 'I'm only allowed to see children at the centre, because of the insurance.'

I said I'd make sure Jodie was there.

The weekend passed, and Jodie showed no improvement. The whole family spoke in whispers, in recognition of her suffering. We took turns sitting with her on the sofa, reading her favourite stories or trying to involve her in games, but not even the *Mary Poppins* video could produce a reaction. All she wanted was to go to bed, where she now spent an increasingly large part of the day, and from which it was a struggle to coerce her in the morning.

I prayed that Dr Burrows would have some answers for us.

Chapter Twenty-Eight

Assessment

On Monday morning I washed and dressed Jodie, then watched as she sat at the kitchen table, staring into space. Eventually I threw away the porridge she hadn't touched, tucked a packet of crisps into my bag and helped her on with her coat and shoes. I had told her we were going to see Dr Burrows, but she was as lifeless as ever. I helped her out of the house, strapped her into her seatbelt and turned up the volume on her favourite singalong cassette. As we drove to the clinic she stared straight ahead at the seat in front of her, and said nothing. She was completely unreachable, and I wondered if she even knew where she was.

We arrived at the clinic and I gave our names to the receptionist, who told us to go straight through to the consulting room. I knocked and entered; Dr Burrows was arranging crayons on the child-size table. As soon as Jodie saw the doctor, her previous lethargy vanished and she erupted into a violent tantrum.

'Don't want to! Go away!' She kicked the small plastic chairs across the room.

'All right, Jodie,' Dr Burrows soothed. 'There's nothing to be worried about. I'm here to help you.'

'Don't want your help! Piss off!' Jodie covered her ears, screwed up her eyes and screamed for all she was worth.

The doctor motioned for me to do nothing, so I stayed where I was, as the cry reverberated around the walls in an agonizing crescendo. Eventually she ran out of breath, and the scream ended as abruptly as it had begun. She lowered her hands and darted to the table, throwing it against the wall. She overturned the toy boxes, kicked the contents across the floor, then turned to the filing cabinet, which had one drawer half open. Dr Burrows intercepted her.

'No. You can't go in there,' she said calmly, placing herself between the filing cabinet and Jodie. 'That's mine and contains important papers. Not in there.'

To my surprise, Jodie accepted this, but her unspent anger turned inwards, upon herself. She grabbed a clump of her hair and tore it out. At this, I got up and restrained her. It might not have been the correct approach in the doctor's eyes, but I wasn't prepared to stand by and watch her harm herself. I held her wrists, then crossed her arms, enfolding her as I did at home. She struggled, spat and then finally went limp. I led her over to the sofa and put my arms around her. Whether Dr Burrows approved or not, I couldn't tell. She sat opposite, and the room was quiet. I looked at the mess; the floor between us was covered in debris, a sea of destruction.

We sat in silence, then Dr Burrows leaned towards Jodie. Her voice was soft and low, and she was searching for eye contact. 'I know you're hurting, Jodie, and I want to try and stop that hurt. You let Cathy help you. Will you let me help you too? It would be really good if you did.'

It was a relaxed, non-threatening approach, which I was sure had worked with countless children before, but although Jodie was quiet, it was a silence I recognized as being withdrawn.

Dr Burrows gave me a reassuring smile, then repeated her request. Jodie didn't move, and gave no indication that she'd even heard. The psychologist tried again, this time rephrasing it. 'Jodie, Cathy has told me about how brave you've been; you've had an awful lot to deal with. But I think you're finding this problem is too big to fix on your own. That's why Cathy's here, and that's why I'm here too. Will you let me help you?'

Jodie continued staring at some indistinct point a yard or so ahead, remaining as closed off and removed as ever.

Dr Burrows sat back, and opened the notepad on her lap. 'Cathy, perhaps you could tell me how Jodie's been since we last met. I know you've been worried about her.'

I assumed this was a strategy to encourage Jodie to share her feelings, so I explained that she'd been doing extremely well, but that horrible memories from her past had been making her unhappy. I gave a couple of examples, to make it clear to Jodie that Dr Burrows knew her history and that she could be trusted. I said that the whole family was very worried; Adrian, Lucy and Paula cared a great deal for Jodie, and didn't like to see her upset. Dr Burrows leaned forward again.

'I see lots of children who are upset and angry because of things that have happened. It's not their fault. I know ways to help. I help them get rid of some of the hurt, so they can be happy again. I'd like to help you, Jodie.'

The nature of our visit appeared to have changed from assessment to therapy, but unless Jodie engaged, and the pathway of communication opened, it would all be in vain.

'I'd like you to help us,' I said, hoping the 'us' might spark Jodie's confidence, but she remained inert, staring straight ahead. Dr Burrows made another note in her pad.

'Would you like to play a game, Jodie?' she asked. 'I could bring in the doll's house.'

I looked at Jodie hopefully, but she made no move.

'How about a drawing? You drew a lovely picture on your first visit. I've still got it.'

Jodie didn't even look up.

'I tell you what.' The doctor rose from her chair. 'Before we do anything, Cathy and I are going to put these toys back in the boxes. We'd like you to help us, please.'

I took my cue, slipped my arm from Jodie and joined the doctor on the floor. Presumably the aim was to engage Jodie in physical collaboration, in the hope that it would ease her into saying something. But as we repacked the toy boxes and picked up the crayons I could see out of the corner of my eye that Jodie wasn't even looking at us, perhaps wasn't even aware of us. A few minutes later we finished, and returned to our seats. Dr Burrows made some more notes in her pad, while I sat with my arm around Jodie. I couldn't begin to guess what she was writing, but I supposed to her professional eye there were indicators, and possibly even a diagnosis, despite Jodie's non-cooperation.

She closed her pad and smiled kindly. 'That's enough for today. Thank you both for coming. I'll be in touch.'

I was taken aback, and wondered if this was another ploy to spark Jodie into communication. The psychologist stood up. 'I'll see you again soon, Jodie.' The session was definitely finished.

I looked at Jodie, who was still motionless, wearing the same impenetrable stare.

'OK, sweet, we can go home now.' I took her hand and lifted her from the chair, as the doctor opened the door. As we walked out into the daylight I had an awful sense of foreboding.

Chapter Twenty-Nine

Therapy

My sense of foreboding persisted through the following day. Jodie and I sat on the sofa as I read her one of her favourite rhymes by Shirley Hughes. 'Bathwater's hot, seawater's cold. Ginger's kittens are very young, but Buster's getting old.' In the past she had turned the pages eagerly, repeating the words, enjoying the pleasant sound of the rhyme. Now she seemed impervious; deaf and mute.

Jodie's disturbance had reached a new level and I knew that what I could offer was grossly inadequate. There was something frightening as well as deeply saddening about watching her distress. How far could a personality fracture before it was impossible to put it back together? Where would all her misery and hurt take her in the end? It seemed as though it was leading her to a place of darkness and silence where, finally, no one would be able to reach her. I knew she needed help urgently. But what kind of help? And how could I comfort her?

I put the book down and held her close, as I replayed the previous day's session with Dr Burrows in my head.

I hadn't expected a miracle cure, but I had hoped for at least a hint of progress. Instead the session had only served to demonstrate how disturbed Jodie was, and how powerless even the psychologist was to reach or help her. I stroked a few strands of hair from her forehead, and looked at her pale, unresponsive face. Was it possible that she would be trapped like this forever?

'I feel so helpless, Jodie,' I whispered. 'I wish I could do something. I wish I was a fairy godmother and I could wave a magic wand so all your troubles would go away.'

I looped my arms under her shoulders, eased her on to my lap and rocked her gently. She remained impassive. My gaze drifted to the window as a rogue snowflake floated past. It was followed by another, and then another. They drifted down as if from heaven, and then melted as they touched the patio.

'Look, Jodie!' I raised her head towards the window. 'It's trying to snow and it's April!'

She looked up, and her eyes seemed to focus for a second.

'Shall we go outside and have a look? You like snow, don't you? Please look.'

But the moment passed, and she turned her head back to the floor, showing no emotion or recognition.

I put her to bed at seven and, with the girls at their piano lessons and Adrian coming home much later, I had the house to myself. I tried to read, but I couldn't concentrate. I put on a CD of classical music, but it only made me sad. In the end I sat watching TV, keeping the volume low so I could hear if Jodie stirred. I went to bed early and, as I lay awake, I prayed for the first time in thirty years.

In the morning I fancied there was some small improvement. Jodie came downstairs on her own, and managed a few spoonfuls of Weetabix. Sadly, though, it didn't last. Half an hour later she was curled foetally on the sofa again, silent and withdrawn.

Jill phoned at 9.30. The new team leader had called an emergency planning meeting for 11.00, and my presence was required. She didn't know exactly why the meeting had been called, but said it suggested things might be starting to move. Dr Burrows may have recommended that therapy start immediately. Alternatively, if we dared hope, new evidence might have emerged that would finally put Jodie's abusers behind bars. Jill's colleague, Lisa, had offered to babysit, and would arrive in about an hour. Finally, some action, I thought. I looked down at Jodie, and felt my hopes begin to rise.

Lisa arrived in good time, and I introduced her to Jodie, who did at least manage to look in her direction. I showed her where the coffee and biscuits were, then left, as she began reading a Barbie magazine to Jodie. I'd changed into my smart 'meetings' suit, and my spirits continued to lift as I drove to the Social Services. Perhaps something good was going to come out of this; finally other people had begun to understand what I had known for some time – that the extent of Jodie's troubles was extraordinary and that she needed specialist help and immediate therapy. Someone had to know how to unlock her and restore her to life.

I parked in the multi-storey car park nearby, and took the lift down to the street with ten minutes to spare.

The ornate stone building, which had once been the old town hall, was now surrounded by high-rise flats, and retained only the façade of its previous gentility. I heaved open the double doors and walked in. As usual, it was full. People of all ages and nationalities were sitting, standing or pacing as they waited anxiously for their numbers to appear on the electronic display suspended from the ceiling. As I walked through the mêlée a toddler grabbed the hem of my skirt, before his mother whisked him back on to her lap, smiling an apology.

I approached the reception desk. 'Cathy Glass,' I said, as the receptionist slid the glass partition just far enough to hear. 'I'm here for the eleven o'clock meeting in respect of Jodie Brown. I'm her carer.'

With stoic resignation she ticked my name off a printed list, then handed me a stick-on security pass, with 'Visitor' printed in large black letters. I pressed it on to my coat.

'Room seven,' she said. 'Through the double doors, up the stairs, and it's on your left.' The partition slid shut before I or anyone else could poke a head in.

I knew the layout of the building, having attended many meetings here in the past. Room seven was one of the largest, and as I climbed the stairs I realized that it was also where Jodie's pre-placement meeting had taken place almost a year earlier. It was hard to believe that it had been so long. I thought back to that day and cringed at my cavalier assumptions at the time. Back then I had been in no doubt that all any child needed was care, firm guidelines, encouragement and attention, and I had had no doubt that this Jodie would end up as another success. I had been so confident that I would reach Jodie just as I had reached so many troubled children and helped to put them back on the road to recovery and as normal a life as possible. But for once my tried and tested methods had failed me. At least I wasn't alone in not being able to reach the source of Jodie's torment. Nevertheless, I wondered if anyone in room seven would show their disappointment.

Jill, Sally and Gail, the new team manager, were already seated along two sides of the polished mahogany table. They smiled as I walked in, and Gail introduced herself. I exchanged a 'Good morning' with Sally, and sat next to Jill.

'We're just waiting for Dr Burrows and Mary from finance,' Gail said. 'Eileen's on leave, I'm afraid. And Jodie's headmaster won't be coming, but he has submitted a report.'

I slipped off my coat, draped it over the back of my chair, and took heart from the fact that finance had been invited. Usually, finance people were only present when funding needed to be found. And funding would be required in order to embark on therapy.

'How is she?' Jill asked quietly.

'Pretty much the same. But once she's in therapy I'm sure things will start to improve.'

'Let's hope so,' she smiled.

The door opened and Mary rushed in, clutching a thick wad of papers; she apologized for being late. She sat opposite me, and I was dying to ask how much therapy their budget would stretch to, but I knew it would be poor protocol to do so before the meeting had even started. Gail and Mary spoke quietly between themselves, discussing a different case. Then the door opened again, and Dr Burrows appeared carrying a briefcase, looking more like a city worker than a psychologist in her smart grey suit. 'Sorry to keep you waiting, but the cab was late.'

Gail waited for her to sit down, and then opened the meeting. She thanked us all for coming, minuted the date, the time, and the names of those present, and then asked us to each introduce ourselves.

After the introductions she looked down the length of the table. 'We're here to assess the present situation with regard to Jodie, and to decide how best to proceed. I think it would be helpful to start with you, Cathy, then, Sally, if you could go next. I'll read out the school's report, and perhaps if you would conclude, Dr Burrows.'

We murmured our agreement.

I'd rehearsed what I was going to say during the drive over. I was going to be positive about Jodie's initial progress, without minimizing her need for help. I took a deep breath, and began.

'As you know, Jodie showed very challenging behaviour when she came to me, to such a degree that she had been through five carers in four months. She was extremely aggressive and confrontational, and suffered from delayed development. She had poor bowel control and very low self-esteem. She exhibited sexualized behaviour towards men and women.

'Over time, she settled into our household routine and began to respond to the clear boundaries I set, and the positive encouragement. As her anxiety decreased she became less violent and was learning to manage her anger. However, as she began to feel safe she started to disclose. The extent of the sexual abuse she has suffered at the hands of her family is horrendous.

'As the disclosures continued, her progress halted, and she became increasingly disturbed. Since that time she has suffered from night terrors, vivid hallucinations, and her personality seems to be fragmenting.

'Over the last two weeks, as you know, Jodie's condition has deteriorated further, and faster. Despite all my encouragement and reassurance, she now spends large parts of the day in bed, and takes virtually no interest in what is going on around her. She rarely speaks or eats, and I often find her crying silently to herself. In January she joined the Abbey Green Primary School, where she was supported by a full-time assistant. Initially she made some progress, but since her deterioration she's been unable to attend. She's missed more than three weeks in total.'

I looked them in the eye as I spoke, and saw concern and disquiet reflected back. 'I admit I am at a loss to know how to reach Jodie, and help her come to terms with her experiences. In my view she needs the help of a professional psychotherapist. Given our earlier success, I'm optimistic that once therapy has begun we can resume making progress.'

Gail thanked me, and handed over to Sally, the guardian ad litem. Sally listed the dates when she'd visited, and praised my success in gaining Jodie's trust, which had allowed her to disclose. She said that while she hadn't had the chance to observe Jodie recently, she had been in close contact with Dr Burrows and Eileen, and was thus fully abreast of the current situation. She'd seen Jodie's parents, and made them aware of how badly Jodie had been affected by the disclosures. Jodie's father had been unmoved and was still adamant that Jodie was making it up, but Mrs Brown had broken down in tears. She said nothing more about Jodie's parents – and with her professionalism, there was no question that she would – but there was an inference that there was not much doubt of their joint culpability in what had happened to Jodie.

I felt no sympathy on hearing that Jodie's mother had broken down; my immediate reaction was that it was a sham, to cover up her own guilt. I had no doubt that what Jodie had told me was the truth. There was no other way a child of her age could know the things she knew and describe the things she had described; and I only had to look at her disintegration to know that what she had said had happened.

I could hardly bear to think about her parents. I hated the thought that they were free to continue their daily lives and whatever degradations they got up to, while their daughter was imprisoned inside the pain and suffering they had caused. What they had inflicted on Jodie had condemned her to a life sentence.

'Jodie is a very badly damaged child,' Sally concluded, 'and my recommendations will be wholly in line with Dr Burrows' findings.'

There was silence, as Gail made a note, then she took a sheet from her file and read out the headmaster's report. At the time of writing, Jodie had attended a total of seventy-two days, and Mr West had based his observations on both her academic ability and how she interacted with her peers. At present she was learning to sequence the alphabet and the numbers up to twenty. She had no sight vocabulary but had been working on a target of learning five new words a week. Her concentration was very limited, and she was being encouraged to spend longer on tasks, and to work independently. She had found difficulty in making friends, largely due to her erratic and strange behaviour. The test results showed she was at about the average level of a four-year-old in terms of reading and writing. His concluding sentence summed it up perfectly:

'Jodie's education and social development are being severely restricted by her experiences, and until these have been addressed I feel her achievements will be negligible.'

Gail filed away the report, and I felt my pulse quicken as Dr Burrows opened her file. She would be the final speaker, and after she had given her recommendations Mary would do her sums and then funding would be confirmed, so that we could start Jodie on the path to recovery. I only hoped it would be adequate. My feeling was that she needed at least two one-hour sessions a week.

'As you know,' Dr Burrows began, 'I have been appointed by the court to assess Jodie in respect of the full care proceedings. While this was originally intended to determine the feasibility of her returning to live at home, what has come out since confirms that returning home is impossible, so I am now addressing the issue of her present mental health.' She proceeded to give a clinical appraisal of Jodie's condition, making reference to our last two appointments. I appreciated that Dr Burrows' presence and her report indicated just how seriously everyone was now taking this matter. The psychologist was only supposed to submit her comments at the final proceedings later in the year, but she had stepped outside her remit from the court to give her analysis earlier. What she had observed about Jodie had caused her such concern that she knew immediate action had to be taken – hence her presence at this meeting, despite her extremely busy schedule.

I looked along the table at the others, as they took detailed notes. The doctor drew to a close.

'It is therefore my recommendation that Jodie requires nothing less than intensive, long-term therapy with a paediatric psychotherapist experienced in child sexual abuse.'

Thank God, I thought. All we need now is the funding.

'What level of therapy do you have in mind?' Gail asked. Mary slid her calculator in front of her.

'Jodie has learning difficulties,' said Dr Burrows, 'and functions at the level of a much younger child. As a result she has difficulty in engaging with concepts and retaining them. In view of this, and the severe nature of her condition, I do not think even a high level of sessional therapy would be of any help. It is therefore my professional opinion that for therapy to have any effect in Jodie's case it must be constant and immediate. I therefore recommend the best chance of recovery would be in a therapeutic residential unit.'

I heard the last two words, but it took a moment to sink in. The room fell silent, as the others finished writing. I could feel my pulse pounding in my neck, and my stomach churning. Jill touched my arm.

'Thank you, Dr Burrows,' Gail said. 'That was very helpful.'

I could feel their eyes on me, as I stared down at my notepad.

'Cathy,' said Sally, 'how do you feel about this? I know you've become very close to Jodie.'

I lifted my head and swallowed. My voice was uneven, and I was struggling to hold back the welling tears. 'It's difficult. I wasn't expecting this. I was hoping that once Jodie started regular therapy we'd be able to see her through.' I paused for a second. 'To be honest, I feel it's all been for nothing.'

Sally looked at Dr Burrows, who gently shook her head.

'Even before this present crisis,' said the doctor, 'I doubt Jodie could have functioned successfully in a normal family. She's deeply traumatized, and it's affecting all aspects of her life. Very few carers would have invested as much as you have, and it's to your credit that she's come this far.'

Gail, Sally and Jill all muttered their agreement.

I shrugged despondently. 'Would it not be worth trying sessional therapy for, say, six months?'

They looked again at Dr Burrows.

She looked over at me sympathetically. 'In my opinion, no. Not only would it not be effective, but it could exacerbate her condition. Jodie's personality is disintegrating, and the longer it's left, the more profound the long-term damage may be.'

I said nothing.

'What time scale are you looking at?' Gail asked.

'If I make a recommendation immediately, she could be in within a month.'

I flinched.

'Do you have somewhere in mind?' Gail continued.

The doctor delved into her briefcase, and brought out some coloured pamphlets which she distributed along the table.

'It's called High Oaks, and it's run by Dr Ron Graham and his wife Betty. They're practising child psychologists. You may have heard of them. They're well respected in their field.'

Jill opened the pamphlet between us, and I stared at the first page. All I could see were blocks of fuzzy print, juxtaposed with pictures of smiling children. I blinked and tried to focus.

The doctor continued her explanation. 'They've been established for twelve years and have built up an excellent reputation. It's a lovely old manor house set in an acre of wooded parkland on the outskirts of Cambridgeshire. The Grahams live on site, together with a support staff of highly trained therapists. The children are taught by qualified teachers who come into the schoolroom in the morning. They cover all the curriculum subjects up to GCSE. The afternoons are given over to recreational activities and one-to-one therapy. At weekends they do what other families do, outings to the cinema, swimming and so on, and of course they take them on holiday. I've had close links with the Grahams since they first opened, and they have a very high success rate. Ninety per cent of the children eventually move on to live in a family. But of course it doesn't come cheap.'

'How much?' Gail asked.

'It depends on the package, but for someone with Jodie's needs it will be approximately four thousand pounds a week. I would make an initial recommendation for three years, but of course that would be under regular review.'

I glanced up, Mary tapped some figures into her calculator and showed the result to Gail, who made a note.

'Would she be able to receive visitors?' Jill asked, knowing that's what I would have asked if I had been thinking straight.

'Absolutely,' replied Dr Burrows. 'In fact, it's essential. If a child has no family then High Oaks arranges for a befriender. It's very important that the children maintain ties with the outside world.'

'And Cathy, you'd want to continue contact?' asked Sally.

'Yes, of course,' I responded automatically.

Gail looked along the table. 'We'll have to take it to panel, but as it's your recommendation it's likely to be approved. Is there anything else?'

Dr Burrows leaned forward. 'Only to thank Cathy for all she's done, and the offer of contact in the future.'

The others concurred, and immediately began gathering together their papers. They dispersed quickly, leaving Jill and me alone. I placed my hands palm down on the table, and took a deep breath.

'How am I going to explain this to Jodie? She trusted me, and now I've got to tell her she's going. She'll think I've rejected her like the others. What's that going to do for her mental health?'

Jill touched my arm. 'I know, I'm so sorry, Cathy.

Listen, I wouldn't say anything to her just yet. In my experience, these organizations tend to have a set procedure for introductions. I'll contact High Oaks and see how they want to handle it. We'll take it from there.'

I sighed and stood up. 'OK. I'd better be getting back, she'll wonder where I am.'

Jill joined me in the corridor. 'It may not seem like it now, but it is for the best. You couldn't have done any more. You'll be keeping in touch, so she'll know you haven't rejected her. And who knows: three years down the line...?'

'Yes, I know what you're saying. I understand that it's for the best. The question is, will she?'

I walked out of the building fighting my feelings of failure. Jodie was going to leave me in a worse condition than she'd arrived in – that was a first for any child who'd been placed with me. I could tell myself all I liked that it wasn't my fault, but it was hard not to feel that it had all been a waste of time – all those sleepless nights, the endless draining days of tantrums and violence, the scenes in public, the awful mealtimes, the disruption to my children's lives. Now, after everything we'd suffered, Jodie was going to be moved on again.

I knew intellectually that Jodie needed proper help and intensive therapy of the kind I simply couldn't offer, not with all the love, kindness and common sense in the world. But still, I felt like I'd let myself down. And, most importantly of all, I'd let Jodie down.

How could I tell her that she had to leave?

Chapter Thirty

Green Grass and Brown Cows

That night, while the rest of the house slept, I took out the photo album containing pictures of all the children I've fostered; I call it my Rogues' Gallery. I flicked through the photographs. Some of them were posed, others captured unaware, on an outing to the coast or running round the garden. There were children of all ages and races, from little Jason who was only two days old when he arrived, to Martha, an angry and defiant seventeen-year-old, who went on to become a doctor.

I'd lost contact with some of them, but many still wrote to me and phoned. Four of them had stayed with me for a year or more, and all four now visited regularly, and had become part of our extended family. As I turned the pages, remembering the children's various personalities and problems, there wasn't one that I felt I'd failed. At least, not until now. There were no pictures of Jodie yet, but when I did come to add them I knew they would be the last. Whatever aptitude or ability I'd had seemed to have been lost. My confidence was shattered and I decided I wouldn't foster again.

Three days passed before I heard anything further, and all the while Jodie remained shuttered and distant. I didn't even raise the possibility of school any more; there was no point, she was in a world of her own. Somehow, we got through the days. I read to her, cuddled her and tried to tempt her to eat, while Adrian, Lucy and Paula made their own efforts to try and cheer her up.

I had sat the children down not long after I'd returned from the emergency meeting and told them that Jodie would be leaving us. They didn't say much but their solemn expressions and quiet acceptance told me that they already knew how serious Jodie's condition had become. It was always a sad moment when a child left us, but usually it was in the knowledge that they were going forward in a positive way – back to their families, or on to an adoptive family – and they left us better than they had arrived. With Jodie there was no such comfort; despite our best efforts, we had not managed to help her, and no one was unaffected.

'Don't blame yourselves,' I said, echoing Jill's words to me. 'We've done our best. That's all we can do.'

But it sounded as hollow to them as it had done to me, and I knew that they shared my sense of failure.

Four days after the meeting a letter arrived from Ron Graham. Inside the envelope there was a letter for me, and a second envelope, addressed to Jodie. In my letter, Ron introduced himself and wrote that he would phone soon to arrange a visit. In the meantime, would I give Jodie the enclosed? I handed her the envelope as she picked at her lunch. She took it from me suspiciously, then peered at her name on the front. Suddenly her eyes brightened. 'For me? Who's it from?'

'You'd better open it and find out. It looks very important.'

I moved her plate away as she carefully picked open the flap and unfolded the pale yellow sheet. It was typed in bold red print, with a little smiley face in one corner; it was immediately appealing.

'For me?' she said again.

'Yes. Shall I read it?'

She held it between us protectively, and I pointed to the words as I read.

Dear Jodie
My name is Ron and my wife is called Betty. We have lots of children living with us, in a big house in the country. We sort out their problems and have lots of fun too. We are good at sorting out problems and we'd like to come and tell you about us.
We look forward to meeting you.
Bye for now,
Ron and Betty

It was a simple but cleverly crafted introduction, and she was thrilled at having a letter of her own. She asked me to read it to her again, and then a third time.

'When are they coming?' she asked, showing more enthusiasm than she had done in weeks.

'I don't know yet. They're going to phone.'

'I hope it's soon. They sound nice, don't they, Cathy?'

'Yes, they do, sweet.'

She tucked the letter back into the envelope, and carried it around with her for the rest of the day. When Adrian, Lucy and Paula arrived home, she got them to read it to her, and they were as surprised by her enthusiasm as I had been. None of us actually said so, but we were all feeling a little bit slighted. How had one letter from strangers succeeded, where months of care from us had failed?

That night when Jodie was in bed, Ron phoned. I told him about her positive reaction.

'Children like Jodie very rarely form attachments,' he said, instinctively registering my unspoken feelings. 'It's no indictment of you, Cathy.' He asked about the make-up of my family, and how Jodie had interacted with everyone. He explained the introductory procedure: it started with the letter, and would continue with a visit from him and his wife the following week.

'We never rush the introductions,' he said. 'Jodie has put her trust in you, and now we have to transfer some of that trust to us.'

As he spoke, I was impressed by how much of Jodie's background he had at his fingertips; he must have read the file from cover to cover, and we were on the phone for over an hour. It was a relief to talk to someone who seemed to know what they were doing and to be fully conversant with the case. It made such a difference.

Although Jill had done all she could, she was just a small cog in an enormous wheel, with very little power to change anything. She could only make suggestions and ask questions. Eileen, Jodie's supposedly dedicated social worker, had proved uncommitted, inefficient and, if I was honest, negligent in the handling of the case. After a year she still didn't seem to know the details of Jodie's file, neither had she taken the trouble to get to know Jodie, or fulfilled her statutory duties. It was only when I talked to Ron that I felt some of the burden I had carried for so long beginning to lift from my shoulders. I hadn't realized how lonely I had felt. For so long, it had been Jodie and me struggling along together as best we could while the system ground slowly on, hampered by its vastness and bureaucracy. Now, at last, I felt as though someone was truly interested in her.

When I asked what I should tell Jodie about their visit, he said to tell her as little as possible, but to write down any questions she had, and to reassure her that they would be answered when Ron and Betty arrived.

I went to bed feeling happier than I had done in a long while; Jodie had responded positively, and Ron seemed to be sensitive and direct. Perhaps everyone was right, and this was for the best.

The following morning, when the others had left for school, I told Jodie about Ron's phone call the night before.

'What's he want?' she snarled, pushing away the porridge she'd just asked for.

I wondered if she understood that Ron was the one who had sent the letter. 'To find out how you are. He wrote you that lovely letter, remember? They're going to come and see you next week.'

'Don't want to. Shut up. Go away.'

'Jodie ...?' I started, but I decided not to pursue it. I'd do as Ron had asked, and take my cue from her.

She didn't mention Ron, Betty or the visit for the rest of the day, and remained silent and withdrawn. At bedtime I found the letter torn into pieces, scattered across the floor. It would have been ridiculous to ignore this, as I knew Jodie well enough to realize that this was her way of communicating anger. I gathered together the scraps of paper and sat on the edge of the bed.

'I know it's difficult, sweet. It's difficult for all of us. Can you tell me how you're feeling? What your thoughts are? Maybe I can help.'

Her face crumpled and she threw herself into my arms. I held her close, her head pressed against my chest, as she cried pitifully.

'What is it, Jodie? Try and tell me, please. I do really want to help.'

She thought for a few seconds, then blurted out, 'They'll do what the others did. I don't want to. It hurt. You said it wouldn't happen again.'

'Oh, sweetheart, no. They're good, kind people. They'd never hurt you, honestly.'

But Jodie's perception was very different to mine. In her world, a new adult usually meant someone new who would abuse and hurt you, with only a handful of exceptions. The idea of any new adult must have been terrifying for Jodie. Ignoring Ron's advice to say as little as possible, I tried to explain.

'Ron and Betty are like me. They help children who have been hurt, only they can do it better than me. They know the right things to say. They've helped hundreds of children, and they want to help you. I'll be with you the whole time they're here. All they want to do is to talk. They're going to tell us about the house where they live, and the other children who stay there.'

She sniffed. 'They won't go in my bedroom, will they? And I don't want to go in their car.'

'No, of course not.' I turned her to face me. 'Look, Jodie, you've met lots of new people since you've been with me, and none of them has hurt you. I wouldn't let them come here if I didn't think it was for the best. You do trust me, don't you?'

She nodded. 'Then please trust me on this, sweet.' She let me dry her tears with a tissue, but I wasn't sure that she'd accepted my assurances. After all, her time with me had been relatively short, compared with the eight years beforehand. In Jodie's experience, my world was still the exception, not the norm.

I read her a story, and settled her for the night. As I came out of her room I heard Amy telling Jodie, 'You can trust Cathy. Really, you can.'

As the day of the visit drew nearer, Jodie became increasingly unstable. She lapsed in and out of the Reg and Amy characters, and in between she offered little else. Occasionally I saw the real Jodie, and I tried to make the most of it, but she quickly retreated back into her shell, and I was again met with that blank, unrelenting stare. School remained out of the question and, apart from essential shopping expeditions, we hardly left the house.

On the morning of Ron and Betty's visit she was no different, and I was anxious that she'd deteriorate further with strangers coming into the house. Betty phoned from the car to say they'd be with us in fifteen minutes, and I warned her of my concerns.

'You've done well to see it through,' she said, as positive and perceptive as her husband. 'Once we're in the house, and she's met us, it will become easier.'

I wasn't convinced.

I returned to the lounge, where I'd started a jigsaw in the hope of trying to entice Jodie into doing something. 'That was Ron and Betty,' I said brightly. 'They'll be with us shortly. Shall we start this puzzle?'

To my amazement she slid off the sofa, picked a piece and passed it to me. I put it into position, and the face of a cat took shape.

'Where's our cat?' she asked suddenly.

'Toscha's asleep in her basket by the radiator.'

'Have they got a cat?'

'I don't know. That's something we could ask.'

She passed me another piece, and I snapped it into place. When the doorbell rang, Jodie was still on the floor, to all appearances playing contentedly like any other child.

I took Ron and Betty's coats, and showed them into the lounge. They were a well-built couple in their late forties, smartly dressed in country casuals, with warm, likeable faces.

'Hi, Jodie,' Betty said brightly. 'It's very nice to meet you.' She bent down to examine the jigsaw. 'That's good. Do you like puzzles?'

Jodie nodded.

'This is my husband Ron.'

Jodie looked up and smiled, as Ron sat unobtrusively in the armchair a short way from her.

'Jodie was wondering if you had a cat,' I said.

'Not a cat,' replied Betty, 'but behind the house is a field with lots of cows.'

'Cows?' said Jodie, suddenly interested.

'Yes. In the morning you can hear them mooing, and then the farmer comes and takes them for milking. The children love to watch that. Sometimes the cows come right up to the fence, and you can stroke them.'

'Really?' She was beaming now. I slipped into the kitchen and made some coffee.

Toscha, hearing new voices, rose languidly from her basket and went in to take a look. I heard Jodie introduce her.

'This is Toscha, but she's smaller than a cow.'

'That's right,' said Betty. 'A lot smaller.'

Jodie must have seen something in Ron and Betty, because she was so unlike the child I'd described, I felt my account could have been called into question, if there hadn't been all the other reports.

I carried the tray through, as Betty helped put the finishing touches to the jigsaw. I sat and admired the result. Jodie passed around the plate of biscuits, then sat beside Betty on the sofa.

'Tell me what other games you like, Jodie,' said Ron, gently introducing himself into the conversation. He was softly spoken, and could never have been described as intimidating.

'Painting, I like,' she said, 'and going to the park.'

'That sounds good.' He smiled at her, and Jodie smiled back.

We spent some minutes talking about the park, then Ron subtly drew the conversation to High Oaks, and the activities and outings they did there. He took a leaflet from his pocket: it was a children's version of the one I'd seen at the meeting, and we gathered around Jodie as we read through it. As Jodie turned the pages, Ron described their daily routine, and mentioned some of the other children. Jodie asked if they had a television, and what time they went to bed.

Ron and Betty stayed for nearly two hours, talking and playing, and showed us a short video of High Oaks, which included the rooms and the grounds. Once they were satisfied that Jodie was ready, they suggested we make a date to visit High Oaks the following week.

'I want to go now,' laughed Jodie, jumping up.

'Oh no,' Betty smiled. 'We want to have your room ready, so you can see it when you come.'

This was the first time any of us had mentioned 'her' room, or the possibility of her living there, and I watched Jodie to see her response.

'Can Cathy come?'

'For the visit? Of course,' replied Ron. 'She'll bring you in the car, and you'll both see your room and meet everyone. Then the next time you come, you can stay the night, and Cathy will come home and pick you up the following day.'

'Will I stroke a cow?' she asked.

'You'll certainly see one,' said Betty. 'Whether you stroke it or not depends on how close it comes to the fence.'

I smiled to myself. Cows had clearly replaced cats in Jodie's affections, as surely as Ron and Betty were replacing me. We saw them out and waved goodbye, and Jodie remained lively and excited for the rest of the afternoon. She spent some time painting in the conservatory, and when I came in to check on her she grinned proudly as she showed me her latest work. It was a bright, colourful picture of a big red house, set in a green field, with three brown cows.

Chapter Thirty-One

High Oaks

A week later there was an air of hushed expectation as we pulled into the drive at High Oaks, and the imposing manor house came in view. Jodie had spent much of the long drive dozing, or talking to Julie, her life-size doll. As we approached High Oaks she fell silent and pulled herself forward for a better view. We recognized the house from the video, but I was surprised at its size close up. It was enormous, with fourteen bedrooms stretching out over two wings, and an annex to the right, which had once been the servants' quarters and was now the therapy and 'quiet' room. The roof was gabled, dipping over an arched brick porch, which was draped with ivy. I guessed the buildings had been built in the mid-nineteenth century.

'This is very grand,' I said. 'We'll have to make a appointment to speak to you.'

Jodie grinned, not quite understanding what I'd said, but appreciating that it was special, and that it applied to her.

I parked behind a line of three cars on the carriage drive and opened Jodie's door to let her out. She slipped her hand in mine, and we crunched across the gravel towards the oak door. I pulled the brass bell cord, and we heard the bell echo inside.

'Me do it,' she said, and gave it another three sharp tugs.

The door opened and Betty appeared, smiling. 'Do you like our bell, Jodie? We thought about having a modern one fitted, but everyone voted to keep it.'

Jodie immediately swapped my hand for Betty's, and I was surprised, as that morning she'd claimed she didn't even know who Betty was. We walked into the hall, which was decorated by white-painted panels with stencilled rosettes in the centre of each square, giving the space a light, cheery feel. Ron appeared from within the house. 'Hi Jodie, hi Cathy. Did you have a good journey?'

'Yes, thank you,' I answered for us both. Jodie took refuge behind Betty.

Ron had phoned the previous evening, and I'd updated him on Jodie's state of mind. There had been no change, and Jodie hadn't raised the subject of the visit. We'd only discussed it once, the day before, when I'd reminded Jodie that we were going, and Reg had replied that he 'fucking wasn't'.

'This way to the lounge,' said Betty, leading Jodie down the hall. 'The children are out for a walk, which is why it's so quiet. They'll be back later.'

The lounge was at the back of the house, and it must have been three times the size of ours at home. Through the French windows was a concrete patio area, and beyond that there were swings, a climbing frame, a seesaw and a magnificent tree house. Beyond the fence at the back I could see the field, which was at present empty of cows. The lounge was furnished practically, with four sofas around the walls, as well as two armchairs and half a dozen beanbags, arranged at angles facing the widescreen television.

'We use this room in the evenings and weekends,' Ron said, 'when we're all together. We'll show you the rest of the house later.'

Jodie sat next to Betty on one of the sofas and propped her doll between them. I sat on the adjacent sofa, and Ron took the large armchair. We were like Goldilocks and the Three Bears, with the father bear having the largest. Betty offered us a drink, but we declined, having stopped on the motorway for breakfast.

'We have ten children with us at present,' said Ron, looking at Jodie, 'and nine carers to help. Clare and Val will be your special adults. You'll meet them next visit. Betty and I are always here, so is the housekeeper, Shirley. She makes our meals, then we all help clear away. I know you like helping, don't you, Jodie?'

She didn't answer but smiled sheepishly, and inched into Betty.

Ron continued to explain how the children had turns in choosing what they wanted for the evening meal; meanwhile I glanced around the room. I wondered how they kept it so clean and tidy with so many children, and supposed it must be down to the housekeeper.

'Now, have you thought of any questions?' asked Ron.

'Where's the cows?' she said, becoming more confident, and wriggling to the edge of the sofa.

'At this time of day they're usually in the upper fields. You'll be able to see them from your bedroom. Would you like to look round now?'

She nodded vigorously, and slid off the sofa. With the doll clutched under her arm, she followed Betty into the dining room, which also overlooked the garden and had a long refectory table and fourteen chairs. Next to this was the office, which the children were not allowed to go into without knocking first. Next door was the playroom, which was as big as the lounge and brimming with toys, beanbags and equipment. There were three computers, various small plastic tables, and cupboards stacked with games, soft toys and books. There was also a 'home corner', which was equipped with a toy cooker, a sink, a microwave, a settee and a cot. Around one little table sat half a dozen teddy bears, with plastic cups and plates neatly laid out in front of them. Jodie pointed at it excitedly.

'We had a teddy bears' picnic last night,' said Betty. 'I bet your dolly would like to join in next time.' Jodie shook Julie, so that the doll appeared to be nodding. 'Good, then we'll lay an extra place.'

We moved on to the kitchen, where a woman was busy at the sink.

'Shirley, this is Jodie,' Ron said, 'and her carer Cathy.'

Shirley was a rotund woman in her late fifties with a kind, open face. She wiped her hands on her apron and came over. 'Hello, Jodie, nice to meet you. And who's this?' She was referring to the doll, but Jodie had hidden her behind Betty's back.

'I'm sorry,' I said, shaking her hand.

'No problem. I expect she'll show me next time.'

'Now your bedroom,' Betty said, sensing Jodie's eagerness to move on. Jodie released her hand and took mine, and we followed Ron up the winding staircase with an impressive balustrade, along the landing to the door second from last.

'You go in first, Jodie,' Betty encouraged. 'This is your room, and we're your guests.'

Jodie proudly turned the handle and went in, and we heard her gasp with delight. The room had been freshly decorated in two-tone peach, with complementary flowered curtains and a matching duvet. A new pine bed was against one wall, with a matching wardrobe, chest of drawers and bookcase against the other.

Jodie was at the window. 'Over there! I can see cows!'

I stood behind her, as we looked out on half a dozen Friesians gathered around a massive oak tree to the right of the property. 'Cows at last,' I said, as much to Betty and Ron as to Jodie. But it was a beautiful view, with the grounds stretching to the field on one side and rolling hills on the other. I couldn't have imagined a better start to Jodie's recovery than opening the curtains every morning and gazing on such tranquillity.

She stood staring for a while, then turned to explore her room. She opened and closed all the drawers, investigated the wardrobe and then sat heavily on the bed.

'Next time you come,' Betty said, 'you could bring one of your toys and leave it in your room if you like.'

'I can leave the doll now,' she exclaimed, holding her up by the arm.

'Are you sure? If she's your favourite, you won't see her again until next week.'

'I want her to stay,' she said determinedly.

Betty and I exchanged approving glances, as Jodie pulled back the duvet and tucked Julie in. Clearly, this was a positive sign.

We moved on to the bathrooms, which were each shared by three children. We then walked past the other bedrooms, but we didn't go in; Betty explained to Jodie that these were private. As we headed downstairs, the front door opened, and the children returned from their walk. The quiet house suddenly erupted into excited chattering, and Jodie grabbed my hand and froze.

'It's OK,' I said. 'There's nothing to worry about.'

'We'll say a quick hello,' said Betty encouragingly, 'then I think that's enough for today. You've done very well, Jodie.'

I coaxed her down the rest of the stairs but, confronted with so many new faces, she stayed hidden behind me. The children began taking off their muddy boots and hanging up their coats. They all had their own pegs and shoeboxes.

'This is Jodie and Cathy,' Ron said.

There was a chorus of 'hi's and 'hello's, but Jodie said nothing and stayed where she was.

'Is the hot chocolate ready?' one boy asked.

'Shirley's doing it now,' replied Ron. It seemed that a long walk followed by hot chocolate was a regular routine, and the children streamed off in the direction of the dining room like one big family returning from an outing. With the hall now clear, Jodie came out from her hiding place.

'Have you thought of any more questions?' Betty smiled.

Jodie shook her head and moved towards the front door.

'OK, well if you do think of anything, you can tell Cathy. We'll give you a ring tomorrow, and then see you next week.'

I thanked them as we left, and they waved until we were out of sight.

Jodie, having risen to the occasion, was now physically and emotionally exhausted. She lay on the back seat moaning, then stuck her thumb in her mouth, curled into a ball, and was asleep within five minutes. I phoned home to say we were on our way, and told the children the visit had gone well.

'So she's definitely going then?' Paula asked. I could hear the sadness in her voice.

'Yes. You know, it really is the best place for her, and I think she knows that. I'll tell you all about it later.'

I settled in the traffic on the southbound carriage, at a steady 65–70 miles per hour. Every now and then I glanced in the mirror, as Jodie slept on the back seat. She'd been so calm and normal today, I was tempted to overlook the months of disturbed behaviour, and believe once again that she could possibly have stayed with us.

Maybe with regular therapy, love and patience she could recover and learn to function within a family. In my mind I replayed Dr Burrows' diagnosis, and wondered if she was ever wrong. Did she make mistakes? Was her conclusion 100 per cent certain, or just the best guess she could make at the time? We were the only family Jodie had, and however good High Oaks might have been, it was still a children's home. I turned Radio Four on quietly, and focused on the car in front.

Twenty minutes from home, Jodie woke with a cry. She was desperate for the toilet. 'I can't wait, Cathy. I'll wet meself!' This was at least one area where she clearly had improved; a year ago she would have simply done it on the back seat.

I pulled off the motorway and found a quiet lane, then I spotted an entrance to a field. I pulled in and led Jodie behind a clump of trees. 'You can squat here. No one can see.'

She lifted her skirt and grinned. 'Do you want to watch?'

'No. Of course not.' I turned my back.

I heard the stream of water, then her voice. 'My daddy did. I had to pee on his face. He said it was the drink of the gods, warm and sweet.'

I said nothing. Hiding my revulsion had become as much a part of caring for Jodie as showing love and affection.

Chapter Thirty-Two

Overnight Stay

Jodie's normality was short-lived, and it took all my energy to see her through the following days. The morning after the visit, she woke up expecting to see cows out of her bedroom window, and became angry when I told her that they were at High Oaks, and that she'd see them again the following week.

'You've taken them,' she sneered. 'It's your fault. You hate me.'

'I don't hate you, Jodie. I like you very much.'

'Give me the cows, then,' she persisted. 'I want them now.'

'I can't, sweet. They're not here. It's impossible.'

I wondered if her confusion was due to the impending move. Bringing her to a realization that she would be going was a subtle and gradual process. I had obviously never said, 'You are going to leave us, Jodie,' which would have made her feel rejected and negated the positive feelings about High Oaks that we had carefully been nurturing. Instead, we worked on bringing her to an understanding that she would be going to High Oaks in the near future, first for a visit where she would have her own room and stay the night and have lots of fun. It all had to be very positive, which it was. It was moving on, not leaving behind. She appeared to listen as I emphasized all the progress she had made during her stay with us, how much she would enjoy herself at High Oaks with Ron and Betty, how we would all miss her, and that we would still visit.

'Will my mummy and daddy visit?' she asked.

'No. Definitely not.' But whereas in the past this would have given her some comfort, she now seemed to see it as another rejection.

'You lot! You're all the same. I hate you. Get out!' Reg suddenly appeared and lunged at me, spitting abuse. I hurried out and shut the door, then hovered on the landing. Ten minutes later the door swung open. Amy appeared, with her thumb in her mouth and a wet stain down the front of her pyjamas.

And it was a measure of how strange and distorted our lives had become that I was pleased to see Reg and Amy back. It meant that some level of 'normality' had been regained.

As the days brought us closer to Jodie's next visit to High Oaks, she flipped between acute lethargy and violent anger, so I was administering sympathy and discipline in equal amounts, sometimes within the same minute. I was also struggling to come to terms with my own feelings about her leaving, as well as having to try to keep the rest of the family's spirits up. I felt I was being stretched in all directions.

Wednesday morning finally arrived, and we found ourselves at High Oaks again, this time with Jodie's overnight bag. Jodie rang the bell enthusiastically, and Ron and Betty answered. They'd advised me to keep my goodbye as short as possible, but in practice I was given no choice in the matter. Jodie wanted nothing to do with me, instantly transferring her affections and attention to Betty.

'Bye, then, Jodie,' I said cheerfully. 'Have a lovely time and I'll see you tomorrow.'

She said nothing, and met my offer of a kiss and a hug with sullen refusal. Betty gave me a sympathetic smile, as if to say 'don't take it personally', but that didn't stop the pang of rejection I felt. Jodie and I had been together almost constantly for a year and I felt that everything we'd been through had bonded us and brought us close. It was hard seeing her turn her back on me and walk away without a second thought.

It was not her fault, I reminded myself. Her ability to form attachments was yet another piece of her personality numbed and stunted by the abuse. I was the normal one, not her, and I ought to be grateful to have the capacity to love and miss other people. On the way home, though, I had to stop for a strong black coffee and some quiet time to help me recover.

By the time I arrived back, there wasn't much of the day left. I made dinner for the children, cleared up the plates, and then collapsed in front of the television.

After a fitful night's sleep, I returned to collect her at 1.00 p.m. However, as much as our first visit had been a success, this one had not. Ron took me aside on the gravel drive and updated me.

'She had a couple of tantrums, which weren't entirely unexpected. Betty had to restrain her once after she attacked one of the boys. But please don't worry, Cathy. This move is obviously going to cause a reaction. We're well prepared for it.'

Jodie was due to move there permanently in only five days' time, and I now had misgivings about the timetable. 'Do you think we ought to consider pushing the move back, to give her more time to adjust?' I asked.

'No,' he replied firmly. 'In my experience, delaying it now would only confuse her and make it worse.'

We stepped into the hall, and Betty and Jodie appeared from the playroom. Jodie wasn't happy. 'What you doing here?' she scowled. 'Why do you always stop me having fun?'

'It's time to go home, Jodie,' I replied patiently.

'But I want to stay here. Why won't you let me stay?'

The same old Jodie, with her unfathomable switch-arounds and contrary behaviour.

'You can stay very soon, Jodie, but just not today, OK? Now come on, we have to get going.'

Ron and Betty saw her into the car with her bag.

We were up most of the night. Jodie was scared and disoriented, and adamant that there were people in her room. The next morning I was exhausted, but I was kept busy by a battery of phone calls from the various professionals involved with Jodie's case, all wanting updates, and arranging their final visits. Sally the guardian came round to say goodbye. Her report was now complete, so her practical involvement with Jodie was over. As she explained this to Jodie, I could see that Sally had developed a genuine affection for her. I realized how difficult her job must be, always having to say goodbye. Jodie, however, couldn't remember who Sally was, and told her to fuck off.

Jill arrived the next morning and gave Jodie a present for her new bedroom. It was a pretty china ornament of a cat, and Jodie seemed pleased, and even thanked her.

Now that Jodie was leaving me, Jill would end her connection with the case, so she had wanted to come round and say a proper goodbye to Jodie. It was not only that she was a nice person – it's good social work practice to say goodbye to children when you are no longer going to see them. For a child who is constantly moving and meeting lots of new adults, it can be disorienting if people simply vanish from their lives with no explanation, and it can make them feel even more abandoned and out of control. So when children leave me, there are always visits and goodbyes and a little farewell party.

'Goodbye then, Jodie,' Jill said, as she left. 'Lots of luck.'

'Say goodbye to Jill,' I said, and Jodie obediently waved her off. However, as soon as Jill had gone, Jodie threw the china cat on the floor, smashing it into pieces.

Dr Burrows phoned that afternoon, and said she would need to see Jodie one last time before filing her assessment in court. To my relief, she added that she would prefer to leave it until Jodie had relocated to High Oaks, so she could include this in her report.

The final visitor, two days before the move, was Eileen, who breezed in more than an hour late, again offering no apology. In her case it was not goodbye, as Eileen would continue being Jodie's social worker and should visit Jodie and monitor her progress. I felt a little sad that the only person who was going to stay in official contact with Jodie was the one who seemed to care least about her – but there was not much I could do about that.

'Are you looking forward to going?' she asked insensitively. 'You'll be living with other boys and girls just like you.'

'I'm going to kill them all!' Jodie thundered, rising to the occasion. 'I'm going to rip their heads off. And yours. You bleeding cow.'

Eileen declined my offer of coffee, and was with us for just fifteen minutes, as usual. It was probably the last time I was going to see Eileen – another social worker might have continued the connection and kept me informed out of courtesy, but I had a feeling that wouldn't happen in this case. And I couldn't stifle a sense of relief that I wouldn't have to deal with her any more myself.

I showed her to the door, and she turned round with a cheery and unconcerned, 'Bye then!' There were no words of thanks or gratitude for the hard work I had put into Jodie over the past year, or any sense that we had been bonded by this tragic little girl.

'Goodbye, Eileen,' I said. If anyone had needed a damn good social worker it was Jodie, but maybe, between the rest of us – Dr Burrows, Sally, Jill and myself – we had done our best to make up for it.

After Eileen left it took me an hour to calm Jodie down again, and I promised her she wouldn't be seeing much more of Eileen. Given Eileen's performance to date, this was probably true.

Despite Jodie's negative outbursts about High Oaks, she also said on more than one occasion that she wanted to 'go and live with the cows'. The following afternoon I found her in the kitchen, trying to open the cupboard doors.

'What are you looking for, Jodie?'

'Carrier bags,' she muttered, as if it was none of my business.

'Can you tell me why? I might be able to help.'

'I need to pack,' she answered wearily.

I took her upstairs, fetched the suitcases from the top of my wardrobe, and carried them through to her room. We worked slowly, side by side. 'It's like going on holiday,' she said, stuffing handfuls of toys into the holdalls.

'Yes, a little. Have you ever been on holiday, Jodie?'

She looked at me blankly, and I realized that, like many deprived children, she'd probably never had a proper holiday, but was simply repeating what she'd heard at school or on TV.

'This is more like moving home,' I added, which was something she could relate to. I felt a pang of regret, for, if things had been different, I could have taken her on her first holiday.

During these last few days, Adrian, Paula and Lucy were unusually quiet, and showed enduring patience in the face of Jodie's tantrums and insults. I knew that they, like me, were finding Jodie's departure more difficult than that of any other child we'd fostered. To say goodbye when a child is returning to parents who have overcome their problems has an optimistic feeling of success. Even those children who can't return home, and are found adoptive families or long-term foster placements, leave with a fresh start and the knowledge that they will be welcomed and loved by a new set of parents. The only consolation in Jodie's case was that she'd be in safe hands, and would finally receive the therapy that I hoped would set her on the path to recovery.

Chapter Thirty-Three

Goodbye

On the morning of the move Jodie refused breakfast and sat at the kitchen table, waiting impatiently. I finished my coffee, then began stacking her cases in the hall. She stood at the bottom of the stairs watching me, but turned her back when I asked her if she wanted to help. Eventually all the bags were piled up in the hallway, just as they had been a year before.

'Where are we going?' asked Jodie, trying to reach her coat.

I lifted it down. 'To High Oaks. Remember? You're going to your new home.'

'Oh goody. Is it today? I thought it was next year.' Next year, next week, it was all the same to Jodie.

Adrian, Lucy and Paula got up early so they could see us off before going to school. They gathered in the hallway, uncertain what to say. Paula took the lead and tried to give Jodie a hug, but she stuck out her tongue and turned sideways.

'We'll miss you, Jodie,' Lucy said, 'and we'll speak to you soon.' Jodie just shrugged. She seemed to be quite indifferent to the parting, even though it was obvious Paula and Lucy were quite upset. The three of them helped me load the car, then stood on the doorstep waving.

'You going home?' asked Jodie, as we pulled out of sight.

'I will be once I've settled you, yes.'

'Good. Don't want you. I've got Betty. You can go home, Cathy.'

I knew this was her way of dealing with the separation. She was feeling an emotion, but couldn't acknowledge what it was, or even that she was feeling it.

'I'll phone you on Saturday,' I said. 'And when Betty and Ron tell me it's OK, we'll all come and visit.'

'Don't want to,' she said again. 'Hate you all.'

She'd only been awake for an hour, but she was soon asleep again. She had been reasonably quiet in the night but, as I glanced back at her, lying on the back seat, I wondered how well she could have slept. I turned the radio on low, then switched it off again; the busy string quartet only added to my gloom. I concentrated on driving, and reminded myself of all the positive aspects of where Jodie was going. Nonetheless I kept returning to the guilty question that made me feel hollow inside: had I really done all I could to help her?

When we arrived at High Oaks, Jodie still had her eyes closed, but I sensed that she wasn't asleep.

'Jodie, pet.' I gently rocked her shoulder. 'We're here. Shall we go and find Ron and Betty?'

Her eyelids flickered, then opened, and she smiled directly at me. She gave me her hand, and I helped her scramble out. Ron and Betty appeared on the doorstep, but Jodie dashed straight past them and up to her room. The three of us went inside, and had coffee in the lounge. As it was a weekday, the children were having lessons in the playroom and I could hear the steady hum of their voices as we talked. We completed the paperwork and I handed over Jodie's bank book, where I'd been depositing five pounds a week. The allowance from the Social Services that is supposed to cover pocket money and treats is minuscule, so I made it up with my own money to a half decent sum to provide a little fund for the future. It was the only money of her own Jodie would have.

I also handed over the book in which I had kept a record of the things we had done, and which I knew would be part of her life story work.

'This looks good,' said Ron, flicking through the pages and seeing photographs of us all and the places we had been, pasted-in drawings, bus tickets, train tickets, pamphlets and other memorabilia from days out. I had written a few lines under each entry, with an explanation and the date.

'Great,' he said. 'This will really help with the life story work, and of course we'll be continuing it here as well. It's one of the best I've seen. So many foster parents don't seem to have the time to do it, and it's so important for these children to have evidence of their past, particularly when they start therapy. Hopefully Jodie's social worker will be able to give us some things as well, from the time before she came to you.'

Don't count on it, I thought, but said nothing.

Ron smiled. 'You've done magnificently for Jodie, you really have. Thanks, Cathy. She couldn't have asked for better.'

I welcomed Ron's praise. I already greatly admired the work he and Betty did at High Oaks, and a compliment from him was valued and much appreciated.

Before I knew it, it was time to leave, and Ron advised me to make my departure as brief and low key as possible. While Jodie played in her room we unloaded the car and stacked the cases in the hall. When we were finished I stood there uncertainly, wondering if I should just slip out.

'I'll fetch her,' Betty said, sensing my indecision. 'It's important to say goodbye.'

I waited with Ron while Betty disappeared upstairs. A child's voice erupted in the playroom, followed by the soothing tone of the teacher.

'Try not to worry,' Ron said. 'Really, she'll be fine.'

Betty appeared on the landing, holding Jodie's hand, and as they descended they counted down the steps together, just as we had at home. 'Eleven, twelve, thirteen ...' Jodie hesitated.

'Fourteen?' I offered.

'That's right, Cathy, but let Betty do it. It's her job now.'

I couldn't help but smile. 'I'm going now, Jodie. Will you give me a hug goodbye?'

She rolled her eyes, then held out her arms sullenly,

waiting for me to come to her. I walked over, bent down and put my arms around her. She was stiff and unwilling, but then as I moved to pull away I suddenly felt her arms tighten round my waist. Her head pressed against my stomach. I stroked her hair and blinked back my tears. This would be the last time I hugged her like this, I knew that. I tried to put everything I could into that last embrace: how much I cared for her, how I hoped that she would get better – and how sorry I was that I hadn't been able to help her in the way she needed. She had been the most testing of all the children I'd fostered, and yet that had brought a bond of such closeness that it was difficult to let go, even though I knew it was for the best.

After a few moments I eased her away and drew back. 'OK, sweet, I'll be off now and leave you to unpack. I'll phone in a couple of days.'

'Where you going?' she asked, frowning.

'Home, pet. I have to do the housework, then make Adrian, Lucy and Paula their dinner. You'll be busy too.'

She moved towards Betty, looping her arm around her waist, and snuggled into her side. 'OK, Cathy, I understand. This is my home now, and Amy's. You go. Bye.'

I glanced at Betty, then turned towards the door. Jodie was behind me, repeating her explanation to Amy. 'Betty looks after us now.'

Ron opened the front door, and I crossed the gravel towards the car. I didn't look back until I was in my seat. The three of them gave a little wave, then disappeared inside.

Chapter Thirty-Four

Progress

The house was quiet save for the intermittent ringing of the phone. I listened as the answer phone clicked in, then turned over and closed my eyes. Was it the same person, or a number of different callers? It didn't matter. I'd deal with it in my own time.

It was the day after Jodie had left. I'd gone back to bed after seeing the children off to school, and although I didn't sleep, the enveloping warmth of the duvet safely embraced and cocooned me. Had she slept, I wondered, or had she been plagued by nocturnal demons? What was she doing now? It was mid-morning. Was she in the playroom, out for a walk, or finishing her unpacking? Was she happy? Or had she been taken over by one of her characters? How was she engaging with the other children? That was my biggest concern. Would they be more tolerant, having had similar experiences to hers? Or would their anger and bitterness turn on the stranger in their midst? I feared for her, but I knew I had to let go.

The phone rang again and I snatched it up.

'Cathy?' It was Jill. 'Sorry to disturb you, but I thought you'd want to know. The police have picked up Jodie's parents, and three of the granddads and uncles, and they're going to charge them. The Smiths have accused them of abusing their daughter, and the police have got evidence this time.'

My mind snapped into focus as I pulled myself up the bed. 'The Smiths.'

'You remember. Jodie's neighbours? They stopped their daughter, Louise, going round to play.'

'Yes, yes, I know, but I thought they wanted to give the parents a character reference?'

'They did, until all this came out. DNA has identified Jodie's father and others. The police raided the house, and found thousands of photographs. It is a paedophile ring, and it looks pretty widespread.'

I stared at the curtains, with the floral pattern illuminated by the morning sun. The enormity of what was happening suddenly hit me. The burden of proof had at last swung in Jodie's favour. There was a chance that she would get justice and that the vile people who had abused her would be punished.

'Eileen wants to know if you'll give evidence. I said I was sure you would. And they'll need your log. I'll arrange to have it collected.'

I was still staring straight ahead, as the peonies on the curtains glowed fiery red. 'Yes, of course, anything. Oh, thank goodness. Do they know when it started? Have they got any idea?'

'They're still investigating, but apparently some of the photos show Jodie very young.'

I paused. 'Eighteen months. That's when her development stopped.'

'Yes. And there's some before that. I'll keep you posted.'

I replaced the receiver and remained sitting up in bed. I thought of poor Louise Smith, who had suffered despite her parents having been warned, because they'd failed to take action. How many others had had their lives ruined because Jodie had been ignored? All those years she had been on the at-risk register, supposedly receiving regular visits from social workers, yet no one had noticed anything untoward.

I thought of Jodie's parents, and remembered something I'd been told during training on sexual abuse, some years before. The speaker had said that paedophiles were harder to catch than other criminals, because they didn't believe they were doing anything wrong, so they didn't act guilty.

Heaving myself out of bed, I walked along the landing and into Jodie's room. The emptiness was stark, compared with the cluttered chaos of before. The room still smelled of Jodie, that personal scent which individualizes us all, the most evocative reminder of an absent friend or relative. I stared at the bed, which hadn't been touched since she'd left. Dust motes hung in the shaft of sunlight. I stood silently, taking in the lingering presence of Jodie, still palpable, as though at any moment she could have reached out and touched me. As I turned to leave, I caught sight of an envelope propped on the chest of drawers behind the door. 'Cathy' was printed on the front, in what appeared to be Paula's handwriting. I picked it up and opened it. Inside was a sheet of lined paper, torn from an exercise book.

Dear Cathy,
Paula is writing this as I don't know my words. It was kind of you to look after me and I wish I could have stayed. I'm sorry for all the bad things I did. I can't help it. Something makes me. You are the only person who has looked after me and not got angry. I think you understand. I hope you forgive me. Adrian, Lucy and Paula are very lucky. When they have made me better can I come and live with you? Will you be my new mummy? I don't want my old one.
Love,
Jodie

She'd signed her name herself, and the rest of the page was filled with kisses in red crayon. I looked up, and my eyes brimmed. Somehow I had reached her. It made everything worthwhile. It helped to assuage some of my sense of failure.

Yes, Jodie, of course I will. Whenever you're ready, pet.

Epilogue

Initially Jodie found the move very difficult. She had two full-time carers, Clare and Val, who were allocated solely to her, working in shifts. I wasn't told very much about her progress, as I no longer had an official role; I wasn't a relative, or her carer, I was just a visitor. Nonetheless I gathered that she had often been violent and disruptive, and had continued with roughly the same patterns of behaviour as during her last months with me.

In those first few months she would phone regularly. Clare or Val would make the call, we'd have a brief chat, and then they'd hand the phone over to Jodie. Usually she was calling to complain about Clare or Val, because they weren't letting her do exactly as she wanted. I would listen patiently as that familiar voice shouted, 'I'm bleedin' going to kick 'em!', and then I'd try to reason with her, to get her to understand that her carers' requests were for her own good, just as mine had been.

Although we were frequently in touch, Jodie rarely gave us any sign of affection. I could tell she felt rejected and upset about the move, and she made this clear every time we visited. As we prepared to leave I would try to hug her, but instead of returning the affection she would wallop me on the arm or, worse, stand sullen and silent.

What we did during our visits varied, depending on Jodie's mood. If she was reasonably stable we might go bowling, or to the park, or some local site of interest, usually followed by lunch at Pizza Hut, which had become her favourite. If she was having a bad day we'd stay in the house, playing in the home corner, with Jodie making dinner on the toy oven or remonstrating with her baby doll.

But however hostile she'd been she would always ask when our next visit was going to be, and phone within the week. After about six months she managed to say goodbye properly at the end of a visit, without thumping me, and it felt like a breakthrough. We praised her immensely. Jodie never spoke of her feelings, except of the hatred she still felt for her father, so all we could do was to try and interpret the few clues she gave. She never told me she resented me or felt rejected. Equally, she never said she missed us or looked forward to seeing us. I felt that her finally being able to say goodbye was a good sign, as it suggested she was reconciled to being at High Oaks, if nothing else.

During this time there was some discussion about whether to start contact between Jodie and her brother and sister, who had been found an adoptive family. In the end the decision was made to leave things as they were. Jodie hardly ever mentioned her siblings, except during therapy, and the general feeling was that they weren't close, so it would be best to allow Ben and Chelsea to have a fresh start. In many respects Jodie had lost her childhood, but they still had theirs, having been taken into care that much younger and, it was thought, having escaped the kind of abuse Jodie had suffered.

Jodie did make progress at High Oaks, but her therapy and recovery were hampered by her learning difficulties. A CAT scan revealed brain damage, which had probably been caused by repeated blows to the head when she was an infant. Perhaps as a result of this, there was little progress in Jodie's education, speech or motor skills, even though her behaviour did show some improvement.

Jodie put on a lot of weight at High Oaks, and quickly. She had been overweight when she had come to me, but I had managed to stabilize it. At High Oaks, however, some of the children were anorexic, so the house policy was to allow the children to eat pretty much what they liked. Jodie, given a free rein, had two helpings of everything, and within months the rolls of fat had reappeared round her middle and thighs.

In the months after Jodie left, the two court cases took place: the final care hearing, and the criminal prosecution of the abusers. The care hearing came first, and resulted in Full Care Orders for Jodie, Ben and Chelsea, which in practice meant that they all remained where they were.

During the care hearing my logs were requested by the judge to be used as evidence, but I didn't have to attend in person.

A few months later the criminal case was heard. The crimes against Jodie weren't actually included in the charges, as there was felt to be insufficient evidence.

Instead, Jodie's father and the other men were charged in respect of another child, and the possession and making of indecent photographs. Again, I had no involvement in the court case, and I only found out the outcome from Jill. Jodie's father and two other men were found guilty on all charges. Jodie's mother, and two other defendants, were acquitted. The three convicted men were all given custodial sentences.

Jodie had been on the at-risk register since birth, and by the time she was taken into care she'd had more than fifty visits to casualty, with injuries including broken bones, burns, scalds and cuts. Jodie's Social Services file was apparently so large that it filled two suitcases.

Jodie's case history was a catalogue of errors, and a shameful indictment of the failings of the Social Services. For Jodie to have been on the at-risk register for eight years was bad practice in itself. Children are placed on the register to allow Social Services to monitor and investigate; either an investigation should take place, or Social Services should satisfy themselves that everything is in order, with the child then being removed from the register. In Jodie's case, neither course was followed.

One reason for this appears to have been the high turnover of social workers: there had been over twenty involved in Jodie's case. It appears that Jodie's social workers had avoided making visits to the house, or had allowed themselves to be intimidated into not asking the proper questions. As a result of this intimidation, the family were frequently passed on to new social workers.

As bad as this sounds, I did have some sympathy. The majority of social workers are women, and they are expected to visit violent households on their own. They are frequently attacked, but they hardly ever press charges, because their job requires them to try to build a relationship with these parents. As a result, parents who know the system know that they can treat social workers with impunity. In this context it's no wonder that some social workers avoid visiting aggressive families, or accept unconvincing excuses.

As the Brown family were passed from one weary social worker to the next, their file at Social Services quickly expanded – social workers are plagued by paperwork. The file soon became prohibitively large, in that its sheer size meant that no one involved in the case seemed to have time to read the whole thing. If anyone had seen the overall picture, including all of Jodie's hospital visits, they would surely have acted sooner. However, Jodie's case isn't the first to be overlooked in this way, and, sadly, I doubt it will be the last.

Today, three years on, Jodie continues to make slow, limited progress. Much of her anxiety has gone, and she's probably as happy as she's ever going to be. The intensive therapy has helped her to bring the various parts of her personality together, and Amy and Reg now make only rare appearances. She feels safe at High Oaks, and knows that the protection of those identities is no longer needed.

Jodie is now in a special school. As she has grown older her learning difficulties have become increasingly apparent. When I take her out, people now treat her like a disabled child, going out of their way to speak to her, behaving with exaggerated kindness. She's very overweight, and this makes her even more cumbersome and accident-prone. Her delayed development and poor speech are also obvious, and every year she falls further behind her peers. At some point, perhaps quite soon, she will reach her ceiling in terms of what she can learn, and her disability will become even more pronounced in contrast to her peers.

She rarely mentions her parents now, other than in the context of her ongoing therapy. She does exchange birthday and Christmas cards with Ben and Chelsea, and she has spoken to them on the phone once. This phone call, however, was not a success, and is unlikely to be repeated, as she became very confused and hostile. Much of what happened to Jodie remains deeply buried, and will probably stay buried indefinitely. Only time will tell.

The children and I still visit Jodie, making the return trip of two hundred miles every four to six weeks. We also speak to her on the phone most weeks. On our most recent visit, Paula and I took her to a steak house (as a change from pizza) and while we waited for our order to arrive Jodie suddenly looked directly at Paula and said, 'I like your top. It's very pretty.' We were delighted. It was the first compliment we'd ever heard Jodie offer, and it suggested real progress, as it showed the beginnings of empathy: Jodie had complimented Paula because she wanted to make her feel good, and because she wanted us to like her.

I still find it hard to understand what happened to Jodie. I can somehow accept that there are parents who neglect their children, through drink or drugs or mental illness, and whose cruelty is a side-effect of other problems. But the dreadful abyss that Jodie lived in is a mystery of such darkness and evil that it beggars belief. When I look at my own children and, thank goodness, the majority of children, who are loved and cared for and nurtured, it is hard to comprehend the mindset of parents who seem to care nothing for their child, and do not simply neglect her but actively set about destroying her for their own perverted gratification.

Jodie is a damaged child. She has been vandalized. Her mental processes and her emotions have been destroyed. I doubt she will ever recover sufficiently to lead a normal life, and she will never get the pleasure from life that should have been hers. She has been condemned to an endless punishment by the very people who should have cared for her the most. To me, that is the worst crime imaginable.

I still visit Jodie at High Oaks. Many of the children who were there when Jodie arrived have now left, having recovered enough to move on to long-term foster families. Whether Jodie will ever be able to do the same remains to be seen, but if ever she can, and I'm not too old, my offer stands. And I am still fostering. There's always another child out there who needs help.

SUGGESTED TOPICS FOR READING-GROUP DISCUSSION

Cathy says that children in care are rarely 'orphan Annies'. What do you think she means by this? How does a child's past experience shape their behaviour?

What were the initial indicators that suggested Jodie was a highly disturbed child?

There are some practices and rules in foster carers' homes that might not be found in other homes. What are they, and why do you think they are necessary?

With hindsight, Jodie should have perhaps gone straight to a residential therapeutic home, rather than being placed with Cathy. What, if anything, did Jodie gain from staying with Cathy and her family?

It is understandable that Jodie's behaviour in public attracts stares and comments. What strategies does Cathy use to manage Jodie's behaviour at home and outside?

Jodie is in a constant state of high alert for the first part of the book. Why do you think this is?

Some children (and adults) become desensitized as a result of their shocking experiences, and abuse can become almost normalized. Discuss with reference to Jodie.

As Jodie discloses what has happened to her, she becomes increasingly disturbed instead of starting to heal. Her personality fragments. Why do you think disclosing has this effect on her?

Damaged couldn't be said to have a happy ending, but is there at least closure?

The Saddest Girl in the World

Prologue

This is the story of Donna, who came to live with me when she was ten. At the time I had been fostering for eleven years, and it is set before I had fostered Jodie (*Damaged*) or Tayo (*Hidden*), and before I had fostered Lucy, whom I went on to adopt. When Donna arrived, my son Adrian was ten and my daughter Paula was six; the impact Donna had on our lives was enormous, and what she achieved has stayed with us.

Certain details, including names, places, and dates have been changed to protect the child.

Chapter One

Sibling Rivalry

It was the third week in August, and Adrian, Paula and I were enjoying the long summer holidays, when the routine of school was as far behind us as it was in front. The weather was excellent and we were making the most of the long warm days, clear blue skies and the chance to spend some time together. Our previous foster child, Tina, had returned to live with her mother the week before and, although we had been sorry to see her go at the end of her six-month stay with us, we were happy for her. Her mother had sorted out her life and removed herself from a highly abusive partner. Although they would still be monitored by the social services, their future looked very positive. Tina's mother wanted to do what was best for her daughter and appeared to have just lost her way for a while – mother and daughter clearly loved each other.

I wasn't expecting to have another foster child placed with me until the start of the new school term in September. August is considered a 'quiet time' for the Looked After Children's teams at the social services, not because children aren't being abused or families aren't in crises, but simply because no one knows about them. It is a sad fact that once children return to school in September teachers start to see bruises on children, hear them talk of being left home alone or not being fed, or note that a child appears withdrawn, upset and uncared for, and then they raise their concerns. One of the busiest times for the Looked After Children's team and foster carers is late September and October, and also sadly after Christmas, when the strain on a dysfunctional family of being thrust together for a whole week finally takes its toll.

It was with some surprise, therefore, that having come in from the garden, where I had been hanging out the washing, to answer the phone, I heard Jill's voice. Jill was my support social worker from Homefinders Fostering Agency, the agency for whom I fostered.

'Hi, Cathy,' Jill said in her usual bright tone. 'Enjoying the sun?'

'Absolutely. Did you have a good holiday?'

'Yes, thanks. Crete was lovely, although two days back and I'm ready for another holiday.'

'Is the agency busy, then?' I asked, surprised.

'No, but I'm in the office alone this week. Rose and Mike are both away.' Jill paused, and I waited, for I doubted she had phoned simply to ask if I was enjoying the sun or lament the passing of her holiday. I was right. 'Cathy, I've just had a phone call from a social worker, Edna Smith. She's lovely, a real treasure, and she is looking to move a child – Donna, who was brought into care at the end of July. I immediately thought of you.'

I gave a small laugh of acknowledgement, for without doubt this prefaced trouble. A child who had to be moved from her carer after three weeks suggested the child had been acting out and playing up big time, to the point where the carer could no longer cope.

'What has she done?' I asked.

It was Jill's turn to give a small laugh. 'I'm not really sure, and neither is Edna. All the carers are saying is that Donna doesn't get along with her two younger brothers. The three of them were placed together.'

'That doesn't sound like much of a reason for moving her,' I said. Children are only moved from a foster home when it is absolutely essential and the placement has irretrievably broken down, for clearly it is very unsettling for a child to move home.

'No, that's what I said, and Edna feels the same. Edna is on her way to visit the carers now and see what's going on. Hopefully she'll be able to smooth things over, but is it OK if I give her your number so that she can call you direct if she needs to?'

'Yes, of course,' I said. 'I'll be in until lunchtime, and then I thought I would take Adrian and Paula to the park. I'll have my mobile with me, so give Edna both numbers. I assume that even if Donna has to be moved there won't be a rush?'

'No, I shouldn't think so. And you're happy to take her, if necessary?'

'Yes. How old is she?'

'Ten, but I understand she is quite a big girl and looks and acts older than her years.'

'OK, no problem. Hopefully Edna can sort it out if it's only sibling rivalry, and Donna won't have to move.'

'Yes,' Jill agreed. 'Thanks. Enjoy the rest of your day.'

'And you.'

She sighed. 'At work?'

* * *

I returned to the garden to finish hanging out the washing. Adrian and Paula were in the garden, playing in the toy sandpit. While Paula was happy to sit at the edge of the sandpit and make little animal sand shapes with the plastic moulds, Adrian was busy transporting the sand with aid of a large plastic digger to various places on the lawn. There were now quite sizeable hills of sand dotted on the grass, as if some mischievous mole had been busy underground. I knew that the sand, now mixed with grass, would not be welcomed back into the sandpit by Paula, who liked the sand, as she did most things, clean.

'Try to keep the sand in the sandpit. Good boy,' I said to Adrian as I passed.

'I'm building a motorway,' he said. 'I'm going to need cement and water to mix with the sand, and then it will set hard into concrete.'

'Oh yes?' I asked doubtfully.

'It's to make the pillars that hold up the bridges on the motorway. Then I'm going to bury dead bodies in the cement in the pillar.'

'What?' I said. Paula looked up.

'They hide dead bodies in the cement,' Adrian confirmed.

'Whoever told you that?'

'Brad at school. He said the Mafia murder people who owe them money, and then put the dead bodies in the pillars on the motorway bridges. No one ever finds them.'

'Charming,' I said. 'Perhaps you could build a more traditional bridge without bodies. And preferably keeping the sand in the sandpit.'

'Look!' he continued, unperturbed. 'I've already buried one body.'

I paused from hanging up the washing as Adrian quickly demolished one of the molehills of sand with the digger to reveal a small doll caked in sand.

'That's mine!' Paula squealed. 'It's Topsy! You've taken her from my doll's house!' Her eyes immediately misted.

'Adrian,' I said, 'did you ask Paula if you could borrow Topsy and bury her in sand?'

'She's not hurt,' he said, brushing off the sand. 'Why's she such a baby?'

'I'm not a baby,' Paula wailed. 'You're rotten!'

'OK, OK,' I said. 'Enough. Adrian, clean up Topsy and give her back to Paula. And please ask your sister next time before you take her things. If you want to bury something, why not use your model dinosaurs? Dinosaurs are used to being buried: they've been at it for millions of years.'

'Cor, yes, that's cool,' Adrian said with renewed enthusiasm. 'I'll dig in the garden for dinosaur fossils!' On his hands and knees, he scooped Topsy up in the digger and deposited her in Paula's lap, and then headed for the freshly turned soil in a flowerbed that I had recently weeded. I thought that if Edna couldn't smooth over the sibling rivalry between Donna and her younger brothers and Donna did come to stay, she would be in very good company, and would soon feel most at home.

I made the three of us a sandwich lunch, which we ate in the garden under the shade of the tree; then I suggested to Adrian and Paula that we went to our local park for an hour or so. The park was about a ten-minute walk away, and Adrian wanted to take his bike and Paula her doll's pram. I asked Adrian to go to the shed at the bottom of the garden and get out the bike and doll's pram while I took in the dry washing and the lunch things, and closed the downstairs windows. Since my divorce, Adrian, in small ways, had become the man of the house, and although I would never have put on him or given him responsibility beyond his years, having little 'man' jobs to do had helped ease the blow of no longer having his father living with us, as did seeing him regularly.

It was quite safe for Adrian and Paula to go into the shed: anything dangerous like the shears, lawn feed and weedkiller was locked in a cupboard, and I had the key. Apart from being necessary for my own children's safety, this was an essential part of our 'safer caring policy', which was a document all foster carers had to draw up and follow, and detailed how the foster home was to be kept safe for everyone. Each year Jill, my support social worker, checked the house and garden for safety, as part of my annual review. The garden had to be enclosed by sturdy fencing, the side gate kept locked, drains covered and anything likely to be hazardous to children kept locked away. The safety checklist for the house itself grew each year. Apart from the obvious smoke alarms, stair gates (top and bottom) if toddlers were being fostered, the locked medicine cupboard high on the wall in the kitchen, and the plug covers or circuit breaker, there were also now less obvious requirements. The banister rails on the stairs had to be a set distance apart so that a small child couldn't get their head, arm or leg stuck in the gap; the glass in the French windows had had to be toughened in case a child ran or fell into them; and the thermostats on the radiators had to be set to a temperature that could never burn a young child's delicate skin. It is true to say that a foster carer's home is probably a lot safer than it would be if only the carer's own children were living there.

'And don't forget to close the shed door, please, Adrian,' I called after him. 'We don't want that cat getting in again.'

'Sure, Mum,' he returned, for he remembered, as I did, the horrendous smell that had greeted us last week after a tomcat had accidentally got locked in overnight; the smell still hadn't completely gone, even after all my swabbing with disinfectant.

'Sure, Mum,' Paula repeated, emulating Adrian, having forgiven him. I watched as Adrian stopped and waited for Paula to catch up. He held her hand and continued down the garden, protectively explaining to her that she could wait outside the shed while he got her pram so that she wouldn't have to encounter the big hairy spiders that lurked unseen inside. Ninety per cent of the time Adrian and Paula got along fine, but like all siblings occasionally they squabbled.

Half an hour later we were ready to go. The bike and doll's pram, which we had brought in through the house to save unpadlocking the side gate, were in the hall. I had my mobile and a bottle of water each for the children in my handbag, and my keys for chub-locking the front door were in my hand. Then Paula said she wanted to do a wee now because she didn't like the toilets in the park because of the spiders. Adrian and I waited in the hall while she went upstairs, and when she returned five minutes later we were finally ready for off. I opened the front door, Adrian manoeuvred his bike out over the step, and Paula and I were ready to follow with her doll's pram when the phone on the hall table started ringing.

'Adrian, just wait there a moment,' I called, and with Adrian paused in the front garden and Paula waiting for me to lift the pram over the step I picked up the phone. 'Hello?'

'Is that Cathy Glass?' It was a woman's voice with a mellow Scottish accent.

'Speaking.'

'Hello, Cathy. It's Edna Smith, Donna's social worker. I spoke to Jill earlier. I think you're expecting my call?'

'Oh yes, hello Edna. I'm sorry, can you just wait one moment please?' I covered the mouthpiece. 'It's a social worker,' I said to Adrian. 'Come back inside for a minute.' He left his bike on the front path and came in, while I helped Paula reverse her pram a little along the hall so that I could close the front door. 'I won't be long,' I said to the children. 'Go into the lounge and look at a book for a few minutes.' Adrian tutted but nevertheless nodded to Paula to follow him down the hall and into the lounge.

'Sorry, Edna,' I said, uncovering the mouthpiece. 'We were just going out.'

'I'm sorry. Are you sure it's all right to continue?'

'Yes, go ahead.' In truth, I could hardly say no.

'Cathy, I'm in the car now, with Donna. She's been a bit upset and I'm taking her for a drive. I had hoped to come and visit you, just for a few minutes?'

'Well, yes, OK. How far away are you?'

'About ten minutes. Would that be all right, Cathy?'

'Yes. We were only going to the park. We can go later.'

'Thank you. We won't stay long, but I do like to do an initial introductory visit before a move.' So Donna was being moved, I thought, and while I admired Edna's dedication, for doubtless this unplanned visit had disrupted her schedule as it had ours, I just wished it could have waited for an hour until after our outing. 'I should like to move Donna to you this evening, Cathy,' Edna added, 'if that's all right with you and your family?'

Clearly the situation with Donna and her brothers had deteriorated badly since she had spoken to Jill. 'Yes, we'll see you shortly, then, Edna,' I confirmed.

'Thank you, Cathy.' She paused. 'And Cathy, you might find Donna is a bit upset, but normally she is a very pleasant child.'

'OK, Edna. We'll look forward to meeting her.'

I replaced the receiver and paused for a minute in the hall. Edna had clearly been guarded in what she had said, as Donna was in the car with her and able to hear every word. But the fact that everything was happening so quickly said it all. Jill had phoned only an hour and a half before, and since then Edna had seen the need to remove Donna from the foster home to diffuse the situation. And the way Edna had described Donna – 'a bit upset, but normally … a very pleasant child' – was a euphemism I had no difficulty in interpreting. It was a case of batten down the hatches and prepare for a storm.

Adrian and Paula had heard me finish on the phone and were coming from the lounge and down the hall, ready for our outing. 'Sorry,' I said. 'We'll have to go to the park a bit later. The social worker is bringing a girl to visit us in ten minutes. Sorry,' I said again. 'We'll go to the park just as soon as they've gone.'

Unsurprisingly they both pulled faces, Adrian more so. 'Now I've got to get my bike in again,' he grumbled.

'I'll do it,' I said. 'Then how about I get you both an ice cream from the freezer, and you can have it in the garden while I talk to the social worker?' Predictably this softened their disappointment. I pushed Paula's pram out of the way and into the front room, and then brought in Adrian's bike and put that in the front room too. I went through to the kitchen and took two Cornettos from the freezer, unwrapped them, and took a small bite from each before presenting them to the children in the lounge. They didn't comment – they were used to my habit of having a crafty bite. I opened the French windows and, while Adrian and Paula returned to the garden to eat their ice creams in the shade of the tree, I went quickly upstairs to check what, tonight, would be Donna's bedroom. Foster carers and their families get used to having their plans changed and being adaptable.

Chapter Two

So Dreadfully Sad

No sooner had I returned downstairs than the front door bell rang. Resisting the temptation to peek through the security spy-hole for a stolen glance at my expected visitors, I opened the door. Edna and Donna stood side by side in the porch, and my gaze went from Edna, to Donna. Two things immediately struck me about Donna: firstly that, as Edna has said, she was a big girl, not overweight but just tall for her age and well built, and secondly that she looked so dreadfully, dreadfully sad. Her big brown eyes were downcast and her shoulders were slumped forward as though she carried the weight of the world on them. Without doubt she was the saddest-looking child I had ever seen – fostered or otherwise.

'Come in,' I said, welcomingly and, smiling, I held the door wide open.

'Cathy, this is Donna,' Edna said in her sing-song Scottish accent.

I smiled again at Donna, who didn't look up. 'Hello, Donna,' I said brightly. 'It's nice to meet you.' She shuffled into the hall and found it impossible to even look up and acknowledge me. 'The lounge is straight ahead of you, down the hall,' I said to her, closing the front door behind us.

Donna waited in the hall, head down and arms hanging loosely at her side, until I led the way. 'This is nice, isn't it?' Edna said to Donna, trying to create a positive atmosphere. Donna still didn't say anything but followed Edna and me into the lounge. 'What a lovely room,' Edna tried again. 'And look at that beautiful garden. I can see swings at the bottom.'

The French windows were open and to most children it would have been an irresistible invitation to run off and play, happy for the chance to escape adult conversation, but Donna kept close to her social worker's side and didn't even look up.

'Would you like to go outside?' I asked Donna. 'My children, Adrian and Paula, are out there having an ice cream. Would you like an ice cream?' I looked at her: she was about five feet tall, only a few inches shorter than me, and her olive skin and dark brown hair suggested that one of her parents or grandparents was Afro-Caribbean. She had a lovely round face, but her expression was woeful and dejected; her face was blanked with sadness. I wanted to take her in my arms and give her a big hug.

'Would you like an ice cream?' Edna repeated. Donna hadn't answered me or even looked up to acknowledge my question.

She imperceptibly shook her head.

'Would you like to join Adrian and Paula in the garden for a few minutes, while I talk to Cathy?' Edna asked.

Donna gave the same slight shake of her head but said nothing. I knew that Edna would really have liked Donna to have gone into the garden so that she could discuss her situation candidly with me, which she clearly couldn't do if Donna was present. More details about Donna's family and what had brought her into care would follow with the placement forms Edna would bring with her when she moved Donna. But it would have been useful to have had some information now so that I could prepare better for Donna's arrival, anticipate some of the problems that might arise and generally better cater for her needs. Donna remained standing impassively beside Edna at the open French windows and didn't even raise her eyes to look out.

'Well, shall we sit down and have a chat?' I suggested. 'Then perhaps Donna might feel more at home. It is good to meet you, Donna,' I said again, and I lightly touched her arm. She moved away, as though recoiling from the touch. I thought this was one hurting child, and for the life of me I couldn't begin to imagine what 'sibling rivalry' had led to this; clearly there was more to it than the usual sibling strife.

'Yes, that's a good idea. Let's sit down,' Edna said encouragingly. I had taken an immediate liking to Edna. She was a middle-aged woman with short grey hair, and appeared to be one of the old-style 'hands-on' social workers who have no degree but years and years of practical experience. She sat on the sofa by the French windows, which had a good view of the garden, and Donna sat silently next to her.

'Can I get you both a drink?' I asked.

'Not for me, thanks, Cathy. I took Donna out for some lunch earlier. Donna, would you like a drink?' She turned sideways to look at her.

Donna gave that same small shake of the head without looking up.

'Not even an ice lolly?' I tried. 'You can eat it in here with us if you prefer?'

The same half-shake of the head and she didn't move her gaze from where it had settled on the carpet, a couple of feet in front of her. She was perched on the edge of the sofa, her shoulders hunched forward and her arms folded into her waist as though she was protecting herself.

'Perhaps later,' Edna said.

I nodded, and sat on the sofa opposite. 'It's a lovely day,' I offered.

'Isn't it just,' Edna agreed. 'Now, Cathy, I was explaining to Donna in the car that we are very lucky to have found you at such short notice. Donna has been rather unhappy where she has been staying. She came into care a month ago with her two younger brothers so that her mummy could have a chance to sort out a few things. Donna has an older sister, Chelsea, who is fourteen, and she is staying with mum at present until we find her a suitable foster placement.' Edna met my eyes with a pointed look and I knew that she had left more unsaid than said. With Donna present she wouldn't be going into all the details, but it crossed my mind that Chelsea might have refused to move. I doubted Edna would have taken three children into care and left the fourth at home, but at fourteen it was virtually impossible to move a child without their full cooperation, even if it was in their best interest.

'Donna goes to Belfont School,' Edna continued, 'which is about fifteen minutes from here.'

'Yes, I know the school,' I said. 'I had another child there once, some years ago.'

'Excellent.' Edna glanced at Donna, hoping for some enthusiasm, but Donna didn't even look up. 'Mrs Bristow is still the head there, and she has worked very closely with me. School doesn't start again until the fourth of

September and Donna will be in year five when she returns.' I did a quick calculation and realised that Donna was in a year below the one for her age. 'Donna likes school and is very keen to learn,' Edna continued positively. 'I am sure that once she is settled with you she will catch up very quickly. The school has a very good special needs department and Mrs Bristow is flexible regarding which year children are placed in.' From this I understood that Donna had learning difficulties and had probably (and sensibly) been placed out of the year for her age in order to better accommodate her learning needs. 'She has a good friend, Emily, who is in the same class,' Edna said, and she looked again at Donna in the hope of eliciting a positive response, but Donna remained hunched forward, arms folded and staring at the carpet.

'I'll look forward to meeting Emily,' I said brightly. 'And perhaps she would like to come here for tea some time?'

Edna and I both looked at Donna, but she remained impassive. Edna touched her arm. 'It's all right, Donna. You are doing very well.'

I looked at Donna and my heart went out to her: she appeared to be suffering so much, and in silence. I would have preferred her to have been angry, like so many of the children who had come to me. Shouting abuse and throwing things seemed a lot healthier than internalising all the pain, as Donna was. Huddled forward with her arms crossed, it was as though Donna was giving herself the hug of comfort she so badly needed. Again I felt the urge to go and sit beside her and hug her for all I was worth.

At that moment Adrian burst in through the open French windows, quickly followed by Paula. 'I've brought in my wrapper,' he said, offering the Cornetto wrapper; then he stopped as he saw Edna and Donna.

'Good boy,' I said. 'Adrian, this is Donna, who will be coming to stay with us, and this is her social worker, Edna.'

'Hello, Adrian,' Edna said with her warm smile, putting him immediately at ease.

'Hi,' he said.

'And you must be Paula?' Edna said.

Paula grinned sheepishly and gave me her Cornetto wrapper.

'How old are you?' Edna asked.

'I'm ten,' Adrian said, 'and she's six.'

'I'm six,' Paula said, feeling she was quite able to tell Edna how old she was herself. Donna still had her eyes trained on the floor; she hadn't even looked up as Adrian and Paula had bounced in.

'That's lovely, isn't it, Donna?' Edna said, trying again to engage Donna; then, addressing Adrian and Paula, 'Donna has two younger brothers, aged seven and six. It will be nice for her to have someone her own age to play with.' This clearly didn't impress Adrian, for at his age girls were something you dangled worms in front of to make them scream but didn't actually play with. And given the difference in size – Donna was a good four inches taller than Adrian – she would be more like an older sister than one of his peer group.

'You can play with me now,' Paula said, spying a golden opportunity for some girl company.

'That's a good idea,' Edna said to Paula. 'Although we won't be staying long – we've got a lot to do.' Placing her hand on Donna's arm again, Edna said, 'Donna, you go in the garden with Paula for a few minutes, and then we will show you around the house and go.'

I looked at Donna and wondered if she would follow what had been an instruction from Edna rather than a request. Edna, Adrian and Paula looked too.

'Come on,' Paula said. 'Come and play with me.' She placed her little hand on the sleeve of Donna's T-shirt and gave it a small tug. I noticed Donna didn't pull away.

'Go on, Donna,' Edna encouraged. 'A few minutes in the garden and then we must go.'

'Come on, Donna,' Paula said again and she gave her T-shirt another tug. 'You can push me on the swing.'

With her arms still folded across her waist and not looking up, Donna slowly stood. She was like a little old woman dragging herself to do the washing up rather than a ten-year-old going to play in the garden.

'Good girl,' Edna said. We both watched as, with her head lowered, Donna allowed Paula to gently ease her out of the French windows and into the garden. Adrian watched, mesmerised, and then looked at me questioningly. I knew what he was thinking: children didn't usually have this much trouble going into the garden to play.

'Donna is a bit upset,' I said to him. 'She'll be all right. You can go and play too.'

He turned and went out, and Edna and I watched them go down the garden. Adrian returned to his archaeological pursuits in the sandpit while Paula, still holding Donna's T-shirt, led her towards the swings.

'Paula will be fine with Donna,' Edna said, reading my thoughts. 'Donna is good with little ones.' While I hadn't thought that Donna would hit Paula, she was so much bigger, and it had crossed my mind that all her pent-up emotion could easily be released in any number of ways, including physical aggression. Edna gave a little sigh and returned to the sofa. I sat next to her so that I could keep an eye on what was happening down the garden.

'I've had a very busy morning,' Edna said. 'Mary and Ray, Donna's present carers, phoned me first thing and demanded that I remove Donna immediately. I've had to cancel all my appointments for the whole day to deal with this.'

I nodded. 'Donna seems very sad,' I said.

'Yes.' She gave another little sigh. 'Cathy, I really can't understand what has gone so badly wrong. All the carers are saying is that Donna is obsessively possessive with her brothers, Warren and Jason, and won't let Mary and Ray take care of them. Apparently they've had to physically remove her more than once from the room so that they could take care of the boys. Donna is a big girl and I understand there have been quite a few ugly scenes. Mary showed me a bruise on her arm, which she said Donna had done last night when she and Ray had tried to get her out of the bathroom so that the boys could be bathed. They are experienced carers, but feel they can't continue to look after Donna.'

I frowned, as puzzled as Edna was, for the description she had just given me of Donna hardly matched the silent withdrawn child who had slunk in unable even to look at me.

'The boys are staying with Mary and Ray for now,' Edna continued. 'They all go to the same school, so you will meet Ray and Mary when school returns. They are both full-time carers; Ray took early retirement. They are approved to look after three children and have done so in the past, very successfully, so I really don't know what's gone wrong here.'

Neither did I from what Edna was saying, but it wasn't my place to second guess or criticise. 'Looking after three children has probably been too much,' I said. 'It's a lot of work looking after one, let alone three, particularly when they have just come into care and are upset and still adjusting.'

Edna nodded thoughtfully and glanced down the garden, as I did. Donna was pushing Paula on the swing, but whereas Paula was in her element and squealing with delight, Donna appeared to be performing a mundane duty and was taking no enjoyment whatsoever in the task.

'Is Donna all right doing that?' I asked. 'She doesn't have to push Paula on the swing.'

'I'm sure she is fine, Cathy. She's showing no enthusiasm for anything at present.' Edna returned her gaze to me. 'I've been working with Donna's family for three years now. I have really tried to keep them together, but her mum just couldn't cope. I put in place all the support I could. I have even been going round to their home and helping to wash and iron the clothes, and clean the house, but by my next visit it's always filthy again. I had no alternative but to bring them into care.' Edna looked at me with deep regret and I knew she was taking it personally, feeling that she had failed in not keeping the family together, despite all her efforts. Edna was certainly one conscientious and dedicated social worker, and Donna was very lucky to have her.

'You obviously did all you could,' I offered. 'There can't be many who would have done all that,' and I meant it.

Edna looked at me. 'Donna's family has a long history with social services, and mum herself was in and out of care as a child. Donna's father is not supposed to be living at the family home but he was there only last week when I made a planned visit. The front door had been broken down and Rita, Donna's mum, said Mr Bajan, Donna's father, had smashed his way in. But he was sitting happily in a chair with a beer when I arrived and Rita wasn't exactly trying to get him out. I made arrangements to have the door repaired straight away, because there was no way they could secure the house and Chelsea is still living there.'

I nodded. 'What a worry for you!'

'Yes, it is. Chelsea hasn't been in school for months,' Edna continued, shaking her head sadly. 'And she told me that Mr Bajan hadn't been taking his medication again. He's been diagnosed as a paranoid schizophrenic, and if he doesn't take his medication he becomes very delusional and sometimes violent. I explained to him that he must keep taking it and that if he didn't I would have to have him sectioned again. He was very cooperative, but I don't suppose he will remember what I said. When he is taking the tablets he functions normally, and then because he feels better he thinks he doesn't need the tablets any more, he stops taking them, and becomes ill again.'

I thought what a lot Donna and her family had had to cope with, and I again glanced down the garden, where Donna was still laboriously pushing Paula on the swing.

'Donna's mum, Rita, has a drink problem,' Edna continued, following my gaze, 'and possibly drug abuse, although we don't know for sure. The house is absolutely filthy, a health hazard, and I've had the council in a number of times to fumigate it. Rita can't keep it clean. I've shown her how to clean, many times, but there's always cat and dog mess on the floors, as they encourage strays in. Instead of clearing up the mess, they throw newspaper down to cover it. The whole house stinks. They have broken the new bath I had put in, and the cooker I gave Rita a grant for has never been connected. There is no sign of the table and chairs I had delivered, nor the beds I ordered. The children were sleeping on an old mattress – all of them on one. There's nothing on the floors but old newspaper, and most of the windows have been smashed at one time or another. Rita phones me each time one is broken and I have to make arrangements to have it repaired. There is never any food in the house, and Warren and Jason, Donna's brothers, were running riot on the estate. Neighbours have repeatedly complained about the family, and also about the screaming and shouting coming from the house when Mr Bajan is there.'

I nodded again, and we both looked down the garden, where Donna was still pushing Paula on the swing.

'Mr Bajan is Donna's father and also the father of Warren and Jason, according to the birth certificates, although I have my doubts,' Edna said. 'Chelsea has a different father who has never been named, but she looks like Donna – more than Donna looks like the boys. Mr Bajan has dual heritage and his mother is originally from Barbados. She lives on the same estate and has helped the family as much as she can. I asked her if she could look after the children, but at her age she didn't feel up to it, which is understandable. She's not in the best of health herself and goes back to visit her family in Barbados for some of the winter. She's a lovely lady, but like the rest of the family blames me for bringing the children into care.'

Edna paused and let out another sigh. 'But what could I do, Cathy? The family situation was getting worse, not better. When I first took Donna and her brothers into care they all had head lice, and fleas, and the two boys had worms. I told their mother and she just shrugged. I can't seem to get through to Rita.'

'So what are the long-term plans for the children?' I asked.

'We have ICOs' – Edna was referring to Interim Court Orders – 'for Donna and the boys. I'll apply to the court to renew them, and then see how it goes. Having the children taken into care might give Rita the wake-up call she needs to get herself on track. I hope so; otherwise I'll have no alternative but to apply for a Full Care Order and keep the children in long-term foster care. I'm sure Rita loves her children in her own way but she can't look after them or run a house. I wanted to remove Chelsea too, but she is refusing, and in some ways it's almost too late. Chelsea is rather a one for the boys, and mum can't see that it's wrong for a fourteen-year-old to be sleeping with her boyfriend. In fact Rita encourages it – she lets Chelsea's boyfriend sleep with her at their house and has put Chelsea on the pill. I've told Rita that under-age sex is illegal but she laughs. Rita was pregnant with Chelsea at fifteen and can't see anything wrong in it. She's spent most of her life having children – apart from Chelsea, Donna, and the boys she's had three miscarriages to my knowledge.'

I shuddered. 'How dreadfully sad.'

'It is. It would be best if Rita didn't have any more wee babies and I'm trying to persuade her to be sterilised, but I'm not getting anywhere at present. She has learning difficulties like Donna and Chelsea. Warren and Jason are quite bright – in fact Warren is very bright. He taught himself to read as soon as he started school and had access to books.'

'Really? That's amazing,' I said, impressed.

Edna nodded, and then looked at me carefully. 'You won't give up on Donna, will you, Cathy? She's a good kid really, and I don't know what's gone wrong.'

'No, of course I won't,' I reassured her. 'I'm sure she'll settle. I've taken an immediate liking to Donna and so has Paula by the look of it. ' We both glanced down the garden again. 'Although from what you've said Donna is going to miss her brothers,' I added.

'I think Donna is blaming herself for the three of them being taken in care,' Edna said. 'Donna was the one who looked after Warren and Jason, and tried to do the housework. Chelsea was always out, and mum sleeps for most of the day when she's been drinking. But you can't expect a ten-year-old to bring up two children and run a house. Donna blames herself, and the rest of the family blame me. Rita hit me the last time I was there. I've told her if she does it again I'll call the police and have her arrested.' Not for the first time I wondered at the danger social workers were expected to place themselves in as a routine part of their jobs.

We both looked down the garden. Paula was off the swing now, talking to Donna, who was standing with her arms folded, head cocked slightly to one side. She had the stance of a mother listening to her child with assumed patience, rather than that of a ten-year-old.

'Donna and her brothers will be seeing their parents three times a week,' Edna said. 'Monday, Wednesday and

Friday, five to six thirty, although I've cancelled tonight's contact. I'm supervising the contact at our office in Brampton Road for now, until a space is free at the family centre. Do you know where that is?'

'Yes.' I nodded.

'Will you be able to take and collect Donna for contact?'

'Yes, I will.'

'Good. Thanks. Rita is angry but you shouldn't have to meet her. I'll bring the placement forms with me this evening when I move Donna. It's going to be after six o'clock by the time we arrive. Ray wants to be there when Donna leaves in case there is a problem. He doesn't finish work until five thirty. And Mary has asked that I keep Donna away for the afternoon. She said she will pack her things and have them ready for five thirty.' Edna sighed again. 'Donna will have to come with me to the office for the afternoon, and I'll find her some crayons and paper to keep her busy. Really, Cathy, she's a good girl.'

'I'm sure she is,' I said. 'It's a pity she can't come with us to the park this afternoon.' But we both knew that couldn't happen, as until all the placement forms had been signed that evening I was not officially Donna's foster carer.

'I think that's all then, Cathy,' Edna said. 'I can't think of anything else at present.'

'Food?' I asked. 'Does Donna have any special dietary requirements?'

'No, and she likes most things. There are no health concerns either. Well, not physical, at least.' I looked at her questioningly and she shrugged. 'Mary said she thought Donna was suffering from OCD.'

'OCD?' I asked.

'Obsessive Compulsive Disorder.'

'Oh, I see,' I said, surprised. 'Why does she think that?'

'Apparently she keeps washing her hands.' Edna gave one of her characteristic sighs. 'I don't know, Cathy. You seem pretty sensible. I'm sure you'll notice if there is anything untoward.'

'It's probably just nerves,' I offered.

'Yes. Anyway, we'll leave you to go to the park now. Thanks for taking Donna and sorry it's such short notice. I know I have to phone Jill and update her later.'

'Yes please. Would Donna like to look around the house before you go?'

Edna nodded. 'We'll give her a tour, but don't expect much in the way of response.'

'No,' I said, smiling. 'Don't worry. I'm sure she'll soon thaw out when she moves in.' Edna seemed to need more reassurance than I did, and I thought that over the three years she had worked with the family she had probably built up quite a bond with the children. She appeared to have a particularly soft spot for Donna, and I could see why: Donna was crying out for love and attention, although she didn't know it.

I stood and went to the French windows. 'Paula!' I called from the step. 'Donna has to go now.'

I saw Paula relay this to Donna, who was still standing, arms folded and head lowered, not looking at Paula. Donna didn't make a move, so I guessed Paula repeated it; then I watched as Paula slipped her hand into Donna's and began to lead her up the garden and towards the house. It was sad and almost comical to see little Paula in charge of, and leading, this big girl, and Donna walking a pace behind her, allowing herself to be led.

'Good girls,' I said, as they arrived.

Paula grinned but Donna kept her eyes down and carefully trained away from mine.

'Cathy is going to show us around now, Donna,' Edna said brightly. 'Then we must be going.'

'Can I come to show Donna around?' Paula asked.

'Yes, of course.' I smiled at her, and looked at Donna, but she didn't look up, and sidled closer to Edna, taking comfort in her familiar presence in what was for her an unfamiliar house. I could see that Donna thought a lot of Edna, as Edna did of Donna.

I gave them a quick tour of the downstairs of the house and pointed out where all the toys were. As we entered each room Edna said, 'This is nice, isn't it, Donna?' trying to spark some interest. Donna managed a small nod but nothing else, and I wasn't expecting any more, for clearly and unsurprisingly she was finding all this very difficult. She didn't raise her eyes high enough to see any of the rooms we went into. As we entered what was to be her bedroom and Edna said, 'This is nice, isn't it?' Donna managed a small grunt, and I thought for a second she was going to look up, but instead she snuggled closer to Edna, and it was left to Paula to comment on the view out of the bedroom window.

'Look, you can see the swings in the garden,' Paula called, going over to the window. 'And next door's garden. They've got children and they come round and play sometimes.'

Donna gave a small nod, but I thought she looked sadder than ever. I wondered if that was because she was going to have to settle into what would be her third bedroom in under a month; or perhaps it was because of the mention of 'children' and the realisation that she wouldn't be playing with her brothers on a daily basis.

'It will look lovely when you have your things in here, Donna,' Edna said encouragingly. Donna didn't say anything and Edna looked at me. 'Thank you for showing us around, Cathy. I think it's time we went now. We've got a lot to do.'

Edna led the way out of the bedroom with Donna at her heels, and Paula and me following. Paula tucked her hand into mine and gave it a squeeze; I looked at her.

'Doesn't she like her bedroom?' Paula asked quietly, but not quietly enough; I knew Donna had heard.

'Yes, but I'm sure it must seem very strange to begin with. You're lucky: you've never had to move. Don't worry, we'll soon make her feel welcome.'

Paula came with me to the front door to see Edna and Donna out. 'Say goodbye to Adrian for me,' Edna said. 'Donna and I will see you as soon after six o'clock as we can make it. Is that all right with you?'

'Yes. We'll be looking forward to it.'

'Bye, Donna,' Paula said as I opened the door and they stepped out. 'See you later.'

Edna looked back and smiled, but Donna kept going. Once they had disappeared along the pavement towards Edna's car, I closed the door and felt relief run through me. Although Donna wasn't the disruptive child I had thought she might be, kicking, screaming and shouting abuse, the weight of her unhappiness was so tangible it was as exhausting as any outward disturbing or challenging behaviour.

Paula followed me down the hall and towards the French windows to call Adrian in. 'Do you think Donna will want to play with me?' she asked.

'Yes, I am sure she will, love. She's a bit shy at present.'

'I'll make her happy playing with me,' she said. 'We can have lots of fun.'

I smiled and nodded, but I thought that it would be a long time before Donna had genuine and heartfelt fun, although she might well go through the motions and cooperate with Paula, as she had done when pushing the swing. Despite all Edna had told me about Donna's family, the circumstances for bringing her and her brothers into care and now moving her to me, I was really none the wiser as to why she was having to move and why she was so withdrawn. But one thing I was certain of was that Donna carried a heavy burden in her heart which she wasn't going to surrender easily.

Chapter Three

Donna

With Adrian pushing his bike along the pavement, and Paula her doll's pram, we made a somewhat faltering journey to our local park. I always insisted that Adrian wheel his bike until we were away from the road and in the safety of the park with its cycle paths. Paula stopped every so often to readjust the covers around the 'baby' in the pram, although in truth, and as Adrian pointed out with some relish, it was so hot that it hardly mattered that baby was uncovered as 'it' was hardly likely to catch cold.

'Not again,' Adrian lamented as our progress was once more interrupted by Paula stopping and seeing to baby. 'Give it to me,' he said at last, 'and I'll tie it to my handlebars. Then we can get there.'

'It's not an it,' Paula said, rising to the bait.

But that was normal brother and sister teasing, and I thought a far cry from whatever had been happening between Donna and her brothers. As nothing Edna had said had explained how the situation between Donna and her brothers had deteriorated to the point of her having to move, I came back to the possibility it could be an excuse from her carers. Perhaps Mary and Ray hadn't been able to cope with having three children, all with very different needs and who would have been very unsettled, and as experienced carers they had felt unable to simply admit defeat and say they couldn't cope, and had seized upon some sibling jealousy to effect the move. I didn't blame them, although I hoped that Donna hadn't been aware that she was the 'culprit'; Edna had referred to the situation as Donna being 'upset', which shouldn't have left her feeling in any way guilty.

Once in the park, Adrian cycled up and down the cycle paths, aware that, as usual, he had to stay within sight of me. 'If you can see me, then I can see you,' I said to him as I said each time we brought his bike to the park. Even so, I had one eye on him while I pushed Paula on the swings and kept my other eye on 'the baby' in the pram as Paula had told me to.

I thought of Donna as Paula swung higher and higher in front of me with little whoops of glee at each of my pushes. I thought of Donna's profile as I had seen her at the bottom of our garden, slumped, dejected and going through the motions of entertaining Paula. I would have to make sure that Paula didn't 'put on' Donna, for I didn't want Donna to feel she *had* to entertain or play with Paula, or Adrian for that matter, although this was less likely. Something in Donna's compliance, her malleability, had suggested she was used to going along with others' wishes, possibly to keep the peace.

Paula swapped the swing for the see-saw, and I sat on one end and she on the other. As I dangled her little weight high in the air to her not-very-convincing squeals of 'Put me down', I felt a surge of hope and anticipation, an optimism. I was sure that when Donna came to stay with us, given the time and space, care and attention she clearly so badly needed, she would come out of her shell and make huge progress, and I could visualise her coming here to play. I also thought that Donna was going to be a lot easier to look after than some of the children I had fostered. She didn't come with behavioural difficulties – kicking or screaming abuse, for instance – and certainly wasn't hyperactive; and if Mary did have a bruise on her arm, I now smugly assumed it was because she and Ray had mishandled the situation when they had been trying to bath the boys. Had they allowed Donna to help a little, instead of trying to forcibly remove her from the bathroom, I was sure the whole episode could have been defused. Like so many situations with children, fostered or one's own, it was simply, I thought, a matter of handling the child correctly – giving choices and some responsibility, so that the child felt they had a say in their lives.

I had a lot to learn!

We ate at 5.00 p.m., earlier than usual, so that I could clear away and be ready for Donna's expected arrival soon after 6.00. We'd had chicken casserole and I had plated up some for Donna, which I would re-heat in the microwave if she was hungry. After she had spent the afternoon with Edna in her office they were returning to Mary and Ray's only to collect her belongings and say goodbye, so there was a good chance she wouldn't have had dinner. Children always feel better once they've eaten their first meal in the house, and spent their first night in their new bedroom. I had also bathed Paula early, and she was changed into her pyjamas; her usual bedtime was between 7.00 and 7.30, but that was when I would be directing my attention to Donna tonight. Adrian, at ten, was used to taking care of his own bath or shower, and could be left to get on with it – he didn't need or want me to be present any more.

At 6.00 p.m. the children's television programmes had finished; the French windows were still wide open on to the glorious summer evening and Adrian was sitting on the bench on the patio, playing with his hand-held Gameboy with Paula beside him, watching. I'd told Paula that she could go outside again, but as she'd had her bath I didn't want her playing in the sandpit and in need of another bath. I was sitting on the sofa by the French windows with the television on, vaguely watching the six o'clock news. I doubted Edna and Donna would arrive much before 6.30, by the time they had said their goodbyes to Mary and Ray (and Warren and Jason) and loaded up the car with Donna's belongings. I wondered how her brothers were taking Donna's sudden departure. They had, after all, been together for all their lives, albeit not in very happy circumstances, so they would be pretty distressed, I thought.

Jill, my support social worker, was present whenever possible when a child was placed with me; however, I wasn't expecting her this evening. She had left a message on the answerphone while we'd been at the park, saying that she'd been called away to an emergency with new carers in a neighbouring county, and that if anything untoward arose and I needed her advice, to phone her mobile. I didn't think I would need to phone, as the placement of Donna with me would be quite straightforward; Edna was very experienced and would bring all the forms that were needed with her.

Five minutes later the doorbell rang and my heart gave a funny little lurch. I immediately stood and switched off the television. Welcoming a new child (or children) and settling them in is always an anxious time, and not only for the child. I must have done it over thirty times before but there was still a surge of worry, accompanied by anxious anticipation, as I wanted to do my best to make the child feel at home as quickly as possible. Adrian and Paula had heard the doorbell too; Adrian stayed where he was, intent on his Gameboy, while Paula came in.

'Is that Donna?' Paula asked.

'I think so.'

Paula came with me down the hall, and I opened the front door. I could tell straight away that parting hadn't been easy: Donna was clearly upset. She had a tissue in her hand and had obviously been crying; she looked sadder than ever and my heart went out to her. Edna looked glum too, and absolutely exhausted.

'Come in,' I said, standing aside to let them pass.

'Thank you, Cathy,' Edna said, placing her hand on Donna's arm to encourage her forward. 'We'll sit down for a while, and then I'll unpack the car.'

'Go on through to the lounge,' I said as they stepped passed me into the hall, and I closed the door. Paula walked beside Donna and tried to take her hand, but Donna pulled it away. I mouthed to Paula not to say anything because Donna was upset.

'You go with Adrian for now,' I said to Paula as we entered the lounge. She returned to sit beside him on the bench outside, where he was still engrossed in his Gameboy.

'It's one of those Mario games,' I said to Edna as she glanced out through the French windows at Adrian. Edna smiled and nodded. Donna had sat close beside Edna on the sofa and her chin was so far down that it nearly rested on her chest.

'Is everything all right?' I asked Edna.

She nodded again, but threw me a look that suggested they had had a rough time and that she would tell me more later, not in front of Donna. 'Mary and Ray gave Donna a goodbye present,' Edna said brightly, glancing at Donna.

'That's nice. Can I have a look?' I asked Donna. Children are usually given a leaving present by their foster carers, and also a little goodbye party, although I assumed that hadn't happened here. Donna was clutching a small bright red paper bag on her lap, together with the tissue she'd used to wipe her eyes. 'What did you get?' I tried again, but she shrugged and made no move to show me. 'Perhaps later,' I said. 'Would you like a drink, Donna? Or something to eat? I've saved you dinner if you want it.'

She gave that slight shake of the head, so I assumed she didn't want either now.

'I'll do the paperwork,' Edna said, 'and then I'll leave Donna to settle in. She's had a very busy day and I expect she'll want an early night.'

I nodded. 'What time do you usually go to bed, Donna?'

Edna glanced at her and then at me. 'I'm not sure, but she's ten, so I would think eight o'clock is late enough, wouldn't you?'

'Yes,' I agreed. 'That sounds about right. Adrian is the same age and usually goes up around eight and then reads for a bit.' I looked at Donna as I spoke, hoping I might elicit some response; it felt strange and uncomfortable talking about a girl of her age without her actually contributing.

Edna took an A4 folder from her large shoulder bag and, opening it, removed two sets of papers, each paper-clipped in one corner. 'I think I've already told you most of what is on the Essential Information Form,' she said, flipping through the pages and running her finger down the typing. 'I've only included the names and contact details of Donna's immediate family; there are aunts and uncles, but Donna sees them only occasionally. She had a medical when she first came into care and everything was fine. Also Mary and Ray took her to the dentist and optician, and that was all clear too.' It is usual for a child to have these check-ups when they first come into care.

'That's good,' I said, and I glanced at Donna, who still had her head down. She'd cupped the little red bag containing the present protectively in her hands as if it was her most treasured possession in the world.

Edna checked down the last pages of the Essential Information Form, and then leant forward and handed it to me. This would go into the file I would start on Donna, as I had to for all the children I looked after, together with the paperwork I would gradually accumulate while Donna stayed with me, and also the daily log which I had to keep and which Jill inspected regularly when she visited.

'The Placement Agreement forms are complete,' Edna said, flipping through the second set of forms. 'I checked them before we left the office.' She peeled off the top sheets and, taking a pen from her bag, signed at the foot of the last page. She did the same for the bottom set of forms, which was a duplicate of the top set, and then passed both sets of forms to me. I added my signature beneath hers on both copies and passed one set back. The Placement

Agreement gave me the legal right to foster Donna and I was signing to say I agreed to do this and to work to the required standard. One copy would be kept by the social services and my copy would go in my file.

'Nearly finished,' Edna said, turning to Donna.

I glanced through the open French windows at Paula and Adrian, sitting side by side on the bench. Adrian was still intent on his Gameboy and Paula was looking between the game and Donna, hoping Donna might look up and make eye contact.

'Here's Donna's medical card,' Edna said, passing a printed card to me. 'Will you register her at your doctor's, please? She's outside the catchment area of Mary and Ray's GP.'

'Yes, of course.'

'I think that's about it then,' Edna said, closing the folder and returning it to her bag. She placed her bag beside the sofa, glanced first at Donna and then looked at me. 'Do you have any plans for the weekend, Cathy?'

'Not especially. I thought we would have a relaxing weekend, and give Donna a chance to settle in. I will have to pop up to the supermarket tomorrow for a few things. Then on Sunday we could go to a park; the weather is supposed to be good.'

'That sounds nice,' Edna said. 'Donna is good at shopping. She likes to help, don't you, Donna?' We both looked at Donna and she managed to give that almost imperceptible nod. 'You will be able to tell Cathy what your favourite foods are when you go shopping,' Edna continued, trying to spark some interest. 'I am sure Cathy will let you have some of them.'

'Absolutely,' I agreed. 'You can help me choose, Donna.'

Edna's gaze lingered on Donna and I knew she was finding it difficult to make a move to leave. I wondered if Donna had been this quiet and withdrawn all afternoon, while she'd been with Edna at the office. Sitting forward, Edna said, 'OK, Cathy, could you give me a hand unpacking the car then, please?'

'Yes, of course.' I stood and went to the French windows. 'I'm just helping Edna unload the car,' I said to Adrian and Paula. 'You're all right there for now, aren't you?'

They nodded, Adrian without looking up from his game and Paula with her eyes going again to Donna.

'You can stay there, Donna,' Edna said, 'or you can go in the garden if you like with Paula and Adrian.'

Donna shrugged without looking up, and Edna left the sofa and began towards the lounge door. 'I'll come back in to say goodbye,' she said, pausing and turning to look at Donna. Donna shrugged again, almost with indifference, as though it didn't matter if Edna said goodbye or not; but I knew for certain that it did matter. The poor girl had spent the last hour saying goodbye – to Warren and Jason, to Mary and Ray, and now to Edna. I could only guess at what must be going through her mind as her social worker, to whom she was obviously very close, and with whom she had spent all day, was about to depart and leave her with strangers, albeit ones with good intentions.

I followed Edna down the hall and she stood aside to allow me to open the front door. She gave one of her little heartfelt sighs. 'I'm sure Donna will be fine by the end of the weekend,' she said. 'I'll phone on Monday and arrange to visit next week.'

'I'll look after her, Edna,' I reassured her. 'Don't worry. Has she been this quiet all afternoon?'

'She wasn't too bad until we went to say goodbye.' Edna lowered her voice and leant towards me in confidence. 'It was awful at Mary and Ray's. Donna was so upset to be leaving Warren and Jason, but the boys couldn't have cared less.'

'Really?' I said, shocked. 'Why?'

'I don't know. I had to make them say goodbye. They told Donna to her face that they were pleased she was going, and that they didn't want her to come back.'

'But that's dreadful!' I said, mortified.

'Yes, I know.' Edna shook her head sadly. 'I don't know what's been going on. Mary and Ray said Donna had being trying to dominate the boys and boss them around, but I'm sure it was only her way of caring for them; Donna has spent all her life trying to look after the boys as best she could. But Warren and Jason, only a year apart in age, are glued to each other and present a united front. As they are so much brighter than Donna I wouldn't be surprised if they have been bullying her. I've seen them play tricks on her and use their intelligence to poke fun at her. I've told them off for it before. All the same, Cathy, I have to say, I was shocked by their attitude tonight. Donna loves them dearly and would do anything for them. It's probably for the best that they are being separated, for Donna's sake. She's not fair game for the boys. She's got a big heart, and I know she's a bit slow, but you would have thought brotherly love might have counted for something.'

'Is Donna close to her older sister, Chelsea?' I asked.

'No. Chelsea and Mum are thick as thieves, and I'm beginning to think that Donna was out on a limb. You never really know what's going on in families behind closed doors. We brought the children into care because of severe physical neglect but emotional abuse is insidious and can be overlooked.' She paused. 'Anyway, Cathy, I'm sure Donna will be fine here. And when she does open up to you, I'd appreciate you telling me what she says.'

'Yes, of course I will.'

'Thanks. Let's get the car unpacked, and then I must get home to my hubby. He'll be thinking I've deserted him.'

Edna was truly a lovely lady and I could imagine her and her 'hubby' discussing their respective days in the comfort of their sitting room in the evening.

We made a number of journeys to and from the car, offloading a large suitcase, some cardboard boxes and a few carrier bags. Once we had stacked them in the hall, Edna said, 'Right, Cathy, I'll say a quick goodbye to Donna then go.'

We returned to the lounge, where Donna was as we had left her on the sofa, head down and with the red paper bag containing her present clasped before her.

'I'm off now,' Edna said positively to Donna. 'You have a good weekend and I'll phone Cathy on Monday; then I'll visit next week. If you need or want anything, ask Cathy and she will help you. And I think Paula is dying to make friends with you, so that will be nice.'

Edna stood just in front of Donna as she spoke but Donna didn't look up. 'Come on,' Edna encouraged kindly. 'Stand up and give me a hug before I go.'

There was a moment's hesitation; then, with a small dismissive shrug, Donna stood and let Edna give her a hug, although I noticed she didn't return it. As soon as Edna let go, Donna sat down again. 'Bye then, Donna,'

Edna said; then leaning out of the French windows, 'Bye Adrian, Paula, have a good weekend.'

They both looked up and smiled. 'Thank you.'

Edna collected her bag from where she'd left it beside the sofa and with a final glance at Donna – who was once more sitting head down with the present in her hands, and I thought trying hard to minimise Edna's departure – walked swiftly from the room.

'Take care and good luck,' Edna said to me as I saw her to the front door. 'I'll phone first thing on Monday. And thanks, Cathy.'

'You're welcome. Don't worry. She'll be fine,' I reassured her again.

'Yes,' Edna said, and with a quick glance over her shoulder towards the lounge, went out of the door and down the path towards her car.

I closed the front door and returned to the lounge. 'All right, love?' I asked Donna as I entered.

She slightly, almost imperceptibly, shook her head and then I saw a large tear escape and roll down her cheek.

'Oh love, don't cry,' I said, going over and sitting next to her. 'It won't seem so bad in the morning, I promise you, sweet.'

Another tear ran down her cheek and dripped on to the red paper bag in her lap, and then another. I put my arm around her and drew her to me. She resisted slightly, then relaxed against me. I held her close as tear after tear ran down her cheeks in silent and abject misery.

'Here, love, wipe your eyes,' I said softly, guiding her hand containing the tissue towards her face. She drew it across her eyes, then slowly lowered her head towards me, where it finally rested on my shoulder. I held her tight, and felt her head against my cheek as she continued to cry. 'It's all right,' I soothed quietly. 'It will be all right, I promise you, love. Things will get better.'

Paula came in from the patio and, seeing Donna crying, immediately burst into tears. I took hold of her arm with my free hand and drew her to sit beside me on the sofa. I encircled her with my right arm while my left arm stayed around Donna.

'Why's Donna crying?' Paula asked between sobs.

'Because a lot has happened today that has made her sad,' I said, stroking Paula's cheek.

'I don't like seeing people cry,' Paula said. 'It makes me cry.'

'I know, love, and me. But sometimes it's good to have a cry: it helps let out the sad feelings. I think Donna will feel a bit better in a while.' I remained where I was on the sofa with an arm around each of the girls, Paula sobbing her heart out on my right, Donna on my left, crying in silent misery, and me in the middle trying hard not to join in – for, like Paula, I can't stand seeing anyone upset, particularly a child.

Chapter Four

Silence

Adrian was not impressed. The phone had started ringing and, feeling unable to simply stand and desert the girls, I hadn't immediately answered it.

'The phone's ringing,' he said helpfully, coming in from the patio, with his Gameboy in his hand. He stopped as he saw the three of us and pulled a face, suggesting he didn't fully approve of this collective display of female emotion.

'I'll answer it now,' I said, throwing him a smile. 'Everyone will be OK soon.' This reassurance was enough for Adrian and he smartly nipped off into the garden, grateful he didn't have to be party to what must have appeared to a boy of his age to be blubbering nonsense.

I eased my arms from the girls and went to answer the phone on the corner unit. It was Jill.

'You took a long time to answer. Is everything all right, Cathy?'

'Yes. Donna is here.' I glanced over to the sofa as Paula took up the gap I had left and snuggled into Donna's side. Donna lifted her arm and put it around Paula. 'Yes, everything is fine,' I said.

'Cathy, I won't keep you now, as it's getting late. I just wanted to make sure Donna had arrived and there weren't any problems.'

'No, no problems,' I confirmed. 'Edna only left ten minutes ago. She's going to phone you, and me, on Monday. She brought all the forms.'

'Good. Well, enjoy your weekend. If you do need to speak to someone, Mike is back, and on call over the weekend; dial the emergency number.'

'OK, Jill, thanks.'

'And I'll phone on Monday, and visit as soon as I can next week.'

'Fine,' I said. We said goodbye and I hung up.

I glanced at the carriage clock on the mantelpiece. It was 7.40 p.m., after Paula's bedtime and getting close to Adrian and Donna's. I crossed over to the girls; they had both stopped crying now and Donna still had her arm around Paula. Both were sitting very still, as though appreciating the moment, although Paula was the only one to look at me.

'Girls,' I said gently, drawing up the footstool and squatting on it so that I was at their level. 'Are you feeling a bit better now?'

Paula nodded and, with her head still resting against Donna, looked up at her. Donna had her head down and rubbed away the last of the tears from her cheeks with the tissue. I put a hand on each of their arms. 'I think we will all feel better after a good night's sleep, and it is getting late,' I said. Paula looked up again at Donna for her reaction, but there wasn't one: Donna remained impassive, head lowered, with the little red paper bag in her hand. 'Donna, love, would you like something to eat?' I asked again. 'I have saved you dinner.' She gave her head a little shake.

'What about a drink before bed then?'

The same small shake of the head.

I hesitated, not really sure how to proceed. In many ways it was easier dealing with a child who was angry and shouting abuse: at least the pathway of communication at some level was open and could be channelled and modified. With so little coming back from Donna – she hadn't said a word yet – it was difficult to assess or interpret her needs. I hadn't thought to ask Edna if Donna had eaten, but even if the answer had been no, I could hardly force her to have dinner. 'Are you sure you don't want anything to eat?' I tried again. 'Not even a snack?'

The same shake of the head, so I had to assume she wasn't hungry, and if she hadn't eaten she could make up for it at breakfast. 'I'd love to see your present,' I said, looking at the little bag. 'So would Paula. Will you show us?'

Paula raised her head from Donna's side for a better view and Donna withdrew her arm. 'What did Mary and Ray buy you?' I asked. 'I bet it's something nice.'

Very slowly and not raising her head, and with absolutely no enthusiasm, Donna moved her fingers and began to open the top of the paper bag. Paula and I watched as she dipped in her fingers and gradually drew out a bracelet made from small multi-coloured beads.

'Oh, isn't that lovely,' I said. 'What a nice present.'

Donna cupped the bracelet in the palm of her hand, and I continued to enthuse, grateful for this small cooperation, which I viewed as progress. 'Can you put it on your wrist and show us?'

Donna carefully slipped the bracelet over the fingers on her right hand and drew it down so that it settled around her wrist. As she did, I thought of Warren and Jason's parting shot, when they had told Donna not only that were they pleased she was going but not to go back. I felt so sorry for her.

'That's beautiful,' I said. I could tell that Donna was proud; she supported the wrist with the bracelet with her other hand, as though displaying it to its best advantage. It wasn't an expensive bracelet; it was the type of 'infill' present that one child gave another at a birthday party. The beads were painted plastic, strung together on elastic so that the bracelet fitted most-sized wrists. But if Paula thought the gift wasn't as precious as Donna did, she certainly didn't say so.

'That is pretty,' Paula said, touching it. 'I like the red and blue ones.' And I thought if anything typified the gaping chasm between children who had and those who did not, it was the bracelet. In our wealthy society with its abundance of acquirable material possessions, the gap between children from poor homes and those who enjoy all its advantages was widening. Paula had a couple of these bracelets, possibly three, and also a bedroom packed full of similar treasures which she'd received for Christmas and birthday presents, and treats from grandparents; but I knew from the way Donna cradled the bracelet that she certainly did not.

'We will have to find a safe place for it in your bedroom,' I said. Donna nodded.

I glanced at the clock again; I really had to start getting all three children upstairs and into bed. There was no way I was going to attempt Donna's unpacking now; it was too late, and we would have plenty of time the following day. 'Now, love,' I said, placing my hand on Donna's arm again. 'We're going to take just what we need for tonight from your bags and sort out the rest in the morning, all right? Once you've had a good night's sleep everything will seem a lot better. I'd like you to come with me into the hall and tell me which bag has your nightwear and washing things.' Then it occurred to me that Donna probably didn't know what each bag contained, as Edna had said Mary had done the packing that afternoon while Donna had been with Edna. 'Do you know what's in each bag?' I asked her.

Donna shrugged. 'Wait there with Paula a minute,' I said, 'and I'll take a look, unless you want to come and help me?'

She shook her head, and I left her sitting with Paula, who was still, bless her, admiring the bracelet, while I went down the hall, hoping I wouldn't have to unpack every bag and case to find her night things. I peered in the various carrier bags and found that Mary had put everything Donna needed for the night in one plastic bag, presumably guessing it would be too late for us to unpack properly. Picking up this carrier bag, I returned to the lounge.

The girls were still together and Donna was slipping the bracelet from her wrist and returning it to the paper bag. 'I've found what you need for tonight,' I said. I went over and, opening the bag, showed her inside. 'Nightdress, wash bag and teddy. Is there anything else you need, love?'

She shook her head.

The French windows were still open and Adrian was outside, now at the end of the garden having a last swing before he had to come in. It was nearly 8.30 p.m. and the air temperature was just starting to drop. 'Adrian,' I called from the step. 'Five minutes, and then I want you to come in and get changed.' He didn't say anything, but I knew he had heard me, for this scenario had been repeated most nights since school had broken up – I had left him playing in the garden, sometimes with the neighbour's children, while I got Paula ready for bed.

'OK, girls,' I said. 'Let's go up and get you settled. Are you sure you wouldn't like a drink before you go, Donna?'

She shook her head.

With a different child on their first night I would probably have put Paula to bed and spent some time talking to the child and getting to know them before settling them for the night. However, because Donna was not communicating I felt, as Edna had done, that she was exhausted. I was now dearly hoping that I would have Donna's cooperation in going to bed, but I was starting to feel a bit uneasy. If Donna didn't move and ignored my requests, or answered them with a shrug or shake of the head, what was I supposed to do? She was far too big for me to carry upstairs as I might have done with a little one, and if she didn't respond to my cajoling and persuading there was virtually nothing I could do. It crossed my mind that maybe that was how Mary had received the bruise to her arm – perhaps Donna had refused to cooperate despite all their efforts, and Mary and Ray had resorted to physically moving her; but I quickly let that thought go, for if that was so, then I was in big trouble, as I had no 'Ray' to help me.

'Right,' I said, using an assertive tone. 'I have got all you need for tonight, Donna. The three of us will go upstairs together. Donna, while I help Paula, you can get changed, ready for bed.' I had said it as though I meant it, as a request not open to debate. Paula immediately stood and came to my side, aware she was going to bed later than usual and not wishing to overstep the mark. Donna remained where she was on the sofa, impassive, head down and once more clutching the little bag with her present. 'OK, Donna, are you ready?' I said, and I felt another twinge of anxiety. She still didn't move and I saw Paula look at me questioningly, also worried by Donna not doing as I'd asked.

'Come on, Donna,' Paula said in her little voice. I looked at Paula and shook my head to indicate to her not to continue. Her request had sounded like a plea and I needed Donna to do as I had asked as a matter of course; I wasn't going to plead with her.

I took Paula's hand and gave it a reassuring squeeze, and with Donna's carrier bag in my other hand, I turned away from the sofa, ready to leave the room. There was a limit to how many times I could politely say that I wanted her to go upstairs before I started to look ineffectual and lose my credibility and authority. 'Right, we're going up now, Donna,' I said and, still holding Paula's hand, I began slowly and steadily towards the lounge door. As I went I was frantically searching for plan B if she didn't follow me, which vaguely centred around taking Paula up and coming down and trying again. But I knew that was likely to be even less successful than the first time, and I couldn't have Donna sitting down here all night. As a last resort I would have to phone the fostering agency and ask for help, although practically I wasn't sure what they could do either.

To my great and utter relief, as Paula and I stepped from the lounge and into the hall, Donna stood and began to follow us. I waited for her to catch up and then continued down the hall. I didn't praise her, for I had to give the impression that I expected her to follow my instructions and requests. Although I felt dreadfully sorry for Donna, and my heart went out to her, she was only ten and like all children she had to do as she was told.

Paula and I went up the stairs first with Donna a step or two behind. At the top of the stairs I said to Paula, 'You go into the bathroom and do your teeth while I show Donna to her bedroom.' I wasn't sure what was going to happen next with Donna, and I didn't want Paula being party to any sudden outburst. Donna was so quiet and withdrawn it was unhealthy, and I had the feeling, as I had done when she'd first visited and gone down the garden with Paula, that she was like a tinder box waiting to ignite and go up in flames – you can only suppress so much emotion before something gives. While Edna had reassured me that Donna was 'a good girl', social workers, no matter how efficient they are, don't see the child on a daily basis as Mary and Ray had done, and they'd had problems with Donna.

Paula did as I asked and went to the bathroom while I continued round the landing to Donna's bedroom, with Donna following me in silence.

'All right, love,' I said, kindly but firmly. 'Here is your nightdress, teddy bear and wash bag.' I took the items from the carrier bag and set them on the bed. 'I'll leave you to get changed, and then I'll show you into the bathroom. We won't worry about a bath tonight. If you want the toilet, it is right next to your bedroom.' I pointed out towards the landing. 'I'll be back shortly.'

Without looking at her, and thereby not giving her room for refusal, I came out and closed the bedroom door; whether she did as I asked or not remained to be seen. I went round the landing and into the bathroom, where Paula was cleaning her teeth. I waited until she had finished and then went with her to the toilet, where I waited, as I did every evening at bedtime, outside the toilet door. The toilet, at the other end of the landing to the bathroom, was the room next to Donna's, and as I waited for Paula I listened, but I couldn't hear any movement. I prayed Donna was doing as I had asked and getting changed.

When Paula came out of the toilet I went with her into her bedroom and drew the curtains. Once she was in bed I took a book from her bookshelf and propped myself on the bed beside her with my feet up, as I did every evening, as part of our bedtime routine. 'I'm only reading one story tonight, love,' I said, 'as I need to get Donna settled.'

I had chosen a short story, but a favourite of Paula's – *The Very Hungry Caterpillar*, which I had been reading to her since she was a toddler. Paula knew it by heart and could also read most of the words. She joined in as I read, poking her finger through the hole in each page where the caterpillar was supposed to have eaten. At the end, where the caterpillar changes into a beautiful butterfly, I said, as I always said when I read this book, 'You are my beautiful butterfly.' Paula grinned and snuggled her head into her pillow, and I kissed her goodnight. 'Thanks for helping to look after Donna,' I said. 'I'm sure she'll be better tomorrow.'

Paula looked concerned. 'Mum?' she asked. 'Does Donna talk?'

I smiled. 'Yes, love, but she's finding it difficult at present because of everything that has happened to her. I am sure she will start talking to us soon.'

'Good. Because I don't like her being so quiet. It's a bit scary.'

'I know, love, but don't you worry.' I got off the bed and kissed her goodnight again. 'Everything will be all right. Now, it's late and I want you to go straight off to sleep.'

'Is Adrian coming in soon?' Paula asked.

'Yes, just as soon as I've got Donna settled.'

'Will she go to bed at the same time as me every night?'

I smiled. 'No, she's older than you, and it's well past your normal bedtime.'

'I know.' Paula giggled and buried her head under the sheets.

'Night, love,' I said again. 'Sleep tight.' Coming out, I blew her one last kiss and drew the door to but left it slightly ajar as she liked it. I went round the landing and knocked on Donna's door. There was no reply, so I knocked again, then slowly opened the door and put my head round. Donna had changed into her nightdress and I inwardly breathed a sigh of relief. She was sitting on the bed with the red paper bag in her hand. 'Do you want to put your present in this drawer for now?' I said, going in and opening one of the drawers in the wardrobe. 'It will be quite safe in there.'

She shook her head and clutched the bag tighter.

'OK, but you will have to put it down when you have your wash or else it will get wet.' I picked up her wash bag containing the flannel and toothbrush, and in my firm but kindly tone said, 'This way to the bathroom, love.' I turned and left the room decisively as though I expected her to follow, which she did.

In the bathroom I put her flannel on the towel rail with ours and her toothbrush in the mug with ours. 'The toothpaste is there,' I said. 'That tap is the hot water and that one is the cold.' Obvious to us, but less obvious to a newcomer because the red and blue marks on the taps had worn away with use. 'This is your towel,' I said, pointing again to the towel rail. 'Do you need anything else?' Donna shook her head. 'OK, when you have finished, go to the toilet and then I will come and say goodnight.'

I came out, and went downstairs and into the lounge. The light was fading now at nearly 9.00 p.m. and there was a nip in the air. I stood at the French windows and called Adrian in, and unusually he came with the first calling.

'Good boy,' I said. 'Now straight upstairs and change into your pyjamas. Donna will be finished in the bathroom by the time you are ready to go in. You can leave your shower until the morning as we're late.'

'Cool,' he said, which was his favourite expression, used to denote most things that met with his approval.

'And not too much noise when you go up: Paula is going off to sleep.'

'I'll have a drink first,' he said, and he went through to the kitchen, while I closed and locked the French windows.

Leaving Adrian to pour himself a glass of milk, I returned upstairs, taking a couple of Donna's carrier bags with me, which I placed in her bedroom. The water had stopped running in the bathroom and I went round and knocked on the bathroom door, which she had left ajar. 'All right?' I asked, going in. She nodded. 'Have you had your wash and done your teeth?' I noticed she was once more clutching the red paper bag. She nodded again.

'Good girl. Straight into bed then. It's after nine o'clock.'

She followed me silently round the landing and into her bedroom. I pulled back the sheet – there was no need for a duvet, as it was too hot – and I stood aside and waited for her to get into bed. 'Do you have your teddy bear in bed with you?' I asked, picking up the clearly much-loved threadbare soft toy.

She nodded.

'Has he or she got a name?'

She shrugged and laid her head on the pillow. I tucked the teddy in beside her and then draped the sheet over her. I drew the bedroom curtains and returned to stand beside the bed. 'We'll unpack all your things tomorrow,' I said, leaning slightly forward. 'Have a good sleep and you can have a lie-in if you wish: there's no rush tomorrow. If you need me in the night, you know where my bedroom is. Just knock on the door. I'm a light sleeper, so I will hear you.' I hesitated and looked at her. She was on her side, facing out into the room. She was staring straight ahead and had one arm around the teddy. There wasn't much else I could say or do that night, although I felt there was plenty I should be saying and doing to help her. 'Sleep tight, love, and see you in the morning. Would you like a goodnight kiss?' I always ask the fostered child this when they first arrive; it's an intrusion in their personal space to just assume they want a kiss.

She nodded slightly and I leant further forward and kissed her forehead. 'Night, love, sleep tight. We'll have a good day tomorrow. We'll unpack first – it's nice to have all your things around you. I'm so pleased you have come to stay with us.'

I hesitated again, hoping, wishing, she would say something, some verbal acknowledgement that she was all right and not in need of anything. But there was absolutely nothing.

'Night, love,' I said again. 'Would you like your bedroom door open or closed?' She gave a small shrug. 'OK, I'll close it a little.'

With a final glance at her I came out and pulled the door to without shutting it fully. Adrian was in the bathroom, having changed into his pyjamas, and was now finishing his washing and teeth brushing. I waited on the landing until he came out, and then I saw him into bed. 'If you're reading tonight, it's only for a short while,' I said. Although we didn't have to be up early for school in the morning, if Adrian didn't have enough sleep, he was not at his best, to put it mildly. Kissing him goodnight, I left him reading by the light of his lamp and came out and shut his bedroom door right to, as he liked it. I looked in on Paula, who was fast asleep; then I listened outside Donna's door. There was no sound, but I didn't go in in case I disturbed her. I would check on her later on my way to bed.

I went downstairs, locked the back door, and then flopped on to the sofa in the lounge and put my feet on the footstool. I was absolutely exhausted, and it seemed incredible that only ten hours had passed since I had received Jill's call about Donna. It wasn't only anxious anticipation of Donna's arrival, and welcoming her, that had drained me, but the relentless effort to get any form of acknowledgement from her, and the worry about what was really going on inside her head. As I sat on the sofa and slowly, gradually, began to relax, I realised that even though I had fostered over thirty children, Donna was the first to have spent an entire evening in the house and gone to bed without uttering a single word. I wondered just how long she could keep it up.

Chapter Five

Cath-ie

Donna maintained her vow of silence, if that is what it was, for the whole of the weekend. Not having slept well on Friday night, I rose early on Saturday morning, and went downstairs for a coffee. At 8.00 I heard movement coming from Donna's bedroom and I went up, knocked on her door and entered.

She was in her nightdress, sitting on the edge of the bed and staring at the carpet. I asked her if she had slept well and if she needed anything, and was met with the same shake of the head. I left her to get dressed, and she finally came down at nearly 10.00, by which time Paula and Adrian had long since eaten their breakfasts and were playing in the garden. I asked Donna what she would like for breakfast and gave her the options – a choice of cereal, toast or egg and bacon. But there was no response other than a shrug, so, unable to decipher her preferred menu, I gave her the safe bet of cornflakes, followed by toast and honey, with a drink of juice, which she ate slowly and in silence, alone at the table. I had taken my coffee to the table as I gave her the breakfast, but she seemed so uncomfortable with my presence that eventually I busied myself in the kitchen and left her to eat alone. When she had finished, I told her to go and brush her teeth and have a wash, which she did without comment, while I cleared away her breakfast things.

If I had thought it was hard work the previous evening, it got steadily worse during the day, and not wishing to be unkind, it was like having a zombie in the house. Her downcast face, her stooped shoulders, her slowly lumbering gait would have suggested depression had she been an adult, and I thought that if she didn't improve over the weekend I would phone Jill and Edna first thing on Monday and suggest I take her to the doctor.

After Donna had finished in the bathroom I told her we would unpack her things. I had already carried up all the bags and boxes and stacked them on the landing. I now pulled the large suitcase into her bedroom and, setting it on the bed, opened it. 'We'll hang up these clothes in the wardrobe,' I said, and I began unfolding her jeans and joggers and draping them on to the hangers. Then I took the jumpers and T-shirts and laid them in neat piles in the drawers of the wardrobe. Donna stood by in silence, her head slightly lowered and her arms loosely folded in front of her, watching me but not helping, although I encouraged her often.

It was obvious which clothes Mary and Ray had bought – they were new – and which had come with her from home – a selection of worn and faded joggers and T-shirts which not even a jumble sale would have taken. I stacked the old clothes at the bottom of the wardrobe, although clearly she would be wearing the new ones, and those I bought for her. There is a great temptation for foster carers to throw out all the rough stuff children bring with them when they come into care, but these are familiar things for the child in an otherwise unfamiliar and strange environment, and it is important they are kept until the child feels comfortable about letting them go; which was why Mary had packed them and sent them with Donna.

There were two pairs of plastic trainers with the toes out and the laces missing, which I placed at the bottom of the wardrobe, leaving the new trainers and sandals beside her bed. There were a few pieces of very old school uniform – a bobbled sweatshirt and a torn T-shirt, both with the school's logo, and a badly stained skirt. Donna had come into care right at the end of the summer term, so Mary and Ray hadn't replaced her school uniform; I would do so at the start of the next term. There were half a dozen pairs of new pants and socks, and a few pairs of white faded grey, which I packed at the bottom of the wardrobe. There was a badly stained and ripped anorak, which I assumed had been Donna's coat before coming into care, and also a new lightweight summer jacket, which I hung in the wardrobe. As I worked, separating and sorting the clothes, Donna continued to stand a little way from me, either shaking her head or nodding if I asked her something that required a yes or no answer, or shrugging if my question needed a choice.

I talked as I worked, and continually sought her opinion and advice on where things should go, in the hope of getting her to join in. 'Shall we put this in here? This is a pretty top – where did you get it from? We'll make this the drawer for your underwear,' and so on, but there was absolutely no response. Once the suitcase was empty, I heaved it on to the top of the wardrobe out of the way and asked Donna to bring in the last of the bags and boxes from the landing, which she did. These appeared to contain her personal things – two worn books, a torn magazine, a bare and grubby doll, a new story CD, and a crayoning book with felt-tip pens. I told Donna I would leave her to put those things away, and I opened the empty drawers, and also pulled out a store-away box from under the bed.

One of the carrier bags which I had looked in and put to one side seemed to contain an assortment of what looked like old rags. I now picked it up, and I felt Donna watching me from under her lowered eyes as I pulled it open for a closer look. There were a couple of very old vests and pieces of what looked like torn-up sheets. I wondered if these were comforters – I'd had children of Donna's age and older arrive with chewed and torn security rags and blankets which they obviously needed to keep with them until they were no longer needed. But these were very dirty and I thought that Mary would have washed them if Donna had to have them close to her, and one smelled distinctly of disinfectant.

'What are these for?' I asked lightly. But there was no reply, not even a shrug. 'Shall I get rid of them?' Donna shook her head rigorously, with more enthusiasm than she'd shown in response to any of my previous questions. 'I'll put the bag in the wardrobe then,' I said. I slid open the door at the bottom of the wardrobe, which was a separate compartment, and placed the bag inside. I had a feeling that Donna was still watching me intently, although for the life of me I couldn't imagine why this bag of old and dirty rags was of any importance to her.

'I'll leave you to unpack that last box,' I said, 'then come down, and we'll have a drink and a snack before we go to the shops.'

I went downstairs, where I made up some fresh lemonade, dropped in some ice cubes and prepared a plate of cheese on crackers, which I placed on a tray. I called Donna, who came down straight away, and I carried the tray into the garden, where Adrian and Paula joined us at the table on the patio. As they gathered round the table I poured the lemonade and placed the cheese and biscuits in the centre for everyone to help themselves. Adrian and Paula delved in and then watched as Donna finally, slowly and laboriously took one. I saw Adrian and Paula surreptitiously watch her, and whereas Paula had been all over Donna the day before she was now slightly guarded and kept a small distance between them. If I was finding Donna's unremitting silence daunting and unnerving, how much worse must it have been for a child of Paula's age? Paula was used to trusting and reaching out to people, and usually made friends easily with the children who stayed with us, even those who were noisy and rude. This was something completely new to her, as it was to Adrian and me.

The day was heating up quickly and I wanted to get what I needed from the shops before the car became uncomfortably hot. The quick trip to the supermarket that I had mentioned to Edna the day before, which had seemed very positive when Edna had told me that Donna liked shopping and liked to help, now loomed as something else to overcome with one-sided conversation and a large measure of patience. Once we had finished the snack I bundled everyone into the car, showing Donna where to sit and checking her seatbelt was on. At their ages, all three children had to be on booster seats by law and in the rear of the car, and there wasn't an awful lot of room.

Paula, the smallest, was in the middle, with Donna and Adrian either side. There was the usual elbowing between Adrian and Paula when they first got in and fastened their seatbelts. Once they were settled, I started the car, fed in the sing-along cassette and began the ten-minute journey to the supermarket. Normally Paula would have joined in the catchy rhymes but she sat, as did Adrian, in unnatural silence, further intimidated, I thought, by Donna's withdrawn and now close presence.

At the supermarket I took a small trolley and went up and down the aisles, dropping in what we needed. Adrian and Paula, as usual, chose a couple of 'treats' each, which was their reward (or bribe) for enduring another shopping trip. Donna, despite Edna's assurance of her liking shopping, walked beside the trolley, head down and taking no interest whatsoever. I repeatedly asked her if she liked this or that, lingering at the displays of unhealthy but tempting biscuits and crisps, but there was nothing beyond a shrug, or on one occasion a brief nod. Even at the ice-cream cabinet she barely raised her eyes, and certainly didn't express a preference. Over the years I've taken many children to the supermarket and I have experienced many different reactions – from a child stealing when I wasn't looking to a full-scale tantrum (often) when I wouldn't buy all the sweets that had been demanded – but never before had I experienced complete and utter silence and indifference.

Arriving home, I gave everyone a carrier bag and we made one journey into the house and took them through to the kitchen. Adrian and Paula went straight out into the garden, while Donna hovered, arms loosely folded in front of her and head hung down. I asked her if she would like to help me unpack. She shrugged without looking up and continued to stand, a haunted silhouette in the doorway of the kitchen.

'Donna, love,' I said at last, 'you can do what you like, play in the garden, help me, or look at a book, but find something to do until lunchtime, pet.' She moved away and, head down, shuffled off. Presently I saw her appear in the garden and sit on the bench on the patio, watching Adrian and Paula playing in the sandpit. I viewed the fact that she had actually gone outside as a positive sign, and I watched her for a few moments longer; then I stopped unpacking the bags and went to offer some encouragement.

'Donna, would you like to play in the sandpit too?'

She shook her head.

'What about the swings?'

The same shake of the head.

'Do you want a bat or ball, or a bicycle out of the shed?'

Nothing, so I returned inside and finished the unpacking.

I made sandwiches for lunch and, with a packet of crisps for each of us, carried the tray outside to the table. We ate under the sunshade and in silence. Adrian and Paula were even quieter now – the unhealthy and oppressive silence was contagious, and like a smog it seemed to hang in the air.

'I thought we would spend the rest of the day in the garden,' I said. 'Then tomorrow shall we have a day out somewhere?'

'Sure,' said Adrian, without his usual enthusiasm and suggestions of where we could go.

Paula looked up at Donna for her input and predictably was met with nothing. Paula continued eating her egg sandwich and crisps in silence, and as soon as she and Adrian had finished they scuttled off; I remained where I was at the table, opposite Donna. I looked at her. Here we were in the garden on an idyllic summer's day, surrounded by flowers in all their colourful glory, with a gentle breeze faintly stirring the trees, and Adrian and Paula without a care in the world, and Donna was in abject and withdrawn misery. I reached out and touched her hand.

'Donna, love,' I said gently. 'You are going to have to start talking to me some time. It's too lonely for you otherwise.' She withdrew her hand from mine and shrugged. 'I know it's difficult for you, sweet, but you can trust me. I want to help you, but I need you to start talking to me. Adrian and Paula were looking forward to you coming to live with us, and they want to be friends with you.'

She shrugged again and, leaving the rest of her sandwich, got up from the bench and went to sit in the lounge. I sighed. My prognosis of a good night's sleep making all the difference now seemed laughable. And if I was honest, part of me was becoming irritated by her continual rejection of my best efforts, for I was sure she had some control over this unrelenting front she was hiding behind. I knew she was suffering, but she must have been talking at Mary and Ray's; otherwise they would have raised the alarm and Edna would have certainly told me. I could only assume that it was as a result of being separated from her brothers, and having to move, but how on earth I dealt with it was another matter. I decided the best course of action was to carry on as much as was possible with normal family life and include Donna, but not expect her to participate, in the hope that eventually she would feel comfortable enough to drop the barriers and join in. If nothing had changed by Monday morning, I would phone Jill and Edna and ask for help.

I took Paula and Adrian to one side and tried to explain the position to them, because I couldn't just ignore Donna's persistent silence: it was like ignoring the elephant in the room. 'Carry on as normal,' I said. 'Talk to Donna but don't expect her to reply or join in.' They said they would try, but clearly it was difficult for them. Later Paula made a few brave attempts to include Donna in her play but with no success.

That evening I ran a bath for Donna while she stood by me in silence, and then I left her to wash and change into her nightdress. I said goodnight and told her that the following day we would go out somewhere. I kissed her goodnight, said sleep tight, came out and pulled the door to. I consoled myself that while Donna wasn't engaging with me at any outward level at least she was cooperating and doing what I was asking. The day before I had been worried that she might stubbornly refuse to do anything, which would have been even more difficult, if not impossible to deal with.

Sunday evening approached. We had spent the day at a small adventure park, where Donna had sat and watched Paula and Adrian enjoying themselves with all the other children but not joined in once. I knew I would have to phone Jill and Edna first thing in the morning. I would ask them how to handle the situation because clearly my strategies were not working. I began the bedtime routine, and I left Donna to change into her nightdress and have her wash and do her teeth while I went downstairs and wrote up my log notes. Paula was already asleep and Adrian was getting changed into his pyjamas in his bedroom.

When I heard the bathroom door open and Donna return to her bedroom, I went upstairs to say goodnight. She was in bed with her arm around the teddy and had closed the bedroom curtains. I was half inclined to say a brisk goodnight and come out, for I was finding it difficult not to take her refusal to speak to me personally. I felt very frustrated and not a little hurt that she was making no attempt to communicate at all. But something stopped me from taking this line, and instead I went to her bed and knelt beside it.

I stroked her forehead and she didn't pull away. 'Donna, love,' I said, 'I know you are hurting but you must start talking to me. I can't help you if you don't.' I paused and continued to stroke her head. I really didn't know what else to say. 'I'm here to help you, and we all want to see you happy. Can you tell me what the matter is?'

She shook her head.

I hesitated, stopped stroking her head, and stood. 'OK, love, you get off to sleep.' I moved away, but as I went to the door I heard her voice, so faint I could have missed it.

'Cath-ie,' she said, pronouncing the two syllables separately. At last! I thought, and I could have jumped for joy.

I immediately returned to the bed. 'Yes, love? What is it?'

'I'm sorry, Cath-ie,' she said in a small voice.

I knelt down again and stroked her forehead. 'There is no need to be sorry, pet. All I want is for you to be happy. Will you try to talk to me tomorrow?'

She nodded.

'And to Paula and Adrian? They would like that.'

She nodded again.

'Is there anything you want to tell me now?' She looked at me for the first time since arriving, her big brown eyes doleful and full of pain. She was an attractive girl, her light brown skin soft and flawless, but her pleasant features were dulled by her inner turmoil. 'Yes?' I encouraged.

'It's my fault,' she said quietly.

'What is, sweet?'

'It's my fault my brothers and me came into care.'

'No, it's not, love,' I said, gently but firmly. 'Not at all. And being in care is not a punishment. It's to help your mum and give her a rest.'

'Mum says it's my fault. She said I should have tried harder.'

'Harder at what?'

'Looking after the house, and Warren and Jason. I did my best, but it wasn't good enough. And Mary and Ray didn't want my help.'

I continued to stroke her forehead. 'Donna, at your age, love, you should not be responsible for looking after the house or your younger brothers. That is the adult's responsibility. It was nice of you to help, but it was your mother's job to look after you, just as Mary and Ray are looking after your brothers now, and I will look after you. Do you understand?'

She nodded.

I paused. 'Is that what's bothering you, or is there something else?'

She gave a slight shake of her head.

'All right, love, we'll talk about this more tomorrow, but I'm very pleased you felt you could tell me.' I smiled and she looked directly at me again and, although she didn't return my smile, I thought I saw a slight lifting of the dreadful melancholy that had frozen her expression into sadness.

'Night then, love.' I kissed her forehead.

'Night, Cath-ie,' she said, again separating the second syllable.

I came out and with huge relief went into Adrian's room to say goodnight.

'Donna's talking,' I said.

'Cool. Now she can play with Paula.' I wasn't sure if this was a comment on Donna's progress or that Paula had been taking up rather a lot of his time recently.

I said goodnight to Adrian and, with my usual warning about not reading until too late, came out and went downstairs. I went into the lounge, where I wrote up my log notes with considerable relief and some small satisfaction that I had got there in the end and Donna was finally talking.

That night I slept very well, after sleeping badly the previous two, and when I went downstairs it was just after 7.00 a.m. At the end of the hall, I was surprised to find the door to the kitchen slightly open – I usually made sure all the downstairs doors were shut before I went to bed. I tentatively pushed the door wider open and went in. As I did, I started and did a double take. I couldn't believe what I was seeing. Donna was on her hands and knees, scrubbing the kitchen floor for all she was worth. She was using the rags that had been in the carrier bag in her bedroom.

Chapter Six

Amateur Psychology

'Whatever are you doing?' I asked, amazed. Donna was in her nightdress, and the floor was awash with puddles of water and the sopping wet rags, which were dotted around her.

She didn't answer, but continued rubbing one of the rags back and forth across the floor.

'Donna?' I said again. I began walking across the wet and now slippery tiled floor, with my bare feet squishing on the tiles. 'Donna?' I went right up to her. She must have heard me, and seen me out of the corner of her eye, but she kept on scrubbing furiously. Both of her hands clutched the rag in front of her and she rubbed it backwards and forwards as though her very life depended on it. In different circumstances I might have seen the funny side of it – a child frantically mopping up a spillage before I could see it, with their well-meant intentions making it a lot worse. But not now. This was no spillage – there was too much water and Donna's work was all-consuming and frantic.

'Donna?' I said again, more firmly; then I placed my hand on her shoulder, hoping to break the motion. My hand jerked back and forth in time with her frenzied cleaning. 'Donna, stop now,' I said loudly. 'You don't have to do this.'

'I do,' she said, and she continued, now pushing the cloth round and round. The water sprayed against my ankles. I thought she must have tipped the washing-up bowl full of water over the floor, for there was far too much water for it to have come from the wet rags alone. She must have left her bedroom and come downstairs very quietly, for normally I heard a child out of bed and on the landing.

'Donna, I want you to stop. Now!' I said, and again I touched her shoulder.

'No! I must clean,' she said, her voice rising in panic. 'I must! I must! I have to clean the kitchen floor.'

'No,' I said, raising my voice above hers. 'You don't have to. Stop it, now! And you are not supposed to be in the kitchen. It isn't allowed.' Which was true: it was a house rule that I didn't have young children in the kitchen, for safety reasons, but I hadn't yet explained the house rules to Donna.

Gradually the frantic scrubbing grew less frenzied, and then came to a halt. Her hands on the rag became still, but she remained on all fours, bent over the rags. 'Don't hit me,' she said. 'I've done my best.'

I stared at her, horrified. 'Of course I'm not going to hit you. I don't hit anyone, and certainly not a child.' I continued to look at her, as I tried to understand what was happening. Keeping my voice even, I said, 'Donna, I want you to stand up, and dry yourself. We need to talk.' My firmness masked my anxiety, as I continued to search for a reason that could have brought Donna down here in the early hours to do this.

I took the hand towel from the rail by the sink and held it out. 'Now please, Donna, stand up and dry your hands and legs. You're soaking.' The front of her nightdress was sopping wet where it had trailed in the water; it dripped as she stood. I passed her the towel and she slowly wiped her hands, then bent down and wiped her knees. I watched her: the frenzied movements of her scrubbing had vanished and she had once more resumed her slow lethargic manner. She finished wiping off the excess water from her legs and handed back the towel. Although her legs and hands were dry, her nightdress was still dripping. 'I think we had better get you changed first before we talk,' I said.

She shrugged.

I reached out and took her hand, and she allowed me to lead her from the wet and slippery floor of the kitchen, across the carpet of the annexe and into the hall. I let go of her hand as I led the way upstairs. Adrian and Paula were still asleep – it was just before 7.30 a.m. I went into Donna's bedroom, took a set of clean clothes and underwear from her wardrobe and laid them on the bed. 'Get dressed, please,' I said. 'I'll be back in a minute. Leave your nightdress in the laundry basket on the landing.'

Donna didn't say anything but made a move towards the clothes. I came out, pulling the door to behind me. I went to my bedroom, where I quickly dressed and ran a brush through my hair. My morning routine having been disrupted, I would have to shower later, after I had spoken to Donna. What had been going through her head to make her rise at the crack of dawn and creep downstairs with her bag of rags and start the ritualised cleaning, I couldn't begin to guess. It hadn't been proper cleaning, as if she had wanted to make a difference; nor had it been a small task, as Adrian and Paula sometimes performed, which I would have to admire with great delight – 'Look, Mum! We've tidied the toy box!' No, Donna's work had been a frenzied attack, almost as if she was acting out something, which hadn't been aimed so much at accomplishing a task as releasing something in her. Edna's almost throwaway comment came back to me – 'Mary thinks she might have OCD.' I knew very little about OCD, other than that it was an obsessive need to do something over and over again; was this how it manifested itself?

I went round the landing and knocked lightly on Donna's door. 'Are you dressed?' I asked quietly, not wanting to wake Adrian and Paula.

Donna's small voice came back. 'Yes, Cath-ie.'

I went in. She was sitting on the bed, hunched forward, arms folded into her waist and head down. The colourful beads from her bracelet were now strewn across the floor.

'Oh dear, have you broken your bracelet?' I asked, wondering if this had anything to do with what had just happened in the kitchen.

She shook her head, and in that movement I saw a small guilt. I was almost certain that the two incidents were somehow connected, and that she had possibly broken the bracelet on purpose.

'Donna,' I said, sitting next to her on the bed, 'can you please try to tell me what's going through your mind?' It was at times like this that I really wished I was a psychiatrist, with a better understanding of what made children tick, rather than a mother and carer who had to rely on intuition, some training, and experience from looking after children.

Donna shrugged again.

'When we were in the kitchen, why did you think I was going to hit you?' I asked gently, taking her hand in mine.

She didn't resist, and I stroked the back of her hand and waited.

She shrugged again.

'Come on, love. I want so much to understand and help you. But I can't unless you try to tell me. Why were you cleaning? You didn't accidentally spill something, did you?'

She shook her head.

'So why did you think I was going to hit you? That worries me.'

Her mouth opened and closed before she spoke; then eventually she said quietly, 'My mum did. If I didn't clean well.'

'Your mum hit you for not cleaning properly?' I asked.

She nodded.

Good grief! I thought, but I kept my voice steady as I asked, 'How often did that happen, Donna?'

She shrugged again, then after a moment said, 'Lots. It was my job to clean the house for when Edna came. Mum said if I didn't keep the house clean Edna would take us away.'

'I see,' I said. 'Thank you for telling me.' The logic of trying to clean the house before the social worker made her visit had a dismal ring of truth about it. Edna had said she thought Donna had felt responsible for them being taken into care, and Donna had admitted to me the night before that she blamed herself, but I doubted Edna knew the extent of Donna's sense of responsibility, or that her mother had made her clean, and had hit her for not doing the job properly. I would have to remember as much as possible of what Donna was telling me so that I could write it in my log notes, then tell Edna when I spoke to her. 'Donna, when you say your mother hit you "lots", what do you mean? Every month? Every week?'

'Every day,' she said in a small voice. 'With a coat hanger.'

'A coat hanger?' I asked, horrified.

'A wire one. She unbended it so it was long. It hurt.'

I inwardly cringed and gently rubbed the back of her hand. 'I'm sure it did hurt, sweet. That was very, very wrong of your mother. No adult should ever hit a child. A mother shouldn't, and I certainly won't.' Obvious, but not necessarily to Donna, who – from what she was telling me – had been beaten on a daily basis.

'The boys used a skipping rope,' she added matter-of-factly.

I stopped rubbing her hand. 'Your brothers hit you too?'

She nodded. 'With the skipping rope. It had a wooden end on it.'

I stared at her, aghast. 'Why did they hit you?'

'When I didn't do the cleaning as good as I should. Mum said they could. And they liked it.' I felt such a surge of anger towards Warren and Jason at that moment that had they been in the room I would have given them a good telling-off, although in reality they were probably as much victims as Donna was, having learned their behaviour in a household that appeared to survive on perverted discipline.

'Donna, love,' I said, 'that was so very wrong of them. People don't hit each other, and certainly not members of the same family. Brothers and sisters, mums and dads should take care of each other, not bully them and cause them pain. I will never hit you,' I said, reinforcing what I had said before. 'Neither will Adrian or Paula.' The notion of which seemed slightly ludicrous, given that Adrian and Paula were much smaller than Donna, but then Warren and Jason were only six and seven.

Donna gave a faint nod, and I continued to look at her downcast profile. 'What about Chelsea and your dad? Did they hit you?'

'Chelsea did, but not Dad. I looked after him when he wasn't well. I tried to get him to take his tablets, so that he would be well. He was kind to me.'

Well, at least that was something, I thought. Donna had one ally in a house of abusers, as long as she reminded her schizophrenic father to take his medication. What a horrendous way to live! 'Did your mother hit your brothers and Chelsea?' I asked. All the information I gathered would help Edna, and ultimately the judge to decide the long-term care plans for the boys and Donna.

'Sometimes Mum hit my brothers,' Donna said softly. 'But not often. Only when the boys were really getting on her nerves. Sometimes Chelsea and Mum had an argument and they hit each other.'

'The boys didn't get hit for not doing things like cleaning?' I asked.

Donna shook her head. 'Mum only hit them when she had been drinking and they got on her nerves. She loves them.'

'I'm sure your mum loves you too, sweet,' I said, finding not for the first time since I'd been fostering that I had to separate parental love and the way the parent behaved, and also wanting to offer Donna something positive. 'Mum has got a lot of problems and I don't suppose the drink helped.'

'She always hit me more after drinking,' Donna confirmed.

I nodded, and looked from Donna to the floor and all the little coloured beads from the bracelet, which were spread around her feet and into the far corners of the carpet. 'Why did you break your bracelet?' I asked gently. 'I thought you liked it very much?'

She shrugged. I noticed a small muscle twitch nervously at the corner of her eye. 'They wouldn't let me clean.'

I hesitated, trying desperately to piece together the few words she was offering and make sense of her actions. 'You broke the bracelet because you remembered you weren't allowed to clean? What, at Mary and Ray's house?'

She nodded.

'Did that make you angry?'

She nodded again.

'What? Angry with Mary and Ray?'

Another nod.

'You must have been up very early this morning. You were asleep when I looked in last night, and the bracelet wasn't broken then.'

'I have to get up early to clean the house.'

'Not here you don't,' I said firmly. 'I see to the cleaning here. You don't have to do it.' I then realised I was taking the same route that Mary and Ray had probably taken in not letting her help at all. 'Donna, you don't have to worry about the cleaning here, but you can help me. I am the adult, and housework is my responsibility, but I can certainly find you some jobs to do.' I didn't know if I was handling this right, or simply repeating what Mary and Ray had said and thereby going down the same path and getting it wrong. 'Is that what Mary said?' I asked.

Donna nodded. 'Well, she was right, in that respect. You don't have to clean now, and you certainly won't get hit for not doing it.'

'I do,' she suddenly blurted. 'I do have to clean. I do!' And again I thought of Edna's mention of OCD, for it seemed Donna was admitting to some form of obsession, though whether it was OCD or not I hadn't a clue.

'OK, Donna,' I said slowly. 'If I understand you, you feel you need to clean, probably because of all the cleaning you had to do at home. I think this morning you needed to let something inside you come out. Some anger? And I think you broke the bracelet because you remembered that Mary wouldn't let you help, and you took your anger out on the bracelet. Is that right?'

Donna nodded, and then, unbelievably, she smiled, her whole face lighting up. 'Can I help you clean here, Cathy?' she asked.

'Yes, of course you can. But I will find you some jobs to do. I don't want you getting up early and flooding the kitchen again.' I smiled, and she actually managed a small laugh. I gave myself a mental pat on the back. I might not have been a psychiatrist, but I had managed to get it right this time.

'And I can help you look after Adrian and Paula?' she asked, still smiling.

'Yes, of course you can, Donna. But remember you don't have to, and it wasn't your fault you and your brothers came into care.'

She leant towards me and planted a little kiss on my cheek. 'Thank you for letting me help, Cathy. You're nice.'

I smiled again, and drawing her to me gave her a big hug. 'So are you, love.'

What I didn't know was that my simplistic solution of agreeing to let Donna help had unleashed something which would quickly gather momentum and have far-reaching effects. It would be outside anything I had experience of, or knew how to deal with.

Chapter Seven

Runt of the Litter

I was feeling pretty pleased with myself when Jill phoned at ten o'clock on Monday morning.

'Yes, we are doing OK,' I confirmed. 'Donna was very quiet and withdrawn to begin with, but she is now talking and starting to join in.' I told Jill about the beating Donna had received at the hands of her family for not cleaning properly, and also about her frenzied floor scrubbing at our house, and the bag of rags she had brought with her, presumably for this purpose.

'The poor kid,' Jill said with a heartfelt sigh. 'It's just as well she has been separated from her brothers, if they have been bullying her to that extent.'

'Yes,' I agreed, and I explained how I was going to give her little jobs to do, so that she could join in and have some responsibility.

'That's how I would handle it, Cathy. And you're obviously keeping detailed log notes? It sounds as though Edna wasn't aware of some of this.'

'Yes, my notes are up to date,' I confirmed, and then I updated Jill. 'Donna has contact tonight; I think she is seeing her whole family. And school begins again a week on Wednesday.'

'Thanks. I'll speak to Edna today, and I'll visit you later in the week. If you need me in the meantime, phone.'

'Will do.' I paused. 'Jill, do you think Donna is suffering from this Obsessive Compulsive Disorder? I really don't know much about it.'

'Neither do I. But I shouldn't think so. There aren't any other symptoms, are there?'

'Such as?'

'From what I know of OCD the person repeatedly performs a task in a ritualised pattern. Like insisting a chair or book is in a particular position before they can leave the room. It has to be exactly right to within millimetres; otherwise the person becomes very anxious. The person can move an object dozens and dozens of times before they are satisfied. We all do it to some extent, for example when we return and double check the back door is locked before we go out, although we know it is. But people suffering from OCD take it to obsessive lengths, and it governs their lives.'

'No, there hasn't been anything like that,' I said. 'Just this one incident of cleaning the floor. And what Mary told Edna.'

'I'm sure it's not OCD. Donna will be fine. You've dealt with it, and she's been able to open up to you and start talking. Well done.'

'Thanks,' I said, grateful for the praise.

When Edna phoned an hour later I updated her as I had done Jill. When I had finished Edna was very quiet.

'Dear me,' she said at last. 'I knew those boys got the better of Donna sometimes but I had no idea they were actually whipping her – with a skipping rope?'

'That's what she said.'

'No wonder the poor kid didn't settle at Mary and Ray's.' She paused again. 'Cathy, as you know we brought Donna and the boys into care because of severe neglect. There was a suspicion of physical abuse but I'd no idea they were all beating Donna, and I have been working closely with that family for over three years now.' She stopped again and I knew Edna was blaming herself for not spotting the depth of the abuse. 'Donna had some bruises on her back and legs when she first came into care and had her medical. She told the doctor she had fallen in the garden at home. I expect she was too scared to say anything else.'

'Yes,' I agreed.

'Dear me,' Edna said again. 'I'm going to talk to her mother, Rita, and also to Mary and Ray, and those boys. I shall also be keeping a close eye on the family at contact tonight. Donna is such a sweet thing. She wouldn't hurt a fly.'

'I know, she's lovely,' I said. 'Edna, this bag of rags she's brought with her – did it come from home or Mary's?'

'I really don't know. Why?'

'It seems a strange thing for a child to bring with her. I mean the rags aren't security blankets or comforters. They're cleaning rags.'

Edna paused. 'Look, Cathy, I've got a lot of questions I need to put to Mary and Ray, and the boys, after what you have told me. I also need to visit Rita and Chelsea as a matter of urgency. Can I phone you back later?'

'Yes, of course.'

'I've given you the details for the contact tonight, haven't I?'

'Yes, thanks.'

There was another pause. 'What is Donna doing now, Cathy?'

'She's in the garden with Adrian and Paula.'

'Good. We'll speak later. Thanks, Cathy. And thank goodness I moved her!'

I hung up and went down the hall and into the lounge, where I looked out of the French windows to check on the three children. They were grouped around the basketball post, taking turns at aiming and throwing. Donna appeared to be in charge and was organising the game, running to retrieve the ball from where it landed and handing it to Adrian or Paula for their turn to take a shot.

I watched for a few moments, and then called, 'Donna, you make sure you have a turn as well.' She smiled sheepishly, almost embarrassed, and then passed the ball to Adrian for his turn. Oh well, I thought, if she was happier organising the game rather than joining in, I'd leave them to it, and Adrian and Paula certainly weren't complaining.

Having had a full day out the day before, we were spending today around the house and in the garden. Entrance fees for children's amusement parks are horrendous now, and yesterday's excursion had cost me over £70 – £10 each to get in and then there had been lunch and drinks. Like many parents, I couldn't afford to provide non-stop entertainment throughout the summer holiday; and nor did the children need it – Adrian and Paula were just as happy amusing themselves in the garden on a fine day.

I made a sandwich lunch, and Donna appeared and asked if she could carry the tray outside. I placed the tray containing the sandwiches and crisps in her outstretched hands, and I followed with a jug of orange squash.

'I'll fetch Adrian and Paula,' Donna said helpfully, setting the tray on the table on the patio.

'Thanks, love.'

I watched her stroll down to the bottom of the garden. She was talking more now she had a role, and it was like having a little mother's helper. 'Adrian and Paula,' I heard her call from a distance, as I sometimes did. 'Come on now, your lunch is ready.'

They both stopped what they were doing and began to run up the garden towards me. I smiled: they had come a good deal quicker than when I called them.

'Are your hands clean?' Donna asked as they sat on the benches either side of the table ready for lunch.

Adrian and Paula turned over their hands to show their palms, as too did Donna. 'I suppose we should really give them a wipe,' I said, 'as you are having sandwiches.'

'Shall I fetch a cloth from the kitchen?' Donna asked.

I was about to say yes please when I realised that I ought to start implementing my policy of not having children in the kitchen. 'No, don't worry. I'll fetch it.'

I went into the kitchen, where I took the carton of Wet Ones from the cupboard and tore off three strips. I handed one to each of them and waited until they'd finished wiping their hands and passed the used tissues back to me.

'Let's have a look?' Donna said, and Adrian and Paula offered their hands for inspection. I smiled again. Donna was certainly more conscientious than I was, and with far better results, particularly from Adrian, who as a young boy did not believe that cleanliness was next to godliness – just the opposite in fact!

A few clouds rolled in that afternoon, but the air was still warm, and with the French windows wide open we spent a lazy afternoon in and out of the garden, pleasing ourselves. Donna organised some running races between Adrian and Paula, and then my neighbour's boy, Billy, who had heard all the excitement, climbed up the tree to see over and asked if he could come round and join in. I told him he could but that he had to ask his mother first. Sue came out of her house and said it was fine, but only for a couple of hours as they were going out later. She helped him clamber over the fence and I introduced him to Donna. Billy joined in the hopping race that Donna was organising while I chatted over the fence to Sue.

'She looks like she's going to be a big help,' Sue said, nodding to Donna.

'Yes, although I would like to see her playing more – you know, joining in and having fun. She has been organising the games all day. She always puts herself last.' I obviously couldn't say anything more to Sue (or any of my other friends and neighbours for that matter) about Donna's situation or background, as these were highly confidential, and Sue appreciated that. She knew I fostered and was used to seeing children suddenly appear and then disappear from my back garden.

During the afternoon I regularly brought out drinks for the children and also offered ice creams from the freezer. Donna didn't want an ice cream to begin with. 'No, let them have them,' she said, nodding to Adrian, Paula and

Billy, as if there weren't enough for everyone and they should have first call.

'Donna, love,' I said, 'there is plenty for everyone. I'm sure you would like an ice cream. There's choc ice, raspberry ripple or an ice lolly.' I offered her the open cartons.

'Oh all right then, if you insist,' she said, and I smiled at the quaint adult term she had used. She quickly dipped her hand into the box of choc ices and took one, as though at any moment the offer might be withdrawn or she was doing something prohibited.

I returned the rest of the ice creams to the freezer and then stood for a moment at the kitchen window, watching her. Adrian, Paula and Billy were sitting on the grass in a small circle, eating their ice creams, but Donna was on the bench on the patio a short distance away, almost as if she was overseeing them. I continued to watch her slow measured movements as she gradually peeled down the wrapper of the choc ice and took small bites, savouring each mouthful as if it was the first and last. It was almost as if an ice cream was a forbidden pleasure for her, and she ate as though it was the first time she had ever tasted one – a precious treat that was not likely to be repeated. By the time she had finished, the last of it had melted away and she came into the kitchen to rinse her fingers.

'Did you enjoy that?' I asked lightly, as she turned on the tap.

She nodded.

'I always have ice cream in the freezer in summer,' I said.

'Do you?' She turned to look at me, her expression one of amazement and surprise.

I passed her the hand towel. 'Yes. And next time we go shopping you can tell me which ice creams you prefer, and choose some food you like.'

'I like anything, really, Cathy. But not coleslaw.'

'Coleslaw?' It was my turn to look surprised, for I would not have associated coleslaw with a child's preference. 'No, I don't think Adrian and Paula do either,' I said. 'I buy it sometimes for myself.'

Donna finished wiping her hands and folded the towel neatly on to the towel rail. She was very methodical and precise when it came to folding items like her clothes or the towel. 'I always had to eat coleslaw at home,' she continued. 'So I'm not too keen on it now.' I smiled again at the adult phrase 'not too keen'. She often used such phrases, which sounded quaint on a child's lips.

'I expect your mum thought coleslaw was good for you,' I suggested.

She nodded. 'We had to buy it because it was on the list. But no one liked it, so I had to have it.'

'Oh, I see,' I said, not really seeing at all. 'What, with salad?'

'No, by itself. I had it for my dinner and tea.'

I looked at her. 'I'm not understanding you, Donna. You can't just have eaten a tub of coleslaw for your dinner and tea?'

She nodded quite matter-of-factly as if I should have known. 'When Mum's giro came through she gave me some money to go shopping. There was a list I had to use each week. I took Warren and Jason with me. There was coleslaw on the list because Edna had told Mum it was good for us. But no one liked it, so when we got home with the shopping everyone took what they wanted from the bags, and there was just the coleslaw left. Warren and Jason are smarter than me, so they got what they wanted from the bags first. Warren always had the custard cream biscuits and Jason had the loaf of bread. Chelsea had the ham and I was left with the coleslaw. Mum didn't eat much. She had beer instead.'

I stared at her, dumbfounded. 'And that was your dinner or tea?'

'Both,' she said.

'What about on the other days, when you didn't have the giro? What did you eat then?'

'What was left. Sometimes the tub of coleslaw lasted two days, and the bread did. Warren always ate all the custard creams on the first day, although I told him not to.'

'Then what?'

'The neighbours fed us. And sometimes we walked to my aunt's. And when we were at school we had breakfast there, and school dinner.'

'And no tea?'

'Not until it was giro day again.'

Bloody hell, I thought. No wonder she liked her food, and ate everything I put in front of her. 'Well, at least the coleslaw was better for you than Warren's choice of biscuits.'

'So you know I don't like coleslaw?' she confirmed.

'Yes, I know, Donna.'

'But I like sitting at the table to eat. Do all foster carers have tables and chairs?'

'Yes, I think so.' Donna certainly wasn't the first child I'd fostered whose family home had never had a dining table and chairs.

'You know, Donna,' I said, 'that wasn't a good diet. It's a wonder you weren't all ill.'

'Chelsea said it gave her spots.'

'She could be right. And Donna?'

'Yes?'

'Have you ever had an ice cream before?'

'Oh yes, of course! Edna bought me one when we came to you for the visit on Friday. It was lovely. I really enjoyed it, and the one you gave me today. That was nice too.'

'So that was your second ice cream just now?'

She nodded. 'I've tried lots of new things since I've been in care.' I smiled sadly. 'I think I might like being in care, Cathy. People are so nice to me.'

Edna phoned again at 4.00 p.m., having visited Warren and Jason at Mary and Ray's. She asked if she could be overheard and I said no: Donna was with Adrian and Paula, watching children's television in the lounge. She said Warren and Jason had admitted to hitting Donna, and when Edna had questioned them further they'd confirmed that they'd used an old skipping rope. Edna had asked them why they'd been so cruel to their sister and they had said it was because Donna hadn't done what Mum had told her to – clean the house properly. The boys also confirmed that their mother had told them to beat Donna, and when Edna had asked where all this had taken place, they'd said usually in the kitchen when Donna was on her hands and knees trying to clear up the cat shit. My thoughts flipped to the morning when I had found Donna on all fours in the kitchen and she'd pleaded, 'Don't hit me. I've done my best.' Edna said that the boys had told her that their mother and Chelsea also regularly hit Donna, and that they wouldn't let her have any new clothes. Edna was obviously appalled and horrified, particularly as Warren and Jason could see absolutely nothing wrong in what they had done and showed no remorse.

'Cathy,' Edna said, 'I asked the boys separately if they hadn't thought what they were doing was wrong, and that it hurt Donna, and do you know what they said? That because Donna was so stupid she wouldn't feel it!'

'She's not stupid,' I erupted. 'And she certainly felt it, although she probably didn't ever say so. And Edna, do you know what the poor girl had to eat when there was money for food? The stuff no one else wanted!' I told her about the coleslaw and the shopping, although I didn't point out that the coleslaw had been at Edna's suggestion. 'I persuaded her to have an ice cream today,' I said. 'It was only the second one she'd ever had in her life. The first one you bought her when you visited us. She's ten years old and living in an affluent society, for goodness sake! And I know not having ice cream doesn't amount to child abuse, but it is indicative of the miserable, deprived existence she led. I expect the boys enjoyed an ice cream when there was the money for treats!'

Edna was silent for some moments. 'I know, Cathy. I remember when I bought her that ice cream she was so grateful. What I didn't know was the level of deprivation and also about the abuse that had been aimed at Donna. Warren called her the runt of the family. Now where on earth did a boy his age learn a term like that?'

'I haven't a clue, but from what I'm picking up on here it sums up how they treated her – like the runt of the litter.'

We were both quiet. I knew I shouldn't have exploded: it sounded as though I was blaming Edna, who, bless her, undoubtedly had done her best, but apparently she hadn't been able to see through the united front presented by the rest of this dysfunctional travesty of a family.

'I'm going to see Rita and Chelsea tomorrow,' Edna said after a while. 'They weren't in today when I called. I pushed a note through their letterbox saying I would call back tomorrow. How has Donna been this afternoon?'

'She has been organising games for Adrian and Paula,' I said. 'And also the boy from next door, who came to play.'

'Good. I'll see you later briefly when you bring Donna to contact.'

'Yes,' I said, and, still subdued from what I'd heard, I replaced the receiver. I then checked in the lounge, where the three children were watching cartoons.

I left them for another fifteen minutes, then told Donna to have a quick wash and change into some clean clothes, ready for contact. At 4.45 p.m. I bundled everyone into the car – with some protest from Adrian, whose programme I had interrupted – and drove to the social services office in Brampton Road. It wasn't the social services' main office but a large Victorian detached house that was used as overspill, and housed the Children and Families team. I pulled onto the driveway and left Adrian and Paula in the car while I took Donna into the small reception area that had once been the hall. I gave our names to the receptionist and she phoned through to Edna, who appeared almost immediately through the security-locked inner door.

'Hello, Cathy, Donna,' she said with her warm encouraging smile. 'I hear you've had a lovely time in the garden today, Donna. And also that you went out for the day yesterday?'

Donna nodded shyly.

'Your mum and brothers are already here,' she continued to Donna. 'Dad won't be coming today, as he's not feeling so well.' I thought I heard Donna give a little sigh and so too, it seemed, had Edna, for she threw me a pointed glance. 'I shall be supervising contact as usual, Donna, so there is nothing for you to worry about.' Then, looking at me, Edna said, 'I'll see you at six thirty. Thank you for bringing Donna.'

'You're welcome. See you later, Donna.' I left the building and drove home, where Adrian managed to finish watching his programme before it was time to return for the end of contact.

Donna didn't say much in the car coming home and I knew Edna would tell me if anything had emerged at contact that I should know about. Once home, I began the bath and bedtime routine – Paula first, then Donna and Adrian.

As I said goodnight to Adrian, and was about to leave him reading, he said, 'Mum, I need to ask you something.'

'Yes, love.' I returned to beside his bed. 'What is it?'

'Is Donna in charge of us?'

I looked at him carefully. 'What do you mean exactly?'

'Well, in the garden today she kept bossing us around and telling us to do things like she was our mother, only not like you do,' he added quickly. 'It was all right to begin with, when she was organising a game, but then she wouldn't let up. She kept telling us and Billy what to do. Paula said she was in charge.'

'No, of course Donna isn't "in charge". I'll have to explain to Paula.'

'And will you tell Donna? I don't want her to keep telling me what to do the whole time,' Adrian added.

'Yes, I understand. I'm sorry. You should have said something to me sooner.'

'It was difficult with her being there the whole time.'

'I'll keep an eye on it tomorrow and if necessary I'll speak to her, OK?'

'Yes.'

I kissed him goodnight again and came out feeling that perhaps he was overreacting, being a bit sensitive to having a child living with us who was the same age, physically bigger and in some respects more mature. But I would watch more closely tomorrow. I had already noticed that Donna could be a little forceful in her desire to organise. When she had been helping me with some chores in the house I had found that more than once she'd tried to take over and tell me how it should be done. And whereas, as an adult, I could laugh it off and subtly direct her to doing something as I wished, at his age Adrian obviously didn't have such resources and had taken it personally. Well, that was how I saw it – until the following morning.

Chapter Eight

Dirty

It was raining in the morning and I suggested we went to the cinema for the eleven o'clock show to see the new Walt Disney film. Adrian, Paula and Donna were upstairs, taking turns in the bathroom to brush their teeth and have a wash while I cleared away the breakfast things. Suddenly there was a cry from Paula, and Adrian came flying down the stairs.

'Mum! Come quick! Donna's hit Paula!'

I dropped the tea towel and flew out of the kitchen, along the hall and upstairs. Paula was in the bathroom, standing beside the basin with her toothbrush in her hand and tears streaming down her face. Donna was standing beside her.

'Whatever's happened?' I asked, taking Paula and cradling her in my arms.

'She hit her!' Adrian said, coming in behind me.

I looked at Donna, who was standing expressionless in front of me. 'Did you hit her?' I asked sternly.

'She did!' Adrian yelled from behind me.

'All right, Adrian. I want to hear it from Donna or Paula.'

Donna said nothing and I looked at Paula. 'Did Donna hit you?'

She nodded, tears still running down her face.

'Where?'

Paula stretched out her left hand and I saw a large red mark on the back of it. 'Did you do this, Donna?' I demanded.

She nodded slowly, not at all abashed. She looked sad, but then Donna always looked sad, even when she was playing, apart from the couple of times she'd smiled yesterday. 'Paula wouldn't do as I told her,' Donna said at last. 'I told her to do her teeth properly and she didn't.'

'That's no reason to hit her!' I said. 'No one in this house hits anyone, ever. I'm surprised at you, Donna! You know how much hitting hurts! Now go to your room while I see to Paula, and then I want to talk to you.'

She hesitated, and in that hesitation I saw the first sign of resistance, an insolence, a 'take-me-on-if-you-dare' look, and I thought of the bruise Mary had received to her arm – from a similar incident, perhaps? 'Now! Donna!' I said, and I held her gaze.

There was another second's hesitation, and my heart pounded as I felt a cold shudder of fear. She was nearly as tall as me and sturdy. I knew that if she'd wanted to she could have done real damage – to people and property. Gone was the downtrodden-victim look and in its place I saw insolence and determination. Then she stamped her foot and pushed past me, knocking into me as she went. She stomped round the landing and then slammed her bedroom door shut. Paula was holding on to me tightly and Adrian was very still and pale.

'It's all right,' I reassured them both. It was one of the few times I'd actually felt threatened by a foster child, and clearly Adrian and Paula had felt so too. I had looked after children before who had kicked and screamed and tried to thump me when they'd been very upset, but they'd been smaller and more easily contained. Again, my thoughts went to Mary and Ray, and the two of them having to struggle with Donna to remove her from their bathroom, after she had done what? I needed to find out. Was this a new development, or a repetition of something that had happened at Mary and Ray's?

I continued to hug Paula, then I put my arm round Adrian and drew him to my side. 'It's OK,' I reassured them once more. 'I'll speak to Donna and make sure it doesn't happen again.' Although in truth I wasn't at all sure how I was going to do this. I didn't know what I was dealing with; Donna had suddenly turned on Paula and for no apparent reason.

'All right, love?' I asked Paula gently, easing her from me and looking at her. She had stopped crying, but her hand was still red. 'That was very naughty of Donna. I'm going to tell her off,' I said, reinforcing the point. I didn't want Paula or Adrian believing that hitting was in any way acceptable. I'd known foster carers whose own children's behaviour had deteriorated in line with a foster child's, rather than the foster child following the example of the carer's 'well brought up' children.

I gave Paula and Adrian another hug, and Adrian said, 'I'm fine now, Mum.'

'Good boy. Will you look after Paula for a bit while I speak to Donna?'

He took her hand. 'Come on, Paula, you can play on my Gameboy.' Which was a real treat for Paula – to be allowed access to the much-coveted 'Super Mario' leaping over obstacles. Pacified, Paula trotted round the landing with Adrian and into his bedroom.

I took a moment, and then went round to Donna's room. I was feeling far from composed. I was going to speak to Donna, and then I wanted to talk to Mary and Ray and try to find out more. If I had a child in my house who could threaten my children, I needed to know exactly what I was dealing with. Edna had dismissed Mary and Ray's failure to look after Donna, as I had done, as it being too much for them to look after three children, with the inherent suggestion that Mary and Ray could have handled it better. Now I had big doubts and I was wondering if I had done them something of a disservice.

Donna's door was shut right to from her having slammed it. I drew myself up, took a deep breath and, knocking briefly on the door, opened it and went straight in. She was sitting on the bed, looking morose, with her arms folded across her chest and rocking back and forth.

'Donna,' I said firmly, ignoring the pang of pity I now felt for her at seeing her so dejected. 'I need to talk to you.' I didn't sit next to her but stood a little way in front. I wanted to keep the height and distance between us, just in case she went for me. 'Donna, you need to understand that in this family, as in most other families, we don't hit each other. I don't hit you or Adrian or Paula or anyone. And children do not hit each other. Do you understand?'

She didn't say anything. Her eyes were trained on the ground and she continued to rock back and forth. In a different situation I would have immediately gone and comforted her, for she looked so lonely and unloved, but now I needed to make sure that she understood her behaviour was totally unacceptable. Although Paula had recovered, and the injury was relatively minor, it had nevertheless been an assault, which would have hurt Paula emotionally, and reduced her trust not only in Donna but in other children. And with Donna twice the size of Paula, who was to say that another attack wouldn't be a lot worse? I needed to keep everyone safe.

'Donna, this is a safe house,' I said in the same firm manner. 'Paula feels safe here, Adrian feels safe here and you are safe here. No one purposely hurts anyone else. I need to hear you tell me that you understand, and that you won't do it again.' I waited. Donna continued looking down and rocking. I waited some more. I wasn't sure how to proceed now. 'Look, Donna,' I said in a less authoritative tone, 'I know lots of bad things have happened to you, but you must try to leave them behind. We all look out for each other here, and you will find if you look after Adrian and Paula they will be just as keen to look after you.'

I paused again, but there was no response; Donna hadn't looked up or stopped rocking. I decided she could do with a few minutes to reflect on what I'd said, before I hugged her and we put the incident behind us. 'OK, Donna,' I said, 'I want you to think about what I've said. Then when you feel able, come down and tell me that it won't happen again. And I also think you need to say sorry to Paula.'

Still nothing. I turned and slowly left the room, drawing the door to behind me, but not closing it. I went downstairs, and to the phone on the hall table, and dialled Edna's number.

'Edna,' I said as soon as she answered. 'It's Cathy, Donna's carer.'

'Hello, Cathy?' I could tell by her tone she guessed something was wrong.

'We've had a bit of a problem here,' I said. 'And I would like some more information.' I explained what had just happened and finished by saying that I thought it would be useful if I could speak to Mary and Ray and find out exactly what had happened there.

I could hear the relief in Edna's voice, for doubtless she had thought that with Donna hitting Paula I would be calling an end to the placement and asking for Donna to be moved. 'Yes, of course, Cathy,' she said. 'I have their telephone number here. I'm so sorry you've had to deal with this. I don't understand what has got into Donna. I've never seen that side of her.'

I waited for her to read out the telephone number, which I wrote on the pad I kept beside the phone in the hall and repeated back to her. 'I'm going to phone them now,' I said.

'Yes, Cathy. I'll speak to them myself later as well. I'm so very sorry.'

I severed the line and keyed in the numbers to Mary and Ray. It was all quiet upstairs – Adrian and Paula were still ensconced in his bedroom with the Gameboy, and I assumed Donna was contemplating, and I hoped taking on board, what I had said, ready to offer an apology to Paula. I listened to Mary and Ray's phone ringing; then a female voice answered.

'Is that Mary?' I asked.

'Speaking.'

'This is Cathy Glass, Donna's carer.'

'Oh, hello.'

'I hope you don't mind my phoning. Edna gave me your number. We've had a bit of an incident here this morning and I felt I needed to speak to you to try to learn more.'

I thought there was a small hesitation before she said, 'Sure, go ahead.' I also heard boys' voices in the background and I assumed they were those of Warren and Jason, playing.

I began positively, and said that Donna was settling in well, but that out of the blue she'd smacked my daughter this morning, and I was wondering if Mary had had any similar incident when Donna had been living with her. I didn't say that I knew Mary had received a bruise, or add any more; I wanted to hear what she had to say. What Mary told me didn't in any way lighten my concern.

'Donna was fine when she first arrived,' Mary began. 'A bit quiet and too compliant, but otherwise OK. She was used to looking after her younger brothers, although they often teased and bullied her. She was more like their mother or carer than an older sister, and I thought I should take some of the responsibility from her. So many of these children come into care having never had a childhood because of all the responsibility they've had at home.' I agreed and knew from what Mary was saying that she was a sensible, level-headed and experienced foster carer, and that what she was giving me was an objective and rational account. 'The problems began when I tried to discourage Donna from continually fussing around the boys. She fussed around them so much that they really resented it. She also tried to discipline them, which they resented, and I stopped it. It was unhealthy; she wouldn't let them be, and she couldn't see that they were making fun of her. They are a bright pair and can easily get the better of her. I was very shocked when they admitted to Edna that they'd beaten her with a skipping rope. You know Edna came here and spoke to them?'

'Yes,' I said.

'The situation quickly deteriorated and really, Cathy, there was no way the three of them could stay together. Donna was trying to control not only the boys' lives but ours as well. My husband is a full-time carer and stood by me. But Donna even tried to order him around and resented either of us doing anything for the boys. She actually started to physically push us away if we went near Warren and Jason. We asked for her to be moved after a particularly ugly scene in the bathroom. Ray and I were trying to get the boys ready for bed. They were a bit hyper but no more so than usual. Donna wasn't having any of it. She came storming in and demanded to know what we were doing. She grabbed my arm and bent it back – I thought she was going to break it. Ray had to drag her off. I've still got the bruise.' Mary stopped as my worst fears were confirmed.

'Thank you, Mary,' I said slowly. 'I'm going to have to think carefully how to handle this.'

'How old are your children?' she asked.

'Six and ten.'

'I only have my seventeen-year-old son living with me now. I'd be very careful if I were you, Cathy. Donna's a big girl and could really hurt someone smaller.' She paused. 'Will she stay with you?'

'I hope so. I don't want her to feel rejected, but I'll have to see how it goes. Donna has obviously come from a highly abusive family, and I know it's not her fault, but I can't have my children placed in permanent danger.'

'No. Quite,' Mary said. 'Ray felt I had been placed in danger.'

I paused. 'Mary, one last thing. Edna mentioned the term OCD. I think you had suggested it?'

'Yes. Donna displayed some strange habits here. She kept washing her hands in a really agitated way, over and over again. I had seen a programme on television about OCD, and it looked very similar to what Donna was doing. Has she done that with you?'

'Not to my knowledge.'

'To be honest, it's the least of her problems. I think Donna is like a firework waiting to go off. Goodness knows what has gone on in that family, but I think Donna bore the brunt of it. I was sorry to see her go, but Ray and I couldn't have looked after her and the boys: it was impossible.'

'Yes, I understand. I'm going to have to make sure she doesn't try to replicate the situation here with my children, which is possible. Thanks for your time, Mary.'

'You're welcome. Please say hello to Donna for me. I've got my fingers crossed for you. I hope it works out. We'll probably bump into each other at school when the term starts.'

'Yes. Thanks,' I said again, and I slowly put down the phone.

As I did, I heard Donna's bedroom door open and she appeared on the landing. Very slowly she came downstairs. Her head was down and her shoulders were hunched forward; her whole stance was dejected, as it had been when she'd first arrived. She came to a halt just in front of me and slowly raised her head. Her large brown eyes were so full of sorrow my heart went out to her.

'I'm sorry, Cath-ie,' she said, pronouncing the two syllables separately. 'I'm sorry I hit Paula. Shall I say sorry to her?'

'In a minute, Donna. First I need to talk to you. Come with me into the lounge, please.'

Compliant and subdued, she followed me down the hall, and we sat together on the sofa. Outside the French windows the rain was sheeting down; today was set for a mixture of sunshine and showers.

I turned to her. 'Now listen, love. It's important you understand why you are saying sorry to Paula.'

'Because I hit Paula,' she said quietly.

'Yes, I know, but do you understand why it was wrong to hit Paula?'

Donna shrugged.

'Hitting hurts, obviously, you know that, but it also it makes that person afraid of you. You felt like that when your mother and Chelsea and your brothers hit you, didn't you?' Donna gave an almost imperceptible nod. 'It's an assault on the whole person and makes that person wary of you. You don't want Paula being afraid of you, do you? You want to play with her like a sister, and Adrian like a brother.'

Donna didn't say anything, so I continued with the second part of what I needed to say. 'Now, love, it's nice that you want to help me look after Adrian and Paula, but that's my job. I would like you to help in the house, but I will tell you what to do. We don't want Adrian and Paula feeling that you are bossing them around, do we? Because it's not nice to be bossed around and made to do things, is it? I'm sure you know that.' I hoped I was making sense.

Donna gave a short nod. 'Shall I say sorry to Paula now?' she asked.

'Yes, that would be nice. I'll call her down. But first let me give you a big hug. I want you to be happy here, just as I do Adrian and Paula, OK?'

Donna let me put my arms around her and I gave her a hug, although she didn't actually hug me back. Then, leaving her in the lounge, I went upstairs to fetch Paula. Whether I was getting through to Donna and could succeed where Mary and Ray hadn't remained to be seen. It appeared that Donna had come from a family that was highly abusive, where they had shown each other absolutely no respect, or kindness. It was a case of trying to undo all that and start over again – the process of socialisation that is begun in healthy families with the child is a toddler and continues through to adulthood.

Upstairs, Paula and Adrian were still engrossed in the Gameboy, the upset apparently receding with each new point scored on the game.

'Donna would like to say she is sorry,' I said. 'I have spoken to her and she understands it must never happen again. And, Adrian, I have also said she mustn't tell you or Paula what to do, and that I'm in charge. I shall be watching her carefully, all right?' I smiled and they smiled back; then Paula scampered off the bed and took my hand, and we went downstairs and into the lounge, where Donna was as I'd left her, on the sofa.

'I'm sorry, Paula,' Donna said as soon as we walked in.

'I forgive you,' Paula said, and she went over and planted a big kiss on Donna's cheek.

'Good girls,' I said.

Donna didn't say any more, so I left it at that and hoped that we could move on and put the incident behind us.

We didn't make the 11.00 a.m. showing of *The Lion King*, but went instead to the next showing of the film at 1.45 p.m. I bought popcorn and sat with Donna on one side of me and Adrian and Paula on the other. I was being careful, and had started the vigilance which I would keep up for as long as was necessary. I hoped that at some point in the future I would be able to relax my guard and the children would be able to play or be together again without me being present. But for the time being if they went anywhere together then I would be close by. I was grateful there was only a week until the start of the new school term, for it was going to be hard work having to be continually aware of where Donna was in the house or garden.

When we returned home after the film it was just gone 4.00 p.m. The sun had come out and the last of the rain had evaporated. The grass was dry enough to play on, and the children went outside, while I watched from the kitchen window as I prepared the vegetables and meat for the evening meal. Donna kept her distance, and once more sat on the bench on the patio while Adrian and Paula played. I hadn't stopped her playing with Adrian and Paula – indeed it would have been nice if she had joined in. But I would make sure she didn't keep organising Adrian and Paula, for then it was only a short step to dominating them, and possibly replicating what had happened at Mary and Ray's, with Donna trying to take over – using force if necessary.

We ate at 6.00 p.m., and then at 7.30 I began the bedtime routine. Leaving Donna in the lounge doing a jigsaw, I took Paula up first. Adrian had popped next door to play with Billy for a while, and when I called him back at 8.30, Donna had already taken her turn in the bathroom. Once Adrian had finished his shower I went in to say goodnight to him, and as I did I heard Donna's door open as she went out and into the toilet. When I'd finished saying goodnight to Adrian, and had also had a look at the illustrations in the book he was reading – *The Magician's Nephew* by C.S. Lewis – I came out and saw that the toilet door was still shut. Donna had been in there for over twenty minutes!

'Are you OK?' I called lightly, not wanting to wake Paula but wondering if Donna was feeling unwell.

There was no reply.

'Donna?' I said again, 'are you all right?'

There was still no reply, but I could hear the tap running. I knocked lightly on the door. Nothing. The locks on the toilet and bathroom doors (as in most foster carers' homes) were out of reach of the children as part of the safer caring policy so that children couldn't lock themselves in, either accidentally or in a fit of pique. 'Donna?' I said again, easing the door open and ready to close it again quickly if she was on the toilet.

But she wasn't on the toilet. She was standing beside the small hand basin, washing her hands. The plug wasn't in, and the hot water tap was on full. She stood with the nailbrush in one hand, roughly scrubbing the back of the other hand.

'Donna?' I asked.

There was no answer, but she kept scrubbing; then, turning her hand over, she continued on the palm and fingers. It wasn't normal washing: it was the same frenzied scrubbing I'd witnessed in the kitchen, only now it was directed at her hands and not the kitchen floor. As I watched, and she appeared oblivious to my presence, she swapped the nailbrush over and began on the other hand, scrubbing her skin with fierce determination and her face set hard.

My first reaction was to close the door and move away – it was as though I had looked in, and stumbled on, some private ritual. I felt I was a voyeuristic intruder, seeing something I shouldn't be party to. But as I looked, I saw that the light brown skin on her hands was now red and angry with scratches from the nailbrush. I knew that what she was doing wasn't healthy and she needed to stop.

'Donna,' I said firmly, 'stop that now.' I didn't want to go too close in case she lashed out at me, as she had done with Mary. 'Donna, don't do that,' I said again. 'You are making your hands very sore.'

She continued. I went closer, and then, risking a thump, I placed my hand on her arm. 'Please stop. Your hands are clean now. You are making them sore.'

'They're not clean,' she suddenly blurted while still scrubbing. 'They're dirty. Mum says I have to get the dirt off.'

'Donna, your hands are clean,' I said, keeping my voice even. 'Please stop it now.' I reached over and switched off the tap, half expecting her to push me, or grab my hand, or hit me. She didn't, nor did she try to turn on the tap again, but she carried on scrubbing her hands with the nailbrush, over and over again. I could see the scratch marks the nylon bristles were making and the angry red weals. 'That's enough,' I said. Then I slowly took the nailbrush from her hands, and reaching for the towel, folded her hands in it. 'Let's dry them,' I said, lightly patting the towel. 'You've made your hands so sore.' I carefully dried her hands, and she didn't resist. Then I returned the towel to the rail and looked at her hands. Both sides of both hands were an angry red; had she gone on scrubbing for much longer I was sure she would have drawn blood. 'Come on, love,' I said. 'Let's get you into bed. It's been a bit of a rough day for you.'

I led Donna into her bedroom and turned back the sheet. She slowly, compliantly, climbed into bed. I sat on the edge of the bed, and she put her head on the pillow and seemed to relax a little. I stroked her forehead. 'What's the matter, love?' I asked gently. 'Can you tell me?'

A tear escaped and ran down her cheek, then another. 'Mum says I have to wash all the dirt off, but it won't come off. I keep trying.'

'Darling, your hands are spotlessly clean,' I said. 'I expect they are even cleaner than mine.' I was trying to put the incident into perspective, lighten her mood, and possibly even diffuse her obsession and raise a smile. I placed my own hands palms upwards on the pillow to show her. 'Look, no one's hands are spotless all the time.' She drew her left hand from beneath the sheet and placed it, palm upwards, next to mine. 'It's not so bad on this side,' she said, referring to her palm, 'but it's the other side. Mine is dirty, not like yours.'

I frowned, puzzled; her hands were perfectly clean, although red from the scrubbing. Mary's suggestion of OCD hung in the air. Donna turned her hand over so that it was palm down and I did the same with mine. Her hand was of course clean, although her skin was a little darker than mine because she was of dual heritage. I looked at our hands side by side on the pillow and was about to reassure her again that her hands were clean when, with a stab of horror, I realised what she meant.

Chapter Nine

Outcast

'And Donna's mother has convinced her that's she's dirty, and has to scrub it off! It's her natural colour, and the poor girl has been trying to get rid of it! It's nothing to do with OCD. Donna is trying to wash away her skin colour!'

I was on the phone to Edna at 9.30 the following morning, so incensed that I was nearly shouting down the phone.

'I've been up half the night trying to convince her it's natural, and something to be proud of. Do you know her mother even gave her wire wool in the bath, and told her to keep scrubbing until she was as white as her! What the hell is wrong with that woman? She wants locking up! And what about the boys? They're dual heritage too, aren't they? Have they been told to scrub off their skin colour?' I could feel my heart pounding and my cheeks flushing.

'No,' Edna said evenly, 'the boys don't do that. Mary would have said.'

'Well? Does Chelsea do it? Has Rita told her she's dirty too?'

'No,' said Edna subdued. 'I don't think so.'

'Edna, Donna has been victimised by that family at every conceivable level – whipped for not doing the housework, made to feel responsible for them coming into care and told she is dirty because her grandmother is black! I assume Rita didn't think Donna's father was dirty when she slept with him! It's just as well I don't have to meet Donna's mother at contact! She has a lot to answer for.' I stopped and wondered if I had gone too far, but I was seething, on Donna's behalf. I took a breath. 'Donna is completely messed up. She has spent her whole life being vilified, and being told she is rubbish. I think you had better get her some therapy fast before it's too late, because I don't know how to deal with this. Someone needs to try to undo some of the damage that has been done to her, and I'm no psychologist!'

Edna hesitated. 'I'll raise the possibility of therapy with my manager,' she said quietly, 'but as you know, Cathy, they don't usually like to put children into therapy until they are settled. After the final court hearing, when we know where Donna will be living, would be the usual time. Donna is on an Interim Care Order and Rita has the right to object to anything we do. If I suggest therapy I'll lose what little cooperation I have from her.'

I seethed some more, but I knew from experience that Edna was right on both counts. While Donna was on an ICO her parents maintained certain rights to her and could raise all sorts of objections. Rita could make life very difficult for all concerned, not least for Donna, who would still be seeing her mother at contact. I also knew that therapists were reluctant to begin therapy until the court had made a decision about the child's future, and the child was settled wherever the judge decided they would be living. It was generally held that to begin therapy before then would be like lifting the lid on Pandora's box and could actually make the child more disturbed.

'I assume Donna won't be returning to Rita's care after all this?' I said.

'At this point we don't know. But it's looking increasingly doubtful.' Which was as much as Edna could say at present, until all the reports had been compiled and put before the judge at the final court hearing.

'Has the date for the final hearing been set yet?' I asked, calming my tone and looking at the practical issues.

'It's provisionally booked for next May,' Edna said, still subdued. 'Can I come to visit you and Donna tomorrow?'

'Yes, please. Jill is coming in the morning. Could you make it after one o'clock so that we can have some lunch?'

'Would two o'clock be all right?'

'Fine. I'll put it in the diary.'

'And I will speak to my manager about the therapy,' Edna finished by saying. 'But in the meantime if there is anything I can do, please let me know. And obviously I'll talk to Donna when I see her and reinforce what you have said.'

'OK, Edna.' There was nothing else I could say, other than asking if Donna could start her life over again in different circumstances, which unfortunately Edna couldn't make happen.

'Thank you, Cathy. See you tomorrow, and say hello to Donna for me.'

'I will do.'

I continued to watch Donna like a hawk, for her benefit as much as for Adrian's and Paula's. I knew where she was at any given moment and also what she was doing. Gone was any thought of simply letting the three of them amuse themselves, so I arranged games which we all played together, although Donna had difficulty 'playing' as such, presumably because she had never played as a small child. But at least she joined in, and went through the motions, and I hoped that by doing so one day she would find real enjoyment in playing. I organised rounders, bat and ball, basketball and, when it rained, Monopoly and jigsaw puzzles. It was obviously important that the children played as naturally as possible, but I hoped my being in charge would help reinforce in Donna's eyes the difference between my adult role and hers as a child.

I would have played with the children anyway, for some of the time, but having to do it continuously was pretty exhausting and meant that I had to catch up on the housework in the evening when they were in bed. However, some of the chores, like preparing the vegetables, dusting and tidying, became a group activity: I gathered everyone together and gave them a task each, while watching that Donna didn't dominate.

I removed the nailbrush from the wash basin in the toilet, and also the pumice stone from the bathroom, which could have done great damage if Donna had set about using it to try to remove her skin colour. When Donna went upstairs to go to the toilet, or when she had a bath, I found an excuse to hover on the landing, and I listened for any sounds that might have suggested she was trying to scrub off her skin. I reinforced to Donna that children weren't allowed in the kitchen when I wasn't there, again separating our roles, and at every opportunity I praised her, and particularly her appearance. We went shopping, and I bought her a new skirt and blouse and told her how pretty she looked, which Paula reinforced. I told Donna I would buy her new school uniform on the first day of the term because, as with most junior schools now, the logoed uniform could only be bought from the school office, to help raise school funds.

How much of my positive encouragement to raise Donna's self-image was getting through to her was difficult to say. Donna met any praise or encouragement with a bashful, very doubtful shrug – hardly surprising considering I was trying to undo ten years of abuse. Her self-esteem and confidence were zero, and if I asked her to do anything her first reaction was 'I can't' or 'I don't know how.'

Jill and Edna came as arranged and by the end of the day I felt we had all been over 'social workered'. It was a relief when Edna finally left at 4.15 p.m., having spent over two hours with us, an hour of it alone with Donna in the lounge. It is usual for the social worker to spend time alone with the looked-after child in case the child wants to raise any issues that they would feel uncomfortable about raising with the carer present. I knew Edna would be talking to Donna about what had happened recently, and also continuing my efforts to improve Donna's self-image.

'You look lovely,' Edna said to Donna, not for the first time, as we finally saw Edna to the door. But Edna's compliment was met with the same self-deprecating shrug that met all my attempts to raise Donna's self-esteem.

Jill had also praised Donna when she'd visited that morning. Jill's primary responsibilities were to check that the placement was progressing as it should and that I had all I needed to care for Donna, and to offer me support and advice where necessary. As I had kept Jill and Edna updated on a daily basis, when Jill checked my log notes there were no surprises. She signed and dated my record, and I returned the file to the locked drawer of my desk in the front room. Jill had also been in regular phone contact with Edna, so both were fully abreast of what was going on.

I had raised the matter of the forthcoming school run with Edna because I had realised that the logistics of dropping Adrian and Paula off at their school, which was in the opposite direction to Donna's and had the same start time of 8.50 a.m., were going to cause me a problem. Foster carers normally take their foster children to school, as they would their own children, but sometimes that was physically impossible, as it would be in this case, without Donna or Adrian and Paula arriving very late. In situations like this approved escorts are used to take the foster child to school, although this is avoided wherever possible: not only is it a heavy call on the social services' budget – approved escorts are very expensive – but it is clearly preferable for the looked-after child to have their carer (*in loco parentis*) standing in the playground with the other mothers rather than being collected by a taxi.

Fortunately my problem was solved when Edna said that Donna enjoyed helping at the breakfast club at her school and would like to continue to do this. The breakfast club started at 8.15 a.m., so I could drop Donna off first and then take Adrian and Paula to their school for 8.50. This arrangement wouldn't be necessary on the first day, however, as Donna's school went back a day before Adrian and Paula's. I asked my neighbour, Sue, if Adrian and Paula could stay with her for an hour while I took Donna to school on that first morning. Sue was happy to oblige: we helped each other out from time to time, although I could never have left a looked-after child with Sue because she wasn't an approved carer.

Donna had contact on Friday, as she had done on Wednesday, and following the same routine I took her in and left her with Edna in reception. As before, Donna was quiet in the car on the way home and I was particularly vigilant for the remainder of the evening. I was aware that, despite Edna supervising the contact, Donna had just seen her family, which could have easily reinforced all her feelings of worthlessness. I felt it wouldn't be long before Donna started to make comparisons between the life she had led at home and the one she led now. When she saw the hurt and injustice that had been inflicted on her I was expecting an explosion of unprecedented anger, for as Mary had said Donna was like a firework waiting to go off.

It was with some relief that I would no longer have to be ever vigilant, and also with some regret that the lazy unstructured days of the summer holidays had come to an end, that on the following Wednesday morning I had everyone up, dressed, washed and breakfasted by 8.00. I took Adrian and Paula next door to be looked after by Sue at 8.20. Donna's school's breakfast club didn't begin until the second day of term, so we left a bit later on that first day. I drove the fifteen-minute journey to Belfont School and arrived at 8.35. I had plenty of time to buy the uniform and introduce myself to the head before the day started at 8.50. I parked in a side road a short distance from the school as a few children in their uniforms strolled past with their mothers.

'OK, love?' I asked Donna, silencing the engine and glancing at her in the rear-view mirror. 'I'm looking forward to meeting your headmistress again. I wonder if she will remember me?'

'Do you know Mrs Bristow?' Donna asked.

'I used to. I looked after a boy a few years ago who went to your school. He won't still be there now, though: he's fourteen and at secondary school.'

'Mrs Bristow is nice.'

'Yes, very,' I agreed. 'It's a good school. I know you are going to do really well this term.'

Donna gave her usual self-deprecating shrug, which she gave at any suggestion she might actually be good at something. I got out of the car and then went round and opened her door, which had the child lock on. She stood beside me on the pavement and looked at the other children heading towards the school. 'Let me know when you see your friend, Emily,' I said, 'and I'll say hello.' Donna nodded.

We went to the end of the road then turned the corner that would take us towards the main gates. As we did, Donna let out a small cry and her face suddenly lit up.

'There's Mum!' she cried. 'And Warren and Jason! And Aunt May, and Granny Bajan!'

I looked, and saw the group standing directly in front of the school gates. Oh dear, I thought, and on our first morning! Foster carers do run into looked-after children's natural families, and in some instances it doesn't matter. Indeed, in the past I had worked closely with children's natural parents, and it was always preferable for the child to see everyone cooperating. But this appeared to be a welcoming party of unprecedented proportions – at least I hoped it was welcoming. To deal with it I would have to put aside my own feelings towards Rita for Donna's sake. I would also have to make Edna aware of this meeting; Donna's contact was carefully supervised and this unscheduled contact clearly would not be.

Donna had quickened her pace and nearly ran the last few steps towards the chatting, laughing throng. As I approached, I searched the gathering of six adults, a teenager and two boys, trying to identify who was who among the adults. Granny Bajan from Barbados, Donna's gran on her father's side, stood on the edge of the group. She was a plump, kindly-looking woman, in her late fifties and very dignified; she greeted Donna with a big hug and then looked at me.

'Hello, I'm Cathy, Donna's carer,' I said.

Mrs Bajan smiled. 'Nice to meet you, Cathy.' Her Caribbean accent caused her words to rise and fall like music. 'But this is so sad,' she added, and I assumed she meant the children being in care.

A smartly dressed middle-aged white couple on my right introduced themselves as Mary and Ray and we shook hands.

'Quite a welcoming committee,' Ray said quietly and I smiled. I looked at Jason and Warren, aged six and seven; with their big brown eyes and sweet open faces, it was very difficult to imagine how they had perpetrated the abuse they had on Donna. But then, at their ages, in a dysfunctional family where morality, respect and kindness were in short supply they had doubtless simply followed the example of their mother and done as she had bade. Removed from that situation and now living with Mary and Ray, and being shown the correct and loving way to behave, they would hopefully eventually change their ways – they were young enough to relearn how good families worked. I felt no anger towards them.

Jason and Warren were all over the person I now took to be their mother, Rita, and she was all over them.

'Is that mum?' I asked Mary and Ray quietly.

They nodded. 'And that woman next to her is Rita's neighbour,' Mary said. 'Not sure yet who the other woman is. We got here just before you.'

I looked at Rita. I knew from the Essential Information Forms that she was in her early thirties, but she could have easily been fifteen years older. She was a short dumpy woman, badly overweight, and with long unkempt thin fair hair straggling around her shoulders. She was wearing a faded cotton T-shirt and a short skirt, both of which were stretched tightly across her stomach and hips. The T-shirt had risen up to reveal a pierced belly button and stretch marks. She had an arm around each of the boys and couldn't get enough of them. I noticed she had completely ignored Donna's arrival. Donna, having received a hug from Granny Bajan, now stood watching her mother and the boys, perhaps waiting for her turn to be hugged, although she didn't seem to be expecting it.

'Hello, Rita,' I said, taking a step forward. 'I'm Cathy, Donna's carer.' Rita ignored me and continued hugging and tickling the boys. I thought they were going to be well hyped up by the time they got into school, and I wondered what the other parents and children who were passing on their way in were making of this noisy gathering.

Beside Rita stood a teenage girl, also badly overweight, and with her stomach showing and revealing a similar piercing. She was chewing gum and staring into space, and

I could see the likeness Edna had spoken of. Without doubt it was Chelsea, and she looked like Donna, more than Donna looked like her brothers, although Donna, Warren and Jason were supposed to have the same father.

'You must be Chelsea?' I said, smiling. She glared at me and continued chewing; I guessed she had assumed her mother's hostility towards me. Apart from the neighbour that Ray had pointed out, another white woman stood on the edge of the group. I took her to be in her forties; she had blonde hair and a walking stick. I looked at her and she made eye contact.

'I'm May, Donna's aunt,' she said. I smiled and nodded, and remembered that Donna had said she went to her aunt's sometimes for her meals; I wondered if this was the same aunt. I didn't know if May and Rita were sisters; I couldn't see any family likeness.

I looked again at Donna, who still hadn't been acknowledged by her mother but was clearly hoping that at some point Rita would leave the boys and at least look at her. I saw Mary and Ray looking at Donna too. I felt dreadfully sorry for her as she stood like an outcast on the edge of the group, while her two brothers competed for, and enjoyed, their mother's attention.

'How are you, Donna?' Mary asked. 'You're looking great.'

Donna gave a shy half nod.

'She is doing very well,' I said, loud enough for Rita to hear. 'I am so pleased with her progress.'

'That's excellent,' Ray and Mary both said. Rita said nothing and didn't even glance up.

It was nearly 8.45 a.m. and I was becoming mindful of the time. I wanted to go into reception before the bell rang to buy Donna's uniform and make sure the school had my contact details, and also hopefully say hello to the head, Mrs Bristow. Donna would see her brothers later in the playground and also at lunchtime, and given that Rita was ignoring her, and no one else seemed in any rush to speak to her now that her gran had given her a hug and Mary and Ray had said hello, I thought there didn't appear to be much point in hanging around. Indeed there was every reason why we shouldn't: with each passing minute, as Donna stood on the edge of the group and was ignored, her rejection seemed more pronounced and pathetic. She looked so sad and I felt the indignation of her exclusion even if she didn't.

'Donna,' I said, 'I think we should go into school now so that I can buy your uniform.' She glanced at me and then looked anxiously at her mother, clearly hoping that her mother would seize this last opportunity to at least say hello, if not hug her, as she was still doing with the boys. Despite the appalling treatment Donna had received at the hands of Rita, Rita was still her mother, and there was doubtless a bond there. Time and time again I had looked after children who had been dreadfully neglected and abused but had still maintained a bond with their parents, and still sought their approval, affection and attention. Only in the absolute worse cases of horrendous (often sexual) abuse did children sever the bond as soon as they could and reject the parents. What I had seen happen, though (and what I thought might happen in Donna's case), was that as time went by and the child started to make comparisons, and judgements on the way they had been treated, they reduced their dependency on their parents and the bond weakened, disappearing altogether if the child was adopted or placed with long-term carers. But for now Donna craved the attention of her mother, and it was pathetic to watch her being ostracised.

'Donna,' I said again, moving closer to her. 'We really need to go now.'

'Yes, and we should be going in too,' Mary said.

It was always difficult ending these impromptu meetings; in contact the start and end times of the session were clearly stated to everyone, and strictly adhered to. 'Come on, Donna,' I said again.

It wasn't Donna who spoke next, but Rita. 'Come on, boys,' she said, 'give me one last hug.' She drew them to her and at the same time, looked over their heads to Donna. 'And you can piss off, you cunt,' she sneered, and then she spat.

I gasped. Ray and Mary looked at each other, horrified, and Granny Bajan said, 'May the Lord forgive you, Rita.' The neighbour remained impassive, as though it was a run-of-the-mill comment that she'd heard before. And Aunt May said, 'Rita,' in a cautionary tone. Chelsea grinned maliciously while Donna simply stood there, as though half-expecting this or something similar.

I touched Donna's arm. 'Come on, love,' I said quietly. 'Let's go in now.'

With a final glance at her mother, who was still cuddling the boys, Donna came with me, and I quickly led the way up the short path to the main entrance. The door opened as we approached and Mrs Bristow appeared.

'I was just coming out,' she said, looking worried. 'Are you all right?'

I nodded. Although Mrs Bristow couldn't have heard Rita's comment, being a very experienced head she would have been aware that the meeting was not advisable at any level, and undoubtedly had had to deal with similar situations with looked-after children before. 'Perhaps I could have a word with you once I've got Donna settled,' I said.

Mrs Bristow nodded, but she was still anxiously watching Ray and Mary through the window in reception. They were trying to persuade the boys away from Rita. After another few moments the boys broke away and ran down the path and round the side of the building towards the playground, followed by Ray and Mary. Rita and her gathering slowly turned and wandered off.

Mrs Bristow let out a quiet sigh of relief and returned her attention to us. 'It's lovely to see you, Donna, and to see you again, Cathy.' We shook hands, and she gave Donna a hug. 'Edna has given me your contact details,' she said to me. 'And I understand you want to buy Donna a new uniform.' She smiled at Donna. 'That will be nice, won't it?'

'Yes,' I said and I smiled too, hoping that an entire new school uniform might in some small way be recompense for her mother's atrocious rejection and comment. I was still appalled and shaken by what I had just seen and heard; I would obviously be logging the details and my observations in my notes when I returned home, and also making Edna aware of it.

Mrs Bristow took us through to the office. Kay, the school secretary, remembered me; we exchanged greetings and she too gave Donna a big hug. 'Good to see you again, Donna,' she said, 'and looking so well.' Kay was lovely, warm and welcoming, exactly what a school secretary should be. I guessed she had a soft spot for Donna and her brothers, as she had done for the last child I'd looked after who had gone to the school. Edna had said that Donna liked school very much; clearly school had been her lifeline. For so many children who have appalling home lives, school is often the one place that can be relied upon to be constant, safe and secure.

Mrs Bristow left us and said she would be back later when I had sorted out the uniform. Kay took us through to the stock room, where I bought two school sweatshirts, three T-shirts to go underneath, two skirts, PE kit and a bag to put the kit in, together with another bag for Donna's reading book and homework; all of it was navy, with the school's logo in red.

Donna changed into the uniform, and Kay and I said how smart she looked; Donna dismissed the compliment with her usual self-effacing shrug. Kay gave me a carrier bag for the clothes Donna had changed out of, and we returned with Kay to the office, where I wrote a cheque for the uniform and accessories. Foster carers receive a grant to cover most of the cost of a new uniform. The bell had rung and Kay suggested Donna now went straight through to join her class. I gave Donna a hug, told her again how smart she looked and said I would be waiting in the playground for her at the end of school. I watched her disappear through the door that would take her to the classroom.

'Poor kid,' Kay said once Donna had left us.

'Yes,' I agreed. 'And do you know what her mother said to her?' I was fuming, at last able to give vent to my fury. 'I can't believe it!'

'I can guess,' Kay said dryly.

'I won't repeat it, but it was foul.'

Kay nodded, and by her expression I could see that she had probably had similar dealings with Rita. 'It's the drink,' she said.

I said nothing; drink or not, it was a dreadful expression to use, especially to a child. I considered it the worst of all swear words, and for a mother to use it to her daughter was abominable.

Kay sorted out and gave me various printed sheets – a list of term dates for the year, forthcoming school events and PTA activities, and a copy of the school's new prospectus. Mrs Bristow reappeared and suggested we went into her office for a quick chat. Her office was as I remembered it from five years before: carpeted in bright red, the walls adorned with children's work, and with an area with toys for young children to play while their parents talked to her.

'I'm still reeling from the way Rita spoke to Donna,' I said as we sat down in the armchairs (I couldn't remember Mrs Bristow ever sitting behind her desk – she was far too 'user-friendly'). 'You will never believe what she called Donna! And she didn't even say hello, let alone hug her.'

Mrs Bristow looked at me, sombre and concerned. 'Donna has been so badly treated by that family,' she said. 'I raised my fears about her and the boys when they first joined the school. I can't tell you how relieved I am that the children have finally been taken into care. Why did Donna have to leave Mary and Ray's?'

'There were some problems between her and the boys,' I said. 'I don't know all the details.' And I left it at that. If Edna hadn't seen the need to give Mrs Bristow all the details, it wasn't incumbent on me to do so. Although Mrs Bristow was a caring and highly professional head, I didn't want Donna's reputation in any way sullied at school by my describing her aggressive behaviour at her previous foster home. Donna had moved on from that and I was dealing with her aggression and other issues at my home. At school Donna could just be Donna, a ten-year-old who would improve and make the most of her education. I felt sure that if there were any issues at school in respect of Donna's behaviour then Mrs Bristow would tell me. I doubted there were, though, because, as with many children like Donna, she had been operating a double standard – between acceptable behaviour at school and what went on at home.

'I want to help Donna all I can with her school work,' I said. 'I understand she is in the year below the group for her age?'

'Yes,' Mrs Bristow confirmed. 'Donna has mild learning difficulties, but to be honest I think a lot of her poor learning ability has been a result of her home life. Now she's settled with you I'm sure she'll make huge progress.' Which was exactly my feeling. Then Mrs Bristow spent some time telling me about Donna's strengths and weaknesses in her school work, and said that she would give me a copy of Donna's PEP (Personal Education Plan), which all looked-after children have. It would help me to work alongside the school and reinforce the work her teacher was concentrating on.

'Do you think Rita will be outside the school again?' Mrs Bristow finished by asking.

'I've no idea,' I said. 'I hope not. Donna and her brothers have supervised contact on Mondays, Wednesdays and Fridays. We can do without that every morning.'

'I'm thinking it might be better if you and Mary and Ray used the staff entrance to enter and leave by. It's at the rear of the school and is security locked. I could give you the pass number. Rita has already been warned by Edna that she is not allowed on the school premises or else I will call the police, which is presumably why she waited outside this morning and not in the playground.'

'I would appreciate that,' I said. 'It was very unpleasant for Donna. I understand Donna helps out at breakfast club, so we will be coming early in future.'

'Yes, at eight fifteen. I'll update the class teacher, Beth Adams. She's hoping to meet you briefly at the end of school.'

Mrs Bristow wrote down the security code for the staff entrance on a piece of paper; we said goodbye and I left the building. Outside there was no sign of Rita, but then she had come to see the boys, not Donna and me.

I drove home, now even more aware of the dreadful injustice that had been inflicted on Donna by her mother, and telling myself it was little wonder Donna behaved as she did sometimes. I collected Adrian and Paula from my neighbour, and then the three of us spent a leisurely afternoon in and around the house and garden. And it would be dishonest of me not to admit that it was a lot easier to have just Adrian and Paula, and not have to be continually vigilant. However, I remained hopeful that, given time, Donna would improve to the point where I could trust her again with Adrian and Paula.

When I returned to collect Donna at the end of school, I took Adrian and Paula with me; they were keen to see Donna's school and also I didn't feel I could ask my neighbour to look after them again. They were most impressed when I drove into the staff car park, and even more so when I keyed in the security number and let us in through the staff gate. We waited in the playground with the other parents for Donna's class to come out, and when Donna appeared and saw the three of us I thought she looked just a little bit proud. She came over and said 'Hi,' to Adrian and Paula, as other children were greeting their younger siblings.

Beth Adams, Donna's class teacher, followed Donna out and came over and introduced herself. She was in her twenties and very pleasant; she told me she was from New Zealand, and was here on a year's contract with her husband. I said again that I wanted to help Donna with her school work, and she said she would put extra work sheets in Donna's reading folder, and also that there would be set homework, and Donna was expected to read her book every night. I thanked her for all she was doing for Donna, and the four of us then left the school by the staff entrance, with the children feeling somewhat aloof at their new elevated status.

That evening over dinner I casually asked Donna if Aunt May, whom I had met that morning, was the same aunt she had sometimes visited for her meals.

Donna nodded. 'She uses a walking stick because she's got a plastic foot. Warren used to run off with the foot and hide it.'

I smiled at this childish, if not a little unkind, prank.

Adrian giggled. 'Why has she got a plastic foot?' he asked, while Paula sat there looking nonplussed, having no idea what a plastic foot was.

''Cos her other one got burnt off when she was a baby,' Donna said. 'Her mum hung her over the fire and it got burnt off.'

We stopped eating. 'No! Surely not?' I said. 'That sounds to me like the story of Pinocchio, who sat too close to the fire.' Adrian nodded, Donna shrugged and the subject was left at that.

Later Paula asked me what a plastic foot was and I explained about prostheses and how some people didn't have limbs, without going into too much detail, which could have been upsetting for a child of six. The following day when I spoke to Edna and told her, among other things, about the 'welcoming party' at school, she confirmed Donna's account of how Aunt May had lost her foot. As a baby it had been so badly burned when her mother (who was also Rita's mother) had held May over a coal fire that it had had to be amputated. The family had a history of abuse that went back three generations.

Chapter Ten

Tablets

The routine of our school week began in earnest the following day when I woke Adrian, Paula and Donna at 7.00 a.m., and had them dressed, washed and breakfasted and in the car by 7.50. I saw Donna into her school to help with the breakfast club at 8.15; then I drove back to Adrian and Paula's school to arrive at 8.40, which gave us ten minutes to mingle in the playground before the bell went at 8.50. In the afternoon I did the reverse, and first collected Adrian and Paula, who came out at 3.10 p.m., and then made a dash to Donna's school for her dismissal time of 3.30. This arrangement relied on Adrian and Paula coming out exactly on time, and I mentioned to Beth Adams that I might occasionally be a few minutes late, if the traffic was heavy or Adrian and Paula weren't dismissed at exactly 3.10. As it turned out, though, Donna was usually five or ten minutes late leaving the classroom, as she was always the one who volunteered to help clear up if the room was in a mess.

'Donna likes to help so much, doesn't she?' Beth Adams commented to me after school one day. 'She'll even give up her lunchtime if something needs doing; she's always asking me for jobs to do.' I agreed, although I felt that Donna's eagerness to clean and tidy wasn't altogether healthy, and was probably a legacy of her role at her mother's when cleaning had been her responsibility. I would rather have seen her stream out with the other children, not caring a damn about the state of the classroom and happy to leave it to someone else.

After a few days Donna pointed out her friend Emily to me and I introduced myself to her and her mother; they were both aware Donna was in foster care. Emily's mother, Mandy, was very friendly and told me about Emily's learning difficulties, and how she really appreciated Emily having Donna as her friend – someone her own age in the same class. I said it was important we kept their friendship going, and that I would like it very much if Emily could come to tea. Mandy agreed, but said that Emily was a little shy and asked if we could leave it until later in the term when Emily had resettled into the school routine. They were Polish and had spent the entire summer holidays in Poland, and Emily had found the transition back not an easy one. We always chatted briefly when we saw each other in the playground at the end of the school day.

On Mondays, Wednesdays and Fridays I had to do a quick turnaround after school because of Donna's contact. As soon as we arrived home at 4.00 p.m. Donna washed and changed, and then had her evening meal, ready to leave the house again at 4.40 for contact at 5.00. I had started giving Donna her evening meal before contact, as Edna had said that Donna was 'pigging out' on the biscuits at contact because she was hungry, and then feeling sick. Indeed, on more than one occasion when I'd collected her we'd had to drive home with the car window open as she had felt so rough, and then she hadn't wanted her dinner. On these evenings Paula, Adrian and I ate when we returned from taking Donna to contact and before we had to get back into the car to collect her. It was a rush, but Adrian and Paula had grown up being herded in and out of the car for contact, as do other children of foster carers. Contact always takes priority, even to the extent of rearranging and sometimes cancelling one's own appointments.

Our routine of school continued and accelerated towards the half-term holiday in October. The evenings vanished, for apart from the contact, which dominated three of the evenings, there was homework to be done, the evening meal to be cooked and eaten, baths to be had and the children's favourite television programmes to be watched, before we began the bedtime routine. I maintained my vigilance with Donna whenever she was with Adrian, and particularly when she was with Paula, for while we hadn't had another incident of Donna actually hitting Paula, Donna would still try to dominate and chastise Paula and tell her what to do, often repeating my instructions with a lot more authority than I had given them. So if I said to Paula, 'Come on, it's time to do your reading,' Donna would echo, 'Your mother told you to do your reading. Now!' To which I would gently reply, 'It's OK, Donna, I'll tell Paula. You don't have to, love.' I suppose Donna felt chastisement was part of the role of looking after younger siblings, which it had been when she'd been living at home. I hoped that this behaviour, like others, would diminish over time.

I continued to monitor Donna's washing: when she had a bath or went to the toilet I stood on the landing, listening for any sound that might have suggested she was washing with more vigour than she should – trying to rub her skin colour off again; although having removed the nailbrushes and pumice stone I felt there was less chance of her doing real damage to herself with the sponge and flannels that were left. I also remained concerned about Donna's poor self-image – not only in respect of her dual heritage but also with her self-esteem in general, which was non-existent. Mrs Bristow assured me that she was already seeing positive changes in Donna and felt that she was gaining confidence. Her teachers and I praised Donna at every opportunity. I continued to give Donna little jobs to do in the house so that she felt she was helping, but I was gradually reducing these, hoping to wean her off her need for drudgery and subservience. When she performed a task her manner was so servile it was uncomfortable to watch. However, Donna wasn't ready to let go of this role yet, and in order to exorcise her compulsion she discovered a new behaviour which was quite bizarre.

I went up to her bedroom one day to find the whole room littered with hundreds of tiny bits of paper torn from old magazines, which she had bought with her pocket money.

'That's a right mess,' I said, not best pleased. 'And I've only just vacuumed.' The tiny bits of paper were everywhere – all over the floor, the bed, the bookshelves and every available surface.

'I'm going to clean it up,' she said laboriously, and immediately dropped onto all fours and began steadily picking up the tiny scraps of paper. Half an hour later the room was spotless again.

After that it became a regular pursuit: Donna spending thirty minutes tearing up the paper and then another thirty minutes clearing it up. When she had exhausted her own supply of magazines or drawing paper, she asked me if she could have the old newspapers, which I reluctantly gave her. I wasn't at all sure I should be encouraging this, for it seemed it could be reinforcing exactly the behaviour I was trying to persuade her out of – cleaning. I talked to Edna and Jill about it and they both thought that it was a pretty harmless way of her acting out her role from the past, and as long as it didn't escalate, to let her continue. They said that it should slowly disappear over time, but that if it didn't then it could be addressed at therapy when it was started after the final court hearing in May. I asked them if I should let her do more in the house, as it seemed to me that I might have caused this new development by stopping a lot of her 'housework', but they said no, it would be a retrogressive step, and I was handling it correctly. I told Adrian and Paula not to say anything or laugh if Donna's bedroom door was open and they saw her tearing up or picking up the paper for this was her way of dealing with her past.

'She can clean my room,' Adrian said to me with a cheeky grin.

'Absolutely not,' I said. 'That's your job.' But I knew Donna would have done it if he'd asked.

Apart from the times when Donna tried to tell Paula what to do or chastise her, she remained very quiet and compliant – too much so, I thought. Her voice was always flat and expressionless, even when there was a treat to be enjoyed, as though she didn't dare express any excitement or pleasure. I was sure, as Mary had been, that Donna was internalising a lot of her pain, frustration and anger, and that at some point it would explode.

* * *

I was right, and it happened in October, during the week's half-term holiday from school.

Donna's contact continued during half term, so I had to make sure that when we went out for the day on Monday, Wednesday and Friday we were back home relatively early. On Tuesday, when we weren't constrained by contact times, I took the opportunity of having a full day out, and we visited a theme park, which was about an hour's drive away. It was an excellent day, and I knew that Donna had enjoyed it as much as she could enjoy anything, although she hadn't said much and had needed a lot of persuasion to go on the rides.

On the way home Donna reminded me that she had contact the following day. 'I know, love,' I said. 'Don't worry, I won't forget.' She then said that her dad would be going and that he had been there on Monday. Her father had made intermittent appearances at contact, about every fourth one. I had never met Mr Bajan, but I knew he was the only one in the immediate family who hadn't abused Donna, and that his illness – paranoid schizophrenia – prevented him from taking a more prominent role in her life.

'He hasn't been taking his medication,' Donna said reflectively a short while later. 'I told him on Monday to take it. Otherwise Edna will have him locked up.' Donna was referring to her father being sectioned under the Mental Health Act, which seemed to happen a couple of times a year when he stopped taking his medication and began behaving irrationally and sometimes violently.

I glanced at Donna in the rear-view mirror. 'Edna doesn't have him locked up,' I said. 'When your dad doesn't take his tablets he can't cope, so he is taken into hospital. The doctors make sure he has his medicine and then he is well enough to go home again. Don't you worry: I'm sure Edna or your mum will tell him.'

Donna didn't say anything more in the car, but having been responsible for making sure her dad took his medication when she had been at home, she had clearly recognised the signs of him not having taken it, and this was proved the following day.

On Wednesday I took Donna to contact at 5.00 p.m., and I had just returned home when I got a phone call from Edna saying she was terminating contact immediately, and could I collect Donna straight away? Edna spoke quickly and anxiously – a sharp contrast to her usual calm and reassuring manner. She said she'd called the police and an ambulance for Mr Bajan, and that I should wait in the car outside the social services offices and Donna would be brought out to me. I told Adrian and Paula that Donna's father had been taken ill at contact, and we were going to collect her early, and to put on their shoes, which they had only just taken off. With mounting anxiety and no idea what to expect, I drove back to the offices in Belfont Road. As I turned into the road I saw two police cars and an ambulance parked on the forecourt at the front of the building. I pulled into the kerb a little way back and turned off the engine.

'Why are the police here?' Adrian asked.

'I think it's in case the ambulance crew need help,' I said, leaving it at that. I knew that sometimes schizophrenics could suffer from delusional hallucinations and become violent, but to talk about that to the children would have been frightening.

We sat in the car for about ten minutes, and I was expecting to see Donna appear at any minute with Edna.

Instead, after another few minutes the front door of the building suddenly burst open and, as we looked, two uniformed police officers came out, followed by another two, with a man I took to be Donna's father struggling between them. They were holding an arm each. He was a large man and appeared to be very strong. He was shouting and struggling, and trying to fight off the demons that clearly plagued him. 'Fuck off! Fuck off! I've told you! I'll have you crucified like him!' he yelled. He pulled and wrenched from side to side, and it was clear that it was all the officers either side of him could do to restrain him and stop him from breaking free. The officers were talking to him quietly, perhaps trying to reassure him, but I doubted he could hear over the noise of his shouting and wailing.

Behind them came the ambulance crew: two paramedics, one male and one female. There was no sign of Edna, Donna, Rita, Chelsea or the boys, all of whom had attended contact. Adrian, Paula and I watched, mesmerised and horrified by the scene. The female paramedic opened the ambulance doors and lowered the steps.

'Oh no! On no! Oh no!' Mr Bajan wailed. It was truly pitiful and frightening to watch. He struggled and cried out, pulling back from the steps of the ambulance. I thought that when he was well he would have the same dignity as his mother, for despite his illness he seemed a proud man and was smartly dressed in grey trousers and an open-neck shirt.

Adrian was at his side window, enthralled and appalled by what he was witnessing. Paula had slunk low in her seat with her hands pressed over her ears. 'He'll be all right. Don't worry,' I said, trying to reassure them, although I could feel my own heart racing; it was very upsetting. A young couple walking along the street hesitated, and then ran past the end of the forecourt.

Mr Bajan continued shouting as the two police officers guided him to the foot of the ambulance steps, ready to climb up, and then he set up the most dreadful wail. I could see his face contorted with pain and anger as he tried to fight off his internal tormentors. His skin ran with sweat and his eyes bulged. No wonder in bygone days it was thought the mentally ill were possessed. The poor man looked as though he was at the mercy of some unseen evil spirit that was hell-bent on destroying him and would stop at nothing to achieve it.

The other two officers helped, and it took all four of them to slowly manoeuvre Mr Bajan up the two steps and into the ambulance. The paramedics followed them in and closed the rear doors. I don't know what happened then; I assumed he was sedated, because a few minutes later the rear doors of the ambulance opened and all four police officers came out, together with the female paramedic, and it was quiet inside. She closed the ambulance doors and said something to the police officers; then she went to the driver's door of the ambulance and got in. Two of the officers got in one of the police cars, while the other two returned inside the building. The ambulance and police car pulled away from the forecourt and left with their blue lights flashing and sirens wailing.

'Cor,' Adrian said, impressed by the ambulance, as any boy his age would be.

I turned again to Paula in the back. 'It's OK, love. You can take your hands down now.'

She slowly lowered her hands from her ears. 'I don't like shouting,' she said in a small voice.

'No, I know. It's all right now. Mr Bajan was very upset and they are taking him to the hospital. The doctors will make him better.'

We sat in subdued silence for another ten minutes; then Edna appeared with Donna. She saw my car and, as she came over, I got out and stood on the pavement. I could see that Edna was maintaining a calm façade for Donna's sake, but her anxiety showed in her face. She was talking quietly to Donna as they approached, and Donna looked deathly pale.

'I'll phone you later,' Edna said to me, 'when I've finished here. Donna's very upset and I think she just needs to get home now.' She touched Donna's arm, and I opened the rear door of the car and waited while she got in. 'I'll speak to you later, Cathy,' Edna said again anxiously. 'I've still got the boys, Rita and Chelsea inside.'

'All right, Edna. Don't worry.'

She returned into the building as I got into the car.

'Are you all right?' I asked Donna gently.

She shrugged. Paula and Adrian were looking at her with sympathy and concern.

'Let's get home,' I said, and I started the engine.

Donna didn't say anything during the twenty-minute journey home. She sat beside Paula, with her head down and hands clasped tightly together in her lap. When we arrived home and I opened the front door, she went straight up to her bedroom. A minute later I heard a loud bang come from her room, quickly followed by another and another. Telling Adrian to stay with Paula in the lounge, I shot upstairs. Donna was screaming now at the top of her voice; giving a brief knock on her door, I opened it.

She was darting around her bedroom, screaming, and picking up anything and everything that came within reach and hurling it against the walls. 'Donna!' I said loudly. 'Stop that.' She glanced at me but continued screaming and throwing everything that came to hand – the portable CD player, her crayons, books and games, her teddy and the china ornaments she'd started collecting with her pocket money. I stayed by the door, not daring to go further in, in case her anger turned on me. She pulled the sheet off the bed and ripped it, her teeth gritted, her face set hard. 'Donna!' I said again. 'Stop! Donna, now!' She went to the curtains and yanked one down with such force that the rail came out of the wall in a shower of plaster. 'Donna! Stop it! Do you hear me!' My heart was pounding and my mouth was dry.

Suddenly she froze, the screaming stopped, and she dropped to her knees and began sobbing uncontrollably. She was bent forward, clutching her head in her hands and rocking back and forth.

I slowly went in and towards her as her sobbing grew. I knelt beside her, and then tentatively placed my hand on her shoulder. Her head was down and she was rocking and crying. I began lightly rubbing her back. 'It's OK, love,' I soothed. 'I understand. It'll be all right now.' She continued to rock and cry, and I slowly slid my arm around her shoulders. Gradually the sobbing eased. 'Donna, look at me, love,' I said gently and, placing my hands on hers, I slowly lowered them from her face. Her eyes were red and swollen and her breath was coming fast and shallow. 'Everything is all right now.' I drew her to me and she allowed her head to rest on my shoulder.

'I told Dad to take his tablets,' she said between sobs. 'I told him on Monday. Mum doesn't tell him. She's useless. She only thinks about the boys. He needs to take his tablets. It's my fault.' Her body stiffened and she was digging her nails into the palms of her hands.

'Donna, love, I know you told him, but it's not your fault. Your daddy is a grown man. Somehow he will have to find a way to remember to take his tablets. The doctors will help him work it out.'

She gave a dismissive shrug and I felt pretty impotent. I knew from what Edna has said that periods of Mr Bajan not taking his medication had been a pattern of their lives, and with no one at home now to remind him to take them, it was a pattern that was likely to continue. Schizophrenia is a controllable disease, thanks to modern medicine, and it was so sad that Mr Bajan's life and the lives of his children continued to be blighted by something as simple as remembering to swallow some tablets.

'Will I get it, and be like him when I'm older?' Donna said suddenly. She had stopped rocking and turned to look at me.

'No, love. Absolutely not.'

'Mum says it's in his family, and I'll end up as loony as him. She says I already am, and sometimes I think she's right. I think and do weird things.'

'No,' I said firmly again. 'You won't. There's nothing wrong with you, Donna, and there won't be.'

'Mum says I'm a nutter already,' Donna said. 'She says I should be locked up like him.'

I stopped myself from vilifying her mother. 'Donna, that was a very unkind thing for her to say, and it certainly isn't true. Trust me, you are doing fine, and once your dad starts taking his tablets again he will be fine too.'

She seemed to accept this, and I thought that the next time I spoke to Edna I would ask her to reinforce to Donna what I had said. For it is often the case with a medical condition that if you believe you are suffering from it, you can start to imagine the symptoms developing.

'Has that been worrying you?' I asked gently. 'That you might develop the illness your dad has?'

She nodded. 'Mum says I have it, and that's why I'm so odd.'

'And does she say that about Warren and Jason too?'

'No.'

Which I thought was interesting, considering they were supposed to have the same father and therefore the same possible genetic susceptibility.

'Donna, it was a very unkind thing to say, and it certainly isn't true. You are one of the healthiest people I know, and Edna says so too. You have been through so much at home and now you are doing really well.'

'You know Mum didn't want me, Cathy?' she said. 'I was an accident. She tried to get rid of me by poking a knitting needle inside her, but it didn't work.'

I inwardly recoiled, and I wondered if Donna knew exactly what she was saying, but I wasn't about to explain abortion to a ten-year-old. 'That was a cruel thing to say,' I said. 'And I'm pleased it didn't work because otherwise I wouldn't have you here now. I like looking after you and I'm very glad you are living with us.'

She looked at me again, her eyes round and imploring. 'Are you? Are you really?' She was surprised.

'Yes, darling, I am. You are a lovely person and I know you are going to do very well.' I was pleased Donna was finding it easier to talk to me, and I hoped that by talking about her worries and what had happened she would start to find some release. I glanced around at the debris of her trashed bedroom.

'Mum had a hot bath and drank a bottle of gin as well,' Donna added, 'when the knitting needle didn't work. Why did she do that, Cathy?'

I hesitated. Donna clearly knew more than the average ten-year-old, but even so I didn't want to go into the gory details of abortion. 'She was trying to have what's called a termination,' I said. 'But I would like to leave telling you more about that until you are older. It would be easier then. Is that OK?'

She nodded, and then let out a little laugh.

'What is it?' I asked, surprised that anything could be funny in what she had just told me.

'Mum said it didn't work because there wasn't enough hot water. Chelsea had taken it all, so I guess I have to thank her for saving me. And Chelsea doesn't even like me!'

I marvelled at Donna's adult ironic humour. 'Well done Chelsea, I say! Donna, you are a lovely person and whatever happened in the past is gone. Things will be much easier for you now, and that will help you get better at everything.' I put my arms around her and hugged her. She didn't return the hug, but neither did she immediately move away. We sat quietly for some time until she finally eased away.

'I'm tired, Cathy,' she said. 'Can I go to bed? I'll clear up in the morning.'

'Yes, love. Have an early night. And Donna, next time you feel really angry we'll find another way of letting it out. Like hitting a cushion hard, or running round and round the garden. It does help.'

She nodded. 'I'm sorry. I liked my bedroom.'

'OK, love. Now take your nightdress into the bathroom and get washed and changed while I find you a new sheet. The curtains will have to stay as they are for tonight. I'll see if I can fix the rail back on the wall tomorrow.'

'Sorry,' she said again, and taking her nightdress from under her pillow she went through to the bathroom.

I took a clean sheet from the airing cupboard and replaced the old one, which having been ripped in half would be consigned to the rag bag. I collected together all the broken pieces of ornaments and dropped them in the waste-paper basket, which I then put out on the landing ready to take downstairs. I didn't think Donna would use the broken china to self-harm, but I wasn't taking any chances. Although some of her anger had come out I knew there was still a long way to go before she was free of all the hurt, anger and rejection that must still be boiling inside her. I checked there was nothing sharp left in the room, looking under the bed, on the shelves and in the drawers. The portable CD player was miraculously still working, and the crayons and other things could be cleared up tomorrow. I left the curtain hanging off the rail; I'd have to fetch the stepladder from the shed in the morning and see if I could fix the bracket onto the wall with filler.

When Donna returned from the bathroom I tucked her into bed and kissed her goodnight. 'All right now, love?' I asked before I left.

She nodded. 'Night, Cathy. Will you say goodnight to Adrian and Paula for me?'

'Will do, love. Sleep tight.' I came out and closed the door.

I carried the waste-paper basket with the broken china downstairs and tipped the contents into the kitchen bin. I then went into the lounge, where I spent some time talking to, and reassuring, Adrian and Paula that Donna was all right, and so too would her father be now that he was in hospital.

At 8.00 p.m., just as I'd returned downstairs from seeing Adrian and Paula into bed, the phone rang. It was Edna, still at the office in Belfont Road. 'How is she?' she asked, sounding exhausted. I told her about Donna venting her anger on her room, and what she had said about her worries of mental illness, and her mother telling her about terminating the pregnancy. Edna listened in silence, occasionally tutting and sighing in dismay.

'Rita tried to blame Donna tonight for Mr Bajan's behaviour,' Edna said. 'Rita said, "Look what you've done now. It's your fault, you silly cow." I stopped her before she said anything else. I knew Mr Bajan hadn't been taking his medication as soon as he walked into contact. He was speaking on a toy mobile phone – you know, the ones that play ringing noises when you press the buttons. He said he was talking to God, only I don't think God could have got a word in edgeways over his continuous babble. Warren and Jason carried on playing; they're used to their father's behaviour. Rita and Chelsea told him he was a nutter and silly old fool and laughed at him. Donna was the one who tried to talk to him and look after him. I stopped the contact immediately.'

'How long will he be in hospital?' I asked.

'It's usually about three months before he is stabilised, but he might be discharged sooner.'

'Is there no way he can be reminded to take his medication?'

'Not while he is living with Rita. I am going to see if I can find him a place in sheltered accommodation, because this has been going on for too long now and he's having too many relapses. He lived with his mother for a while and she made sure he took his tablets, but she's away for most of the winter, and Mr Bajan keeps gravitating back to Rita. She doesn't remind him about his pills; she's got her own problems with the drink and drugs. The only one who helped him was Donna, and it's hardly the responsibility of a girl her age.'

'No. That's what I told her.'

Edna sighed. 'Anyway, I'm going home now, Cathy. I haven't had anything to eat all day and I've a report to write for another case which is due in court next week. I've been up until midnight writing reports every night for a week. Was there anything else, Cathy?'

'No. I'll tell Donna I've spoken to you.'

'Thanks. Goodnight, Cathy.'

I said goodnight, and as I went upstairs to check that Donna was asleep I thought how conscientious and hard-working Edna was. It was indicative of the huge workload social workers carried that in order to do her job properly Edna spent her days tending to the needs of her clients and her evenings catching up on the paperwork.

Chapter Eleven

A Small Achievement

'Why don't you hit people?' Donna asked on Monday morning in the car on the way to school.

'Because it is an assault on the person; it hurts and makes them afraid of you. Talking is a better way of working out disagreements. It's wrong to hit another person, and certainly very wrong for an adult to hit a child.' I had said similar things to Donna when she'd first arrived and had viewed corporal punishment and physical violence as the norm, but often during car journeys Donna reflected on things and suddenly asked a question unrelated to anything immediate. Adrian and Paula did it too; I think the soporific motion of the car encourages reflection, and indeed my thoughts sometimes wander while I'm driving.

'But what if a child doesn't do as they're told?' Donna said. 'Shouldn't you hit them then?' Again, I had covered this previously, but clearly something was now gelling in Donna's mind.

'No, never. As a parent you have to be very patient and sometimes explain something over and over again. If a child still won't do as they are told, or they are being very naughty, then I find stopping a treat usually works wonders.' I glanced at Adrian in the rear-view mirror: he was sitting so quietly and angelically that he could almost have sprouted wings and a halo. He had recently been on the receiving end of my philosophy, and had lost thirty minutes of television time for continually kicking his football into the flowerbed when I'd asked him to use the goalposts at the bottom of the garden, which were away from the plants.

'My mum hit me,' Donna said, a short while later.

'Yes, I know, love.'

'So did Chelsea, Warren and Jason.'

'Yes, you told me, and it was very wrong of them.'

'Mum didn't hit Warren and Jason much – only when they got on her nerves when she'd been drinking. And when they wouldn't go into her bed.'

I glanced in the rear-view mirror again, this time at Donna. She was sitting back in her seat and gazing through the side window. 'What do you mean, she hit them when they wouldn't go into her bed?'

'Mum liked them to go into her bed sometimes when Dad wasn't there, but they didn't want to.'

'What? To give them a cuddle, you mean?'

I saw Donna shrug. 'She didn't hit them much but she made them go into her bed when they were naughty.' I wasn't sure what Donna was saying. Many children go into their parents' bed for a cuddle but this sounded as if it had been a punishment for the boys.

'I don't understand, Donna. Can you explain?' She shrugged again. I had stopped at a set of traffic lights and I briefly turned to look at her. 'Why did they have to go into her bed when they had been naughty? Didn't they like having a cuddle in bed?'

'I don't know,' she said. 'I was never allowed in. But if they were naughty Mum said, "You'll go into my bed for that." And when they came out sometimes they were crying.'

'Did she hit them?'

'I don't know. I had to stay downstairs.'

I put the car into gear as the lights changed and I pulled away. 'And Warren and Jason didn't tell you what had happened in your mother's bedroom?'

'Mum told them not to tell anyone. She said if they did it would be all the worse for them next time.'

I tried to concentrate on the traffic, at the same time listening to what Donna was telling me. I didn't like what I was hearing, and I was feeling decidedly uneasy. Whatever had gone on when Rita had summoned Warren and Jason to her bedroom certainly didn't sound like a family cuddle. I needed to try to find out more so that I could inform Edna; I would also have to write all this in my log when I got home.

'I see,' I said, thoughtfully. 'How often were the boys made to go into your mother's bedroom?'

'When Dad wasn't there,' Donna said. 'I guess about once a week.' Adrian and Paula were gazing out of the windows, blissfully unaware of any sinister undertones in what Donna was saying. 'They had to go to the toilet when they came out,' she added. 'Sometimes Jason had wet himself.' From what, I wondered? Fear?

'And your brothers didn't ever say what had happened?'

'No. Warren said it was better to be hit with a coat hanger like Mum did to me than go into Mum's bed.'

I braked as the car in front slowed. Good grief, I thought, that's definitely not a cuddle. 'And he never told you why?'

'No. Mum said they mustn't or else.'

'OK, love, thank you for telling me. I'll tell Edna. It doesn't sound very nice to me.'

'No, you can't tell Edna!' Donna said, her usual flat and emotionless voice rising. 'Mum will be angry, and we'll all be in for it. I'll get another beating.'

'No you won't,' I said firmly. 'You are not at home now, and neither are your brothers. And it's important that Edna knows that Warren and Jason were upset because she can make sure it doesn't happen again.'

'Oh yes,' Donna said, and I could hear the relief in her voice. 'I'd forgotten that. She can't be angry with me at contact because Edna stops her.'

'That's right, love. You see, I told you life would get better.' And as I glanced in the rear-view mirror I saw a brief smile of relief and contentment flicker across her face.

Having seen Donna into school, I took Adrian and Paula to their school, and as soon as I arrived home I wrote up my log notes, including what Donna had said, as near verbatim as possible. At this stage it was impossible to know the significance of what she had told me, or its relevance in the light of what might come out in the future. The detailed log notes foster carers have to keep are sometimes requested by the judge for the final court hearing, if he feels their content is pertinent to the case. Although Donna hadn't witnessed first hand what had happened in her mother's bedroom, and the boys hadn't told her, because of Rita's threats, Donna had said enough to leave me with a heavy feeling of unease. Clearly she was starting to reflect on the life she had led with her mother and the one she now led with me – that is, in a normal family – and she was beginning to draw conclusions and recognise the things that hadn't been right at home. Donna, like many children who come into care for similar reasons, had assumed the neglect and abuse she'd suffered were the norm. It was taking time for her to realise that the life she'd led wasn't normal and some things were clearly bad. It never ceases to amaze me what some children believe is acceptable simply because they have grown up with it, and have never known anything different. One girl of five I looked after thought it was perfectly normal to be tied by the legs and arms to the bed and left for a day and night without food or water as a punishment for bad behaviour.

Although I would be seeing Edna briefly before and after contact the following day, I didn't want to discuss what Donna had told me in front of her, so once I'd finished writing up my notes I telephoned Edna. She wasn't in the office; her colleague said she was on a home visit, and I left a message with her asking if Edna could phone me when she returned. What Donna had said played on my mind as I tidied up the living room, vacuumed the carpets and then went outside to do a spot of gardening. It was a fresh autumn day, and as I pruned the bushes, which had become unruly during the summer, I had a growing feeling of disquiet. I thought of Adrian and Paula, who had climbed into my bed at the weekend for a cuddle when they were younger; Paula still did if she woke early. I remembered my brother and me clambering into my parents' bed, and I thought how far removed that was from what Donna had told me about Warren and Jason, who had been made to go to their mother's bed as a punishment and had come out crying and in need of the toilet. In most families the parents' bed is a safe and inviting place for a young child to spend a leisurely hour on a

Sunday morning, but it sounded far from a safe place to be at Donna's house.

I had just come in from the garden at 11.30 a.m. when the phone rang, and it was Edna, returning my call.

'Hello, Cathy. Is everything all right?' she asked as she always did if I phoned her.

'Donna is fine,' I reassured her. 'And this may be something or nothing, but I think you should know what she told me this morning. If you could just hang on a moment I'll fetch my notes so that I can tell you exactly what she said.'

'Yes of course, Cathy. Go ahead.'

I left the phone in the lounge and went through to the front room, where I took my log notes from the drawer of my desk. I returned to the phone, and having explained to Edna that we had been in the car going to school when the conversation took place, I read out my notes. Edna was silent as I finished; then she said, 'I shall speak to the boys after school today, Cathy. I'll phone Mary and Ray and tell them I'm coming. The boys obviously haven't said anything to Mary and Ray, but they wouldn't if they'd been scared into secrecy. I don't like what I'm hearing, Cathy. I know Rita only had eyes for the boys, but if Donna is telling the truth it sounds as if there might be more to it. I've never known Donna lie before, but do you think she is telling the truth? Or could she be trying to get Warren and Jason and Rita into trouble – getting her own back?'

'I don't think Donna is capable of that type of manipulation,' I said. 'But obviously I can't know for sure.'

'No. OK, Cathy. Thanks. I'll speak to the boys later. If Donna says anything else, will you let me know, please, and also could you print out a copy of your notes and let me have them tomorrow at contact. I hope Donna is making this up.'

'Yes,' I agreed. 'So do I.'

Edna phoned that evening from the office at 7.00 p.m., after she had seen Warren and Jason. 'They have been sworn to secrecy,' she said. 'I knew from their faces there was something they weren't telling me. Jason was about to say something but Warren elbowed him in the ribs to make him be quiet. Mary and Ray are going to talk to the boys separately, and see if they can find out anything. I shall also be having a word with Chelsea to see if she can throw any light on this, although I'll have to get her away from Rita first; they're as thick as thieves at present. I take it Donna hasn't said any more?'

'No. If she does know anything further it will come out in her own time.'

'All right. Thanks, Cathy. I'm off home now.'

Every evening after school, Donna, Adrian and Paula did their homework before watching children's television. Paula's homework was usually reading; Adrian had work sheets to complete and sometimes needed help; Donna had reading and work sheets and required more help. She was on a reading scheme designed for the average seven-year-old and starting to make some progress. In addition to the reading and work sheets, she had been asked to start learning her times tables, ready for a test on Friday. The whole class was being tested on the two times table, and I knew that when Beth Adams had told me of this new target she hadn't held out much hope for Donna being able to learn and fluently recite the table. I was determined we would prove her wrong. Donna had mild learning difficulties but it didn't mean she couldn't learn.

Armed with a whiteboard and black marker pen, I took Donna into the lounge after dinner, and we sat on the floor. I slowly recited the two times table as she wrote down the numbers. Beth Adams had given each of the class a printed sheet with the table on it, but what I had in mind would be more visually stimulating, and therefore more likely to be remembered. It would also be more fun than a typed piece of paper. Donna wrote very slowly and meticulously as I repeated the table, rubbing out a number if she wasn't completely satisfied. Her writing was a stark contrast to Adrian's: the same age, he wrote in a flurry, covering pages with writing as his thoughts spilled out. It was quarter of an hour before Donna was satisfied with the columns of figures she had produced, and we then sat either side of the whiteboard and I pointed to each line and we read it together: 0 x 2 = 0, 1 x 2 = 2, 2 x 2 = 4, and so on until the end. We went through it a second time, and then a third time to familiarise Donna with the pattern and rhythm of the table.

'OK, Donna,' I said, 'now we are going to learn it in groups of three. That's easier than trying to learn the whole table to the end.' I covered up the lower nine lines of the table with a sheet of paper, leaving only the top three lines visible, and we read them together: '0 x 2 = 0, 1 x 2 = 2, 2 x 2 = 4.' Then I told Donna to read these first three lines by herself out loud, which she did with some hesitancy. Then a second and third time.

'Good,' I said. 'Now I want you to look away. Look at the wall and see how many of these first three lines you can remember.' This would have been ridiculously easy for the average child of ten, and indeed for a much younger child, but Donna had learning difficulties and I knew she would need more reinforcement and time to learn.

'I can't,' she said flatly, glancing between the wall and the three exposed lines of figures.

'Yes you can,' I said positively. I felt, as Mrs Bristow had, that some of Donna's learning difficulties could well be due to lack of confidence.

'I don't know them,' Donna said, not even willing to try.

'Yes you do. I'll help you to get started. We'll read the first three lines together again, and then I want you to look away and see if you can remember any of them.'

'0 x 2 = 0, 1 x 2 = 2, 2 x 2 = 4,' we chanted together.

'OK, Donna, look away and have a go. 0 x 2 = ' I said, leaving the answer blank.

'0,' Donna said.

'1 x 2 = ' I said.

'2,' Donna supplied, then unaided she said, '2 x 2 = 4.'

'Excellent!' I said. 'Now again from the beginning. 0 x 2 = '

'0. 1 x 2 = 2, 2 x 2 = 4,' she said.

'Well done!' I clapped. 'And again, this time a bit faster.'

'0 x 2 = 0, 1 x 2 = 2, 2 x 2 = 4.' She was smiling now, almost grinning, and surprised at her ability to achieve something she hadn't thought was possible.

'Right,' I said, 'now we are going to look at the next three in the table.' I slid down the paper that covered the whiteboard to reveal the next set of three, and we read them together: '3 x 2 = 6, 4 x 2 = 8, 5 x 2 = 10.' We read them a second and third time, and then Donna read them alone. Then as before I got her to look away and, with less resistance this time, she recited them – to her utter amazement and my great relief and praise. Before we attempted the next set of three I wanted her to consolidate what she had learned so far and hear and see the rhythm of the first six lines. We read the lines together twice, then I got her to look away and she began to recite them from memory. She hesitated and needed prompting but we got there in the end.

So we continued for the next forty minutes, with me releasing three lines at a time and endless repeating and consolidating what she had learned, until we reached 12 x 2 = 24. When it came to putting them altogether and reciting the whole table, Donna's confidence faltered, and she said she couldn't remember any of it. I said we'd recite it together, which we did, with my voice mainly in the background as a prompt. Donna faltered with 6 x 2, 8 x 2 and 9 x 2, got 10 x 2, and then fell away again at the end. I told her how well she had done and she glowed from the praise. 'We're stopping now,' I said. 'That's enough for tonight. You must be tired out.'

The following morning in the car instead of having the radio on I began reciting the two times table. Adrian joined in, and on my second run through so did Donna, very quietly and only offering those she was sure of. I was concerned that Adrian, completely fluent in all his tables (as were most of his class), shouldn't emphasise Donna's learning difficulties by his prowess. After I had dropped Donna off at school I explained to Adrian (and Paula) that Donna could learn as well as anyone but it took her a little longer and perhaps they could curtail their enthusiasm, especially Adrian, when we practised the times tables in the car. Such a conversation was always difficult for me when we looked after a child with learning difficulties, for clearly I had to acknowledge and praise my own children for their achievements, without undermining that of the fostered child, who was finding learning more difficult. That afternoon when I collected Donna from school I set up the chant of the two times table in the car and all three children joined in, with Adrian and Paula, as I had asked them, giving Donna the louder voice.

I went through the two times table again with Donna that evening – just the two of us, seated in the lounge. She was fluent up to 5 x 2 but then stumbled on 6 x 2, 7 x 2, 8 x 2 and 9 x 2, picking up the rhythm again for the last three. And so we continued for the rest of the week, chanting the table in the car and at home at any opportunity. It had turned into something of a game, with Donna now asking if we could run through it just one more time, which I always did, although secretly I was sick of the sound of it, as I'm sure Adrian and Paula were. But I wasn't doing it solely so that Donna knew her table but also to prove to her that she could do it, which would raise her confidence and help her learning and self-esteem in general.

On Thursday evening, the day before she was going to be tested at school, she stumbled a few times on the first run-through, and then managed it word perfect. I praised her immensely and said, 'Donna, there is something I want to try now. Don't worry if you can't do it but just have a go. I'm going to ask you questions on the tables, jump around and see if you know the answers. You have done so well learning them, so let's see how well you can do these.' I began easily with 2 x 2 and she gave the correct answer of 4; then I asked 5 x 2 and she answered 10. I returned to 0 x 2, then 3 x 2 and so on, until I had covered the easy ones; then I began on those that had caused Donna problems.

'6 x 2?' I asked.

'12.'

'Excellent! 8 x 2?' She didn't know, and I saw her confidence immediately tumble. 'Don't worry,' I said. 'Go back to the last one you do know and say the table from there in your head. You know 5 x 2.'

'10,' she said.

'So in your head, go on from there.'

Half a minute later she had come up with the right answer of 16. I clapped and said, 'Great! Excellent!' I knew that in the test she might not have time to go through the whole table to supply the answer, and I hoped she wouldn't panic and forget the lot, so I said, 'If Miss Adams asks you one and you can't remember, don't worry, just leave a space and go on to the next one, which you will know.'

On Friday in the car going to school instead of reciting the table I dotted around with the questions: '3 x 2? 6 x 2? 11 x 2?' I had already primed Adrian and asked him not to answer, and as I glanced in the rear-view mirror I could see him sitting with his lips pursed tightly to stop the answers from spilling out. I smiled at him. Donna couldn't remember 7 x 2 or 9 x 2, and took some moments to go through the whole table in her head until she could supply the answer. With lots of praise and wishes of good luck, I saw her into school and returned to the car, with some relief that I wouldn't have to listen to the two times table again until Paula had to learn it in a year or so.

As I opened the door and got in Adrian and Paula were giggling.

'What's the matter with you two?' I asked with a smile.

'Listen to Paula,' Adrian said.

Paula laughed, and then in a bright clear voice she recited the two times table from beginning to end, word perfect. Without learning difficulties, and having listened to the tables in the car, her brain had automatically picked up and stored the information effortlessly. It highlighted the huge work Donna, or any child with learning difficulties, had to put in to achieve the same result.

'Well done,' I said to Paula. 'I expect it will be the three times next week!'

That evening when I met Donna from school the question that was burning on my tongue was answered as soon as I saw her. Her slow laborious way of walking was nowhere to be seen, and she bounded to my side.

'I got them all right!' she said, her face lighting up.

'You did? All of them!'

'Yes. And when Miss Adams jumbled up the questions I answered them!'

'That's absolutely fantastic!'

Beth Adams was just behind Donna and clearly wanted to speak to me. She stepped round the other children, who were filing out and meeting up with their parents in the playground. 'Donna has done amazingly well,' she said. 'She could write the table, recite it and answer all the questions. She has earned two house points for her team.'

We both praised Donna again, although Donna hardly needed our praise; having achieved something she had thought was impossible was praise enough.

I could tell that Beth Adams was pleased, and astounded. 'It's the three times table next week,' she said. 'I've put the work sheet in Donna's bag.'

'Thank you. We'll make a start on it over the weekend.' I did some quick mental arithmetic myself and calculated that if we had to learn one table a week, by the time we got to twelve it would be past Christmas and into the New Year!

We left, as usual, through the staff exit and crossed to the car, where Adrian and Paula were waiting. As Donna got in, without being asked, she said. 'I got them all right!' Adrian and Paula were as pleased as she and I were.

Learning the two times table typified Donna's ability to learn, and also mild learning difficulties in general. She wanted to learn and could learn, but it just took her a bit longer.

That evening when I took Donna to contact the first thing she said when Edna met us in reception was, 'I've learnt my two times table, and I was tested, and got them all right! I got two team points.' Edna knew the significance of this and was truly and genuinely in awe of Donna's achievement. She praised her immensely, and then thanked me for all the hard work I had put in. I later learnt that Beth Adams had asked Donna how she had learned her tables so well, and Donna had told her what we had done. Beth Adams had then phoned Edna and told her of my input, and also that Donna was starting to learn in other areas with a newfound confidence. I was so very pleased.

However, I also learnt that when Donna had gone into contact that evening, and had told her family of her success, her mother and Chelsea had ignored her and turned their backs. Edna had said, 'Rita, Donna's got some good news. Listen to her.' Donna had repeated her news, and Rita had shrugged, while Warren and Jason said, 'Easy peasy,' and laughed. It was Edna who told me this, not Donna: she had just accepted yet another rejection.

Chapter Twelve

Working as a Family

By the first week in November I was beginning to feel that Donna was making some real progress, and things were going pretty well. Although she still found it almost impossible to play with Adrian and Paula, preferring to watch them or amuse herself, I was finding I could relax a little and be less vigilant when she was in a room with Paula. Donna didn't appear to be trying to dominate and chastise Paula as much as she had done in the past.

The first week in November was a busy one for 'official' visits: Jill and Edna both paid their six-weekly visit, in the evening after school, Jill on Tuesday and Edna on Thursday. I had been in regular contact with both of them since they had last visited – Jill by telephone, and Edna when I saw her briefly before and after contact. Their visits were therefore more perfunctory than they might have been otherwise – just to see Donna at home and make sure everything was going all right. When Edna visited she also took the opportunity of telling me that Warren and Jason still hadn't said anything to Mary and Ray about the 'punishment' (if that was what it was) that they had received in their mother's bed, although, like Edna, Mary and Ray were convinced that the boys were hiding something, and felt that it would take time before they trusted them sufficiently to confide in them. The boys might have been unwilling to betray their mother, as they had been her favourites and they appeared to have a stronger bond with her than Donna did, presumably because their treatment at her hands had been less severe, or their silence might have been based on fear – no one knew at this stage.

The Guardian Ad Litem phoned that week as well and made her first visit the following Tuesday. Her name was Cheryl Samson. She was appointed by the court for the duration of the case and her role was an important one. As the Guardian for the boys and Chelsea as well as Donna, she would visit all the parties involved in the case a number of times, then write a detailed report for the judge, stating her findings and what she believed to be in the long-term best interest for the children. Her final recommendation as to where the children would live permanently would be vital to the judge when he made his decision at the final court hearing in May the following year. Cheryl was an experienced Guardian and quite forthright in her manner. When she arrived she spent some time talking to Donna and me together, and then me alone. She had met all members of Donna's family and was also in regular contact with Edna.

'Donna has been completely rejected and victimised by Rita,' Cheryl said to me, 'to an extent I have never seen before. She has been a scapegoat, blamed for all the family's ills. Why, I don't know, but Rita can't even look at her when they are in the same room. I'm not sure how much good contact is doing Donna, and I shall be looking to reduce it as we approach the final court hearing.'

'For the boys as well?' I asked. If it was just Donna's contact that was reduced it could have appeared to her a further victimisation by singling her out again.

'Absolutely,' Cheryl agreed. 'I can't see there is any way they can return to live at home, so contact needs to be reduced for all the children. Rita can't get off the drink and drugs and she is refusing any help. Edna has put in so much support but there has been no improvement in the home. I do not want Donna and the boys to follow in Chelsea's footsteps. Chelsea is just fifteen and we've now found out she's pregnant!'

'Oh no! Really?'

Cheryl nodded. 'Rita announced it to Edna yesterday after contact, as though it was something to be proud of. Edna has been trying to persuade Chelsea to go into foster care for some time, and Rita told Edna she couldn't move her now she was pregnant. But she's wrong on that count. I want Chelsea moved into a mother and baby unit, assuming she is pregnant and it's not a ruse of Rita's making. Chelsea says she doesn't know who the father is; apparently there's a choice of three.'

I didn't comment; it wasn't for me to pass judgement on Chelsea's morals, although of course it was illegal to have sexual intercourse with a girl under sixteen. 'Will Chelsea keep the baby?' I asked. I remembered that when I had seen Chelsea outside the school gates on that first day of term she'd appeared grubby and uncared for, barely able to look after herself, let alone a baby.

'We'll give her a chance and monitor her closely, which is another reason why I want her in a mother and baby unit.'

I nodded. 'It's Donna's birthday on the sixteenth of November and she would like a bowling party,' I said, lightening the subject. 'We are going to ask her brothers to come, but what about Chelsea? Should we invite her?'

'It's a nice thought, but Chelsea is sure to turn up with Mum, so I think the answer is no. Edna will arrange a birthday tea for Donna at contact, so Chelsea will have the chance to celebrate Donna's birthday then, if she has a mind to.' I knew what Cheryl meant: judging from the reception Donna had been receiving from Chelsea and Rita at contact it was hardly likely they were going to put much effort into celebrating Donna's birthday. One of the reasons I had suggested we invited Chelsea was to try to forge a better relationship between her and her sister, but I would be guided by the Guardian. I couldn't risk Rita, with her bad attitude towards Donna, turning up at the party and possibly ruining it.

'All right,' I said. 'Is there anyone else in the wider family I should invite? Cousins?'

'No. I should keep it to your family, Donna and the boys. And there's her special friend Emily at school?'

'Yes, that's right. We shall be inviting Emily. Donna doesn't find it very easy to make friends, so there will just be the seven of us, including me.'

Cheryl smiled. 'She'll enjoy it. I doubt she will have had a party before, of any description. I don't think she even had presents on her birthday and Christmas last year.' Which unfortunately was true for many of the children I fostered.

On Sunday I helped Donna to write some colourful birthday invitations; on each one she had to fill in the name of the person invited, the time and the venue, and sign it. I had already booked the bowling alley for Sunday

15 November, the day before Donna's birthday. The package they offered included an organiser/entertainer, two games of bowling for each child, a party tea and a 'goody bag' to take home. I had asked Donna sometime before, when I had first brought up the subject of her birthday, what she had done for her last birthday, and she had shrugged and said she didn't know, from which I had guessed that it was nothing, or something so insignificant as not to merit being treasured as a fond memory. Now as we worked side by side on the table in the annexe, and I watched her slide the invitations into the envelopes and then address them with so much care and precision, I casually brought up the topic again.

'You are doing a really good job there, Donna,' I said. 'Have you ever written birthday invitations before?'

She shook her head. 'No.'

'Not all families have birthday parties, but we do,' I said. 'It's nice to have fun.' She didn't say anything but concentrated on meticulously sliding the next invitation, which was to Warren, into the envelope. 'I think it helps you to remember your birthday if you do something a bit special. It is an important day, after all.'

'I can remember my last birthday,' Donna said stoically. 'Very well. I had to do the washing.'

I glanced sideways at her. 'Oh yes?'

'Mum said as it was my birthday everyone could have clean clothes. Dad wasn't there, but Mum, Chelsea and the boys all went and changed and brought me their dirty washing. Then Mum went round the house and gathered up all the clothes and rags that were lying around, and the stuff from her wardrobe, and dumped it in the kitchen. I spent all day washing. We didn't have a washing machine like you do, and it took ages in the sink. Then I had to try and get it dry, 'cos no one had any more clean clothes, and we didn't have a washing line. Mum hit me with a wet towel when I couldn't get it dry, and then told Chelsea and the boys to hit me.'

I looked at her and swallowed hard. Donna had said it so matter-of-factly she could have been telling me how she'd poached an egg; she was now carefully filling in her name on the next invitation, making sure she didn't make a mistake. I couldn't speak for the lump in my throat and I waited for the moment to pass.

'How do you spell Adrian?' she asked glancing up at me.

I swallowed again, and spelt it out. 'Donna, love,' I said, placing my hand on her arm and trying to raise a smile, 'one thing I can guarantee is that you won't be doing any washing on your birthday this year, or at any time in my house.'

She smiled sadly.

When she'd finished writing the invitations I asked Donna again if there was anyone else in her class or the school whom she wanted to invite to her party, but there wasn't; she then gave me my invitation, and Adrian and Paula theirs. We smiled and thanked her. Donna would give out Emily's and her brothers' invitations at school the following day. I opened my invitation and said I would be happy to come to her party and she smiled.

However, at bedtime when I tucked Paula into bed she said in a subdued and embarrassed voice, 'Mum, I don't want to go to Donna's party. Do I have to?'

I looked at her, surprised – that wasn't like her. 'Why not?' I asked. 'What's the matter? There's only us and Warren, Jason and Emily going.'

'Nothing's the matter. I don't want to go,' she said quietly.

I sat on the bed. 'Paula, there is something the matter. You must have a good reason for not wanting to go to something as important as Donna's birthday party?'

'I don't like her,' she said and she looked at me, half-expecting to be told off. This was totally out of character for Paula, and I knew there must be something badly worrying her. I settled myself on the bed for a long chat. Paula wasn't easily fazed, but when something did trouble her it became ingrained and took a while to uncover.

'What made you say you didn't like Donna?' I asked gently. 'I know she doesn't play with you, but she hasn't hit you again, has she?'

Paula shook her head. 'She didn't hit me.'

'So what has made you feel like this?' There was a long pause. 'Come on, Paula, I need to know so that I can put it right. This is important for all of us. If something is going on you must tell me.'

There was another long pause before Paula eventually said, 'Adrian doesn't like her either.'

I was taken aback, and also a little annoyed that I wasn't getting any closer to the root cause of the problem. Clearly there had been a conversation between Adrian and Paula that I hadn't been party to. 'Why doesn't Adrian like Donna?' I asked.

'Same reason as me.'

'Which is?'

'She doesn't like us.'

I gave an inward sigh. I was going round in circles, and I was starting to wonder if it was just a childish falling out, although I couldn't remember an incident taking place that could have led to them 'falling out'; indeed Donna hardly interacted enough with Adrian and Paula for there to have been a tiff.

'What makes you think she doesn't like you, Paula?' I asked. 'I'm sure Donna does like you.'

'No she doesn't,' Paula said adamantly.

'Well, tell me why you think that and I'll try to put it right. I can't do anything unless you tell me. How long have you both felt like this? And why haven't you said anything before?'

'You are always too busy with Donna, and you like her. We didn't want to make you upset.' And I had a sinking feeling, not for the first time since I'd started fostering, that I really wasn't getting it right after all, and I hadn't seen what was going on under my own nose.

'Look, love,' I said, 'I am never too busy to listen to you and Adrian. I thought you knew that. I like Donna, and I feel very sorry for her because of her past, but that doesn't mean I love you less. I had no idea that Adrian and you felt this way, and you should have said something sooner – at bedtime. We always have a chat at bedtime. Now, love, can you please tell me why you think Donna doesn't like you, so that I can do something about it. I know she hit you, but that was a while ago and I thought you'd forgiven her. Has something else happened recently that I should have known about? Has she said or done something to make you think she doesn't like you?'

There was another long pause before Paula said, 'It's not what she's done but the way she looks at us. It's like she's telling us off with her look, without saying anything.'

I paused and considered this. 'Can you explain a bit more, or show me the look?' I didn't dismiss what Paula said as childish sensitivity because I was well aware that control could come in many shapes and forms, and once the seeds of control (or fear) have been sown, a look can reinforce it as much as any words. Parents use the technique as a normal part of child rearing: the look, the warning that the child has done something that has overstepped the mark, and they'd better not do it again – a censorious expression. Although I had been very vigilant, I now wondered if I had missed something. Was Donna trying to control Paula and Adrian by a look? Perhaps along the lines her mother had done at home (and was possibly still doing at contact)?

'I can't make the face she does,' Paula said. 'It's in her eyes, the way she looks, like this.' She widened her eyes and glared at me in an expression of 'I'm warning you: I know what you're up to, and you'd better watch out or else.' 'Adrian can tell you better,' Paula said. 'It's not nice, it frightens me and I don't want to go to her party.'

'All right love,' I said. 'Thanks for telling me. I'll talk to Adrian, and then I'll work out a way to put it right. I just wish you had told me sooner. Next time something bothers you, tell me: don't brood on it.'

She nodded. I lay on the bed next to her and read her a bedtime story; then, reassuring her again that I would put it right, I kissed her goodnight and came out. Donna was in her room, getting ready for bed. I could hear her moving around; it always took her a while before she settled. I went into Adrian's room. He was propped up in bed, reading.

'It's not time to say goodnight yet,' he said.

'No, love, I know. But I need to talk to you about something Paula has just told me.' Once again, I sat on the edge of the bed. Adrian put down his book, and I repeated what

Paula had said. By the time I'd finished, Adrian was nodding furiously. 'She does this,' he said, and widening his eyes, he glared at me with a really angry, accusing, threatening expression; whether it was exaggerated or not I didn't know.

'So why didn't you tell me?' I said. 'You're older than Paula. I would have thought you could have come and told me.'

'You're always so busy with Donna,' he said, echoing Paula's words. 'I was going to, but when I thought about what I could say – "I don't like the way Donna looks at me" – it sounded silly. So I stick my tongue out when she does it to me. But it frightens Paula.'

I looked at him as his gaze fell to his open book. How many times since I had started fostering had I reminded myself to make sure my time was divided equally between all my children – continuously? It was something that was always on my mind. But if I was honest, I could see that when I looked after a child with a high level of needs, as in Donna's case, I had to give the fostered child more than their fair share of attention, to welcome and settle them into our family and ensure all their needs were met – apparently to the detriment of Adrian and Paula.

'Sorry,' I said.

Adrian looked up and shrugged. 'It doesn't matter.'

'It does matter,' I said firmly. 'I realise now how much time I have been putting into Donna. I just assumed you two were all right but now I know, I shall be able to do something about it.' Adrian nodded. 'I will be keeping a close eye on Donna. I like her a lot, but she has been treated very badly by her family. I think she is copying the way she was treated at home. She doesn't know any different, and part of our job is to show her a different way. But I'm not having you and Paula upset. It makes me sad, Adrian. I love you both so much.'

'I know,' he said quietly. 'We love you too.'

'So will you work with me on this? And tell me if anything else crops up in the future?' I couldn't have a sub-plot running in the family, with Adrian and Paula in collusion and not telling me. A foster family is a unit where all members pull together, including natural and foster children, with no double standards; otherwise it's impossible to make it work.

'Yes,' he said.

'Good boy. Thanks, Adrian. I'll leave you to your book now. Hopefully in a week's time, when it's Donna's party, you and Paula will feel comfortable enough to join in, and enjoy it. There's only us, her brothers and Emily going.'

He nodded and picked up his book. I kissed his forehead. 'It's eight thirty. I'll come up again in half an hour to say goodnight.' I left him once more immersed in Roald Dahl's *Revolting Rhymes*, which apparently they were studying at school.

I didn't raise the matter with Donna that night, for when I thought about it, what could I have reasonably said? 'Donna, Paula and Adrian don't like the way you are looking at them. Could you stop it, please?' Such a complaint seemed as 'silly' to my ears as it had done to Adrian's, and also I wanted to see at first hand what exactly they were talking about before I said anything to Donna.

I didn't have to wait long.

The following morning at breakfast I was presented with a classic example. Paula was sitting opposite Donna at the table, with Adrian to her side. The three children were eating, and I had just made some fresh toast and was carrying it through to take my place at the end of the table. A cornflake dropped off Paula's spoon on to the table and I saw Paula immediately look up at Donna, as though expecting censure. She was well rewarded: Donna's eyes widened and she stared at Paula – an all-in-one package of anger, chastisement and a warning that it shouldn't happen again, or else!

'It's only a cornflake,' I said to Donna, 'and there's no need for you to tell her off.'

Donna looked at me, shocked and surprised by my sudden insight. 'I didn't say anything,' she said.

'No, you didn't have to. Does your mother look at you like that?'

Donna looked doubly shocked by my second stab of insight and stopped eating her wheat flakes.

'Does she?' I asked. 'Because if so it's not nice.'

She didn't say anything but remained very quiet and still, as did Paula and Adrian. I didn't think that Donna was particularly concerned about the cornflake being dropped and making a (small) mess; it was that she was reverting to learned behaviour, seizing any opportunity to discipline, blame and punish a family member as had happened to her at home.

My voice was even but firm, as I buttered my toast and continued, 'Harsh words are bad, but harsh looks are equally bad,' I said. 'They can make you feel uncomfortable and threatened. There is a saying – a picture paints a thousand words, and your look just now, Donna, painted a picture of anger with a punishment to follow.' I looked around the table. 'We are a family here – all four of us,' I said, 'and we work together as a family. If anyone has a problem they come to me, and I will try to put it right. I am the adult, the parent here, and if any one of my children – Adrian, Paula or you, Donna – needs correcting in any way, I shall do it. I will not have anyone else trying to tell another family member what to do, either through words or looks. It's a form of bullying. And no one bullies anyone in this family, or anyone outside it.' They were quiet and I felt the atmosphere weigh heavy, for rarely did I speak so harshly, and to everyone. Normally I dealt with the little incidents that arose individually, but clearly this was a whole family matter and needed direct, collective and immediate input.

'So now we will finish our breakfast and get ready for school,' I said. 'And I don't want to see any more looks or tongue poking from anyone. Do I make myself clear?'

Adrian and Paula nodded, very subdued. Donna remained quiet and still. I picked up my toast and continued eating. Adrian finished first and left the table to go to the bathroom and brush his teeth. I looked between Donna and Paula.

'You know, Donna,' I said more gently. 'Paula could be like a little sister to you. You never had a younger sister at home and she's dying to play with you.'

Paula looked hopefully at Donna, and we both waited, but still feeling bruised by my lecture, Donna wasn't about to give anything away just yet. After a moment she shrugged and then picked up her spoon and began eating again. When Paula had finished she left the table to take her turn in the bathroom. I looked at Donna again. 'That look you have been giving Paula and Adrian – is that what your mother has been giving you at contact? I know your mum can't say horrible things to you at contact because Edna stops her, but a look is easy to hide and just as hurtful. Particularly if it has a history and makes you remember hurtful things that happened in the past.'

Donna gave a small nod. 'She always does it.'

'OK, I'll speak to Edna. You should have told me. Your mum shouldn't behave like that, and you mustn't do it here any more. Now go into the bathroom when Paula has finished and do your teeth. We're going to give out your invitations to Emily, Warren and Jason today,' I added brightly.

Donna left the table without saying anything, and sulking. But now that I'd spoken directly and firmly the matter was dealt with and would be put behind us, although obviously I would still be vigilant. Old habits die hard and Donna had spent all her life learning this behaviour, so it wasn't going to disappear overnight.

After I had taken the children to school I telephoned Edna and explained what had happened. Edna treated the matter with the seriousness I had done, well aware that fear and control come in many forms. She said she would watch Rita closely, and asked me to tell her immediately if Donna said she had experienced the look again at contact. I also told Edna that Donna was giving out party invitations today – to Warren, Jason and Emily – but in view of the Guardian's advice we wouldn't be giving one to Chelsea, with which Edna agreed.

'Donna's birthday is on a Monday,' Edna said, 'so I'll do a special tea at contact that evening, and I'll remind Rita and Chelsea to buy a present. In fact I think I'll buy presents for them to give to Donna, because Rita will say she hasn't any money. If I give her money it's sure to go on something else – drink. Have you got any suggestions for presents?'

'Donna likes making things,' I said. 'How about some sort of craft set? A jewellery-making set or basket weaving? We've bought her a bike. She's never owned a bike before.'

'That's very generous of you, Cathy,' Edna said. 'Is the birthday money enough to cover it?' She was referring to the allowance that is paid to foster carers towards the cost of the looked-after child's birthday present and party. It wasn't enough to cover it, but if foster carers kept only to the allowance, children would have pretty meagre birthdays.

'No problem,' I said. 'It has helped towards the cost.'

By the time I collected Donna from school that afternoon the heavy atmosphere of the morning had lifted, and she told me she had given out her invitations and Emily had immediately said she could definitely come.

The following day, without the quick turnaround necessary for contact, I made a point of seeing Emily's mother, Mandy, and confirmed the arrangements for Sunday. Emily hadn't been to tea yet – I had left an open invitation with Mandy – and Mandy was very pleased that Emily would be going to Donna's party, for like Donna, Emily found it difficult to make friends. I told Mandy who would be going to the party, and she said she would drop Emily off at the bowling alley at 2.30 p.m., and then collect her at the end at 5.00. She also asked what Donna would like for a present. I said I'd give it some thought, but I was sure Emily could suggest something; as her best friend she would know what Donna liked.

* * *

The week as usual ran away with us, and very quickly it was Friday and Donna's party was two days away. However, this took a back seat on Friday morning when Donna went into school to be tested on her three times table. We had been practising the three times all week, as we had done the previous week with the two times table, and I wished her luck, as did Adrian and Paula. We'd had only two incidents of Donna giving that 'look' to Paula, and I'd dealt with it by saying a firm 'No' to Donna. Adrian and Paula seemed more relaxed in her company now that they were aware I was dealing with the situation. Donna had accepted my 'No' and spent only a short while sulking, for she was too excited about her party to sulk for long.

It was only when I arrived home on Friday morning, having dropped the children off at school, that I realised I hadn't had confirmation from Mary and Ray that Warren and Jason would be coming to Donna's party, although I'd assumed they would be. Occasionally I saw Mary and Ray going in or coming out of school, but not often, and I wouldn't have the chance to seek them out in the afternoon because I had to do the quick turnaround for contact. I thought I would give them a ring, just to confirm that the boys had shown them the invitations and would be at the bowling alley at 2.30 p.m. for Donna's party. I phoned at lunchtime, Mary answered, and I knew immediately something was wrong.

Chapter Thirteen

The Birthday Party

'Cathy,' Mary said slowly, as though gathering her thoughts. 'I was going to phone you. I have been putting if off, in the hope that the boys could be persuaded to change their minds.' I didn't say anything, and waited as Mary paused again before continuing. 'I'm sorry, Cathy, but Warren and Jason are saying they won't come to Donna's party. I have been trying to persuade them all week, but they are stubbornly refusing.' She stopped, and I could tell she was as uncomfortable and disappointed to be giving me the news as I was to be receiving it.

'Why not?' I asked. 'There's only Warren, Jason, Emily and us going. There's nothing for them to be worried about. You can stay with them if they want you to.'

'No, it's not that,' she said, and she paused again. I thought, what on earth is it then? This is the boys' sister's birthday we're talking about! 'Look, Cathy, I don't know if the boys have been got at by their mother or whether it's a continuation of their behaviour towards Donna from the past. But they are both saying they won't come to the party, and have rightly pointed out that Ray and I can't force them to go. I told Edna yesterday, and she asked me to talk to them again to see if I could find out what the problem was, and if I could get them to change their minds. I can't. Edna said she was going to speak to you later today.' Mary stopped and there was a very awkward silence.

'Donna will be very disappointed,' I said at last. 'She has been planning this party all week. It's all she talks about. It won't be much of a party with just Emily and us there.'

'I know,' Mary said sadly. 'That's what I told the boys, but they just shook their heads and wouldn't budge.'

'And they haven't said why they don't want to come?'

'Not exactly, although Warren said, "Mum wouldn't like it," which is why I'm pretty certain it's come from Rita. The boys went to a friend's birthday party last Sunday with no problem; they're not shy. I'm sure Rita has told them not to go.'

'That's dreadful,' I said, appalled. 'If that is so, then Rita is still managing to victimise Donna, even from a distance! It could only have happened at contact. Somehow Rita has got at them.'

'I know. That's what Edna said. Although she's no idea how. I didn't push it with her, because she's such a dear and I know she feels it personally. Edna never leaves them alone at contact, but of course she only has to turn her back for a second and Rita could have easily whispered in Warren's ear. Jason does as his older brother says.' I thought that with this, and the looks she had been slyly giving Donna, Rita was running rings around Edna at contact.

'All right,' I said, sad and deflated. 'I'll have to try to think of a way to tell Donna, although goodness knows what I'm going to say.'

'Do you want to tell her the boys are ill?' Mary asked. 'I wouldn't normally suggest lying, but I can't think of anything else.'

'I don't know. I'll phone Edna and see what she thinks. If the boys do change their minds, will you let me know?'

'Yes, of course, but I don't think they will. They are adamant. I'm so sorry, Cathy. I know how you must be feeling. I have bought a nice present for the boys to give to Donna, and also one from Ray and me. I'll send them with the boys to contact on Monday.'

'Thanks,' I said, no less disappointed. 'Let me know if they do change their minds, even if it's on Sunday morning.'

'I will do, but honestly Cathy, they wouldn't dare go against their mother, even now.'

'No,' I said. 'I know.'

We said goodbye and I put the phone down, my heart heavy and my plans for Donna's party falling apart. What mother does that to their daughter, I thought? It was vindictive to an unprecedented extent. Not only had Rita made Donna's life a misery for all the years she had been at home but she was now finding ways to continue doing so. By stopping the boys going, Rita was not only reinforcing her rejection and control, but also continuing to reinforce Donna's brothers' rejection of her. It was unbelievable. Rita must have known how much Donna's party would mean to her, particularly as it was the first one she'd ever had, and now she was sabotaging it! It was only ever going to have been a small affair because Donna only had one proper friend, and Rita couldn't even allow her that. I silently cursed the woman who, as far as I was concerned, had absolutely no claim to the title of mother apart from that of having given birth to her. I sincerely hoped she got her comeuppance one day.

I hovered by the phone, my mind frantically searching for any way to salvage Donna's party. There was no one else in her class she wanted to ask, and it was probably too late anyway to start issuing more invitations now. I considered phoning around my friends who fostered and inviting them and their children to the party, but what would have been the point in that? A party of strangers was hardly likely going to recompense Donna for her brothers' refusal to go. No, we were just going to have to do our best and make the most of it.

Just as I walked away from the phone it rang again and for a moment I thought it might be Mary, phoning back to say she'd thought of a way to persuade the boys to go.

'Hello?' I said, my spirits briefly rising. They fell again instantly. It was my ex-husband, John.

'Hello, Cathy,' he said, suitably subdued, aware that I hadn't fully appreciated his running off with a woman half his age three years previously. 'How are you?'

'Fine,' I said, which was what I usually said.

'I was due to see the children Sunday week,' he continued, 'but something's come up. Could I bring my visit forward to this Sunday?' That's all I need, I thought!

'I'm sorry,' I said. 'Adrian and Paula are going to a birthday party this Sunday. They are free on Saturday, though.'

'No can do Saturday. I've got tickets for the theatre in the evening – it would be too much of a rush.' Suit yourself, I thought, but didn't say. 'Couldn't they miss the party?'

'No, I'm afraid not. It's someone close.' He didn't have to know the details; he knew I still fostered, but my business was none of his concern now, unless it was related directly to Adrian and Paula.

'OK,' he said. 'I'll have to shift my visit back. I'm on holiday for a couple of weeks, so I'll see them a month on Sunday.'

'Fine,' I said. 'I'll put it in the diary. I'll tell Adrian and Paula you phoned.'

'Thanks.'

Curt possibly, but I hadn't been rude. I put down the phone and wondered what other bad omen was going to blow my way this Friday. It was just as well it wasn't Friday the 13th or else I could have been persuaded into feeling superstitious. Not only did I now have to tell Donna that her brothers wouldn't be coming to her party, but I also had to tell Adrian and Paula that their father was postponing his visit and wouldn't be coming for another month. They looked forward to seeing him, and although I had my own thoughts about his irresponsibility in deserting his family, I had kept them to myself and not let them get in the way of the children's relationship with him. The time they spent with their father was limited – one day a month (his decision) – and Adrian and Paula looked forward to his visits. The last time he had postponed, Adrian in particular had seen it as a personal rejection – 'He doesn't have to come at all if he doesn't want to,' he'd said moodily. It had taken me some while to persuade Adrian that his father did want to see him and that the postponement had been unavoidable.

Edna phoned five minutes before I was due to leave the house to collect the children from school.

'I'm sorry,' she said. 'I didn't realise the time.' She apologised again for the boys not wanting to go to Donna's party, feeling that it was her fault that the boys had been 'got at', as she put it. 'Cathy,' she said, 'I'm going to try to find a colleague to help me supervise the contact in future. You need eyes in the back of your head when Rita and Chelsea are together. They're a devious pair, and I know how cruel they can be to Donna, but I'm shocked they have stooped this low. Trouble is I'm finding it difficult to get someone to commit to staying until six thirty three nights a week.'

I could see her problem; I doubted many of her colleagues would want to extend their working days into the evening, one of the evenings being a Friday. In my experience Edna's commitment was well beyond the norm, and proof of her dedication and love of her work.

'What will you tell Donna?' she asked.

'I really don't know yet. I think it might be the truth. If I lie to Donna and tell her the boys are ill, and she finds out they aren't, it's going to undermine her trust in me. I'm not sure yet what to say. I'll give it some more thought. I'm sorry, Edna, I'm going to have to go now or I'll be late collecting the children from school.'

'Yes, of course. Sorry, Cathy,' she said, finishing as she had started.

I left Adrian and Paula in the car in the staff car park while I went in to collect Donna from school. It was pouring down and the rain had a cold biting edge to it, which said winter was just around the corner. I was so preoccupied with the bad news of the day that I had completely forgotten about the three times table test, and I wondered why Donna was bounding towards me, and why Beth Adams was close behind her, clearly wanting to see me.

'I remembered them all!' Donna exclaimed. 'And got all the test right!'

'She did,' Beth Adams confirmed.

It took me a moment to realise what they were talking about. 'Excellent,' I said. 'That's fantastic news. Well done, love.'

'I have earned another two team points,' Donna said, beaming.

'She deserves it,' Beth Adams said. 'The three times table is a tricky one, and only half the class got all the test right. Donna was one of them!'

I congratulated Donna again, and thanked Beth Adams. It was the best news I'd had all day, and also proved that with time and a lot of hard work Donna could learn as well as anyone. I thought that Beth Adams was going to have to readjust her expectations of what Donna could achieve, for if this was an indication of what Donna was capable of, then she had only just begun!

That evening when Donna was in the bath I told Paula and Adrian that I needed to talk to them. Without making a big issue of it, and thereby hopefully minimising their disappointment, I told them that unfortunately their father had had to postpone his visit planned for the following Sunday. Paula didn't say anything, which didn't surprise me, for if I was honest she had less of a bond with her father than Adrian did; she'd been only three when John had left and didn't remember a time when he'd lived with us. Adrian had been seven, and remembered a different family where his father had been present, and perhaps also because he was a boy, he had suffered more when his father had suddenly gone. Predictably, now Adrian was the one who made the comment 'What is more important than seeing us?' And as I was put in the position of having to defend my ex for the sake of Adrian maintaining a positive image of his father, I felt that familiar stab of irritation.

'He didn't say exactly why he couldn't come,' I said. 'But he made a special point of asking me to tell you that he is sorry. And that he misses you both and loves you very much.' Which softened the blow a little, as it had done in the past when he'd postponed a visit. I moved swiftly on. 'I'm afraid there is another piece of disappointing news,' I said. 'And I'm going to need your help on this one. Both of you.' They looked at me questioningly. 'It's not about your father,' I added quickly. 'But I have learnt this afternoon that Donna's brothers won't be coming to her party.'

'Why?' they asked together.

'It's something to do with her mother,' I hedged.

'What?' Adrian said. 'We'll look after them if that's what she's worried about.'

I wish, I thought. 'No, I'm afraid it's more to do with the bad way she treated Donna at home, and her not wanting Donna to have a good time.'

'That's horrible,' Paula said.

'It won't be much of a party if no one's coming,' Adrian said. 'I had twelve at mine.'

'I know, love. And that is why I'm going to need your help. I'm not going to say anything to Donna yet: I'm still hoping her brothers' carers can persuade them to change their minds. But if they can't, then the three of us and Emily must make sure Donna has a wonderful time. I'm sure we can do it.'

Paula nodded and Adrian said, 'I could ask some of my friends to come?'

I smiled. 'That's sweet of you, and I had thought of that, but I don't think it will be the same for Donna. She doesn't really know them, does she?'

'But why doesn't Donna's mum want her to have a good time?' Paula asked, her naïve and unsullied innocence making it impossible for her to grasp the concept of such nastiness from a mother to a daughter.

'Donna's mother treated Donna very badly,' I said, 'which is why she came into care. I think she's still trying to do it from a distance. By making her feel rejected and unloved.'

'I love Donna,' Paula said, looking very sad, and my heart gave that little lurch. 'We'll make sure she has a good time. You don't need lots of people. It's the ones close to you who count.'

'Exactly,' I said, smiling at Paula. 'I couldn't have put it better myself.'

Over the weekend, when we weren't learning the four times table, Adrian and Paula paid Donna extra attention, and went out of their way to talk to her and suggest games she might like to join in. They clearly felt the rejection that Donna would be feeling if her brothers didn't change their minds and come to the party. It was at times like this that I was most proud of Adrian and Paula: I was always proud of them, but the tenderness and concern they showed for Donna highlighted their empathy and insight into Donna's plight, feeling as most children from normal families would have done. However, in making these friendly advances towards Donna, Paula and Adrian had left themselves wide open, and I had to remind Donna a few times over the weekend not to try to boss Adrian and

Paula or discipline them. It wasn't Donna's fault; she was simply reverting to the example of how her family had treated her in the previous ten years. Adrian and Paula, now more aware of what Donna had been through, and with her party looming, were even more forgiving.

By 12.00 noon on Sunday, when I hadn't heard anything from Mary and Ray, I had to finally admit that Warren and Jason wouldn't be coming, and I braced myself to tell Donna.

She was in her bedroom, already sorting through her wardrobe of clothes, trying to choose what to wear for the party, although there was plenty of time – we didn't have to get ready until 1.00 p.m. at the earliest, to leave the house at 2.00. Her bedroom door was open and, giving my usual knock, I went in. Donna turned to look at me, new trousers in one hand and pink sweatshirt in the other.

'I think I'll wear these,' she said, holding them up. 'I was going to wear a skirt. But when I bend over to bowl I might show my knickers in a skirt.' She gave a small laugh.

'I think that's a good choice, and you haven't worn either of them yet. It's nice to wear something new for a party.' I hesitated, as Donna again looked at the clothes, clearly considering if this was going to be her final decision. Best get on with what I had to say, I thought. 'Donna, I'm afraid that Warren and Jason won't be coming today, so you'll celebrate your birthday with them tomorrow at contact.'

She moved towards the wardrobe and looked in again. 'No, I will wear these. I'm not going to change my mind again,' she said.

'I think they are fine,' I said again, and paused. 'Donna, did you hear what I said, love? The boys can't make it this afternoon.'

'I heard. I expect Mum told them not to come.'

I was taken aback, and also quietly relieved that I'd been saved the awful job of telling her the reason, although I wasn't going to make it worse by confirming it with detail. 'It's possible.' I said. 'Mary doesn't know for sure.' I paused, waiting for some kind of reaction as the information sunk in.

'It's their loss,' she said after a moment. 'They are the ones missing out, not me.' And so saying, Donna put the clothes she had chosen on her bed and closed the wardrobe door. 'Will you help me do my hair when I've changed? I want it to look nice for the party.'

'Of course, love,' I said. 'Give me a shout when you're ready. We'll use those new hair braids I bought, shall we?'

She nodded, her face lighting up.

'Come here and give me a hug,' I said. 'You're a lovely person.'

She came over and I put my arms round her and gave her a big hug. For the first time since she had arrived I felt her arms tighten around my waist as she returned it. After a moment she eased away. 'I'm going to get changed now,' she said. 'I'm so excited. This is going to be my best birthday ever! Thanks for giving me the party, Cathy. I can't wait to get there!'

I smiled, and felt my eyes well. 'You're welcome, love.'

While I had spent the entire weekend angsting over our depleted numbers, aware how Adrian and Paula would have felt if they'd been in Donna's position with having only one friend and us attend, Donna, bless her, having never had a birthday party before and therefore having no expectations, had simply accepted the non-attendance of her brothers in her usual stoical manner.

I left Donna to change and went downstairs.

'Donna's fine,' I said to Adrian and Paula, who were in the lounge looking very concerned, aware that I had gone upstairs to break the 'bad' news.

'Good on her!' Adrian said.

'I told you,' Paula said. 'It's not how many who go to your party, but who.'

I nodded, and hugged them both, my spirits lighter than they had been since I'd received the news on Friday. And as I acknowledged the sensible rationale of all three children, I felt that as an adult I could probably learn a lot from them.

By 1.45 p.m. the four of us were changed into our party best and in the hall ready to leave. I had braided Donna's hair; she'd inherited dark brown and slightly curly hair from her father and with the new braids she looked very pretty. I arranged the children in a semi-circle in the hall and took a photograph of them before we left, and then another as they got into the car. I wanted a record of Donna's party and birthday; there would be a copy for her and one for my album. I had no idea if Donna would be with us for her next birthday; that would depend on the outcome of the court case.

I took another photograph of the three children going into the bowling alley, and then two more as we went inside. Adrian was getting embarrassed by now – having to stand still and pose between the girls. It was 2.15 p.m., but we weren't the only ones who had arrived early, for as

I tucked my camera into my handbag Emily appeared with her mother.

'Happy birthday!' Mandy called as they came over. Donna smiled sheepishly. 'You look nice, all of you.' Mandy had met Paula and Adrian in the playground on the occasions when they had come into the school with me.

Emily gave Donna a small box-shaped present, gaily wrapped and tied with ribbon. 'Happy birthday,' she said, giving her a kiss on the cheek.

'Thanks,' Donna said. She took the present and then held it as if it was the first one she'd ever received in her life, which it might well have been. She would be having her presents from us on her actual birthday the following morning.

Emily and Donna began chatting and laughing excitedly, glancing at the bowling lanes and pointing. It was lovely to see Donna so relaxed, and happy, and with her friend.

'There's just going to be us,' I said quietly to Mandy. 'Donna's brothers can't come.'

'Oh dear,' she said. 'That's a pity, but I'm sure Donna will have a good time. Emily hasn't stopped talking about this party all weekend. She was changed and ready by twelve thirty.'

I laughed. 'Same with Donna.' And we both glanced at the girls, giggling and whispering excitedly. 'Emily must come to tea, if she feels ready now,' I said, renewing my invitation.

'Yes, I'm sure she'll be fine now,' Mandy said. 'And Donna must come to us too. We'll arrange something next week.' Mandy confirmed she would return to collect Emily at 5.30 p.m., and we said goodbye. 'Have a lovely time!' she called to the children as she left, and Emily gave a little wave.

Leaving the children in a small group, I went over to the reception desk a couple of yards away and gave my name. 'I've booked for seven including me,' I said. 'But there will only be five of us, four children. Unfortunately two can't come.'

'No problem,' the girl on reception said. 'I'll introduce you to your party organiser. Lisa,' she called to a girl who was tidying the bowling shoes at the far end of reception. 'Lisa, this is Cathy Glass,' she introduced. 'The party is for Donna, who will be eleven.'

Lisa smiled brightly at me. She was about eighteen and had a light and fun manner. 'Is everyone here?' she said glancing at the clock. 'Because if so we can make a start.'

'Yes, unfortunately two children can't come,' I confirmed again.

'So it's four children and yourself?'

'That's right.'

'We'll have lots of fun. First we'll bowl, and then we'll have some games, then the party tea and then another game of bowling. How does that sound?'

'Sounds good to me,' I said.

'If you could bring the children over, I'll sort out their bowling shoes first.'

I waved to the children to come over, and they ran to my side; from then on Lisa took charge, and I did as I was told. She asked us what shoe size we were and handed us each a pair of bowling shoes, storing our own shoes in a rack at the end of the reception area. Then she gave us each a large name badge. It was about three inches across and decorated with pictures of multi-coloured balloons, with the name of the person printed in red in the centre. As Lisa led us over to lane twenty, which was set aside for the party, my anxieties about Donna having less than the best party finally evaporated. Large balloons in every colour imaginable hung in bunches from the ceiling the entire length of the bowling lane, and a massive banner declaring 'HAPPY BIRTHDAY' stretched from one side to the other.

'Look!' Donna exclaimed as we approached the lane. 'That's for me!'

'It is,' Lisa said, 'especially for you! It's your special day.'

We grouped at the end of the lane as Lisa gave us a brief talk on how to bowl safely – that is, without dropping the bowl on our toes, falling over it or getting our fingers stuck in the holes. 'I hope you're listening to this,' Adrian said to me with a laugh.

Then, with Donna naturally going first, we began the game. There was a lot of cheering and jumping up and down as Donna's ball swerved and rolled down the lane towards its target, knocking three pins over with the first ball and two with the second. Emily went next, then Adrian and Paula, and I went last. And it was pure fluke, for I am the world's worst at bowling, but somehow my ball went on target (probably helped by the sides being up), and I scored nine with my first ball and then felled the tenth with my second. Everyone clapped and cheered, and Adrian good-humouredly yelled, 'Fixed!'

Lisa didn't bowl but gave an exciting running commentary as we took our turns, and also helped Paula, who was struggling, even with the lighter children's ball. Our excitement grew as the game continued and the scores mounted on the display board, until there was only a few points' difference between the two leaders – Donna and Adrian. I saw the family who were playing on the lane next to ours glance across; so too did Donna, and she beamed. Possibly for the first time in her life she was the centre of attention in a positive way, and she was loving every minute of it. And while Adrian was the stronger bowler (having had lots of practice in the past) I noticed that his skill suddenly fell away with the final round, so that Donna was the winner. 'That was nice of you,' I said quietly, and he shrugged with a boy's embarrassment. In truth, though, I didn't think it would have mattered to Donna whether she won or lost, for the whole experience was so new and exciting to her, it was a winner in itself.

After we had congratulated Donna on her win, Lisa led us through to the party room for drinks and some games. The party room was gaily decorated with a large mural of clowns running round the walls, more bunches of balloons and another large 'HAPPY BIRTHDAY' banner strung across the ceiling. We played musical chairs and then various guessing games, designed to quieten the children down before their tea. Tea was a choice of pizza, chicken nuggets or burger, all with chips; then there was jelly and ice cream – as much as anyone could eat – and a birthday cake with eleven candles. I had bought another birthday cake to have at home on Donna's actual birthday the following day.

We finished with another game of bowling, which Donna won again; then Mandy arrived to collect Emily, and Lisa gave all the children a party bag. I thanked Lisa for all she had done and tipped her £5. She wasn't going to accept it to begin with, but I insisted. 'You've made the party a great success,' I said. 'I'm very grateful. Thank you.'

We exchanged our bowling shoes for our own and, with more thanks, finally said goodbye to Lisa. Outside I reminded Donna to thank Emily and Mandy for the present; she was still clutching it protectively and had carried it everywhere with her, only putting it down to bowl and eat her tea. She hadn't yet opened it, wanting to save it for her actual birthday. 'Thanks,' I added to Donna's, as we said goodbye to Emily and Mandy in the car park outside.

There was silence in the car as I drove us home and also, I thought, a small anti-climax as happens at the end of a good time. Donna was sitting with Emily's present cupped on her lap, and as I glanced in the rear-view mirror I saw Paula rest her head on Donna's shoulder and begin to doze.

That night I said everyone had to be in bed exactly at their bedtimes, as I would wake them early so that Donna had time to open her presents in the morning before we went to school. All three children were asleep within ten minutes of going to bed, exhausted by the day's excitement. Paula had gone to sleep with her thumb in her mouth, Adrian with his book open on his bed and Donna with her hand under her pillow clutching Emily's unopened present.

Chapter Fourteen

No Dirty Washing

I had been touched by Donna's innocent and accepting pleasure of all aspects of her little party, and I was doubly touched the following morning when she began to open her presents. Before I had gone to bed I had taken her presents into her room and placed them on the floor beside her bed so that she would see them as soon as she woke. There was the bike from me, which I had wrapped in yards and yards of wrapping paper, a cycle helmet from Adrian and Paula, a present from my parents, and another from my brother and his wife; and of course there was the present from Emily, which was still tucked under Donna's pillow.

As soon as I heard Donna stir, I went to her room. 'Happy birthday,' I said, kissing her forehead. I woke Adrian and Paula so that they too could watch Donna open her presents – it was a family tradition that we all grouped around the person's bed on the morning of their birthday to watch them open their presents. This was a whole new experience for Donna and, as I looked at her, I became increasingly convinced that she had never opened presents in her life before.

She stared at the large gift-wrapped frame of the bike. 'I wonder what it is?' she said, not daring to believe her eyes, although its shape made identification pretty obvious.

'You'll have to open it to find out,' I said, encouraging her. Donna appeared to want to savour being surrounded by the brightly wrapped presents and I knew we hadn't got unlimited time – at some point we had to get washed and dressed, ready for school.

Finally Donna sat on the edge of her bed and, sliding Emily's present from under the pillow, she carefully and very slowly began untying the ribbon. She picked off the sticky tape even more slowly, then peeled off the paper, not ripping it off as Adrian and Paula would have done. It was a jeweller's box. 'I wonder what it is,' she said again, and Adrian and Paula watched in awe as she slowly lifted the lid. Donna's eyes widened, and her whole face shone as she looked inside, but didn't remove the gold necklace with a pendant in the shape of the letter D.

'Isn't that lovely?' I said, as Adrian and Paula moved closer for a better look. 'What a beautiful present!' It was very generous of Mandy. Donna gazed at the necklace and touched it, clearly believing that at any second it might disappear.

'Shall I put it over here, while you open the rest?' I said, again mindful of the time. She carefully closed the lid on the box and handed it to me. I placed it on top of the chest of drawers. She gazed at the other presents, finding it impossible to choose which one to open next. 'How about this one?' I suggested, passing her the large box from my brother and his wife. Donna was now sitting on the floor, with Adrian and Paula kneeling either side of her. Once again she started picking at the sticky tape; then very slowly and carefully, she unwrapped the present. It was a large boxed compendium of games – Snakes and Ladders, Ludo, playing cards, dice for performing tricks and so on.

'Cor, that looks good,' Adrian said. Donna glowed from being the owner of something valued and admired by Adrian.

She opened the present from my parents next, which I knew was a fashionable denim skirt – my mother had asked me Donna's size and sent the receipt so that Donna could change it if it didn't fit or she didn't like it. There was no need to worry on the last score: her face beamed, and standing, she held it up against herself. 'Just what I always wanted,' she said. Paula and I admired the skirt while Adrian was more interested in Donna opening the next two presents.

'Here,' he said, passing her the present from him and Paula. 'It's from us. Happy birthday.'

'Happy birthday,' Paula said.

With the same painstaking precision Donna peeled off the sticky tape and unwrapped the present – a bright pink very fashionable cycle helmet. 'Now I wonder why you have been given that?' I said, smiling.

Donna grinned, and, setting the box on her bed, knelt down and began steadily unwrapping the bike. It had taken me ages to wrap it; I had wound the gift paper around the crossbars and handlebars, and fully over both wheels, so that the whole bike was entirely covered. It took Donna equally long to unwrap it as, trying not to tear the paper, she picked off the sticky tape a little at a time and unwound the paper. Although it had been obvious from the bike's shape what it was even before she'd begun unveiling it, it wasn't until she had completely removed the last piece of paper, folded it, and placed it on top of the pile of other wrapping paper that she allowed her excitement to show.

'Is it mine to keep?' she asked, looking at me.

'Of course, love. All the presents are. You can ride it in the garden after contact tonight. Then at the weekend when we have more time, we'll go to the park for a long ride.' I knew Donna could ride a bike because she'd used an outgrown one of Adrian's in the garden in the summer.

Donna looked wistfully at the bike and then ran her hand over the length of it, almost caressing the shiny metal bars, black leather seat and handlebar covers. The trimmings and wheel guards were in two-tone pink and the bike was the latest Raleigh model for girls; I had wanted Donna to have the best. It had a bell on the handlebars, and also a small saddlebag at the back in matching pink.

'And I can keep it for always?' she asked again.

'Yes, love, it's your present. Of course you can keep it. I'm not going to take it back, am I?' I saw her face tighten and register pain.

'Mum gave me a present once,' she said slowly, still running her hands over the bike as if at any moment it might disappear. 'It was a doll.'

'Oh yes?' I said.

'But when it was Ruby's birthday, she was the girl next door, Mum took it back and gave it to Ruby as a present. It was brand new and I never saw it again.'

Adrian and Paula looked at me, absolutely horrified, and I fought to hide my own shock as my eyes misted. 'Donna, the bike is yours to keep, love, as are all the presents. They are yours and only yours. People don't give presents and take them back – well, not nice people, anyway.'

Apparently there was no depth Rita hadn't stooped to in order to make Donna feel worthless and unloved. I thought that emotional sadism like this was more hurtful and damaging than any beating: the scars ran deeper and lasted longer. Who knew what else Donna had suffered? She'd said very little really.

Another of our little family traditions is to sing 'happy birthday' in the morning after the presents have been opened, usually to the person's embarrassment. We would sing it again to Donna in the evening when the birthday cake was lit and before she blew out the candles. I now struck up the first note, and Adrian and Paula joined in. It sounded like the alleycats' tea party, but Donna didn't mind. 'Thanks,' she said as we finished (not all at the same time). 'Thanks for giving me a birthday. I've never had a birthday before.'

I think at that point Adrian and Paula realised that what they had enjoyed and had assumed to be the norm in respect of birthdays clearly wasn't, and unfortunately didn't apply to everyone. It was as much a shock to them as it would have been for the average child, and it served as a stern reminder that even in our country some children are deprived of what we assume to be a basic ingredient in every child's life.

I had to encourage everyone to get washed, dressed and ready for school, as we were running late. In fact we arrived at Donna's school fifteen minutes late – at 8.30 a.m. instead of 8.15. I went with her into the dining room where the breakfast club was held to explain the reason for our lateness. But there was no need. Miss Warren, who ran the breakfast club, apparently had known it was

Donna's birthday and guessed she might be late. 'Happy birthday!' she called in front of all the children as we went in. Donna smiled, embarrassed. I kissed Donna goodbye and told her to have a good day, and passed her the carrier bag of variety chocolate bars, which I'd bought for her to give to her class to mark her birthday.

'Do you think Donna's mum really gave her present to the girl next door?' Adrian asked as I returned to the car.

'Yes,' I said.

'But that's evil,' he said.

'Very, but Donna is having a good birthday with us now.'

However, I had grave reservations about the contact that night, for even with Edna there, I knew with sly underhand comments and evil looks Rita could still easily sabotage Donna's birthday.

Edna phoned just after 10.00 a.m. to ask how the party had gone on Sunday, and I told her. 'I'll be keeping a close watch on Rita tonight,' she said, 'and I have managed to enlist a colleague to help. She can't stay to every contact but she's available this evening. I've bought the presents for Rita and Chelsea to give to Donna, and wrapped them. All they have to do is to sign the gift card and give Donna the presents. Rita isn't going to get the better of me or Donna tonight, that's for sure.'

As it turned out, Rita did get the better of Edna and Donna, or so she thought: she didn't turn up for contact, and neither did Chelsea. What mother doesn't see her daughter on her birthday? It said it all. But if Rita thought she was causing Donna any suffering she was wrong.

Donna was wearing the new denim skirt my parents had bought her and a pale blue blouse for contact. She was looking forward to what she called her 'second birthday party'. When I dropped her off Edna quietly told me that the boys had arrived a few minutes before us, with their presents, but Rita and Chelsea hadn't arrived yet. Edna said she had tried phoning Rita's mobile but it was switched off. She assumed they were running late and she was expecting them at any moment, which was my expectation too. Donna's father would not be attending, as he was still in hospital; however, his mother, Donna's grandma, was waiting inside as a surprise. Edna had gone into the contact room early and, armed with sandwiches, biscuits and cake, had laid out a party tea.

When I collected Donna at 6.30 p.m., Edna, her colleague, Mrs Bajan and the boys all came out to the car, helping Donna carry her presents. They were in high spirits and I said hello to Mrs Bajan and Edna's colleague. I opened the car boot for the presents, and Edna quietly told me that Rita and Chelsea had boycotted the birthday contact; they hadn't sent a message, and couldn't be contacted. 'Wait until I see them,' Edna hissed under her breath. 'That Rita had better have a damn good excuse,' although Edna thought, as I did, that Rita's absence had been intentional; we would have both been very surprised if she'd had a genuine reason for her and Chelsea not coming.

'Not that Donna appeared very bothered by their absence,' Edna added as I closed the car boot. 'She's had a good time. I organised games for her and the boys. My colleague, Kate, and I joined in. I tell you, Cathy, we're both exhausted.'

I smiled at Edna and Kate. 'That was nice of you,' I said. 'And so many presents! I'm sure all in all it's been Donna's best birthday ever.'

Edna nodded. 'That's what Donna said, and she thanked me, bless her, for making it happen.' I could see that Edna was deeply touched by Donna's gratitude.

It took a good five minutes for everyone to say goodbye to each other. Donna kissed and thanked Edna again, then her gran, her brothers and Edna's colleague, Kate. The escort car to return the boys to their carers drew up on to the forecourt beside us, and then had to wait as the boys wanted to give Donna a final kiss on her birthday, and also wave her off. Left to their own devices, away from the influence of their mother, Warren and Jason seemed completely different – reasonably loving and affectionate towards Donna. Eventually we were all in the car. With the windows down and arms waving, and to the shouts of 'Happy birthday' and 'Bye', I slowly drove off the forecourt and up the road, finally raising the windows when we were out of view.

'You've had a smashing time,' I said, glancing in the rear-view mirror at Donna. 'What a lovely surprise to see your gran there! I know it's a long way for her to travel on the bus.'

'I love my gran,' Donna said. 'She told me she'd seen Dad and he's doing well.'

'Excellent. I said the doctors would make him better, didn't I?'

'Did you have another birthday cake?' Adrian asked.

Donna nodded.

'We've got one for you at home as well. That makes three you've had,' Adrian said admiringly.

'I know,' said Donna. 'Aren't I lucky?'

Adrian and Paula agreed, not at all begrudging, as they knew how much the birthday meant to Donna, and what dreadful ones she'd had in the past.

I wasn't going to raise the subject of Rita and Chelsea's absence with Donna, but I felt that it hung in the air. Donna had obviously had a really good time without them, and I wasn't going to sully it by mentioning them unless Donna did. Her face, her whole body language reflected pure enjoyment and delight, and like yesterday at her party when her brothers hadn't come, she had simply and unreservedly made the most of every moment without any preconceived expectations.

'It was nice of Edna to do me a party tea,' Donna said after a while. 'And I've got so many presents. I've even got one from Mum and Chelsea. They've never bought me a present before.' No, I thought, and little do they know that they have now.

Donna must have reflected on this during the journey home, or possibly she had entertained suspicions from the outset as to who the actual buyer of the presents was, for when we arrived home and were unloading the presents from the boot, she suddenly said, 'Cathy, I don't think Mum and Chelsea bought the presents, although the card had their names on.'

I closed the front door and hoped this was an observation rather than a question, but a minute later as we sat in the lounge and admired her presents, Donna said, 'I wonder if Mum and Chelsea really bought the presents? They're very good presents.'

I guessed they were too good. The present Edna had bought for Rita to give was a table tennis set. When I had first seen it I thought that it was a clever choice, designed to encourage Donna to play with others rather than alone – you can't play table tennis by yourself. Now I was faced with the dilemma of either lying to Donna, or telling her the truth and undermining Edna's good intentions of making sure Donna had a present from her mother and sister.

'Mum's never bought me a present before,' Donna said again reflectively, while I was still considering what to say. 'Neither has Chelsea. I think Edna or Gran had something to do with it.'

I paused from reading her cards and looked straight at her. 'Donna, I think Edna is such a kind person that she wanted to make sure you had the best birthday ever. If she did have something to do with it, then I think that makes your present even more special, doesn't it?'

Donna nodded, and then a smile lit up her whole face.

'What is it, love?' I asked. Adrian and Paula were looking too, wondering, as I was, why Donna was smiling if she believed her mother hadn't even managed to buy her a present.

'I'm glad Edna chose it,' Donna said. 'Otherwise my present might have been another load of dirty washing.'

I laughed. Despite everything Donna's humour had surfaced again. 'Absolutely!' I said.

The four of us continued to admire Donna's presents. Apart from the table tennis set there was a jewellery-making set from Chelsea, a fashionable girl's handbag with a matching purse from Warren, a large boxed set of scented and coloured bubble baths from Jason, a beautiful silver bracelet from Mary and Ray, a basket-making set from Edna, and a £10 note in a card that was signed 'Gran and Dad'.

Leaving the children in the lounge gloating over Donna's presents, I went into the kitchen and lit the candles on the chocolate birthday cake. I carefully carried it through, and Adrian, Paula and I sang 'happy birthday' again (no more in tune than the first time). I took another photograph of Donna blowing out the candles. She was becoming quite proficient at blowing out candles now and blew out all eleven candles with one breath. I handed her the knife and she carefully cut the cake and served us each with a slice on a plate. It was raining now and dark at 7.00 p.m., so I suggested to Donna that she left trying out her bike in the garden until the following day, when hopefully it would be dry and, without contact, we would be home earlier.

'You can take your bike into the garden as soon as we get home from school tomorrow,' I said.

'Is it still there?' she asked.

'Your bike? Of course. It's in your bedroom where you left it this morning, with your other presents.' Even now Donna didn't fully believe me when I said that her presents were hers to keep. I had arranged her cards on the mantelpiece in the lounge, but I had left the presents in her room. Adrian and Paula always liked to keep their presents in their bedrooms for a week or so after their birthdays so that they could see them each morning when they woke.

After we had eaten the cake and had a glass of lemonade we had a few games of table tennis. Then it was time for bed. Paula, Adrian and I helped Donna carry her presents upstairs to join the others in her room. Like Adrian and Paula, she liked the idea of having her presents close to her.

'My bike!' she exclaimed as we walked into her bedroom, apparently surprised to see it still here.

* * *

'Donna,' I said after Adrian and Paula had gone to wash and change, ready for bed, 'I know your mum didn't buy you presents when you were living with her, but didn't Granny Bajan ever give you something on your birthday? Or send you a card? She seems a lovely lady.'

Donna was again slowly running her hands over the length of the bike, apparently still not fully convinced it wouldn't evaporate into thin air. 'She tried to,' she said, 'but Mum stopped her.'

'What do you mean, "stopped her"?'

'Mum told Gran not to send me anything, and Gran didn't like to upset Mum 'cos she took it out on Dad.'

I looked at her carefully. 'How did your mum take it out on your dad? He's a big man and your mum isn't any taller than me.'

'She hid his tablets and wouldn't let him have them. So he would lose his mind and be locked up. Gran worried about that.'

I stared at her, amazed and shocked. 'How do you know this?'

'Mum told me, and so did Gran. Mum said Gran was an interfering bitch because she talked to Edna about our family. If Mum wanted to get at Gran or Dad, she stopped him from having his tablets, so he went mad. Sometimes I found the tablets again when Mum was drunk or asleep, and I gave them to Dad. But Gran worried what Mum would do if she disobeyed her, so she didn't send me any presents. I didn't mind. I just wanted Dad to be well.'

'Yes,' I said, absently, contemplating this new disclosure of deviousness. 'I'm sure your dad will be well soon, now he is in hospital. I'm going to let Edna know what you said about his tablets; then perhaps she can think of a way of making sure he has his medicine.

'Thanks, Cathy,' Donna said. 'It would be great if Edna could help him. And thanks for my birthday. It's been lovely. And no dirty washing!' We both laughed.

Chapter Fifteen

Mummy Christmas

A week later Donna put the yards of gift paper I had used to wrap her bike to good use. Together with the other sheets of wrapping paper and an old magazine, she tore it up and littered her entire bedroom. Hundreds and hundreds of tiny pieces were once again strewn on every available surface. She did this less often now; it used to be three times a week but recently it had been about every ten days. As usual Donna had spent a productive and silent thirty minutes tearing up the paper and then sprinkling it over her room, ready to clear up later.

'Very pretty,' I said dryly as I went into her room. 'It looks as though it has been snowing coloured paper.' I could be fairly relaxed about this behaviour now, and even joke about it with Donna. I was aware that this was her way of acting out, and dealing with, her role of cleaner and general dogsbody when at home, and I knew that eventually it would be addressed in therapy.

What I wasn't so relaxed about was Donna's ongoing need to try to dominate and chastise Adrian and Paula, and also trash her bedroom. Her treatment of Adrian and Paula was slowly improving, but despite my earlier optimism, I found that if I relaxed my vigilance and didn't remind Donna not to speak to Adrian and Paula so harshly, her earlier behaviour quickly resurfaced, and she reverted to chastising them in imitation of the vicious pecking order that had existed at her house. Both Jill and Edna had witnessed Donna 'sniping' at and trying to control Adrian and Paula on their visits, and agreed that it was something that would take a long time to go and was something else that should be addressed in therapy after the final court hearing. But the final court hearing wasn't until May, and even then I wasn't expecting a miracle cure. Children can be in therapy for years before there is any sign of improvement.

Trashing her bedroom was something else that I really needed quicker results with, and Jill and Edna both advised me that I should start applying sanctions. Donna had trashed her room four times by the beginning of December and on each occasion it was after contact. Apart from the mess, which I now insisted Donna helped clear up, she had torn down the curtains each time and they were now irreparably ripped, as was a new duvet cover. Anything that could be smashed was, and on the last occasion Donna had thrown the portable CD player so hard against the window that it had chipped the glass; had it been thrown with much more force it would have shattered the window. It was also frightening to witness Donna's loss of control, not only for me but for Adrian and Paula. I always told them to stay downstairs when it happened, but they could still hear Donna shouting and screaming, and the sound of things breaking as they were hurtled against the walls. Donna was so out of control at these times that had her anger turned towards a person instead of property she could have done them real harm. I always waited by her bedroom door, gently talking to her and persuading her out of the anger before I went in.

Jill had suggested that, as well as making Donna help clear up (which was no great punishment, given her need to clean), I stopped her pocket money to help towards some of the cost of replacing the items that she had destroyed or damaged. I'd had to get Edna's permission to stop Donna's pocket money because there was a small amount included in the foster carer's allowance for pocket money; it was designated as the child's and could not be withheld without the permission of the social worker. Edna fully concurred with Jill's suggestion and we agreed that I would stop two weeks' pocket money each time Donna trashed her bedroom. The small weekly amount was hardly likely to cover the damage she'd done, but its withdrawal was designed to give Donna the message that her actions had a knock-on effect, and that she was culpable and therefore had to take responsibility for her actions and learn to control them.

Having trashed her room twice in a four-week period, she went for a month without any pocket money, but I'm not sure how much good stopping it did. A sanction is more effective if it is applied immediately, but if Donna trashed her room on a Wednesday (as had happened on the previous occasions), she didn't feel the loss of her money until Saturday, which was pocket money day. Also, since her destruction of her room always happened after contact, I felt it was directly related to seeing her mother and having all the bad things that had happened in the past reinforced. But stopping contact wasn't an option, and even reducing it wasn't going to be considered until nearer the final court hearing.

I therefore reverted to the approach I had tried on the first occasion she'd vented her anger on her room: I tried talking her out of it, and then suggested she try to channel her anger in something less destructive, like thumping a cushion or running round the garden shouting. But although Donna was amenable to my suggestions, and when she was calm agreed to try them, when she came in from contact bursting with anger she was invariably in her room, screaming and throwing things, before I had time to intervene and direct her to something else. Once she was out of control it was too late. I could only hope that in time this behaviour might also improve, although I thought the only real improvement would come if contact was stopped.

As far as I was aware, Donna hadn't tried to rub off her skin again when washing, although I knew she retained a poor self-image in respect of her dual heritage. She loved her dad, who was mixed race, and, despite his odd behaviour when he hadn't taken his medication, Donna was proud of him, and of her gran, who was black. But Donna couldn't translate this positive view of their colour to herself. Her mother had been so negative and demeaning of her racial origins that the damage ran deep.

The four of us went shopping together to spend the £10 that her gran and dad had sent her for her birthday, and Donna wanted to go to Boots the chemist to spend it. I assumed she wanted to buy some perfume or even some make-up, as girls of her age often start experimenting with a bit of lipgloss or eye shadow – they were advertised in all the girlie magazines. But once inside the chemist Donna spent ages wandering up and down the aisles without actually telling me what she was looking for. Eventually we stopped at the display of hair removal creams – depilatories as they are called – and she began examining the various boxed tubes.

'What are you looking for, Donna?' I asked. She didn't have excessive hair, and hair removal wasn't something a girl of eleven would normally have contemplated. She shrugged and appeared to be studying the ingredients listed on the boxes, although her level of reading wouldn't have allowed her to make much sense of the long names of the chemicals used in the products. I couldn't even pronounce some of them, let alone identify what they were used for – calcium thioglycolate, lithium hydroxide, disodium lauryl sulfate, to name but three.

'Does it have bleach in it?' she asked after some moments. Adrian and Paula were now becoming restless at this lengthy and unproductive shopping trip.

I looked at the ingredients on the box Donna held, containing the tube of cream designed to 'efficiently and gently remove unwanted hair'.

'Not as far as I can see,' I said. 'But you don't need this. It's for ladies to remove hair from their legs.'

She returned the product to the shelf and picked up a similar one but with a different brand name and manufacturer. 'Does this have bleach in it?' she asked again.

'I don't know,' I said, not looking at the ingredients. 'But you're not going to buy hair-removing cream, Donna. You don't need it at your age.'

'Chelsea uses it,' she said.

'Well, she's older than you. I guess at fifteen she might be removing the hair from her legs, but you haven't got any hair on your legs to remove.' Even at fifteen I would have supervised a girl using these products, as they are very strong and there was a long list of warnings and contraindications on the packet, and details of when and how one should or should not use them.

'It's not for her hair,' Donna said after some moments. Adrian and Paula were really fidgeting now.

I glanced again at the box. 'This product is for hair removal, Donna. What else could she use it for?'

'Whitening,' she said.

I looked up. 'Whitening? Whitening what?'

'Some of the hair-removing creams have bleach in them and it can whiten your skin. Chelsea uses it on her face. It makes her lighter.'

Dear God, I thought! Whatever next? 'Does your mother know she uses it for that?' The answer to which I could have reasonably guessed.

'Mum told her to. I want to buy some. Then I can be lighter like Chelsea.'

Chelsea had a different father and therefore different genes to Donna, but that was hardly the issue. 'Absolutely not,' I said and, returning the box to the shelf, I moved away from the display. 'Donna, there is no way you are going to try to lighten your skin. You have inherited some of your looks from your dad and Granny Bajan, and you look lovely just as you are. Whatever would your dad and gran say if they knew? They'd have a fit, and so too would Edna. No way, Donna. You can spend your money another day on something else.'

I led the way out of the shop with Donna trailing behind, sulking. Adrian and Paula asked me what the matter was, and I said I would explain later. Had I been a black carer it would have been easier to try to persuade Donna to a better self-image because she would have had an immediate and positive example to follow. This is one of the reasons children coming into care are placed with carers who reflect their ethnicity. But there is a permanent shortage of carers from 'ethnic minorities' where I live, despite repeated advertising campaigns. In the past I had successfully fostered black children and those with dual heritage but it was in cases like Donna's, where she had such a negative view of her skin colour, that I had the biggest challenge.

I decided that something I could do was to buy some magazines that were aimed at black women and teenagers, and would show Donna positive images of black women and girls. Donna often bought magazines with her pocket money but she usually chose *Girl Talk*, *Amy* or *Go Girl*, in which the pictures were mainly of white girls. She could still buy these magazines, but together with what I had in mind there would be a better balance.

Having left the chemist, we went up the high street and into the newsagent's, where I sifted through the shelves of magazines. Adrian stood smirking at the magazines on the top shelf, which showed pictures of women with their breasts exposed. I couldn't find any magazines catering specifically for black girls of her age, so I took down and looked through *Ebony*, which was aimed at black women, and *Young Voices* and *Right On*, which were aimed at black teenagers. Although the actual articles were a bit old for Donna, there was nothing inappropriate in them, and they contained lots of pictures and feature articles on black women and teenagers, all very positive. I decided to buy *Ebony* and *Young Voice*, and then I let Paula and Adrian choose a magazine each for themselves (though not from the top shelf), and Donna also wanted the latest edition of *Girl Talk*.

In the car going home Donna had got over her sulk, and all three children were looking at their magazines, and also glancing at each other's. I would explain later to Adrian and Paula why I'd bought Donna two extra magazines, and why they featured only black women and girls, although I doubt they had even noticed. They were unaware of the issue of Donna's colour – to them she was their foster sister and they appeared to take for granted that she had a slightly darker skin tone and hair.

I had a good friend, Rose, who is dual heritage and that evening I phoned her and told her what Donna had wanted to buy in the chemist. 'I didn't even know hair-removing cream had bleach in it,' I said. 'Did you, Rose?'

'Yes. And unfortunately I know some women do use it to lighten their skin. There are also products on the market specifically to lighten skin tone, although I've never seen them in the shops around here. I think they're mail order.'

'Really?' I said, taken aback. 'You don't use them, do you?'

'No, of course not.' She laughed. 'Look, we're overdue for a coffee and a chat. Why don't you and the kids come over on Saturday? Daniel was saying only the other day he hadn't seen Adrian for a while, and Libby can educate Donna; they're about the same age.'

'That would be great,' I said, for obviously Daniel and Libby were well adjusted and proud of who they were and would be a good example to Donna. But I could only do so much, and the rest was a matter of time and giving Donna ongoing praise and encouragement.

* * *

Christmas was fast approaching, and by the end of the second week in December I had done most of the present buying and the four of us had decorated the house. Given what Donna's birthdays with her mother had been like, I hadn't dared ask her about her last Christmas.

Paula asked, though. 'What did you have for Christmas last year?' she said, as they wrote their Christmas cards for their school friends; Adrian had finished his and had left the table where we were working.

'Nothing,' Donna said.

'Nothing?' Paula repeated disbelievingly, although I think even she now understood enough of Donna's life to know that 'nothing' might be possible. 'Didn't you have presents from Father Christmas?' she tried again.

'No,' Donna said.

'What about your dad?' Paula persisted. 'We have presents from Father Christmas and ones from our dad.'

Actually it's Mummy Christmas in this house, I thought, but Donna was shaking her head. 'Edna gave me a present. It was a teddy bear, the one I take to bed.'

Paula was still looking at Donna, her little mouth open and her eyes round in disbelief. I motioned to her not to pursue the questioning. Edna's Christmas present was clearly the only one Donna had received, and I now knew that her gran had probably been stopped from sending Donna a present. I thought that receiving nothing from her mother was at least preferable to the pile of dirty washing she'd received on her birthday.

School broke up the week before Christmas and we relaxed into the festive season. With the three children together for the greater part of each day I renewed my vigilance.

And possibly because Christmas was coming, or perhaps because she was improving anyway, I noticed that when Donna spoke to Paula and Adrian it was with less severity and she appeared to be joining in more. Donna was looking forward to Christmas, and I guessed it would be her first proper Christmas, as it was with so many of the children I had looked after.

Christmas Day was on Sunday and Donna had her usual contact on the Friday before. I had found with the previous children I had fostered that this last contact before Christmas (unless they were seeing each other over Christmas) was used to celebrate Christmas, and presents were exchanged.

Donna had chosen and wrapped presents for her mother, father, gran, Chelsea and brothers, and took them to contact. I had added a present and card for Edna from us all. I knew that Donna's gran wouldn't be at contact because she had gone to stay (as she usually did) with her family in Barbados for a month. Donna's dad was still in hospital, but Edna had said she would make sure that he and her gran got their presents from Donna as soon as was possible after Christmas. Buying all these presents, together with my own shopping, had taken quite a lot of time and organisation, but it is part of a foster carer's role to arrange presents for the looked-after child to give to their family on birthdays and at Christmas, and quite rightly so.

When I collected Donna from contact at 6.30 p.m. I was relieved to see she was carrying a number of presents, all of which were still wrapped and would be put under the tree for her to open on Christmas Day. There was a present from Edna, one each from Warren and Jason, one from

Donna's dad and her gran, which Edna said her gran had sent to her office before she'd gone away, and also one each from her mum and Chelsea. 'I took Rita and Chelsea Christmas shopping,' Edna said to me quietly, as I placed the presents in the car boot. 'I made sure they bought Donna something this year.'

'That's so sweet of you, Edna,' I said. 'You have a lovely Christmas, and a well-deserved rest.'

'And you,' she said. 'And thank you for my present and card.'

'You're very welcome.' Edna was truly an angel. With all her workload, she'd found the time to take Rita and Chelsea shopping to ensure that Donna had a Christmas present from them. And doubtless the money for this had come from the social services budget, for Rita appeared to be permanently broke.

Adrian and Paula saw their father for the day on Christmas Eve, and returned with presents from him to go under the tree. This would be their third Christmas without their father and it still touched a raw nerve with me, as I'm sure it does for any family that isn't complete. But I wished John a merry Christmas and he did me. Paula and Adrian gave him an extra hug and a kiss before they said goodbye, and he returned to spend Christmas with his partner.

Our Christmas followed its usual tradition and on Christmas Eve we went to the family service at our local church. It's a very informal short service and centres around the crib scene and what the Christmas story is all about. We returned home for a late supper, after which the children put a glass of milk in the porch for Santa, together with a carrot for the reindeer (one to be shared between nine because I needed the rest for Christmas dinner). Then Donna, Paula and Adrian hung their pillowcases on the inside of the front door in anticipation of Father Christmas's visit that night, while I took a photograph. The pillowcases would be magically filled during the early hours and appear by their beds in morning. It had never actually been stated in our house how this happened; Paula and Adrian happily accepted, as Donna now did, that it was just part of the 'magic' of Christmas. Aged six, Paula still believed in Father Christmas, and I had asked Adrian a couple of years previously, when he'd started expressing doubts, to keep them to himself, for no child likes to be told that Father Christmas doesn't exist; they want to hang on to the fantasy for as long as possible. Donna embraced the whole concept of Father Christmas unreservedly, although obviously being the same age as Adrian (and aware that Santa hadn't existed in previous years) she must have known the truth.

It was 9.30 p.m. before I finally had the children in bed, and another half an hour before they were asleep. Mummy Christmas then sat up until nearly midnight with a couple of glasses of sherry and a mince pie, watching a late-night film. Only when she was certain that the children were really fast asleep did she resist another glass of sherry and unhook the empty pillowcases from the front door. She then tiptoed up the stairs and into her bedroom, where she took the wrapped presents from her locked wardrobe and packed them into the correct pillowcases. Then, very quietly, she trod round the landing, carefully avoiding the squeaking floorboard, and into the children's bedrooms, hoping they wouldn't wake and see her. She carefully rested the overflowing pillowcases against the bed of each child, then stole from the last bedroom and into her own bed.

And it seemed to her that she had only just gone to sleep when she was woken by the sounds of excited squeals. She opened one bleary eye to look at the clock and saw it was 5.55 a.m.

'Merry Christmas!' came the cries from the landing. 'Can we come in?'

'Yes. Merry Christmas,' Mummy Christmas returned.

And as all three children dragged their pillowcases into her room, as tradition required, then sat on her bed and opened their presents, she saw the look on their faces, and knew that all the hard work and expense had been completely and wondrously worthwhile.

My parents, and my brother and his wife, arrived within five minutes of each other at 11.00 a.m. on Christmas morning, and put their presents under the tree to join the huge pile. We had drinks, nibbles and mince pies, and then played some games – Twister and an old favourite, Hunt the Thimble. We spent over an hour unwrapping Christmas presents, with my father reading the names on the gift tags one at a time and handing them out. We had another drink before I served dinner at 3.00 p.m., and my brother carved the turkey. After the main course we had a break from eating and I organised some 'sitting down' games in the lounge while we digested our meal. We returned to the dining table in the front room for pudding, and my brother poured copious amounts of brandy over the pudding and set fire to it. I had made a trifle because I knew that Adrian and Paula didn't like the rich Christmas pudding, and Donna had a bit of everything. She'd done very well joining in, and although she had been quiet she'd taken part in all the games, and also spent some time talking to my mother, to whom children easily warm. I presented the cheese board in the lounge at 7.00, and although everyone groaned and claimed they 'couldn't possibly eat another thing', either they did, or we'd had a nasty invasion of mice.

We finally said goodbye around 10.00 p.m., and everyone agreed it was the 'best Christmas ever', but then we say that every year. However, for Donna I thought it was probably true, and most likely her only Christmas to date. As the four of us grouped on the doorstep and waved off my parents and my brother and his wife, it crossed my mind what my ex had missed with just him and his partner and no children. I also wondered what Rita and Chelsea had done, for while Donna and her brothers had enjoyed a Christmas with all the trimmings, Rita and Chelsea had presumably spent it by themselves, and I imagined it had been a pretty dismal one. Despite everything Rita had done to Donna, I felt sorry for her and Chelsea, particularly for Chelsea, who had been denied the pleasure and excitement of a child's Christmas for life.

Chapter Sixteen

Winter Break

The children returned to school on 4 January, and when I arrived home I took down the decorations with a severe case of post-Christmas blues. I felt like this every year; I'm sure a lot of people do. There is all the excitement and build-up to the festive season and then January falls flat and cold, with short days, overcast skies and spring seeming a long way off. Adrian's and Paula's birthdays were the next family celebration – 30 March and 7 April – but until then there was a bit of a void. What we really needed was a holiday, a change of scenery, in the February half-term break. Somewhere hot and sunny, I thought, in a hotel where I was waited on hand and foot! We hadn't had a holiday abroad since my husband had left. How much would a holiday for four in February cost, I wondered as I packed away the last of the decorations? There was only one way to find out, and on the whim of the moment I took my coat from the hall stand, picked up my bag, and with that buzz that comes from throwing caution to the wind, I drove to the shopping mall, where I parked in the multi-storey car park and walked to the travel agent's.

Two hours later I came away with the brochure and booking form – proof that the children and I would be spending half term in Morocco, and with my winter blues banished and my savings account just about coping. I'd phoned Edna from the travel agent's, before booking and had obtained her permission to take Donna. She'd given it without hesitation 'What a lovely opportunity for Donna,' she'd said. 'Thank you so much. I'll arrange a passport for her straight away and also check that her vaccinations are up to date.'

It was 2.30 p.m. by the time I was in the car again and I drove straight to collect Paula and Adrian from school. I was bursting to tell them, but I stopped myself: I wanted to wait until we were all together at home. It was Thursday, so without the quick turnaround necessary when Donna had contact, as soon as we arrived home I told the children to go into the lounge because I had something important to say. They were subdued and wide-eyed when I went in, sitting in a line on the sofa and wondering what was so important, and if they had done something wrong.

'I've booked us a holiday,' I announced, producing the brochure and squatting on the floor in front of them. 'At half term we're going on a plane to Morocco!'

'Wow!' Adrian said, and he immediately slid off the sofa and joined me on the floor for a closer look. 'Cor,' he said. 'What type of plane is it?' I hadn't thought to ask. 'I bet it's a Boeing 747,' he said, bubbling over with excitement. 'It's one of the biggest planes in the world – that's why it's called a jumbo jet. It's got four engines and can seat over five hundred passengers!'

'Yes,' Paula knowledgeably agreed, joining him on the floor for a closer look at the brochure.

Donna hadn't said anything.

'Well, what do you think?' I asked. 'Are you happy to go?'

She stared at me in utter amazement. 'Are you taking me?' she asked.

'Yes, of course.' I had thought it would be obvious but apparently it hadn't been. 'Donna, you are part of this family. Of course you are coming with us.'

She too now left the sofa and joined us on the floor, and with the brochure open at the page showing the hotel I read out the details of this luxurious and family-orientated resort. To say they were excited was an understatement; if Christmas had taken Donna's breath away then this left her absolutely speechless.

'Are you all right? Donna,' I asked, for even now she wasn't saying anything. 'There's nothing for you to worry about on the plane. I'll look after you. It will be one big adventure for us all.'

'I don't think Mum will let me go,' she said sombrely.

'I've spoken to Edna and she is going to ask your mother, but if she says no then Edna can make the decision. Edna wants you to come, so you will be coming, I promise you that.'

But later when Edna told me what Rita had said I was still shocked. 'Good riddance to bad rubbish. I hope the plane crashes,' Donna's mother had said.

'Why does Rita hate Donna so much?' I asked Edna, for I had come to believe that 'hate' wasn't too strong a word.

'I really don't know,' Edna said. 'But I have come across cases before where one child in the family is victimised, sometimes when the other children are reasonably well cared for, although that wasn't so here.' No one really knew why Rita hated Donna, but it was very, very sad.

* * *

The weeks flew by to our holiday and before we knew it, it was the last day of the half term and we were going the next morning. When I collected Adrian and Paula from school it appeared that most of their classes were aware of our holiday, and we left the playground to the cries of 'Have a good time!'

When I met Donna from school, the head, Donna's teacher, Emily and her mother, Mary, Ray and the boys all made a point of seeing us and wishing us a happy holiday. Mary and Ray were taking the boys for a few days out over the half-term break, including a trip to the zoo, and I wished them a good time. 'It's a lovely opportunity for Donna,' Mrs Bristow said to me. 'We'll look forward to hearing all about it, and make sure you show us the photos, Donna.'

Beth Adams added that the class had been tested on their twelve times table and, as with the others, Donna had got them all right and received two team points. I was obviously pleased and praised Donna, as I had in all the previous weeks, but I was also quietly relieved that we had finally come to the end of the times tables and that learning them would no longer dominate our car journeys, evenings and weekends. But the result of all the weeks of hard work and repetition was not only that Donna now knew her times tables but that she had proved to herself and her teacher that she could learn as well as anyone, given time. I had high hopes for Donna in the future.

It was a very noisy crew that I drove home that afternoon, and also a very cold one. The temperature had dropped, and although we hadn't had snow, 'flurries' had been forecast and the skies looked full of it. I prayed that nothing would happen over night that could disrupt our travel plans.

As it was Friday, Donna had contact, so we weren't out of the routine yet. I had plated up Donna's dinner as I usually did, and she ate it and then changed out of her school uniform. At 4.30 p.m. we were in the car again, taking her to contact. When I collected her at 6.30, Edna brought Donna out to the car and made a point of wishing us all a good holiday. Edna always took the opportunity at the end of contact to let me know how contact had gone and update me, and tonight was no exception.

Once Donna was in the car with the door closed and out of earshot, Edna said, 'Rita has told the boys that she will take them on a plane to Morocco when they go home to live with her!' Edna raised her eyes, for clearly making unrealistic promises to young children was unfair and could only lead to disappointment. However, on a purely personal and selfish level I felt that if that was all that had been said, then Donna had escaped very lightly.

That evening my parents and my brother phoned to wish us bon voyage, and so too did Paula and Adrian's father, which I thought was decent of him. By the time everyone had had a bath and was changed, it was 8.30 p.m. 'In twelve hours' time,' I announced, 'we shall be in the taxi going to the airport!' They all cheered.

It was difficult to say who was more excited that evening, the children or me; certainly it took me the longest to get off to sleep. Apart from the anticipation of a long overdue holiday, I kept running through a mental checklist of anything I could conceivably have forgotten. I was still tossing and turning at 1.00 a.m., and eventually I got out of bed and double checked that the plane tickets and passports were still in my handbag, which of course they were. At 7 o'clock the alarm went off and I was up, washed and dressed within fifteen minutes. I woke the children and they performed the same feat in ten minutes!

I love take-off – the speed and exhilaration that flattens you into your seat, as you hurtle down the runway, going the fastest you are ever likely to go on land in your life. Then there's that euphoric moment as the wheels lift from the tarmac and you are airborne, actually flying! As at the end of a good ride at the fair, I feel I want to go back and do it again. Just one more go, please! I glanced across at the children and knew they were feeling it too, although Donna and Paula with a little trepidation. The children occupied the three seats that stretched out from the window, while I was on the end of the row directly across the aisle. They were going to take turns to sit by the window. I looked at their happy smiling faces, on the biggest adventure of their lives to date, and I knew I had made the right decision to throw caution to the wind and come on holiday. And just as Christmas had been the best one ever, I felt this holiday would follow suit, and also help confirm to Donna that she was truly an integrated member of the family.

Chapter Seventeen

Final Rejection

My only criticism of the holiday was that it wasn't long enough and before we knew it we were at the airport again for the return flight. But as well as giving us all a wonderful break, the holiday had helped to strengthen our bond as a family. There had been no major disagreement or incidents, despite us all being together for the most part of seven days. I'd only had to tell Donna once not to boss Paula, when I'd asked Paula to get out of the pool, as it was time to get changed for dinner, and Donna had shouted, 'Get out of the pool now!' But she had quickly apologised.

I felt Donna was more accepting of her role as simply that of a child and I didn't anticipate having to continually watch her any more when she was with Paula and Adrian as I had done in the past. I also hoped there would be no more of the violent outbursts of anger which had culminated in Donna trashing her room. I wasn't expecting an angel, for Donna had suffered a lot in her past, but she was making more attempt to talk to me, and I hoped she would therefore be able to verbalise her anger rather than taking it out on her room.

* * *

The following Monday saw us back in the routine, and me with a suitcase full of washing to be done. The children had wrapped the model camels they were going to give their friends as presents, and we took them with us to school. The children looked incredibly healthy: their faces glowed from the sun and fresh air, and we were all a shade darker. The weather wasn't quite as cold as it had been when we had left England, but we wrapped up warmly on that first morning – it was taking a while for us to acclimatise. I saw Donna into the breakfast club, and Mrs Bristow, the head, was waiting for her.

'Come here and tell me all about your holiday,' she said, and she gave Donna a big hug. 'You do look well!'

I didn't have time to chat with Mrs Bristow, as I had to take Adrian and Paula to school, so I left it to Donna to tell the head all about our holiday, which she'd started to do immediately. 'We had loads to eat,' I heard her say as I left the breakfast club, 'and a camel ride, and swimming in the pool and sea.'

A similar reception greeted Adrian and Paula, first from their friends, all wanting to know if they'd had a good time, and then, when the bell rang and the staff came out into the playground, from their class teachers. I said goodbye, and returned home, where I set the washing machine going. I sorted the mail, which I'd opened but hadn't dealt with, then finished unpacking the cases. Edna and Jill phoned to ask how the holiday had gone, and I was able to tell them that it had truly been a holiday for us all.

In the afternoon, half an hour before I was due to leave to collect the children from school, Edna phoned again. And unlike her previous call when she'd asked brightly about our holiday, her voice now sounded strained and anxious.

'Cathy, Donna has contact tonight,' she said, going straight into what she had to say. 'And I've just had a phone call from Rita, telling me she's pregnant.' She paused and, whereas I would normally have offered congratulations on hearing the news of an expected baby, now I didn't know what to say. 'It's due in August,' Edna said. 'Two months after Chelsea's baby is due. I've told Rita not to say anything to the children tonight at contact, but she might.'

'So you don't want me to tell Donna before we go?' I asked.

'No. Hopefully Rita will do as I've asked. I've tried to explain to her how traumatic the news will be to the children, particularly to Donna. She's likely to see it as the final rejection.' I knew what Edna meant: Rita's children had been taken into care and now she had set about replacing them, like a worn-out pair of shoes. 'I want time to prepare Donna for this,' Edna said again. 'And also to be certain that Rita is pregnant. She's phoned me before with these "phantom pregnancies".'

'Has Chelsea's pregnancy been confirmed then?' I asked. 'It hadn't when the Guardian told me.'

'Yes, last week. I'm trying to persuade Chelsea to listen to my advice so that there's a chance she'll be able to keep the baby.'

'Good.'

'Mrs Bajan will find out at some point about Rita, assuming she is pregnant. I know she will be upset. I might tell Mrs Bajan myself before Rita does.' I assumed Edna meant that Donna's gran would be upset because the baby might be mistreated as her other grandchildren had been, but there was a different reason for Edna's comment. 'Mr Bajan can't be the father because he is still in hospital,' Edna said. 'Rita hasn't been anywhere near him all the time he's been in.'

'Oh, I see.'

'There's a strong possibility,' Edna continued, 'that Rita's baby (if there is one) has the same father as Chelsea's. There's a man living on the estate who sees himself as some sort of Casanova and goes round impregnating single women. He's been seen going in and out of Rita's house.' I didn't know whether to laugh or cry. 'Anyway, Cathy, once Rita's pregnancy is confirmed, I'll talk to Donna. There's no point in upsetting her if there is no need.'

'Thank you, Edna. Is Chelsea still attending contact? Donna never talks about contact when she comes home.'

'Sometimes. When Rita has run out of money. She knows that because Chelsea is still a minor I can give her additional allowances, and I'm not likely to refuse to. When Rita is broke, Chelsea appears at contact and asks for money.' She paused and I heard her sigh. 'What a mess! All the support I have put into that family and it's come to this. Sometimes I wonder how efficient I am at my job.' I thought Edna sounded tired and worn out, which was hardly surprising given her workload. She would probably be dealing with another fourteen child protection cases, and being so conscientious, it was obviously taking its toll.

'You do an excellent job, Edna,' I said. 'I'm sure you have made a big difference to a lot of people. I couldn't begin to imagine what Donna's life would have been like had she not come into care. And her brothers are doing well, aren't they?'

'Yes, I suppose so, put like that.' But her voice still sounded flat. 'Perhaps I'm getting too old for this job,' she said. 'Or possibly I'm in need of a holiday. I haven't had a proper one in years. When I take time off from work, I end up writing reports. My hubby is always going on at me to take a holiday. Perhaps I should follow your example.'

'You should, Edna. It wasn't until I got back, feeling so relaxed, that I realised how much I had needed one. Book it tonight!'

She laughed. 'OK, Cathy. I'll speak to my hubby. See you later at contact.'

Chapter Eighteen

Don't Stop Loving Me

Thrust straight back into our routine, I collected the children from school, gave Donna her evening meal and then took her to contact. The children were still talking about our holiday, reliving the highlights and looking forward to seeing the photographs, which I'd yet to send off to be developed. I hoped that Donna would have the chance to talk about her holiday at contact. I knew Edna would obviously be interested, but it was highly doubtful that Rita would. I had worked with parents in the past who'd derived much pleasure from their children being taken on holiday while in care, and selflessly enjoyed hearing about something that they'd never had the opportunity to experience. However, this wasn't to be so here.

When I collected Donna from contact, Edna came up to me and said quietly, 'Rita ignored Donna for the whole evening, apart from telling her news!' I glanced at Donna, who was sitting in the back of the car with Adrian and Paula; unsurprisingly, she looked dejected and morose.

'Not only did Rita tell her that she was pregnant,' Edna said, shaking her head sadly, 'but she told the boys, so that Donna could hear, that the baby would be beautiful, not like Donna.'

I cringed, shocked and appalled, and I looked seriously at Edna. 'Edna, I really think it's time to be reducing contact. I'm sure it's doing Donna more harm than good. How is she supposed to improve when she is subjected to this type of comment three times a week?' I stopped myself from saying more because I could see that Edna was blaming herself.

'I know,' Edna said, looking as dejected as Donna. 'I'm going to speak to the Guardian and see about an application to court.' Because Donna was in care under an ICO Edna couldn't change the level of contact that had been set by the judge without making an application to the court, which meant appearing before the judge and giving good reasons why the contact should be reduced. Parental rights in respect of contact are taken very seriously by the court, sometimes, I feel, to the detriment of the child, who may be trying to move on from the past. There was no point in saying anything further. Edna was as aware as I was of the negative impact contact was having on Donna; whether or not the judge agreed remained to be seen.

I said goodbye to Edna and got into the car. Edna usually spoke to Adrian and Paula, but now she was too preoccupied to ask about their holiday.

'All right?' I asked Donna, turning in my seat to look at her. She shrugged and, with her head down, wrung her hands in her lap. Adrian looked at me questioningly, for the contrast in the Donna who had gone into contact bubbling with her news of the holiday and the dejected child who now sat next to him was obvious to all. Donna still yearned for, and sought, her mother's praise and acceptance, and Edna had told me more than once that it was crucifying to watch Donna trying to ingratiate herself to her mother.

I started the car and headed for home. Adrian and Paula were silent during the journey, sensing and respecting Donna's unhappiness. I had decided that once I had Paula in bed I would try talking to Donna about what her mother had said this evening, and also about some of the issues from her past. I had tried talking to Donna before when she'd returned from contact obviously upset, but I'd come to realise that she preferred to be left alone, and she usually sat in her room for half an hour to unwind. Sometimes she tore up paper, and on four previous occasions she'd trashed her room. But since the bonding of our holiday I felt more confident in approaching her and hoped she would feel able to confide in me.

I parked the car on the driveway, got out and opened the child-locked rear doors. The children followed me up the path to the front door and I unlocked it and let us in. Paula squatted in the hall to take off her shoes. Then suddenly, without any warning Donna let out an almighty roar and thumped Paula in the chest. Paula fell backwards and banged her head on the edge of the partially open front-room door.

'Donna!' I yelled as I went to Paula, who was struggling to right herself. 'My God, are you all right?' I drew Paula to me. Her eyes were watering and she had one hand clutching her head and the other on her chest. I took her onto my lap as Donna ran upstairs. Adrian closed the front door and then stood, looking horrified, his face white. Donna's bedroom door slammed shut; then there was quiet.

I quickly examined Paula's head. There was an angry red lump on the back of it where it had hit the edge of the door, but thankfully the skin wasn't broken. I gently eased up her jumper to reveal a red mark where Donna had thumped her in the chest. As I comforted her, my heart pounded and my anger rose. Donna had hit Paula with such force that she could have easily broken a bone, and I knew at that moment that such an incident must never be allowed to happen again, and I cursed myself that it had happened at all.

I held Paula to me and soothed her. Suddenly the silence in Donna's room was replaced by banging and crashing as she started trashing her room.

'Adrian, will you look after Paula for a moment, please,' I said tightly. 'I need to see Donna.' Adrian took Paula by the hand, and easing her off my lap, led her along the hall and towards the lounge.

I went upstairs, my heart thudding and my body tense. I was furious with Donna. What the hell did she think she was doing! Damage to property was one thing, but damage to my child was something else! I went round the landing to Donna's room. The sound of her screaming and breaking things grew louder. Without knocking, I threw open the door and went straight in. She had her back to me and was throwing everything that came to hand.

'Donna!' I yelled at the top of my voice. 'What the hell do you think you're doing? How dare you! How dare you hit Paula! Stop that now!' My chest tightened and my pulse raced as my voice drowned out Donna's screaming. 'I won't have you doing that!' I shouted. 'Do you hear me? I won't have you hitting Paula! How dare you!' I was right in her room now, only a couple of feet in front of her. I was hot and shaking with anger. I had never been so angry in my life. 'Do you hear me, Donna?' I yelled again. 'How dare you hurt Paula!'

She suddenly stopped screaming and throwing things, and turned to look at me, shocked by my outburst.

'How dare you!' I cried again. 'She's only little! You have hurt her. I won't have it, Donna! Do you understand me! I won't have it in this house!'

She stood very still and stared at me.

I stared back. 'You didn't like it when your brothers hit you. And now you've done it to Paula! I've had enough, Donna. We've just returned from holiday and you've done this! You've gone too far now! You've overstepped the mark!' Fuming, I came out and slammed the door. I needed to put some distance between us before I said something I would regret.

I stood on the landing, my heart pounding and my breath coming fast and shallow. I felt hot and sick. I'd never shouted at anyone like that, ever, let alone a child. Foster carers aren't supposed to shout at the children they look after, and I hadn't, not in all the years I had been fostering, until now.

All manner of things went through my mind as I moved away from Donna's door and round the landing and began going downstairs. How could she have taken it out on Paula like that? Why wasn't I getting through to her? Why couldn't she talk to me instead of unleashing her anger on a child of six? Could I really continue looking after her with the possibility of Paula being hurt again? Was there something wrong in the way I was treating Donna? Why hadn't she made the progress I'd anticipated? I had been so hopeful that we'd turned a corner during our week away, and now this had taken us back to square one, or further. I would have to tell Jill and Edna what had happened, and admit to my outburst, and perhaps also admit defeat. For if this was the point we had come to after eight months, I didn't see how I could be the right carer for Donna. What she needed I didn't know, but clearly it was more than I could offer.

I arrived at the bottom of the stairs, still shaking and with tears forming at the back of my eyes. I went along the hall and into the lounge. Adrian and Paula were sitting together on the sofa, Adrian with his arm round Paula. They were both very pale and looked frightened; they had never seen me so angry or shout like that. I went over and made room between them on the sofa. I put an arm round each of their shoulders and we sat in silence, while I slowly calmed down.

They were as shocked as I was by my shouting, and it is for this reason that foster carers shouldn't shout. It is frightening for a child to witness an adult out of control (and in the case of foster children, very likely replicating the behaviour they've been moved from at home). The fostering family is supposed to set a good example of what family life should be like; if foster carers lose the plot and started ranting and raving, what sort of message does that send out? But I was only human, and I had been furious, not only because of Donna's treatment of Paula, but that after all this time of looking after Donna it appeared I'd done her no good whatsoever.

We sat in silence for some moments as I cuddled Paula and Adrian, and my thoughts slowly settled. It was still quiet upstairs, and I wondered what Donna was doing. I would have to go up and check on her soon, in case her anger turned inwards and she tried to harm herself.

'Are you all right now?' I asked Paula gently. 'Your head isn't cut, but there is a lump. It will be sore for a few days.'

'I'm all right,' she said quietly. 'Are you?'

'Yes, love.' I slid my arms from their shoulders, and again parted her hair and examined her head. The red lump hadn't swollen any larger, but it had obviously hurt a lot. I eased up her jumper again and saw that the red mark on her chest was fading. Donna's attack could have been a lot worse, I told myself, but that was no consolation at all.

'What's the matter with Donna?' Paula asked in a small voice.

'She's angry with her mother and unfortunately she's taking it out on us. I'm sorry, love.'

'It's not your fault,' Paula said.

'I should have realised she was so angry when we came in. I am wondering if Donna wouldn't be better off living with another family.' But even as I said it I knew that wasn't the answer, though what the answer was I'd no idea. I had tried my best, tried to integrate her into the family, and used my well-tested strategies to help her come to terms with her past and hopefully move her on to a better future, and apparently I'd failed.

'Is Donna all right?' Paula asked, her concern for her foster sister outweighing her own hurt.

'I'm going to check,' I said. 'Will you be OK here for a minute, while I try to talk to her?'

Paula nodded. 'Good girl. And thanks, Adrian.' I moved to the edge of the sofa and stood, but before I got any further we heard Donna's bedroom door open, followed by her footsteps on the stairs. I glanced at Paula, who was looking anxious, clearly thinking that if Donna was still angry she might hit her again. 'It's all right,' I reassured her. 'You stay on the sofa with Adrian.' I walked to the lounge door and stood in the entrance, where I waited as Donna appeared. She came slowly towards me along the hall, her shoulders slumped forward and head hung down. Her slow lumbering gate reminded me of when she'd first arrived, when she appeared to carry the weight of the world on her shoulders and even breathing was too much effort.

She stopped a little way in front of me and slowly raised her head. Adrian and Paula were silent in the room behind me. Donna looked at me with large woeful eyes, so full of pain and suffering that the sight of them made my heart sting, despite what she'd done. Yet although I now felt desperately sorry for Donna my concern lay with Paula, who sat on the sofa behind me, hurting from the pain Donna had inflicted, and with her trust in Donna gone.

'Yes?' I said to Donna.

She opened her mouth to speak, and slowly, laboriously the words came out. 'I need to say sorry to Paula,' she said, her gaze falling from me to the floor. 'I need to say sorry. I want to say sorry to Paula so she will love me again. I don't want her to hate me like my family does. I want you all to love me. Please don't stop loving me, Cathy. I need you to love me.'

Tears immediately stung the back of my eyes, and I heard Paula leave the sofa behind me. I was still in the doorway to the lounge, blocking Donna's entrance, and protecting Adrian and Paula, although there seemed no need to now. Donna's anger was spent and I knew Paula was in no danger. Paula came past me and put both her arms around Donna's waist and hugged her tight.

'I still love you, Donna,' she said. I looked at Paula, that much smaller than Donna, with her arms clasped tightly around Donna's waist. 'Don't worry, Donna,' Paula said. 'We won't stop loving you. This family isn't like that.'

If ever I'd needed an example from a child, it was now, and Paula had given one. No, I thought, our family isn't like that. I glanced at Adrian, who, like me, was watching Paula and Donna framed in the doorway, holding onto each other.

'Come and sit down, both of you,' I said at last, 'and then we can talk.'

I saw Paula give Donna a final squeeze; then, taking her hand, she led her to the sofa, exactly as she had done when Donna had first visited and Paula had led her down the garden to the swings.

Emotional scenes happen in any loving family, but even more so in a family that fosters, where dealing with distressing issues is a part of everyday life. Yet as I looked at Paula, so small beside Donna, but taking the lead and comforting her, I didn't think I had ever felt so emotional. Paula, vulnerable by her unreserved and childish love, and Donna, rendered as vulnerable by her desperate need to be forgiven and loved.

'I'm sorry, Paula,' Donna said again, her head resting on Paula's, and tears on her cheeks, as Paula cuddled up to her.

'Don't cry, Donna,' Paula said. 'You hurt my head but I forgive you. I still love you.'

I saw Adrian's face cloud over, even though he was trying to do what he saw as the 'man thing' and view this female emotion with dispassion. Yet while my heart lurched, and I was deeply touched by both Donna's and Paula's words – and I could have gone over and encircled them both and told them that everything would be all right – I knew that if we were to continue as a family I would have to make sure Donna's rage didn't touch Paula again. Paula was a child and couldn't see further than Donna's present apology and unhappiness, as I could.

I crossed to Paula and Donna, who were side by side on the sofa, and drawing up the footstool, I perched on it, just in front of them. Donna had her eyes lowered, her head still resting on Paula's as they hugged each other tightly. I gently eased Paula's arm away.

'Donna, I need to talk to you.' Paula sat back and took one of Donna's hands in hers. Slowly Donna raised her head and looked at me, her cheeks and eyelashes wet from crying. 'Dry your eyes, love,' I said, passing her the tissues. I waited while she took a tissue from the box, wiped her eyes and blew her nose. Paula followed suit. I took hold of Donna's other hand. 'Donna,' I said, gently but firmly, 'I know you're sorry now, and I'm pleased you have apologised to Paula. But love, we have to make sure it never happens again.'

'I won't hit Paula again, I promise.' She sniffed and wiped her tears.

'I know you won't, not while you're like this. But your anger can get the better of you, and then you don't know what you're doing and you're out of control. This evening you were very angry with your mother, but instead of telling me, or letting it out somehow, it all built up until it had to come out like an explosion. I was very angry with you just now, Donna, but I didn't hit you. Something stopped me getting close to that, and that something would always stop me from striking someone. We have to help you do that.'

'I didn't mean to hit Paula,' Donna said, her face crumpling.

'No, I know. That's what I am saying. You were very angry and she was the first person you saw.' I paused. 'Donna, can you think of a way that would allow you to control your anger and stop it from happening again?'

Donna was quiet, thinking about what I'd said. Adrian and Paula were quiet too.

'I will have to try to talk to you,' Donna said at last.

'Yes, that's important, and talking before it builds up. Also letting your anger out in other ways like those we have talked about helps. I know you're hurting inside, because you have been treated badly. Edna has talked to you about finding a counsellor, but it won't be until after the court case in May. Donna, do you think it makes it worse by seeing your mother three times a week?' It wasn't a question I would have asked a very young child because it would have been asking them to make a value judgement about their family, which wasn't right. But I felt Donna was old enough, and had enough insight, to give her opinion. Indeed the Guardian had already asked Donna about her feelings towards her family, although I hadn't been in the room to hear her answers.

Donna shrugged.

'Edna thinks, as I do, that it might be better if the contact was reduced. You would still see your mother and

Chelsea but not so often. You see your brothers every day at school. Mrs Bristow says you have lunch with them in the canteen.'

'I'd rather see my dad,' she said.

'Your dad is still in hospital, but as soon as he comes out I'm sure Edna will arrange for you to see him, perhaps on another evening, separately from your mother.' I paused, scanning my thoughts for what to say next. It was difficult. The truth was that Donna badly needed therapy to help her to come to terms with her anger and her past, and I was no therapist.

Suddenly she looked at me, as though seeing something for the first time, or perhaps viewing it from a different angle. 'Cathy, I think it would help me if I stopped wanting my mum to love me so much. I get angry because I try so hard to get her to love me, and when she doesn't, it hurts and makes me angry. I don't know why Mum doesn't love me. I haven't done anything wrong. I was the one who did all the housework at home, and I tried to stop us going into care. But I was blamed for everything, even those things that weren't my fault. I think there is no point in loving my mum any more. She hates me and she will always hate me. I am right, Cathy, aren't I?'

What could I say? How could I agree with a child that her mother hated her, apparently had always done so and was very likely to continue doing so in the future, and for reasons that no one understood? But in some ways that was what Donna needed to hear, put less severely, so that she could start to come to terms with her past and hopefully move on to a better future.

'Donna, love, you are a good person and your mother has treated you very badly. I don't know why, and neither does Edna. Sometimes in families it happens, though fortunately not very often. Your mother didn't treat your brothers very well, nor Chelsea, but her treatment of you was far worse. Your brothers love you, and so do your dad and gran. You need to remember that: it is important. Some children I look after have never had anyone love them. Your mother is very silly for not loving you as much as she could. It was bad of her to treat you as she did. But it has nothing to do with you as a person, or anything you did or didn't do. It could just have easily have been Warren, Jason or Chelsea she picked on. Sadly it was you. Her comments tonight about the baby were part of all that. I don't know whether she will ever change. But you have your whole life ahead of you, and it will be a good life because you are a good person, Donna.' I finished as I had started, for festering within Donna was the feeling that she was bad and to blame, and her badness had brought it all on. Although my simplification of the situation was grossly inadequate, it was the best I could offer.

Donna slowly nodded. 'I'm sorry, Paula,' she said again. 'I'm really sorry for hurting you. Do you still love me?'

Paula's little voice came out from where she was snuggled into Donna's side. 'Yes, I love you, Donna.'

'I'm sorry, Adrian,' she said, looking at him as he squirmed slightly at the surfeit of emotion. 'Do you still love me?'

He nodded and grunted.

Donna looked at me. 'And you, Cathy? Can you love me like my mum should have done? I love you like a daughter.'

I swallowed the lump in my throat and blinked back my tears. 'Yes, love. I'm sure we can all put this behind us and move on.' We had to. I couldn't give up on Donna now, and I was sure Adrian and Paula wouldn't have wanted me to either.

Chapter Nineteen

Paula's Present

Donna didn't suddenly and miraculously recover from all the trauma of her past, but we did slowly and gradually turn the corner. I was sure it was that recognition Donna had had, that flash of insight which had allowed her to view her mother objectively that was responsible, rather than anything I had said or done. How dreadful was it that a child had to admit that their mother didn't love her, had never done so and probably hated her, before she could start to like herself?

My assertion to Donna, my promise to love her as a daughter was true: I did, while she was with me, but her future was still undecided. The final court hearing was two months away and I couldn't know what the judge's decision would be, or what the care plan drawn up by Edna in conjunction with the Guardian would outline for Donna while she was a child in care, although I knew enough to be certain Donna wouldn't be returning to live with her mother, and neither would the boys. For, apart from the boys being severely neglected, they had begun to say things about their mother to their carers.

Warren and Jason had told their carers that they'd been made to go into their mother's bed when they'd been naughty, but the punishment they began to describe to

Mary and Ray wasn't a smack or even a beating but of a sexual nature. I wasn't told the details by Edna: there was no reason for me to know. It wouldn't have helped my care of Donna to know, and I certainly wasn't going to ask. As a foster carer I hear enough details of degradation and abuse (including sexual abuse) from the children I foster to last me a lifetime; I didn't want more horror stories to plague me at night.

Edna discussed the possibility of reducing Donna's contact (and also that of the boys) with the Guardian, Cheryl Samson, but they decided that with the final court hearing less than two months away, after which contact would be reduced, there wasn't much to be gained. By the time the application had been compiled and gone before the judge there would probably be only about a month left. But Edna suggested that I start arriving late for contact and also collect Donna early for the next couple of months. This arrangement gave Donna about forty-five minutes there. I sat in the car with Adrian and Paula, reading or listening to the radio while Donna was at contact. There was no point in returning home for the ten minutes it would have given us. We all had our evening meal together on our return just after 6.00 p.m.

Aware that Donna seeing her mother had been a catalyst for many of her angry outbursts, I told Donna that I didn't want her going to her bedroom or sitting by herself and brooding immediately after contact. I gave her little jobs to do as I prepared dinner, which redirected her thoughts and also allowed me to keep an eye on her. Donna was a child who internalised her pain and anger to the point where it eventually exploded. I spent a lot of time talking to her and encouraged her to tell me what she was feeling, rather than letting it build up. I would like to say that Donna's self-image dramatically improved, but it didn't: her progress was very slow and piecemeal, for the scars ran deep.

Emily finally came to tea the second week in March and returned the invitation the following week. When I collected Donna from Emily's, her mother, Mandy, said that the girls had played nicely and remarked how polite Donna was. 'I had to tell Emily off, though,' Mandy added. 'I thought I would mention it, as Donna looked very worried.'

'OK, thanks,' I said lightly, not thinking anything of it. But going home in the car, Donna seemed quieter than I would have expected after spending an enjoyable evening at her best friend's.

'Is everything all right?' I asked.

She shrugged, and then, remembering my repeated warnings about not letting worries build up and to tell me instead, she said, 'I got Emily into trouble.'

I glanced at her in the rear-view mirror. 'Did you? How?'

'I showed her how to tear up paper into little bits. And we threw them all over her bedroom. Her mum came in before we cleared it up and Emily got into trouble.'

'I see,' I said. 'Thank you for telling me. Shall I explain to Mandy that it wasn't really Emily's fault?'

'Yes please. Or else Emily might not want to be my friend any more.'

'Don't worry. I'll put it right.'

I had to smile to myself, for what I had come to view as an innocent and harmless way for Donna to release and act out her role from the past Mandy had seen as unacceptable. If I had been a mother without the experience of fostering, and had invited a child to tea and doubtless cleared up and made sure my daughter's bedroom was tidy, I wouldn't have been very pleased either to find it littered with hundreds, possibly thousands, of bits of paper. But as a foster carer I had seen such bizarre and extreme behaviour from the children I'd looked after that I had adapted and modified my judgement of what was a wrongdoing.

The following day I had a quiet word with Mandy in the playground when I collected Donna from school. I thanked her again for having Donna to tea and said how much she had enjoyed it. I then apologised, and said that the mess the girls had made in Emily's room wasn't really Emily's fault. Without breaking confidentiality I briefly explained that this was Donna's way of acting out some of her past, and that I had now told Donna it wasn't acceptable to do it in someone else's house. Mandy thanked me for telling her and said she would square it with Emily, and that Emily had already asked when Donna could come again to tea. But as we said goodbye I wondered what Mandy really thought, for ours must have seemed a strange house to her. Not only did I appear to tolerate such odd behaviour but I accepted it almost as the norm, which it was for Donna. And, I thought, Mandy didn't know the half of it: shredding paper was nothing compared to some of the behaviour I had seen from children who had had to rid themselves of their trauma in any way they could.

Adrian's and Paula's birthdays were two weeks away. I had planned their parties, and they had given out their invitations. Although their birthdays were only a week apart –

30 March and 7 April – as usual they were going to have separate parties, on consecutive Sundays. Adrian wanted a football party that would be organised by, and hosted at, our local football club. Paula wanted her party at home, with jellies and ice cream, and games organised by yours truly. Donna had said to me that she wanted to buy Adrian and Paula a birthday present each, and she had set aside two weeks' pocket money to do this, which was very thoughtful of her. The opportunity for us to go shopping without Adrian and Paula arose the following Saturday, when they were out with their father for the day.

Once I had said goodbye and seen them off at the door, Donna and I went into town to find the gifts, and also for me to buy some wrapping paper and order their birthday cakes. Much to the dismay of Adrian and Paula, I didn't have the cake-making skills of some of their friends' mothers, who annually produced the most amazing scenes of Superman, castles and Winnie-the-Pooh, out of sponge, coloured icing and Smarties (and, I suspected, sorcery).

Donna and I were browsing in the 'pound shop' in the arcade. It was a shop selling low-priced goods including children's toys and games, books and ornaments. I had told Donna that I would add to her pocket money so that she could afford whatever gifts she chose for Adrian and Paula, but she was adamant that she wanted to buy them herself, so that they were 'really' from her. 'I've never been able to buy presents before with my own money,' she said. For like most children who come into care she'd never had pocket money: there simply hadn't been enough in the household budget.

We had been in the pound shop for about ten minutes, and Donna was looking at a little gaily painted jewellery box, which she thought Paula would like, and I agreed. I became aware of someone standing close behind us and I thought they were trying to get past. The shop was crowded on Saturday; it was always popular with those wanting small gifts that were reasonably priced. I took a step forward to allow the people behind us to get by, and continued looking at the box, which Donna was now opening to examine the inside. A woman's voice suddenly came from behind.

'Well! Look what we have 'ere!' The voice was harsh and scathing, and I immediately turned. Rita and Chelsea were standing side by side, hands on hips in a mirror image of each other, glaring at us.

I felt my stomach tighten. Donna didn't turn but remained, head lowered, looking at the jewellery box, although obviously she'd heard her mother.

'Hello, Rita, Chelsea,' I said evenly. 'Nice to see you again.' I hadn't seen either of them since that first day at school in September, and although 'nice' wasn't the term I would have used given what I now knew of the way Rita had treated Donna, I had to remain polite. They were as poorly turned out as before, with very worn matching black nylon jogging bottoms, and stained nylon tops now stretched over their bumps. Chelsea, six months pregnant, had the larger bump, and Rita (who I'd learned from Edna was definitely pregnant) was catching up fast, assisted by already being badly overweight. They were both watching Donna intently, although not in a friendly way. Donna still hadn't turned; she was actually trying to ignore them.

'How are you both?' I asked, trying to deflect their interest from Donna. 'Congratulations,' I added. I wasn't being hypercritical; it was the polite and decent thing to say.

'We're good,' Rita said, while Chelsea chewed on her gum. 'Be better if that nosy parker Edna minded her own bleedin' business.'

I gave a half smile and glanced at Donna. She still had her back to them, and was now nervously fiddling with the jewellery box, opening and closing the lid.

'Ain't ya gonna say hello to your mother and sister?' Rita demanded loudly, and she prodded Donna sharply in the back. I saw a woman standing further up the aisle glance at us.

Donna shrugged but still didn't turn. I felt my pulse rate begin to rise. I could see that this could quickly develop into an ugly scene. I had run into foster children's parents before while shopping and the outcomes had been variable – sometimes a brief 'hi' was enough and we went on our way, sometimes if the parents were amicable I stopped for longer and chatted, but neither of these approaches fitted the present encounter.

'Donna is choosing a present for my daughter's birthday,' I offered, hoping to defuse the situation.

'Is she?' Rita sneered sarcastically. 'D'you 'ear that, Chels? Your sister is buying a present for someone else's kid. Ain't bought us nofing, 'as she?'

Chelsea shook her head and continued chewing her gum. Damn, I thought, now what?

'And why d'you keep bringing her late for contact?' Rita said, turning her attention to me. 'Ain't that bleedin' social worker told ya what time you supposed to be there?' Given that Rita ignored Donna at contact unless she wanted to say something spiteful, I didn't think she could be missing her.

'Edna thought this arrangement would suit everyone better,' I said evenly, swallowing what I would really have liked to have said.

'Did she now?' Rita said sarcastically. 'Wait till I see her. I'll show her what suits me.'

The conversation was going from bad to worse, and I didn't see how it was going to get any better with Donna ignoring them and Rita openly hostile. I was feeling very hot, and as uncomfortable as Donna looked. Rita and Chelsea were making no move to go and seemed to be basking in Donna's nervousness. I thought the only way out was for us to leave the shop, hopefully not followed by Rita and Chelsea.

'Donna,' I said. 'Would you like to say hello to your mother and Chelsea and then we must go.'

Donna shrugged, and still didn't turn. Rita prodded her sharply again in the back. 'D'you hear what your carer said? Say hello to your mother and your sister, you little shit.'

That was it: I'd had enough. Politeness and diplomacy were never going to help Donna when it came to her mother. We needed to just get out of the shop, and fast. 'Come on, Donna,' I said more firmly. 'We're going now.' I touched her arm, and took a step to go, but Donna didn't move. She remained staring at the jewellery box she still held in her hand.

'There!' Rita exclaimed. 'She don't even do what you tell her. Waste of fucking space, that kid! Come on, Chels, don't waste your time on that turd.' Giving Donna another, harder, prod in the back, Rita lumbered off, followed by Chelsea, who threw Donna a look of hate and disgust.

I stood beside Donna and watched the pair of them leave the shop, then I sighed with relief. My heart pounded and I felt upset by what had happened, and Donna must have been feeling far worse than me.

'Are you all right, love?' I asked quietly.

She nodded and carried on examining the jewellery box, once again hiding and internalising her pain and sense of rejection.

'I think Paula will like this,' she said after a moment, turning the box over to look at the base.

I took a breath and looked at her. 'Yes, Donna, I'm sure she will. But we've just had an awful scene with your mother and you are not saying a word. I know what you must be feeling. I feel some of it too. You must be very upset, angry and also, I think, a bit frightened.' I spoke quietly, for there were shoppers all around us, moving down the aisle in the space Rita and Chelsea had left.

Donna slowly closed the lid on the jewellery box and turned and met my eyes. 'I am, Cathy. They make me upset and angry, but they won't change. I'm having fun choosing a present for Paula with my money, and I won't let them spoil it. I won't let them spoil my fun any more.'

I held her gaze and my heart went out to her. She was worth a thousand Ritas, and her response to her mother of not letting her upset her had proved it, and touched me deeply. Donna had been able to rise above her mother in integrity, compassion and everything that makes us socialised human beings, and I felt very humble beside her. 'All right, love. I understand.' I said. 'That's very sensible of you.'

We continued shopping and Donna bought the jewellery box for Paula, and then a book for Adrian, both of which she wrapped with great excitement when we arrived home. If Donna could hold on to her philosophy and rationalise her mother's words and actions, then her future looked a lot brighter. So often abuse in childhood goes on to blight the adult, souring and diminishing anything they achieve. It took a very courageous person to put the past behind and move on, and I hoped Donna had what it took.

Chapter Twenty

The Question

Adrian's and Paula's birthday parties were a great success. Adrian's was all boys and they spent an hour and a half playing football, organised by the coach, had a party tea provided as part of the package, then finished with games, also organised by the coach. Donna, Paula and I watched the football, although Donna could have joined in if she'd wanted to; Paula was a bit too young. We all sat down and joined in the tea, and afterwards Donna and Paula joined in the games. Paula's party was a more sedate affair and required a lot more organisation on my part than Adrian's had, where all that had been required of me was to arrive, watch and enjoy, then pay.

For Paula's I made sandwiches with the crusts cut off, cooked mini pizzas, arranged cocktail sausages on sticks, squirted cream on the individual jellies I had made, and limited the number of chocolate biscuits the children ate so that no one went home feeling sick. I organised games with prizes – Squeak Piggy Squeak, Pin the Tail on the Donkey, Musical Chairs (or rather pillows and cushions, because we didn't have ten dining-room chairs), and then followed this with a sing-along – 'Old MacDonald Had a Farm' and 'The Farmer's in his Den' – before lighting the candles and bringing in the cake. Donna joined in as best she could, for although her ability to play had improved, she still couldn't completely throw herself into games with a child's uninhibited pleasure. She came to me more than once during the party worried about the mess that was being made – 'There's a drink been spilt,' she said anxiously, or 'There's popcorn on the carpet.'

'Don't worry,' I reassured her, as I always did. 'I'll clear it up later. It's a party and I'm not worried about a bit of mess.' I wasn't, for compared to Adrian's party the previous year, which he'd had at home, I was getting off lightly: I had found pieces from the party-poppers lodged in corners of the bookshelves and behind sofas for weeks afterwards; one hadn't been discovered until I'd moved a cabinet to make room for the Christmas tree, eight months later. But Donna's anxiety about mess stemmed from her role of domestic drudge at home, and the guilt that had been heaped on her by her mother, who had made her feel that it was because Donna had failed in her duties she and her brothers had been taken into care. Not that Donna viewed being taken into care as a bad thing now – far from it – but the guilt remained, and would do for a long time to come.

Donna's school work improved dramatically in the summer term. Her reading age went up by two years, from seven to nine. She was still four years behind the average child of eleven, but relieved of the burden that she'd carried at home with its continual degradation, she'd gained confidence in her ability to learn and was going from strength to strength. Mrs Bristow, the head, and Donna's class teacher, Beth Adams, were delighted, and I think surprised – more so than I was. I had looked after children before who had been badly underachieving at school simply because of their appalling home lives. There's nothing left over for studying and learning if you're worried about where your next meal is coming from or when you'll receive the next beating, or worse.

The final court hearing was expected to last for five days and was scheduled to begin on 25 May. Although Donna was aware of the date, largely because her mother was cursing about it at contact, Donna appeared unaffected by its approach. Edna had explained to Donna, as I had, that the hearing would be when the judge made his decision in respect of the best place for her and her brothers to live while they were children. Chelsea was also part of the care proceedings, but I didn't have any details other than that Edna and the Guardian wanted her away from Rita and living in a mother and baby unit. In practice, however, given Chelsea's age and opposition to anything Edna suggested, this was going to be highly unlikely, unless Chelsea had a change of heart and cooperated, for clearly no one could force her to move, even if it was for her own good.

The Friday before the court hearing was due to begin was a dramatic one for news. Edna phoned in the morning to advise me of two developments. Firstly, that Rita had withdrawn her application to the court to have the boys returned to her, so she was no longer contesting the case. She had never made an application for Donna to be returned, but for whatever reason had now decided she no longer wanted to 'fight' for the boys return.

'I would like to think that Rita has finally seen good sense,' Edna said. 'I have spent months talking to her, trying to persuade her that it was best for the boys to remain in care. Perhaps I succeeded, or perhaps she realised there was too much evidence against her and has finally listened to her solicitor.' Or perhaps, I thought uncharitably, with the baby due in three months she's lost all interest in the boys, who were now hard work and not as immediately appealing as a vulnerable baby.

'And Cathy,' Edna continued, 'I have a piece of news of my own that I want to tell you before you hear it from anyone else.' She can't be pregnant too, I thought, for Edna was in her late fifties! 'I've decided that when I've finished with this case I shall be taking early retirement.'

'Oh Edna! I am sorry.'

She laughed. 'I'm not.'

'No, I didn't mean … I'm just sorry to be losing you.'

'Thank you, Cathy. But I've been a social worker for twenty-eight years and I think I've done my bit. Things have changed so much, and I'm getting too old to be up to midnight writing reports. My husband retires this year – he's a bit older than me. We want to enjoy our retirement and spend time with our children and grandchildren in Scotland. Do you know, Cathy, I haven't seen them in over a year?'

'I understand perfectly, Edna. But it will be a great loss.'

'That's nice of you. I will see Donna and the boys through to permanency before I fully retire. I've got a couple of other cases that are nearing the end, so I'll be coming in part-time for a few months.' Conscientious to the last; I could see only too well why Edna was taking early retirement. But I did wonder how easy she would find it to adapt, for social work had been her life, as looking after children had been the greater part of mine. 'And,

Cathy,' Edna continued, 'I've stopped contact for tonight and next week. It will be too much for Rita to handle with the court case. I don't want her anger spilling over. Will you tell Donna, please?'

'Yes, of course.'

'I'll phone you with the outcome as soon the court's made its decision and approved the Care Plan; then I'll come round and see you. I don't think the hearing will last the five days set aside now that Rita isn't opposing the case.'

We said goodbye, and I wasn't expecting to hear from Edna again until the following week. However, she phoned again at 6.00 that evening.

'Chelsea has had her baby, early,' Edna said. 'A little girl. Could you tell Donna, please? She's an aunty now.' I could hear warmth in Edna's voice, for although the social situation the baby had been born into was far from perfect, the birth of a baby is special and always welcomed, whatever else may be going on.

'Yes, of course,' I said. 'Are Chelsea and the baby well?'

'They are now. They're in hospital.' Edna paused. 'Don't tell Donna these details, please, but Chelsea gave birth at home. I didn't hear about it until the police phoned me. A neighbour heard Chelsea screaming early this morning and thought she was being assaulted. She called the police, and when the police and ambulance crew arrived they found Chelsea on the kitchen floor with the baby, still attached by the umbilical cord.'

'Good grief! Poor kid,' I said, horrified. 'Chelsea must have been very frightened. Where was Rita?'

'Upstairs in bed, sleeping off last night's drink.'

My heart went out to Chelsea, who at fifteen had given birth to her first child alone and on the cold kitchen floor.

'I'll try to visit Chelsea after court on Monday,' Edna said. 'I've told the hospital to keep her and the baby there for as long as possible. They've said they won't discharge her while the baby is so small. It was just five pounds. It will give me a chance to persuade Chelsea to go into a mother and baby unit. I've reserved a place for her. Chelsea can't return home with the baby: the place is filthy. The police said there was cat pooh all over the downstairs, even in the kitchen where Chelsea had given birth!'

I cringed. 'How absolutely dreadful! Do you want me to take Donna to visit Chelsea and the baby in hospital?'

Edna paused. 'Not yet. Let's get the court case over with, and then I'll set up a separate contact for Donna to see Chelsea and the baby. If you were to go to the hospital in visiting hours with Donna, Rita is sure to be there, so I think it's better to wait.'

'OK, Edna. Shall I buy a card for Donna to send?'

'Yes, that would be nice. Chelsea is on Maple Ward at the General.'

I jotted it on the notepad by the phone. 'I'll tell Donna the news, and when you see Chelsea, please pass on my best wishes.'

'I will, Cathy. Take care and I'll phone you next week.'

A new baby, a new life, but what a way to start it – born on a filthy kitchen floor! If Chelsea went into a mother and baby unit, then she would stand some chance of being able to look after the baby and keep her. Mother and baby units teach mothers (and fathers if they are parenting) to change nappies, bath the baby, make up bottles and generally look after the baby, as well as how to play with and nurture them. The staff are always on hand to give assistance, as well as monitor the young mother's progress. Only when they are satisfied that the mother knows how to parent the baby safely does the girl leave. The girls are usually found a council flat if there is no suitable home for them to return to, and the staff from the unit, as well as the social worker, continue to visit and monitor mother and baby for as long as is necessary.

It was difficult to know how to pitch the news to Donna, as it was likely to produce conflicting emotions. While the birth of a baby is a joyous event, given the way Chelsea had treated and rejected Donna I was half expecting Donna to be angry. I should have had more faith in Donna, for when I told her, she took the news with stoicism. 'That's nice,' she said, briefly pausing from the jigsaw she was helping Paula to complete. 'I hope Chelsea will be happy now and look after the baby well.'

'She will do,' I said, and I explained to Donna that Chelsea would be receiving a lot of help, both in hospital and then on her discharge, at a mother and baby unit. 'If you want to see Chelsea and the baby, Edna will arrange it in a couple of weeks. In the meantime you can send a congratulations card.'

'OK, Cathy,' Donna said, glancing up again. 'I'll think about that. Thank you for telling me.'

I sat on the sofa and picked up the newspaper, which as usual had remained unread during the day. As I scanned the front page for any news that wasn't doom and gloom, Donna added succinctly (and I could have said with great insight), 'She's a bit of a tart, that Chelsea. I always thought she'd end up in trouble with the boys.'

'Hmm,' I said as I raised the paper to cover my smile. 'I'm pleased you won't be following in her footsteps then.'

'What's a tart?' Paula asked.

'A pastry with jam in,' I said.

'And it can also mean a girl who is free with the boys, and doesn't respect her own body,' Donna added. And I thought that Donna had come a long way in the time she'd been with us; I couldn't have imagined Rita or Chelsea phrasing it so delicately.

We'd had no more incidents of Donna chastising, bossing, bullying or in any way trying to hurt Adrian and Paula, and I was once again finding that I could safely leave the three of them in a room without having to be continually vigilant. Donna was trying to find other outlets for her anger: she sometimes pummelled a cushion when frustrated, and she was also talking to me more. With no contact for the whole week there was less reason for her anger to build up and then explode. All of which was beginning to confirm my thoughts of offering to foster Donna long term – that is, to suggest she become a permanent member of our family.

One of the documents before the judge was the Care Plan, and this would detail the arrangements the social services were planning if the Full Care Order was granted: that is, where and with whom Donna and her brothers would live. If the Care Plan was upheld by the Guardian it was likely the judge would agree to it. Sometimes the Guardian's recommendations were different from those of the social services, and in some cases the children were returned home against the advice of their social worker. But I knew this wouldn't be so here. Both Edna and Cheryl Samson had agreed that the children should not return to Rita's care because, put simply, Rita couldn't look after them, had neglected and abused them, and in all probability would continue to do so.

What I didn't know was what the long-term plans were for where Donna would live. She was eleven and would be in foster care until she was eighteen; so too would the boys, although being that much younger there was a chance that they might be found adoptive parents. Donna was too old to be considered for adoption – most adopters want young children, who are less likely to be emotionally damaged. Sometimes relatives come forward and offer a permanent home to the child, and they are assessed as to their suitability. If they are suitable then this is usually considered the best option for the child – that is, to live with a member of the extended family; it is known as kinship caring.

But as far as I knew no one had come forward to look after either Donna or the boys. Donna's father unfortunately wasn't in any position to look after her, although when he was well he appeared to have a lot of love for Donna, as she did for him. Likewise Donna's gran, Mrs Bajan, was a kind and loving person, but she was not in the best of health, and also spent long periods during the winter with her family in Barbados. Edna had already said that Mrs Bajan didn't feel she could look after any of the children permanently but wanted them to stay with her during some of their school holidays. There was an aunt, whom I had only met once on that first morning at school, but Donna and the boys hadn't seen her since, and no mention had been made of her, so I guessed she wasn't a candidate to look after any of the children. I was almost certain that the court would say the boys should stay together and that Donna should continue to be fostered separately long term. If they were reunited and fostered as a sibling group there was a strong possibility that the problems that there'd been initially between them would resurface. Donna was settled and was achieving, as were the boys.

The question that I considered, therefore, was that if Edna asked if I could look after Donna permanently (which I thought she might) would I agree? And I already knew my answer. I'd always felt very protective of Donna, and in recent months that protectiveness had turned into a strong bond which was quickly turning to love. I was very proud of Donna and what she had achieved, and I wanted to be there for her as she continued her journey through childhood to become an adult. Obviously I would have to ask Adrian and Paula, as it was a life-changing decision and would affect us all. And of course. Donna would be asked, but I was pretty certain I knew what her answer would be. But all this rested on the outcome of the court case and the judge's decision in the final hearing.

Chapter Twenty-one

A Kind Person

The court case ended after two days and the judge gave his decision on the morning of the third. Edna phoned from outside court and said the judgement was as they'd expected, and Donna and her brothers would be staying in foster care.

'Good. Well done,' I said, which was in recognition of the hard work Edna had put in to secure the children's futures.

Edna said she'd like to see Donna and me later in the day, and also that she'd taken a photograph of Chelsea and her baby, Cindy, to give to Donna. 'Will it be all right if I visit at five thirty?' she asked.

'Yes, absolutely.' And my heart skipped a beat at the thought of the question I was sure Edna was going to ask.

Having collected the children from school, I made our evening meal earlier than usual. I knew that what Edna had to say wouldn't take five minutes, and everyone would be hungry if I waited until after she'd gone. I hadn't said anything to Adrian and Paula about the outcome of the court case (or my hopes of Donna staying with us), for Edna should speak to Donna first.

Uncharacteristically Edna arrived nearly half an hour late. 'Sorry, Cathy,' she said, hurrying in out of breath. 'It's been non-stop, all day.'

I offered her a drink and she gratefully accepted a cup of tea. 'I'd like to speak to you before I speak to Donna,' she said. 'Can we go somewhere alone?'

I could guess why.

Edna called 'Hello,' to Donna and Paula who were playing in the front room, and I showed her through to the lounge. Adrian was upstairs, doing his homework in his bedroom.

'Thank you very much,' she said as I handed her the tea. 'It was after three o'clock by the time I got back to the office, and there were two emergencies needing my attention. Roll on retirement!'

I nodded, and, sitting in the chair opposite, waited for the important news she brought.

Edna took a few sips of her tea and then returned the cup to the saucer in her lap. 'So, Cathy,' she said with a small sigh and looking at me. 'We have the Full Care Order on Donna and the boys. The case for Chelsea has been adjourned so that I can assess her with the baby. I've got to go back to court in two months with that.' I nodded. 'I was able to tell the judge how well Donna and the boys have settled, and how much improvement the children have made since coming into care. The judge has upheld my plans for them. We are going to try to find adoptive parents for Warren and Jason, who will be placed together. Failing that it will be a long-term foster placement, but I'm hopeful we can find them an adoptive family. They are young enough to adjust.'

'Yes, indeed. And how nice for them to have a fresh start,' I said, willing her to move on to Donna.

'Absolutely. I want to get that going as soon as possible.' Edna paused and took another sip of her tea, and I wasn't sure if it was my imagination but I thought she looked as though she was hesitating, or perhaps summoning up the courage to tell me something. She returned her cup to the saucer with a small chink, and then looked up and smiled at me reassuringly. 'Donna will remain in long-term foster care, Cathy. And after a lengthy discussion with my manager, we feel that it would be best if she was placed with a black carer or a couple who reflect her ethnicity.'

'Oh,' I said. 'Oh, I see.'

Edna smiled kindly. 'I know, Cathy. Donna has done incredibly well since she's been with you. I'm so grateful to you and your family, but the issue of her cultural identity remains. It wasn't a decision we took lightly, but we really do feel Donna should be found a family who can help her with her cultural identity. You remember when she was trying to rub her skin off?'

'Yes, but she hasn't done that for a long time,' I said, almost as a plea for her to stay.

'No, I know, thanks to you. But I think you will agree that Donna is still struggling with her self-image. Only last week her teacher overheard her telling Emily that she wished she was white like her.'

'Did she?' I asked, taken aback. 'I didn't know.'

Edna nodded. 'You have done so much for Donna and I can't thank you enough, but in respect of her cultural needs the scars inflicted by her mother run deep. The Guardian and judge agreed this would be best addressed in a black or dual-heritage family. I realise this will mean another move for Donna when she is so settled with you, but it's thought it's for the best. I hope I've made the right decision, Cathy. You will of course keep in touch with her; it's important that you do.'

'Yes,' I said, finally coming to terms with what Edna was saying. 'Yes, of course we will. We're going to miss her very much.'

'I know you will, and she'll miss you.'

Although the news wasn't what I'd anticipated, or wanted to hear, I could see the truth in what Edna had said, and if I was honest I suppose part of me had wondered if Donna's cultural identity would come into Edna's plans for Donna's future.

'I shall also be looking for a family where there are no younger children,' Edna added. 'You have coped remarkably well, but I don't want a repetition of what happened here with Paula and Adrian.'

'Donna wouldn't do that again,' I said defensively. 'That's all under control now.'

'I know, and Adrian and Paula have been so accepting of Donna, but Donna does need a lot of attention. I'm hoping to find her a family where the carers' own children are older, or have even left home. Donna is an absolute credit to you, as are Adrian and Paula.'

'Thank you, Edna,' I said, although the praise did nothing to soften my disappointment. 'I'll have to let Adrian and Paula down gently,' I said reflectively.

Edna nodded, then finished the last of her tea while I remained quietly watching her.

'In a minute when I see Donna,' Edna said, 'I'll tell her the outcome of the case, but I'm not going to say anything yet about the proposed move. I have a meeting with the Family Finders team later this week, but as you know it could take months to find a suitable family. I don't want Donna becoming unsettled here. Once we have identified suitable carers I will speak to her and explain.'

'All right,' I said. It was a sensible decision. It wouldn't have helped Donna to know at this point.

'Now to the matter of contact,' Edna said. 'We will be reducing it to once a month straight away for Donna and the boys to see their mother.'

'Good,' I said.

'It will still be supervised, but I will be handing over the supervision to someone else. Once Donna and the boys go on to permanency it will be three times a year.'

I nodded. This was usual for children who wouldn't be returning home. Otherwise, if they were continually seeing their natural parents there was less chance of them settling and bonding with their 'forever families', as they are known.

'Once the children have moved I shall be arranging extra sibling contact,' Edna continued. 'It's not necessary now, as Donna and the boys see each other every day at school. Does Donna want to see Chelsea and the baby?'

'I'm not sure. I told her the news and suggested we bought a card, but Donna said she would think about it. She's still thinking about it as far as I know.'

Edna smiled. 'OK. I'll talk to her about that in a minute. I've brought the photograph.' She placed her cup and saucer on the coffee table and, opening her briefcase, passed me the photograph.

Chelsea was sitting in a chair beside her hospital bed; the iron bedhead and white cotton pillows were to the left of the photo. Baby Cindy, wrapped in a white blanket, was asleep on Chelsea's lap with her head resting on Chelsea's arm. Chelsea wasn't looking down at the baby as many new mothers do but stared into the camera. Her young, vulnerable face seemed to say it all: a mixture of surprise, shock and distance, as though she was struggling to come to terms with what had happened. She looked so lost that my heart went out to her. If ever a girl had needed looking after it was Chelsea.

'She's agreed to go into a mother and baby unit,' Edna said.

'Good,' I said, handing back the photograph. 'Hopefully Chelsea will be able to keep her baby.'

'Hopefully,' Edna repeated. 'I'll see Donna now then, please, Cathy.'

I went through to the front room and told Donna that Edna wanted to see her, and I also told the girls to say goodnight to each other, as it was Paula's bedtime. Leaving Edna with Donna in the lounge, I took Paula upstairs.

'Is Donna staying?' Paula whispered as we turned the landing, for even Paula, at her age, knew that the final court hearing meant decisions.

'Yes, for now,' I said. 'The judge has decided she won't be returning home.'

'Good,' Paula said. 'Her mum is horrible.'

I perched on the edge of the bath and looked at Paula as she washed her face. 'You know, love, Donna's mother wasn't born horrible. I know she's done bad things to Donna but she hasn't always been like that. Perhaps her mother wasn't nice to her. Since Donna has been with us we've shown her a different way to behave so that if she has children one day, she'll know how to treat them and love them properly.'

'Donna will make a good mother,' Paula said, drying her face on the towel. 'She's a kind person. She doesn't get angry with me any more.'

'That's right, love. And she was never really angry with you. It just came out that way.'

'I won't get angry with my children, and Donna won't get angry with hers,' Paula said decisively.

'I know, love, you are both very kind people. And I love you!'

Giving Paula a big hug, I then went with her to her bedroom and saw her into bed. I had just started reading a bedtime story when I heard Edna call from the hall. 'I'm off now, Cathy.'

'I'll finish your story in a minute,' I said to Paula, and kissing her forehead, I went downstairs.

'Everything all right?' I asked Edna as I met her in the hall. Donna was still in the lounge.

'Yes, Donna is fine. I've explained the judge's decision, and given her the photograph. She doesn't want to see Chelsea yet, so I've told her to tell you if she changes her mind. Now I must be getting back to my hubby.'

It was after 7.30 p.m. and I doubted Edna would have finished yet; having spent all morning in court and away from her office, she would doubtless have some reports to write. I opened the front door and wished her goodnight.

'Oh yes,' she said, suddenly remembering something. 'About the therapy.' She lowered her voice so that Donna couldn't hear from the lounge. 'I feel it should wait until after her move. It would be too much for Donna to begin therapy and cope with a move to permanency.'

'Yes,' I agreed. 'And there's no urgency for therapy now. Donna is doing so well.'

'I know,' Edna said with a smile. 'Thanks to you. Goodnight and God bless, Cathy.'

'And you, Edna.'

Chapter Twenty-two

Marlene

Life continued as usual for us while the 'family finding' for Donna went on unseen in the background (and unknown to Donna, Adrian or Paula). I felt very sad sometimes as I watched Donna going about a task, or playing with Paula and Adrian, aware that at some point she would no longer be with us. Edna asked me to send her a full-face photograph of Donna, which was easy, for I had plenty to choose from. This would be used to 'advertise' Donna in fostering magazines, and also on flyers sent to approved foster carers. Beside her photograph would be a small piece about her, and the type of family that was wanted. Advertising a child is an emotive issue but has been shown to be highly effective in finding the right family for a child – for how else can prospective parents be paired with children in need of a family? – although the child is never aware they are being 'advertised'.

I expected the family finding to take some time for Donna, as the social services were looking for quite a distinctive family – black or dual heritage, and with no younger children – which would obviously limit the number of applicants. This was fine with me, for while I recognised Donna needed to be settled with her forever family as soon as possible for her own good, on a purely selfish level, I was pleased we had the extra time with her. It was the middle of September, and Donna had been with us for over a year, when Edna phoned me out of the blue to say Family Finders had found a good match for Donna, and could I attend the 'matching meeting' scheduled for the following Wednesday.

'Er, yes,' I said, quickly coming to terms with what I was being told. 'Yes, of course.' The matching meeting was to make sure the carers, or carer, who'd come forward, wanting to parent Donna, were the most appropriate, before the match was approved by the 'permanency panel' and Donna was told. Having been part of this process before, I knew how it worked, and also that it did work: mistakes were very rare.

'Her name is Marlene,' Edna said. 'She's lovely, but I'll let you be the judge of that.' Which was all I would know about Donna's new carer until I met her at the meeting.

The children had returned to school for the autumn term, the week before – Adrian was in the first year of his new grammar school, Paula had gone up a year in her junior school and Donna was in the final year of her junior school. The matching meeting was scheduled for 10.00 a.m., at the social services office, and I made my way up the various flights of stairs towards the small committee room with no small amount of trepidation. For when all was said and done I was about to meet the person who would be taking over from me and would eventually become as close to Donna as I had been.

Going into the committee room, I smiled at the assembled group, then took a chair at the large square wooden table. Joyce, from the permanency team, whom'd I'd met before, was chairing and opened the meeting by asking us to introduce ourselves. Apart from Joyce, Jill, Edna and myself, there was Marlene, her link worker Carla, and Lisa, a trainee student social worker who would be taking the minutes. Marlene was sitting directly opposite me, and I eyed her suspiciously. She was certainly an attractive and elegant-looking woman, but would she make a good mother for Donna? I tried to remain objective as I scrutinised her, without appearing rude. Her brown skin was almost the same as Donna's, and her hair was black and well oiled, as I'd tried to do for Donna. Her large dark eyes seemed warm as she looked at me and smiled. I guessed she was in her early fifties, and she wore a light pink jumper and black skirt. She sat upright, with her hands folded loosely in front of her on the table. When she spoke, she had the faintest hint of an accent, a milder version of Granny Bajan's Caribbean accent. She must have felt self-conscious, for the meeting centred on her, but she didn't show it and appeared calm and dignified.

Having introduced ourselves, Joyce explained the purpose of the meeting for the minutes, then asked Edna to give us an update on Donna. Edna would have met Marlene at least once prior to this meeting, as well as having read Marlene's details and discussing her application to foster Donna with Joyce from the permanency team. Likewise Marlene would have had the chance to read the details about Donna, and would also have had the opportunity of discussing these with Edna and Joyce. Edna was being asked to bring Marlene up to date, therefore, adding to what Marlene already knew about Donna.

Edna looked at Marlene as she talked about Donna's continued progress – during the summer holidays and now she had returned to school. She described Donna's personality, elaborated on her background before she came into care and described some of the problems we'd encountered in the early days, all of which Marlene would have had some knowledge of from her previous meeting with Edna and Joyce. 'Donna wants to be a nurse when she grows up,' Edna finished by saying.

I nodded and smiled. 'She talks of nothing else,' I said, 'and is always administering medicine to her dolls.' Everyone smiled. The mood of the meeting was relaxed and informal, for this was about the beginning of a new family where Donna had a new mother and Marlene a daughter, unlike some of the meetings I attend, which are very serious and formal and deal with abuse before a child is brought into care.

'Perhaps you would like to continue?' Joyce asked me.

I nodded and took Donna's Life Story book from my bag and passed it across the table to Marlene. I had begun the book when Donna had first arrived and it was now bulging with photographs, paper memorabilia such as cinema tickets and school merit certificates, and with a handwritten commentary from me. I compiled a Life Story book for all the children I looked after and it was an important and ongoing piece of work that the child took with them. For unlike one's own children, who are continuously surrounded by their past in the form of other family members and their shared memories, once the fostered child had left, particularly if they didn't keep in touch, the Life Story book was the only evidence they had of their time with us, together with their own memories.

Marlene turned the pages as I spoke. I began by saying, as Edna had, how much Donna had improved since she'd been with us, and how loved she was by my family. I went over the problems we'd encountered, and how I had dealt with them. It was no good giving Marlene an unrealistic account, for that would have been dishonest, and also left her ill-prepared for any problems that might arise, particularly in the early days when they were still getting to know each other. I told Marlene why I thought Donna had behaved as she had, setting it in the context of her past. So I described her bullying of Adrian and Paula as a result of the bullying and degradation Donna had endured in all the years she'd lived with her mother.

'So when my niece and nephew visit I should keep an eye on them?' Marlene asked, glancing up from the Life Story book. 'They are five and six years old.'

'To begin with, yes, I think so,' I confirmed, and Edna nodded. 'We haven't had an incident for nearly four months now, and I'm sure we won't have another one, but it's as well to be cautious to begin with.'

'Donna could become a little unsettled by the move,' Edna said, 'although I'd put money on it not happening again.'

Apart from any personal responsibility I felt to be honest with Marlene, it was exactly because of the possibility of this type of situation that Marlene had described (her niece and nephew visiting) that it was so important for Edna and me to be honest. There have been incidents recorded where information had been withheld from a carer by a social worker and injury had resulted.

'Does Donna still tear up paper?' Marlene asked with a small smile.

I returned her smile. 'Yes, and I haven't stopped her, although she knows not to do it when visiting other people's houses.'

'It's something that can be addressed at therapy,' Edna said, 'which I intend to start as soon as Donna has settled after the move. I have the funding approved for it.'

Marlene nodded. 'That should help.' She turned the last few pages of the Life Story book and passed it back across the table. 'Donna looks a lovely child and has obviously been very happy with you. I hope I can make her as happy. My family are looking forward to meeting her. I have two grown-up children, a girl and a boy in their twenties, and lots of nieces and nephews. We have large family gatherings most weekends, and I'm sure Donna will get along well with my niece Kerry, who is the same age as Donna. I visit Barbados every year. My grandfather was born in Barbados and I have aunts and cousins who still live there.'

'Really?' I said, surprised and delighted. 'Donna's grandmother is from Barbados. Will you be taking Donna when you visit?'

'Of course,' Marlene said, slightly taken aback that there could be any suggestion she wouldn't. 'Has she ever been before?'

'No,' Edna said. 'Her gran visits for some of the winter, but Donna has never been.'

'She'll love it,' Marlene said. 'We stay with my family and there's always a house full of relatives and neighbours. It's like one big party, the whole time.'

'I'd love it too,' I said, laughing. 'Can I come?'

'And me,' Edna and Joyce chorused.

I was quickly warming to Marlene. She appeared a naturally kind and open person, who had obviously carefully thought through her application to look after Donna long term and the commitment and responsibility that would entail. As Marlene spoke, I learned that she had been fostering for five years, but they had all been short-term placements and she really felt she had more to offer a child on a permanent basis. We talked about Donna's self-image in respect of her race, which Marlene was in an ideal position to address: her mother was black, and her father was white British, although both her parents were now dead. Marlene had no children at home, so she could give Donna all the attention and help she required. She worked part-time as a psychiatric nurse with flexible hours that could be adjusted, so she could take Donna to school and collect her.

Marlene lived fifteen miles from where I did, so us keeping in touch wasn't going to be a problem. Edna had already emphasised, both at the meeting and when she'd met Marlene previously, that it was important we kept in touch with Donna, particularly in the months straight after the move. 'Donna mustn't in any way feel that she has been rejected again,' Edna said. 'And obviously once this match has been approved by the permanency panel I shall speak to Donna and explain the reasons for the move to her myself.'

By the end of the meeting I was certain that Marlene was the right person for Donna. Although I would still be very sad to see Donna go, I had to admit it was a perfect match; indeed, if someone had drawn up a profile of the most suitable person to be Donna's mum, it would have been Marlene. Joyce concluded the meeting, firstly by asking everyone if they had any more questions, which no one did. Then she went round the table asking each of us if we were happy for this match to go before the permanency panel, which would sit again on 5 October. Marlene answered first and said a loud and very positive 'Yes. Absolutely. I'm looking forward to meeting Donna' (which she wouldn't do until after the panel had approved the placement). Marlene's link worker said yes, she felt it was an excellent match, as did Edna, Joyce, Jill and Lisa.

I looked across the table at Marlene as I said, 'Yes, I think Donna will be very happy with you. She's a lucky girl.'

'Thank you, Cathy,' Marlene replied, embarrassed. 'That's very kind of you.'

Joyce wound up the meeting by saying we would all meet again on 6 October, after the permanency panel had given their approval, to plan the move. This was normal procedure: the introduction of Marlene and Donna would be carefully structured. It was likely to take place over a two-week period, resulting in the move at the end of that time if everything was all right, which I felt sure it would be.

As the meeting closed and everyone began to leave, I said goodbye to Jill, who would be visiting us the following week, and I also took the opportunity of asking Edna how Chelsea was. I hadn't spoken to Edna for a couple of weeks, and the last time she had visited us, three weeks before, she'd said that Chelsea and Cindy were doing well in the mother and baby unit. Donna still hadn't wanted to visit her.

'Yes, Chelsea is doing fine,' Edna confirmed. 'Whether she can continue as she has been doing when she moves to the flat remains to be seen.'

'She's leaving the mother and baby unit then?'

'In a month. I'm not on the case now that I'm part-time and semi-retired. But my colleague has found her a nice little one-bedroom flat on View Estate, and will be closely monitoring her and the baby. She wanted to keep Chelsea in the unit for longer, but Chelsea said she would run away if they didn't find her a flat soon.'

'Hopefully Chelsea has learned enough to look after the baby,' I said.

'Hopefully. It's whether she can look after herself as well, and keep the flat clean. At sixteen I'm not sure I could.'

'No,' I agreed. 'Nor me.'

'My hubby says I have to stop worrying about her now she's no longer my responsibility. I'm continuing part-time until Donna and the boys are settled, then we're off to stay with our children in Scotland for a month.'

'Lovely,' I said. 'And what about Rita? Isn't her baby due now? It must be soon.'

Edna's face fell. 'She had it last week.' I looked surprised. 'I haven't said anything to Donna because I didn't want to worry her. Rita has disappeared.'

'What? With the baby?'

Edna nodded. 'She had a little girl. Later the same day Rita walked out of the hospital with the baby. My colleague has taken out an Emergency Protection Order, and the police are looking for her.' She sighed. 'Goodness knows where she's staying. I suppose I should tell Donna – she has a right to know.'

'Do you want me to tell her, Edna? I could keep it low key and reassure her?'

'Yes, please, Cathy, would you? Give Donna my love and tell her I'll phone when I have any news.'

'Will do. I'll put the emphasis on how well Chelsea is doing.'

'Thanks, Cathy.'

When I told Donna that evening about her mother's baby and subsequent disappearance she shrugged. 'Typical,' she said. 'I hope they find the baby soon.'

'They will,' I reassured her.

'At least I'm out of all that now,' she added, and that was all Donna said.

A week later Edna phoned to say that Rita and the baby had been found. Apparently Rita had eventually returned to her house, and a neighbour had heard a baby crying virtually non-stop for twenty-four hours and alerted the social services. The colleague of Edna's who was now dealing with the case went to the house with the police and found it filthy and cold. Rita was drunk in bed with the baby beside her. The baby's nappy was overflowing with faeces, having not been changed for days. On being admitted to hospital the baby was found to have lost weight and be dehydrated. Edna said that as soon as the baby had regained the weight and was well enough to be discharged from hospital she would go straight to a foster carer. It didn't mean there wasn't any chance of Rita having her baby back. The childcare proceeding would begin all over again, and Rita would be assessed to see if she could parent the child, which I had to admit looked far from hopeful. As

I had done so often since I'd begun fostering, I wished I could have waved a magic wand and made everything OK, so that Rita could look after her baby; but realistically only early intervention and education can stop the cycle of abuse and neglect.

Chapter Twenty-three

Lilac

The permanency panel approved Marlene's application to foster Donna, and on 6 October, Edna, Joyce, Marlene, her link worker, Jill, Lisa who was taking the minutes and I once more sat around the table in the committee room to plan Donna's introduction to Marlene, and ultimately her move. Edna had arranged to visit us at 5.30 that evening to tell Donna, and asked me not to say anything to her prior to this.

'How is Donna?' Marlene asked eagerly at the start of the meeting.

'Very well,' I said. 'Her school work has improved tremendously this term.'

Edna looked up. 'School is one of the issues I should like to discuss before we look at the dates of the introduction.'

'Go ahead,' Joyce said.

'Donna is doing so well at her school,' Edna said, 'I should like her to stay at the same school for her last year there. I realise it isn't local to you, Marlene, and the social services are prepared to provide an escort if you can't manage the school run. I appreciate it's, what, twenty miles from you?'

Marlene nodded thoughtfully. 'I would like to take Donna to school for at least some of the time so that I am in contact with the school. But it would be too much for me to take her and collect her each day, as well as my part-time job.' Which was perfectly reasonable. Marlene paused then looked at me. 'Does Donna still help at the breakfast club?'

'Yes, she really likes it. She has to be there at eight fifteen.'

'How about if I take Donna each morning,' Marlene said, looking at Edna, 'and the escort brings her home? I can go into work after I've dropped her off.'

'That's fine with me,' Edna said. 'I think it's a good arrangement.'

'Thanks,' Marlene said. 'That would help me a lot. And presumably when Donna leaves her junior school at the end of the year, you won't mind her going to a local secondary school? We have a very good one only five minutes away.'

'Not at all,' Edna confirmed. 'Indeed, it's important Donna does go to a local school, so that she can make new friends in your area.'

This was agreed, and minuted by Lisa.

'Contact,' Edna said, looking at us all. 'Since the final court hearing this has been reduced to one a month, which has been much better for Donna. From now on it will go to three times a year as per court order. Cathy,' Edna said turning to me, 'there will be no more contact while Donna is with you. The next one will be in December, after she's left you and is settled at Marlene's. Donna will still be seeing her brothers at school, and she doesn't want to see Chelsea at present.'

I nodded.

'Marlene,' Edna said, now turning to her. 'My colleague, Valerie, is taking over the case. She will arrange the date of the next contact nearer the time. It will be supervised and the venue may be changing. Valerie will be in touch once the move is complete.'

Marlene nodded and made a note in her diary.

'OK, that's all from me,' Edna said. 'Other than to say congratulations, Marlene.' Edna was congratulating Marlene on becoming Donna's new 'mum'.

'Yes, congratulations,' everyone added, and I smiled at Marlene.

'Thank you,' she said, embarrassed. 'I have Donna's room ready. It's lilac, with pine bedroom furniture. You said she liked lilac, Cathy.' Marlene looked at me.

'Yes, indeed,' I said, surprised, for it had been one small comment I'd made at the previous meeting when I'd described Donna's likes and dislikes. 'It sounds lovely.'

'Great,' Joyce said. 'Now all we have to do is move Donna into her new room.' Everyone laughed. 'Marlene, did you bring some photographs of you and your family for Edna to show Donna?' Joyce asked.

The photographs would form part of Donna's introduction to Marlene and her family, and they were an important first step. Edna would show them to Donna that evening, talk her through them, and then leave the album with her, so that when the introductions began Donna would already be partially familiar with what was to be her new family and home.

Marlene bent down and delved into her handbag on the floor beside her chair. She took out a little photograph wallet, which she propped open on the table so that we could all see. 'This is my house,' she said pointing to the first page; then, slowly turning the pages: 'my lounge, my kitchen, my garden, and my cat, Harris. This is Donna's bedroom, and this is my immediate family.' The last photo was of a group of ten or more adults and children, all smiling and waving for the photo. They were arranged on and around the sofa in Marlene's lounge and had obviously adopted their best poses for the camera. 'We had a bit of a laugh taking this,' Marlene said with a smile.

'I can imagine,' Edna said. 'Can you tell me who these people are so I can tell Donna?'

Marlene angled the album towards Edna. 'This is my sister and her husband,' she said pointing. 'This is my brother and his wife, and their children. These are my two cousins and their partners, and this is Kerry, the niece I mentioned who is the same age as Donna.' Marlene was divorced, so there was no husband in the photo.

'What a lovely family,' I said.

'Thank you.' Marlene smiled and, closing the album, passed it to Edna.

'Thank you very much, Marlene,' Edna said. 'This will help me a lot when I see Donna.'

And while it was a clearly a lovely family Donna would be going to, I felt what had become a familiar surge of regret and sadness that my own lovely family was soon going to be one short.

'Now,' Mary said, 'let's get down to the dates. Edna, you are going to see Donna this evening?' Edna nodded. 'So I suggest Marlene visits Donna and Cathy tomorrow for an hour. It's Saturday. Is that possible?' Mary looked at Marlene and me, and we both nodded. 'Then could Donna and Cathy visit Marlene on Sunday for an hour?' Once the introductory process is started it quickly gathers momentum, so that the child isn't left for days in limbo between one home and the next, with time to worry and speculate about the partially known.

'I go to church at eleven o'clock on Sunday,' Marlene said, 'so can we avoid that time?'

I nodded. 'You say the time that would suit you. But I will have to bring Paula and Adrian with me as it's a Sunday.' I looked from Marlene to Edna. 'Is that all right?'

'That's fine with me,' Marlene said.

Edna agreed. 'I should think they will quite enjoy it, and it will be nice for Donna as well.' I was relieved. Once before I'd dealt with a social worker who hadn't wanted my children involved in the introductory visits. Not only had I had to make extensive arrangements for my parents to look after Adrian and Paula, but also the children had felt excluded from the process, which wasn't the best way to say goodbye to a child who had effectively been their brother for nearly a year.

With Edna, Marlene and me making notes in our diaries, and Lisa minuting the dates and times, we planned the rest of the introduction, including three nights when Donna would sleep at her new home, before the move two weeks later. There were days in between some of the visits to give Donna, Marlene and my family time out, and for Edna, Marlene and me to speak on the phone and discuss how the introduction was going, and make any necessary alterations to the timescale. If it went according to plan, then Donna would move on Saturday, in two weeks' time. The week after that was the half-term holiday from school and Marlene said she would take the whole week off work so that she and Donna could spend time together before the school routine began again.

An hour later the meeting ended and I drove home, reflective and a little anxious. Although Edna had recognised the need to make sure Donna didn't feel rejected by the move, it was still a monumental step for Donna. She had been with us for just over fourteen months and in many respects if felt longer, so strong was the bond we had formed with her, as I knew she had with us. And while I liked Marlene very much, and had every faith in her ability to successfully parent Donna, I knew it was likely that the move, no matter how well planned, could unsettle Donna, and rekindle some feelings of rejection (and anger) in the short term. But Marlene, Edna and I would have to deal with those as and when they arose.

I met the children from school that afternoon with a heavy heart but careful to keep my feelings to myself. I made dinner and told the children we were eating early because Edna was coming at 5.30 p.m. to see Donna, which didn't seem strange to them, as we always ate early when Edna or the Guardian visited in the evening. But secretly I felt guilty for withholding the information that only I was party to – the real reason for Edna's visit. When Edna rang the doorbell at exactly 5.30 my stomach churned, while the children remained upstairs playing in their respective bedrooms, still blissfully unaware of the true reason for Edna's visit.

'All right?' Edna said with her usual cheerful smile as I opened the front door.

I put on a brave face and nodded. 'Donna is in her room. I'll bring her down.'

'Thank you, Cathy.'

Edna went through to the lounge while I fetched Donna and saw her into the lounge. I asked Edna if she wanted a drink, which she didn't, and I came out, closing the door behind me. Edna had already told me that she wanted to talk to Donna alone first, and I returned upstairs, where I had some talking to do.

'Will you come with me into Adrian's room for a moment?' I said to Paula, poking my head round her bedroom door. 'I need to speak to you both.'

Paula looked at me, wondering what I could want, then put down the doll she'd been playing with and came with me to Adrian's room. I knocked on his bedroom door and we went in. He was still doing his homework, of which there was plenty now he was at the grammar school. 'It won't take long,' I said to him. 'But I have something important I need to tell you both.'

He laid his pen on the table which acted as a desk. 'It's good news, but also sad,' I said, bravely. 'Edna is here to tell Donna that she has found her a forever family. So I'm afraid she will be leaving us.' There was no other way to say it. 'Her new carer is called Marlene. She is very nice and will be visiting us here tomorrow.'

'Oh,' Adrian said, clearly taken aback. Paula didn't say anything but looked as though she was about to cry. I put my arm around her.

'When?' Adrian asked

'If everything goes according to plan she'll move in two weeks.'

'Oh,' Adrian said again, and, picking up his pen, he returned to his school work. This was his way of dealing with loss, and I knew he would want to talk more about it later.

Leaving Adrian to his school work, I took Paula's hand and we returned to her room. 'Shall we play with your dolls while Edna is with Donna?' I asked, thinking this might be a good distraction.

She nodded, and I sat on the floor in front of her doll's house next to Paula, and she picked up the 'mummy' doll she'd been playing with when I'd interrupted. The doll was about three inches high and one of a set of four – two adults and two children. It was the epitome of the 'perfect' mum, with hair drawn into a neat bun and a white apron covering her knee-length floral dress. In one hand she carried a rolling pin, suggesting she was a very accomplished cook, or possibly as Adrian once said (to Paula's horror) it was to 'wallop the kids' with.

'Does Donna have to go?' Paula asked presently in a little voice, walking the mummy doll into the house.

'I'm afraid so, love. You remember like Jasmine did?' Jasmine had stayed with us for six months the year before and been found adoptive parents.

'Will Donna phone and see us sometimes?' Paula asked.

'Yes, I'm sure she will. I have met her new carer, Marlene, and she will help Donna to stay in touch.' Although in truth a balance would have to be drawn between Donna keeping in contact with us and bonding with Marlene and her family.

'Can I see where she's going to live?' Paula asked, giving me the 'daddy' doll.

'Yes, you will on Sunday. We're all going for a visit.' We wouldn't be meeting any of Marlene's family on our first visit: that could have been overwhelming for Donna. The first visit was for Donna to see her new home; meeting Marlene's extended family would come later and gradually over the two weeks.

I stayed in Paula's room, playing with her and the doll's house, although in truth my heart wasn't really in it, and I didn't think Paula's was either. Paula played the 'mummy', and her perfect mummy doll washed the pans in the tiny doll's house sink, and made the little beds, while I, the less than perfect daddy doll, stood watching her, although I did take the dog for a walk and put the garbage out when asked. Every so often Paula stopped her role playing and asked if Donna was all right, and what was Edna telling her.

'I'm sure she's fine, and Edna will be telling her lots of nice things about Marlene, and Donna's new home and family.'

'We're a nicer family,' Paula said defensively, and I smiled.

Nearly an hour passed before I heard the lounge door open and Edna call from the hall, 'Cathy, could you join us now, please.'

'I won't be long,' I said to Paula. Standing, I gave her a reassuring kiss on her cheek, and I left to the sound of Paula telling the mummy doll that she was the 'nicest mummy in the world', which I hoped reflected on me.

In the lounge Edna and Donna were sitting side by side on the sofa. Donna was holding the wallet of photographs that Marlene had prepared for her and given to Edna that morning. It reminded me for a moment of when Donna had first arrived – Donna and Edna together on the sofa. Although of course now Donna wasn't sitting dejectedly, shoulders hunched forward and arms folded into her waist as though protecting herself, but was upright and confident. I sat on the other sofa.

'Donna and I have had a nice long chat,' Edna said. 'And she is looking forward to meeting Marlene when she comes here tomorrow. Donna knows that it will be a bit strange for everyone to begin with, and that she can talk to you about her feelings.'

'I'm sure we will be talking a lot,' I said, smiling at Donna. She wasn't exactly smiling, but didn't seem unhappy, more deep in thought.

'Would you like to see my photographs?' she asked me after a moment.

'Yes please, very much.'

Edna winked at me knowingly. 'I'll leave you to it then. I'll be off now and I'll phone on Monday.'

'Fine,' I said. 'Donna, I'll just see Edna out then we'll look at your photographs together.' I smiled again at Donna and she smiled back.

I went with Edna to the front door. 'It appears to have gone well,' I said quietly.

'Yes, it did, bless her. She's so eager for you to see the photographs, I didn't let on you'd already seen them. But I've told her you've met Marlene and you like her. It's important for her to know that you approve.'

'Yes, thanks, Edna.'

We said goodbye and I closed the front door. Edna was a highly experienced and dedicated social worker, and also very sensitive to children's feelings. I didn't know what exactly Edna had said to Donna, but whatever it was had left Donna in a very positive mood. When I went into the lounge she was still poring over the photographs, eager to show me.

I sat beside her and watched as she carefully turned the pages, describing what was in each picture. When we came to the photograph of her bedroom her eyes lit up. 'It's lilac,' she exclaimed, as doubtless she had done when she'd first seen the photo with Edna. 'It's my favourite colour.'

'It is,' I said, 'and what a lovely room! Aren't you lucky?'

She nodded happily. 'I'm looking forward to seeing it on Sunday. That's when we visit, isn't it?'

'Yes, love, it is.'

Donna turned to the last photograph, of Marlene's extended family, and told me the names of those people she could remember. When Paula appeared five minutes later, Donna went through the photographs again, pointing out the details in each photo with a more elaborate commentary. When Adrian, having finished his homework, came down for a drink and snack twenty minutes later, Donna went through the photo wallet again.

That night when I went into Donna's room to say goodnight, I thought she looked sad. She was in her pyjamas, sitting in bed waiting for a goodnight kiss. The photograph album was closed in her lap. I perched on the edge of the bed and she looked at me with big wondering eyes. 'This time next week, 'she said, 'I shall be sleeping in my new bed for the first time.'

'That's right, love. In your beautiful lilac room with lilac sheets and duvet.' I took her hand between mine.

She thought for a moment, then said softly, 'I'm happy Marlene wants me as a daughter, but it will be a bit strange to begin with, like when I first came here.'

'It will seem a bit strange, yes, because it will all be new, but I don't think it will be like when you first came here, love. Do you remember how you felt then?' She nodded. 'You have come a long way since then, Donna, and I am very proud of you. I know you will be just fine, although we're going to miss you loads.'

'That's what Edna said.' She gave a little wistful smile. 'And we will keep in touch, won't we, Cathy? It's important to me.'

'Of course, love. It's important to us too. We'll all stay in touch for as long as you want, Donna. I promise you.'

She put her arms around me and hugged me tightly. 'For ever, Cathy. You will be my second family when Marlene is my new mum.'

Chapter Twenty-four

Introductions

As one o'clock approached the following day, the time Marlene was due, it was difficult to say who was the more nervous: Donna, who was standing behind the net curtains in the front room watching for the first glimpse of Marlene; Paula, who was making regular trips from the front room to the kitchen to update me; or me, wiping the work surfaces as a displacement for my own nervous energy. Adrian was perfecting his 'Mr Cool' image and, aware that Marlene's visit was soon, was in his room listening to his iPod. However, at 1.10 p.m., when I heard Donna's little voice call 'She's here,' followed by Paula's louder cry of 'She's here!' and I answered the door, it was obvious who was the most nervous – Marlene.

'Do I look all right?' she asked, smoothing her hand over her floral patterned dress and adjusting the small gold chain around her neck.

'Of course. You look fine. Come in.' I smiled and touched her arm reassuringly. 'The girls have been looking out for you.'

'I'm so sorry I'm late, Cathy. The traffic was horrendous, I should have guessed it would be busy on a Saturday.'

'Don't worry. They would have been watching for you whatever time you'd come. Let's go through to the lounge.'

I led the way down the hall to the lounge, at the same time calling, 'Donna, Paula, Marlene is here.' Now the longed-for arrival had happened the girls had gone shy and were hiding in the front room.

'Do sit down,' I said to Marlene. 'Can I get you a drink?'

'No thanks, Cathy. I'm fine. It's a lovely place you have here.'

'Thank you.' I sat on the other sofa. 'Your photographs were a great success,' I said. 'Donna was so proud of them – she must have shown us all at least six times.'

'Were they all right? Thank goodness. I did wonder,' Marlene said, flustered. 'I am pleased.' Although it was a fairly cool autumn day Marlene looked hot and her forehead glistened slightly.

I began making small talk – about the weather and the traffic in the high street; then I told Marlene more about Donna's school. It was better for Donna that we carried on in a natural manner, where there was no pressure on her; she would join us when she felt able. I told Marlene of our evening routine, some of which she could adapt in the first few days after the move to help make Donna feel at home. Then Marlene told me some more about her family. Presently we heard footsteps coming along the hall and Paula and Donna entered the lounge. Paula was holding Donna's hand and leading her, just as she had once led her down the garden in what now seemed a lifetime ago.

'Donna, Paula, this is Marlene,' I said. Marlene stood, and went over and shook Paula's hand, then Donna's. Donna had her eyes trained on the floor, and for the first time since I couldn't remember when, she had her shoulders slightly hunched forward.

'Lovely to meet you both,' Marlene said, and she glanced anxiously at me.

'Come and sit down,' I said to the girls. 'We've been talking about the photographs, and the people in the family group. Marlene is going to see her niece, Kerry, later.'

Paula led Donna to the sofa and they sat beside me. Marlene returned to the other sofa, and we picked up our conversation about Marlene's family for a few minutes, so the atmosphere was relaxed. Out of the corner of my eye I saw Donna gradually raise her head and steal a glance at Marlene, then lower it again quickly. Marlene smiled and continued talking. A moment later our cat, Toscha, sauntered into the lounge.

'Hello,' Marlene said, and Donna glanced between Toscha and Marlene. 'Did you see the picture of my cat, Harris?' Marlene asked.

'Yes,' I said. 'He's quite a bit bigger than Toscha.' Donna looked up, for longer this time.

'Harris is a very lazy cat,' Marlene said. 'All he does is eat and sleep. He's part Persian, so he has long hair and needs a lot of brushing.'

'I brush Toscha,' Donna said, raising her head and speaking for the first time.

'I don't,' Paula said. 'Toscha scratched me once.'

'That's because you poked your finger in her ear, when you were little,' I said to Paula, and she giggled.

'Shall I brush Toscha now?' Donna asked quietly, daring to raise her head for longer.

We didn't normally brush the cat in the lounge because of the hair but I thought it would help 'break the ice' and give us a focal point. 'Yes, if you like. You know where the brush is.'

Donna and Paula went to the cupboard under the stairs to fetch the brush. I smiled at Marlene. 'Don't worry. Donna is slowly thawing out. It's bound to take time. I wouldn't have expected any different.'

'Do you think she likes me?' Marlene asked anxiously.

'Yes, of course. Please don't worry.'

The girls returned with the cat brush, and Donna sat on the floor beside Toscha and began grooming her, brushing her fur from the neck down towards her tail as I had shown her. She had a naturally light touch and a soothing, almost soporific manner, as though caressing the cat with each stroke of the brush. Toscha stretched out and yawned contentedly, making the most of this sudden and unscheduled attention. Paula sat a little away from them, not wholly convinced the cat wouldn't suddenly remember her poking its ear and turn and seek revenge, although I had spent a long time trying to convince Paula otherwise.

Marlene slipped from the sofa and joined Donna on the floor. 'Hello Toscha,' she said gently, then began stroking the cat's forehead while Donna continued her slow leisurely brushing. I thought the cat was going to be very spoilt after all this.

'Harris is going to love you, Donna,' Marlene said. I smiled, and so too did Donna.

Marlene and I kept the conversation going while she continued stroking Toscha's forehead as Donna brushed. I steered the conversation to Marlene's house, and said how much Donna liked the photograph of her bedroom. Marlene said she had redecorated it herself and was about to start redecorating the kitchen. Adrian appeared and I introduced him to Marlene. He went over, and she stood to shake hands.

'How is school?' she asked.

'Good, thanks,' Adrian said, then he disappeared into the kitchen to get himself a drink, before returning to his bedroom. I hoped she didn't think him rude.

'He has a lot of school work,' I offered.

Marlene nodded. 'My son is twenty-two now, and is in his last year at university. He's studying law.'

'That's a good profession,' I said.

A few minutes later I thought the cat grooming had run its course and I suggested to Donna that she did a jigsaw puzzle, with the intention of Marlene and her doing most of it, so that they could continue working together.

'I'm not very good at jigsaws,' Marlene said. 'Are you, Donna?'

'A little,' she said in a small voice.

I went to the toy cupboard and found a jigsaw that could be completed in the twenty minutes that was left of Marlene's visit. Marlene and Donna sat side by side on the floor and began sifting through the pieces, finding the corners and straight edges, with Paula helping. I continued to make light conversation. It wasn't the easiest situation, but I hadn't expected anything different with the first meeting. I hoped that Marlene wasn't disappointed and hadn't expected Donna to rush into her arms and treat her as a new mother. An hour was enough for this first visit, and once the jigsaw was complete, I confirmed the arrangements for the following day. 'Is one o'clock still all right for us to visit you?' I asked Marlene.

'Yes. Would you like me to make some lunch?'

I thought having to sit and eat lunch might be too much for Donna on her first visit to Marlene's. 'No, don't worry about lunch,' I said. 'A drink and a biscuit will be fine.'

Marlene returned to the sofa for a few minutes and Donna fell quiet again. 'OK,' Marlene said after a moment, 'I'll look forward to seeing you all again tomorrow.' She said goodbye to Donna and Paula in the lounge, and I saw her to the door.

'It will be easier tomorrow,' I reassured her, for Marlene did look quite worried.

'Do you think she likes me?' Marlene asked again, as she had done in the lounge.

'Yes, you did fine. Please don't worry. It's a huge step for Donna, and she'll need time to reflect on this meeting. I know her – meeting new people is always difficult for her. Would you like me to phone you this evening?'

'Oh, yes please,' she said, relieved. 'You will tell me if I'm doing anything wrong, won't you?'

'Yes, but I'm sure you're not. Donna is quiet at the best of times.'

'I do hope she likes me,' Marlene said again.

I renewed my assurance and we said goodbye.

For the rest of the afternoon Donna talked about nothing else apart from Marlene and her home: 'Do you think …?' she asked repeatedly. 'Will she have …? Does she like …?' Sometimes I could answer her questions but often I had to say, 'I don't know, but that's something you could ask Marlene tomorrow.' When we sat down to dinner and the questions were still coming, I said, 'Donna, Marlene is the best person to ask, and she would like it if you did ask her questions and talk to her. You might not realise it, but Marlene is just as nervous as you are. She so much wants you to like her.'

'I do like her,' she said quietly. 'It's just all a bit strange.'

'I know, love. I do understand.'

That evening I phoned Marlene while Donna was in the bath and told her that Donna hadn't stopped talking about her all afternoon. 'And she likes you already,' I said.

'Did she say so?'

'Yes, and she's going to try to talk more tomorrow.'

'Oh, that's great. Thank you for telling me. After I left you I bought some more jigsaws, and also a new doll, which I have sat on Donna's bed.' Marlene was trying so hard – I really felt for her.

'That's lovely,' I said, 'but please don't worry. I know this will work out fine. It will just take time.'

That evening after I had read Donna a bedtime story and was saying goodnight to her, she said, 'It feels so strange, Cathy. I think it's because Marlene is different to you.'

'Just as well,' I said, smiling. 'Give yourself time, love. It's strange for Marlene too. She appreciates how you must be feeling.' Donna smiled but was clearly deep in thought. I remained perched on the edge of the bed and stroked her forehead. 'You all right, love?'

She nodded. 'Cathy, do you think Marlene really does want me?'

'Yes, of course, love. Whatever made you ask?'

'My mum didn't want me.'

'Is that what you've been thinking about?'

She nodded, and looked up at me imploringly.

'Donna, love, your mum had so many problems in her life that they stopped her from seeing the beautiful things. She couldn't appreciate you, look after you or love you enough, because of her problems. Marlene and I, and most mothers, are different. You are a lovely person, and I know

Marlene already likes you. I also know that in time she will love you as we do.'

She smiled. As we had thought might happen, the introduction to Marlene had unsettled Donna and brought back the negative feelings and memories from her past. Prior to me, the other person who had been in the mothering role, far from liking Donna, had treated her appallingly. I could only offer so much reassurance; the rest would come when Donna saw for herself that Marlene behaved as I did, with the same respect and love.

As predicted, our visit to Marlene's, the following day, was a lot easier, with everyone far more relaxed. Marlene met us at the door of her three-bedroom semi with its neat front garden, and began a tour of the house. Harris, her large (and lazy) cat, was sprawled on the sofa in the lounge and living up to his reputation. Adrian sat on the sofa next to the cat and stayed downstairs, while Marlene showed the girls and me upstairs. Donna was keen to see her bedroom, and it was even more luxurious than the photograph had suggested. The smell of fresh paint still hung in the air, and the crisp cotton lilac curtains and matching duvet cover were brand new. There were lots of little matching accessories – a pale lilac shaded lamp, a lilac velvet-topped dressing-table stool and the new doll in a lavender-colour dress that Marlene had bought specially sitting on the bed. I hoped Donna appreciated just how much trouble Marlene had gone to.

'Isn't it lovely?' I said to Donna. 'You are a lucky girl.'

Donna smiled, and looked as though she did appreciate it. She and Paula sat on the bed and began playing with the doll. The doll was about twelve inches high and dressed in

Victorian costume with layers of petticoats topped with the lavender-coloured satin dress. It was a lovely doll and I guessed quite expensive.

'Do you want to stay here and play for a while?' Marlene asked the girls. 'Cathy and I can go downstairs.' The girls nodded. 'We'll be in the lounge when you've finished,' Marlene added.

Downstairs Marlene set up the PlayStation for Adrian, and she and I sat in the armchairs at one end of the lounge-cum-dining room and chatted, while Adrian amused himself at the other end. Marlene told me that she had moved to the house three years previously and had had to extensively modernise, and redecorate every room. An elderly couple had lived in the house before her, for most of their lives, and the upkeep of the house had become too much for them. Marlene said that although the house was structurally sound she had been working on it continuously since moving in. I admired Marlene's handiwork and told her of my own decorating.

'When you live by yourself,' she said, 'it's surprising what you can do if you have to. I have even plumbed in the new kitchen sink.'

'Really?' I said, impressed.

The kitchen was the last room that needed work doing to it, Marlene said, and she wanted to show me how far she had got. 'My family give me a hand sometimes,' she said as we went into the kitchen, 'but I don't like to keep asking them.' The new gleaming stainless-steel sink stood out against a backdrop of half-removed tiles. 'They're dreadful to get off,' Marlene said. 'The news ones are over there.' She pointed to a stack of boxes by the wall. 'The next job is to replace the kitchen cupboards,' she continued, happy to have an appreciative audience. 'I've got a local man coming in to help. Then it's the flooring.' She tapped her foot on the torn and faded linoleum. 'I haven't decided what to put down yet.'

'It will be lovely when it's finished,' I said. 'I'm afraid my DIY is limited to painting and wallpapering.'

'I've had enough of it now,' she admitted with a small sigh. 'I'll be pleased when it's finished and I can just enjoy it.'

Marlene made us a cup of tea, then called the girls and Adrian for a drink and biscuits. We sat around the table in the dining area of the lounge and chatted – Adrian about the PlayStation game, and Donna and Paula about Donna's bedroom. Once we'd finished the drinks, Marlene cleared away the cups and glasses and produced one of the jigsaw puzzles she'd bought. Marlene, the girls and I sat at the table and slowly assembled it while Adrian returned to the PlayStation.

Our hour's visit ran over time but it didn't matter; Donna was clearly far more relaxed than she had been the day before, and appeared to be enjoying herself. Marlene was more relaxed too. Once the jigsaw was complete I began to take our leave. I confirmed the details of Donna's next visit, which would take place on Tuesday. I would bring Donna straight from school to Marlene's and she would stay for dinner; then I would collect her at 7.30 p.m. This was to be repeated on Thursday. Then, if everything was going all right, she would stay over on Friday and Saturday night, and I would collect her on Sunday morning. It had been decided at the planning meeting that Donna wouldn't accompany Marlene to church on this occasion as it could be too much for her so soon, and I would collect Donna at 10.00 a.m. on the Sunday. Donna was due to stay the night of the following Wednesday, and Marlene would take her to school in the morning. If everything went well, we would then have a little farewell party for Donna on the Friday, and I would move her to Marlene's on the Saturday. It was going to be a very busy two weeks: apart from the practical aspect of driving Donna to and from Marlene's, I would also be spending a lot of time talking to Donna, and generally keeping an eye on her to make sure she felt comfortable with the pace at which we were going.

The two evening visits, Tuesday and Thursday, went very well – better than I had anticipated – but a problem arose on the Saturday, although I didn't find out until I collected Donna on Sunday morning.

It had been really strange not having Donna sleeping in her bed at home, and a taste of what it would be like when she had moved. Donna's place at the meal table was glaringly empty, and suddenly three seemed a very small number. 'I wonder what Donna is doing,' Adrian and Paula asked more than once on Saturday, to which I replied, 'I expect she is getting to know Marlene,' or 'Playing,' or 'Possibly helping Marlene with her kitchen.' Marlene had already said that she'd appreciate Donna's help in finishing her kitchen. And I wondered if perhaps I hadn't let Donna help enough, and crucified myself thinking of all the things that I could have handled differently – better, if I'd had another chance. But that is the nature of fostering, and child rearing in general – you do what you think is best at the time and try not to repeat your mistakes in the future.

On Sunday morning when we arrived at 10.00 a.m. to collect Donna, Marlene met us at the door, looking very worried. Donna was nowhere to be seen downstairs.

'She's in her bedroom,' Marlene said, 'sulking, I'm afraid. Would Adrian and Paula like to play in the lounge while I speak to you in the kitchen?'

I motioned for the children to go into the lounge, where Adrian immediately picked up the controls to the PlayStation and began explaining to Paula what she had to do. I followed Marlene into the kitchen, wondering what Donna could have done. I felt my anxiety rise.

'I've dealt with it as best I could,' Marlene began. 'But I've had to tell Donna off, and she's not happy with me.' I looked at Marlene and waited as she shifted uncomfortably from one foot to the other. 'We had a really good Friday evening, and a good day yesterday,' she continued. 'When I said goodnight to Donna last night she seemed fine. But she must have got out of bed after I was asleep, and she tore up the magazines I'd bought for her yesterday. I went in this morning and found her room covered with paper. I wasn't worried, because you'd told me to expect this, and Donna said she would clear it up later. While she was in the shower I thought I would save her the bother and I got out the hoover and quickly went round her room. I thought I was doing her a favour, but when she saw what I'd done she was so angry. She shouted at me, then called me an interfering bitch.'

'Did she indeed!'

'I told her off and she's been sulking ever since. That was about an hour ago. I've tried talking to her, but she's not having any of it. I'm sorry, Cathy. I've clearly done something very wrong.'

I could see immediately what the something was but it certainly wasn't Marlene's fault. 'It's part of Donna's ritual to clear up the mess she makes,' I said gently. 'To her the clearing up is the most important part of the ritual. But that's no excuse for shouting or swearing at you.' Marlene looked at me, still upset and shaken by the whole experience, and now blaming herself. 'Because of her cleaning role at home,' I continued, 'Donna needs to clean and tidy; it's her acting it out. When she does it again, leave her to clear up the mess. But I'm not having her being rude.'

'I'm sorry,' Marlene said again. 'I should have realised.'

'No, you shouldn't. Donna could have explained to you rather than bursting into anger. She's been living with me for over fifteen months and she knows that type of behaviour isn't acceptable. Shall we go and see her together? I think it might be useful.'

Marlene readily agreed, and leaving Paula and Adrian playing on the PlayStation in the lounge, we went to Donna's bedroom. I could see that Marlene was still upset, and I guessed she'd also been frightened by Donna's anger, as I had been when she'd first come to live with me. Her rage could be very threatening.

I knocked on Donna's door and opened it. She was sitting on the edge of her bed, quite clearly sulking. Her face looked like thunder and it was so severe that it looked almost fake – an adopted pose to make Marlene suffer. Had it been me she was directing it to I would have laughed and cajoled her out of it, but it wasn't, and Marlene didn't know Donna well enough to have the confidence to risk humour. She had been frightened and compromised by Donna's outburst and it wasn't fair on her.

'Donna,' I said firmly, raising my voice slightly in indignation, 'I don't know what you think you're doing, but you need to apologise to Marlene. Now. '

She glanced up at me, slightly taken aback, perhaps expecting my sympathy. 'How dare you speak to Marlene like that?' I continued in the same authoritative tone. 'You know that type of language is unacceptable. You don't swear in my house and you certainly don't here either.' She lowered her head again, but the sulk wasn't as emphasised now that she realised it wasn't going to have much effect. 'Marlene made a mistake in clearing up your bedroom,' I said. 'She thought she was being helpful; she wasn't to know you liked doing it. It was no reason to shout and swear at her, was it?' Donna sat with her head lowered but said nothing, clearly digging her heels in.

'What should you have done?' I continued. 'What have I taught you to do if there is a problem, rather than getting angry or sulking?'

I waited, and Marlene waited too; we were both looking at Donna, who was still perched on the edge of the bed.

'Talk,' she said at last in a small voice.

'Exactly,' I said. 'So why didn't you talk to Marlene? You should have explained to her that in future you would like to clear up your mess. It would have been the adult and sensible thing to do. It is what I have spent fifteen months teaching you to do, Donna. Please don't forget it all now and let me down.' But of course in the new situation of Marlene's house Donna had simply reverted to her learned behaviour from the years before. 'Right, young lady,' I said, finally, 'apologise to Marlene now please.'

Again, Marlene and I waited, and I knew quite a bit hung in the balance. These two weeks were a difficult period because Donna was slowly transferring not only her allegiance and feelings from me to Marlene, but also her trust, and the respect she had for my authority.

'Well?' I said. 'I'm waiting.'

'Sorry, Marlene,' she said slowly and in the same small voice. 'I should have talked to you. I will next time.'

'Thank you, Donna,' Marlene said. 'I hope you feel you can talk to me, as you do to Cathy.'

Donna nodded.

'Good girl,' I said. 'Now we will say goodbye and let Marlene get off to church. I bet she feels she needs it.' I glanced at Marlene and she smiled. But Donna's apology had been the best possible outcome, and I was quietly pleased. She could have burst into another furious rage and said she hated Marlene (and me) and wasn't going to come here ever again. But she hadn't, her anger had been confined to the one incident and we had dealt with it.

As we said goodbye in the hall, Donna apologised again to Marlene, 'Sorry. I've had a nice time really.'

I saw Marlene's spirits lift. 'Good. I've enjoyed it too. And I'm looking forward to seeing you again on Wednesday. I'll cook you your favourite dinner.'

Donna smiled, but I could have scowled, for it was a stark reminder that very soon Marlene would be cooking all Donna's favourite meals, and she would soon be the most important person in her life.

Later that day I reinforced to Donna how important it was for her to talk to Marlene if she felt there was a problem, and she promised me she would. Donna had progressed sufficiently since living with me to be able to rationally explain her feelings, rather than let them bottle up until they exploded as she had done in the early days. I wondered how much of Donna's anger had been simply to test Marlene's reaction.

When Edna phoned on Monday we agreed that, given the enormity of the changes Donna was having to accommodate, the incident was minor, and the introduction and move would go ahead as planned. Donna spent Wednesday night at her new home, and Marlene took Donna to school on Thursday morning and met some of the staff. When I collected Donna at the end of school Beth Adams and Mrs Bristow told me how proud Donna had been when she had introduced Marlene to them. I was pleased, but I also experienced that now very familiar sadness that my role in Donna's life was slowly being transferred to Marlene. I knew I would have to let go quicker than I had been doing, for Friday night was Donna's last with us, and on Saturday I would be moving her.

Chapter Twenty-five

Moving On

During the rest of the week I found myself stealing little glances at Donna and trying to imagine what life was going to be like without her. I thought that Adrian and Paula were doing likewise, and also making the most of the time they had left with her; Paula hardly left her side. While Donna was at school on Friday I packed most of her belongings. I had suggested to Donna that I did this, as we were going to have a little leaving party on Friday evening and there wouldn't be much time; also, packing to say goodbye was a sad business for an adult, let alone a child. Donna had readily agreed to let me do it.

When I collected Donna from school on Friday I said goodbye to all the staff and thanked them for what they had done. This would be my last visit to the school, as my involvement there had now finished, although as Mrs Bristow said, 'We might see each other again in the future with another child.' I gave her a large box of chocolates to be shared among the staff, and thanking them again, said an emotional farewell.

That evening we had our leaving party for Donna. My parents, my brother and his wife, Sue and family from next door, Emily and Mandy (they were saying goodbye to me, for they would still see Donna at school), and Jill, arrived at 6.00 p.m. They all brought presents for Donna, which she opened. 'It's like my birthday again,' she said brightly, 'or Christmas come early.' I smiled to hide my regret. Donna wouldn't be with us for Christmas, although I knew she would have a good time with Marlene. Paula, Adrian and I had bought Donna a leaving present, but we were going to give it to her on Saturday, last thing before we took her to Marlene's.

I had prepared a buffet and set it on the table in the breakfast room, and Donna's leaving party was a happy affair, despite our sadness at her going. The adults chatted, everyone helped themselves to food and I organised some games at the children's request. Our guests said goodbye just after 8.30 p.m., wishing Donna good luck and telling her to write when she had a chance. The house suddenly fell quiet and Donna thanked me for her party. 'You're more than welcome, love,' I said, and I gave her a big hug.

While the children went upstairs to change, ready for bed, I cleared away the remainder of the buffet and loaded the dishwasher. I fed Toscha, and then went up to say goodnight. Paula was nearly asleep; it was 9.30 p.m. and well past her bedtime. I kissed her goodnight then went into Adrian's room; he said he was going to read for half an hour. Donna was in bed, with her leaving presents on the floor beside her. There was a china ornament which looked like Toscha from my parents; a framed family photograph of all of us from my brother; a book from my neighbour; a pink purse from Emily; and a gift voucher from Jill.

'We'll have to remember to pack those in the morning,' I said, perching on the edge of her bed. I had taken the cases and boxes containing the rest of Donna's belongings downstairs and stacked them in the front room, which we hadn't used during the evening.

'And my bike,' Donna said. 'Don't forget that.'

I smiled. 'No, love, I haven't forgotten that. I've put it in the boot of the car already. I wanted to make sure it fitted in.'

'You think of everything,' she said with a grin.

'I wouldn't say that, love, but I try my best.' I paused and looked at her. She was snuggled beneath the duvet, her eyes heavy with sleep but content. 'Donna,' I said gently, 'I want you to remember that Marlene will be trying to do her best too. She might not always get it right, but that's where you can help, isn't it?'

She nodded. 'I know. By talking to her and telling her how I feel.'

'That's right. Good girl.' I continued to look at her, and stroked away a strand of hair from her forehead. I didn't want to get all emotional, but I was finding it difficult to say goodnight for what would be the last time. 'And Donna, remember it's going to be a bit strange to begin with, until you get used to your new home. I know we've talked about this but if you give yourself time I know things will just get better and better for you.' I paused and smiled, still reluctant to say goodnight and pull myself away. 'OK, love,' I said after a moment. 'You get some sleep. You must be exhausted. It's been a busy day.'

'Yes. And thanks again for everything, Cathy. I've loved being here. Adrian and Paula are very lucky.'

My heart lurched. 'I feel very lucky to have known you, Donna. It's been a privilege looking after you. But this isn't goodbye. You promised to keep in touch, and I shall look forward to hearing all your news. Marlene thinks she's very lucky too.' Donna smiled, and then yawned. 'Goodnight love, sleep tight.'

'Night, Cathy.'

I kissed her forehead and, coming out, swallowed the lump in my throat. Saying goodnight to Donna for the last time was one of those heartfelt moments that I knew would stay with me for ever.

The following morning Donna was up early and very excited. 'It's like going on holiday,' she said, taking her presents downstairs and packing them in the case I had left open. Adrian and Paula were up and dressed earlier than was usual on a Saturday and joined in Donna's excitement, although I could see they were putting on brave faces to mask their sadness at Donna leaving. We had pancakes for breakfast – Donna's favourite – and I then put her nightwear and wash bag into the case and zipped it shut. The four of us loaded the car, arranging and rearranging the bags and boxes until they all fitted in. By the time we'd finished, the boot lid only just closed and the passenger seat was full, as were the foot wells. The children would also have some of the smaller bags on their laps; any more luggage and I would have had to have made two trips.

Before we set off, I checked Donna's bedroom for anything that could have been missed; then we gathered in the lounge, where I presented Donna with her present from Adrian, Paula and me. As she carefully peeled off the wrapping paper I took the final photograph – of the jeweller's box appearing, and her face lighting up.

'It's a proper watch!' she exclaimed. 'An adult one! Thank you so much. That's great!'

'You're very welcome, love,' I said. 'I thought that now you can tell the time you should have a decent watch.' It was a nice watch: I had chosen it carefully from the jeweller's, a ladies' watch not a child's, set in a silver bracelet. Donna put it on her wrist and we all admired it.

'I'm going to keep it in the box for now,' she said, carefully sliding it off and returning it to the box. 'I don't want it getting scratched.'

'You won't be able to tell the time with it in there,' Adrian teased.

'Typical boy!' Donna returned.

We piled into the car and Donna sat with the present held protectively in her lap. As I drove, I repeatedly glanced in the rear-view mirror at her. I was reminded of when she'd first arrived, clutching the present from Mary and Ray. How different she was now: brighter, more upright, more confident and happy, and much taller. She must have grown four inches in the time she'd been with us; I'd had to replace her jeans and shoes every couple of months. All three children were quiet as I drove to Marlene's, gazing out of the windows, and I saw that Paula was holding Donna's hand.

Marlene must have been looking out for us, for as soon as we drew up outside her house at 11.00 a.m., the front door opened and she came out, smiling and waving.

'Hi!' she called. 'Welcome. I hope you're hungry. I've made Donna's favourite – pancakes for us all.'

I smiled, and so too did the children. 'I'm sure you can all manage another one,' I said quietly to them.

We unloaded the car; with all five of us helping it didn't take long. We carried the boxes, cases and bags through the hall and straight up to Donna's bedroom. Marlene wheeled the bike into the conservatory. By the time we'd emptied the car, Donna's room was full.

'I know what we shall be doing today,' Marlene said to Donna.

'Unpacking,' Donna said, and she put her arms around Marlene's waist and gave her a big hug. Marlene beamed, so very pleased.

We sat around the table in the lounge and Marlene served us pancakes, with a choice of toppings – syrup, icing sugar, ice cream, honey and grated chocolate. I managed to eat one, Paula and Donna two, and Adrian three.

'These are amazing,' Adrian said, helping himself to more ice cream and chocolate. I agreed. 'They're different from the ones you make,' he added (for 'different' read 'better'), and I agreed again.

I knew it wasn't in anyone's interest to prolong our leaving, so once we'd finished our 'second breakfast', I said we had better be off. We all helped to clear the table, leaving the plates and cutlery in the kitchen sink, then we began a slow path down the hall and to the front door. Our goodbyes needed to be quick and positive, with the reminder that we would phone in two weeks. It had been decided at the planning meeting that I should allow two weeks before phoning, so that my call didn't unsettle Donna while she was still bonding with Marlene in the early days. After that it was up to Donna (and Marlene) how often she wanted to phone.

'Right then,' I said positively, as I stood by the front door with Adrian and Paula beside me. 'We'll leave you to get on with your unpacking. I'll phone in two weeks, Donna.'

Marlene smiled and nodded, while Donna gave a half nod. She was standing next to Marlene, with her eyes lowered and her shoulders slightly hunched forward.

'Come on, love,' I said. 'I want to see a big smile and have a hug before I go.'

Without raising her eyes, Donna came to me and, putting her arms around me, hugged me hard.

After a moment I gently eased her away and looked at her. 'Where's that lovely smile then?'

She looked into my eyes and managed a smile, but I could see her eyes welling.

Paula stepped forward and threw her arms around Donna's waist and gave her a big squeeze. 'I'll miss you,' Paula said.

Donna kissed her cheek. 'I'll miss you too.'

I glanced at Adrian and he pulled a face. 'I don't do girly cuddles,' he said. 'But I'll shake your hand, Donna.' Marlene and I smiled as Donna and Adrian shook hands.

'Take care,' I said to Donna and Marlene, and I opened the front door.

'And you,' Marlene said. Donna was concentrating on the floor again.

'Come on then,' I said to Adrian and Paula, for no one was moving.

I stepped out of the front door with Paula holding my hand and Adrian following a little behind. I didn't look back as I went down the path; only when we were in the car, and I had opened the windows so that we could wave, did I look at them. Marlene and Donna were framed in the doorway, standing side by side. Marlene had her arm around Donna's shoulders, and Donna was wiping the back of her hand across her eyes. I started the engine and, stifling my own tears, gave a little wave, and gradually pulled away. Paula and Adrian waved from their windows until the house was out of sight; then I raised the windows.

As I pulled to the T-junction at the end of the road, I glanced in the rear-view mirror. Adrian and Paula were silent and close to tears. I saw how empty the back seat looked without Donna in her usual place by the window. 'I've got to stop at the shops on the way home,' I said, 'then I thought we would go to the cinema.' Aware we were all going to need something to cheer us up, I'd already booked the tickets.

'Good,' Adrian said with no real enthusiasm.

'I wish Donna was coming,' Paula said. 'I miss her.'

'I know, love.'

We went home after the supermarket shopping, as the film didn't start until 5.00 p.m., and as I entered the hall, I saw that the light on the answerphone flashing, signalling a message. Paula and Adrian, still subdued, took off their shoes and coats and went into the lounge, while I pressed 'play' on the machine. The message was from Jill, timed half an hour before: 'Hi, Cathy, I hope the move went all right. I'll phone on Monday to catch up. And Cathy, we've had a referral through for a five-year-old boy. They are looking for a foster home for him in a week's time. I'll tell you more on Monday. Have a good weekend. Bye, and thanks for all you did for Donna. It's much appreciated.'

I deleted the message, and began down the hall and towards the lounge. By Monday I might be able to consider taking a new child, but not yet. Now, I just needed time with Adrian and Paula, and we all needed time to reflect on Donna. We would have to adjust to being a family of three again before we could consider welcoming a new child. I knew that for the next few days we would be sharing many fond memories of Donna and her time with us – a collective healing process, as we remembered all the good times that had made up our family life. Only then could we begin to consider the five-year-old boy, whose problems would doubtless be very different from Donna's, but no less urgent and demanding.

Wouldn't it be lovely, I thought again, if I could wave my magic wand and make every child wanted and cared for, and every parent capable of caring for and loving their child? But practically, all I could do was the best for the children I looked after, and hope I gave them something positive to take with them. And if Donna had learned something from my family, so had our lives been enriched from knowing her: to have suffered the abuse and degradation she had done and not be consumed by hate said a lot about her. I doubt I would have fared so well.

Epilogue

Eight years have gone by since Donna moved, and we are still in contact with her. She is nineteen now, a very attractive girl who braids her hair and wears a little make-up and likes fashionable clothes. When I first phoned her, after the two weeks, she was pleased to hear from me and sounded settled, and she had lots of news about her home and family. Paula and Adrian spoke to her too, mainly about school and their respective cats – Toscha and Harris. I also talked to Marlene, who confirmed that Donna was doing well, and that there had been no major problems. We said goodbye and Marlene and Donna promised to keep in touch.

It was six months before we heard from them again; Marlene made the call and spoke to me first before she passed the phone to Donna. Marlene apologised for not phoning sooner but said that they'd had a bit of a 'rocky time'. She explained that Donna had been in therapy for four months and it had unleashed a lot of painful memories, which had resulted in her becoming unsettled and angry – she had twice trashed her bedroom. Marlene said that although Donna was still in therapy (and would be for some years) she was a lot calmer now, and was slowly coming to terms with the hurt and rejection from her past.

Marlene felt that the worst was behind them. I said that I understood, and I was pleased to hear from her now, as we had often talked about Donna and wondered how she was doing. I could hear the warmth in Marlene's voice as she spoke of Donna, and also the concern about what had been a very worrying period.

When Donna came to the phone it was so lovely to hear her voice again. She sounded older, more mature and also very positive. She told me all about her home life, school and the holiday she was going on with Marlene in August to Barbados. As she spoke she referred quite naturally to Marlene as 'Mum', and her extended family as aunts, uncles and cousins. She talked a lot about Kerry, Marlene's niece who was the same age as Donna, and said Kerry had become her 'second best friend' after Emily. When we had finished speaking I passed the phone to Adrian and Paula, and between us we were on the phone for nearly two hours, catching up with all Donna's news.

After that phone call Donna (and Marlene) continued to phone us every couple of months, and we began seeing them twice a year. We took it in turns to visit each other's houses, and one Christmas we all went to a pantomime together. Now Donna is nineteen she visits us alone, although she still lives with Marlene, who always sends her warmest wishes.

Donna is a lovely girl who has now managed to let go of a lot of her anger, and much of her negative self-image, helped by therapy and Marlene. She smiles a lot, looks you in the eyes when she speaks and only occasionally hunches her shoulders forwards – when something really bothers her. Her self-effacing and placid nature has continued, though, but this has become a positive attribute. It's like a breath of fresh air to be with Donna. She is a warm, gentle and caring person who speaks slowly and takes life in her stride. Nothing seems to faze her, for as she says, 'I've seen the worst of life and now it just gets better and better.' And I think some of that is to do with her new boyfriend, Robert, whom she brought with her last time she visited. He is a tall and good-looking lad whom she met at college, where Donna is studying to be a nurse and Robert a mechanic. I liked Robert, and was touched that Donna had wanted us to meet him. He treats her with much respect and they clearly think a lot of each other. How much of her past she has told him I don't know.

And what of Donna's family – the family who were responsible for so much of her unhappiness? I know only what Donna has told me. The supervised contact three times a year was stopped when Donna was fourteen, at her request, although Donna now visits her mother, whom she refers to as Rita, once a year. Rita's baby stayed in foster care until the court process was complete, and then she was adopted by a childless couple in their thirties. Donna has never seen the child, although the adoption order stipulates that the child should be made aware of her natural family when she is of a suitable age. Chelsea's baby, Cindy, despite all the support and help, both in the mother and baby unit, and when Chelsea moved into her flat, was eventually taken into care. Chelsea couldn't parent the child alone and moved back in with her mother, where Cindy quickly became badly neglected. When the social worker went with the police to remove the baby, Cindy was nowhere to be seen. Eventually, after searching the house and garden a second time, they found Cindy hidden under a pile of filthy rags in a crumbling shed at the bottom of the garden.

A year later Chelsea was pregnant again, and then she suffered a miscarriage after being beaten up by the person she claimed was the father of the baby. She moved out from her mother's house and hasn't been seen or heard of since. Rita is still drink and drug dependent, and Donna says the house is filthy and there is never any food there because Rita drinks and doesn't eat. Donna said the last time she visited, Rita looked like an old woman. From what Donna had learnt in her nursing studies, she thought that Rita would be dead in a year if she didn't stop drinking. Donna has never taken Robert to meet Rita and has no plans to.

Donna sees her brothers once a year, around Christmas time. They were found adoptive parents together and are doing very well, both at home and at school. Donna doesn't say much about them; I think her visits are more to stay in touch rather than prompted by any deep sibling bond. Whether Warren and Jason have suffered any remorse or guilt for the way they treated Donna when they were little, I don't know, but they were old enough at the time to remember that dreadful period. It would be nice to think that at some point in their lives they apologise to Donna, although Donna doesn't bear them any grudge. She wouldn't: it would never enter her head to bear anyone a grudge, such is her gentle and forgiving disposition.

When the supervised contact stopped, Donna began visiting her dad at his flat, first accompanied by Marlene and then for the last three years going alone. Edna found Mr Bajan a council flat before she retired, and he lives by himself and has no contact with Rita. Donna visits him every two weeks, on a Sunday, and cleans and tidies his flat and cooks him dinner. He knows exactly where his tablets are in the kitchen cupboard, and remembers to take them each morning and night. He has had only two relapses in the last eight years, and he joined his mother on a trip to Barbados for one winter. Donna also visits her gran, Mrs Bajan, who is not in the best of health. Donna takes three buses every month to spend a day with her. She cleans and tidies her flat and makes sure she has enough food in the fridge. Donna loves her gran and dad; together with Marlene they are her family, and the most important people in her life.

Therapy and having Marlene as her mother have helped Donna along the path to becoming a well-adjusted and successful adult. Donna tells me that just occasionally, if she is frustrated by something or someone, she goes to her bedroom and quietly tears up a magazine, and then clears it up. She and Marlene laugh about it, and if tearing up paper helps then there is no reason for her to stop it. We all need some release from life's little downers, and on the scale of things, shredding paper is no great problem; I might try it some time.

Donna will qualify as a nurse in two years' time and is looking forward to starting work and earning a wage. She officially came out of care when she reached the age of eighteen and therefore no longer has a social worker. She still sees a therapist every so often, at her request, when she feels she needs to talk to someone outside the family. Although she has made new friends at college, she is still in contact with Emily whom, together with Kerry, she regards as her 'best buddy'. Emily left school at sixteen and works as a sales assistance in a department store. Donna, Emily and Kerry go out together in the evening and also on extended shopping expeditions; being the age they are, they love to shop. They have also discussed the idea of renting a flat together when Donna and Kerry finish their education and start earning.

Despite the years that have passed, Donna vividly remembers the time when she lived with us, and has many fond memories. She also remembers the hurt and trauma she was going through inside at that time, and how I continually encouraged her to let it go by talking. She has thanked me more than once for being so patient and understanding, and has also apologised to Paula and Adrian for being so 'horrible', as she puts it. I have reassured her that there is no need either to thank me or to apologise, and that she wasn't horrible, just a child in crisis. Paula and Adrian have only good memories of her time with us, especially of Christmas and our holiday together. We still look at the photographs, and remember – Donna, who was once the saddest girl in the world, but blossomed into a wonderful young woman. Well done, love.

suggested topics for reading-group discussion

When children come into foster care, sibling groups like Donna's are kept together wherever possible. In what circumstances do you think sibling groups should be separated? Is it important that they keep in contact, and if so, why?

Edna, Donna's social worker, has a very positive relationship with Donna: she is warm and reassuring, but firm when necessary. How does she achieve this?

Children who have been neglected or abused show it in different ways. How does Donna's past come out in her behaviour? Why does she want to chastise Adrian and Paula?

Donna's negative behaviour can't be changed all at once. If you were her foster carer, what would you prioritise? How does Cathy work with Donna to achieve more positive behaviour?

It appears that Donna needs to keep some of her obsessive compulsive behaviour. Why do you think this is, and how is it accommodated?

There are other cases documented where a mother has rejected one child but looked after the others in a family. What reasons could there be for this? In what circumstances might it happen?

Many children who come into care, like Donna, have missed out on their childhood. Apart from neglect, what other reasons could there be for this? How would you try to give such a child a childhood? Why is this important?

Donna's self-esteem improves while living at Cathy's. How is this achieved?

Although Donna is settled at Cathy's, the decision is made to move her to a foster carer who matches Donna's ethnicity. Do you think this was the right decision? What reasons do you think lay behind that decision?

If Donna had stayed with Cathy, what could she have done to encourage her towards a positive cultural identity? Why is this important?

How were the lives of Cathy and her family enriched by knowing Donna? What did she teach them?

The Silent Cry

PROLOGUE

The room is dark, although it's daylight outside. Strangely dark and eerily quiet. Not a sound when there should be noise. Crying and screaming, that's what she was expecting to hear. And the room seems smaller now too, as though the walls are gradually closing in and crushing her, crushing her to death.

She sits huddled at one end of the sofa, too scared to look around. Scared of what she might see in this unnaturally dark and quiet room that is threatening to squeeze the air out of her and squash her to nothing. Scared, too, of what lies ahead if she stands and goes to the telephone to make that call, and tells them what she's done. They will come and take her baby for sure if she tells them that she has given birth to the devil.

CHAPTER ONE

A FUNNY TURN

Everyone loves a newborn baby and wants a little look. Even those who protest that they are not 'baby lovers' can't resist a peep at the miracle of a new life. I joined the other mothers grouped around the pram in the school playground as we waited with our children for the start of school.

'Congratulations, he's gorgeous,' I said, adding my own best wishes to the many others.

'Thank you,' Laura (the new mum) said quietly, a little bemused by all the attention.

'How old is he now?' I asked.

'Two weeks.'

'Aah, he's adorable.'

'Make the most of every moment,' another mother said. 'They grow up far too quickly.'

My own daughter, Paula, aged thirteen months, was sitting in the stroller and wanted to have a look too, so I unclipped the safety harness and lifted her out so she could see into the pram.

'Baby,' she said cutely, pointing.

'Yes, that's baby Liam,' I said.

'Baby Liam,' she repeated with a little chuckle.

'You were that small once,' I said, and she chuckled again.

'He's my baby brother,' Kim, Laura's daughter, said proudly.

'I know. Aren't you a lucky girl?' I said to her, returning Paula to her stroller.

Kim nodded and touched her baby brother's face protectively, then planted a delicate little kiss on his cheek.

The family had moved into the street where I lived about a year before. Laura and I had got to know each other a little from seeing each other on the way to and from school. My son Adrian, aged five, attended this school but was in a different year to Kim, who was seven. Living quite close to each other I kept meaning to invite Laura in for a coffee and develop our friendship, but I hadn't found the opportunity, what with looking after my own family, fostering and studying for a degree part-time. I guessed Laura had been busy too, especially now she had a baby.

Amid all the oohings and aahings over little Liam the Klaxon sounded the start of school and parents began saying goodbye to their children.

'Bye, love,' I said to Adrian, giving him a kiss on the cheek. 'Have a good day. Make sure you eat your lunch, and have a drink.' He'd only been in school a year and I still fussed over him.

'Bye, Mum. Bye, Paula,' he said, and ran over to join his class who were lining up, ready to go in.

'Bye, little Liam,' Kim said, leaning into the pram again to give her brother one last kiss. She clearly didn't want to leave him. 'See you later. Be a good boy for Mummy.' I smiled.

'Cathy,' Laura said suddenly, clutching my arm. 'I feel a bit hot. I'm going to get a drink of water. Could you stay with the pram, please?'

She turned and walked quickly towards the water fountain situated in an alcove at the far end of the building. Kim looked at me anxiously.

'Don't worry, love. I'll make sure your mum is all right. You go into school.'

She hesitated, but then ran over to join her class, who were going in. I could see Laura at the fountain, leaning forward and sipping the cool water. I thought I should go over in case she was feeling faint. She'd only given birth two weeks before and I could remember how I'd sometimes suddenly felt hot and dizzy in the first few weeks after having both of my children. Pushing Paula's stroller with my right hand and Liam's pram with my left, I steered them across the playground to the water fountain. 'Are you OK?' I asked Laura as we approached.

'Oh, yes, thank you,' she said, straightening and wiping her mouth on a tissue. 'I came over a bit funny. I'm all right now.'

I thought she looked pale. 'Why don't you sit down for a while? The children are going in.' There were a couple of benches in the playground that the children used at playtime.

'No, I'm all right, honestly. I just felt a bit hot and panicky. I think it was all the attention, and it is warm today.'

'Yes, it is warm for May,' I agreed. 'But make sure you don't overdo it.'

She tucked the tissue into her pocket and shook her hair from her face. 'My husband and mother-in-law said it was too soon for me to be out and about. I guess they were right. But I was getting cabin fever staying at home all the time. I needed a change of scenery.' She put her hands onto the pram handle ready for the off.

'Are you going straight home?' I asked. 'I'll walk with you.'

'Yes, but there's no need. I'll be fine.'

'I'd like to,' I said. 'I walk by your house on the way to mine.'

'All right. Thanks.' She flicked her hair from her face again and we began across the playground to the main gate. Laura was a tall, attractive woman, whom I guessed to be in her mid-thirties, and she was very slim despite recently giving birth. She had naturally wavy, shoulder-length brown hair, which was swept away from her forehead.

'Is Liam sleeping and feeding well?' I asked, making conversation as we walked.

'Baby,' Paula repeated, pointing to his pram travelling along beside her.

'Yes, that's right,' I said to her. 'Baby Liam.'

'I'm up every three hours at night feeding him,' Laura said. 'But you expect that with a newborn, don't you?'

I nodded. 'It's very tiring. I remember craving sleep in the first few months. If someone had offered me a night out at a top-class restaurant or seven hours unbroken sleep, I would have gone for the latter without a doubt.'

'Agreed,' Laura said with a small smile.

We were silent for a few moments as we concentrated on crossing the road, and then we turned the corner and began up our street. 'How do you like living here?' I asked, resuming conversation.

'Fine. It's nearer Andy's – my husband's – job, and his family. My mother-in-law only lives five streets away.'

'Is that the lady I've seen in the playground, collecting Kim from school?' I asked out of interest.

'Yes. Geraldine. She's very helpful. I don't know what I'd do without her.'

'It's good to have help,' I said. 'My parents help me out when they can, but they live an hour's drive away, and my husband's family are even further away.'

'Yes,' Laura said, looking thoughtful. 'My mother lives over a hundred miles away. You foster, don't you?'

'I do, although I'm taking a few months off at present to finish my degree. After our last foster child left my husband accepted a contract to work abroad for three months, so it seemed a good opportunity to study. The social services know I'm available for an emergency or for respite care, but I'm hoping I won't be disturbed too often.'

'What's respite?' Laura asked, interested.

'It's when a foster carer looks after a child for a short period to give the parents or another foster carer a break. It might just be for a weekend or a week or two, but then the child returns home or to their permanent carer.'

'I see. It's good of you to foster.'

'Not really. I enjoy it. But I must admit I've been struggling recently to study and foster, with Paula being so little. Hopefully I'll now have the chance to complete my dissertation.'

'What are you studying?'

'Education and psychology.'

She nodded. We'd now arrived outside her house, number 53, and Laura pushed open the gate. 'Well, it's been nice talking to you. Cathy, isn't it?'

'Yes – sorry, I should have said.'

'Thanks again for helping me out in the playground. I hope I haven't kept you.'

'Not at all. If ever you want me to collect Kim from school or take her, do let me know. I'm there every day with Adrian.'

'Thanks, that's kind of you, but Geraldine, my mother-in-law, always does it if I can't.'

'OK. But if she can't at any time you know where I am. And perhaps you'd like to pop in for a coffee one day when you're free.'

She looked slightly surprised. 'Oh, I see. That's nice, but I expect you're very busy.'

'Never too busy for a coffee and a chat,' I said with a smile. 'I'll give you my telephone number.' I began delving into my bag for a pen and paper.

'Can you give it to me another time?' Laura said, appearing rather anxious. She began up her garden path, clearly eager to be away. 'Sorry, but I'm dying to go to the bathroom!' she called.

'Yes, of course. I'll see you later in the playground. I can give it to you then.'

'Geraldine will probably be there,' she returned, with her back to me, and quickly unlocking the door. 'Push it through my letterbox.'

'OK. Bye then.'

'Bye!' she called, and going in closed the front door.

'Baby Liam,' Paula said, pointing to the house.

'Yes, that's where he lives,' I said.

'Out!' Paula now demanded, raising her arms to be lifted out of the stroller.

'Yes, you can walk, but remember you always hold my hand.'

I undid the safety harness, helped her out and took her little hand in mine. 'We always hold hands by the road,' I reminded her. I didn't use walking reins but insisted she held my hand.

'Baby Liam,' Paula said again, looking at his house.

'Yes, that's right.' I glanced over. A woman, whom I now knew to be Laura's mother-in-law, Geraldine, was looking out of the downstairs window. I smiled and gave a little wave, but she couldn't have seen me for she turned and disappeared into the room.

'Home,' Paula said.

'Yes, we're going home now.'

We continued haltingly up the street with Paula stopping every few steps to examine something that caught her interest, including most garden gates, walls, fences, lampposts, fallen leaves, every tree in the street and most of the paving slabs. But I knew that the exercise would tire her out and that once home, after she'd had a drink and a snack, she'd have at least an hour's sleep, which would give me the chance to continue researching and writing my dissertation: 'The psychological impact being in care has on a child and how it affects their educational outcome.'

That afternoon, before I set off to collect Adrian from school, I wrote my telephone number on a piece of paper and tucked it into my pocket ready to give to Laura. She wasn't in the playground and for a while it appeared that no one had come to collect Kim, for I couldn't see Geraldine either. The Klaxon sounded for the end of school and the children began to file out, and then Geraldine rushed into the playground at the last minute and went over to Kim. Adrian arrived at my side very excited because his class was going on an outing. He handed me a printed sheet with the details of the outing and a consent form, and I carefully tucked it into my bag. I looked around for Geraldine, but she'd already gone. We joined the other parents and children filing out of the main gate and then crossed the road. As we turned the corner into our street I could see Kim and her grandmother a little way ahead. Kim turned and gave a small wave. We waved back. I was half-expecting Geraldine to turn and acknowledge us, or maybe even wait for us to catch up and fall into conversation, but she didn't. She kept on walking until they arrived at number 53, where she opened the garden gate and began up the path. As we drew level she was opening the front door.

'Excuse me!' I called. She turned. 'Could you give this to Laura, please?' I held out the piece of paper. 'It's my telephone number. I said I'd let her have it. Is she all right now?'

Geraldine nodded, straight-faced, and tapped Kim on the shoulder as a signal for her to collect the paper.

Kim ran down the path and smiled at me as she took the paper. 'Thank you,' she said politely.

'Say hi to your mum,' I said.

'I will.'

With another smile she ran back up the path to her grandmother, who'd now opened the front door and was waiting just inside, ready to close it. I smiled at her but she didn't return the gesture, and as soon as Kim was inside she closed the door. With her short grey hair and unsmiling features Geraldine came across as stern. I was slightly surprised by her coldness, and it crossed my mind that she'd very likely seen me that morning through the front-room window and, for whatever reason, had chosen to ignore me.

CHAPTER TWO

VERY CONCERNED

I saw Geraldine in the playground every day for the rest of that week – in the morning when she took Kim to school, and in the afternoon when she collected her – but she didn't acknowledge me or make any attempt to start a conversation. Neither did she have anything to do with any of the other parents waiting in the playground, which was unusual. It was a relatively small school, and friendly, so that eventually most people started chatting to someone as they waited for their children. But Geraldine didn't; she hurried into the playground at the last moment and out again, aloof and stern-looking. By Friday, when Laura still hadn't reappeared, I began to wonder if she was ill. She'd had a funny turn earlier in the week, on her first outing with Liam – perhaps she'd been sickening for something and was really poorly. Although Geraldine apparently didn't want anything to do with me, Laura hadn't been so hostile, and given that we lived in the same street and our children attended the same school I felt it would be neighbourly of me to ask how she was. If you are feeling unwell and someone asks after you it can be a real pick-me-up. So on Friday afternoon when Geraldine collected Kim from school I intercepted her as she hurried out of the playground.

'I was wondering how Laura was,' I said. 'I'm Cathy. I live in the same street.'

'Yes, I know who you are,' she said stiffly. 'Laura is fine, thank you. Why do you ask?' Which seemed an odd question.

'When I last saw Laura she wasn't feeling so good. She came over a bit hot and wobbly. I wondered if she was all right now.'

'Oh, that. It was nothing,' Geraldine said dismissively. 'It was far too soon for her to be going out and she realizes that now.'

I gave a small nod. 'As long as she's not ill.'

'No, of course not,' she said bluntly.

'Good. Well, if she ever fancies a change of scenery and a coffee, she knows where I live.'

'Oh, she won't be up to that for a long while,' Geraldine said tartly. 'I've told her she's not to go out for at least another four weeks, possibly longer. That's the advice we had after giving birth.' Taking Kim by the arm, she headed off.

Not go out for another four weeks! You could have knocked me down with a feather. Wherever had she got that from? It was nearly three weeks since Laura had given birth and as far as I knew there was no medical advice that said a new mother had to wait seven weeks before going out, unless Geraldine was confusing it with postpartum sex, but even then seven weeks was excessive if the birth had been normal. More likely, I thought, Geraldine was suffering from empty-nest syndrome and she liked being the centre of the family and having Laura rely on her. It would make her feel needed, and if that suited Laura, fine. It was none of my business. I'd been reassured that Laura wasn't ill, and I had my family to look after and work to do.

* * *

It was the weekend and the weather was glorious, so Adrian, Paula and I spent most of Saturday in the garden, where the children played while I read and then did some gardening. On Sunday my parents came for the day and after lunch we were in the garden again. In the evening after they'd gone, my husband, John, telephoned from America where he was working. He'd got into the habit of telephoning on a Sunday evening when it was lunchtime where he was. We all took turns to speak to him and tell him our news. Even little Paula 'spoke' to him, although she was bemused by the workings of the telephone and kept examining the handset, trying to work out where the voice was coming from, rather than holding it to her ear.

On Monday the school week began again, and as the weather was fine we walked to and from school. I only used my car for school if it was raining hard or if I had to go somewhere straight after school. Geraldine continued to take Kim to school and collect her, and continued to ignore me and all the other parents. Perhaps she was just shy, I thought, although she had a standoffish, austere look about her. Each time I passed Laura's house, number 53, which was four times a day (on the way to and from school), I glanced over. But there was never any sign of Laura or baby Liam, so I assumed Laura was making the most of having Geraldine in charge and was relaxing indoors or in the back garden. Sometimes Paula pointed to the house and, remembering that Liam lived there, said, 'Baby.' If she was out of her stroller and walking, she tried the gate – and most of the others in the street!

On Thursday afternoon, once we'd returned home from school, we hadn't been in long when the telephone rang. It was a social worker asking if I could do some respite and look after a little boy, Darrel, aged three, for that night and all day Friday. His mother, Shelley, a young, single parent, had to go into hospital as a day patient and the person who was supposed to have been looking after Darrel had let her down at the last minute. She had no one else she could ask at such short notice, and I said I'd be happy to help and look after Darrel.

'Shelley's a young mum but she's a good one,' the social worker said. 'She'll bring Darrel to you at about six o'clock this evening. She said she'd bring everything he needs, but she's fretting that she's run out of meatless sausages. She's a vegetarian and she's bringing up Darrel the same. Apparently he loves meatless sausages for lunch, but she hasn't got time to go into town and buy more. I've told her you'll be able to cook him something else vegetarian.'

'Yes, of course I will, but tell her I'll see if I can get some of the sausages. If she's not bringing Darrel until six, I've got time to pop down to our local supermarket. I'm sure I've seen some there.'

'Oh, you are good. I'll tell her. It's the first time Darrel has been away from her overnight and she's getting herself into a bit of a state. It's understandable.'

'Yes,' I agreed.

'She has to be at the hospital at eight o'clock tomorrow morning and she should be discharged later that afternoon. If she does have to stay overnight or doesn't feel up to collecting Darrel on Friday evening can he stay with you for a second night?'

'Yes, of course.'

'Thank you. I'll phone Shelley now and reassure her, and give her your contact details.'

'I'll see her about six then.' We said goodbye and I hung up. I hadn't been told what was wrong with Shelley and I didn't need to know. But I could appreciate why she was anxious at being separated from her son and was fretting because he would miss his favourite food. I'd seen the meatless sausages in the freezer cabinet at the supermarket a few weeks before when I'd been looking for something else. I just hoped they'd still have some in stock. But it's strange the way things work out sometimes, as if it's meant to be, for had I not offered to go to the supermarket I would probably have remained ignorant of what was really going on in Laura's house.

'Sorry,' I said to Adrian and Paula. 'We've got to pop down to the shop.'

Adrian pulled a face. 'We've only just got in and I wanted to play in the garden.'

'You can play as soon as we return,' I said. 'We won't be long. We're looking after a little boy tonight and he likes a special type of sausage. I want to see if I can buy some.'

Adrian was growing up with fostering, as was Paula, so it didn't surprise him that a child could suddenly appear and join our family. It was when they left that he didn't like it. Neither did I, but as a foster carer you have to learn to accept that the children leave you, and you take comfort from knowing you've done your best to help the child and their family, and then be ready for the next child.

'Can I have an ice cream from the shop then?' Adrian asked cannily.

Usually the answer would have been, 'No, not before your dinner,' but given that he was having to come out again and go shopping rather than playing in the garden, I thought a little reward was in order.

'Yes, a small one that won't spoil your dinner,' I said.

'Yippee, ice cream!' Adrian said.

'Ice cream,' Paula repeated.

'Yes, you can have one too.'

As Adrian put on his trainers I fitted Paula's shoes and then lifted her into the stroller, which I kept in the hall.

The local supermarket was at the bottom of my street, to the right, on the same road as the school. While it wasn't suitable for a big shop it was very useful for topping up, and I often popped in if we were running short on essentials. If they didn't have the sausages in stock I would tell Shelley I'd tried and then ask her what else Darrel liked to eat. I was sure I'd be able to find something else he liked. Although he was only staying with me for a day or so, it was important the experience was a good one for him and his mother, and that included meeting his needs and accommodating his likes and dislikes where possible. I would also ask Shelley about Darrel's routine, and I'd keep to it as much as possible to minimize the disruption to him. Even so, despite everything I was going to do, he was still likely to be upset – a three-year-old left with strangers. Had this not been an emergency respite placement he could have come for a visit beforehand to meet us, so it wouldn't be so strange for him.

As we walked down the street Adrian asked, 'Will Darrel go to my school?'

'No, he's not old enough for school yet,' I said.

'Oh, yes, of course,' Adrian said, with an embarrassed grin. 'I knew that really. I am a muppet.'

'Muppet,' Paula repeated.

'You're a muppet,' Adrian said, teasing his sister and ruffling her hair.

'Muppet,' she said again, giggling.

'You're a muppet,' Adrian said again. And so we continued down the street with the word 'muppet' bouncing good-humouredly back and forth between the two of them.

'So how do we cross the road safely?' I asked Adrian as we arrived at the pavement edge.

'Think, stop, look and listen, and when it's all clear walk, don't run, across the road,' he said, paraphrasing the safety code that they'd been taught at school.

'Good boy.'

We waited for the cars to pass and then crossed the road and went into the supermarket. I took a shopping basket and we went straight to the freezer cabinet. To my relief they had three packets of meatless sausages; I took one and placed it in the basket. Adrian then spent some time selecting ice creams for him and Paula and put those in the basket too. Paula reached out and began whining, wanting her ice cream straight away. 'I have to pay for it first and take off the wrapper,' I said.

We headed for the checkout. As we turned the corner of the aisle we saw Kim with a shopping basket on her arm, looking at a display of biscuits. 'Hello, love,' I said. 'Are you helping your mum?'

'Yes,' she said, a little self-consciously. I glanced around for Laura but couldn't see her. 'Where is she?' I asked her. 'I'll say hello.'

'She's at home,' Kim said.

'Oh, OK. Tell her I said hi, please.'

Kim smiled and gave a small nod.

I wasn't going in search of her grandmother, whom I assumed was in one of the other aisles, to say hello, so we continued to the checkout. There was a woman in front of us and as we waited another joined the small queue behind us. Then, as we stepped forward for our turn, I saw Kim join the queue. The cashier rang up our items and placed them in a carrier bag, which I hung on the stroller. I paid and before we left I looked again at Kim and smiled – she was still waiting in the queue, without her grandmother.

Outside the shop I parked the stroller out of the way of the main door and gave Adrian his ice cream, and then removed the wrapper from Paula's. I glanced through the glass shop-front and saw that Kim was now at the till. 'Surely Kim isn't here alone?' I said out loud, voicing my concerns.

Adrian shrugged, more interested in his ice cream.

I threw the wrappers in the bin but didn't immediately start for home.

'Can we go now?' Adrian asked impatiently. 'I want to play in the garden.'

'Yes, in a minute.'

I watched as Kim packed and paid for her shopping and then came out. 'Are you here alone?' I asked her.

She gave a small, furtive nod, almost as if she'd been caught doing something she shouldn't.

'We can walk back together,' I suggested.

She gave another small nod and we crossed the pavement and waited on the kerb. I was surprised and concerned that Kim was by herself. She was only seven, and while there is no law that states a child of seven shouldn't go out alone I thought it was far too young. She wasn't in sight of her house, she was by herself and she'd had to cross quite a busy road. A foster child certainly wouldn't have been allowed to make this journey alone at her age, and neither would I have allowed my own children to do so.

'Is your mother all right?' I asked Kim as we began up our street. I wondered if there had been an emergency, which had necessitated Kim having to buy some items.

'Yes, thank you,' she said politely.

'Where's your gran?' I asked, trying not to sound as though I was questioning her.

'At her house,' Kim replied.

'And you've been doing some shopping for your mother?' She nodded. 'Do you often do the shopping?' I asked after a moment, for she appeared quite confident in her role.

'Yes, sometimes, since Mum had Liam.'

'Does your gran not do the shopping then?'

'Sometimes, but Mum doesn't always like the things Gran buys.'

So why not ask her to buy the things she does like? I thought but didn't say.

'And your mum didn't want to walk down with you?' I asked as we walked.

'She's got a bad headache. She's in bed, and Dad won't be home until later.'

'Oh dear.' I could see Kim looking enviously at Adrian's and Paula's ice creams and I wished I'd thought to buy her one. 'So who's looking after Liam?' I asked.

'He's in the pram, asleep. I wanted to bring him with me, but Mum wouldn't let me. If she's not up later I can make him a bottle,' Kim added proudly. 'I know what to do.'

I smiled and hid my concerns. This wasn't making sense. If Geraldine liked to help, why wasn't she helping the family now when they needed her? Laura was in bed, unwell, and Kim's father wasn't home. Why not phone Geraldine and ask for help? She only lived five streets away. We were drawing close to Laura's house now.

'What time does your dad get in from work?' I asked her. 'Do you know?'

'I think it's usually about seven-thirty or eight,' Kim said.

That was three hours away. 'Does he know your mum is unwell and you had to go to the shop?' We'd arrived at her garden gate.

'No,' Kim said, and opened the gate. If I hadn't been expecting Shelley and Darrel, I would have gone in and asked Laura if there was anything I could do.

Kim paused on the other side of the gate as she looped the carrier bag over her arm and took a front-door key from her purse.

'Kim, will you please tell your mother I said hello and to phone me if there is anything I can do? She has my telephone number.'

'Yes. Thank you,' Kim said sweetly, and then hesitated. With a slightly guilty look she said, 'You won't tell Dad or Gran you saw me, will you?'

'No, but is there a reason?'

'They wouldn't like it,' Kim said. With a little embarrassed smile she turned and continued up the path to her front door.

I watched her open the door and go in. There was no sign of Laura. The door closed and we continued on our way home.

'Why is Kim doing the shopping?' Adrian asked, having heard some of the conversation.

'Her mother isn't feeling well.'

'Would I have to do the shopping if you weren't well?' he said through a mouthful of ice cream.

'No. You're too young.'

'So who would do the shopping while Dad's away if you were ill?'

'I'd ask Sue [our neighbour], or another friend, or Nana and Grandpa. But don't you worry, I'm not going to be ill.' I knew Adrian was anxious about his father working away, and he occasionally asked who would do the jobs his dad usually did, like cutting the grass, or about other 'what if' scenarios, and I always reassured him.

I paused to wipe ice cream from Paula's mouth and hands, as it was melting faster than she could eat it, and then we continued up the street towards home. Perhaps it was from years of fostering that I instinctively sensed when a child might be hiding something, and I felt that now with Kim. What she might be hiding I didn't know, but I had a nagging doubt that something wasn't right in her house. I decided that the following week, at the first opportunity, I would make a neighbourly call and knock on Laura's door – unless, of course, she was in the playground on Monday, which I doubted.

CHAPTER THREE

LULLABY AT BEDTIME

We'd just finished dinner that evening when the doorbell rang, and Adrian and Paula came with me to answer the door. Although it was still light outside I checked the security spyhole before opening it.

'I'm Shelley and this is Darrel,' the young woman said, with a nervous smile.

'Yes, I've been expecting you, love. Come in.'

'This is the lady I told you about,' Shelley said, bending down to Darrel. He was standing beside her, holding her hand, and now buried his face against her leg, reluctant to come in.

'He's bound to be a bit shy to begin with,' I said.

'I know. I understand how he feels,' Shelley said, clearly anxious herself. 'Look, Darrel, Cathy has children you can play with.'

'This is Adrian and this is Paula,' I said.

But Darrel kept his face pressed against his mother's leg as she gently eased him over the doorstep and into the hall. I closed the front door. Adrian, two years older than Darrel and more confident on home territory, went up to him and touched his arm. 'Would you like to come and play with some of my toys?' he asked kindly.

'That's nice of you,' Shelley said, but Darrel didn't look up or release his grip on his mother.

Then Paula decided that she, too, was shy and buried her face against my leg.

'Do you want to leave your bags there?' I said to Shelley, pointing to a space in the hall. 'I'll sort them out later.'

She was carrying a large holdall on each shoulder and, unhooking them, set them on the floor. She was also carrying a cool bag. 'Could you put these things in the fridge, please?' she said, handing me the cool bag. 'There's a pot containing his porridge for breakfast. I made it the way he likes it, with milk, before we came, so you just have to heat it up.'

'OK, that's fine, thank you.'

'And there's some yoghurt in there as well, and diced fruit in little pots. He has them for pudding and snacks. I've also put in a pint of full-cream milk. He prefers that to the semi-skimmed. I give him a drink before he goes to bed. I forgot to tell the social worker that and I didn't know if you had full-cream milk here.'

'I've got most things,' I said, trying to reassure her. 'But it's nice for Darrel to have what you've brought.'

'Oh, the sausages!' Shelley exclaimed.

'Yes, I got some. Don't worry.'

'Thank you so much. I am grateful.' Then, bending down to Darrel again, she said, 'Cathy has got your favourite sausages. Isn't that nice?'

But Darrel kept his face pressed against his mother, and Shelley appeared equally nervous and anxious.

'Try not to worry. He'll be fine soon,' I said. 'Come and have a seat in the living room, while I put these things in the fridge.'

Shelley picked him up and held him tightly to her. I thought he was probably sensing her anxiety as much as he was nervous and shy himself. I showed them into the living room. Adrian went in, too, while Paula, slightly unsettled, came with me into the kitchen. At her age it was more difficult for her to understand fostering.

'Baby?' she asked as I set the cool bag on the work surface and unzipped the lid.

'No, Darrel is older than you. He's three. He's sleeping here for one night. You can play with him.'

I began putting the contents of the cool bag into the fridge as Paula watched. Shelley seemed to have thought of everything, and I recognized the love, care, concern and anxiety that had gone into making up all these little pots so that Darrel had everything he was used to at home. Each pot was labelled with his name, what the pot contained and when he ate the food – so, for example: *Darrel's porridge, breakfast, around 8 a.m.*, and *Darrel's apple and orange mid-morning snack, around 11 a.m.* Once I'd emptied the cool bag I returned to the living room with Paula and placed the bag near Shelley. 'All done,' I said.

'Thank you so much,' she said gratefully. Darrel was sitting on her lap, with his face buried in her sweater. 'I've written down his routine,' she said, passing me a sheet of paper that she'd taken from her bag.

'Thanks. That will be useful.' I sat on the sofa and Paula sat beside me. Adrian was on the floor, playing with the toys and glancing at Darrel in the hope that he would join in.

'I'm sure he'll play with you soon,' I said. Then to Shelley: 'Would you and Darrel like a drink?'

'No, thank you, we had one before we left. He had warm milk, and he has one before he goes to bed too. I put the milk in the bag.'

'Yes, I saw it, thanks. Although I've got plenty of milk here. Has he had his dinner?'

'Yes, and I gave him a bath this morning so there is no need for him to have one this evening. I thought it would be better for him if I did it rather than him having to have a bath in a strange house. No offence, but you know what I mean.'

I smiled. 'Of course. Don't worry. I'll keep to your routine. I'll show you both around the house before you leave, so it won't be so strange.'

'Thank you.'

I guessed Shelley was in her early twenties, so she could only have been seventeen or eighteen when she'd had Darrel, but she obviously thought the world of him, and, as the social worker had said, she was a good mother. She was slim, average height, with fair, shoulder-length hair and was dressed fashionably in jeans and layered tops. She had a sweet, round face but was clearly on edge – she kept frowning and chewing her bottom lip. I knew Darrel would pick up on this. Paula, at my side, was now chancing a look at Darrel as if she might be brave enough to go over to him soon. Shelley saw this. 'Come and say hello to Darrel,' she said. 'He's just a bit shy, like me.'

But Paula shook her head. 'In a few minutes,' I said.

'I think I've packed everything Darrel needs,' Shelley said. 'His plate, bowl, mug and cutlery are in the blue bag in the hall. I've put in some of his favourite toys and Spot the dog. He's the soft toy Darrel takes to bed. Darrel is toilet trained, but he still has a nappy at night. I've put some nappies in the black bag, but he only needs one. I didn't have room to bring his step stool, but he needs that to reach the toilet.'

'Don't worry. I have a couple of those,' I said. 'They are already in place in the bathroom and toilet.'

'Thanks. I've put baby wipes in the blue bag too. His clothes and night things are in the black bag, but I couldn't fit in his changing mat.'

'Don't worry,' I said again. 'I have one of those too. In fact, I have most things children need.'

'Oh, yes, of course, you would have,' Shelley said with a small, embarrassed laugh. 'You have children and you foster. Silly me.'

She was lovely but so anxious. 'I promise I'll take good care of Darrel and keep him safe,' I said. 'He'll be fine. How did you get here with all those bags and Darrel?'

'On the bus,' she replied.

'I wish I'd known. I could have come and collected you in the car.'

'That's kind, but we're pretty self-sufficient. I like it that way. You can't be let down then.' She gave another nervous little laugh and I wondered what had happened in her past to make her feel that way.

Toscha, our lovable and docile cat, sauntered into the room and went over to Adrian.

'Oh, you've got a cat!' Shelley exclaimed. For a moment I thought she was going to tell me that Darrel was allergic to cat fur and it could trigger an asthma attack, which was true for some children. Had this not been an emergency placement I would have known more about Darrel, including facts like this. Thankfully Shelley now said excitedly, 'Look at Cathy's cat, Darrel. You like cats. Are you going to stroke her?' Then to me: 'Is she friendly?'

'Yes, she's very friendly. She's called Toscha.'

Toscha was the prompt Darrel needed to relinquish his grip on his mother's jersey. He turned and looked at the cat and then left her lap and joined Adrian on the floor beside Toscha. Paula then forgot her shyness and slid from the sofa to join them too.

'Toscha likes being stroked,' I said. Which was just as well, as three little hands now stroked her fur and petted her while she purred contentedly. Now Darrel was less anxious I could see Shelley start to relax too. With a small sigh she sat back in her chair.

'I know I shouldn't worry so much,' she said. 'But coming here brought back so many memories.'

I smiled, puzzled. 'Oh yes? What sort of memories?'

'Going into a foster carer's home for the first time. I was in care for most of my life and I had so many moves. I hated having to move. New people and new routines. It was so scary. I felt scared most of my early life. I thought I'd got over all of that, but bringing Darrel here today brought it back.' Which I thought explained at lot of Shelley's apprehension and anxiety. 'I'd rather die than let my little boy lead the life I had,' she added.

'He won't,' I said. 'You'll make sure of it. You're doing a great job. Your social worker told me what a fantastic mum you are. I'm sorry your experiences in care weren't good. It was wrong you had to keep moving, very wrong, but try not to worry about Darrel. He'll be fine here with me and you'll see him again tomorrow.' My heart went out to her. Whatever had the poor child been through?

'Thank you,' she said quietly. 'I worry about him so much. He's all the family I have. I nearly wasn't allowed to keep him when he was a baby. I had to prove to the social services that I could look after him.'

'And you've done that,' I said firmly. 'Admirably.' But I could see she was worried, and I understood why she had overcompensated. 'Do the social services still have any involvement with you and Darrel?' I asked, which again would have been something I'd known if the placement had been planned.

'Not since Darrel was eighteen months old,' Shelley said. 'That's when their supervision order stopped. It was a great relief. I was going to cancel my hospital appointment tomorrow when my friend let me down and said she couldn't look after Darrel. But I knew I'd have to wait ages for another appointment and my teeth really hurt. I've got two impacted wisdom teeth and they're taking them out under general anaesthetic tomorrow. I was really nervous when I phoned the social services to ask for help. I hung up twice before I spoke to anyone. Then I got through to my old social worker and told her what had happened. She was lovely and asked how Darrel and I were. She said she'd see what she could do to arrange something for Darrel so I didn't have to cancel my appointment.'

I nodded sympathetically, and not for the first time since I'd started fostering I realized just how alone in the world some people are. 'So who is collecting you from hospital tomorrow?' I asked.

'No one. I'll get a cab here.'

'I can come and collect you,' I offered.

'That's nice of you, but I'll be fine, and I don't know what time I'll be discharged.'

'You could phone me when you know and I'd come straight over. The hospital isn't far.'

She gave a small shrug. 'Thanks. I'll see how it goes.' And I knew that given her comment about being self-sufficient she'd have to be feeling very poorly before she took up my offer of help.

Toscha had sauntered off and the children were now playing with the toys I'd set out. It was after six-thirty and at some point Shelley would have to say goodbye to Darrel and leave, which would be difficult for them both. The sooner we got it over with the better, and then I could settle Darrel before he went to bed.

'I'll show you around the house before you go,' I said to Shelley.

Her forehead creased and she looked very anxious again. 'I was thinking, if you don't mind, is it possible for me to stay and put Darrel to bed? Once he's asleep I'd go, and he wouldn't be upset.'

Each fostering situation is different, and foster carers have to be adaptable to accommodate the needs of the child (or children) they are looking after, and also often the parents too. There was no reason why she couldn't stay.

'Yes, that's fine with me,' I said. 'But we will need to explain to Darrel what is happening. Otherwise he'll wake up in the morning expecting to find you here, and be upset when you're not.'

'Darrel, love,' Shelley said, leaving her chair and going over to kneel on the floor beside him, 'I've got something to tell you.'

He stopped playing and looked at her, wide-eyed with expectation and concern.

'It's nothing for you to worry about,' she reassured him. 'But you remember I explained how you would be sleeping here for one night while I went into hospital?'

Darrel gave a small nod.

'Well, I am not going to leave you until after you are asleep. Then, in the morning when you wake up, Cathy will be here to look after you until I come back. I'll be back as soon as I can tomorrow. All right, pet?'

'Yes, Mummy,' he said quietly.

'Good boy.' She kissed his cheek.

I thought Shelley had phrased it well, and at three years of age Darrel would have some understanding of 'tomorrow'.

'Shall we have a look around the house now?' I suggested. 'You can see where you will be sleeping,' I said to Darrel.

'Yes, please,' Shelley said enthusiastically, standing. Darrel stood, too, and held her hand. He looked at Adrian and Paula, now his friends.

'Yes, they will come too,' I said. They usually liked to join in the tour of the house I gave each child when they first arrived, although obviously there was no need, as they lived here. 'This is the living room,' I began. 'And through here is the kitchen and our dining table where we eat.'

As we went into the kitchen Darrel exclaimed, 'There's the cat's food!' and pointed to Toscha's feeding bowl.

'That's right,' I said, pleased he was thawing out a little. 'It's empty now because Toscha has had her dinner.'

'I've had my dinner,' Darrel said.

'I know. Your mummy told me. What did you have? Can you remember?'

'Stew,' he said. 'With dumplings.'

'Very nice. Did you eat it all up?'

'Yes.'

'He's a good eater,' Shelley said. 'He likes my bean stew. I learned to make it from a recipe book. I put in lots of vegetables and he eats it all.'

'Very good,' I said, impressed, and thinking I should make stew and dumplings more often.

We went down the hall and into the front room. Given that Darrel was only young and here for one night, I didn't go into detail about what we used the rooms for; I was just showing him around so he was familiar with the layout of the house and would hopefully feel more at home.

'We'll bring the bags up later,' I said as I led the way upstairs. We went round the landing to Darrel's room.

'It's not like my room at home,' he said, slightly disappointed as we went in.

I smiled. 'I'm sure your bedroom at home is fantastic, and it'll have all your things in it, but this will be fine for tonight.'

'Yes, thank you, Cathy,' Shelley said, frowning at Darrel. 'It's very nice.'

I then briefly showed them the other rooms upstairs, including the toilet and bathroom where the step stools were already in place. I made a point of showing Darrel where I slept so that if he woke in the night he knew where to find me. It helped to reassure the child (and their parents), although in truth I was a light sleeper and always heard a child if they were out of bed or called out in the night.

'Thank you very much, Cathy,' Shelley said, and we began downstairs.

We returned to the living room and the children played with the toys again. Shelley sat on the floor with them and joined in, childlike and enthusiastic in her play. She carefully arranged the toy cars and play-people in the garage and sat the attendant behind the cash desk. I thought that, like many children from neglected and abusive backgrounds, she'd probably missed out on her childhood and had grown up fast to survive. After a while she left the children to finish their game and joined me on the sofa. I took the opportunity to explain to her that I would have to take Darrel with me to school in the morning when I took Adrian. I said that if he couldn't manage the walk there and back I had a double stroller I could use.

'He'll be fine walking,' Shelley said. 'It's not far, and he walks everywhere with me. I don't have a car and I sold his stroller six months ago as I needed the money.' I appreciated it must be difficult for her financially, bringing up a child alone.

It was nearly seven o'clock and I said I usually took Paula up for her bath and bed about this time.

'It's nearly Darrel's bedtime too,' Shelley said. 'Can I give him his drink of warm milk now?'

'Yes, of course. I'll show you where everything is in the kitchen.'

Leaving the children playing I took Shelley into the kitchen, showed her around and then left her to warm Darrel's milk, while I took Paula upstairs to get ready for bed.

'Baby bed?' Paula asked.

'Darrel will be going to bed soon,' I said, guessing that was what she meant. My reply seemed to satisfy her, for she chuckled.

I gave Paula a quick bath, put her in a clean nappy and then, after lots of hugs and kisses, tucked her into her cot bed. 'Night, love,' I said, kissing her soft, warm cheek one last time. 'Sleep tight and see you in the morning.'

Paula grinned, showing her relatively new front teeth, and I kissed her some more. I said 'Night-night' again and finally came out, leaving her bedroom door slightly open so I could hear her if she didn't settle or woke in the night, although she usually slept through now.

Downstairs Darrel had had his milk and Shelley was in the kitchen, washing up his mug while Darrel played with Adrian in the living room. Shelley looked quite at home in the kitchen and I asked her if she'd like a cup of tea, but she said she'd like to get Darrel to bed first. We went into the living room where she told Darrel it was time for bed. 'Say goodnight to Adrian,' she said.

'Goodnight,' Darrel said politely, and kissed Adrian's cheek. Adrian looked slightly embarrassed at having a boy kiss him, but of course Darrel was only three.

'I'm sorry,' Shelley said, seeing Adrian's discomfort. 'He always kisses me when we say goodnight.'

'It's fine,' I said. 'As Mrs Clause says in *Santa Clause: The Movie*, "If you give extra kisses, you get bigger hugs!"'

'That's lovely,' Shelley said, clasping her hands together in delight. 'I'll have to remember that – "If you give extra kisses, you get bigger hugs!"'

Adrian grinned; he loved that Christmas movie and the saying, as I did.

Shelley and I carried the holdalls upstairs and into Darrel's room, with Darrel following. Having checked she had everything she needed, I left Shelley to get Darrel ready for bed and went downstairs. I'd got into the routine of putting Paula to bed first and then spending some time with Adrian. He usually read his school book, then we'd play a game or just chat, and then I'd read him a bedtime story and take him up to bed. It was our time together, set aside from the hustle and bustle of him having a younger sister and fostering. Now, as I sat on the sofa with my arm around him, we could hear Shelley moving around upstairs while she saw to Darrel.

'It's strange having another mummy in the house,' Adrian said.

'Yes, it is,' I agreed. 'But it's rather nice.' It was touching and reassuring to hear another mother patiently and lovingly tending to the needs of her child.

Once I'd finished reading Adrian his bedtime story, he put the book back on the shelf and then went over to say goodnight to Toscha as he did every night. She was curled on her favourite chair and he gently kissed the top of her furry head once and then twice. 'Remember, Toscha,' he said. '"If you give extra kisses, you get bigger hugs!"'

'That's right,' I said. 'Although I'd be very surprised if she got up and hugged you.' Adrian laughed loudly.

'Mum, you are silly sometimes.'

We went upstairs and while Adrian went to the toilet I checked on Paula. She was fast asleep, flat on her back, with her arms and legs spread out like a little snow angel. I kissed her forehead and crept out, again leaving her door slightly open. Shelley was in Darrel's room now and through their open door I could hear her telling him that she would only go once he was asleep, and then she'd come back for him as soon as possible the next day. There was anxiety in her voice again, and I hoped it wouldn't unsettle Darrel, for it could take hours before he went to sleep.

I ran Adrian's bath and waited while he washed – even at his age I didn't leave him unattended in the bath for long. I also washed his back, which he often forgot about. Once he was out, dried and dressed in his pyjamas, I went with him to his room. Following our usual routine, he switched on his lamp and I switched off the main light, then I sat on his bed while he snuggled down and settled ready for sleep. He often remembered something he had to tell me at this time that couldn't wait until the morning. Sometimes it was a worry he'd been harbouring during the day, but more often it was just a general chat – a young, active boy delaying the time when he had to go to sleep. But tonight we heard Shelley talking quietly to Darrel in the room next door.

'Will Darrel still be here when I come home from school tomorrow?' Adrian asked.

'I don't think so. His mother is hoping to collect him in the early afternoon.'

'He's nice, isn't he?' Adrian said.

'Yes, he's a lovely little boy, just like you.'

Adrian smiled and I stroked his forehead. 'Time for sleep,' I said.

Then we both stopped and looked at each other in the half-light as the most beautiful, angelic voice floated in from Darrel's room. Shelley was singing him a lullaby and her soft, gentle voice caressed the air, pitch perfect and as tender and innocent as a newborn baby – it sent shivers down my spine. First Brahms's 'Lullaby' and then 'All Through the Night':

'Sleep, my child, and peace attend thee,
All through the night,
Guardian angels God will send thee,
All through the night ...'

By the time she'd finished my eyes had filled and I swallowed the lump in my throat. It was the most beautiful, soulful singing I'd ever heard, and I felt enriched for having been part of it.

CHAPTER FOUR

SHELLEY

'You've got a lovely voice,' I said to Shelley when she finally came downstairs from settling Darrel for the night.

'Thank you. I wanted to become a professional singer, but that won't happen now.'

I was in the living room with the curtains closed against the night sky, reading the sheet of paper Shelley had given to me on Darrel's routine. 'Would you like that cup of tea now?' I asked her.

'Yes, please. Shall I make it?'

'No, you sit down,' I said, standing. 'You've had a busy day. Milk and sugar?'

'Just milk, please.'

'Would you like something to eat now too?' I asked. 'It's a while since you had dinner.'

'A biscuit would be nice, thank you,' Shelley said. 'I usually have one with a cup of tea when I've finished putting Darrel to bed.'

I went through to the kitchen, smiling at the thought of Shelley's little evening ritual, not dissimilar to my own, of putting the children to bed first and then sitting down and relaxing with a cup of tea and a biscuit. I guessed parents everywhere probably did something similar.

I made the tea, set the cups and a plate of biscuits on a tray and carried it through to the living room. 'Help yourself to biscuits,' I said, putting the tray on the occasional table and passing her a cup of tea.

'Thank you. You've got a nice home,' she said sweetly. 'It's so welcoming and friendly.'

'That's a lovely compliment,' I said, pleased.

'Do you find it hard with your husband working away?' Shelley asked, taking a couple of biscuits.

'I did to begin with,' I said. 'But we're in a routine now. And my parents will always help out if necessary.'

'I wish I had parents,' she said.

'Where are they?' I asked. 'Do you know?' It was clear that Shelley wanted to talk, so I felt it was all right to ask this.

'My mum's dead, and I never knew my dad. I think he's dead too,' she said without self-pity.

'I am sorry.'

She gave a small shrug. 'It was a long time ago. It happened when I was a child. They were both heavy drug users. It was the drugs that killed my mum and I think my dad too. I remember my mum from when I was little, but not my dad. I never saw him. I have a photo of my mum at home. I keep it by my bed. But even back then you can see she was wasted from the drugs. When the kids at secondary school started boasting that they'd been trying drugs I used to think: you wouldn't if you saw what they did. My mum was only twenty-six when she died, but she was all wrinkled and wizened, and stick thin.'

'I am sorry,' I said again. 'You've had a lot to cope with in your life. And it must be difficult bringing up a child completely alone. Although you are doing a good job,' I added.

Shelley gave a small nod and sipped her tea. 'I was a week off my eighteenth birthday when I had Darrel,' she said, setting the cup on the saucer. 'All my plans had to be put on hold. I had great plans. I wanted to be something. Go to college and study music and try to become a professional singer. I thought I'd get a good job, buy a house and a car, and go on holidays like other people do. But that's all gone now. I know other young single mums and, although we all love our children, if we're honest we'd do things differently if we had our time over again – get a job and training first, meet someone, set up home and then have a family. You can't do that if you have a child.'

'It is difficult,' I agreed. 'You're not in touch with any of your foster carers?'

'No. I was moved so often I can't even remember most of their names. Some of them were nice, others weren't. The only one I really felt was like a mother to me was Carol. I was with her from when I was fourteen to when I was seventeen. She was so nice. She helped me through a really bad time. But when I was seventeen the social worker said I had to go and live in a semi-independence unit ready for when I left care. Carol tried to stay in touch – she phoned and put cards through my door – but I never got back to her.'

'That's a pity. Why not?'

Shelley shrugged. 'Not sure. But I was dating then and I sort of put my trust in him.'

'Have you thought about trying to contact Carol now?' I asked. 'I'm sure she'd be pleased to hear from you.'

'It's been over three years,' Shelley said.

'Even so, I still think she'd be pleased if you did get in touch. I know I am when a child I've fostered leaves and we lose contact, and then they suddenly phone or send a card or arrive at my door. Foster carers never forget the children they look after, but once the child has left the social services don't tell us how you are doing.'

'I didn't realize that,' Shelley said, slightly surprised. 'I'll think about it.' She took another biscuit.

'Are you sure I can't make you something proper to eat?' I asked.

'No, really, I'm fine. I must go soon.' But she didn't make any move to go and I was happy for her to sit and talk. 'When I found out I was pregnant,' she continued, 'Darrel's father had already left me. I told the social worker getting pregnant was an accident, but it wasn't a complete accident. I mean, I didn't plan on getting pregnant – I wanted to go to college – but neither did I take any precautions. I was pretty messed up at the time, and I sort of thought that having a child would give me the family I'd never had. I wanted to be loved and needed.'

'We all want that,' I said. 'It's such a pity you weren't found a forever family. I don't understand why the social services didn't look for an adoptive family for you, with both your parents dead.'

'They did,' Shelley said in the same matter-of-fact way. 'I was adopted. But it didn't work out.'

'Didn't work out?' I asked, dismayed. 'Adoption is supposed to be for life. In law, an adopted child is the same as a birth child.'

'I know. They even changed my surname to theirs. I was with them for two years, from when I was nine. But then the woman got pregnant. They thought they couldn't have kids and when the baby was born they were all over it and I was pushed out. That's what it felt like. So I started playing up and being really naughty. I remember doing it because I felt like no one loved me, so they put me back into care.'

'That's awful,' I said. 'I am so sorry to hear that.' It was such a sad story, but Shelley didn't appear bitter.

'That's life,' she said with a dismissive shrug. Draining the last of her tea, she returned the cup and saucer to the tray. 'I'd better be going. Thanks for listening. I hope I haven't kept you.'

'Of course not. I've enjoyed having your company. And please don't worry about Darrel. I'll take good care of him. I hope the operation goes well.' The clock on the mantelpiece showed it was nearly ten o'clock. 'Shelley, I don't really want you going home on the bus alone at this time. Can I call a cab? I'll pay for it.'

'That's kind of you. I'm not usually out this late,' she said with a small laugh. 'I'm usually at home with Darrel. But is it safe for a woman to be alone in a cab? I mean, you read bad stuff in the papers.'

'It's a local firm I know well,' I said. 'They have at least one lady cab driver. Shall I see if she's free?'

'Yes, please. I'll pop up to the loo while you phone them.'

I called the cab firm and the controller said they had a lady driver working that night, so I booked the cab. He said she would be with us in about fifteen minutes. Shelley had been right to be concerned, a young woman alone in a cab, but I was confident she'd be safe using this firm or I wouldn't have suggested it. I heard her footsteps on the landing, but before she came downstairs she went into Darrel's room. A few moments later she returned to the living room. 'He's fast asleep,' she said, joining me on the sofa. 'He should sleep through, but he'll wake early with a sopping wet nappy. I'm trying to get him dry at night, but it's difficult.'

'You could try giving him his last drink in the evening earlier,' I suggested. 'Perhaps with his dinner, or just after. That's what I did with Adrian and the children I've fostered who were still in nappies at night. After all, what goes in must come out!'

She smiled. 'Yes, very true. I'll give it a try.'

I told her the cab was on its way and, taking out my purse, I gave her a twenty-pound note to pay the fare.

'It won't be that much,' she said. 'I'll give you change.'

'No. It's OK. Buy yourself something.'

'Thank you. That is kind.'

We continued chatting, mainly about Darrel and being a parent, until the doorbell rang. I went with her to the front door and opened it. The lady driver said she'd wait in her cab.

'Good luck for tomorrow,' I said to Shelley. 'And phone me if you change your mind about a lift back from the hospital.'

'All right. Thanks for everything,' she said, and gave me a big hug. 'How different my life would have been if I'd been fostered by you,' she added reflectively.

I felt my eyes fill. 'Take care, love, and see you tomorrow.'

I waited with the door open until she was safely in the cab, and then I closed and locked it for the night. Shelley's unsettled past was sadly not a one-off. Too many children are bounced around the care system (for a number of reasons) and never have a chance to put down roots and have a family of their own. These young people often struggle in adult life, and feeling unloved can lead to drink and drugs or abusive relationships. Since I started writing my fostering memoirs I've been heartbroken by some of the emails I've received from young men and women with experiences similar to Shelley's. Far more needs to be done to keep children in the same foster family or adoptive home so that they grow up and meet the challenges of adulthood with the confidence and self-esteem that comes from being loved and wanted.

Before I went to bed I checked all three children were asleep, leaving their bedroom doors ajar so I would hear them if they called out. I never sleep well when I have a new child in the house. I'm half listening out in case they wake and are upset. As it happened, Darrel slept through, but I woke with a start at six o'clock when I heard him cry, 'Mummy!'

I was immediately out of bed and going round the landing in my dressing gown. The poor little chap was sitting up in bed, his round face sad and scared. 'Where's Mummy?' he asked.

'She's gone to the hospital to have her tooth made better,' I said, sitting on the edge of the bed. 'I'm Cathy. Do you remember coming here yesterday? You're staying with me while Mummy is at the hospital, then she'll come and collect you.'

But he wasn't reassured. His face crumbled and his tears fell. 'I want my mummy.'

'Oh, love, come here.' I put my arm around him and held him close. It was only natural for him to be upset, waking in a strange bed and being separated from his mother for the first time.

'It's all right,' I soothed, stroking his head. 'I'll look after you until Mummy comes back.'

'I want my mummy,' he sobbed. 'Where's my mummy?'

I felt so sorry for him. 'She's not here, love. She's at the hospital. You'll see her later.'

But he wouldn't be consoled. 'Mummy! Mummy!' he called out with rising desperation. I knew it was only a matter of time before he woke Adrian and Paula.

Sure enough, a moment later Adrian's feet pitter-pattered round the landing and he came into Darrel's room in his pyjamas, looking very worried.

'It's OK,' I reassured him and Darrel. 'Darrel will be fine soon.'

'Don't be upset,' Adrian said, coming over to Darrel and gently rubbing his arm. 'We'll look after you. You can play with my best toys in my bedroom if you like.'

'Wow. Did you hear that, Darrel?' I said to him. 'Adrian says you can play with his best toys.' He kept them in his bedroom out of harm's way, as Paula at thirteen months was still rather clumsy.

The offer to play with an older boy's best toys was too good to refuse, and far more comforting than my well-meant words of reassurance. Darrel's tears stopped and he climbed out of bed. 'I have to take my nappy off first,' he said to Adrian.

I knew from Shelley's notes that she used baby wipes to clean Darrel in the morning, and then he went to the toilet. So once he was clean and dry, he stayed in his pyjamas and went into Adrian's room where Adrian had already set out some toys for them both to play with. With the boys occupied and Paula still asleep, I took the opportunity to shower and dress. By the time I'd finished Paula was awake and jumping up and down in her cot wanting to be 'Out! Out!' so I got her dressed. I took her with me into Adrian's room, thanked him for looking after Darrel and left him to dress while I helped Darrel in his room. Aged three, Darrel could mostly dress himself but needed some help, especially with his socks, which are difficult for young children – he kept getting them on with the heel on top.

By the time we arrived downstairs for breakfast Adrian was Darrel's best friend and he wouldn't let him out of his sight. I had to push his chair right up close to Adrian's at the table so they were touching, and he chatted away to Adrian. I warmed up the porridge Shelley had made for him and poured it into a bowl. Before Darrel began eating he asked Adrian if he'd like some. 'Mummy won't mind,' he said cutely.

'That's OK, you have it,' Adrian said. 'I've got wheat flakes.' In truth, Adrian had gone off porridge and didn't eat it at that point.

Paula was sitting on her booster seat at the table, opposite Darrel, and was far more interested in watching him than she was in feeding herself. He was a new face at the table and she didn't understand why he was there. I was sitting beside her and kept filling her spoon from her bowl of hot oat cereal and reminding her to eat. Darrel finished his porridge and I gave him the fruit his mother had prepared. He gave us a grape each, which we thanked him for and ate. 'Very nice,' I said.

Mindful of the time ticking by, I shepherded everyone upstairs and into the bathroom to brush their teeth and wash their faces. It was quite a logistical exercise getting three small children ready to leave the house on time, but eventually they were all in the hall with their jackets done up and their shoes on. Paula wanted to walk, but there wasn't time, so I told her she could walk on the way back from school and lifted her into the stroller and fastened her safety harness before she had a chance to protest. Outside she wanted to hold Darrel's hand as he walked beside her stroller and he was happy to do so, finding the novelty of a little one quite amusing. The boys talked to each other as we walked and Darrel told Adrian he would be starting school in September when he was four.

We arrived in the school playground with a few minutes to spare and I glanced around for any sign of Kim, but she wasn't there. The Klaxon sounded for the start of school and Adrian began saying goodbye to us all. Although I'd already explained to Darrel that Adrian would have to go to school, I don't think he understood the implications, for he suddenly looked very sad. 'Don't leave me,' he said. I thought he was going to cry.

Adrian looked at me anxiously. 'You go in,' I said. 'Don't worry. Darrel will be fine.' It was possible they might see each other at the end of school, but I couldn't promise, as that would depend on what time Shelley was discharged from hospital and came to collect Darrel.

Saying goodbye, Adrian ran over to line up with his class and I turned to Darrel. 'I could do with your help,' I said to distract him. 'Paula's going to walk back and she obviously likes holding your hand. When I let her out of the stroller could you hold one of her hands, please, and I'll hold the other? She doesn't understand about road safety yet, so it's important she holds our hands.'

Darrel rose to the occasion. 'I'm good at helping,' he said proudly, looking less sad. 'I help my mummy.'

'Excellent.'

I undid Paula's harness and helped her out of the stroller. As I did I saw Geraldine rush into the playground with Kim. Neither of them looked at me as they were concentrating on getting Kim into school on time. I still intended to call on Laura the following week if she didn't appear in the playground. With Darrel on one side of Paula and me on the other, we made our way out of the main gate and began our walk home. It was a slow walk – very slow – but it didn't matter, as it kept Darrel occupied and distracted him from worrying about his mother. He found Paula's habit of stopping every few steps to examine something in detail very funny. 'What's she looking at now?' he said, laughing. 'It's a twig, Paula!' Or, 'It's another stone. You are funny.' It was nice to see him happy, and Paula was enjoying his company, although I don't think she understood why her behaviour was amusing. At one point Geraldine overtook us on the opposite said of the street, although she didn't look in our direction.

Paula paused as usual outside number 53 and rattled the garden gate. 'Baby,' she said, recognizing the house.

'Yes, baby Liam lives there,' I said. I glanced at the windows, but there was no sign of anyone.

She took another couple of steps up the street and then stopped to examine a weed that was sprouting between the paving slabs.

'It's a weed,' Darrel said. 'There are lots of them!'

And so we continued our meandering journey home.

CHAPTER FIVE

A VERY STRANGE PHONE CALL

Once home, I kept Darrel and Paula entertained with various games and activities, and then at eleven o'clock I gave both children a drink and a snack, before putting Paula in her cot for a little nap. While she slept I read to Darrel from books he chose from our bookshelves, and then we had a few rounds of the card game Snap, which he was learning to play. He asked about his mummy a couple of times and I reassured him that she was being well looked after and he'd see her before too long, so he wasn't upset. I knew from Shelley's notes that he had his lunch at about 12.30 p.m., so once Paula was awake I got her up and cooked vegetarian sausages, mash and peas for us all. I'd just set the food on the table when the doorbell rang.

'Mummy?' Darrel asked.

'I think it's a bit early yet,' I said. 'Stay here and I'll check.'

Leaving the children at the table, I went down the hall to answer the door. To my surprise it was Shelley, looking very pale, with one side of her face swollen and a bloody tissue pressed to her lips.

'Oh, love,' I said, concerned and drawing her in. 'Whyever didn't you phone me to collect you? I hope you haven't come on the bus.'

'I got a cab,' she mumbled, stepping in and barely able to speak. 'I used the rest of the money you gave me.' It obviously hurt her when she spoke.

'Have you taken something for the pain?' I asked.

She nodded. 'Paracetamol.'

'Mummy!' Darrel cried, having heard his mother's voice. He left the table and ran into the hall but stopped dead when he saw her swollen face.

'It's all right,' I reassured him. 'Mummy's mouth is sore, but she'll be better soon. I think she needs looking after.' I took her hand and led her down the hall and into the living room. As we passed Darrel she managed a wonky smile, but he looked very concerned. 'Mummy's going to have a quiet sit down while you have your lunch,' I said, settling her on the sofa.

'Thank you,' she said, sitting back with a small sigh.

'Can I get you anything?' I asked.

'A glass of water, please.' She winced as she spoke and put her hand to her face.

'You sit there and I'll fetch it,' I said. Then to Darrel, 'Come with me. We'll leave Mummy to have a rest.'

He hesitated.

'Go on, love,' Shelley said. 'Good boy.'

He slipped his hand into mine and I took him to the dining table, where Paula was still seated and making a good attempt to feed herself using her toddler fork and spoon. 'Good girl,' I said, returning the peas to her plate.

Darrel picked up his knife and fork and began eating, while I went into the kitchen and poured Shelley a glass of water. I added a straw to make drinking it a little easier, then took the glass through to the living room.

'Thank you,' she said gratefully, and gingerly took a few sips before handing it back to me. She sighed and rested her head back on the sofa.

'Would you like to go upstairs for a lie down?' I suggested.

'I'll just sit here for a bit if that's all right.'

'Yes, of course.' I set her glass of water on the coffee table within her reach and also a box of tissues. 'Do you want anything else?' I asked. She shook her head and her eyelids began to close. 'Call me if you need anything,' I said. She nodded and I came out closing the door behind me so the children and I wouldn't disturb her. I thought a sleep would do her good; having an anaesthetic can leave you feeling very tired.

'Mummy is having a rest,' I said to Darrel as I returned to the table. 'She'll be all right soon, so you have your lunch and when she wakes we'll tell her what a good boy you've been.'

He looked concerned but continued eating. Paula dropped a lump of mashed potato in her lap and tried to pick it up. She laughed as it squashed between her fingers, which made Darrel smile too. He ate all his meal and Paula ate her mash and peas but left some of the sausage. It was the first time she'd had a vegetarian sausage, so it was a new taste and texture for her, but at least she'd tried it. Darrel had one of the yoghurts his mother had brought for his pudding and Paula had a fromage frais. Once they'd finished I went into the living room to check on Shelley. She was fast asleep with her head resting on the sofa back and her mouth slightly open. I crept out and quietly closed the door. I suggested to Darrel that the three of us play something at the table so we wouldn't disturb his mother. 'Do you like Play-Doh?' I asked him. I'd never met a child who didn't.

'I have Play-Doh at my house,' he said enthusiastically.

I cleared the dishes from the table, covered it with a protective plastic tablecloth and took out the Play-Doh set. Once they were both occupied I went into the kitchen, where I could still see them, and cleared up, then I joined in their play at the table. Darrel was concentrating on feeding blue Play-Doh through the toy machine and creating different shapes. Some of it came out as long, thin strands like spaghetti and he pretended to eat it, which made Paula laugh.

I checked on Shelley again, but she was still fast asleep. If necessary I could leave her sleeping and take Darrel with me when I collected Adrian from school, but that wasn't for another hour. When Darrel and Paula had tired of the Play-Doh we packed it away and I showed Darrel the toy cupboard and let him choose something else to play with. He picked a jigsaw puzzle of a farmyard scene and I took out an early-years puzzle for Paula. The three of us sat at the table assembling the puzzles. When Darrel had completed his I praised him and he packed it away and took out another one. Five minutes later I heard the door to the living room open and then Shelley came in carrying her empty glass of water. 'How are you feeling, love?' I said. Darrel looked at her anxiously.

'A bit better now, thanks,' she said, trying to raise a smile. 'I need to take a couple more paracetamol. Can I have another glass of water, please?'

'Yes, of course. Sit down. I'll get it.'

She sat at the table and as I poured the water I could see Darrel looking at her anxiously. It's difficult for a child to see their usually strong parent compromised and vulnerable. 'That's a good puzzle,' she said, trying to divert his attention. 'See if you can finish it before we go.'

I handed her the glass of water and she took two tablets. 'Could you manage something to eat now?' I asked. 'Soup? I could break up some bread to put in. That would be easy to eat.'

'Oh, yes, please,' she said gratefully. 'I couldn't have anything before the operation and I am hungry. But are you sure I'm not keeping you?'

'Not at all. I don't have to collect Adrian for three-quarters of an hour, and you're more than welcome to stay here while I get him. I can take you home in the car after.'

'The doctor said I mustn't have anything too hot,' she added as I went into the kitchen. 'Because of the stitches.'

'Stitches?' Darrel asked, worried.

'Yes, to help make my mouth get better,' Shelley said, reassuring him.

She sat at the table and watched the children playing as I warmed some cream of tomato soup, buttered some bread and cut it into small chunks to dunk in the soup. I carried it through and set in on the table with a spoon.

'Thank you,' Shelley said again. 'You are kind to me.' Bless her, I thought. She was such a sweet kid. I wished I could have done more for her.

I played with the children while she ate, and once she'd finished she thanked me again and then to my horror said: 'I feel well enough to go and get the bus now.'

'There's no way you're going home on the bus,' I said, dismayed. 'If you don't want to wait until I return from collecting Adrian, when I can take you in the car, then I'll call a cab.'

'I'd really like to get home and get settled, and then have an early night,' she said, which I could understand.

'OK, I'll call a cab then,' I said, standing. Without waiting for further protest I went to the phone in the living room and booked the cab with a lady driver, then, returning to Shelley, I gave her money for the fare. Needless to say, she thanked me profusely.

While Shelley stayed with the children I quickly went round the house gathering together Darrel's belongings and packing them into his bags, which I put in the hall. Fifteen minutes later the cab arrived and the driver helped Shelley with the bags while I took Darrel and Paula to the car. Shelley and Darrel climbed into the rear of the cab and Shelley fastened their seatbelts. 'Thank you so much,' she said again.

'You're welcome, love. Take care.'

'Say goodbye and thank you to Cathy,' she told Darrel.

'Bye, and thank you,' he said adorably.

'We've all enjoyed having you to stay,' I said.

'Thanks for everything, and thank Adrian for playing with Darrel,' Shelley said.

'I will.'

I closed the cab door and Paula and I waved until the cab was out of sight. Although Darrel was obviously pleased to be going home, Paula looked sad. But goodbyes are part of fostering, and it was important that Paula was included in this, for a good farewell is as important as welcoming a child when they first arrive. Yet I'll admit I felt sad too. Even if a child is only with you a short while, as Darrel had been, they touch your life and you don't forget them. I would remember Darrel and Shelley in the years to come and wonder how they were doing. If I saw them again then that would be a huge bonus, but it couldn't be guaranteed, and as a foster carer I had to accept that.

* * *

I returned indoors with Paula and then it was time to collect Adrian from school. I persuaded her into the stroller with the promise that she could walk some of the way back. As we waited in the playground I saw Geraldine arrive in good time and then as usual stand alone, separate from the other parents, as she waited for school to end. The Klaxon sounded and Adrian ran out amid the hubbub and excitement of Friday afternoon and the start of the weekend. But as he neared I could see him looking for Darrel.

'He's just gone home with his mother,' I said. 'They said to say goodbye and thank you for looking after Darrel.'

'Oh, OK,' he said. 'Pity I couldn't have said goodbye.'

'I know.' Then I distracted him by talking about the busy weekend we had coming up. We were going to visit my parents on Saturday and then Adrian had been invited to a friend's football birthday party on Sunday. I reminded him that the present needed wrapping and the card had to be written and suggested we did it that evening.

Once we'd crossed the road and entered our street I let Paula out of the stroller. There was no sign of Geraldine and Kim ahead of or behind us. Perhaps they'd stopped off at the shop. However, as we passed number 53 I saw that their front door was wide open. I glanced in but couldn't see anyone in the hall. We continued our slow, faltering walk past and then a few steps further up I heard a loud bang as a door slammed shut behind me. I instinctively turned. A middle-aged man in a suit and tie was storming down the front garden path of Laura's house. He was clearly annoyed – his face was set and his body tense as he thrust a fob at the car parked in the kerb outside their house. He jumped in, immediately started the engine and the car tyres screeched as it pulled away and sped past us.

'That car's going far too fast,' Adrian remarked.

'Yes, it is,' I agreed.

I had no idea what Laura's husband looked like – I barely knew her – and if it was her husband and they'd had an argument then it was none of my business. Or was it? How many neighbours when interviewed after a tragic domestic incident exonerate themselves by saying that the family seemed pleasant but kept themselves to themselves. I already had some concerns about Laura, and perhaps as a result of fostering and having to piece together snippets of information from children who were trying to tell me what they had been through (they rarely tell the full story all in one go), I'd become more adept at looking at the wider picture. But on the other hand you can't jump to conclusions and phone the social services just because you have a suspicion that all is not well in a family. You need some evidence.

Half an hour later, after we'd arrived home, the telephone rang. I wasn't thinking about Laura at that moment and I didn't make the connection when I heard a female voice say rather loudly, 'Is that Cathy?'

'Yes?' I said tentatively.

'You don't recognize me, do you? It's Laura from number 53.'

'Oh, hello. How are you?' I was completely thrown. It didn't sound like her at all.

'I'm fine,' she said. 'Really good. I thought I'd give you a ring. Do you remember you left your phone number with my mother-in-law and said to phone for a chat?'

'Yes, of course.' But it was an odd time to phone for a chat. Most parents with a young family were occupied at this time making dinner or seeing to their children. 'Is everything all right?'

'Yes, fine, good. How are you? I haven't been going to school. Geraldine's been taking and collecting Kim. She says I have to rest. My husband Andy says so too. They agree about most things. So I'm doing what I'm told. Like a good girl. That's why you haven't seen me. But I'm fine. We're all fine ...' And her words continued, fast and furious, fired at me in short, staccato sentences and not 'chatty' at all. She sounded hyper, agitated. 'So Geraldine, my mother-in-law, is looking after us all,' she continued. 'Me, Kim, Andy and little Liam. She's doing a great job.'

'How is Liam?' I asked, forcing a gap.

'He's fine. Well, like a baby. Eating, sleeping, crying. But Geraldine takes care of that. Many thanks to Geraldine, I say. She's a natural with children. I think some people are, don't you?'

'Is Geraldine with you now?' I interjected.

'Who?'

'Geraldine. Your mother-in-law. Is she with you now?'

'Yes, of course. Why do you ask? She's here most days while Andy is at work. Andy is my husband. Sometimes she stays after he comes home to make sure he has his dinner. But that's mothers for you. They never stop fussing over their little boys. Although what would I know? Kim is a girl. But Geraldine is great. In fact, it was she who suggested I phone you. She thought I should.'

'Why?'

'Oh, you know. For a chat. To tell you I'm OK. In fact, we're all OK. Me, Andy, Liam and Kim. We're doing fine. I believe you saw Kim at the shop? She's a good girl, helps me out sometimes. But we won't mention that, will we?' And she gave a small, high-pitched laugh.

'Is there anything I can do?' I asked.

'No, nothing you can do.'

'I was thinking of popping in to see you next week.'

'Oh, I see. Well, you can if you like, but really there's no need. I'm fine. We all are. Couldn't be better.'

'What day suits you?' I began.

'Not sure. Have to go now. Bye.' The line went dead.

I stood for a moment, completely bemused, then slowly returned the handset to its cradle. It was one of the strangest telephone calls I'd ever received. Whatever was all that about? Why had she phoned? I had no idea. The Laura I'd spoken to while walking back from school had been quiet, shy and a little withdrawn, whereas this Laura was gushy and completely over the top. It didn't sound like the same person. I didn't think she was drunk, although she had sounded confused and had repeated herself. But Geraldine was with her, presumably helping her, so I put Laura out of my thoughts for the time being and concentrated on my family.

After dinner I played some games with the children and then began Paula's bath and bedtime routine. Later, when she was asleep, I lay propped on Adrian's bed and we had our little chat before he settled for the night. He suddenly asked, 'I wonder what Darrel is doing now.'

'I expect he's asleep,' I said.

'Do you think his mummy sings to him every night?'

'Yes, although maybe not tonight, as her mouth is sore.'

'What's that tune called?' Adrian asked. 'The one that goes like this.' He began humming one of the lullabies Shelley had sung.

'Brahms's "Lullaby",' I said. 'It is beautiful, isn't it?'

'Yes. I wish you could sing it like Shelley,' Adrian said.

'So do I.' I smiled. 'She's got a lovely voice. Perhaps we could hum it together? Let's try.'

I put my arm around him and in the light of the lamp we began humming the haunting melody of the lullaby, which has become a classic for children everywhere. It didn't sound too bad at all. And I hoped that the sentiment in our tune carried through the night air and touched Shelley and Darrel, so that they knew we were thinking about them.

'Night, Shelley and Darrel,' Adrian said as we finished. 'Night, Mum.'

'Night, love. Sleep tight.'

'Love you.'

'Love you more.'

CHAPTER SIX
USELESS

On Monday morning I was going to ask Geraldine if it would be convenient for me to pop in and see Laura on the way back from school, but she left the playground before I had a chance to speak to her. Laura's phone call on Friday had played on my mind over the weekend and I wanted to just say hi to her and make sure she was all right. I decided I'd stop by anyway, and if it wasn't convenient I could arrange to go back another time. I bought a bunch of flowers for Laura from the local supermarket and once we'd crossed the road I let Paula out of her stroller to walk. It was 9.40 by the time we arrived outside number 53.

'Baby,' Paula said as I opened their gate.

'Yes, that's right. We are going in to see if we can visit baby Liam and Laura,' I said. Paula grinned.

I parked the stroller to one side of the porch and, holding Paula's hand, pressed the doorbell. It was answered almost immediately by Geraldine, who didn't seem unduly surprised to see me.

'Laura's up, but not dressed,' she said rather brusquely.

'Would you give these flowers to her, please?' I said, assuming from her comment that it wasn't convenient for me to go in.

'You can give them to her yourself,' she said equally bluntly.

'Are you sure? I don't want to intrude.' But Geraldine was already holding the door wider for us to go in.

'She's in the living room,' Geraldine said in the same terse manner and nodding down the hall. 'Sorry about the telephone call on Friday. Laura wasn't herself.'

'Oh. That's OK,' I said, surprised that she'd mentioned it. 'How is she now?'

'Fine,' she said, and led the way down the hall and into the living room. Laura was sitting on the sofa in her dressing gown breastfeeding Liam, and she did appear fine.

'Lovely to see you,' she said, looking up and smiling.

'Baby,' Paula said.

'He's gorgeous,' I said. 'Absolutely beautiful.'

'Thank you. Hi,' Laura said to Paula. Paula hid her face shyly against my leg.

'A few flowers for you,' I said, offering the colourful bouquet.

'That is kind of you. Thank you,' Laura replied easily.

'I'll put them in a vase,' Geraldine said, stepping forward. I passed her the flowers. 'Would you like a coffee?' she asked.

'Only if you are making one.'

'I don't drink coffee,' she replied curtly.

'I'd like one,' Laura said.

Geraldine gave a stiff nod and went out of the room.

'Are you sure you don't mind me dropping by like this?' I asked Laura.

'No, of course not. I'm pleased to see you. I wasn't going anywhere. Sit down, and thanks for the flowers.'

'You're welcome.'

I slipped off my jacket, took Paula's jacket off and draped them over the back of a chair. As I sat down Paula scrambled onto my lap.

'He is a beautiful baby,' I said.

'He looks like his dad,' Laura said.

'I can see you in him too. He's got your nose and chin.'

She smiled. 'Mum said that as well.' Laura seemed more like her old self – the person I'd walked back from school with – quietly spoken, pleasant, unassuming and a little on the shy side. Liam stopped feeding and she began to wind him, gently rubbing his back until he burped. Paula giggled.

'So how are you doing?' I asked Laura.

'OK. Sorry about last Friday. I nearly phoned back to apologize. I'd had a blazing argument with Andy, and Geraldine said you'd seen it all. I was in a right state when I phoned you, but I'm fine now.'

'No worries. We all have family upsets.'

'I suppose so. Although I'm rather sensitive at present and tend to take things personally and get upset. But I'm fine now. How are you? How's the fostering? Geraldine said she saw you in the playground with a little boy.'

'Yes, he's gone home now. He was just with me for a day and a night to help out his mother.'

Laura nodded. As we talked we could hear Geraldine moving around in the kitchen and then go down the hall. Presently she came in with two cups of coffee and a plate of digestive biscuits on a tray, which she placed on the coffee table.

'Thank you,' I said.

She gave a stiff nod. 'I've put the flowers in the front room,' she said to Laura. 'If he's finished, I'll put him in his cot.'

Laura wrapped the shawl around Liam and carefully passed him up to Geraldine, who carried him out of the room.

'He sleeps now,' Laura said. 'Help yourself to coffee and biscuits.'

I moved Paula from my lap and onto the seat beside me so I could drink my coffee. She was still shy and kept close but pointed to the biscuits. I passed her one. There weren't any toys in the room; I guessed Kim probably kept hers in her bedroom and Liam wasn't really old enough for toys yet.

Laura took a sip of her coffee and then leant back on the sofa with a small sigh. 'I guess it's normal to feel exhausted when you've had a baby.'

'Absolutely,' I said. 'I was. Up every three hours at night for feeding, and all the hormones rushing around.'

'Yes, those hormones,' she said with another sigh. 'Andy says it's the hormones.'

'But Geraldine is a big help?' I asked.

'Yes.' She glanced at the door as though checking Geraldine couldn't hear, and then lowered her voice. 'I know this sounds really ungrateful, but sometimes I resent her being here. I mean, I need her help, but I wish she wasn't so bloody right the whole time. I guess that's mother-in-laws for you.'

I smiled understandingly.

'Did you feel low after you'd had your babies?' Laura now asked, looking at Paula.

'I was very tired, but thankfully I didn't get the baby blues,' I said. She took another sip of her coffee but kept her eyes down. 'Why? Are you feeling depressed?' I asked.

She gave a small nod and set her cup carefully in the saucer. 'Sometimes, then at other times I'm as high as a kite. Irrational and ridiculously happy. Do you think that's the hormones too?'

'It could be. Have you seen a doctor?'

'No. I'm not ill, just a bit down. That's why Geraldine spends so much time here.'

I nodded. 'And you don't think you should see the doctor or tell the midwife? They might be able to suggest something to help.'

'No. I'll be OK. I got over it last time with Kim. I guess it's the luck of the draw. Geraldine never had it with any of hers, but my mother did.' She stopped, as Geraldine could be heard in the hall and then came into the room.

'You're not overdoing it, are you?' she said to Laura, and I wondered if she'd overheard.

'No!' Laura said, with the briefest flash of resentment.

'I think it's time you showered and dressed,' Geraldine said to her.

'In a moment,' Laura replied. 'There's no rush. It's not as if I have to be anywhere.'

I thought it was time to go. 'I'll be making a move then,' I said. Geraldine hovered as I quickly finished my coffee and then returned the cup and saucer to the tray. 'Thanks for the coffee,' I said to her and, standing, I took our jackets from the chair back.

'Will you come again soon?' Laura asked, with a plea in her voice.

'Yes. I'd like to. When is convenient?' I helped Paula into her jacket.

'Any day. I'll be here. Every day if you like,' Laura said with a small laugh.

'But we do have things to do,' Geraldine said flatly, looking at her.

'What about Thursday or Friday afternoon?' I suggested.

'Yes, Thursday,' Laura said quickly. 'I'll look forward to it.'

'You can come to me if you wish,' I said, putting on my jacket.

'Best if you come here,' Geraldine said. 'One o'clock on Thursday should be convenient.'

I looked at Laura for confirmation and she nodded resignedly.

'I'll see you Thursday then,' I said. I assumed I wouldn't be seeing Laura in the playground before then.

Leaving her sitting on the sofa, I took Paula's hand and we went down the hall. Geraldine saw us out.

'Thank you for the flowers,' she said before she closed the door.

I lifted Paula into the stroller and fastened her safety harness. 'Baby,' she said.

'Yes, baby Liam is having a sleep,' I said.

'Bye,' she said.

'Good girl.'

I pushed the stroller down the front garden path and onto the pavement. I feel there is a fine line between assisting someone in a positive way when they need help, and completely taking over, so the person loses confidence and comes to rely too heavily on their caregiver. It was something I was aware of in fostering and strove to avoid. While I was sure Geraldine meant well in looking after her family, from what I'd seen she was doing far too much for Laura and had taken over, dominating her and making decisions for her. True, I hadn't taken an immediate liking to the woman, but that may have been a personality clash. What concerned me now was that she appeared to have reduced

Laura to a childlike state so that she relied on her for everything, and Laura was starting to resent this, understandably. I liked Laura – she was the type of person I'd want to be friends with – and clearly she'd wanted me to visit again. It was a pity I couldn't persuade her to visit me on Thursday. I felt that not only would the change of scenery have done her good, but it would also have given her a break from her mother-in-law.

When I collected Adrian from school that afternoon Geraldine made a point of nodding in my direction but didn't speak. I returned a pleasant smile. She left the playground as soon as she had Kim, and they were nowhere in sight when we began the slow walk up our road. At home I found a message on the answerphone from Shelley's social worker, thanking me for looking after Darrel at such short notice. She said she'd spoken to Shelley that morning and her mouth felt a lot better now. I was grateful she'd found the time in her busy work schedule to let me know. Not all social workers would have done that and it was very thoughtful of her. Adrian, who'd heard the message, was also pleased Shelley was feeling better.

'So she'll be able to sing to Darrel tonight,' he said.

'Yes, I'm sure she will.'

With no foster child to look after, I made the most of any free time I had to continue writing my dissertation – when Paula had her morning nap, and also in the evening when she and Adrian were in bed. The subject of my dissertation, education and children in care, was a subject I felt passionately about, as so many children in the care system failed to reach their full academic potential. I was exploring the reasons why this should be so and what could be done to reverse the trend. It was a big subject, although one that had received surprisingly little research and had only seldom been addressed. I worked on my dissertation again on Thursday morning while Paula had her nap. After lunch I put some of her toys in the 'baby bag', together with her trainer cup and a change of nappy, and explained to her that we were going to see baby Liam and his mother, Laura.

'Lawwah,' Paula said, making a good attempt at pronouncing her name.

'Yes, Laura.'

'Lawwah, Lawwah,' she repeated, and then broke into fits of giggles. I kissed her cheek.

It was a fine, sunny day, so we didn't need our jackets. I let Paula walk down the street to number 53, but I took the stroller nonetheless. I didn't know how long I'd be staying at Laura's, so I wasn't sure if I'd have time to return home first or if I'd have to go straight to school to collect Adrian.

'Baby,' Paula predictably said as I pushed open the garden gate.

'Yes, we are going to see baby Liam and Laura.'

'Lawwah, Lawwah,' she said, chuckling.

I parked the stroller on one side of the porch, unhooked the baby bag and then pressed the doorbell, but no one answered. I waited and pressed the bell again. 'She did say Thursday,' I said out loud, wondering if I'd got the wrong day.

'Fursday,' Paula repeated, not knowing what I meant.

The door suddenly opened and Geraldine stood before me, looking uncharacteristically flustered. 'I was going to phone you to cancel, but I couldn't find your number.'

'Oh. Do you want me to come back another day? Laura has my phone number.'

'I know, but she wouldn't give it to me – I mean, she couldn't find it,' she quickly corrected herself.

I wasn't sure if I was being admitted or not. Paula stood beside me, holding my hand.

'Well, you may as well come in now you're here, I suppose,' Geraldine said tersely, opening the door wider. 'Or she won't be pleased. But best keep your visit short. Laura hasn't been up long.'

'Oh dear. Is she ill?' I asked, concerned and feeling this was the most likely explanation for someone staying in bed all morning. She didn't reply, so I helped Paula over the doorstep and into the hall.

'She's in the living room,' Geraldine said.

She turned and I followed her down the hall with some apprehension, not knowing what to expect. I sensed an atmosphere, although I wasn't sure why. Laura was sitting on the sofa, gazing into space. I thought she looked pale and tired, and had possibly been crying. There was no sign of Liam.

'Hello,' I said, smiling as we entered.

'I'll leave you to it then,' Geraldine said stiffly, and went out, leaving the living room door wide open.

'Are you all right?' I asked, going over to Laura.

She shook her head, but didn't speak. Standing, she crossed to the living-room door and pushed it shut so hard it slammed. Paula jumped; it made me start too. She returned to the sofa and burst into tears.

'Oh, love, what's wrong?' I asked, going over and sitting beside her.

'Everything,' she sobbed. 'Everything.' Paula stood close to me, looking very worried

'It's OK,' I reassured Paula. 'You can play with your toys while I look after Laura.' I quickly took the toys I'd brought with us from the bag and settled her on the floor, close by my feet. I put my arm around Laura's shoulder and tried to comfort her as she silently wept. I was half expecting Geraldine to reappear – she must have heard the door slam – but she didn't.

'It's all right,' I said to Laura.

I held her until she was calmer and then she took out a packet of tissues she had tucked beside her on the sofa. 'Sorry,' she said, peeling a tissue from the packet and wiping her eyes. 'I'm having a bad day.' Fresh tears formed.

'I understand,' I said, gently rubbing her arm. 'Is there anything in particular upsetting you? Anything I can help you with?' I appreciated how easily things can get on top of you if you are tired and feeling low; even the ironing can seem like an insurmountable task.

She shook her head. 'No. If only it was that simple.' She twisted and pulled at the tissue. 'I feel so useless the whole time. I can't seem to do anything right. I get stressed about the simplest of things, even making a cup of tea or answering the phone, so I don't do anything, because I can't cope. I feel tired the whole time and I can't be bothered to move. Last night I lay in bed listening to Liam crying to be fed, but I didn't have the energy to get up and feed him. Andy had to get up and bring him to me, and then, when he'd finished feeding, he changed him and settled him back in his cot. We agreed I'd do the night feeds, as he has to go to work, but I couldn't. I just couldn't. Then this morning when Geraldine arrived at seven he told her.'

'She arrives that early?' I asked, slightly surprised.

'Yes, that's when Andy has to leave for work. They make sure one of them is here with me the whole time.' She gave a small sob and Paula looked up at her. I threw her a reassuring smile. 'I know I'm useless,' Laura said. 'But Andy and his mother don't help. They talk about me behind my back, and she tuts when I do something wrong. Or maybe it's me being oversensitive, I don't know. I'm sorry, I shouldn't be going on at you like this – you haven't come here to hear this – but I'm so miserable I don't know what to do.' She wiped away more tears.

'It's all right,' I soothed. 'Don't feel embarrassed. We all feel down sometimes, but I am concerned. Have you seen a doctor yet?'

'No. It will pass eventually. It did last time. I just have to get a grip. That's what Geraldine says: "Get a grip."' She sniffed.

'I'm not sure that's the best advice,' I said. 'Sometimes we need help getting over these things. And there may be a physical reason why you're feeling low. A friend of mine developed a thyroid problem after having her second child. She felt really low, with no energy, and she lost her appetite. She worried for weeks before she saw her doctor. He sent her for tests and the thyroid problem showed up. She was put on medication and within a week she was back to her old self. I really think you should see your doctor.'

Laura shrugged despondently. 'I don't know. I'd have to phone the doctor to make the appointment, and I struggle making decisions about anything right now. I couldn't even decide which babygrow to dress Liam in this morning. I mean, how daft is that? It was a choice between white or blue, and I panicked and froze. I just stood there, with him not dressed and getting cold. Then Geraldine heard him crying and came in. She wasn't pleased. She said I should have called her sooner. She dressed him while I went back to bed. I like being in bed, asleep. It's nice being unconscious. I think they like it too. I'm such a burden. I'm sure they'd all be better off without me. Sometimes I think I should do them a favour and kill myself.'

CHAPTER SEVEN

UPSET

I looked at Laura, more concerned than ever now. This was more than feeling down or having a bad day. It sounded to me as though she could be severely depressed.

'I really think you should see a doctor,' I said again. 'I don't understand what's stopping you. You could be suffering from postnatal depression.'

'Yes, I could be,' she said. 'But I don't want it on my medical records. I got through it before with Kim without the doctor, and I will again.'

'How long did it take then?' I asked.

'Not sure. I think I was back to normal when Kim was a year old.'

'A year!' I said, astonished and dismayed. 'That's far too long to be feeling like this. And why should it matter if it's on your medical records? Lots of people suffer from depression at some time in their lives. I remember reading that it was as much as twenty per cent of the population. Shall I make the appointment for you if you don't feel up to doing it yourself? I could phone now from here and you could decide when you wanted to go.' I thought this might help, as everything seemed such an effort for Laura right now, which of course was a sign of depression.

'No, it's OK,' she said. 'I can tell my doctor at my six-week check-up. I think it's the week after next. I'll tell her then.'

'Will you definitely tell her?' I asked.

She nodded.

I couldn't really say any more. Laura was an adult and as such I had to respect that she could make her own decisions, although I was no less worried. 'Have you been out of the house at all?' I asked.

'Not since I was taken ill in the playground. That shook my confidence.' Her eyes welled again.

'Oh, love,' I said, touching her arm.

'Don't worry, I'm not always this low,' she said. 'I'm having a bad day. Some days I'm almost normal, whatever that is.' She gave a small, stilted laugh and wiped her eyes. 'But how rude of me. I haven't offered you a drink. Let's go into the kitchen and make a drink now. I told Geraldine I wanted to do it this time.' She immediately stood.

I took Paula by the hand and we went with Laura into the kitchen. Her house had a similar layout to mine, with the living room and kitchen at the rear, overlooking the garden. 'You've got a lovely garden,' I said. 'Is it your work?'

'It used to be. But I haven't touched it this year. Andy's been keeping it tidy. What would you like to drink? Tea or coffee?'

'I don't mind. Whatever you're making.'

She tensed. 'Could you tell me, please, to make it easy? I don't know what I want.'

'Coffee, please,' I said.

'Good. I'll have the same,' she said, relieved. 'Now, first the mugs.' She turned to the sink, took a mug from the draining board and began drying it on a tea towel. Slowly, carefully, as if it took all her concentration. She set it down and began drying the next.

'Shall I fill the kettle?' I asked, trying to be helpful.

'Oh, yes, good idea. You do that, while I find the coffee.' Clearly making coffee was no longer second nature to her, as it is for most of us.

I filled the kettle and plugged it in as Laura placed the dry mugs on a tray and then opened one of the cupboards and took out a jar of instant coffee. She was like a child asked to perform a task by their mother – meticulous and wanting to get it right. But I saw her hands tremble as she spooned a teaspoon of coffee into each mug. Even a simple task like this appeared to cause her anxiety.

'I don't know what biscuits we have,' she said, now looking in the cupboards. 'Geraldine's been buying them.'

'I'll just have a coffee,' I said. 'No biscuit for me, thank you.'

'Are you sure?'

'Yes, I've been eating too many.' I smiled.

'Do you take milk?' she asked intensely.

'Yes, please.'

With the same profound concentration she opened the fridge door, took out the milk and set it on the work surface beside the tray. A plume of steam rose from the spout of the boiling kettle before the sensor switched it off. I kept Paula at my side, away from the boiling water, as Laura carried the kettle to the mugs and then carefully poured in the hot water and returned it to its stand. She added the milk. All her movements were slow, controlled and precise.

'Ready,' she said with a small sigh, and returned the milk to the fridge.

She carefully picked up the tray and Paula and I followed her back into the living room where she set it on the coffee table. I was going to ask Laura if I could fill Paula's trainer cup with water, but she flopped on the sofa and, throwing her head back, began crying again.

'What's wrong?' I asked, very concerned and going to her.

'I've spilt some,' she said, pointing to the tray.

I glanced at the tray; there was a tiny slop of coffee on it, really small. 'It doesn't matter,' I said. 'I can wipe it up if it's bothering you.'

But, of course, in Laura's fragile state it did matter, a lot, and her tears fell silent and uncontrollable. My heart went out to her. To be so wretched and upset over something so small was pitiful. 'It doesn't matter, really,' I said, trying to reassure her. 'Shall I fetch some kitchen towel and wipe it up?' I thought this might help.

She shook her head but wouldn't be consoled. It was heartbreaking to see a grown woman reduced to this state over something so trivial. Paula must have felt it too for she climbed onto my lap and wanted a cuddle. I sat with one arm around Laura and the other around Paula.

'I'm sorry,' Laura said through her tears. 'I've upset your daughter now.'

'Don't worry. It's you I'm concerned about.' More tears fell.

Geraldine must have heard, for she came in. 'I think it's best if you go,' she said.

I nodded. My presence didn't seem to be doing Laura any good, but I thought I should hear from Laura that she wanted me to leave.

'Shall I go?' I asked her gently. 'And come back another time?'

'Yes, I'm so sorry. I'll have a sleep now.' Fumbling for the packet of tissues, she stood and walked quickly from the room calling 'Sorry!' again as she left.

I looked at Geraldine. Her face had finally lost its stern, almost condescending expression and she looked worried. 'It's a pity you've had to see her like this,' she said. 'But she'll feel better after she's had a lie down.'

I didn't point out that Laura had been in bed all morning and had only just got up. 'Don't you think she should see a doctor?' I asked.

'If we think it's necessary then of course we will consult a doctor,' she said, her usual terseness returning, and clearly resenting my suggestion.

'And you don't think it's necessary now?' I asked as I began returning Paula's toys to the baby bag.

'No. And I'd appreciate it if you didn't discuss it with your friends in the playground,' she said. 'I know you like a chat.'

I was mortified. I stopped what I was doing, straightened and looked at her. 'I wouldn't dream of discussing Laura, but I am very concerned for her.'

'So are we,' she said tartly.

She waited, watching me, while I finished packing away Paula's toys, almost as if she was on guard. Then she led the way to the front door.

'I'll let you know when Laura feels up to having visitors again,' she said as we went out.

'Thank you.' The door closed behind me.

I breathed in the warm spring air, relieved to be out of the crushing, depressive atmosphere in the house but also very worried. It wasn't time to collect Adrian from school yet and I didn't feel like going home, so I put Paula in the stroller and told her we were going to the park. She clasped her hands together in glee. As I walked I went over what I'd seen and heard at Laura's. Was she suffering from postnatal depression, also known as postpartum depression? I didn't know. What were the symptoms? I wasn't sure. My friend with the thyroid problem had confided in me that she'd felt 'low', and another friend had told me she'd felt 'down' after the birth of her first child – a dose of the baby blues, she'd said, and had put it down to tiredness and having to adjust to a new baby. But that was surely very different from what Laura appeared to be going through: constant tears, wanting to sleep all day and talking of suicide. That must be more than the baby blues or a 'bad day'? Thankfully I'd escaped all of this – other than feeling tired, I'd been fine when I had my children. We arrived at the park and I let Paula out of her stroller and then lifted her into one of the toddler swings where I pushed her gently.

If it had been Shelley or someone who had social services' involvement suffering as Laura was, I would probably have telephoned their social worker and discussed my concerns. But Laura didn't have a social worker – there was no reason why she should – and she had her husband and mother-in-law looking after her. From what Laura had said, they'd brought her through a similar episode after she'd had Kim, so I had to assume they knew what they were doing, although I still thought a year was too long to wait if Laura didn't feel significantly better very soon.

I was still thinking of Laura, or rather worrying about her, when twenty minutes later I returned Paula to her stroller and headed towards Adrian's school. It was a sunny day in late May and he had the following week off school for the spring bank holiday. If the weather stayed fine we'd make the most of it in the garden, visiting parks and so on. I arrived in the playground with five minutes to spare and kept a look-out for Geraldine, wondering what, if anything, she'd say to me. But she hurried in just before the Klaxon sounded, collected Kim and walked swiftly out again without looking in my direction. Adrian arrived at my side, excited by the prospect of only one more day of school before a week off, and gave his sister a big kiss, which as usual made her chuckle. Having had plenty of exercise in the park she was happy to stay in the stroller, so our walk home was much quicker than usual. As we passed number 53 I glanced at the house, but there was nothing to be seen. I saw Paula look too and her little face clouded over. She didn't have the vocabulary to express how she was feeling, but she'd seen Laura crying and I knew that it had probably upset her. It had upset me too. 'I'm sure Liam's mummy will be better soon,' I said, reassuring her.

As I made dinner that evening and then played with the children my thoughts returned to Laura, and I wondered what she was doing with her evening. Had the lie down done her good, as Geraldine had said it would? If so, perhaps she was making dinner for her family or playing with Kim or nursing Liam. I hoped so. Although I knew very little about postnatal depression, I instinctively felt that what Laura was suffering from would need more than a lie down, and I doubted that the instructional phrase her mother in-law used of 'Get a grip' would help either. When Adrian and Paula were in bed asleep I decided to consult the fount of much knowledge on motherhood and telephoned my dear mother.

She wasn't surprised to hear from me; we often spoke during the week and always at weekends if we weren't seeing each other. Having asked how the other was and after catching up on our news, I said, 'Mum, do you know anything about postnatal depression?'

'Oh, love,' she said, immediately concerned, 'you're not suffering from that, are you?'

'No. I'm well, but someone I know with a young baby is feeling very low.'

'The poor dear,' Mum said. 'She has my sympathy. I felt like that for a while after having your brother.'

'Did you?' I asked, surprised. 'You've never mentioned it.'

'Well, you don't, do you? I mean, it was a long time ago and we just got on with it back then. Now I think you can get pills if you're really low. I remember feeling very tearful and crying for no good reason, but I put it down to being permanently tired – having a toddler and a baby to look after.'

'Do you remember what it felt like? Apart from crying, did you have any other symptoms?'

'I don't think so. I really can't remember. Tearful and tired summed it up for me. It passed after about three months.'

'And you didn't go to the doctors?'

'Good gracious, no, dear. I wouldn't have bothered the doctor with something like that. They've got better things to do.' My mother was of a similar age to Geraldine and like many of her generation didn't consult the doctor unless it was absolutely essential and couldn't be treated from the pharmacy or by having a rest. 'But I wouldn't have called it depression,' she added. 'Not like some people get depressed. It was more feeling down. I think they call it the baby blues.'

We chatted for a while longer and then I talked to Dad before saying goodnight to them both. Interesting that Mum had never mentioned suffering from the baby blues before, I thought. How many other women had had similar experiences but never mentioned it? Perhaps they were ashamed to admit it at a time when everyone around them was overjoyed by the arrival of a new baby. It seemed a bit of a taboo subject, although as Mum had said there was a big difference between feeling down (the baby blues) and depression.

The following day was Friday and that morning I was delighted to receive a telephone call from Shelley.

'Hello, love,' I said. 'What a nice surprise. How are you?'

'Back to normal and no toothache,' she said.

'Great. And how's Darrel?'

'He's good. He often talks about you, Adrian and Paula.'

'We've been talking about you too,' I said. 'Have your ears been burning?'

'No, why? What have you been saying about me?' She laughed.

'Nice things. Adrian and I have been saying what a beautiful voice you have. We've started humming the lullabies you sang that night. We can't sing well, so we hum them.'

'Aww, that's sweet. I'll think of you then the next time I sing to Darrel. The reason I'm phoning is that I was wondering if you'll be in on Saturday morning. I've bought you a little something to say thank you.'

'You shouldn't have done that,' I said. 'You should keep your money. But of course we're always pleased to see you. Come for some lunch if you like.'

'That would be terrific. Thank you. Darrel will love playing with Adrian again.'

'Shall we say twelve o'clock?"

'Fantastic. See you then.'

* * *

I hadn't long finished talking to Shelley when the telephone rang again. It was a social worker from the children's services department of the local authority. 'Your name is on the white-board,' she said. 'I'm looking to place a child on respite for a few days next week and I see you are free.' The whiteboard was on a wall at the far end of the social services' open-plan office and showed the names of foster carers in the area who were free to take a child. When a social worker was looking for a carer, either because they were bringing a child or children into care, or they were looking for a respite placement, they checked on the board to see if a suitable carer was free. If not, they approached one of the independent fostering agencies. It's a basic method, but it works well and many local authorities use it.

'Yes, I am available for respite,' I confirmed.

'Good. The little boy is called Samson. He's six. I need respite care to give his gran a break. She's the main caregiver in the family. It's the half-term holiday next week and she doesn't feel she can cope with Samson for the whole week. She's not in the best of health and struggles as it is.'

From this I learned that Samson was living at home and being brought up mainly by his grandmother, but his situation was being monitored by the social services.

'Yes, OK. Which days do you want?' I asked.

'Wednesday to Friday. You will need to collect him and return him to Gran, as she doesn't drive. I'll put all the details in the post to you.'

'All right, thank you.' And we said goodbye.

I thought three days of the half-term break would work out fine, so that afternoon when I collected Adrian from school I had two pieces of good news to tell him.

'Darrel and his mother are coming for lunch tomorrow,' I said. 'And then on Wednesday we're looking after a six-year-old boy for three days.'

'Nearly the same age as me!' Adrian said, delighted.

I thought he'd be pleased, for while Adrian obviously loved his sister dearly, nothing can beat having a playmate of a similar age. The background information on Samson that I needed was being posted to me, and I was looking forward to a relatively relaxing week out of the school routine with the children playing contentedly. What could possibly go wrong?

CHAPTER EIGHT

A PLAYMATE?

At exactly twelve o'clock the following morning Shelley and Darrel arrived, both smiling broadly, as pleased to see us as we were to see them. Shelley presented me with a beautiful potted plant.

'Thank you so much, love,' I said, kissing her cheek. 'But you really shouldn't have.'

'I wanted to give you something to say thank you, and I noticed you like plants.'

'I do. That's kind of you. It's lovely.'

She also gave me three packets of chocolate buttons for the children to have after lunch. Adrian took Darrel's hand and rushed him through to the living room where he'd already set out his train set for them to play with. Paula toddled after them and Shelley came with me into the kitchen to make some drinks. Toscha was there and Shelley stroked and fussed over her as I set the plant on the windowsill and then poured juice for us all. I carried the tray of drinks into the living room and Shelley and I settled on the sofa. For a few moments neither of us spoke as we watched the children playing, then Shelley lowered her voice and said quietly to me, 'Darrel would love a brother or sister, but that's not going to happen now.'

'Why not?' I asked. 'You're young. You could meet someone and fall in love.'

She smiled reflectively. 'That would be nice, but I won't hold my breath. It would take someone very special who would love Darrel as his own. I've no idea how I would meet him, as I never go out anywhere to meet people.' She gave a small, dismissive laugh. 'Although I am hoping to get some training and a job when Darrel goes to school, so who knows?' She ended with a shrug.

'Exactly,' I said. 'Many relationships start in the workplace. I'm a great believer in chance meetings, if it's meant to be.'

She smiled and took a sip of her drink. 'I do have news, though – good news.'

'Oh yes?'

'You remember I told you I was trying to get Darrel dry at night and you said to give him his last drink earlier in the evening?'

'Yes.'

'Well, it worked. It only took two nights and he's dry now.'

'That's fantastic,' I said. 'Well done.'

'It's a big saving on nappies; they're so expensive. He's pleased he's dry too.'

'Yes, he's a big boy now,' I said, glancing at Darrel, although he was concentrating on playing with the train set.

'I have another piece of good news,' Shelley said, now turning to me with a glint of excitement in her eyes. 'And it's because of you again.'

'Really?' I asked tentatively, wondering what I was being held responsible for.

'You know we were talking about my experiences in foster care and I said the only foster carer I regretted not keeping in touch with was Carol? And you said she'd still be pleased to hear from me even after all this time?' I nodded. 'Well, I gave it some thought and I asked the social worker if she could find Carol's telephone number for me. I explained I was thinking of trying to contact her. She said she'd look into it, but if they did have her number on file she'd have to check with Carol first before she gave it to me. She phoned back a few days later and had spoken to Carol. She's still fostering and said she'd love to hear from me, so I called her yesterday.' Shelley's face lit up and my eyes rounded too.

'Fantastic. Well done.'

'She was over the moon to hear from me,' Shelley continued. 'It was great hearing her voice. It brought back some really good memories of my time with her. She couldn't talk for long as she had to collect a child from contact, but she's invited me over there next Sunday. Her own children will be there. They're grown up, but they want to see me again, so it will be a family reunion. That's what Carol said – "a family reunion" – like she still thinks of me as family. I couldn't believe it.'

'I'm sure she does think of you as family,' I said. 'You were with her for three years. That's a long time.'

Shelley's eyes glistened. 'It feels so good. So a big thank-you. If it wasn't for you I would never have thought of contacting her.' She gave me a big hug.

'I expect Carol will want to keep in touch in the future now you've made contact,' I said.

'I hope so. That would be wonderful. I've never had a family of my own.'

Shelley was a lovely person who, despite being badly let down by her parents and the social-care system, wasn't at all angry or bitter, which said a lot about her.

We continued talking as the children played, then Shelley suddenly turned to me again in earnest, a serious expression on her face. 'Cathy, there's something I would like to ask your advice about if you don't mind.'

'No, of course not. Go ahead. I'll help if I can.'

'It's about my singing. I saw a card on the noticeboard in the library about a local amateur choir. They meet once a week in the evening to practise and then give little concerts in the community hall. I saw them singing at Christmas – they were very good, and since then I've been thinking, well, that maybe I'd like to try and join them.' She stopped and looked at me hesitantly.

'Yes, that sounds good. What's stopping you? A babysitter for Darrel?' I was ready to offer to look after him so she could attend the choir.

'No. My friend would do that. She's offered before. It's more ...' She hesitated again. 'Two things really. I'm not sure if I'm good enough – they may not want me – and I don't know anyone there.'

'Shelley,' I said, looking at her carefully, 'I'm sure you are good enough, but you won't know unless you try. And I fully understand how daunting it can be to walk into a room full of strangers, but if you want it enough you'll do it. Go for it, I say. I think it's a fantastic idea. You love singing and I'm sure they'll be pleased to have you.'

She gave a little shrug. 'I'll think about it,' she said, not wholly convinced.

'Is there a telephone number for you to call or do you just turn up for an audition?'

'Either,' she said.

'If it was me, I'd telephone first and have a chat with the

organizer. Then, if you decide to go for an audition, you'll already know them, so it will be a bit easier.'

'And you think I stand a chance of getting in?'

'Yes. Absolutely.'

'Hmm. I'll think about it,' she said again.

Self-effacing and a little short on confidence, Shelley didn't fully appreciate what a lovely singing voice she had, but I didn't say anything further; it was her decision, and I now had to put the finishing touches to lunch. I left Shelley in charge of the children while I went into the kitchen. Meatless sausages, chicken dippers, quiche and jacket potatoes were already cooking in the oven, and I now warmed some baked beans and set salad and coleslaw on the table. When everything was ready I called them to the table and we served ourselves, with Shelley helping Darrel and me helping Paula. Adrian served himself. There was rather a lot of giggling from the children, as they were excited, but they also ate, so it didn't matter. Once we'd finished I suggested we went into the garden as the weather was good. Toscha, not wanting to be left out, came with us. I took the children's garden toys from the shed and arranged them on the lawn. Paula began pushing the walker up and down while Adrian and Darrel kicked a football. Shelley and I stood watching them for a while and then sat on the bench by the tree where we could see them as we chatted. Toscha quickly settled between us. We talked intermittently as Shelley absently stroked Toscha, and it wasn't long before she was telling me about Carol again, and the time just after she'd left her.

'I don't know why I didn't keep in touch and answer her phone calls,' Shelley said. 'I should have done. I certainly needed her support. I was in a bad place when I first left care and had to go into lodgings, and then when Darrel was born it got even worse. We were living in the bed and breakfast and I had no one. I was isolated and got really low. The room was damp and smelly and I had to share a bathroom with other families, which didn't help. Then I was up at night with Darrel and got tired and depressed. Everything was such an effort, even getting dressed. Sometimes I didn't get dressed and stayed in for days on end. Thankfully my social worker knew what to do.'

'Which was what?' I asked, glancing at her.

'Go to the doctor's. He gave me some tablets. I didn't want to take them at first, because I thought I might get addicted to them, but my social worker told me I should, as the doctor had prescribed them. I'm glad I did. I started to feel better almost straight away and I came off them after six months.'

'What sort of tablets were they?' I asked, interested.

'Anti-depressants. It's what they give you if you have post-natal depression.'

'Is that what you had?'

Shelley nodded. 'The doctor said I should have gone to see him earlier, but I was worried that it might affect my chances of keeping Darrel. The social services were monitoring me then to see if I could cope. I thought if I admitted I was depressed they would think I couldn't and would take Darrel away.'

'Clearly that didn't happen,' I said.

'No. My social worker was great. She said one of her sisters had had postnatal depression, so she knew what to do.'

I nodded and obviously thought of Laura. 'Did you have any other symptoms apart from feeling very low and finding everything an effort? If you don't mind me asking ...'

'I cried the whole time. If something didn't go right – even something small, like changing a nappy – I'd burst into tears. I cried for no reason too. I felt a complete failure, worthless, and no good to anyone. I thought others were getting at me and I even started to think that Darrel would be better off without me. It seems awful now, but then I felt overwhelmed and everything seemed pointless. It was like I was in a deep, dark pit with no way of getting out. The doctor also arranged some counselling for me, which helped too. I dread to think what would have happened if I hadn't gone to see the doctor. It was just as well I had a good social worker.'

'Yes, it was,' I said thoughtfully. 'Although you may have gone to the doctors in the end anyway.'

'I'm not so sure.'

I stood and went over to Paula, who'd taken a tumble and was looking as though she might cry. Adrian and Darrel got to her first and helped her up. I brushed her down and she was soon smiling again.

We stayed in the garden for another hour or so, talking and playing with the children, and then we returned indoors for the pudding, which we'd been too full to eat at lunchtime. Apple crumble with custard or ice cream (or both). We all had both, the combination of melting ice cream, warm custard, the sweet, crunchy topping and slightly tart apple was too good to resist, so we all had seconds too.

Shelley and Darrel stayed until nearly six o'clock and then, with a reluctant sigh, Shelley said they had better be going. I offered to take them home in the car, but she insisted they'd be fine on the bus. As she pointed out, it was still daylight, she had fully recovered from the operation and didn't have any heavy luggage, so I was persuaded to let her go on the bus. We all went to the front door to see them off. I told Shelley to stay in touch and that I hoped to see them again before long.

'Yes, I'd like that,' she said. 'We both would.'

'Have a good time at Carol's,' I added. 'And don't forget to phone that choir leader.'

Shelley smiled, but changed the subject. 'I'll think about you this evening when I'm singing to Darrel,' she said.

'We'll think about you too,' I said.

We hugged and kissed goodbye and then stood on the pavement and waved until they were out of sight.

'I'm having a lovely time,' Adrian said as we returned indoors. 'First Darrel, and then on Wednesday that other boy is coming. I'm so lucky.'

'Yes,' I agreed. But lucky wasn't the term I would be using by the end of the week – stretched to the limit was more like it.

The next day, Sunday, the first day of June, we went to my parents. On Monday we were mainly at home and on Tuesday we went to a local adventure park. I find that during the school holidays a combination of days out and time spent playing at home works well for the children. The paperwork for Samson had arrived in Monday's post and I'd read it that evening. Respite information for carers is less detailed than the placement information a carer usually receives when a child is staying for longer. It is a brief résumé of what they need to know. It contained Samson's full name, date of birth, home address, his grandmother's name and telephone number, then lines for additional information. *Medication: none. Special dietary requirements: none. Religion: Catholic.*

Other significant adults: Samson lives with his gran, aunts and uncles, and has some contact with his father but not his mother. There was also space to include any special needs and challenging behaviour, and beside this was typed: *Samson can show challenging behaviour at times* – but with no details. I didn't think much of this, as many of the children I'd fostered had shown some challenging behaviour, and given that Samson was being brought up by his grandmother, whom the social worker had said wasn't in good health and was finding it difficult to cope, I assumed it would be a matter of putting a few boundaries in place and keeping Samson happily occupied.

Adrian was so excited on Wednesday morning, planning all the games he and Samson were going to play, that he could hardly eat his breakfast. I intended to take Adrian and Paula with me to collect Samson rather than ask a friend to babysit. The note from the social worker that had come with the information had said I should collect Samson at ten o'clock. I knew the estate where he lived; it was about a twenty-minute drive away, so we left in good time at 9.30 a.m. The estate was a mixture of private and social housing, and had a complicated and confusing series of criss-cross walkways designed to keep cars out of the central residential area. I found the designated car park for flats 15–27 (Samson lived in flat 17) and opened the back doors of the car, which were child-locked, to let the children out.

I held Paula's hand and with Adrian on the other side of me we began down the path to the communal entrance to the flats. It was a three-storey block identical to others on the estate. It was a warm day and many of the residents had their windows wide open. The sounds of life filtered out, converging and echoing in the central courtyard: a television blaring, a baby crying, children shouting, music, a dog barking, as well as various cooking smells. Adrian gave a little skip of happiness and Paula tried to copy him. As we approached the main entrance the net curtain at the window of the ground-floor flat on our left was suddenly pulled back and a boy with a shaved head and piercing blue eyes yelled, 'Are you the foster carer?'

Adrian stopped dead beside me.

'Yes,' I said.

'Gran, she's here!' the boy yelled at the top of his voice. And the net curtain was flung back into place.

'Is that Samson?' Adrian asked quietly, moving slightly closer.

'I think it might be,' I said.

Someone in their flat must have released the security lock on the main door, for it clicked open. With a child on each side I went in and turned left to number 17. Although the occupants clearly knew we'd arrived no one came to the door, so after a few moments I pressed the bell. Noise immediately erupted from inside. The claws of a very heavy dog pounded down the hall and then scratched furiously at the other side of the door as it barked loudly. Adrian darted behind me and I picked up Paula. There'd been no mention of a dog in the information I'd been sent, and I was not pleased. Social workers often have to insist that a dog is shut away before they enter premises, but it would be awkward for me to make the same request.

'Get down, Bruno!' a male voice now yelled from inside the flat. There was more angry barking and scratching, then a yelp, and the door opened. I took a step back.

A boy in his late teens with a shaved head held the Doberman by its studded neck collar. It strained to be free. 'Stop it!' he shouted, yanking on its collar, then looked at me.

'I've come to collect Samson,' I said.

'Gran!' he yelled over his shoulder. 'The social worker's here.'

'Foster carer,' I corrected.

'Foster carer!' he yelled.

'Shut him away, will ya?' a woman's voice came from down the hall.

The lad tugged hard on the dog's collar and managed to turn it around and drag it down the hall, its claws scratching on what was left of the lino.

'Take no notice of him,' the woman who now appeared said. 'His bark is worse than his bite.'

I assumed she was referring to the dog. 'Is the dog shut in a room now?' I asked.

'He will be,' she said. 'I'm Samson's gran.'

'Hello,' I smiled. 'I'm Cathy, the foster carer.'

'Jason! Is Bruno shut in?' she yelled over her shoulder.

There was no reply, but the silence seemed to suggest that he was and she beckoned us to go in. Still carrying Paula and with Adrian holding tightly onto the back of my jeans, we went in. 'I hope you don't mind me bringing my children,' I said.

'No, not at all. I like kids.' She closed the door. 'Come through.'

We followed Samson's gran slowly down the short hall. She was badly overweight and her heavily veined legs and swollen ankles looked painful, causing her to hobble rather than walk. She used the wall to steady herself. Little wonder she struggled to look after Samson, a high-spirited and energetic six-year-old, I thought.

We went into a cramped and cluttered living room where she collapsed into an armchair, out of breath from the exertion of coming to the front door. A large, middle-aged man with a mug of tea balanced on his stomach sat in the other armchair, staring at the television. Naked to the waist, he had the name of a football club (presumably the one he supported) tattooed across his chest. I assumed he was one of Samson's uncles referred to in the information sheet. He looked up and nodded in my direction, then returned his attention to the television. Controlling the television with the remote and sprawled on the sofa beneath the window was the boy we'd already seen at the window. 'You've met Samson,' his gran said, nodding towards him.

'Hello, Samson,' I said brightly. 'How are you?' Adrian peeped out from behind me.

Samson ignored me and continued pressing the remote to channel hop.

'Say hello to your foster carer,' his gran said sternly.

'Say hello, boy,' the man repeated gruffly. 'And leave the bleedin' control alone.'

'Hello,' Samson said, without taking his eyes from the television.

'Will you leave that thing alone and get your stuff,' his gran now said to him.

'Give it here,' the man demanded, reaching out for the remote.

Samson jumped up, tossed the remote into the man's lap and ran out of the room. At the same time two women in their early twenties, hair ruffled from sleep and dressed in pyjama shorts and T-shirts, sauntered in carrying a mug of tea each. They seemed unfazed and indeed uninterested that I, a stranger, was in the room, and with barely a glance in my direction wandered over to the sofa where they sat down and gazed at the television.

'Aren't you gonna offer her a cup of tea then?' Samson's gran said to them.

'It's OK,' I said, smiling. 'I'm fine. We're going as soon as Samson is ready.'

'You know to bring him back at six o'clock sharp on Friday,' Gran said to me.

'Yes.'

'He must be here for six or I'll catch it from his dad. He goes out with his dad every Friday at six o'clock.'

'I'll have him back in plenty of time,' I confirmed.

Samson reappeared with a small backpack. 'Are we going then?' he demanded.

'You got everything, mate?' his gran asked him, from which I assumed Samson had done his own packing.

'Yeah, what do you take me for?' he returned cheekily. No one corrected him, so I guessed that was how he usually spoke to his gran, and possibly to the other adults too.

'Give us a kiss then,' his gran said.

Samson went over and kissed her cheek and then, navigating his way around the clutter on the floor, he continued round the room, giving the two women a kiss on their cheeks and slapping the man on his shoulder. It wasn't an emotional parting; saying goodbye seemed perfunctory, and the adults hadn't taken their gaze from the television screen.

'See you Friday then,' his gran called after him as he shot from the room. 'Be good.'

'Yeah, see ya,' he returned.

I went after him. It appeared we were seeing ourselves out and I called goodbye as we left. I was still carrying Paula, and Adrian was staying close beside me. Samson was already at the door with his hand on the doorknob ready to open it. 'Bye, Bruno!' he yelled at the top of his voice.

From somewhere in the flat the dog barked furiously.

CHAPTER NINE

SAMSON

Poor Adrian, his face was a picture and said it all. This wasn't the playmate he'd envisaged and had been hoping for.

'Where's your car, missus?' Samson demanded as we left the path that led from the flats and approached the designated parking area.

'It's that sliver Ford there,' I said, pointing the fob at my car.

He sneered, unimpressed. 'That ain't much of a car. My last two carers had four-by-fours.'

'Very nice,' I said.

'Give me the key then,' he said, making a grab for the fob. 'I'll unlock it for you.'

'It's OK,' I said. 'Thank you anyway, but I can manage.' I wasn't putting Samson in charge of anything yet until I knew what he was capable of.

'I'll sit in the front then,' he said, yanking the passenger door open.

'No. Children ride in the back,' I said, closing the door.

'I always ride in the front in my uncle's car,' he protested.

'Things are a bit different with me,' I said, opening the rear door. 'The law states that children have to ride in the back of a car with an age-appropriate seat and harness. We don't want to break the law, do we?'

'No. Blimey. We don't,' he said. 'I'll have to tell my uncle. He don't need more trouble with the law.'

I hid my smile. With his streetwise, cheeky manner Samson reminded me of the Artful Dodger in the Dickens classic *Oliver Twist*, but it was already clear to me he was going to be hard work. I adjusted my previous expectations of putting in place 'a few boundaries' and the children all playing happily together, just as Adrian must have been adjusting his. Once I had all three children secured under their seatbelts in the rear of the car I began the drive home. It was a very lively journey. Samson talked non-stop at the top of his voice about anything and everything that came into his head, to the point where I was wondering if he was hyperactive.

'Have you had breakfast today?' I asked over his babble.

'Yeah, of course. I always have breakfast. Our teacher says we must, so Gran makes me. I take it to my room and eat it.'

'What did you have?' I asked, glancing at him in the rear-view mirror.

'Me usual. What I always have. A bowl of dry Chocca cereal and a Mars bar.'

'And to drink?'

'Lemonade. I like lemonade. Lemonade and Coke are me favourites.'

Little wonder he was buzzing, I thought, with all that sugar in his blood. Most parents will agree that food with a very high sugar content can make a child hyperactive. The effect is even more pronounced if eaten on an empty stomach, but once the sugar rush is over the child can easily become irritable and crave more sugar. I didn't say anything, but I could foresee a confrontation looming when he didn't have his sugary cereal and chocolate bar for breakfast. He resumed his chatter: why he didn't like school, the horror films he watched with his (hero) dad, his boring aunts who were only interested in make-up and men, and then what he could see through his window. Adrian was very quiet; he didn't say a word. I could see him in the rear-view mirror looking concerned, and Paula was staring at Samson open-mouthed and in awe, not sure what to make of him. As I pulled onto our driveway Samson was asking Adrian if he had a PlayStation.

'No,' Adrian replied quietly. 'I'm not old enough.'

'Of course you're old enough, boy!' Samson exclaimed. 'Who said you weren't?'

'Me,' I said, saving Adrian the embarrassment.

'Jesus, missus! I had my PlayStation when I was three. It's in me bedroom and I have it on when I like. Anything to keep me quiet.'

Doubtless Samson was repeating what one of the adults in the flat had said, and I appreciated why keeping Samson quiet with the PlayStation was an attractive option. Gran, the main carer, had very limited mobility, so she wouldn't be able to take Samson out and give him the exercise a boy of his age needed. In the small, overcrowded flat, having Samson out of the way and entertaining himself must seem like a blessing. He clearly needed some exercise now to burn off all that excess sugar so that he calmed down.

'It's a lovely day, so you'll be able to play in the garden,' I said as I opened the rear door to let the children out. 'We've got bikes, footballs and plenty of other garden toys and games.'

'But I always watch television in the morning,' Samson said, disgruntled.

'We don't usually have the television on in the day,' I said. 'But you can watch some this evening for a while.'

'What's a while?' he asked, turning to Adrian.

Adrian shrugged.

'About an hour,' I said.

'Fucking 'ell. That ain't much telly, missus.'

Adrian stared at him, dismayed, aware that he'd said a really bad word. 'Samson, we don't swear,' I said as I helped Paula from the car. 'And please call me Cathy.'

'OK,' he said easily.

I locked the car and took hold of Paula's hand, and we all walked up the path to the front door.

'Do you often stay with foster carers?' I asked Samson as I unlocked the door.

'Yeah. It's cos me gran can't cope with me,' he said. 'I don't think the other carers coped with me either, cos I never saw them again.' Out of the mouths of babes, I thought, as I opened the door. He shot in ahead of me and down the hall. By the time I arrived in the living room he was sprawled on the sofa, backpack and shoes still on, with the remote control aimed at the television.

'Samson,' I said, taking the remote from him, 'I said we weren't watching television right now.'

'Ain't fair,' he said, giving the sofa a kick.

'And we take our shoes off in the house.'

'But you said I was going in the garden, and I need me shoes out there, don't I?' he replied cheekily.

I crossed to the patio doors, released the catch and slid one door open. 'Take off your backpack and you can go outside.

See if you can run fifteen laps of the lawn. Do you know what a lap is?'

'Yeah, of course. I ain't silly. I've seen the runners do it on the television.' He grinned, delighted by the challenge, and immediately stood. Slipping off his backpack he threw it on the floor and ran to the door.

'On the count of three then,' I said. 'And no cheating. I'll be watching. A lap is right round the edge of the lawn.'

'Yeah. I'm ready,' he said, adopting a sprinter's starting position.

'One, two, three, go!' I cried.

With a flying leap he was out of the door, running across the patio and then around the edge of the lawn on his first lap. Adrian and Paula joined me on the patio to watch him. Samson's face was set in concentration and his arms worked at his sides as he pounded around the imaginary track. 'That's one lap,' I called as he passed. 'Keep going.' Our garden is rather long and narrow and mostly lawn, so one circuit was about 250 feet (or 76 metres) – a fair challenge for a six-year-old. 'Two laps! Well done!' I called a few moments later as he completed a second circuit. He was smiling broadly and waved as he went past as though on a victory run. 'Good boy.'

Adrian, standing beside me, was still looking anxious. 'Don't worry,' I said, giving him a hug. 'He'll be fine, and I'll keep a close eye on him.'

Although Adrian and Samson were of a similar age, that was where any similarity began and ended. Samson was thickly set, appeared to be physically strong and I guessed liked nothing more than play fighting, given the opportunity. Like many children I'd seen come into care he was self-sufficient from having largely brought himself up and meeting his own needs. He therefore assumed that he was in charge, not only of himself but everyone else, which wasn't healthy for a six-year-old. It wasn't his fault, but I knew that if these three days weren't going to be a foster carer's nightmare I needed to establish that I, the adult, was in charge, not him – in the nicest possible way, of course.

'Three!' I called as Samson sped past, his arms bent and fists working the air beside him. 'Well done.' I continued counting and praising him as he completed each lap until he reached fifteen. 'Excellent!' I said. He ran over to us and flopped onto the patio, exhausted.

'I need a drink,' he gasped, clutching his throat dramatically.

'Of course. Take off your trainers and come inside.'

He kicked off his trainers and I led the way into our kitchen-cum-diner. 'This is where you will sit at the table,' I said, drawing out a chair.

He threw himself into it as though collapsing from exhaustion. 'I'm knackered,' he said.

Adrian silently took his place opposite Samson and I helped Paula onto her booster seat. She was mesmerized by Samson; I think he was the best entertainment she'd had in a long while.

'What would you like to drink?' I asked Samson. 'Water, milk, juice or squash?'

'Ain't you got no fizzy drinks?' he asked, his cheeks flushed from the exercise.

'We only have fizzy drinks on special occasions, like birthdays,' I explained.

'Jesus, this ain't much fun.'

'The blackcurrant squash is nice,' I suggested. 'That's what Adrian has.'

'OK, give me one of those,' he said as though ordering a shot in a bar.

'Would you like something to eat?' I asked him. 'Adrian and Paula usually have a snack mid-morning.'

'A biscuit. Chocolate if you've got them.'

'I think you've had enough sweet things for the time being,' I said. 'Would you like a sandwich, or cheese on biscuits, or some fruit?'

'Yeah. Cheese sandwich and crisps,' he ordered. Then, looking at Adrian, he said, 'It's just like at the other carers' with this "good" food and having to eat at the table.'

I smiled and thought that would at least make my life a little easier. While carers usually try to give the child what is familiar to them and keep to their routines as much as possible, I knew it was highly unlikely that the previous carers would have indulged his high-sugar diet or allowed extreme negative behaviour. We were therefore all coming from the same place, which would help, as Samson would already have some experience of my expectations.

I prepared the snacks and then sat at the table with the children while they ate. Samson didn't have any table manners, but he did have a good appetite and thoroughly enjoyed the sandwich, crisps and squash, talking as he ate. As soon as he'd finished, before he'd swallowed the last mouthful, he leapt from his chair, ran into the living room and switched on the television. Leaving Adrian to keep an eye on Paula, I went after him.

'I did say we weren't watching television in the day,' I said, taking the remote from him.

'So what am I going to do with no telly or PlayStation?' he asked. These had clearly been his life.

'I'm going to show you around the house, and where you will sleep, and then I'll organize a game in the garden.'

I hid the remote control out of sight, collected Adrian and Paula, who were still at the table but had finished eating, and began a tour of the house. Although Samson was slightly calmer now, he still entered each room like a spring uncoiling, dashing in, touching things, firing comments and then running out and into the next room. Paula had taken a shine to him and wanted to hold his hand, which he did for a while. He was gentle with her, so I felt that although he gave the appearance of being ready for a fight with boys his own age or older, he wouldn't harm a toddler. I was more concerned about Adrian.

'Can you kickbox?' Samson asked Adrian on the landing, thrusting his foot in his face.

Adrian flinched and took a step back.

'No. We don't kickbox,' I said.

'My dad's teaching me. Have you got a dad?' he asked Adrian.

'Yes,' Adrian said quietly. 'He's working away.'

'My dad works away too sometimes,' Samson said. 'Gran says it's for Her Majesty's pleasure.' Being detained 'at Her Majesty's pleasure' is a euphemism for being in prison, but I didn't comment. As we entered Samson's bedroom he suddenly turned and bolted out again. 'I'll get me bag!' he yelled, pounding down the stairs. He returned a moment later with his backpack, which he threw onto the bed. Jumping on top of it, he unzipped it, pulled out the contents and stuffed them all in the nearest drawer. 'I know you carers like us kids to unpack so we feel at home,' he said.

It was true, but I usually helped the children unpack. It was sad that he'd had so much experience of being in respite care that he knew the routine. But then again, if having regular respite meant that his gran could cope and Samson could remain living at home, that was preferable to him having to live in care permanently. No one wants to see a family split up; it's the last resort.

Having seen all the rooms upstairs we began downstairs, and Samson asked me what we were going to do now. Before I had a chance to reply he said, 'Are you going to take me on outings like the other carers did?'

'I was thinking of a day out tomorrow,' I said, aware that this would no longer be a surprise.

'Where?' he demanded.

'Well, there are lots of interesting places not too far away.' I began listing them: 'There's the castle ruins, Merrymoor Farm, the zoo, the activity centre …'

But after each one Samson said, 'Been there! Done it!' as though he was winning some unnamed game.

Five minutes later I'd exhausted the list. He'd visited every place of interest within a fifty-mile radius. Many of the places Adrian and Paula hadn't been to. Samson had had far more outings than an average child. Of course, it was the well-meaning foster carers who'd taken him, but sadly the regularity of the outings meant that they weren't treats any more, but something he had to go along with as part of the package of respite care.

'What would you like to do then?' I asked. We were in the living room. He scratched his stubbled head in thought and then gazed down the garden.

'Do more laps in the garden,' he said, smiling.

'Really? Well, we could,' I said, 'if you don't want to go on an outing.' But then I had an idea. 'Samson, you're obviously good at sports so let's have a mini sports day of our own.'

'Yeah!' he cried, jumping up and down. 'Like at school. I love sports day.'

Well done me, I thought. I took Paula's hand and we all went out into the garden again. Samson and Adrian helped me organize what we needed for our sports day while Paula toddled after them. We began with running events – sprinting, circuits and relay. Then I balanced a garden cane across two stacks of bricks for the high-jump event, raising it after each go until the boys reached their maximum. Using the play sandpit, we held a long-jump event, and then egg and spoon races, using table-tennis balls balanced on dessertspoons. Paula joined in as best she could. For the sack race the boys and I had a dustbin liner each to hop in, and I gave Paula a carrier bag, as she was much shorter. It was fun and I was pleased that Adrian was enjoying it as much as Samson. A few times I had to curtail Samson's enthusiasm when he became too boisterous, and I steered him away from his idea of sharpening a garden cane for a javelin event and throwing bricks for shot put.

I took everyone indoors for lunch at one-thirty and then we continued the sports day in the afternoon. I promised a little prize-giving ceremony on Friday, the last day Samson was with us, which would give me a chance to put together some prizes. By the end of the afternoon everyone was exhausted and I settled the children in front of the television while I made dinner. Samson was worn out and no trouble, and I felt comfortable leaving him sitting on the sofa with Adrian and Paula, although I looked in regularly to check on them. After we'd finished eating I trusted Samson enough to leave him playing a board game with Adrian while I took Paula upstairs to bed.

'Samon?' Paula asked, making a good attempt at pronouncing Samson's name.

'Yes, Samson will be here in the morning,' I said, tucking her in.

I took the boys upstairs to bed at 7.30 p.m., oversaw their washes and teeth cleaning and then, leaving Adrian in his bedroom, I saw Samson into his.

'Can we have another sports day tomorrow?' he asked as he climbed into bed.

'Yes, if that's what you would like to do.'

'Yeah, I do. It was fun. Will you give me a goodnight kiss like I ask me gran to?' he said.

'Of course.' Despite all his bravado, he still liked his goodnight kiss and hug.

I tucked him in and reminded him where my room was if he needed me in the night.

'I'm not scared of the dark,' he said, his cheeky little face peering up at me from under the duvet. 'But I have me light on.'

'That's fine,' I said. I adjusted the dimmer switch until the light was how he liked it. 'Good night then, love.'

'Night,' he called as I came out. I drew the door to, but didn't close it completely so that I could hear him if he called out or was out of bed.

I checked on Paula, who was sound asleep, and then I went into Adrian's room and sat with him. I praised him for helping me make Samson's day enjoyable and the sports day a success, for I couldn't have done it without his cooperation.

'I guess Samson is OK really,' Adrian said. 'He just tries to be tough.'

Which I thought summed him up quite perceptively.

The following morning Samson was awake and out of bed at 5.30. I quickly threw on my dressing gown and went round the landing to his room. Quietening him down I told him he had to stay in his room and play until I was ready to go downstairs. I never leave young children unattended downstairs.

'That's why you need to get a PlayStation,' he said cheekily. 'To keep me quiet.'

'There are lots of other enjoyable things you can do,' I said. 'Stay there.'

I hurried downstairs and brought up one of the toy boxes containing puzzles and cars, which I placed on his bedroom floor. I told him to play quietly until I was dressed. But 'quietly' wasn't a word Samson was familiar with, and I could hear his brum-brumming as he played with the toy cars from the bathroom, although he did stay in his bedroom. By six o'clock Adrian and Paula were awake too, and I got Paula up as Adrian dressed himself. We were all downstairs having breakfast at seven – unheard of on a day when we didn't have to be up for school. If Samson had been staying with me for longer I would have settled him into a better routine, insisting that if he woke early he amuse himself quietly in his room until seven o'clock when I would come in and tell him it was time to get dressed (using rewards and sanctions to achieve the goal). But because he was only with me for a short while it was impossible to achieve very much, which I'm sure the other respite carers who'd looked after Samson had found too.

Samson was eager to hold another sports day and Adrian was happy to go along with this, but by mid-morning the novelty had clearly worn off and Samson was becoming disruptive and in need of a new activity. I took the children indoors and arranged various board games, then Play-Doh modelling and crayoning, all of which Samson enjoyed, although he couldn't be left to play unattended, even for a short while – he needed constant supervision. By lunchtime, when he was growing fractious again, I realized a change of scenery was required. There wasn't enough time for a full day out, so I suggested that after lunch we went to a fairground that was in the area for the half-term holiday. Although predictably Samson had been to fairgrounds before, he was more than happy to go again and quickly pointed out that I'd have to give him money to spend at the fair. Adrian had only been to a fair once before, so it was a treat for him, and Paula had never been. It was a successful outing and I gave each boy £5 to spend, although I had to keep a close eye on Samson, who darted off as soon as a ride ended.

We had another early start on Friday morning, although Samson was quieter once I'd resettled him with some toys, and then after breakfast we went into the garden again, this time playing fairgrounds. The bikes, tricycle, skateboard and roller skates were the fairground rides, and we had various sideshow stalls: throw three balls in a bucket for a prize, knock the tin can off the wall (using tennis balls), hook the duck and so on, using anything we had. The boys and I were quite inventive. That afternoon, as promised, I arranged a little prize-giving ceremony, where I stood on the patio and presented each child with a few small gifts for the races they'd won. We applauded after each presentation and Paula had a prize for making a good attempt.

Samson had to be home by six o'clock that evening, as he kept reminding me: 'I see me dad at six on Friday and you can't be late.'

I left our house in plenty of time and we arrived at the flats at 5.45. I wanted to give Samson's gran some feedback on how the respite had gone, which was usual practice. The window of Samson's flat was slightly open and as he ran past he banged on the glass and yelled 'Bruno!' at the top of his voice, which set the dog barking manically.

We went in the main entrance, but no one was at the door of Samson's flat, so he banged on the wood and yelled, 'I'm home!' The dog went frantic.

Then a man's voice shouted, 'Shut up, Bruno!'

The barking stopped and the door was opened by the man I'd previously seen in the living room with a mug of tea. 'You're back then,' he said flatly to Samson as he shot in. 'Thanks,' he said to me and closed the door. So I didn't get the chance to give his gran feedback or to say goodbye to Samson, which was a pity.

However, I felt that the three days had gone reasonably well, although looking after Samson had been hard work. I hadn't done any laundry or housework, let alone worked on my dissertation, as my time had been completely taken up with Samson. Had he been staying for longer, or if I had him again on respite, I would start encouraging him to play independently. So often children who spend a lot of time in front of a screen for their entertainment (PlayStation, television, handheld consoles, etc.) never learn how to play creatively and amuse themselves, which is important for social development, problem solving and decision making now and in later life.

That evening after Adrian and Paula were in bed I had a good tidy up and then sat in the living room and enjoyed the peace and tranquillity. There's never a dull moment in fostering, and while I loved the challenge each new child brought I knew I really needed time to complete my dissertation. I decided that if I was asked to do more respite I'd have to be firm and say no for the next month or so. However, as it turned out it wasn't a foster child who occupied me, but someone much closer to home.

CHAPTER TEN

THE DEVIL'S CHILD

School resumed on Monday after the half-term break and the air temperature rose dramatically by ten degrees, as it can do in England, catching everyone unawares and causing the weather reporter to pronounce a heat wave. The sun shone in a cloudless sky and the air was alive with birdsong and the scent of summer flowers. We didn't need to wear our jackets to walk to school that morning.

Adrian was pleased to see his friends again and they ran around in the playground before school began. Parents chatted to each other, catching up on their news and asking each other if they'd had a nice holiday, and sharing what they'd done. Some families had spent the week at home just relaxing, pleased to be out of the school routine, while others had been more energetic, going out most days, and a couple of lucky families had been abroad for the week. As I talked to my friends I looked around for any sign of Laura, hoping she was now feeling well enough to bring Kim to school, but I couldn't see her. Then just before the start of school Geraldine walked into the playground, with Kim beside her pushing the pram. Kim was looking around her, proud to be in charge of her baby brother, while Geraldine kept her gaze straight ahead, her face expressionless. I assumed therefore that Laura still didn't feel up to coming out, or possibly she was just having a lie-in. I'd ask Geraldine how she was if I got the opportunity.

When the Klaxon sounded the children said goodbye to their parents and then lined up ready to go into school. The little groups of parents began dispersing, making their way towards the main gate. I looked over to where Geraldine had been standing. She was now walking briskly towards the exit. She was always one of the first out, slipping out ahead of everyone else, but this time her progress was slowed by the pram. I caught up with her as she waited for her turn to pass through the main gate.

'Good morning,' I said. Paula was holding my hand and toddling beside me.

Geraldine threw me her usual tight smile.

'Baby,' Paula said, pointing to the pram.

'Yes. Baby Liam. How is he doing?' I asked Geraldine. I could just see his little face over the cover, sleeping.

'He's well,' she said.

'And how's Laura?'

'These things take time.'

'She didn't feel up to coming here today then?' I asked.

'No.'

We were now through the main gate and on the pavement outside and it was clear Geraldine didn't want to walk with us.

'Give her my love,' I said.

She nodded stiffly and then, head down, she set off, pushing the pram at a brisk pace.

'Baby Liam,' Paula said again.

'Yes,' I said absently. 'With his grandmother.'

As we passed number 53 Paula and I both glanced at the house, but there was no one to be seen, and we continued our haltingly slow journey home. It didn't matter that it took us ages; it was a beautiful day and Paula was finding plenty to interest her along the way: ants scurrying across pavements, a cat basking on a sun-drenched wall, front gardens with an array of brightly coloured flowers, all of which were wonderfully new and inspiring to the enquiring young mind of a small child. I wished I had Laura's telephone number – I could have phoned her; just a friendly call to see how she was, for I didn't feel I could simply arrive on her doorstep. The last time I'd visited, Geraldine had made it clear that she'd let me know when Laura was up to having visitors again.

Once home, Paula and I went straight into the garden and I played in the sandpit with her. It was nice being able to give her some one-to-one time again, and she enjoyed it. Mid-morning I settled her for a nap and continued my dissertation. I wondered if Samson's social worker would telephone for feedback on Samson's respite, but she didn't. However, at lunchtime Shelley's social worker telephoned to ask if I could foster a four-month-old baby they were bringing into care the next day. Reluctantly I had to say no, and I explained about my degree.

'OK. Good luck with it,' she said. 'I'll make a note on the whiteboard.'

'Thank you.'

That afternoon Geraldine was in the playground again with Liam in the pram, and as usual she stood by herself with her eyes fixed firmly ahead. When the children came out I saw

Kim pushing the pram towards the exit, but they were well ahead of us by the time we left the playground, as Paula wanted to walk. The next day was the same: Geraldine brought Liam to school in the morning and the afternoon. I didn't know what this said about how Laura was feeling, but I had to believe that Geraldine and Laura's husband, Andy, knew what was best for her, as they were close to her and had helped her through a difficult time after the birth of Kim. There's a fine line between being friendly and neighbourly and being intrusive and a nosy parker, so I felt any further enquiry from me about Laura at that time would be unwelcome and probably resented. If Laura had been an old friend it would have been very different, but for now I just had to accept that Geraldine was in charge and knew best.

However, all that changed the following morning.

It was another fine day and we were walking to school. Paula, as usual, was in her stroller with the promise that she could walk back. As we passed number 53 the front door suddenly burst open. Kim ran out and down the path as Geraldine stood in the doorway. 'Gran says can you take me to school today,' Kim said. 'She has to stay with Mum.'

'Yes, of course,' I said. I looked towards the open door, but Geraldine gave a cursory wave and closed it.

'Is your mum all right?' I asked Kim.

'I don't know. She had a bad night. Gran didn't want to leave her alone, and my daddy had to go to work. We've been looking out for you.'

'Is your mum sick?' I asked, worried. I had no idea what a 'bad night' meant in this context.

'Not really,' Kim said, and looked uncomfortable. I knew not to question her further. She was only seven and I didn't want to place her in an awkward position by asking questions that she couldn't or didn't want to answer.

'I gave Liam his bottle this morning,' Kim said proudly, brightening, as she fell into step beside us.

'Well done. That was a big help,' I said.

'I don't like helping to change his nappy, though,' she said, pulling a face.

'Yuk!' Adrian agreed. '*She* still poos in a nappy,' he said, pointing at Paula, and dissolved into laughter. He was at an age when he and his friends found toilet talk hilarious.

'Baby Liam?' Paula asked, leaning out of her stroller for a better look at Kim.

'Hi,' Kim said sweetly. 'Liam's at home.'

She took hold of Paula's hand and we continued down the street with Kim on one side of the stroller and Adrian on the other. Adrian and Kim began talking about school and then a popular children's television programme, while I thought about Laura. Why didn't Geraldine want to leave her alone? It didn't sound good, and I thought maybe this was the excuse I needed to call in on the way home.

Once in the playground I let Paula out of the stroller and she immediately crouched down and began examining the tarmac, poking her finger at a couple of loose chippings. It's incredible what little ones can spot and play with. A mother approached me with a child of a similar age to Kim. I knew her slightly from seeing her in the playground.

'You've brought Kim,' she said. 'Is Laura all right? I'm Fran. Our girls are friends. How is she?'

'I'm not sure,' I said honestly. 'Her mother-in-law asked me to bring Kim to school this morning.'

'I'm worried about her,' Fran confided. 'I've tried phoning

and I've left messages, but she hasn't got back to me.' The two girls took skipping ropes from their bags and began skipping.

'I'm thinking of stopping by her house on the way back this morning,' I said. 'We live in the same street. I'll tell her you were asking after her.'

'Oh yes, please do.' She hesitated. 'I hope I haven't done anything to upset her. We were both relatively new to the area and seemed to hit it off as friends. But I haven't seen or heard from her since she was in the playground that morning weeks ago.'

'I'm sure it's nothing like that,' I said.

Clearly I didn't know how much Laura had confided in Fran, and Geraldine's words about not discussing Laura in the playground rang in my ears – although, of course, we were only concerned for her wellbeing.

'Give her my best wishes,' Fran said. 'And tell her I hope to hear from her soon.'

'I will.'

The Klaxon sounded and I said goodbye to both Adrian and Kim and watched them line up. 'We're going to see baby Liam on the way home,' I told Paula, taking her hand.

'Baby Liam,' she said and chuckled excitedly.

I wasn't excited, I was very apprehensive, partly from having to confront the formidable Geraldine again, but also because I wasn't convinced I was doing the right thing in just dropping by. Perhaps I was turning into the busybody up the road – 'You know, that woman, the foster carer who thinks she knows everything.' But on the other hand I had a gut feeling that I should stop by and try to see Laura, and sometimes I think it's best if we follow our instincts or intuition.

With the promise of visiting baby Liam, Paula walked

faster than usual and didn't stop to examine every little thing that caught her eye. 'Baby Liam,' she said every so often with a smile.

'Yes, I hope we can see him.' For obviously we might not be invited in.

Undaunted, Paula continued at her best toddling pace along the street until we arrived at Laura's house. 'Baby Liam,' she announced, trying to open the gate.

I lifted the latch, opened the gate and we went up the front path. I parked the stroller in the porch and pressed the doorbell. I felt my pulse speed up a notch and my stomach tighten. I had no idea what to expect, and as we waited for the bell to be answered I prepared myself for most eventualities, including the door not being opened or opened and then shut in my face – most eventualities except … Geraldine answering the door in tears.

'Oh. I'm sorry,' I said, embarrassed and completely taken aback. 'I've called at a bad time.'

She looked at me, a tissue pressed to her lips and despair in her eyes. I didn't know what to do. My instinct was to hug and comfort her, but given her previous hostility I didn't think she'd want my comfort, yet I couldn't just walk away.

'Is there anything I can do?' I asked awkwardly. Paula looked at her, also concerned.

Geraldine shook her head and wiped her eyes, but fresh tears formed. Usually so capable, determined, even hard, her vulnerability shocked and deeply saddened me. With a heartfelt sigh she turned from the door and walked down the hall, leaving the front door wide open. I assumed she wanted me to go in, so I helped Paula over the doorstep and then once in the hall I closed the door. The house was quiet – unnaturally quiet considering there was another adult and a baby inside. There was a stale smell of burning as though food had caught fire. Geraldine had disappeared down the hall and into the living room. Still holding Paula's hand, I followed her. Paula had fallen silent, perhaps sensing the atmosphere.

In the living room Geraldine was standing with her back to me, gazing through the glass patio doors. There was no sign of Liam or Laura, but there were a few of his soft toys propped on the sofa and, dropping my hand, Paula went over to them. I crossed the room and stood beside Geraldine. She was staring, unseeing, down the garden.

'Is there anything I can get you?' I asked after a moment. 'A drink of water or a cup of tea?'

She wiped her eyes and shook her head. 'It'll take more than tea to put this lot right, Cathy,' she said.

She'd never used my name before and I sensed a shift in her attitude towards me. 'Do you want to talk about it?' I asked gently, touching her arm.

'It wouldn't do any good,' she said, her eyes filling again.

Then a terrible thought struck me. 'Are Liam and Laura all right? They're not hurt?'

'No. Laura is in bed upstairs and Liam is asleep in his cot in the front room.'

I remained standing beside Geraldine, not sure what to say or do but feeling I should stay. Paula began playing silently with the soft toys as Geraldine and I gazed down the garden, the joy of the summer outside now at odds with the unhappiness inside. Sometimes silence is more empathetic than words, so I stood quietly beside Geraldine, close but not touching. I sensed she wanted to talk, possibly to confide; that was why she'd left the front door open for us to come in. With her guard down she was less hostile to me, but she was finding it difficult, almost impossible, to know where to begin. I'd seen this before in children I'd fostered who were trying to disclose and tell me about something dreadful that had happened and which they'd kept a secret for a long time. They needed to tell but were fearful of the consequences, so I did now what I did then and waited until they found the strength to start.

After some minutes Geraldine took a deep breath and, still looking straight ahead, said faintly, 'We moved Liam's cot downstairs last week. Andy and I are taking it in turns to sleep on the sofa in the front room so we can keep an eye on him. It's no longer safe for him to be upstairs with his mother.'

An icy chill ran down my spine. 'Why not?' I asked gently.

'Because Laura thinks he's the devil's child. My little grandson, the work of the devil! I ask you, Cathy, it would be laughable if she didn't believe it.' Her face crumpled and she wiped away fresh tears.

I'd heard many terrible disclosures in the past from abused children and I knew it was important that I hid my shock and remained outwardly calm and in control to give them the strength they needed to continue.

'Shall we sit down?' I suggested.

She nodded, and we crossed to the sofa, where I moved Paula to one end to make room for us. 'Good girl,' I said quietly to her, for she was looking worried.

Geraldine sat upright on the sofa and stared straight ahead. 'It's worse this time,' she said. 'Far worse than when Laura had Kim. She seems to be losing touch with reality, and she's started threatening me.'

'Laura is threatening you?' I asked, shocked.

'Yes. She doesn't want me here. She resents me, but she

can't manage on her own, and Andy has to work. She rarely sleeps. She's up most of the night and often doesn't know where she is. She's started having weird waking dreams, like she's hallucinating. She wanders around. Last night I smelled burning and found her in the kitchen, making toast. It was two o'clock in the morning and she kept saying she didn't like the toast I made, as I didn't toast it enough. So she kept putting the same slice of toast back into the toaster until eventually it caught fire. I threw it in the sink and she became aggressive. I had to fetch Andy to put her back to bed. I try not to wake him, but she could have burned the house down.' She took a deep breath and wiped her nose. 'I'm sorry.'

'Don't be. It's all right,' I said, touching her arm.

'She's started doing other irrational things and talking a lot of nonsense,' Geraldine continued, keeping her eyes down. 'Liam has a birthmark on his back. It's not very big, but Laura read somewhere that in ancient times they thought birthmarks were put there by the devil, so the child belongs to the devil and does his work. It's ridiculous, obviously, but she seems to believe it. She's wary of him and I'm frightened she could do him harm. You won't tell anyone, will you?' she said, suddenly turning to me.

'No, of course not, but Laura does need help. More than you and Andy can give her. What did the doctor say?'

'She won't go. She hasn't been. Now she's got worse she doesn't think there is anything wrong with her. When she was just depressed she agreed to tell the doctor, but now she refuses to believe there is anything the matter with her. She says we're ganging up on her and making it up.'

'She was going to talk to the doctor at her six-week post-natal check-up. Did that not happen?'

'I don't think so. I took her to the appointment, but she wouldn't let me in when she saw the doctor. I can't force her to tell a doctor. And to be honest I'm worried that the same thing could happen to her as to her mother. She spent over six months in a psychiatric hospital following the birth of Laura.'

'Oh, I see,' I said. 'Laura mentioned her mother had suffered from postnatal depression, but I didn't realize it was that severe.'

'We don't talk about it. Laura's parents didn't have any more children after Laura,' Geraldine said. 'She and Andy weren't going to have another one after Kim. But then it happened and we all hoped for the best. I read somewhere that because a woman has been depressed after having one baby it doesn't mean it will happen again. But it has. And it's getting worse.' Geraldine shrugged with despair. 'I thought we'd be able to cope and that I could help them through like I did last time. I've only done what I thought was right, Cathy, but it seems I've made things worse – far worse.' Her face creased and, holding her head in her hands, she wept openly.

Now I had no hesitation in putting my arm around her shoulders and comforting her. Gone was the stern-faced, domineering mother-in-law who was firmly in charge and knew best no matter what, and in her place was a frail, broken woman, overwhelmed by the crisis unfolding in her family and not knowing what to do.

I lightly rubbed her back and also took hold of Paula's hand, for she was looking at Geraldine as though she, too, might cry. 'It's all right, love,' I said gently to her.

'I'm sorry,' Geraldine said, raising her head. 'I'm upsetting everyone.'

'There's no need to be sorry,' I said. 'You have a right to be upset. You've been carrying a huge burden.'

She wiped her eyes. 'Thank you for taking Kim to school this morning. Was she all right?'

'Yes. She met up with a friend. I stayed until it was time for them to go in.'

'I couldn't leave Laura alone this morning. She was in such a state. And Andy had to go to work.'

'I'm happy to help any time,' I said. 'I can bring Kim home from school this afternoon if you wish. But I think Laura needs to see a doctor. If she won't go to the surgery then perhaps you could arrange a home visit.'

Geraldine shrugged despondently and reached for another tissue. 'I don't know. I'd have to explain to the receptionist what was so urgent.'

'The surgery staff are bound by confidentiality,' I said. 'Or, if you don't want to talk to the receptionist, you could make an appointment to see the doctor yourself.'

'That won't be necessary,' a voice suddenly said.

Geraldine and I started as Laura came into the room, barefoot and in her dressing gown.

'Oh, you're up,' Geraldine said, shocked and immediately standing.

'Yes. Is that allowed?' Laura asked caustically. 'I'll shower and dress later.'

'How are you?' I asked, feeling I had to say something.

'Very well, thank you. So there's absolutely no need for me to see a doctor.'

And my first impression was that Laura did indeed look well and completely normal.

CHAPTER ELEVEN

TRYING TO HURT HIM

'I'm gasping for a coffee. Would you like one?' Laura asked me, lightly running her hand through her hair.

'Yes, please, if you're making one.'

'I'll do it,' Geraldine said. 'And I'll check on Liam.'

With her cloak of efficiency firmly back in place, Geraldine walked swiftly from the room. Laura sighed and sank into one of the armchairs. 'She won't let me do a thing, it's so frustrating. And she fusses over Liam constantly. She's even got him sleeping downstairs with her now.'

'I think she's just trying to help,' I said awkwardly.

We heard Geraldine go into the front room to check on Liam and then into the kitchen.

'Fran sends her best wishes,' I said. 'She said to phone her when you have a chance.'

'Yes, I must phone her. I keep meaning to. But you know how the time flies when you have a baby. The days just seem to disappear. I'll put it at the top of my to-do list,' she added with a smile.

I smiled too and we were silent for some moments, both gazing at Paula who was playing with one of Liam's soft toys. It was difficult to know what to say. I didn't want to make things worse by saying the wrong thing, but I was amazed at how well she looked – not at all what I'd expected after what Geraldine had just told me. Her cheeks had colour and there was no sign of her previous anxiety or depression. She seemed relaxed and, apart from being irritated by Geraldine, happy.

'It's a lovely day outside,' I said, glancing towards the garden.

'Yes. I was thinking I might collect Kim this afternoon and take Liam, if *she* lets me.'

'Good idea,' I said, ignoring her jibe at Geraldine. I felt uncomfortable; I'd just been sympathizing with Geraldine and now I was being asked to take Laura's side against her. Yet Laura's resentment at having her mother-in-law make her decisions was understandable, as she appeared rational and capable of making her own decisions.

'See how you feel later,' I suggested. 'I can bring Kim home if it helps.'

'You can help me by removing the mother-in-law from hell from my house,' Laura said with a sigh, unable to resist another dig. 'She's outstayed her welcome. Do you know, I'm not even allowed to make myself tea and toast when I feel like it? I fancied some last night. Then the next minute she's in the kitchen saying I'm going to burn the house down. Just because I overcooked the toast! I mean, Cathy, tell me who hasn't burned toast? Then she wonders why I snap at her. I get hungry breastfeeding.'

'Yes, I did too,' I said. 'It's important to eat and drink regularly when breastfeeding.'

'She likes to give him a bottle of formula at night,' she said, and glanced at the wall clock. 'He'll be awake soon for his ten o'clock feed. You don't mind if I bring him in here to feed him, do you?'

'No, of course not.'

'*She* does,' Laura said, again lambasting her mother-in-law. 'She doesn't think it's proper to breastfeed in front of others, especially at the meal table. She told me she fed all of hers in the privacy of her bedroom. Well, good for her, I say. Times have changed. I'll see if he is awake.'

Laura stood and began towards the living-room door as Geraldine came in carrying a tray of coffee and biscuits.

'Where are you going?' she asked Laura.

'To see if Liam's awake for his feed,' Laura replied with attitude. 'Is that OK?'

I felt embarrassed. Keeping her eyes down, Geraldine hurriedly set the tray on the occasional table and went down the hall after Laura. I heard their hushed voices coming from the front room in what sounded like a sharp exchange, and then a few moments later Laura returned carrying Liam in her arms. She raised her eyes in exasperation, which I pretended not to see, and she returned to her armchair.

'Baby,' Paula said, pointing.

'Yes. He's going to have his breakfast,' I explained.

'The second one today,' Laura said with a smile, putting him to her breast.

I watched Paula's face. It was a picture. As Laura fed Liam I sipped my coffee and we talked. Paula took a few steps closer to her for a better look. Laura didn't mind. I saw the love that was in Laura's eyes as she gazed at her son suckling contentedly. It was impossible to imagine what Geraldine had told me. Far from being wary of him as the devil's child, Laura held him close, protectively. I'm sure she would have died for him rather than let any harm come to him, as most mothers would. Her tenderness and compassion were obvious, but why would Geraldine have made all that up?

When Liam finished suckling on one side Laura gently turned him round to finish feeding on the other side, all the time smiling down at him, full of love and kindness. Once he'd finished she winded him and then drank her now-lukewarm coffee. We continued talking, about babies, the school and fostering, which so many people are interested in and ask questions about, then I said I should be going, as I had things to do.

'Thanks for stopping by,' Laura said. 'Can you see yourself out?' Liam was fast asleep in her arms.

'Yes, of course. Take care, and I hope to see you in the playground this afternoon.'

'Yes.' Paula clambered down from the sofa and we quietly left the room so we wouldn't wake Liam. As we approached the front door Geraldine suddenly appeared from the front room. I had the feeling she'd been waiting there for me to leave.

'If I'm not in the playground this afternoon, can you bring Kim home, please?' she said quietly.

'Yes, but Laura seems fine now,' I said. 'She's talking about collecting Kim herself, and taking Liam.'

'We'll see about that,' Geraldine said stiffly, all vulnerability gone. 'She may seem fine now, but her moods can change very quickly. It will ease my mind to know that you will collect Kim if I'm not there.'

'Yes, of course,' I said. Although it seemed she'd already ruled out any possibility of Laura collecting Kim.

'Thank you,' Geraldine said flatly as she opened the front door.

I helped Paula out and over the step and the door closed behind us.

With Paula holding one hand, I pushed the stroller with the other and we walked slowly down the garden path and then along the street towards home. I was perplexed, worried and bemused by what had taken place and began to wonder if Geraldine was the one with issues, for I'd seen no evidence of the paranoia she'd described in Laura. Indeed, Laura had acted perfectly rationally, had talked in positive terms and seemed well balanced and the picture of health. True, she resented her mother-in-law big time, but who could blame her if she was trying to control and dominate her? But then again, why would anyone in their right mind make up such dreadful stories about their daughter-in-law? I didn't know who or what to believe.

Once I'd settled Paula for her nap I took out my books, but I didn't get very far with my research or writing. My thoughts kept returning to number 53 and the awful atmosphere that must pervade there, especially when Laura and her mother-in-law were there alone. Did they try to talk civilly to each other, or did they continuously argue or avoid each other by occupying different rooms? What a dreadful atmosphere for Kim to come home to, though perhaps they made an effort when she was there. I wondered what Andy, Laura's husband and Geraldine's son, made of it all. He must have felt as though he was caught between a rock and a hard place, with his mother and wife feuding. Surely he would take the necessary action, either by ensuring that Laura saw a doctor, if what Geraldine had said was true, or if it wasn't then sending his mother home? Laura had needed help when she'd been depressed, but if Geraldine was now trying to create that need then it really fell to Andy to sort out the mess, difficult though it may be.

I was half expecting to see Laura in the playground that afternoon, as she'd seemed confident that she would be collecting Kim, but she didn't arrive. Then, as the Klaxon sounded for the end of school, I realized that Geraldine wasn't in the playground either. I moved closer to the door where the children would come out and watched carefully for Kim. Adrian's class was out first and then Kim's. When she emerged I went over to her.

'Your gran asked me to collect you,' I said.

'Is Mum all right?' Kim asked, immediately concerned.

'Yes. I saw her and your brother this morning,' I said with a cheery smile. It was all I could say, as clearly I didn't know what had happened in the interim.

On the walk back home Kim baby-talked to Paula, which I guessed she did to her brother. It was sweet and Paula loved the attention. Then Kim told us about her class's project on the Vikings. Their teacher had asked them all to take in as many cardboard boxes as they could the next day, as they were going to make a big model of a Viking boat, big enough for all the class to sit in and row.

'That sounds great,' I said. 'How exciting.' Children's learning is so much fun now.

'I'll have to go to the shop if we haven't got any boxes big enough,' Kim said thoughtfully.

'Do you still go shopping for your mum sometimes?' I asked.

'Not really. Gran's there now.'

I would have liked to hear Kim's views on what was going on at home, but it wasn't appropriate for me to question her. We continued towards her house with Adrian joining in the talk about Viking boat building and Paula trying her best to say 'Vi-King', making it sound like a person.

I intended to walk Kim right up to her front door, but Geraldine must have been watching out for us, for as we stopped at her garden gate the front door opened and Geraldine appeared. Kim said goodbye to us and ran up the path. Geraldine gave a perfunctory wave of thanks and as soon as Kim was inside she closed the door, so I had no idea how Laura was.

We continued home and the evening passed as most school nights do, with the children playing while I made dinner, followed by Adrian's homework, some television and then the children's bath and bedtime routines. But Laura wasn't far from my thoughts, and I wondered how their evening was progressing. That night, as Adrian and I hummed Brahms's 'Lullaby', my thoughts turned to Shelley and Darrel. I hoped she'd let me know how her visit to her old foster carer, Carol, had gone, and whether she'd plucked up the courage to audition for the choir. But even if I never heard from her again I would still remember them both, as I was sure Adrian would.

I was in bed by ten-thirty and asleep before eleven, but then I was jolted wide awake by the telephone ringing. I grabbed the handset from my bedside cabinet with my heart thumping loudly and my mouth going dry, convinced a tragedy had befallen a loved one. It was the only reason I could think of for someone calling at this time, and with my husband, John, working abroad, the chances of it being bad news seemed dramatically increased.

'Yes? Hello?' I said, my voice shaking.

'Cathy? Is that you?'

'Laura?'

'Yes, you sound different. Hope you don't mind, but I thought I'd phone you for a chat.'

I looked at my bedside clock; it was 11.40. I heaved myself up the pillow and tried to calm my racing heart.

'You don't mind me calling, do you?' Laura asked.

'No. It's just rather late. I was asleep.'

'I'm sorry. I didn't realize the time. Shall I call you back another time?'

There didn't seem much point now that I was awake. 'It's OK. Are you all right?'

'Yes, I'm fine. It was nice of you to drop by today. I enjoyed your visit. I haven't seen many people recently because I felt so down, but now I'm better I'll catch up. I've just finished talking to Fran. We were on the phone for ages.' She gave a small laugh.

'That's good,' I said. I hoped Fran was a night owl.

'I told her I'd be in the playground tomorrow.'

'Great, although I thought I might see you there today.'

'I intended to go, but then I nodded off on the sofa and Geraldine didn't like to wake me or just slip out. You know how she fusses. Thanks for bringing Kim home.'

'You're welcome. Did she find some cardboard boxes for her class's Viking project?'

Laura laughed. 'Yes, lots. We had loads in the loft from when we moved. Andy went up there and got them down when he came home from work. I won't go in the loft – there are spiders up there and I hate spiders.'

'Yes, so do I.'

Our conversation continued – a perfectly normal chat between friends, if it hadn't been so late. Laura did most of the talking, and I saw the clock ticking off the minutes to midnight. Then, at 12.15 a.m., I said, 'I'm going to have to go now, Laura, and get some sleep. Why don't you come to me tomorrow for a coffee after you've taken Kim to school?'

'Yes, that would be lovely, thank you. I'll let you sleep now. Sorry to have woken you. See you tomorrow.'

We said goodbye and I hung up. Yes, a perfectly normal conversation apart from the timing. No one with young children telephones a friend just for a chat in the middle of the night, but I assumed it was as Laura had said – that she'd lost track of time while talking to Fran. Thankfully the phone ringing hadn't woken Adrian or Paula, but it took me a while to get back off to sleep.

As Laura was planning to take Kim to school the following morning I kept a lookout for her as we walked down our street. Parents with children who attended the local school left home more or less at the same time, so we often saw others walking the same route. That morning the children in Kim's class were all carrying cardboard boxes, but there was no sign of Kim with her mother, either ahead of or behind us. They weren't in the playground either, but Fran was and she came towards me with a cardboard box under each arm. Her daughter was carrying another two boxes. 'Did Laura telephone you late last night?' Fran asked me.

'Yes.'

'Oh dear. I am sorry. She told me she was planning on phoning you when we'd finished and I tried to persuade her not to. It was so late.'

'Don't worry. It was nice to hear from her, although it was late.'

'It must have been. We were about to get into bed when she phoned me and we were talking for ages. My hubby wasn't amused, although I explained I hadn't heard from her in a long while. Laura said she'd been depressed but was all right now. I invited her for coffee this morning.'

'So did I,' I said, smiling, and again looking around for any sign of Laura. 'I wonder where she is.' There were others arriving with cardboard boxes of all sizes. Some of the children were carrying them on their backs like tortoise shells. It was comical.

'She might have slept in,' Fran said, also glancing around. 'Laura told me she can't sleep at night, and then sleeps in late or nods off during the day. Oh look, there's her mother-in-law with Kim and the baby. So Laura hasn't come. I'll go over and see how she is.'

I turned as Fran went over and saw Geraldine with Kim pushing the pram. She was carrying a couple of cardboard boxes and had another one balanced on the pram. Geraldine was straight-faced as usual and, avoiding eye contact, kept her gaze ahead. I saw Fran say something to Geraldine and she responded with a curt nod and what looked like a very short reply. Fran then went over to speak to another mother, so I guessed she hadn't learned much. The Klaxon sounded and I kissed Adrian goodbye. I saw Geraldine with the pram, speeding towards the exit, but I didn't try to catch up. Fran looked at me and shrugged. 'Not sure,' she said as we left the playground. Then we went our separate ways.

I didn't knock at number 53 on the way home. There was no reason to, and to do so would have crossed the line between good neighbourliness and intrusiveness. But of course I speculated on what exactly was going on.

Laura didn't come for coffee, and I wasn't surprised. Something told me that if she wasn't up to taking Kim to school then she wouldn't be coming to me. Maybe she'd gone to Fran's instead, but I doubted it.

Laura wasn't in the playground that afternoon either, and it was only after the children had come out of the building that I realized with a stab of horror that Geraldine wasn't there either. Kim was waiting with her teacher as they were told to do if a parent or carer didn't arrive to collect them. Grabbing Paula's hand, and with Adrian in tow, I shot over to them.

'I'm so sorry,' I said to her teacher. 'I'm taking Kim home.'

'No problem,' she said, and Kim came with me.

But there *was* a problem. I knew then that I needed to clarify the arrangement I had with Geraldine for collecting Kim. I would ask her to telephone me when she wanted me to collect her. If you do something every day it becomes part of your routine, or if you're asked to do something specifically it's at the forefront of your mind. But this loose, *ad hoc* arrangement where I was expected to collect Kim if Geraldine (or Laura) wasn't in the playground could easily lead to me forgetting Kim, as I'd just shown. Fortunately no harm had been done on this occasion.

I didn't get the chance to speak to Geraldine when I saw Kim home that afternoon, as she opened and closed the front door just long enough to let Kim in. I decided I would either catch her in the playground the following morning or, if not, I'd knock on their door on the way home when I just had Paula with me. I would tell Geraldine that I was more than happy to take Kim to school and bring her home, but that I'd appreciate it if she could telephone me before I left to let me know. It seemed a reasonable request.

That night I'd just got into bed when the telephone rang. It was 10.45 – earlier than the previous night's call, so I wasn't asleep, but it was still late for a chat. I knew straight away there was something wrong.

'Cathy,' Laura said in a whisper. 'I need your help. Can you come? Geraldine is downstairs with Liam and she's trying to hurt him.'

CHAPTER TWELVE

VERY SERIOUS

'I can't tell Andy because he's on his mother's side,' Laura whispered. 'But you're my friend. You understand, don't you? You must come here and help me.'

As a foster carer I'd faced many unusual and difficult situations, sometimes having to make a snap decision on whether someone was telling the truth, but nothing had prepared me for this, in either my fostering experience or my personal life.

'Why do you think Geraldine is trying to harm Liam?' I asked, my thoughts whizzing and my senses on full alert.

'Why?' asked Laura, raising her voice above a whisper. 'I don't know. But she's barricaded herself in the front room with Liam and won't let me in.'

'But how do you know she's harming him?' I asked.

'I can hear him crying. And she won't let me in to see him. I'm in the hall outside the front room. I'm going to wait here until she comes out and then I'll rush in. Do you think I should phone the police?'

If what Laura thought was true, the short answer was yes. If a child is in immediate danger then the police needed to be called as an emergency, but I wasn't convinced Liam was in danger. 'Where's Andy?' I asked.

'Upstairs. Settling Kim,' Laura said. 'All the shouting and screaming has woken her. I'm sorry I've upset her, but I have to protect my baby.'

'Is Liam crying now?' I asked. For Laura had said she was outside the front room but I couldn't hear him crying.

There was a pause when I guessed she was listening out for him, then she screamed: 'No! Oh my god! I can't hear him. He's dead!'

I heard the phone clunk as she either dropped or threw it down, but the line was still open. I heard her shouting and banging frantically on what I assumed was the front-room door. 'Let me in, you evil witch! What have you done to my son?' Then there was nothing to be heard but her hysterical screaming.

I sat on the edge of my bed, rigid with fear. I wondered if I should call the police, but then I heard a man's voice, presumably Andy's, take control.

'That's enough, Laura,' he said firmly. 'Liam is fine. I'm taking you back to bed now.'

The shouting, screaming and banging on the door suddenly stopped and was replaced by the sound of Laura whimpering like a wounded animal. It was heartbreaking to hear, but she must have allowed Andy to take her upstairs and see her to bed, for the whimpering faded into the distance and then there was silence. I kept the phone pressed to my ear, my knuckles white from gripping it so tightly. It must have been ten minutes before I heard another sound – Andy's voice close by, asking, 'Mum, are you and Liam all right? You can come out now. Laura's calmer. I've put her to bed.'

I heard the door to the front room open and then Geraldine's trembling, desperate voice. 'Oh, son, what are we going to do? This can't go on.'

There was no reply, but Andy must have spotted that the telephone was out of its cradle, for I heard him say, 'Who was Laura talking to, Mum? Do you know?'

Geraldine replied 'No.'

There was a small noise as the phone was picked up and then Andy's voice came on the line. 'Hello. Is there anyone there?' he asked tentatively.

I was very tempted to just hang up.

'My name is Cathy,' I said. 'I'm a friend of Laura's. I live further up the street.'

'Jesus!' he exclaimed. Then to Geraldine, 'It's a friend of Laura's – Cathy?'

I couldn't hear what she said, but a moment later Andy came back on the line, his voice tight and controlling. 'I don't know what Laura has told you, but whatever it was just forget it, please. She's very upset tonight and not herself.'

That was the biggest understatement I'd heard in a long while, I thought, but I knew from what I'd just overheard that I couldn't stand impotently by any longer.

'I'm sorry, I can't just forget it,' I said. 'I'm assuming that your mother wasn't harming Liam as Laura said, in which case Laura needs help.'

'I'm aware of that,' he said defensively. 'That's why my mother has moved in with us.'

'I think Laura needs more help than you and your mother can give her,' I said as gently as I could.

There was silence, and then I heard him sigh resignedly. 'I know. You're right. She attacked my mother tonight because she thought she was harming Liam. Mum had to shut herself in the front room. It's a nightmare. I'll take the morning off work tomorrow and make sure she sees a doctor.'

'I think that's for the best. If you need help taking Kim to school or collecting her, or someone to look after Liam, let me know. I'm a registered foster carer and I have two children of my own. My son and your daughter go to the same school.'

'Thank you. Do we have your telephone number?' he asked more conciliatorily.

'Laura does. Shall I give it to you too?'

'Yes, please. Let me get a pen.' Then, 'Thanks, go ahead.'

I gave him my telephone number.

'Thank you,' he said, all trace of resentment now gone. 'I'm sorry you've had to hear all this and be drawn into it.' So I guessed he didn't know of my previous involvement.

'Take care,' I said. 'Give Laura my best wishes. And phone if you need me.'

'I will.'

We said goodnight and I replaced the receiver. My heart was racing and I felt queasy from shock, but at least I'd said what I had to. I got back into bed, but I knew I couldn't sleep. I sat upright, propped up on my pillow, and by the small light coming from the street lamp I stared across the bedroom as my thoughts somersaulted. I took some relief from the fact that Andy was now going to make sure Laura saw a doctor the following day. I sincerely hoped he meant it and would keep his word. Cleary he and his mother had been complicit in trying to deal with Laura's illness – for that was how I now saw it – and had kept it to themselves long after they should have sought professional help. Andy said that Laura had attacked Geraldine, which was bad enough, but if she'd been holding the baby at the time the outcome could have been much, much worse. There was also Geraldine's concern that Laura could intentionally harm Liam, which was the reason she was sleeping with him downstairs and didn't leave him alone with her. I knew the symptoms of postnatal depression included feeling low and experiencing mood swings, anxiety and irritability, but did they include wanting to harm others? I didn't think so.

It was after midnight by the time I fell asleep, and then I was wide awake again at five o'clock, thinking and worrying about Laura and her family. Perhaps it was because of the nature of fostering that I was getting involved, although I doubted that many would have walked away.

I didn't receive a telephone call that morning to take Kim to school, so I continued our routine as normal. Geraldine arrived in the playground with Kim just before the Klaxon sounded. I assumed Andy was with Laura and Liam. She threw me a cursory glance, but that was all. She then rushed off as soon as Kim had gone into school. But from that brief glimpse I'd had of her I could see she was tired and tense, and seemed to have aged in the last week. Little wonder, I thought, with all that she had to cope with. She may not have been the warmest person and clearly thought she knew best, but without doubt she was acting in what she believed was her family's best interests.

That afternoon after lunch I put Paula in the stroller and took her to our local library, or 'lie-rabry' as Paula called it. I had some books I wanted to return, but I also wanted to see if they had any books on postnatal depression. I felt I needed to know more: what the symptoms were and the treatment. Inside the library I let Paula out of her stroller and then parked it in the foyer with the other strollers. She held my hand as I began browsing the shelves, trying to work out where the books I wanted were. The Dewey classification system libraries use in England for arranging books on shelves has always flummoxed me, but eventually I found two books in the social sciences section that looked hopeful. I carried them over to the area for young children and sat on one of the bean bags, while Paula toddled around looking at the brightly coloured and enticing early-years books displayed on the low-level stands.

The first book I opened was too theoretical for what I wanted, with lots of references to postgraduate research. The second was more user-friendly, and it wasn't long before I'd found what I wanted: a list of the symptoms of postnatal depression, also known as postpartum depression. I was surprised by the length of the list, but as the author (a doctor) pointed out, the majority of women only experienced a few of the symptoms. Apart from the ones I already knew about – feeling very sad, crying easily, lethargy, inability to cope, anxiety and low self-esteem – others included feelings of hopelessness and despair, suicidal thoughts, guilt, insomnia, flashbacks, fixating on bad things that have happened in the past, worrying excessively about the baby, panic attacks, problems interacting with others and strange thoughts. The author said that if a new mother experienced three or more of these symptoms or they were particularly acute then she should seek medical help, as it was likely she was suffering from postnatal depression.

The author distinguished between the 'baby blues' and postnatal depression. The baby blues were far less severe, with mothers feeling low and tired for a few weeks after the birth but then recovering, usually of their own accord. The treatment for postnatal depression was usually a course of anti-depressants and sometimes counselling or therapy.

Reassuringly, with treatment, recovery was usually quick, although the longer the condition was left untreated the longer it took, which wasn't such good news if this was what Laura had. Yet while the symptoms listed had included strange thoughts, there was no mention of what Laura was now experiencing – believing the baby had the mark of the devil and that her mother-in-law was harming him, or being physically aggressive.

Then I turned the page and began to read the next section, headed 'Postpartum Psychosis', and I had a cold, sinking feeling. Although postpartum or postnatal psychosis is a relatively rare condition, many of the symptoms fitted Laura: strange beliefs, delusions, paranoia, suspiciousness, hallucinations, as well as some of those also found in postnatal depression, such as insomnia, anxiety and despair. The onus again lay on seeking medical help early, and treatment usually included anti-psychotic drugs, therapy and sometimes admission to hospital if the patient was critical. I read that a woman's chances of developing the condition were increased if her mother had suffered from it after giving birth, or the woman had developed it after a previous birth. Both of which applied to Laura. The author wrote that if there was a history of postpartum psychosis then the woman should be carefully monitored and supported throughout her pregnancy and after the birth. If she was, the outcome was very good, with the majority of women not developing the condition. But of course Laura hadn't been monitored, because her doctor hadn't been told of the problems she'd experienced after the birth of Kim. I guessed her doctor hadn't been told that her mother had spent time in a psychiatric hospital after having Laura either. I realized then that in keeping it to themselves and trying to deal with it in the family, Geraldine and Andy had inadvertently stopped Laura from receiving the help she desperately needed and had probably worsened her condition.

I continued reading until Paula had tired of amusing herself. I returned the books to the shelves and helped her pick some storybooks to check out and take home. I could have checked out the book I'd been reading, but I felt I'd read enough about postnatal depression and psychosis. And while I knew it was dangerous for people without medical training to diagnose (and I would never have voiced my thoughts to anyone, especially Laura and her family), as I left the library and began the walk home, deep in thought, I was almost certain that Laura was suffering from postnatal psychosis, and it was very serious indeed.

When I returned home I wasn't wholly surprised, therefore, to hear Andy's message on the answerphone. 'Cathy, it's Andy, Laura's husband. We're all at the hospital.' His voice was tight and tense. 'I may need to ask you to collect Kim from school today. I'll phone you in about an hour when I know for certain. Thank you.' It was timed half an hour previously. I didn't know if they'd been to the doctor's first or had gone straight to the hospital. An anxious thirty minutes followed, and then fifteen minutes before I had to leave to collect Adrian the phone rang again.

'Cathy, it's Andy. Did you get my message?'

'Yes. How is Laura?'

'Not good. They've sedated her.' His voice caught. 'She's been admitted to St Mary's [our local hospital] for the time being, but they're trying to find a place in a hospital with a mother-and-baby unit so she can keep Liam with her. I don't know how long this is going to take and I can't leave Mum here to deal with this alone. Can I ask you to collect Kim from school, please, and then take her back to your house for a couple of hours? I'll be with you as soon as I can. Is that possible?'

'Yes, of course. I'll give Kim dinner. She can stay the night if necessary. Don't worry.'

'Thank you. Please tell her that her mum is being well looked after and I'll see her soon. The poor kid has been through so much.' His voice broke.

'I'll explain and reassure her,' I said. 'Try not to worry.'

'It's a nightmare.'

'But Laura is getting the help she needs now,' I said, trying to reassure him.

'Yes, I hope so.' We said a quick goodbye and I replaced the receiver.

Five minutes later I locked the front door and left for school in plenty of time. When Kim came out of school I was waiting for her and explained what her father had said. Her face clouded at the thought of her mother being in hospital, but then she brightened a little when I reassured her that her mother was being well looked after and she could play with Adrian and Paula, and have ice cream for pudding. Although Andy and Geraldine would have done their best to protect Kim from all the upset of Laura's illness, as Andy said she had been through a lot, for what affects one member of a family obviously impacts on the rest – adults and children.

Once home, I made a cold drink and a small snack for us all, which we had in the garden, and then I took the toys out of the shed. I stayed in the garden playing with the children until it was time for me to go indoors and make dinner. I asked Adrian and Kim to keep an eye on Paula, although I could see them through the kitchen window as I worked. Kim popped in once to ask if her daddy had phoned yet and I told her I'd let her know as soon as he did. Once the meal was ready I brought the children indoors. Quiche, new potatoes and sweetcorn, followed by tinned fruit and the promised ice cream, with a choice of chocolate or strawberry topping. Adrian had both.

'Yuck,' Kim laughed as Adrian stirred the deep red and brown sauces together into the melting ice cream.

'Yummy,' he retaliated, smacking his lips.

Paula looked on bemused, not really sure what was funny but laughing anyway.

After dinner storm clouds closed in and we just had time to put the toys in the shed before the first drops of rain splattered large on the patio. A minute later it was pouring down and the sky had darkened so much that I had to switch on the lights. I suggested we could play a game of cards or a board game, but Adrian and Kim wanted to watch a Walt Disney film and chose one from our collection. I'd already mentioned to Kim that there was a chance she might be staying the night but that her daddy would telephone and let us know for certain. As the time ticked by her staying the night seemed increasingly likely, but then just before seven o'clock Andy telephoned.

'I'm just about to leave the hospital. I'll be with you in half an hour.'

'OK, I'll tell Kim. Do you know which house I live at?' I thought to ask.

'No, sorry, I'm not thinking straight.'

I gave him my house number.

'Thanks. Tell Kim I'll see her soon.'

I returned the phone to its cradle and told Kim what her father had said, and she met the news with a mixture of relief and disappointment, for most children like a sleepover. Also, I think being away from the very difficult and upsetting atmosphere that must have prevailed at home in recent months had given her some light relief.

'You can come and stay overnight another time,' I said.

'Yes, when Mummy is better,' she said, and returned to watching the rest of the film.

It was really Paula's bedtime now, and I knew it would be too late if I left putting her to bed until after Andy had collected Kim, so I told Paula it was time for bed and to say goodnight. She wasn't pleased. 'No!' she said, screwing up her face, wanting to stay with Adrian and Kim. But she was tired – she'd had a busy day with going to the library as well – and I knew that, like most children, she'd become fractious if she grew overtired.

'Say goodnight,' I said a little more firmly. Taking her hand, I led her first to Adrian and then Kim, who both said goodnight and kissed her.

'Night,' she said, giving in to a yawn.

We went upstairs and she yawned again as I washed and changed her ready for bed, then she fell asleep almost immediately. I'd just returned downstairs when the doorbell rang. It was Andy.

'Cathy?' he asked, for we hadn't actually met.

'Yes, come in.'

'What a day,' he sighed, stepping in. He looked drawn and tired and was wearing a suit, so I guessed he'd originally planned to go to work after he'd taken Laura to the doctor, but clearly that hadn't happened.

Kim heard his voice and rushed into the hall. 'Daddy, Daddy!' she cried and ran into his arms. 'Where's Mummy?'

'She's at the hospital,' Andy said. 'Having a sleep now. The doctors and nurses are looking after her, so don't you worry.' He hugged her hard.

'Where's Liam?' she asked.

'With your gran. She's taken him home. I need to talk to Cathy and then we'll go home too.'

Clearly Andy wanted to talk away from the children. 'Kim, you finish watching the film with Adrian while I speak to your daddy,' I said. I led the way down the hall and into the living room where Andy said hello to Adrian. Kim returned to sit beside Adrian on the sofa.

'Would you like a tea or coffee?' I now asked Andy, showing him through to the kitchen-cum-diner.

'Coffee, please.'

He sat, or rather collapsed, into one of the chairs at the table, while I went into the kitchen and filled the kettle.

'What a day,' he said again with a heartfelt sigh, running his fingers through his hair. 'Thanks for looking after Kim. I might need your help again tomorrow if that's all right.'

'Saturday? Yes. I haven't any plans.'

He sat back in the chair and stretched out his legs as though forcing himself to relax. 'There's been so much going on,' he said. 'I'll try to explain, although from what Mum has told me I think you know some of it.'

'I know Laura hasn't been well,' I said, glancing at him.

He nodded. 'But we didn't realize how ill she was. We should never have let it go on for so long, I know that now. We should have got help sooner instead of letting it get to crisis point. Mum and I were up most of last night with Laura and I telephoned the doctor first thing this morning. He agreed to see Laura as an emergency, but then she wouldn't leave Liam with Mum, so we all went. She was still acting odd in the surgery, saying ridiculous things and shouting and crying. When the doctor saw her he said she needed to see a psychiatrist and to go straight to hospital. We had to wait ages there and Laura got more and more confused and agitated. She was convinced everyone was out to get her, and we couldn't calm her. She began screaming and then locked herself in the toilets with Liam. They had to use the emergency key to unlock the door and get her out. I wanted Mum to take Liam home, but Laura clung to him and started shouting that Mum was trying to steal her baby. Then the psychiatrist came. He examined her and has made an initial diagnosis. I'm sure you won't have heard of it – I hadn't. It's called postpartum psychosis.'

I set the two cups of coffee on the table and sat opposite Andy.

'It's very serious then?'

'Yes, very.'

CHAPTER THIRTEEN

WORRY

'The psychiatrist wanted to know Laura's medical history,' Andy continued, resting his elbows on the table for support. 'I was honest and told him she'd suffered from depression after the birth of Kim. He questioned me as to why she hadn't received medical help back then, and why we'd left it so long before going to the doctor's now. He was very concerned and seemed to blame me. I guess I am to blame. I just let Mum get on with it. She helped Laura after she'd had Kim, so I assumed it would be OK now.' He sighed. 'He asked about Laura's mother too, and I told him she'd once had a mental breakdown many years ago – after having Laura. I didn't realize its significance until today. It wasn't something we ever talked about.' He sighed again and paused to drink his coffee.

He was a tall man with broad shoulders that were now hunched forward under the burden of worry. I could see the likeness to his mother, and I thought he was probably used to being in control too, but he now looked a broken man.

'It seems that a lot of this could have been avoided if we'd been honest with the doctor from the start,' he said, returning his cup to the saucer, 'instead of trying to hide it and deal with it ourselves. I should have been more involved and insisted Laura saw the doctor earlier, rather than going off to work each day and leaving Mum to deal with it.' He sighed again and ran his hand absently through his hair, beating himself up over what should have been.

'So Laura is staying in St Mary's for now?' I asked.

'Just for tonight. She's in the psychiatric wing, but they're going to try to move her tomorrow. St Mary's doesn't have the facilities for a baby to stay, that's why Mum and I had to bring Liam home. Laura fed him before we left. We'll go back first thing in the morning. He's used to having formula sometimes, so that shouldn't be too much of a problem.'

'And Laura didn't mind you bringing Liam home without her?' I asked, mindful that Andy had said she wouldn't be separated from him.

'She was asleep by the time we left, sedated. We didn't have a choice. He couldn't stay there.'

I nodded and drank some of my coffee.

'The psychiatrist explained that a few hospitals have specialist mother-and-baby units for women suffering from this type of condition,' Andy continued. 'But the admission has to be planned. You can't just turn up. He's making a referral today, so hopefully she can go tomorrow. It's an hour's drive away, but he's assured us that it's the best place for Laura to receive the specialist help she needs. As I say, it would probably never have reached this point if we'd got Laura help earlier. She could have stayed at home with medication and therapy.' He drained his coffee and stared past me, deep in thought.

'They'll soon have her better,' I offered. 'Tell me how I can help.'

He returned his gaze to me. 'Yes. Mum and I will go to St Mary's with Liam tomorrow, as soon as we've fed and changed him. We've been told not to get there before nine o'clock and to take a bag of clothes and essentials for Liam and whatever Laura needs. I'll have to make a list. We don't know what time she'll be transferred and I don't want Kim there hanging around all day. Also I don't want her seeing her mum if she's still very disturbed. It's frightening. So could you look after Kim from about eight-thirty tomorrow morning? I know it's asking a lot.'

'Of course. No problem.'

'Thank you. Assuming Laura is calmer, I'll take Kim to visit her on Sunday at the mother-and-baby unit. Kim is going to miss Liam and her mum, but there's no other way round it.'

'She's a sensible girl,' I said. 'She'll understand once you've explained to her why her mother is there, and that you'll be taking her to see her regularly. Do you know how long Laura will be kept in?'

He shook his head. 'We should know more in a few days when a full assessment has been made. Which reminds me, I need to phone Laura's mother as soon as I go home to tell her what's happened.'

'She doesn't know?'

'No. She lives out of the area and works full-time. She saw Liam when he was a few days old but hasn't seen him since. Laura has spoken to her on the phone, but I don't think she's told her how bad she's been feeling. And recently we've been stopping her from phoning when she was distraught and saying ridiculous things.' He sighed again. 'Thanks, Cathy. I'd best be off now.' He drained the last of his coffee and stood.

We went into the living room where the film had finished and Adrian was proudly showing Kim his toy car transporter complete with cars. She was looking suitably impressed.

'Come on, love, time to go home,' Andy said to her.

She stood and went over to her father and, tucking her arm through his, rested her head against him. Adrian came with us to the front door to see them out. The evening had grown dark early as fresh storm clouds rolled in. 'See you tomorrow,' I said. 'Take care.'

We watched them go down the path and then I closed the front door as the first clap of thunder sounded in the distance.

That night Adrian and I had to hum Brahms's 'Lullaby' a little louder over the noise of the storm, and I thought of Laura, alone in her hospital bed, and prayed she would get better very quickly.

I was up and dressed the following morning earlier than usual for the weekend and ready for Kim's arrival. The storm had passed in the night and the sky was clear, promising a fine day. Adrian and Paula were up too but still in their pyjamas when Andy arrived with Kim. Geraldine stayed with Liam in the car, parked outside, but looked in my direction with an almost friendly nod. I smiled.

'I won't come in,' Andy said. 'Kim understands that we need to get to the hospital as soon as possible. She's brought some of her favourite toys and books.'

'That's great,' I said, smiling at Kim. She came in with a small rucksack on her back, looking very sad. I touched her shoulder reassuringly.

'She didn't want any breakfast,' Andy said.

'Don't worry. I'll fix her something when she's ready.'

'I've no idea what time we'll be back, but I'll phone you with an update as soon as I know something.'

'OK. I might take them to the park later if the weather holds, so leave a message on the answerphone if I'm out.'

'Will do. Bye then, love,' he said to Kim. 'Give me a kiss.'

He bent down and Kim wrapped her arms tightly around his neck and smothered his face in kisses. He kissed her cheek and then gently unwrapped her arms from his neck and straightened. 'Be good for Cathy,' he said.

'See you later,' I said, taking Kim's hand. I could see she was close to tears.

I didn't prolong their goodbye but closed the door as soon as he'd returned down the path to his car.

'It's lovely to have you with us for the day,' I said positively to Kim with a cheerful smile. 'Are you going to show us some of your toys? Then I'll make you something to eat. We haven't had our breakfast yet.'

Kim gave a small, brave nod and slipped the rucksack from her shoulder, but then I saw her bottom lip tremble and her tears began to fall. 'I want my mummy,' she sobbed.

'Oh, love,' I said, putting my arm around her. 'Don't cry. The doctors and nurses are looking after your mummy. There's no need to worry.' But seeing a child upset is heart-breaking, and I felt my own eyes fill. Adrian and Paula were looking sad too.

'Let's go and have a seat in the living room,' I said, and I took the three of them through. I sat Kim on the sofa beside me. Adrian and Paula stood a little in front of us, looking at her.

'I know I have to be brave for my daddy,' Kim said through her tears. 'But I can't.' I swallowed hard as Adrian's eyes misted and Paula rubbed her eyes.

'You two find something to do until Kim is better,' I said to them. I didn't think watching her was doing them or Kim any good. They sat on the floor by the toy box.

'Why can't Mummy and Liam come home?' Kim asked with a sob. 'I miss Mummy.'

'Of course you do, love.' I was sure her father would have explained the situation, but clearly Kim needed more reassurance. 'Your mummy isn't well at present,' I said gently, taking her hand in mine. 'She's staying in hospital so the doctors can make her better.'

'What's wrong with Mummy? Daddy said she was ill, but that you couldn't see she was ill because it was inside. Not like if you get a rash or have a cold. You can see those.'

'That's right,' I said. 'Mummy has an illness that has made her very unhappy. Perhaps you've seen her crying and staying in bed?'

Kim nodded. 'And she said some horrible things to Daddy, Gran and me. Daddy said that was because she was unwell.'

'Yes, that's right. So Mummy is staying in hospital while the doctors make her better. They'll give her some medicine and then when she comes home she'll be your old mummy again.' Adrian glanced over and I threw him a reassuring smile.

'Is it Liam's fault Mummy is ill?' Kim suddenly asked, wiping her eyes on her hand. I passed her a tissue. I guessed she'd either made this connection from something she'd overheard, or her father had tried to explain her mother's illness, which was very difficult for a child to understand.

'No, it's not Liam's fault,' I said. 'When a woman has a baby lots of changes happen inside her body. They are caused by hormones, and sometimes some women have a bad reaction to all the hormones and changes. It's no one's fault. It's just something that happens, and once the doctors know they can put it right.'

'Like when I eat strawberries, I come up in a rash?' Kim asked, brightening a little.

I smiled. 'Yes, it is a bit like that. You had a reaction to eating strawberries.'

'Mummy says I mustn't eat strawberries, but Gran forgot and gave me some. I don't think Mummy should have any more babies if it makes her ill.'

'Well, if your mummy does have another baby the doctors will know what to do next time to stop her from being ill,' I said. 'It's nothing for you to worry about. Your daddy and gran are making sure your mummy is well looked after and has all the help she needs.'

'I heard Daddy and Gran talking last night,' Kim said, her brow furrowing. 'They thought I was asleep. I think they were arguing, because Daddy's voice sounded angry. He told Gran she should have told him sooner about the things Mummy was saying and doing. You know, the angry and frightening things she said sometimes. But I don't want Daddy telling off Gran. I don't like it.'

'Your daddy was very worried last night, and tired,' I said. 'Sometimes when people are worried and tired they can say things they don't really mean, and they are sorry afterwards. Your daddy and gran are friends this morning, aren't they?' She nodded. 'So don't worry. Is there anything else you want to ask me?'

'I hope Mummy and Liam can come home soon.'

'I think it will take a while,' I said. 'The doctors will want to make sure your mummy is completely better, but your daddy is hoping to take you to see her and Liam tomorrow.'

She nodded and managed a small smile. 'I know. He told me that.'

'Good girl.' I took a fresh tissue and wiped away the last of her tears. 'Are you ready for some breakfast now? I'm going to make a cooked breakfast.'

'I'm not really hungry,' she said.

'What about some cereal or toast or a piece of fruit?' She shook her head. 'I think you need something.'

'Can I have a banana, please?' she said quietly.

'Of course. And perhaps you'll have something else when it's ready. Now, you could show Adrian and Paula the toys and books you've brought with you while I make breakfast.'

Kim picked up her rucksack and opened it as Adrian and Paula moved closer for a better look. I left the three of them sitting in a circle on the floor as Kim proudly showed them a new book and a game of Guess Who? In the kitchen it wasn't long before Toscha was purring around my legs as the enticing smell of bacon rose from the grill. I cooked extra in case Kim changed her mind and wanted some, and I also slipped a rasher into Toscha's bowl. I scrambled eggs, lightly fried some sliced tomatoes and popped some bread in the toaster. Once it was all ready I called everyone to the table and told Kim there was extra if she wanted some, but she just had a banana and a drink of milk. She was quiet at the table but did say that her daddy liked a cooked breakfast at the weekend too when he had time to eat it.

After breakfast the children played first in the house and then in the garden. I took out drinks and a small snack of cheese and biscuits mid-morning, and Kim had some. She asked a couple of times during the morning if her daddy had telephoned and I said I thought it was too soon, but that we could hear the telephone ring from the garden. Although Kim hadn't eaten much breakfast, she ate a reasonable lunch of cheese pasta and salad, and after lunch I suggested we go to our local park. Kim knew the park from living in the same street; her parents took her there. It was about a fifteen-minute walk. Just before we left – at a little before two o'clock – Andy telephoned.

'The paperwork for the transfer has only just been completed,' he said. 'So we'll be leaving St Mary's shortly to go to the mother-and-baby unit. I'll phone you once Laura is settled and before we leave to come home. Can I speak to Kim, please?'

'Yes, of course.'

I passed the handset to her and she listened carefully while her daddy spoke. He must have told her something about her mother, for she asked, 'Can I speak to her?' She was silent again and then replied, 'Tell Mummy and Liam I love them.' She then said goodbye, replaced the handset in its cradle and looked at me with a small smile. 'Mummy told Daddy to tell me she loves me loads. And I'm definitely going to see her tomorrow.'

'That's fantastic,' I said. I guessed Laura was less distraught now or Andy wouldn't have confirmed the visit.

Our trip to the park was a success. Adrian and Kim played on all the apparatus while I took Paula into the adjacent toddler section, which had smaller swings, a low seesaw and rocking horses. I bought us all a drink, and ice creams for the children, from the park café, and it was about four o'clock when we started for home. The children were pleasantly tired from playing in the park and, once home, collapsed on the sofa. I let them watch some television while I fed Toscha and made our dinner. I didn't know what time Andy and Geraldine would be returning to collect Kim, so I was carrying on my day as usual.

It was a little after six o'clock and we'd just finished eating when Andy telephoned again. 'Laura is settled in the unit,' he said. 'It's a nice place. We'll be leaving soon. We should be with you at about seven o'clock. I won't speak to Kim now, but tell her we're on our way and Mummy sends her love.'

'I will,' I said. Andy sounded far less stressed.

I told Kim what her father had said and she looked at the clock. 'That's about an hour,' I said.

She returned to the game she was playing with Adrian and I took Paula up for her bath and bed. It was a while before Paula settled, but Andy was later than he'd thought and didn't arrive until 7.30 p.m. By that time I was downstairs again in the living room, watching Adrian and Kim playing another game of Guess Who? Kim came with me to answer the front door, eager to see her father again. Geraldine was with him.

'Come in,' I welcomed.

Kim fell into her father's arms. 'I've missed you,' she said.

'I've missed you too,' he said, scooping her up and kissing her cheek.

'I've missed you more,' Kim said, covering his cheek in kisses.

Geraldine looked on, slightly disapproving of this open display of affection. I thought she may have been brought up differently, where the expression of feelings and emotions wasn't encouraged.

'Can I finish my game of Guess Who?' Kim asked her father as he set her down.

'Yes, as long as it doesn't take too long.'

'Would you like a tea or a coffee?' I asked as we went down the hall to the living room.

'No, I'm fine, thanks, Cathy,' Andy said. 'What about you, Mum?'

'No, thank you,' she said stiffly. Perhaps she wanted to go straight home.

Geraldine and Andy sat on the sofa and I took an easy chair as Kim returned to finish the game. She and Adrian were perched on stools either side of the coffee table. From where I was sitting I could see the game from both sides. Kim was clearly winning, but I didn't say anything.

'So the transfer to the mother-and-baby unit went all right then?' I asked Andy and Geraldine.

'Yes,' Andy said. 'It's a lovely place, set in the grounds of a teaching hospital. There are only six bedrooms and each one is like a small studio flat, with a bed, cot, baby-changing facilities, shelves, carpet and curtains. There's a call button in each room if the woman needs help and they are supported and monitored day and night. They share a kitchen, bathroom and laundry room. And there's a communal lounge with a television. The staff are very friendly and there's always at least two nurses on duty. The doctor and psychiatrist are on call and they see the patients regularly. It's not home, obviously, but much better than the hospital, and of course Laura can have Liam with her. She was so pleased to see him this morning.'

'I bet she was,' I said.

'We had a short meeting with the doctor before we left. I'll see him and other members of the care team next week for an update after the assessment. They encourage family to be involved, so we can visit any afternoon and evening. But I have to work and they understand that. We'll spend all tomorrow afternoon there, but Mum doesn't drive, so next week we'll have to go as soon as I'm home from work.'

Kim looked up at her father. Although she'd been concentrating on the game, I knew she'd been taking in every word. 'Am I going to visit Mummy in the evening as well?' she asked, concerned.

'Yes, of course, love,' Andy said. 'That's as important as me seeing her.'

'It's going to be a lot of driving for you, going every night after work,' Geraldine said to him.

Andy shrugged. 'It can't be helped, Mum. I'll leave work early. They'll understand. The average stay in the unit is about two months, so hopefully Laura won't be in for long, although women can stay for up to twelve months if necessary.'

Kim was looking serious again. 'Twelve months is a year, Daddy,' she said.

'Yes, but Mummy will be better before then,' he said.

Reassured, Kim returned her attention to the game.

'The staff are very supportive,' he said to me. 'They're specialists and know how to deal with odd or distressing behaviour. Mum and I feel far more positive now than we did yesterday. Laura's a bit drowsy from the medication, but the doctor explained that it would be adjusted and then reduced as she recovers.'

I nodded. 'Are you sure you wouldn't like a tea or coffee?' I offered.

'No, thank you, we must be going,' Geraldine said.

'Once Kim has finished her game, Mum,' Andy replied firmly. I saw Geraldine's lips tighten.

'When you see Laura tomorrow please give her my love,' I said. 'I've bought her a few chocolates.' I passed him the box I'd bought on the way back from the park.

'Thank you, that's kind of you,' Andy said, and Geraldine nodded stiffly.

'Do you want me to tell Fran what's happened?' I asked. 'She's a close friend of Laura's and she's been worried about her.'

Geraldine looked pointedly at Andy, cautioning him that she shouldn't be told, but Andy said, 'Yes, Laura's mentioned Fran, and I've met her a couple of times. Please explain, and tell her Laura will phone her when she feels up to it.'

'I will,' I said. 'And if Laura would like a visit from me, do let me know.'

'I will. Although I'm hoping she won't be in for long.'

Geraldine was sitting upright with a sanctimonious, disapproving look on her face, but gone were the days when mental-health problems went unacknowledged and the sufferer was shut away. Of course Fran, as Laura's friend, would want to know how she was, and doubtless she'd want to visit her too, just as I did.

'Winner!' Kim cried, revealing the last tile on the game.

'Well done,' I said. 'Well played, both of you.'

Geraldine immediately stood, eager to be off, and told Kim to quickly help pack away the game.

'It's all right,' I said. 'I'll do it later.'

Andy and Kim also stood and I saw them out. It was nearly eight-thirty and time for Adrian to go to bed. Adrian is a sensitive child, but like many boys he often hides his feelings. It wasn't until I was lying on his bed beside him and we were having our little chat last thing at night that he confessed something that had been worrying him. Even then, he didn't come straight to the point.

'Is it only mummies with very young babies who have what Kim's mummy has?' he asked.

'Yes,' I said.

'So you wouldn't have to go into hospital? Paula's too old.'

'No. It wouldn't happen to me now.'

'Are you sure?' he asked. 'Because Daddy is working away and there wouldn't be anyone here to look after us like Kim's daddy is doing.'

'Adrian,' I said, hugging him, 'stop worrying. If I had to go into hospital for any reason, your daddy would come straight home. And what about your nana and grandpa? Have you forgotten them? They'd look after you if I wasn't well, wouldn't they?'

'Oh yes, silly me,' he said with an embarrassed smile.

'I'm glad you told me what was on your mind,' I said, holding him close.

But I was reminded how easily a young child could worry and fret, even if they felt secure and well loved.

CHAPTER FOURTEEN

GINA

On Sunday we went to my parents' house for the day. We tend to take it in turns – they come to us and then we go to them. They're the archetypal loving grandparents who dote on their grandchildren and spoil them with their time and affection. They also welcome into their home and hearts any child or children I am fostering. As was usual for a Sunday, Mum cooked a full roast for dinner, followed by her delicious homemade apple pie with melt-in-your-mouth pastry, served with lashings of warm custard. We ate ourselves to a standstill. The weather wasn't so good, but we managed a short walk after dinner and then spent the rest of the afternoon playing games indoors. My parents have endless enthusiasm and patience for even the most trivial and repetitive of children's games, whether it is pushing a line of toy cars around and around the living-room floor, creating domino runs and watching them fall, or role-playing superheroes – Batman and Robin, and so forth.

We left around six o'clock after a sandwich tea and returned home in plenty of time for John's phone call from America. He spoke to Adrian first, then Paula and me. His contract had eight weeks to run and then he would be home, hopefully for good. Five minutes after we'd finished speaking to him the phone rang again. 'We're popular tonight,' I said to Adrian as I picked up the handset in the living room. It was Shelley.

'Hi, love, great to hear from you,' I said. 'How are you both?'

'Fantastic. Couldn't be better.' She sounded really upbeat. 'I thought you'd like to know how my visit to Carol's went.'

'Yes, indeed. I have been wondering.'

'It was perfect. Carol is lovely, just like I remember her. She was so pleased to see me, and so were her family. They were all there when we arrived and they kissed and hugged Darrel and me as we went in like we were family. I said I was sorry that I hadn't kept in touch, but they were OK about that. They said they'd often thought about me and wondered how I was doing. I was really touched. Carol is still fostering and she's looking after a really stroppy teenager at present, Chantelle. She was there and she had a right face on her. She's fourteen and reminded me of how I was at her age. I told her she needed to lighten up and appreciate all Carol was doing for her. Carol was nearly in tears when I said that.'

I knew exactly how Carol must have felt.

'Chantelle said she wanted a baby like me, so when Carol was out of the room I gave her a good talking to. I told her that although I love Darrel loads I wish I'd waited to have him until I had a career and flat of my own. I don't know if she was listening, but I had to say something. I know how she feels – that having a baby will make you feel loved – but it's not the answer, and I told her how difficult it was bringing up a child alone.'

'That was sensible,' I said.

'Maybe she was listening, I don't know. Carol's own kids are all grown up and her eldest daughter was there with her fiancé. They're both teachers and they're getting married next year. She said I could go to her wedding, as long as I kept in touch. Which of course I will do.' Shelley chuckled. 'I feel like I've got a family. I've never had a family of my own. Carol even said I could go there next Christmas. I know it's a long way off – seven months – but I'm already looking forward to it. I told her Darrel and I had spent Christmas alone last year and she was sad and said that would never happen again. I'm going to start buying one present a week for Christmas. I can afford that and I want to give them all a little something.'

'That's very kind of you,' I said. 'Although I'm sure Carol won't expect it.'

'No, she was over the moon with the box of chocolates I gave her. Thank goodness I got back in touch. Thanks to you.'

'Thanks to you,' I said, 'for making that phone call. Well done.'

'I've made another important phone call too,' Shelley said, bubbling with excitement. 'To the lady who runs the choir.'

'Excellent. Tell me what happened.'

'I'm going for the first time next week. It took me a while to pluck up the courage to phone, but Jenny, the choir mistress, sounded really nice. It's not an audition; you just have to go each week and be able to sing. Jenny said they could do with some more young voices in the choir, as some of their members are getting on a bit.' She laughed. 'It's Tuesday. I'm nervous, but I will go. I've promised myself I will.'

'Good. I'm sure they'll be really pleased to have you, Shelley. You've got a beautiful voice. Are you all right for a sitter for Darrel?'

'Yes. My friend is going to stay with him. It's only from seven o'clock till nine, so I won't be too long. I'm nervous, but I'm also looking forward to singing with others. Do you and Adrian still sing the lullabies?'

'I wouldn't call it singing,' I said with a laugh. 'But we do our best. We always think of you and Darrel when we hum Brahms's "Lullaby".'

'That's nice. We think of you too. Darrel is here beside me. Can he speak to Adrian? He's learning to use the phone.'

'Yes of course.'

I passed the handset to Adrian.

'Hello,' Adrian said.

There was a long pause before Darrel said hello, and thereafter the conversation was rather one-sided, with Adrian, that much older and more confident in using the telephone, doing most of the talking. After a few minutes they said goodbye. Not wanting to be left out, Paula asked to 'speak' to Darrel too, so Shelley put him on again. There was silence. 'Say hello to Darrel,' I encouraged.

'Hello,' she said in a small voice.

'Hello,' Darrel replied.

Satisfied that she'd spoken on the phone, she returned the handset to me and I finished talking to Shelley and wished her good luck for Tuesday.

'Thanks,' she said. 'I'll keep in touch.'

And I was sure she meant it.

I wasn't expecting to hear any more from Andy until Laura felt well enough to have friends visit her, when I hoped Andy or Geraldine would remember to tell me. Neither was I expecting Geraldine to go out of her way to give me updates on Laura's progress, although it would have been nice. When she brought Kim to school on Monday morning she managed a nod in my direction, while Kim smiled and waved at us. Once the children had gone into school Geraldine, as usual, walked swiftly out of the playground ahead of everyone else, while I stayed behind to talk to Fran. I asked her if Laura had telephoned her again and when she said no I explained that at the weekend Laura and Liam had been admitted to a mother-and-baby unit, where Laura was being treated for acute post-natal depression, and that Andy would let us know how she was getting on.

'Oh, the poor dear,' Fran said, immediately concerned. 'I'll visit her as soon as I can.'

I explained that the unit was some distance away and Andy was going to let us know when Laura felt up to having friends visit.

'OK. I'll give him a ring later and see how she is,' Fran said. 'And if there is anything I can do to help. I'll ask him for the address so I can send some flowers and a get-well card.' Which was a really nice thought. 'I hope she's better very soon.'

'Yes,' I agreed. 'Andy said she was being well looked after.'

Talking about Laura wasn't playground gossip as Geraldine had suggested; friends are naturally concerned when someone is unwell and rally together in an emergency. I thought how pleased Laura would be to know her friends were thinking about her and to receive a get-well card and flowers from Fran.

* * *

I had it in my mind that if Geraldine hadn't told me by the end of the week how Laura was doing then I would summon my courage and ask her. Approaching Geraldine felt a little like going to see the bank manager or headmistress. I wasn't expecting Andy to telephone me with an update – he'd be far too busy going to work, dashing home and then driving backwards and forwards to visit Laura each evening. However, that Monday afternoon, as I walked down our street to collect Adrian from school and we neared number 53, a woman I hadn't seen before came out. Early fifties, I guessed, with fair, shoulder-length wavy hair, she was wearing a pretty floral summer dress with a pale blue cardigan. She continued someway ahead of us to the bottom of the road. I didn't know who she was and I didn't give it much thought until I saw her again in the playground. Perhaps she was another friend of Laura's – a parent with a child at the school – although I couldn't remember seeing her here before. But then when Kim came out of school she rushed to her and greeted her with a big hug.

'That's Kim's other gran,' Adrian told me.

'Oh, I see. Laura's mother. That's nice. I expect she's come to help.'

'Kim told me at playtime she might be coming,' Adrian said. 'She was well excited. She likes this gran more than the other one.'

As I looked over I could see how at ease Kim was with Laura's mother. They were holding hands now, both of them smiling and chatting as they crossed the playground towards the main gate. There was a relaxed lightness in Kim's step that I hadn't seen on her recent walks to and from school when she'd been rushed in and out of the playground by

Geraldine. Kim was looking at us as we waited for our turn to go through the gates, proud to be with her gran, then she whispered something to her. She turned and looked at me.

'Hello,' I said with a smile. 'I'm Cathy, a friend of Laura's.'

'Hi, so pleased to meet you,' she said. 'Kim's just told me who you are. You live in the same street, don't you?'

'Yes, that's right.'

'I'm Gina, Laura's mother. Andy mentioned that Kim had spent Saturday with you. Thanks for helping out.'

'You're welcome. How is Laura?'

'Comfortable, as they say,' Gina said. 'I haven't seen her yet. I'm going this evening. I phoned her earlier. She sounded a bit groggy, but that would be the tablets.' I nodded. 'Not sure why no one thought to tell me about all this sooner, but at least I'm here now, and I'll be staying for as long as necessary. I've sent Geraldine home for a rest,' she added with a smile.

We paused at the kerb and then all crossed the road together. Paula began agitating to be let out of the stroller. 'I usually let her walk from here,' I explained to Gina, stopping the stroller. 'It takes us a while, so do go on ahead if you want to.'

'It's OK. There's no rush. Andy won't be home until five and I've got dinner ready.' She smiled at Paula as I let her out, and then we continued walking up the street with Kim and Adrian slightly in front.

'You foster, don't you?' Gina asked me.

'Yes, although I haven't got a child at present.'

'Andy mentioned it when he telephoned me on Saturday evening. He said Kim had stayed with you a couple of times and you were a foster carer. It's a nice thing to do, but it must be difficult to say goodbye.'

'Yes, I'm afraid that's the downside of fostering,' I said. 'Although some of the children keep in touch.'

'Good, must be nice to hear how they are doing.'

'Yes,' I agreed. 'It is.'

I'd taken an immediate liking to Gina. She came across as warm and open, with a bubbly personality that reached out to others, and she was very easy to talk to. I could see the family likeness between her, Laura and Kim, and of course she was a very different character to Geraldine, who had a far more serious demeanour and kept her distance.

'Do you know Geraldine well?' Gina asked as we walked.

'Not really. I've only known her since Laura has been unwell.'

'I have to bite my tongue sometimes,' Gina confessed. 'But I was hurt that no one contacted me sooner, when Laura started to slide. I work, but you take time off when there's a family emergency, don't you? When I told my boss my daughter and baby grandson were in hospital he said I could take as much time off as I needed. I caught the train down this morning and I'll stay until Laura is well on the way to recovery. But I feel guilty that I didn't spot the signs sooner. I should have done, having been through something similar myself. Anyway, she's in the best place now.'

'Yes, she is,' I said. 'They'll soon have her right, I'm sure. Please give her my love when you see her this evening. And let me know if there is anything I can do.'

'Thanks, Cathy. I'll tell you tomorrow how she's getting on.'

* * *

The following morning Gina was already in the playground with Kim when I arrived with Adrian and Paula, and as soon as they saw us they came straight over, both of them smiling.

'I saw my mummy and brother last night,' Kim told Adrian happily, and they began talking between themselves.

'Laura was so pleased to see us,' Gina said. 'It made me cry. She wanted lots and lots of hugs and held my hand like a little child for nearly all the time we were there. She seemed to want me rather than Andy, but I think he understood. She's obviously got a long way to go yet, but Andy could see an improvement already. She gets confused sometimes and we had to explain why she and Liam were in the unit, as she wanted to come home. She said some other things, too, that showed she wasn't completely with it. After we'd left, Andy and I explained to Kim that it was part of Mummy's illness, and that it would go once she got better.'

I glanced at Kim. 'Yes, it must be difficult for her to understand.'

Gina nodded. 'Unfortunately, Laura's had to stop breast-feeding, because of the medication getting through to the baby. It's a pity, but it can't be helped. She's on quite a strong dose at present. And she tires easily – I think that's from the tablets too – so we didn't stay too late. We'll see her again this evening and every evening. But how things have changed since I was in hospital! No long psychiatric wards now. Her room is lovely, bright and airy, and she's encouraged to mix with the other mums. They have individual therapy, group therapy and occupational therapy, so there's a lot going on. They're expected to look after their babies too, although the nurses help when necessary. Andy and I have to go to a team meeting there on Thursday afternoon, so Andy is going to take time off work.'

'Let me know if you want me to collect Kim from school,' I offered.

'Thanks, Cathy, but Andy has already said he's going to ask his mother. It's important she's still involved.'

'Yes, indeed,' I said.

'I told Laura you sent your love, and she said to thank you for the chocolates. She's worrying about Fran. She wants me to tell her that she's really sorry she hasn't been in touch and she'll phone as soon as she can. Do you know who Fran is?'

I looked around the filling playground and spotted her talking to another mother. 'Over there,' I said, pointing.

'Thanks. I'll catch her now if you don't mind. Then I'm going into school to see Kim's teacher. Andy and I think she should know what's going on in case Kim is upset in school.'

'Yes, good idea.' I knew from fostering that the school liked to be informed if there was a crisis in the family so they could help support the child in school.

'I'll see you later then,' Gina said. And, taking Kim's hand, she went over to speak to Fran.

Thereafter Gina made a point of seeing me every day to tell me how Laura was doing, either on the way to school, in the playground or walking home from school. We didn't just talk about Laura, but lots of other things as well. Gina liked a chat and was very easy to get on with. We had a laugh too. She obviously didn't know anyone in the area apart from her family and she said she was pleased to have my company. At home that week I continued with my dissertation whenever I had the chance, and made the most of fine days by playing outside with Paula and taking her to the park. It was early July now and like many summers in the UK the weather was changeable, with a beautiful, warm sunny day that seemed like it could go on forever followed by a drop in temperature and thick cloud cover that saw us reaching for our jackets and umbrellas.

On Thursday afternoon Geraldine collected Kim from school, as Andy and Gina were at the meeting at the unit. She gave me a perfunctory glance as she rushed in and out of the playground. Then on Friday morning Gina was in the playground again and she told me that the meeting the previous day with the mental-healthcare team had been very useful. They'd gone over Laura's healthcare plan and had answered their questions. Some of the team would continue to support Laura once she was discharged from the unit and went home.

'It was a lot of rushing around for Andy,' Gina admitted. 'After the meeting we came back, he gobbled down his dinner, which Geraldine had ready, and then she went with him and Kim to see Laura while I cleared up. He was exhausted when he got back. It's a pity neither Geraldine nor I drive. It'll be less of a rush at the weekend when we're all going.'

That afternoon when Kim came out of school she was carrying a giant get-well card for her mother, which the class had made and all signed. It was a lovely thought and I could see how proud Kim was. Not only would Laura appreciate it, but it would also give Kim a boost to know she had the best wishes of her class. Although Kim appeared to be coping, she must have been missing her mother and Liam dreadfully. We all walked home together, with Kim and Adrian carrying the card between them.

Adrian, Paula and I had a relaxing weekend with a trip to the park on Saturday and games at home on Sunday. Sometimes it's nice to just chill out at weekends, otherwise they can become as hectic as weekdays with shopping, outings and visiting family. The long summer holidays were in three weeks' time, but I hadn't booked for us to go away as John wouldn't be home until the end of the school holidays, so I was planning on days out instead, including a day trip to the coast. On Monday Gina and Kim came out of their house just as we passed on the way to school, so we all walked together. Having spent a large part of the weekend with her mother and Liam, Kim was full of it.

'My brother is growing bigger,' she told us. 'And he's awake more now. I gave him his bottle and I helped one of the other mothers too. Her baby has a trainer cup and Liam will have one when he's older. Then my daddy helped Mummy cook a meal in the kitchen there and we all had dinner together at the table. When Mummy feels better we can go out.'

'Fantastic,' I said. 'You had a great weekend by the sound of it.' Then to Gina I said, 'So everything's going well?'

'Absolutely. I've started to see an improvement in Laura.'

That afternoon as I passed number 53 the front door opened again and Gina came out, but I could see straight away that she was worried and had probably been looking out for me. Her usual smiling face was tense. 'Are you all right?' I asked as she opened the gate to join me.

'Not really. I need to ask you something. You might know, as you deal with the social services.'

'I'll help if I can,' I said.

She fell into step beside me. 'You remember I told you that there was a social worker at that meeting last Thursday?'

'Yes.'

'Well, she telephoned me this afternoon. She says she has to visit us – to do a home visit.'

I nodded. 'That would be standard procedure,' I said.

'That's what she said, but I didn't like her tone. She told me Andy had to be there, and when I said I didn't think that would be possible, as he had to work, she got on her high horse. She said she had to see us all to write her report and that it was important we made the time. She also said she would have to look around the house during her visit. When I asked her why, she said it was part of the assessment, as she needed to be certain it was a safe environment for when Liam returned. I went ballistic. How dare she! Of course it's a safe environment. Who does she think she is?'

'Gina, it's standard practice,' I said. 'Don't worry. She just phrased it badly.'

'Do you think so?' Gina asked, turning to me. 'It's worried me. It was like she was suggesting he might not be safe with us. So you think I should let her snoop around the house then?'

'Yes. Show her around and then she'll be able to write in her report that all is well. The social services have to be ultra-careful where children are concerned. I know it feels like an invasion of your privacy. When I'm fostering the child's social worker always looks at the child's bedroom at every visit, and then at my annual review the whole house is checked.'

'You're good to put up with all that,' Gina said. 'I'm sure I wouldn't. I'll tell Andy what you said. If he can't get time off work I'll ask Geraldine to come round. We'll present a united front.'

While I liked Gina, I could see she was feisty – not necessarily what was required when the social worker visited. I hesitated and chose my words carefully. 'Gina, my advice would be to cooperate fully. Remember, the social worker is just doing her job. Answer her questions, show her around and I'm sure all will be fine.'

CHAPTER FIFTEEN

EVERLEY

It is sometimes said that social workers are 'damned if they do and damned if they don't', meaning that they'll be criticized whatever course of action they take. I knew that the social worker was following procedure to ensure that Liam and Kim were safe at home. I also knew that it was in everyone's interest to cooperate. So often when the social services are involved a 'them and us' situation develops, with the family on one side, feeling threatened and going on the defensive, and the social worker, who in this instance may not have been sufficiently diplomatic, on the other. I hoped that once Gina had calmed down she would feel less hostile.

On Tuesday morning as we all walked to school together Gina told me that Andy had managed to book the following afternoon off work so he could be present when the social worker visited at one o'clock. Gina said they'd also asked Geraldine to be present. 'She's helped a lot,' Gina said. 'So it's important she's there. We want the social worker to see that we're all working together.' Which was a sensible approach. I also thought that having Andy and Geraldine present, who were more reserved in temperament, would be a calming influence on Gina, so there would be less chance of her going 'ballistic', as she'd put it, at the social worker as she had done on the telephone. She was still quite indignant that the visit had to happen at all.

On Wednesday morning as we walked to school I wished Gina luck and told her again not to worry, that it was procedure and everything would be fine. That afternoon I had one eye on the clock as I made lunch for Paula and me and one o'clock approached – the time the social worker was due to arrive at number 53. Then I spent a fair bit of the afternoon wondering how the visit was going in between doing some housework and playing with Paula. I was expecting to see Gina in the playground that afternoon, but it was Andy who strode in to collect Kim. Dressed in a suit, with his tie loosened, he saw me and came straight over.

'So you're meeting Kim today,' I said with a smile. 'She will be pleased.' I knew how delighted children were when fathers who were usually at work suddenly came to meet them.

'Yes,' he said absently, frowning. 'It'll give Mum and Gina a chance to recover. We had the social worker visit this afternoon. She's only just left.'

'How did it go?' I asked.

He rubbed his forehead. 'Not too good, to be honest. It feels as though we're being investigated – some of the questions she asked. Mum was in tears at one point.'

'Why?' I asked, shocked.

'Mum believes it's her fault all this has happened, although I keep telling her it's not. The social worker asked a lot of questions around why we hadn't sought medical help for Laura sooner. We tried to explain that we thought Laura would get better like she had last time, after having Kim, but the social worker said her symptoms were less severe then, and even so her recovery had taken almost a year. She said she had concerns that if Liam and Laura came home and Laura needed help we would "cover it up again". That was the term she used. Mum took it personally. Granted, she didn't want people to know, but she thought she was doing what was best. And the way the social worker was talking it sounded as though Laura and Liam might not come home – well, not in the short term at least. She has to complete an assessment first.'

'An assessment is normal practice,' I offered, trying to reassure Andy, for although he was calm he was clearly very worried.

'That's what the social worker said,' Andy replied, digging his hands into his pockets. 'She asked who would be the main caregiver when Laura and Liam came home, as Gina would have to return home to go to work. Mum said she would be, so the social worker questioned her again about seeking appropriate help for Laura if it was needed. She implied that as Mum had hidden the seriousness of Laura's condition before, even from me, she couldn't be trusted to get help if Laura needed it in the future. That made Mum cry.'

'Poor Geraldine. It sounds as though it wasn't put very well at all.'

'The social worker did apologize. She said she hadn't meant to upset Mum, but she had to be certain Laura would receive appropriate help and support from professionals in the future if it was necessary.' I nodded. 'Then she started talking about concerns around Liam. She said that Laura's medical condition had included hallucinating about the baby and this had placed him at risk. I told her Liam hadn't ever been at risk as Mum had slept downstairs with him when things got really bad. I don't think that helped. She wrote it down, and then she asked about the impact Laura's illness was having on Kim, and we said Kim had been protected as much as possible.'

'Yes, that's very true,' I said.

'But as she pointed out, Kim must have seen at least some of what was going on, living in the same house. She then started talking about bonding. She said some mothers with severe postnatal depression or psychosis fail to bond properly with their children, especially if treatment is delayed. Mum was close to tears again, blaming herself, but I said Laura and Kim were very close, and she wrote that down. Then she said she wanted to see Kim this afternoon, but I said we had to do a quick turn-around to go and see Laura and Liam. So she's going to see her on Friday after school. It seems she's going to be talking to the school too.'

'That's usual,' I said. 'And the school will confirm what you've said – that Kim is a happy and well-adjusted child.'

'I guess,' Andy said, no less worried. 'But the social worker said they might consider applying to the court for a supervision order, which would include Kim. If they got it, we would be monitored by the social services for up to two years. Gina had a right go at her then and said she'd be better off leaving us alone and spending her time working with families who were abusing their children instead.'

'It sounds as though the social worker has put it all very badly,' I said, my reassurance now sounding less effective.

Andy sighed. 'I asked her how long she thought it would be until Laura and Liam could come home and she said she didn't know. It would be a decision made by the mental healthcare team – of which she is a part. Gina was fuming by then and said that if it went on too long she'd bring Laura and Liam home anyway. The social worker said that although Laura was in hospital voluntarily, if she tried to discharge herself and Liam before she was considered well, the social services could apply for an order under the Mental Health Act to keep Laura in hospital and even take Liam into care. Mum was in tears again.' He stopped.

The Klaxon had sounded while he'd been talking and now the children were streaming out. 'Here comes Kim,' he said. 'Mum or Gina will tell you what I've forgotten.' He set his face to a smile, ready to greet Kim, and she ran into his arms. 'You won't mind if we dash off,' he said. 'We're going straight over to see Laura.'

'No, of course not, you go on ahead,' I said. 'Give my love to Laura and try not to worry.'

He nodded stiffly, a little like his mother did, but I could see the pain behind his eyes. His family was under threat and he was very worried. So was I, from what he'd said. After I'd hugged Adrian we began home, and I thought of what Andy had said and how different his family's experience in dealing with the social services had been compared to Shelley's when she'd been suffering from postnatal depression. From what she'd told me her social worker had been highly sensitive, non-threatening and very supportive in getting her the help she needed. I knew Shelley's condition had been less serious than Laura's, but even so I felt that Laura's social worker had been heavy-handed. Families are very fragile at times of crisis and can easily misinterpret what they're being told, seeing a threat where there is none intended. Social workers don't always realize the power they hold, and as a result can unintentionally scare the family, causing a lot of unnecessary worry.

Having said that, what Laura's social worker had told them was true. By not seeking medical help for Laura sooner Andy and Geraldine had unwittingly placed Liam in danger, and of course the social worker had to be certain that if Laura and Liam came home it couldn't happen again. The word *if* haunted me, as I was sure it did Andy, Gina and Geraldine. Here was a loving family who now faced the possibility of having their children taken into care and their mother sectioned under the Mental Health Act. If only they'd sought help sooner, I was sure none of this would have happened.

The following morning Gina was still seething, although she didn't say anything until the children were in school. 'Did you know the social services hold meetings about families without any family member being there?' she asked, her eyes blazing.

'Yes.'

'It's shocking. How do you know that what they're saying isn't a pack of lies? It shouldn't be allowed.'

'There does need to be more transparency in the system,' I agreed.

'Andy's going to get some legal advice. Meetings about us that we're not invited to! And now that bloody social worker – excuse my language – says she has to talk to Kim without us being there. We've tried to protect her as much as possible. How dare she?'

'It's normal practice, Gina,' I said tentatively. 'All the children in the family are usually seen by the social worker. When I'm fostering the child's social worker always spends time alone with the child in case they want to say something they might not feel comfortable saying in front of the carer.'

'But those are foster children who've been abused!' Gina said indignantly. 'Not one of your own who's loved and cared for.'

'As part of my annual review Adrian is asked what he thinks about fostering, without me being in the room,' I said. 'Paula will be asked, too, when she's old enough.'

'Little wonder they're short of foster carers!' Gina snapped.

'Did she look around the house?' I asked, on a lighter note.

'No. She didn't have time. She's going to do that on Friday, after she's seen Kim.'

'And how was Laura when you saw her last night?'

'All right,' Gina said, calming down. 'Obviously we didn't tell her what the social worker had said, and we hid how worried we are. She asked when you and Fran could visit, so she must be feeling a bit better. I said I wasn't sure, as you had the kids and your husband works away. It's an hour in the car. Visiting is any time after one.'

'Could I take Paula?' I asked.

'I don't see why not.'

'Adrian has been invited to a friend's for tea tomorrow,' I said. 'I wonder if I could visit her then. I don't have to be back to collect Adrian until six o'clock.'

'Give the unit a ring and check it's OK,' Gina said. 'Come into the house and I'll write down their details for you. I'll make us a coffee as well.'

'Thank you.'

We'd arrived outside number 53 and I explained to Paula that although we were going into baby Liam's house he wouldn't be there.

'Bay-bee Lee-am, Bay-bee Lee-am,' she said, a little disappointed.

Indoors, Gina showed us through to the living room and produced some toys for Paula to play with and then went into the kitchen to make coffee. It was strange being in Laura's home without her and Liam. I thought how difficult it must be for Kim when she came home from school not to have her mother or brother here. She was being taken to visit them each evening, but it wasn't the same as having your mum at home. The framed family photographs on the walls that had been there on my previous visits now seemed to underline that the family was separated. There were some smaller photographs of Laura cradling Liam propped on the mantelpiece, taken, I guessed, when Liam was a few days old – lovely pictures, but another stark reminder that they weren't here. Through the patio windows I could see the garden, which had been Laura's domain when she'd been well but was now starting to look unkempt. I guessed none of them had the time or inclination to tend it as Laura had done.

Gina told me a bit about Everley, the specialist mother-and-baby unit, as we talked and drank our coffee and Paula played. When I'd finished my coffee I said I needed to go as I had things to do. She wrote down the contact details of Everley and also the telephone number of their house, which I hadn't been given before. I think Gina would have liked me to stay longer, as she admitted she worried more when she was alone in the house and often walked into the High Street just to get out. I appreciated what she meant. With Laura and Liam not there the house felt like a mausoleum, with the images of loved ones displayed but no longer present.

At home I telephoned Everley and explained to the lady who answered that I was a friend of Laura's and would like to visit her the following afternoon, but that I would have to bring my fifteen-month-old daughter with me. She said that should be fine, but she'd need to check with Laura first. She took my name, address and telephone number and said that if I didn't hear anything further from her to assume it was all right to go. That afternoon in the playground I told Fran I was going to visit Laura the following day and I asked if she'd like to come, but it was too short notice for her to arrange childcare for her daughter after school, so she said she'd visit another day and to send Laura her best wishes.

No one from Everley called back, so by Friday morning I assumed my visit was going ahead. I saw the mother of the friend Adrian was going to have tea with in the playground and confirmed I would collect him from her house at six o'clock. On the way home I stopped off at our local supermarket to buy a bunch of flowers for Laura. I didn't put Paula down for her nap that morning in the hope that she would sleep in the car. An hour's journey can be tedious for a young child and I needed to concentrate on driving and finding my way there. I made us an early lunch and explained to Paula that we were going in the car to see Liam, and she clasped her hands together in delight. 'Bay-bee Lee-am, Bay-bee Lee-am.' Then she 'helped' me pack a bag of things she would need, including a change of nappy, her trainer cup, a small snack and some of her toys. Just after twelve-thirty we set off with my notes on the route and the flowers on the passenger seat beside me. I tuned the radio to a station playing soft classical music, guaranteed to send most children off to sleep, and five minutes later Paula's eyes had closed. She didn't wake until I pulled into the car park at the front of Everley.

It had been an easy journey. I'd known my way to the neighbouring town and from there the hospital, in the grounds of which Everley stood, had been clearly signposted. It was a two-storey 1950s brick building, which I guessed had originally served a different purpose. Now modernized, it was surrounded by a small fenced landscaped garden.

'We're here,' I said to Paula as she blinked and rubbed her eyes, still heavy with sleep.

'Bay-bee Lee-am,' she said, puzzled and peering out of her side window.

'Yes, we've come to see baby Liam but in a different home.'

I went round and opened her car door, undid the safety harness and helped her to clamber out. I'd put the stroller in the car but we didn't need it, as the main door was only a short walk away. With the bag looped over my shoulder, the flowers in one hand and holding Paula's hand with the other, we went to the wooden gate where I slid the bolt. A short, paved path led to the security-locked main door and I pressed the buzzer. No one answered, so I pressed it again, and then a female voice came through: 'Yes, can I help you?'

'I telephoned yesterday, Cathy Glass. I've come to see Laura –'

'Come in. I'll open the door.'

The security lock released and we went in. A nurse in a uniform of a white top and navy trousers greeted us. 'Could you sign the visitor's book, please? Laura is in the lounge, down that corridor on the left.'

'Thank you.' I could smell food, so I guessed someone was cooking their lunch.

With Paula toddling beside me we went down the corridor and I knocked on the door marked LOUNGE before opening it. Laura was sitting on the sofa with Liam in a bouncing cradle at her feet. She was alone and immediately stood and came over, smiling. 'Hello, Cathy. Thanks for coming.' She kissed my cheek and hugged me.

'You're looking very well. A few flowers,' I said, passing her the bunch. 'They match your blouse.'

She laughed, for the deep cerise of some of the flowers in the bouquet was the same shade as her top. 'Thank you so much. I'll put them in my room later.'

'This is a lovely place,' I said, glancing round. The lounge was spacious, bright and airy, and furnished with two sofas, bean bags, scatter cushions, bookshelves and a television and sound system, which stood on a cabinet. The gaily patterned curtains matched the cushions on the sofas.

'It's OK,' she said with a shrug. 'But it's not home. The other residents are in their rooms. I can show you my room later if you want.'

'Yes, I'd like that.'

Paula had toddled over to where Liam sat in his bouncing cradle and was kneeling beside him, peering at him intently. He looked a bit startled.

'Nice and gently,' I said to her, going over.

'Would you like a drink?' Laura asked. 'And I'll find a vase for the flowers.'

'Yes, please, if you're making one.'

'I need a drink. The tablets make me thirsty. Tea or coffee?'

'I don't mind. Whatever you're making.' I tensed and could have kicked myself as my thoughts flashed back to a similar scene at Laura's home when I'd given the same reply.

Then, unable to cope with making a choice between tea or coffee, Laura had gone to pieces.

But it was different now. 'Tea then,' she said easily. 'Can you watch Liam while I'm in the kitchen?'

'Yes, of course. Could Paula have some water as well, please?' I took the trainer cup from my bag and handed it to her.

I joined Paula on the floor beside Liam where we made some weird and wonderful coochie-cooing noises. He was a gorgeous baby, round-faced with big blue eyes. He grinned and gurgled contentedly, oblivious to the rocky start he'd had in life. At his age he wouldn't be missing home as Laura was; as long as he was warm, well fed and cared for he didn't mind where he was.

Laura returned with two mugs of tea and Paula's cup of water on a tray, which she placed on one of the small occasional tables. 'I've put the flowers in a vase,' she said. 'I'll take them up to my room later. Thanks again. Everyone is being so kind to me.'

I smiled. 'You're welcome.'

Paula drank some of her water and then squatted down beside Liam again as I sat next to Laura on the sofa. 'You don't take sugar, do you?' she said, passing me one of the mugs of tea.

'No. That's perfect, thanks.'

There was then an awkward silence as we both sipped our tea and occupied our gazes by watching the children.

'Liam's grown since the last time I saw him,' I said.

'Yes. He's doing well. They're very pleased with him here.'

There was another silence and then I commented on the weather and what a lovely view there was through the lounge window. Laura agreed. She didn't attempt to initiate conversation and if I'm honest it was a bit difficult, as I didn't know which subjects were safe and what I should avoid, which was silly really, I suppose. So I asked about Liam – if he slept well and so on, and I told Laura that Fran sent her best wishes and was hoping to visit soon. 'That's nice of her,' she said.

I mentioned that Adrian, Paula and I often walked to and from school with her mum (Gina) and Kim, and that Kim always told us what she'd been doing the evening before when she visited. 'It sounds as though she's a big help here,' I said as I finished the last of my tea.

'Yes. Kim's made friends with the other mothers. They all like her.'

I then said again how comfortable the lounge was, how easy the journey here had been and a bit about Kim and Adrian's school.

'The schools break up soon,' Laura said. 'I've told my doctor I want to be out of here and home in time for the summer holidays.'

I nodded. I didn't know how realistic this was – the end of term was only two weeks away. Laura seemed well enough in many respects; there was no sign of the gnawing anxiety and debilitating depression that had plagued her before coming here, yet there was still something. Her conversation was slow and faltering, and she'd lost spontaneity, which I guessed could be another side effect of the medication – slowing her thought processes as it calmed them. She seemed to be aware of this; a couple of times when she was trying to think of a word and it just wouldn't come she said, 'Sorry, my brain's stopped functioning.' She gave a small laugh.

'Mine stopped a while back too,' I said, and she smiled.

Presently Liam grew bored with being in the bouncing cradle and having Paula amuse him and he began to grizzle. Laura picked him up and soothed him. 'There, there,' she said, gently rocking him. He immediately stopped crying.

'Would you like to see my room now?' she offered. 'I usually put Liam in his cot for a sleep about now. But we need to return the cups to the kitchen first. House rules.'

I clipped the lid on Paula's trainer cup and put it in my bag and then, with Paula toddling beside me, I carried out the tray with the mugs as Laura carried Liam.

'Just leave it in there,' Laura said, nodding to a door marked KITCHEN. 'I'll wash them up later.'

I went in. There was no one else in the kitchen and I left the tray by the sink, with some other mugs waiting to be washed.

Laura's room was up one flight of stairs and, like the lounge, it was bright and well furnished. A single bed and a cot in white wood stood against one wall, with a matching white wooden chest of drawers and chair against the other. Laura's and Liam's clothes and personal belongings were dotted around the room, so it looked quite cosy. 'Have a seat while I change him,' Laura said, moving a baby shawl from the armchair.

I sat in the chair and Paula stood beside Laura watching, intrigued, as she laid Liam on a changing mat on the bed and saw to his nappy. 'He's going to have a little sleep now,' Laura told Paula when he was clean and dressed again. Laura carefully laid him in his cot and drew up the side. Paula peered through the wooden slats and Liam chuckled and waved his arms towards her. He didn't look like he was going to sleep to me. Laura perched on the bed and there was silence. 'It's a nice room,' I said. 'Do you sleep well?'

'Much better now, thank you,' she said. 'I still get anxious sometimes, especially that something might happen to him in the night – you know, a cot death. But some of the other mothers worry about that too.'

'I used to when they were little,' I admitted. 'Sometimes a baby's breathing is so shallow you can't see it. I used to give Adrian and Paula a little poke to make sure they were still breathing.'

Laura smiled. 'One woman here used to force herself to stay awake all night, she was so worried something would happen to her daughter – not only a cot death, but also other stuff, like she could hurt herself or be taken away. She's getting better now.'

Laura fell silent again and I had the feeling she was tiring, physically and mentally, more so than Liam, who was still chuckling and waving his arms at Paula. We'd been here for nearly an hour and an half and I thought we should probably leave soon. 'We'll go shortly,' I said. 'I expect you could do with a rest before your family visit tonight.'

'Yes, I sometimes have a lie down while he has a sleep,' she admitted. 'I do get tired. It's a side effect of the tablets. They're going to start to reduce the dose soon, so it should improve.'

'That's good,' I said. 'You look very well.'

'Thanks. I hope to be discharged soon.'

I told Paula we were going and to say goodbye to Liam. She blew him a kiss through the bars of the cot. Laura asked if we could see ourselves out, as she couldn't leave Liam in his cot unattended. We kissed goodbye and she stood at the door to her room and watched us go, and then called, 'Bye!' and gave a little wave as we turned into the stairwell.

'Bye. Take care, and see you soon,' I returned.

'Bye,' Paula called, and I heard Laura's door shut behind us.

Downstairs I signed out of the visitor's book. It was 3.05. School would be ending soon and Adrian would be getting excited about going to his friend's home to play and have tea. Gina would be on her way to school to collect Kim, and once home their social worker was coming to speak to Kim. Laura hadn't mentioned her visit, so I assumed they hadn't wanted to worry her with it. The social worker's visit was procedure, but it was important that the family cooperated and Gina kept her cool.

CHAPTER SIXTEEN

HOME AGAIN

Gina had given me Laura's home telephone number and I felt I now had a reason to use it. Having spent Friday afternoon and evening wondering/worrying how the social worker's visit had gone, I decided on Saturday morning that it was acceptable for me to telephone and ask without it seeming intrusive or like I was interfering. I think friends often have to make a judgement on whether to say nothing and wait for news or to step forward. I left it until ten o'clock to telephone – a reasonable time for a family to be up at the weekend. Andy answered.

'It's Cathy,' I said. 'I hope I haven't disturbed you but I was wondering how the social worker's visit went yesterday.'

'That's very thoughtful of you,' he said. 'It went well. We'd worried unnecessarily. She only talked to Kim for about fifteen minutes. Kim told us later that she'd asked about her mum and how she felt with her living away. Then she looked around the house. That was it, really. She was in and out in under an hour.'

'Good. I'm pleased.'

'So were we. And thanks for visiting Laura yesterday. She really appreciated it.'

'It was great to see her,' I said. 'She's looking well.'

'Yes. She's much improved. The healthcare team are meeting next week to decide if she is ready to come home. Fingers crossed. She'll still have to take tablets and attend therapy, but at least she'll be home.'

'That's fantastic,' I said. 'I'll look forward to seeing her again soon then. I won't keep you. I'm sure you've got lots to do, but do let me know if I can help out at all.'

'Thanks, Cathy. Have a good weekend.'

'And you.'

Great news, I thought. It was all very positive. The social worker's visit had gone well and Laura would hopefully be discharged soon. I was so pleased I'd telephoned. I could stop worrying and enjoy the weekend, and it was a busy weekend. An old friend of mine, now a single parent, came with her children on Saturday afternoon and stayed for tea, and then my parents came for lunch on Sunday. The weather was fine for the whole weekend and appeared settled, which boded well for the approaching school holidays. On Monday when I saw Gina in the playground she said she thought that Laura would be home by the end of term; they were just waiting for confirmation from the healthcare team. I could see how pleased she and Kim were.

That week the school staged an end-of-term production, an annual event where all the children dressed up and played a part. This year the production was a story about a journey into space, and the school hall was packed with the children's families and friends, who'd come to watch. Andy had taken the morning off work and he, Gina and Geraldine were seated a couple of rows behind us. Paula and my parents were with me. The children had been practising their lines for weeks and despite last-minute nerves their performances were amazing. I'm sure I wasn't the only parent in the audience to be misty-eyed as they watched their child stand proudly on the stage and deliver their well-rehearsed lines. At the end, all the children came on stage to take their final bow and the audience rose to give them a standing ovation, clapping, cheering and whistling. Then the head teacher said a few words about how well they'd done, thanked us all for coming and wished us a good summer holiday. Before we left the hall I introduced my parents to Kim's family, and then we went our separate ways. Andy was going to work, Gina and Geraldine to their respective homes, and Mum and Dad were coming back with Paula and me for some lunch before driving home.

The following Wednesday, with two days to go before the end of term, Adrian was beside himself with excitement at the thought of six whole weeks off school. Kim was excitedly looking forward to her mother's homecoming, although they were still waiting to hear when exactly this would be. I hoped it had definitely been decided that Laura *was* coming home or Kim would be bitterly disappointed. I knew from fostering how tempting it is to give a child who is continually asking when they can live with their mummy again the good news they crave, but I'd learned to be very cautious. I didn't ever tell a child I was fostering any news about seeing their family or going home until it was a hundred per cent certain and had been confirmed to me by their social worker, even if all the signs were positive. Perhaps it was because the arrangements for Laura's return home were vague that I had a sense of foreboding. Unfortunately my fears were confirmed later that morning when I answered the telephone to hear Gina upset and angry.

'Cathy, that bloody social worker has stopped Laura from coming home! Laura's just telephoned me. She's distraught. I've phoned Andy and he's going to Everley now to try to speak to the doctor. Laura was so upset she couldn't tell me properly what they'd said. Wait until I see that witch of a social worker. She'll get a piece of my mind. God knows what we're going to tell Kim. She'll be devastated.'

What could I say? *You should have waited until after the meeting and a definite date had been confirmed for Laura's home-coming before telling Kim?* But that wasn't going to help; the damage had been done.

'Gina, I am sorry,' I said. 'I suppose the social worker felt Laura wasn't ready to be discharged yet.'

'That's what Laura seemed to be saying, but the nurse thought she was ready to go home.' I couldn't comment. I had no idea what had taken place in the team meeting, but I did know that the social worker wouldn't have delayed Laura's discharge without a good reason.

'Gina, wait and see what Andy says when he's seen the doctor. It may be easier to explain to Kim when you have the reason for the delay. Have they given Laura a date when she will be going home?'

'I don't know. I don't think so. Laura was too upset to tell me.'

'I'd wait to see what Andy has to say. I know it's very disappointing, but Laura will be home at some point. It's just been delayed.'

'Because of that social worker!' Gina fumed. 'I'll have to tell Geraldine. I think I'll walk round to her place now rather than phone. I could do with some fresh air and we've been getting on better lately. Having to deal with all of this has brought us together.'

So that was one positive to come out of it, I thought.

That afternoon as I waited for Adrian to come out of school Andy arrived in the playground to collect Kim. Dressed in smart-casual clothes rather than his office suit, I guessed he'd gone home after seeing the doctor instead of returning to work. He saw me and came straight over.

'Gina told you what happened?' he asked.

'Yes. Did you manage to speak to the doctor?'

'No. But I did see the nurse in charge. She was at the team meeting too. Laura and I spoke to her. She's very reassuring and understanding. It seems that the main reason Laura's discharge has been delayed is because of issues with the transfer of her care. Although her social worker will be the same when she leaves Everley, the community mental health team will take over and be responsible for her once home. Because it's the start of the school summer holidays a lot of people are on leave and the community care team is running with a skeleton staff, so realistically there wouldn't be anyone available to support Laura and give her help if she needs it.'

'I see,' I said.

'I asked if the delay had anything to do with us not seeking help sooner, but the nurse said it hadn't and that Laura wasn't the only one to have their discharge delayed. Laura had blamed the social worker because she'd been the one to raise it at the meeting. They're going to review the situation in two weeks, so hopefully she'll be coming home then.'

'Well, that's good news then,' I said positively. 'Laura hasn't had a setback.'

'No, that's right. But the bad news is that after Gina telephoned you this morning she phoned the social worker and had a right go at her.'

'Oh dear,' I said.

'To be honest, I'm not overly keen on that social worker. She's not like the staff at Everley. But it's no good Gina sounding off at her; she's only doing her job. Gina has a very short fuse when it comes to social workers. I think it's because of the way she was treated when she was admitted to a psychiatric hospital after having Laura. Gina doesn't talk much about it, but I know she had a bad time and holds her former social worker responsible. She once said she felt like she'd been locked up and the key thrown away. But times have changed, and Gina agrees that the care Laura is receiving is second to none. I've told Gina to phone the social worker now and apologize. It won't do us any good to make an enemy of her. If she's not in her office she can leave a message on her answerphone.'

I nodded. Andy seemed very positive and in control, and also optimistic after being reassured by the nurse in charge. The children came out. Kim rushed into her father's arms and smothered him in kisses, while Adrian greeted me with a typical boy's reserve: a 'Hi, Mum,' accompanied by a cheeky smile.

We began towards the exit. I thought that Andy might want to go ahead and talk to Kim in private, so I held back, but he waited for us to catch up and we began walking home together.

'I've seen Mummy and her doctor today,' he said easily to Kim. 'They've decided it would be best for Mummy to wait a few more weeks before she comes home.'

Kim frowned. 'Why? That's not fair. You said she'd be home soon, so did Mum.'

'I know, and we were wrong to tell you that. It's what we were hoping would happen, but it wasn't definite.' He then explained about the transfer of care to the community, using age-appropriate words so that Kim could understand, and finished by saying there was going to be another meeting in two weeks' time.

'So Mummy will be home in two weeks?' Kim asked fervently.

'We hope so, but we'll tell you when it's definite – as soon as we know. Now, Nanny Geraldine and Gina are both at home waiting for us. We're not going to have dinner before we see Mummy tonight because we're all going out for a meal.'

'With Liam and Mummy too?' Kim asked excitedly.

'Yes.'

'Yippee!' she cried. Hanging onto her father's arm, she skipped for joy.

'You remember that restaurant we keep passing when we visit Mummy?' Andy continued. 'The one with the children's play area?' Kim nodded. 'We're all going there for dinner. You, me, Mummy, Liam, Nanny Gina and Nanny Geraldine.'

'Yes! I'm so happy!' Kim cried, delighted. 'All my family together again.'

I smiled. 'Well done, Andy,' I said quietly. 'Nicely handled.'

'Thanks, Cathy.'

* * *

School broke up early on Friday and the atmosphere in the playground was electric as the children rushed out, overjoyed at the prospect of six weeks of freedom ahead of them. Adrian, like most of the other children, was clutching carrier bags full of his completed school exercise books and art and craft work, including some models, which he was allowed to bring home. I looped the bags we couldn't carry over the handles of the stroller. Parents and children were now calling their goodbyes to friends and wishing them a happy holiday. Gina and Kim left the playground ahead of us as I continued to say goodbye to my friends and also arrange some play dates for Adrian. I'd already told Gina that if she and Kim wanted to pop in to see us during the holidays they'd be very welcome, and she'd said they'd be in touch. Not knowing exactly when Laura and Liam were returning home, they hadn't made plans to go away, but Andy was taking time off work so they could have some days out together. Gina had also told me that once Laura was home she would need to think about returning to her house and to work. Her boss was being understanding, but she was having to take unpaid leave, so it couldn't go on indefinitely, although she said that in the future she'd be seeing a lot more of Laura and her family at weekends than she had done in the past.

Adrian chatted excitedly on the way home about the fun things they'd done at school for their last day: games organized by the teachers rather than lessons, and a film shown on a big screen in the assembly hall, followed by party food. Once home, he immediately changed out of his school uniform and with great satisfaction deposited it ceremoniously into the laundry basket, declaring that it wouldn't be needed again for six weeks! Then he proudly showed Paula and me some of his schoolwork before going into the garden to play. While I made dinner, John, aware that it was the last day of term and Adrian would be excited, telephoned to wish us a happy holiday and confirmed he would be home at the end of August.

'Why not sooner?' Adrian bemoaned.

'Because my work needs me here,' John replied.

'Tell your work I need you more,' Adrian said, which must have touched John's heart as much as it did mine.

We were late rising on Saturday morning and had a leisurely cooked breakfast, then Shelley telephoned. To begin with all I could hear was her sweet voice running up and down the musical scales, pitch perfect, before she burst into laughter. 'The choir always starts with a warm-up,' she said. 'I do them at home too.'

I laughed. 'So the choir is going well?'

'Perfect. I'm so pleased I joined. It's great fun and everyone is really nice. I was a bit anxious about leaving Darrel to begin with, but he knows my friend well and he was fine after I'd gone.'

'That's good.'

'Cathy, the reason I'm phoning is that in September we're starting rehearsals for our Christmas concert and I want you all to come. There'll be two performances, one in the afternoon and one in the evening, so you could bring the kids to the afternoon one. I don't have the date yet. I'll let you know as soon as I do. I'm going to ask Carol as well. You will come, won't you?'

'Yes. As soon as you have the details, tell me and I'll put it in the diary.'

'Thanks. It will be my best Christmas ever!'

It was half a year until Christmas, but I'd found before that many young people from deprived backgrounds who'd never experienced the joys of Christmas as children look forward to the occasion immensely, wanting to create the magic they'd missed out on as children.

Shelley and I chatted for a while longer and then we made an arrangement for her and Darrel to come for lunch the following week.

The children and I quickly relaxed into the holiday routine; they got up later and often had breakfast in their pyjamas before they washed and dressed. I continued rising at my usual time, which allowed me to put the finishing touches to my dissertation so I didn't have to work on it during the day and could play with them. With a combination of days out and time spent at home, the first week of the school holiday quickly disappeared. Shelley and Darrel came for lunch the following Tuesday and after lunch we went to the local park. She reminded me again about the Christmas concert, and she also talked about the choir, specifically about a lad in the choir who was a couple of years older than her. Did I detect a sparkle in her eyes and a quickness to her breath every time she mentioned his name? I didn't embarrass her by asking. Shelley also mentioned that with Darrel starting school in September she was hoping to find a job, preferably part-time to fit in with school hours, and she'd signed up for a return-to-work programme at the employment centre, which was all very positive.

On Wednesday two significant events occurred, both of which gave me much relief. I finished my dissertation and sent it off. And Laura came home. Having not seen or heard from Gina since school broke up, I didn't know exactly when she was coming home, so it was a lovely surprise when I picked up the telephone to hear Laura say, 'Hi, Cathy, I thought you'd like to know that I'm home.'

'Wonderful! I am pleased. Great to have you back.'

'Thanks. It's great to be back. I was discharged yesterday. Mum's going home on Friday, so I was wondering if you and the children could come over tomorrow to say goodbye. We'll have some cake and coffee.'

'I'd love to, thank you. What time?'

'Shall we say after lunch – about two o'clock?'

'That's fine with me. I'll look forward to it.'

'See you then.'

We said goodbye and I hung up.

Should I have asked Laura how she was feeling? I would have done had she been suffering from a physical illness – how is your leg/stomach/arm/back? Are you feeling better? But that awkwardness that can surround mental illness had got in the way. It was silly of me really, because Laura had been very open with me when she'd been ill, but now I felt that maybe she would want to forget it, put the past behind her and move on, and would be embarrassed if I mentioned it. I'd play it by ear the following day and ask her how she was feeling if it seemed appropriate and she wanted to talk about it.

When I told the children that Laura and Liam were home and we were going to see them the next day they were pleased.

'Kim will be so happy to have her mummy back,' Adrian said.

'Baby Liam home!' Paula cried, delighted.

* * *

Having now finished my dissertation there was no reason why I shouldn't put my name on the whiteboard again to foster, so I telephoned the social services and said I was available. They must have written my name on the board straight away, for no more than thirty minutes later Samson's social worker telephoned and asked if I could look after him for respite the following week, from Monday morning to Wednesday evening. I said I could. Sometimes a carer only looks after a child once on respite, or it can become a regular arrangement to give the main caregiver, in this case Samson's grandmother, a break.

'Thanks, Cathy,' she said. 'I'm afraid Samson's behaviour hasn't improved since the last time you saw him. His gran is really struggling now he's off school for the holidays. We arranged a play scheme for him to go to, but he got excluded in the first week – for knocking another child unconscious, although he said it was an accident. I hope you can cope.'

So do I, I thought.

CHAPTER SEVENTEEN

PROGRESS

The following day I bought a bunch of flowers to give to Laura as a welcome-home gift.

'Thank you so much,' she said, smiling and kissing my cheek as we went in. 'My house is starting to look like a florist. Lovely to see you all again. Hi, Adrian, Paula.'

Kim was standing in the hall just behind her mother and smiling broadly. Gina appeared too. 'Hi, gang!' she called. 'Come on in. I'll put those flowers in water, they're beautiful. You see to Cathy and I'll put the kettle on.'

Laura smiled, passed the flowers to her mother and we followed her down the hall into the living room. Liam was sitting contentedly in his bouncing cradle, wide awake and playing with the mobile attached to the cradle, tapping the brightly coloured toys so that they rattled and spun. Paula went straight over to him and, kneeling down, said cutely, 'Baby Liam home.' Which made us smile.

Kim and Adrian stood by, looking slightly awkward. 'Can Adrian and I play in the garden?' Kim asked her mother.

'Yes, of course, love. We'll bring out some drinks and cakes shortly.'

They shot out of the patio doors, eager to be outside. 'Everyone has been so kind,' Laura now said to me, waving to the flowers and cards arranged around the room. The giant get-well card from school was propped by the hearth, and four smaller get-well cards stood on the mantelpiece between two vases of flowers. Another larger arrangement of flowers was in one corner of the room on a small occasional table. 'Those are from Andy, Kim and Liam,' she said. 'And those on the mantelpiece are from Mum and Geraldine.'

'Beautiful,' I said. 'You can never have too many flowers. Your garden's looking good too.'

'Thanks.' We both looked towards the garden. 'Andy cut the grass at the weekend ready for my homecoming, and Mum's been weeding. I was out there this morning too. I'll soon have it back to normal.'

'It looks really nice,' I said.

Gina appeared briefly at the door of the living room carrying my flowers in a vase. 'Shall I put these in the front room?' she asked Laura. 'We haven't any in there.'

'Yes please, Mum. Do you want any help in the kitchen?'

'No, you chat with Cathy.'

'Shall we sit in the garden?' Laura asked me.

'Yes, I love being outside.'

'Me too.' Laura went over to Liam and Paula. 'Let's take Liam in the garden, shall we?' she said to Paula. Paula nodded shyly, and then came over and held my hand.

We went out onto the decking. A white wrought-iron garden table with four matching chairs stood under a sun umbrella.

'This is perfect,' I said.

Laura smiled. 'We're using it a lot this year. Making the most of every day of sunshine.' Vibrant, happy, at ease with herself and others, I could see a huge improvement in Laura even in the few weeks since I'd visited at Everley.

She placed Liam's cradle in the shade of the sun umbrella and Paula squatted down beside him. Laura and I sat on the two chairs facing the garden so we could keep an eye on Kim and Adrian, who'd begun a game of children's croquet.

'It's a beautiful day,' Laura said, taking in a deep breath of fresh summer air. 'Just right. Warm, but with a slight breeze. I'm learning to appreciate the present rather than worry about the future or the past.'

'You look very well,' I said, feeling comfortable saying this, given her last comment.

'I'm getting there,' she said, gazing down the garden. 'They told me at Everley that it would take time and I shouldn't rush myself. But I can see the light at the end of the tunnel now. It's difficult to describe what it's like if you haven't been there. A bit like swimming up through layers of murky water, slowly reaching the surface. I take it a day at a time. I have some blips, but I'm getting there.'

'I suppose that's true for many illnesses,' I said.

'Yes, but with PND (postnatal depression) acknowledging you are ill in the first place is the first big step and part of the recovery process. I now realize that pretending nothing was wrong was the worst thing we could have done. Andy and Geraldine realize that too. It helps so much to have it out in the open so I can talk about how I'm feeling. I know I can ask for help if I need to, instead of trying to be Supermum.' I looked at Laura and nodded. 'The support group and the therapist at Everley have helped me enormously,' she said. 'And the tablets. I'm on a lower dose now, but I'll keep taking them for a few more months. The doctor reassured me that eventually I won't need them and I'll be my old self – maybe even better!' She laughed and then leaned slightly over the side of her chair, closer to Paula. 'You know you don't have to keep Liam amused,' she said to her kindly. 'You can play with your brother and Kim if you like.' But I could see that Paula was enjoying herself, tapping the mobiles and making Liam chuckle.

'She's fine,' I said.

'That's OK then.' Laura straightened and took another deep breath and gazed down the garden. Clearly she was happy to talk and share her experiences, and I felt comfortable listening. 'Andy's been so good,' she said. 'Really supportive. Some of the women in the group said that their partners and family weren't, and gave them the impression that they just had to get over it and it was all in their heads. Which it is, in a way,' she added with a small laugh. 'But dismissing how rough you feel only makes it worse. It can drive you mad. When I think back to that terrifying place I go cold. I don't ever want to be back there again. It was dreadful.'

'You won't,' I said. 'You will continue to go from strength to strength.'

'I hope so.'

Gina appeared carrying a tray containing a white bone-china teapot, matching milk jug, side plates, cups and saucers, a jug of lemonade and children's plastic beakers, which she set on the table.

'I'll fetch the cakes,' Laura said, standing. She went into the kitchen and returned with two plates of the most delicious-looking homemade cakes: a jam-and-cream-filled sponge and a selection of iced and decorated cupcakes.

'Someone's been busy,' I said. 'They look gorgeous.'

'It's Mum,' Laura said, smiling at her mother.

'I used to love baking when Laura was at home,' Gina said. 'It's nice to have a reason to do it again.'

Kim and Adrian had spotted the arrival of the cake and now ran up the garden. Laura gave them a plate each and they helped themselves to a cupcake and she poured the lemonade. Paula chose a cupcake and I put it on a plate for her and then helped her sit on the doorstep where Adrian and Kim were comfortably perched with their plates on their laps and the beakers of lemonade beside them. At four months old Liam wasn't ready for cake and lemonade yet, but he seemed very interested in what everyone else was eating. Laura poured the tea and I chose a slice of sponge cake.

'Hmm, delicious,' I said as I took the first bite.

'I'm glad you like it,' Gina said. 'I've made you one to take home, to say thank you for all you've done.'

'That's very kind of you.' I was really touched. 'It's so light. It melts in your mouth.'

'The secret is in the whisking,' Gina said. 'The more you whisk the lighter the sponge. I'll let you have the recipe, if you like.'

We continued talking as we ate the cake and sipped our tea. It was a perfect English summer scene – ideal weather with tea and cake on the decking. When the children had finished the three of them went down the garden to play, while Laura, Gina and I drank a second cup of tea and chatted. Gina said she was sorry to be leaving, but she had to get back to work. She said how much she'd enjoyed taking Kim to and from school and being part of the family, but she knew Andy and Laura needed time alone now to get back to normal family life. 'They know where I am if I'm needed,' she said. 'And of course I'll be visiting at weekends.'

We stayed for nearly two hours, during which time Laura gave Liam his bottle and Paula held him for a while – seated on the lawn with Laura and me on either side of her to stop Liam rolling off. When it was time to leave, Gina presented me with the sponge cake in an airtight container, which I said I'd return, and a copy of the recipe. Then they all saw us off at the door, Laura with Liam in her arms. I'd already told Laura I hoped she and the children would visit us in the summer holidays, and she said she'd phone me. It was sad saying goodbye to Gina. Although I hadn't known her for very long, we'd shared quite a journey together through Laura's illness and recovery, and I liked her feisty manner. She was someone I would have continued a friendship with had she lived closer, but fostering had shown me that sadly life is full of goodbyes. 'I hope to see you again one time when you visit Laura,' I said. 'Take care.'

'You too, Cathy.' We kissed and hugged goodbye.

I took Adrian and Paula swimming on Saturday and then on Sunday we met my parents at a well-known beauty spot where we had a picnic lunch. Monday loomed and with it Samson. I'd be lying if I said I didn't have reservations about him staying, especially after his social worker's comment about his behaviour having not improved (read: deteriorated). While his previous stay had gone reasonably well, it had been very hard work. I'd had to keep him occupied the whole time and have eyes in the back of my head to ensure he wasn't getting up to mischief. I wasn't the only one with misgivings.

'Can't we have Darrel to stay instead?' Adrian asked when I told him Samson was coming.

'Fostering doesn't work like that, love,' I said. 'We look after children who need a home. Darrel is fine with his mother and I'm sure we'll see them again. But Samson's grandma needs a rest from looking after him.'

'I'm not surprised!' Adrian said, already developing a dry sense of humour.

'I hope that dog isn't there,' Adrian said anxiously the following morning as we clambered into the car to go and collect Samson.

'Don't worry,' I reassured him. 'I'll make sure Bruno is shut away before we go into the flat. I don't want to be eaten any more than you do.' He managed a small smile.

Paula, that much younger, appeared unperturbed by Samson's visit, but of course at her age she was largely unaware of the problems associated with his visit, or of how much effort and constant supervision it took to keep everyone safe while he was with us.

As it turned out Bruno didn't pose a threat, because we didn't have to go into Samson's flat. As we walked up the path to the main entrance of the flats, Paula holding my hand and Adrian snuggled in close behind me using me as a shield, the net curtain at the open downstairs window of Samson's flat was suddenly and roughly yanked aside. Samson's cheeky face grinned at us. 'They're here!' he yelled at the top of his voice over his shoulder. Then, pushing the window as wide open as it would go, he put one leg over and began to clamber out. His backpack got caught on the hinge of the window and he was stuck half in and half out. 'Someone help me!' he yelled dramatically. 'I can't get out!' Adrian and Paula laughed and I smiled. He did look comical.

'Hi, Samson,' I said, going over. 'How are you?'

'I'm bleedin' stuck,' he said, pulling against the straps and trying to free himself.

'All right. Hold still and I'll get you unstuck.' I unhooked the strap from the hinge and he jumped clear. Bruno barked loudly from somewhere inside the flat and Adrian looked concerned.

'Bye, Bruno!' Samson yelled at the top of his voice. 'Shut your face up!' He went over to Adrian. 'Hello, mate, how are you?' he asked, clapping him on the back.

'I'm all right,' Adrian said, putting on a brave face.

'Where's your gran?' I asked Samson. 'We need to say goodbye to her.' I could hardly just go without letting her know; surely she'd wonder where Samson was?

'She's in there,' he said, referring to the lounge he'd just clambered out of.

I returned to the window and pulled aside the net curtain. I could see her sitting on the sofa in her dressing gown with her legs stretched out in front of her, a plate of toast on her lap and a mug of tea in her hand. She was watching television.

'We're going now,' I said. 'I'll bring Samson back at six o'clock on Wednesday.'

'Thanks, dear,' she said, without taking her eyes from the television. And that was it.

'How have you been?' I asked Samson as we began towards my car.

'Better since school finished,' he said, grinning. 'No hassle from the teachers and no work!' Adrian grinned too.

'So what have you been doing in the holidays?' I asked him, making conversation.

'I dunno.' He shrugged. 'Watching telly, PlayStation, I guess. And getting on Gran's nerves.' I laughed. You couldn't help but like him, he was such a character.

'So what would you like to do while you're with us?' I asked him as I unlocked the car and opened the rear door. 'Any suggestions?'

'Sports day,' he said, climbing in. 'Like we did before. I've been practising since I knew I was coming to you, so no one can beat me. I was good then, but I'm even better now. And I've got some prizes for all of us in me bag.'

'Have you?' I asked, surprised and touched. 'That's very kind of you.'

'They're me toys I don't want, so we can have 'em as prizes. I know you gave us some before, but we need lots and lots.'

'OK. That's nice. We'll use them as prizes, but then you must take them home with you afterwards,' I said. 'They are yours.' I helped Paula into her car seat as the boys fastened their safety belts.

'Nah. You can keep 'em,' Samson said. 'I don't want 'em. Me dad gave 'em to me, so I ain't bothered.' Which I thought was strange. Usually gifts from an absent parent are valued and treasured.

I fastened Paula in her car seat, checked the boys' belts, and then closed the rear door.

'So we can have a sports day today,' I said, getting in. 'What would you like to do tomorrow?'

'Go to the cinema,' Samson said without hesitation, clearly having planned it. 'Gran can't take me cos her legs are bad.

She can't bend them to fit in the seat. And me dad's girlfriend says it's too expensive to take me to the cinema.'

'I'll check to see what is showing,' I said. 'There's sure to be plenty of children's films, as it's the summer holidays.'

'I want to see the new *Death of the Avenger* film,' Samson said. 'But I don't suppose you'll take me to that. It's full of blood and guts.'

'No. It's an adult film and not one I'd want to see anyway. It's horrific.'

'I watch them at home,' he said, which I didn't doubt. And then parents wonder why their child is then being aggressive or having nightmares! I knew enough about this series of films to know they contained shocking scenes of violence and certainly weren't suitable for children. But of course it's the parents who have to censor what is shown in the home, and not all parents appreciate the effect these films can have on young minds.

Samson accepted that he wouldn't be watching that type of film with me, either at the cinema or at home, but was now telling Adrian (and Paula) about some of the scenes in the previous films – blood spurting from the necks of severed heads and eyeballs popping out – so I told him we'd talk about something else.

'Like what?' he asked, giving the back of the passenger seat a couple of good kicks, which I ignored.

'You can tell us what else you have been doing since we last saw you,' I said.

'Nothing,' he said. Then turning to Adrian, 'Why? What have you been doing?'

Adrian looked a little uncomfortable, but then began telling Samson about some of the outings and activities he'd enjoyed, including the end-of-term production at school, day trips and the recent birthday parties he'd been to.

'Cor, I wish I got invited to birthday parties,' Samson said enviously. 'I've never been to one. No one asks me.' I felt sorry for him, although I could appreciate why his unruly behaviour might limit his social calendar. 'What do you do at parties?' he now asked Adrian. It was sad he didn't know. Adrian explained about the football party, and also parties at his friends' homes that he'd been to with games and prizes and a party tea.

'I know, missus!' Samson exploded, giving the seat back another kick.

'Cathy,' I corrected. 'Yes?'

'Instead of having another sports day, we'll have a party! We'll give the prizes I've brought to the winners of the games.'

I glanced at him in the interior mirror. 'If that's what you'd like to do, fine, but there will just be the four of us.'

'That's OK,' he said. 'Can you make jelly and ice cream, like Adrian said?'

'I should think so.'

'Good on you!' He was so excited that a volley of kicks now hit the back of the seat, sending dust motes into the air.

'Samson, don't kick the seat, please,' I said.

'Sorry, missus – I mean, Cathy. I won't do it again. I know I have to behave myself with you.'

'Excellent.'

CHAPTER EIGHTEEN

CHILD ABUSE

It's very sad, I think, that while many children enjoy regular birthday parties – going to them and holding them – other children do not. It doesn't take much to give a child a little birthday party, an experience they'll enjoy and remember to mark their special day. You don't need an expensive professional entertainer, an elaborate dressing-up theme or a costly outing; just a few balloons, a sandwich tea and lots of enthusiasm from the organizer. I was determined that we'd make Samson's party as authentic as possible, given the short notice and the fact that there'd just be the four of us and it wasn't his birthday.

Once home, I sent Samson and Adrian into the garden to run some laps, as Samson was now higher than ever at the thought of his party. While the boys ran off some energy I took Paula with me into the kitchen where I quickly made some jellies and put them in the fridge to set. I knew I had ice cream in the freezer. We'd have to pretend with the birthday cake, but I could put together a party tea with some sandwiches, crisps and biscuits. I called the boys in and made us all a drink and a snack, then with the children still seated at the table I produced some sheets of coloured card and crayons and showed them how to make party invitations, which I explained to Samson was the first step in having a party – inviting people to come. As it was going to be Samson's birthday party, I said he would need to give Adrian, Paula and myself an invitation each. 'Yeah, I've seen the kids at school give them out,' he said cheerfully, and my heart went out to him.

This activity kept everyone occupied for half an hour – I helped Paula make hers. I then gathered together the invitations and told Samson what he needed to write in each card and how to spell our names. To begin with he didn't understand why he shouldn't give himself an invitation, so I explained that as it was his party he would know the details – the date, time and place. This wasn't obvious to him, as he'd never had a party before. Once the invites were written, he carefully slid them into the envelopes, printed our names on the outside and ceremoniously gave them out. We opened them with excited exclamations of 'Wow!' and said we'd love to go to his party, which was at two o'clock that afternoon.

I then set up a board game at the table to keep Samson amused while I found a spare birthday card, which, out of sight of Samson, Adrian and I wrote in. I helped Paula write her name. I hung 'Happy Birthday' banners in the living room, which was to act as Samson's house where the party would take place. Adrian helped me blow up balloons and I pinned a couple of them to the door of the living room to show where the party was being held. We then wrapped up some small gifts – I always had a few spare. After lunch I sent Samson for another run in the garden (he was getting hyper again) while I prepared some party food. At one-thirty he began counting off the minutes until two o'clock when he bellowed at the top of his voice: 'It's time for me party!' He ran into the living room, slamming the door to 'his house' behind him so hard in his excitement that the building shook. Holding a present each, Adrian, Paula and I knocked on the door.

'Who is it?' he yelled from the other side.

'Cathy, Adrian and Paula,' I replied.

'What do you want?' he demanded.

Adrian laughed, for of course this wasn't how you greeted guests coming to your party, but Samson wasn't to know – he'd never done it before.

'We've come to your birthday party,' I said through the door. 'We're all very excited. Can we come in?'

'I'll think about it,' Samson said, which made Adrian laugh even more. Samson then asked, 'Have you brought me a present?'

'Yes,' I said as Adrian giggled.

'OK. You can come in then.' The door quickly opened and he relieved us of our gifts. 'Cor, proper presents!' he said, taking them to the sofa to unwrap them. 'These aren't the ones I brought.'

'Happy Birthday,' Adrian and I said as Samson began tearing off the wrapping paper.

His face was a picture. 'Cor, thanks,' he said, after opening each gift. He had a Batman jigsaw puzzle from Adrian, a word-search book from me and a small, boxed car from Paula, who was looking rather bemused by what was going on. After the door had slammed Toscha had fled to the bottom of the garden and taken refuge on top of the shed. Samson opened the card and I helped him read what we'd written:

To Samson,
Have a lovely party.
Best wishes from Cathy, Adrian and Paula.

'We usually stand our cards on the mantelpiece,' I said to Samson. He handed me the card and I put it in pride of place in the centre.

'Now can we play games and win prizes?' he asked.

'Yes,' I said.

I'd already thought of some games that would work with just the few of us – musical chairs, hunt the thimble, pass the orange, musical statues and sleeping lions. I had some little prizes ready (from my emergency store), but Samson wanted to use the ones he'd brought with him when Adrian, Paula or I won a game. I was therefore able to express genuine surprise when I opened my prize to find a toy ambulance with three wheels missing and half a stale biscuit in the rear. Adrian had a pick-up truck for a prize and Paula a small toy horse. Indeed, many of the prizes we opened were from a toy farm-yard set, including a dog-chewed farmer, bales of hay with teeth marks and a scarecrow with a leg missing. We thanked Samson – it was thoughtful of him, although I'd have to make sure he took his toys home with him. As a foster carer I knew difficult situations could arise if parents discovered their child's possessions were missing, even if the child had given them away. But for now his prizes were part of our play and we were as delighted with ours as Samson was with his – which he would be keeping.

Tea was a success, especially the jelly and ice cream, and cake. I still had over half the cake Gina had given to me, so I decorated it with six candles and set it on the table with the round side facing Samson. He knew it had a piece missing, but it didn't matter. It was the fun of the experience that counted. We sang 'Happy Birthday', he blew out his candles and we all cheered. Samson enjoyed blowing out the candles so much that I had to relight them three times. I helped him cut the cake into four slices. I asked him if he'd had a birthday celebration when he had been six, but he shrugged and changed the subject, so I guessed he hadn't.

'What happens now?' he asked as he crammed the last mouthful of cake into his mouth.

'Well, at the end of a party the host usually sees the guests out and thanks them for coming.'

'Can we have some more games?' he asked, not wanting the party to end.

'All parties have to end some time,' I said. 'And then you have the happy memories to look back on.' We'd been playing at parties for over three hours. 'One more game of sleeping lions and then you can say goodbye to your guests.'

It actually turned into three games of sleeping lions and another of hunt the thimble before Samson announced it was time for us to go. Grabbing Adrian's arm, he began pulling him roughly towards the living-room door.

'No, Samson,' I said, intervening. 'You don't treat your guests like that. You have to be gentle and see them out nicely or they won't want to come again.'

Fortunately Adrian saw the funny side of it and was laughing rather than looking worried. In fact, I'd noticed that Adrian had generally seemed more relaxed around Samson during the afternoon, I think possibly because he'd seen Samson's vulnerable, childlike side when he'd been so involved in enjoying his party.

'You just walk to the door with them,' I said to Samson. 'Thank them for their present and say goodbye.'

Which he now did. Having let Adrian out of the living room, I kept hold of Paula's hand while he saw us out. 'Thank you for my party,' he said.

'You're welcome,' I said. 'Thank you for asking us.'

It hadn't taken much, but I could see it had meant a lot to Samson, and doubtless he would have some happy memories of playing parties that afternoon. Later, I left the boys doing a word-search puzzle while I took Paula up for her bath and bed. Once she was settled, I brought the boys up and then discovered that Samson, having done his own packing, had very little in his backpack apart from the prizes he'd brought with him and his wash bag. I found some pyjamas that fitted him in my spares and a change of clothes for the following day. All foster carers keep spare clothes of different sizes for both sexes for emergency use. As the boys had done a lot of running around and were quite sweaty I thought they should both have a bath, so I settled Samson in his room where he continued the word search while Adrian had his bath. Then Adrian went to his room while I ran Samson's bath. Although Samson had good self-care skills, I made sure the water was the right temperature, then I waited by the bathroom door to check he climbed in safely. As he did I saw a large, angry bruise on his right buttock. My immediate thought was that it must have happened today while he'd been playing. He was so boisterous in his play he often literally threw himself into a game, landing on his knees or bottom. Foster carers have to log any accidents that happen to a child they are looking after and make a note of even minor injuries. I would also need to tell his grandmother what had happened when I returned him.

'That's a big bruise,' I said as he sat in the water. 'Do you know how you did it?'

'Where?' he asked, examining his arms and legs. Like many boys his age they were dotted with small, fading bruises from tumbles during play.

'No, the one on your bottom,' I said.

He turned to try and see but it was out of view. 'Dunno,' he said, disinterested, and began splashing water on himself.

'Do you remember when you could have done it?' I asked. 'Did you sit down very heavily in the garden, or on the patio?'

He shrugged. 'Dunno.'

'OK. Wash yourself. I'll wait here.'

I stood on the landing by the bathroom door to give him some privacy while he washed himself. I knew he wouldn't be long; most boys his age don't linger in the bath or shower. I didn't think playing musical chairs could have given him the bruise – we'd used cushions – and I couldn't imagine that sitting heavily on the carpeted floor could have caused it either. I therefore assumed it must have happened in the garden or possibly before he'd come to me. I'd still have to make a note of it and mention it to his gran.

Samson had a predictably quick bath and clambered out. Drying his front, he stood with his back to the mirror and then craned his neck round to look over his shoulder to see the bruise.

'Oh, that,' he said nonchalantly. 'Me dad's girlfriend did that. She's always whacking me.'

'Is she?' I said. 'That doesn't sound right. With what?'

'Whatever she has,' he said matter-of-factly. 'The broom handle did that. It blimmin' hurt.' He continued towel-drying himself.

'I'm sure it did hurt,' I said. 'She shouldn't be hitting you.'

'I shouldn't have been naughty,' he replied.

'It was still wrong of her to hit you,' I said. While the law in England at present allows a parent to give a child a small slap or tap on the hand when chastising them, hitting the child so it leaves a mark is illegal. It's also child abuse and cruel. Foster carers, childminders, teachers and other childcare workers are not allowed to smack a child, and personally I have never slapped my own children. I use sanctions – the loss of a privilege – and firm talking to curb negative behaviour.

'When did it happen?' I asked Samson as he began pulling on his pyjamas.

'Friday,' he said. 'When I saw me dad. I don't like her, but he lives in her flat so I'm supposed to show her respect.'

Pity she hadn't shown Samson some respect, I thought. 'Does your dad know she hits you?'

'Yeah, of course, he's there,' Samson said, as though it was a daft question.

'Have you told your gran?' I asked.

'Nah. I'd get into more trouble if she found out I'd been rude. Although she doesn't beat me.'

'It's very wrong to hit people,' I said. 'And no one should hit a child. How often does it happen?' I wondered if it was a one-off and she'd lost her temper, although that wouldn't justify it. The severity of the bruise suggested she'd really lashed out and lost control.

'Every time I see her,' Samson said. 'I hate her and she hates me. Do I have to brush my teeth again? I did 'em this morning.'

'Yes please, you should brush your teeth every night and morning.' He gave a groan but picked up his toothbrush and toothpaste from where I'd left them ready on the basin. 'What's your dad's girlfriend's name?' I asked.

'Tanzy,' he said, squirting a very generous measure of paste onto his toothbrush.

'I'll need to tell your social worker so she can stop it happening.'

'That's OK with me,' he said. 'I don't want to see me dad any more when she's there.'

I waited while he brushed his teeth and then I saw him into bed. I tucked him in, dimmed the light, as he liked it, and then gave him a kiss and hug as his gran did.

'What are we seeing at the cinema tomorrow?' he asked as he snuggled down.

'There's a cartoon film showing about dinosaurs,' I said.

'Do they fight each other and eat people?' he asked, his eyes widening in anticipation.

'I wouldn't be surprised,' I said, although I hoped the film wouldn't be frightening, as Paula would be with us. I'd chosen a film with a Universal rating that was suitable for all ages of children and with a subject matter that would appeal to Samson and Adrian. 'Night then, love,' I said, smiling at him.

'Night,' he said, and then looked at me thoughtfully as though he had something to say.

'Yes?' I asked.

'While you're telling me social worker about Tanzy hitting me with a broom you'd better tell her about the other stuff too. Like when I stay there and she shuts me out of her flat. And locks me in the bathroom when her and Dad go to the pub. Gran never does that. And the time she really lost it and tried to strangle me. Me dad stopped her. Just as well or I'd be bleedin' dead.'

I looked at him carefully. 'She did all those things?' I asked, appalled and trying to hide my shock.

'Yeah.'

'That's very wrong,' I said. 'I will tell your social worker and I expect she'll want to talk to you about what happened. She'll want the details, so it's important you tell her, all right?' It was best if I left further questioning to his social worker who, having worked with the family for some time, knew the case well.

Samson nodded. 'It is wrong of her to do these things, isn't it?'

'Yes. Very wrong.'

'I told me dad she shouldn't be treating me like that, but he said if I made trouble she'd chuck him out and he'd have nowhere to live.'

'He's an adult,' I said. 'He can look after himself. He'll find somewhere else to live if necessary. Where he lives isn't your problem. And as your father he should be protecting you and keeping you safe. Not letting you get hurt.'

'I wish me mum had stayed,' Samson said thoughtfully. 'But I guess that's life.' With a shrug he turned over, ready for sleep.

I touched his shoulder. 'Night then, love. Sleep tight, and see you tomorrow.'

'Night,' his voice came from under the duvet. 'Thanks for me party.'

'You're welcome, love.'

Sad and worried, I came out, closing the door behind me. I believed what Samson had told me about his father's girlfriend. His matter-of-fact resignation to being punished and his childlike description convinced me it was true, but it would be for the social services to investigate. I'd telephone his social worker first thing in the morning. The poor kid, I thought, and I wondered how much of his bad behaviour resulted from the abuse he was suffering. He must be angry, and in children anger often comes out in challenging behaviour.

I went into Adrian's room, spent some time lying with him, then said goodnight and checked on Paula. She was sound asleep. Downstairs, I wrote notes on what Samson had told me and then I finished washing the dishes and tidying up from the party, although I left Samson's birthday card on the mantelpiece. With my dissertation finished I didn't feel guilty watching some television, then after the ten o'clock news I let Toscha out for a run and went up to bed. I didn't sleep. As soon as I started to drift off my thoughts went to Samson and what he'd suffered, and would still be suffering if something wasn't done. I appreciated how much patience it took to look after him, even for a short while, but there was no justification for hitting him or locking him in or out of the flat. My anger rose, not just towards the girlfriend, but also towards Samson's father, who'd put his own needs first and failed to protect his son. By standing by and doing nothing he'd been an accomplice in the abuse and was as much to blame as his girlfriend.

It was after midnight before I finally fell asleep and then the following morning Samson was wide awake at six o'clock. I settled him in his bedroom with some toys while I showered and dressed. After breakfast, and as soon as the social services' offices opened at nine o'clock, I told Samson and Adrian that I needed them to look after Paula while I made an important telephone call. Samson rose to the responsibility and held

Paula's hand, which was sweet. I left the three of them seated on the floor in the living room playing with a selection of games, while I went into the hall to make the call. I could hear them from there. I think Samson knew what the call was about, but there was no need for me to tell Adrian; he was used to me making and receiving important calls in connection with fostering.

Samson's social worker was at her desk and she went very quiet as I described the bruise and what Samson had said. Then she gave a heartfelt sigh, which seemed to say, 'Not more suffering … When will it end?'

'We've had concerns about the level of care Samson has been receiving for some time,' she said. 'But this is new. I'll need to speak to him. I can't make it today or tomorrow. My diary is full. I'll see him on Thursday morning when he's home. Does he know you're telling me?'

'Yes. I told him I'd tell you.'

'Good. Reassure him he's done the right thing in telling you and I'll see him on Thursday. I think I'll need to set up supervised contact at the family centre for Friday so he can still see his father, but I'll explain that to him on Thursday. How is he?'

'Not too bad. He wasn't upset when he told me. He seemed to think he deserved being treated like that because he was naughty.'

'The poor kid. And how is his behaviour generally with you?'

'Very manageable.'

'So if we do need to bring him into care, you could foster him, rather than just do respite?'

'Yes.'

'Thank you, Cathy.'

We said goodbye and I put the phone down and returned to the living room. Just in time! Samson was pretending Paula was Superwoman and had stood her on the coffee table and was now telling her to leap off.

'That's not looking after her,' I said to both boys as I lifted her off.

'Sorry, Mum,' Adrian said guiltily. Samson glared at me.

'Can't have any fun here,' he grumbled. And from then on the day went downhill. Perhaps it was because he knew that what he'd told me would have repercussions, or maybe he was just testing me, I didn't know, but he spent the entire morning trying to wind me up, teasing Adrian and Paula, and unable to settle to anything for more than five minutes. Eventually, although I didn't like doing it, I said that unless his behaviour improved we wouldn't be going to the cinema, and he settled down – until we were in the cinema. Then, with limited sanctions available in the cinema to curb his behaviour, he made the most of it by throwing popcorn, kicking the back of the seat in front, jumping up and down, whooping, shouting, giving a running commentary on the film at the top of his voice and generally making a spectacle of himself. Those around us kept turning and shushing him. Adrian looked embarrassed (as I was) and even told him to sit down and be quiet. Some of Samson's behaviour was natural exuberance – excitability – but most of it wasn't. He was testing the boundaries to the limit. The word 'manageable' I'd used earlier to describe his behaviour to his social worker came back to haunt me and I wondered what on earth I'd done by offering to foster him more permanently.

'Samson,' I eventually hissed in his ear. 'You have to settle down, now. Do you understand me? You're spoiling it for others.'

'Don't care,' he said rudely.

'Well, I do, so sit still, stop kicking the seat and shouting or we'll have to leave, and you'll miss the rest of the film.' Indeed, I didn't know why a member of staff hadn't asked us to leave already. Perhaps no one had reported us yet.

'You wouldn't do that,' he challenged me. 'You paid for the tickets. It would be a waste if we didn't see the film.'

'Try me,' I said, meeting his gaze.

He did, and kicked the seat in front so hard that the boy sitting in it jolted forward. 'I'm so sorry,' I said to his mother, who'd turned round and glared at me, annoyed. Then to Samson I said, 'Right, that's it. You've been warned. We're going now.' I picked up my handbag from the floor and moved to the edge of the seat.

He looked shocked. 'Not really?' he asked incredulously.

'Yes. I've warned you so many times.' I turned to Paula, ready to help her off her seat.

At that point Samson finally realized that I meant what I said. 'All right, I'll be good,' he said in a loud whisper.

'No. You've had your chances. It's not fair on the others here.' I made another move to go.

'I promise,' he pleaded. 'Really, I won't do it again.' I looked at him and hesitated. 'Pleeeeze,' he said.

'This will be your very last chance,' I said. 'One more naughty thing and we go home.'

'Will you be quiet?' the woman in front said, turning again.

'Sorry,' I said. Although a bit of patience from her wouldn't have gone amiss – she could see I was dealing with a difficult situation.

Samson sat back in his seat and I tried to relax back in mine. My heart was racing and I felt completely stressed. I held Paula's hand in the dark and waited for Samson's next outburst, when we would leave straight away. But it didn't come. He sat back as good as gold for the rest of the film, and eventually I relaxed too. Samson had tested the boundaries, tested me to the limit and had finally accepted my guidelines for good behaviour – in this situation at least. I knew that if I brought him to the cinema again he'd remember how to behave and it would be that little bit easier.

CHAPTER NINETEEN

UNWELCOME NEWS

When I took Samson home on Wednesday evening it was raining and the window to his flat was closed. We went in through the main entrance and I pressed the doorbell to his flat – number 17. Bruno immediately started barking loudly on the other side and pounded down the hall, landing heavily against the back of the door. Adrian jumped back and I reassured him again that we wouldn't go in until the dog was safely shut away.

'Bruno!' Samson yelled at the top of his voice, banging his fists on the door and winding up the dog even more. I picked up Paula just in case someone opened the door before the dog was shut away. He was so big he would have knocked her flying.

Eventually someone dragged him away and his barks subsided. As we waited for the door to be opened Samson put down his backpack and took out the birthday card and presents we'd given to him, ready to show his family. It was his gran who opened the door.

'Look what I've got! Birthday presents!' he cried, holding them up for her to see.

'It's not your birthday, you silly bugger,' she said, leaning heavily against the wall for support.

'I know that!' Samson cried indignantly. 'But we pretended it was. I had jelly and ice cream and we played games and won prizes. They're in me bag.'

Most parents or grandparents would have said something like, 'That sounds great. Come in and tell me all about it.' But Samson's gran said, 'Are you coming in or what, you daft bugger? I can't be standing here all day. Me legs are killing me.'

I don't think she meant to be unkind, it was just her way, but I saw the look of disappointment on Samson's face. I was now expecting him to assume his usual tough exterior and run indoors shouting, without giving us a second thought, as he'd done before. But he didn't. He stayed where he was and looked up at me. 'Thanks for me party,' he said sweetly. 'It was nice of you to go to all that trouble.'

I could have cried. 'You're very welcome, love,' I said, and touched his shoulder. 'We all enjoyed it.'

Then, turning to Adrian, he said, 'Bye. Thanks for sharing your toys.'

'That's OK,' Adrian said.

Samson reached up to Paula who was still in my arms, wanting to say goodbye to her, so I set her on the ground. 'Bye, Paula,' he said, gently tickling her under the chin. She chuckled. 'Thanks for coming to me party.' I swallowed hard. All that bravado and underneath he was a kind-hearted, thoughtful child who had so much appreciated our pretend party. I felt guilty, and silently renewed my promise that if he ever needed a permanent foster home, I would look after him. It would be hard work, but I'd manage.

We weren't invited into the flat. Gran said to him, 'Now you've said goodbye, boy, you'd better get tidying ya room – ya social worker's coming tomorrow.'

He shrugged and disappeared down the hall.

'He's been fine,' I said to her.

'That makes a change,' she said, and shifting uncomfortably from one foot to the other she began to close the door.

We said goodbye and as we turned the door closed behind us. Bruno barked loudly from inside, which set off another dog in a neighbour's house. It was unlikely I'd hear the outcome of the social worker's visit, or what decisions were made regarding Samson's father and girlfriend, unless I looked after Samson again. Foster carers are told what they need to know about a child's situation while they are fostering them, but once they've left their care they're rarely given updates, which is a pity, as we often think about them and wonder how they're getting on.

We were now already halfway through the summer holidays and making the most of every day. John was due home in two weeks and the date was circled on the calendar on the wall in the kitchen, although we didn't need a reminder. The following day one of Adrian's friends came to play and stayed for dinner, and then on Friday I took the children swimming again. The week after followed a similar pattern of days out and time at home, and included a day trip to the coast with my parents. I hadn't seen Laura since I'd been invited to her house for tea to say goodbye to Gina. I assumed all was well. It had crossed my mind a couple of times to telephone her for a chat in the evening, but then the time had disappeared and it was too late to phone. Although I didn't have another foster child, I was on standby. A social worker had telephoned and said she was trying to bring a teenager into care but she'd run away. She'd asked if I could take her at short notice when they found her – they would bring her straight to me – and I said I could. I'd be told more once she was found and was with me.

It was early on the Saturday evening at the end of that week and I was in the living room with Adrian and Paula. We were on the floor playing Snap. Adrian and I were trying to teach Paula the game. She was too young really, but she wanted to join in. The telephone rang and I answered it in the living room. There was a short silence before a half-familiar voice said, 'Cathy, I'm sorry to disturb you. It's Geraldine.'

'Oh, hello,' I said, surprised. 'How are you? Is everything all right?'

'I'm sorry to bother you on a Saturday night,' she said, 'but I need your advice.'

'Yes,' I said, puzzled. 'I'll help if I can. Is it urgent? Or could I phone you back once the children are in bed?'

There was another pause before she said, 'I was wondering if I could come and see you. It would be easier to talk face to face rather than over the telephone.'

'Yes, of course,' I said, concerned. 'Is Laura all right?'

'It's partly about Laura, yes, but I'll explain when I see you.'

'All right. Would you like to come here this evening? About eight o'clock?'

'If that is convenient with you.'

'Yes. I'll have the children in bed by then. I'll see you at eight.'

'Thank you, Cathy,' she said stiffly, and hung up.

It was clear from her tightly controlled manner that she'd carefully planned what she needed to say. Given that she was not a person who easily shared her feelings or asked for help,

I appreciated that whatever she wanted to talk about must be very serious indeed.

I returned to sit on the floor and play with the children, but my mind wasn't on the game as I ran through the possible reasons for Geraldine wanting to see me. She'd said it was 'partly' about Laura, and I hadn't pressed her as I respected that she preferred to talk in person, which I understood. At seven o'clock, when we finished playing, I took Paula upstairs for her bath and bed, and once she was settled I fetched Adrian. As I lay propped on his bed beside him, having our little goodnight chat, I told him that Kim's grandma, Geraldine, was coming later, just in case he heard the door go and wondered who it was.

'Is she your friend then?' he asked, slightly surprised. I sometimes had a friend round in the evening.

'More like an acquaintance,' I said. 'She wants to talk to me about something – I don't know what exactly.'

'I hope Kim's mummy isn't in hospital again,' he said.

'I don't think she is or Geraldine would have said, but it's nothing for you to worry about.' Like me, Adrian was a bit of a worrier and could fret over things that shouldn't have bothered him.

'I won't worry,' he said cheerfully, snuggling down ready for sleep. 'Dad's phoning tomorrow and he'll be home in a week.'

'That's right. So you think about nice things while you go off to sleep and I'll see you in the morning.'

I kissed him goodnight and came out, then checked on Paula before I went downstairs. I gave the living room a quick tidy ready for Geraldine's arrival and then sat on the sofa. It was now 7.45 and still light outside. Toscha wandered in and settled beside me on the sofa.

At exactly eight o'clock I heard a little tap on the front door. I went down the hall and checked in the security spyhole before opening the door.

'I didn't use the bell,' Geraldine explained apologetically. 'I thought it might wake your children.'

'Come in,' I said. 'They're in bed.'

She was dressed smartly but reservedly as usual, in a knee-length skirt, button-up blouse and cardigan. Her short grey hair was neatly trimmed.

'I haven't seen you for a while,' I said, making conversation as I showed her through to the living room. 'How have you been?'

'Oh, me? I'm all right,' she said dismissively, as though her welfare was of no concern.

'Do sit down. Would you like a drink?'

'No, thank you. I won't keep you longer than I have to. I'm sure you have things to do.' She sat in one of the armchairs and I returned to the sofa. She had an air of businesslike formality about her.

'I'll come straight to the point,' she said, sitting upright and looking directly at me. 'Laura's had a setback.'

'Oh dear, I am sorry. She was doing so well. Is she in hospital?'

'No. She's at home, but she's been very upset and is now depressed again. She knows I'm coming to see you; so does Andy. We haven't worried Gina with it yet.'

I nodded. Clearly it was their decision what or when they told Gina, although I thought it should be sooner rather than later.

'The reason I've come to see you is to ask if it is possible to change social workers. I thought you might know, as you work with them. Are people allowed to change their social worker?'

'Well, yes, sometimes,' I said. 'Are you thinking of asking for Laura's social worker to be changed?'

She nodded stiffly. 'But we don't want to cause trouble and make things worse for Laura. Would it be held against her?'

'No. It shouldn't be. Can I ask why you are thinking of requesting a change of social worker?'

'We believe she's responsible for Laura's a setback,' Geraldine said.

I met her gaze. 'How?'

'What she says and the way she speaks to Laura is all wrong. Laura is sensitive at present, she's vulnerable, and the woman doesn't seem to understand that. It's not only Laura who thinks this; Andy and I do too. We thought the woman was going to help support Laura, but she's doing more harm than good. You know that Gina had a couple of blazing arguments with her a while back. Then Andy and I thought it was Gina who was in the wrong and had overreacted, but not any longer.'

'I see,' I said thoughtfully. 'Something certainly seems to have gone badly wrong for you all to feel this way.'

'Every time she speaks to Laura, Laura ends up in tears. And when she's not there Laura worries about what she's saying about her – the reports she writes and the meetings she has with her manager, which Laura isn't invited to. Laura says she feels her life is slipping out of her control again, because of this woman. She was doing so well. Do you think we have a good reason to ask for a change of social worker or will they say we're causing trouble?'

'I know of cases where there has been a change of social worker,' I said. 'Either because the social services felt it was appropriate, or the client requested it.'

'So it does happen?'

'Yes. Sometimes.'

'Do you think we should say it's a personality clash, rather than blaming the social worker?'

'I suppose it would be more diplomatic, although I think she needs to know how you all feel. She'll probably have no idea of the harm she's doing. Have you spoken to her about it?'

'No.' Geraldine shook her head.

'Would you feel comfortable discussing it with her?'

'I think that would be very difficult,' she said, her brow creasing.

'Then you will probably need to speak to her manager.'

'And we wouldn't be considered trouble-makers, for going behind her back?'

'No. You have valid concerns.'

'So if we request a change of social worker, can we ask for one by name? And if so, can you recommend one, or is that not allowed?'

'Not really,' I said. 'But I've worked with a lot of excellent social workers. What's happened here is unfortunate. If it's decided that a change of social worker is appropriate, it will depend on caseload and experience as to who takes over Laura's case.'

'I see,' Geraldine said, and wrung her hands in her lap. 'This is so difficult. Should we phone, write or make an appointment to see someone? Who do we ask for? Do you know the name of her manager?'

'No, I'm sorry, I don't offhand.' I hesitated and then said, 'Would it help if I telephoned the social services and found out who you should speak to? And confirmed what the correct procedure is?'

'Oh, yes. Would you? We'd be so grateful. We feel completely out of our depth. We don't want to say the wrong thing and make it worse.'

'Don't worry. I'll phone on Monday. But if they ask who it is in connection with, do I have permission to tell them?'

She hesitated. 'Yes, if it helps. I'll leave it to your discretion. Do what you think is necessary.'

'And Laura and Andy are happy for me to telephone?'

'I'm sure they will be. I'll ask them when I get back. Thank you so much, Cathy. I am grateful. I'll let you get on then.' Adjusting her cardigan, she stood ready to leave.

As I saw her out she thanked me again and said she'd phone as soon as she'd discussed what I'd said with Andy and Laura. She was going there now. I asked her to pass on my best wishes to Laura and to remind her that if she felt like dropping by I'd be very pleased to see her.

'I'll tell her,' she said.

Having seen her out, I closed the front door and returned to the living room, deep in thought. I could understand why Geraldine, Andy and Laura felt the way they did: viewing the social services as a vast, secretive, impenetrable organization with immense powers, ultimately to take your children away. Many feel this way, and until there is complete transparency in the system, with court cases accessible to the public, this view won't change. Sadly it seemed that Laura's social worker had compounded this perception. I suppose the family saw me, a foster carer, as a halfway point, a stepping stone, between them and the social services, and to a certain extent I was. Because of my role I had greater insight into the workings of the social services and possibly more accessibility. However, I didn't know whom I should contact to ask advice about a change of social worker; it wasn't something I'd ever been involved in before. Recently, I'd been working with two very good social workers, albeit for respite care only: Samson's and Shelley's. Of the two I'd found Shelley's more approachable. Shelley had spoken highly of her social worker, and I remembered she'd said she'd been very supportive of her when she'd been low after having Darrel. I decided she was the person to ask for advice and I decided I would telephone her on Monday, assuming of course that Andy and Laura agreed with Geraldine that I should phone.

They did. At nine-thirty, three-quarters of an hour after Geraldine had left me, Andy telephoned.

'Thanks, Cathy. Geraldine's told us what you've said and we'd like to accept your kind offer. Please go ahead, but could you emphasize that we're not making a complaint; we just feel Laura would benefit from a change of social worker.'

'I understand,' I said.

I then asked after Laura, and Andy said more or less what Geraldine had said. I finished by saying I'd let them know as soon as I'd spoken to someone at the social services on Monday.

'Thanks again,' he said.

I find that bad news never seems to come alone, and having heard that Laura had suffered a setback, I was shortly to receive more unwelcome news. On Sunday evening the children and I were in the living room; I was reading a story to them while we waited for John's weekly telephone call from

America. He always called about the same time on a Sunday and Adrian answered it. Aged five, this was the only time he was allowed to answer the phone, as I knew who it would be. He loved this small responsibility. 'Hello, Daddy,' he always said proudly, as soon as he picked up the handset, without waiting to hear his father's voice. Then John usually said, 'Hi, Son, how are you?' And they'd start chatting. Tonight, however, with John due home the following weekend, Adrian's excitement was bubbling over. He snatched up the handset and cried all in one breath, 'Hi, Dad, I'm going to see you soon! I can't wait.'

He went very quiet and I watched his little face fall, then he said quietly, 'Why not? You promised.'

Close to tears, he passed the handset to me. 'Dad wants to speak to you,' he said. 'He's not coming home next weekend.'

I put the phone to my ear. 'John?'

Both children watched me carefully as I listened to what John had to say. Paula wasn't old enough to understand what was happening, but she sensed the atmosphere had changed.

'I'm sorry, love,' John said. 'I know you're all disappointed. But the project I'm working on has developed a problem. I've had to cancel all leave and keep everyone on site until it's sorted out.'

'How long is that likely to take?' I asked, trying to adopt the sensible, adult approach.

'I'm hoping we'll get it fixed in a couple of weeks, but it could take longer.'

'And you have to be there?' I asked. 'Someone else couldn't manage it?'

'No. I'm in charge of this project, so it's my responsibility. I'm to blame, if you like. Trust me, I'd much rather be at home.' I heard the stress in his voice and knew he needed my support, not a guilt trip.

'I understand,' I said. 'I'll explain to Adrian, but he's bound to be disappointed.'

'I know. Let me talk to him again. I am sorry.'

I set my expression to an encouraging smile and passed the phone to Adrian. 'Daddy will be home before too long, he's just been delayed,' I said.

I couldn't hear what John was saying, but I could see from Adrian's expression that gradually, as his father spoke and reassured him, he accepted that the delay couldn't be helped and his dad would be home as soon as possible. He then brightened a little and told his father about some of the activities we'd done during the last week. When Adrian had finished talking to his father he passed the phone to Paula. She was able to say 'Hello' and 'Goodbye, Daddy', and in between she giggled and kept looking at the phone to see where his voice was coming from. John always finished by saying goodbye to Adrian and then me.

'Take care,' I said. 'And come home as soon as you can.'

'Of course I will,' he said.

That evening as I lay beside Adrian and we had our good-night chat and hug, I reassured him again that his father would be home as soon as possible.

'I know,' he said. 'At least my daddy lives with us most of the time. Some of the kids at school don't have that.'

'That's right,' I said, pleased he was adopting a positive approach. 'And in a few weeks' time he should be home for good.'

CHAPTER TWENTY

WAITING IN

At 11.30 on Monday morning I settled Adrian and Paula in the living room with their toys and took the phone into the hall where I telephoned Shelley's social worker. It was the second time I'd tried to call her that morning. When I'd phoned her previously a colleague had said she was out of the office and would return around 10.30. I guessed she was very busy on a Monday morning, but now she answered.

'It's Cathy Glass. I looked after Darrel,' I said, feeling slightly guilty for bothering her with a non-urgent matter.

'Yes, of course, hello. How are you?'

'I'm fine, thank you. I'm sorry to trouble you, but I need some advice and I thought you'd be a good person to ask.'

'Is it about Shelley and Darrel?' she asked, a little concerned.

'No. Not at all. I'm really phoning on behalf of a friend.' I then quickly explained Laura's situation – her postnatal depression and psychosis, her admission to hospital, discharge and the problems she was now facing with her social worker, without giving any names. I finished with, 'Shelley mentioned you'd helped her after she'd had Darrel, so I thought you might be able to give me some guidance that I can pass on to the family on the best way to approach this.'

'I see, well, normally the social worker would be the person to approach in the first instance when a client has concerns, but it seems to have gone past that point, so they would need to speak to the social worker's manager. If you tell me who the social worker is I can tell you which manager the family needs to speak to.'

'Thank you. That's rather what I thought.' I told her the social worker's name.

There was a short pause. 'Does this refer to Laura and Liam?' she asked.

'Yes,' I said, slightly surprised.

'I know their social worker, we're in the same team and share the same manager. I'm sure she has no idea of the effect her words are having.'

'No, I'm sure she hasn't,' I said. 'And the family are keen that this isn't treated as a formal complaint. They might still have to work with her.'

'Yes, I understand, but our manager is very approachable. I'm sure she'll be able to help. Her telephone number is –' I wrote it down. 'I have a meeting with her this afternoon. Shall I tell her what you've said so she's expecting a call from the family?'

'I think that would be helpful. Thank you.'

'But you know, it's strange that they feel this way. From what I know of the case, Laura is doing very well.'

'She was,' I said. 'I don't know all the details.'

'All right. I'll speak to my manager. And please tell Laura not to worry. I'm sure we can work something out.'

'Thank you so much. I am grateful.' We said goodbye.

Before I made the next call – to Laura's home – I checked on Paula and Adrian, who were still playing, then I stepped into the hall again. I was half expecting Laura's telephone to be answered by Geraldine, but it was Kim who said a very polite, 'Hello, who's calling, please?'

'Hi, love, it's Cathy, Adrian's mum. How are you?'

'I'm very well, thank you. Did you want to speak to Mummy?'

'Yes, or Geraldine.'

'She's not here. Mummy is in charge. Granny Geraldine only comes here sometimes, when Mummy asks her to.' Which sounded positive.

'OK. I'd like to speak to Mummy then, thank you.'

'Mum!' Kim shouted. 'It's Cathy.' A moment later Laura came to the phone.

'Hello, have you spoken to the social services?' she asked slightly anxiously.

'Yes, just now. They told me to tell you not to worry, that something can be worked out.' She gave a long, heartfelt sigh; not so much from relief, I thought, but more as though it was all too much for her. 'Laura, would you prefer it if I called back later with the details when Andy is home?' I asked.

'No, I need to face this. I can't just hide.' I heard her sigh again.

'All right, if you're sure.'

'Yes, go ahead.'

'I've emphasized that you're not making a complaint but that you'd like to discuss certain issues relating to your social worker. As I thought, you need to speak to your social worker's manager. I have her name and number here.'

'Just a minute while I fetch a pen and paper.'

I waited, and when she came on the line again I gave her the manager's details. 'She's expecting your call,' I said.

'Is she?' Laura asked, now sounding alarmed. 'You told her I'd phone?'

'Not necessarily you. But I said one of your family would – Geraldine or Andy.'

'Oh yes, sorry. I see. I thought you meant I had to phone them. I couldn't do that right now. Or perhaps I should and push myself.' She sounded very tense, so different from the last time I'd seen her when we'd sat in her garden chatting and drinking tea.

'It's up to you who phones, but try not to worry,' I said. 'The social worker I spoke to was very helpful, and confident something could be worked out. You're not the only person to ever have had issues with their social worker.'

'Aren't I?' she said. 'She makes me feel like I am. If she'd just leave me alone I could get on with looking after Liam and Kim. I'm sure I'd do better then. As it is I feel like she's breathing down my neck the whole time, and one wrong move will put me back in hospital, and the children on the child protection register.'

'She didn't say that, surely?' I asked, horrified.

'No, but that's how she makes me feel.'

Cleary Laura's relationship with her social worker had broken down irretrievably, and I hoped the manager would act quickly before Laura lost any more confidence.

'So how are you and the family generally?' I asked, wondering if she'd like a chat.

'The kids are OK. I'm up and down and trying to stay positive,' she replied honestly. 'Sorry I haven't been to see you.'

'That's OK. Come when you feel like it.'

'I will. Thanks for phoning the social services. I'll tell Andy when he calls at lunchtime. He'll know what do to. I'd better go now and see to Liam.'

Laura didn't want to chat so we said goodbye. I felt very sorry for her. Although it appeared she hadn't gone back to those really dark days of psychosis, she did sound very down and anxious. I supposed that was the depression resurfacing. I'd done all I could to help, so, forcing aside my worries for Laura, I returned to play with the children.

Life is never dull as a foster carer, and crises in families that require social services' intervention can develop at any time, so carers have to be very adaptable. At around 12.30 that Monday the children and I were making the most of the good weather and the last week of the school holidays by enjoying a picnic lunch in the garden. When the telephone rang I went into the living room to answer it. I could still see the children from there. It was the social worker of the runaway teenager I'd been put on standby for, and after a pleasant, 'Hi, how are you, Cathy?' she told me that the girl, Tracy, had been found and she would bring her to me later that afternoon, together with the paperwork I'd need – essential information and placement forms. She didn't know what – if any – clothes or toiletries Tracy would have with her, so I reassured her that I had spares she could use. She couldn't give me an exact time of arrival, but guessed it would be in a couple of hours. She said she'd phone later when they were on their way. Tracy had been found at the home of a friend by the girl's mother. They lived two doors away from Tracy and she'd been hiding in her daughter's bedroom.

I returned to the garden and had to tell Adrian (and Paula) that we couldn't go to the park that afternoon as we'd planned because Tracy was on her way. To minimize their disappointment I said we would fill the paddling pool, which they loved to play in. But before I did I checked the spare bedroom and changed the duvet cover to one that would appeal to a teenager. Adrian and Paula then helped me to clear away the picnic and fill the pool. The water was cold but that added to their shrieks of delight. I joined in, paddling and splashing, although I was also listening out for the telephone that would bring further news of Tracy. I told Adrian that when they did arrive he and Paula would have to come indoors as I couldn't leave them unattended by the pool. However, the afternoon went by without Tracy arriving, so when they'd had enough of playing in the pool I emptied it, as I always did for hygiene and safety.

It was nearly five o'clock before the social worker telephoned again, and it wasn't good news.

'Tracy's done another runner,' she said. 'By the time we got to her friend's house she'd gone. Tracy's mother has given us a couple of addresses of other friends where she might be hiding, so we'll need to check those.'

'She's not coming today then?' I asked.

'Not sure yet. The police are going to visit the addresses soon. If she is found then they may bring her to you later this evening or tonight. They've got your address and telephone number.' Which I had to accept. But this meant that not only had I spent the entire afternoon on tenterhooks waiting for news of Tracy's arrival, but that this was now set to continue into the evening and night. I'm not always sure social workers fully appreciate just what carers go through when they are on standby waiting for a child to arrive. If you're a police officer or social worker involved in the case you know exactly what's going on, but the foster carers are often left sitting at home, unable to go out, with little to do but speculate and worry. And the nature of accepting emergency placements, as opposed to long-term fostering, means that this can happen at any time. I love fostering, but it can be very disruptive and makes planning ahead difficult.

Eventually, having heard nothing by eleven o'clock that evening, I went to bed, but I only dozed fitfully as I was aware that the telephone could ring at any time, or even the doorbell if the police just arrived with the child, which had happened before. At 6 a.m., after a restless night, I declared the night over and switched on my bedside radio. I had no idea if Tracy had been found and was on her way to me, or if she was still missing. At 6.30 I showered and dressed just in case she arrived. Then, once Adrian and Paula were up, I had to tell Adrian we were still expecting Tracy so we couldn't go out. Thankfully he was happy to play in the garden again and Paula just went along with her older brother. The morning passed with no news and then, just before midday, the telephone rang.

'I'm going to collect Tracy now,' her social worker said with a sigh. 'We should be with you by three o'clock.'

'Good,' I said, relieved. 'I'll see you later.'

She didn't offer details of where Tracy had been found this time, and I didn't ask. She sounded pretty fed up. Little wonder, I thought, with the run-around Tracy had given her. So the children and I settled in for another day of playing at home, which meant that effectively we'd been in waiting for Tracy for two days. However, by 4.45, when there was still no sign of her, I was frustrated and Adrian was asking if we could take his bike to the park. I waited until five o'clock, then telephoned the social services and asked to speak to Tracy's social worker.

'She's not in the office,' her colleague said. 'She's been out on a case all day. Can I help you?' I assumed the case was Tracy.

I gave her my name, said that I was a foster carer and I'd been expecting Tracy to arrive nearly two hours ago, but I hadn't heard anything.

'Is Tracy still going into foster care then?' she asked.

'As far as I know,' I said. 'I was told by her social worker to expect her at three o'clock. I've been waiting in all day,' I added for good measure.

'I'll see if I can get hold of Tracy's social worker,' she said. 'If I can I'll ask her to phone you.'

'Thank you.'

Another hour passed before Tracy's social worker finally telephoned. 'Sorry, I haven't had a chance to update you. It's been manic all day. Tracy is staying with her older sister for now, so we won't be needing the foster placement. I'll inform the office.'

'OK. Thanks for letting me know,' I said, with only a touch of sarcasm, and we said goodbye.

What a waste of time and resources, I thought. Apart from the police and social worker's time, I'd been on standby when I might have been looking after another child. There is always a shortage of foster carers. But as I said, you have to be flexible in fostering and sometimes bite your tongue. Now I was no longer needed for Tracy, my name would be put on the white-board again at the social services' office, but which child would arrive and when I didn't know. It's a sad fact that there is usually a bit of a lull in the number of children taken into care during the long summer holidays, and when the schools return and teachers start to notice bruises or a child behaving oddly or even disclosing abuse, the number of referrals rises. But for now I would make the most of the rest of the week – the last few days of the summer holidays.

'Who would like to go to the zoo tomorrow?' I asked Adrian and Paula.

'Meeeeeee!' Adrian cried in excitement.

'Meeeee!' Paula repeated, with no idea what she was agreeing to.

Adrian told her: 'They have grizzly bears with big teeth and claws, snakes that can strangle you, alligators and lions that eat you. Grrrr!' he said, clawing his hands and stalking her.

'Grrrrr,' she repeated, laughing, and not the least bit scared.

I sincerely hoped that I didn't receive a telephone call from the social services to say a child was in need of a home, for it's very difficult to say no, yet I couldn't bear the look of disappointment on the faces of Adrian and Paula if another outing had to be cancelled.

That evening, after the children were in bed and there'd been no phone call from the social services, I telephoned a friend of mine whose son was a friend of Adrian's (he went to his birthday party), and whose daughter was a similar age to Paula. I asked her if she'd like to join us on our trip to the zoo. She jumped at the opportunity as she had no other plans, and we made arrangements to meet in our cars at the end of my road at 9 a.m. The following morning when I told Adrian they were coming too, he was delighted, as I knew he would be – having a friend for company adds to the fun of any outing, even grocery shopping! Before we left the house that morning

I checked I'd switched on the answerphone so that if the social services did telephone they could leave a message. If there was an emergency placement then they'd have to find another foster carer. Today I was concentrating on my family.

My friend's car was already waiting at the end of the road and I parked behind her and got out. After a quick discussion on the best route to the zoo she said she'd follow me, as she wasn't sure about some of the route. The zoo was about a forty-five-minute drive away. We returned to our cars and headed off. As I drove Adrian kept watch through the rear window to make sure we didn't lose them, although of course I could see their car in my mirror, but it was part of the fun. Paula kept turning to look too, but being that much smaller she couldn't see over her car seat. The journey went well and when we arrived we parked in the zoo's car park, let the children out and then, armed with the strollers and bags containing nappies and so forth for the girls, we paid at the turnstile and amid great excitement went in.

The weather was perfect for a day that involved lots of walking outside – warm, but with some cloud cover so it wasn't too hot, although we still put sunscreen on the children. The zoo is set in acres of countryside so the animals are free to roam in large enclosures, which is much kinder than keeping them in cages and replicates their natural habitats as much as possible. Cars aren't allowed in the grounds so it's a safe place for children, and the boys ran ahead (although they knew they weren't to go out of our sight), while the girls toddled beside us. My friend and I chatted in between admiring the animals and discussing the facts we learned about them with the children. There were information boards dotted around the park by the enclosures, and I think we all learned something new. The apes, monkeys and chimpanzees were of course fascinating with their human-like characteristics, and we spent a long time just standing and watching them; they held eye contact with us, which was a bit unsettling. But when the female baboons turned around to expose their bright-red bottoms the boys fell about laughing, and the girls were pointing. Of course it's guaranteed with any visit to see animals that at some point a pair will become amorous. Today it was the goats' turn – one buck was very persistent and enthusiastic in trying to mount a doe, but she wasn't interested.

'Look, Mummy,' Adrian's friend said loudly. 'That goat wants to play piggyback but his friend won't let him.'

'I know the feeling,' a man beside us quipped. My friend and I laughed, but his wife told him off.

'They're trying to make babies,' my friend explained quietly to the boys.

The boys glanced at each other, looked embarrassed and then dissolved into laughter. The girls had no idea what was funny but laughed too.

We stopped for lunch in the zoo's café at one o'clock and then continued going round the rest of the enclosures. By five o'clock we'd seen most of the animals and everyone was exhausted; the girls were now asleep in their strollers, so we decided to head for the exit. We stopped off at the gift shop and bought a small souvenir each and then returned home in our convoy of two cars. At the top of my road we parted company, tooting our car horns and with all the children waving vigorously. We'd had a really good day out and despite feeling tired I felt refreshed from the change of scenery after two days at home.

As soon as we stepped into the hall I saw that the answerphone light was flashing, signalling a message. 'Perhaps it's Daddy,' Adrian said hopefully.

'I doubt it. He'll be at work,' I said. He didn't usually phone during the week because of the time difference. But Adrian was still looking at the phone expectantly, so I pressed the play button. Samson's social worker's voice came through: 'Cathy, could you give me a ring, please?' Adrian immediately lost interest and went down the hall while I listened to the rest of the message. 'We're going to court next week for an order to bring Samson into care. I wanted to check that you are still happy to look after him. Could you phone when you are free, please?'

It was too late to telephone now – their offices would be closed – so I'd phone when they opened in the morning. Although I was still happy to look after Samson, I was sad that it had come to this and he had to be brought into foster care. It meant that, despite all the support the social services and other agencies had put into the family, their situation had deteriorated, and there was now no alternative but to bring him into care for his own good – assuming, of course, that the judge granted the order. Unlike under a Section 20 (of the Children's Act), also known as Accommodated, when parents agree to place their child in care voluntarily and there is no court case, the fact that the social services were going to court meant that Samson's family didn't agree with their decision and were fighting to keep him. And who could blame them? I knew Samson's home life wasn't perfect, but they were his only family, and to remove any child from home and split up the family is heartbreaking and a decision that is never taken lightly.

* * *

That evening when the children, tired from all the walking, were in bed asleep and I was thinking of going to bed soon, Shelley telephoned. 'I thought you'd like to know how the choir is going,' she said.

'Yes, please.' I sat up and shook off the sleep.

'It's great! I love singing with all the others and I've met someone! I'm dating!' I could hear the excitement in her voice and knew this was the real reason she'd telephoned.

'That's fantastic,' I said. 'I am pleased for you. Tell me all about him.'

'He's a really, really nice person, Cathy, and good-looking. I can't believe my luck. He hasn't met Darrel yet; I'm waiting until I'm completely sure of him. But I have met his parents. They're lovely too and they all sing. I think they liked me.'

'Is this the lad from the choir?' I asked.

'Yes. How did you know?'

'I think you might have mentioned him the last time I saw you.'

'Yes, possibly. I thought he was cool right from the start. I guess I was hoping he'd ask me out. He's two years older than me and he works for an IT firm, so he knows lots of stuff about computers. He has a car and he collects me from my flat and ...' Shelley continued telling me *all* about him: his work, hobbies, favourite food, tastes in and love of music, the football team he supported and that he went to church. When she'd finished I felt I knew as much about him as she did. I could tell it was serious and that she was falling in love.

'I'm going to tell Carol all about him when I see her on Sunday,' Shelley added.

'She'll be as pleased as I am,' I said. 'I'll look forward to meeting him when you're ready.'

'Oh yes, you and Carol will be the first to meet him. Well, my friend has already met him, but that's different because she babysits for me and he gives her a lift home after. I can't believe how my life has changed in the last six months! I'm so happy, Cathy.'

'You deserve it,' I said. 'You're a lovely person and by the sound of it he is too. You make a good match.'

'Thank you. He is really nice. But enough of me and what I've been doing. How are you guys?'

'We're all fine, thank you. Getting ready for going back to school. How's Darrel?'

'He's good. He starts school next week.'

We chatted for a while longer and then wound up. 'Give Adrian and Paula my love,' Shelley said.

'I will, and wish Darrel well on his first day at school. We'll be thinking about him.'

'Thank you. I'm more nervous than he is. It'll be strange not having him around during the day, but I'm sure he'll be fine.'

We said goodbye and I replaced the handset, still smiling and happy for her. Shelley was such a kind, good-natured, gentle person, she deserved all the happiness on offer. By the sound of it her young man was a genuinely nice guy, so I hoped their relationship would develop. I hadn't told her I'd spoken to her social worker earlier in the week, as it would have raised the question why, and of course my conversation about Laura had been confidential. I wondered if Andy or Geraldine had telephoned the social services and, if so, how they'd got on, but I wouldn't phone and ask them. If they wanted me to know they'd tell me, and before long I'd have my hands full looking after Samson.

CHAPTER TWENTY-ONE

LAST RESORT

I didn't have to telephone Samson's social worker in the morning as I'd planned to do; she phoned me as soon as she was at her desk, at 8.45. 'You got my answerphone message?' she asked.

'Yes. I can look after Samson,' I confirmed.

'Good. I need to show the judge that I have a suitable foster carer ready if the court grants the order. Can I confirm a few details with you? You're married, and you have two children. What are their ages?'

'Adrian is five and Paula is sixteen months.'

'And you'd be able to take Samson to school and collect him? He's been going to breakfast club, so he could continue with that if it helps.'

'Yes, that would help. I could take him first and then take Adrian after. We'll have to work something out for the end of the day.'

There was a pause as she wrote. 'At present Samson has supervised contact with his father once a week, on a Friday, at the family centre. We'll have to make separate contact provision for him to see his gran and possibly the aunts too. It would take place after school at the centre, so you'd be able to take and collect him?'

'Yes.' This was expected of foster carers and was one of their roles.

'If necessary, you'd be able to keep Samson long term?' she asked.

'Yes, although I'd need to check with my husband, but I can't see a problem. I'll mention it to him the next time he phones.'

She wrote again. 'And you can obviously manage his behaviour.'

'I will do my best,' I said. She gave a small laugh. 'Can I ask why you've decided to bring Samson into care?' I now asked.

'His gran's poor health and lack of mobility means she can't meet his needs or cope with his behaviour. There is no one else in the immediate family willing to take responsibility for him or look after him, so he's just been left to run riot. The police have been logging complaints from residents on the estate when he's been out at night causing trouble. Last week they picked him up with a gang of older youths armed with tools for breaking into houses. We're also concerned that no one in the family spotted the abuse by his father's girlfriend. It had been going on for some time. So generally the whole situation has deteriorated. We're going to court next Wednesday and, assuming the order is granted, we're planning to move him to you after contact on Friday.'

'All right, I'll be ready.'

'Thank you. I'll phone beforehand.'

With only three days before the start of the new school term, I checked Adrian's school uniform and games kit and that his book bag was ready. I'd already bought him new school shoes.

It's always a wrench returning to school after the long summer holidays, and while Adrian was looking forward to seeing his classmates again he was understandably anxious at the prospect of a new class teacher with different ways of doing things. I knew Paula would miss having him at home to play with, and I'd miss him too, as well as the relaxing routine of the holiday. The weather seemed to sense that the school holidays were drawing to a close and the autumn term was about to begin. On Saturday the temperature dropped and a chilly north-easterly wind began to blow, bringing rain. We spent the day indoors, and then on Sunday my parents came for dinner. We had a pleasant day, although they didn't stay late, as they knew we had to be up reasonably early for school the following morning.

Adrian took a long while to go to sleep that night; I think he was worrying about school, although he wouldn't tell me. Then on Monday morning he took ages getting dressed and didn't want his breakfast because he said he had a tummy ache. I knew it was a nervous tummy ache, so I gave him a big cuddle and reassured him that all his friends would be feeling the same way and once he was there he would be fine. I said we'd be thinking of him and that the day would fly by and before he knew it he would be home again. He managed a small, unconvincing smile, ate a little of his breakfast and then went very quiet as he brushed his teeth and put on his school shoes. The weather didn't help – it was raining again, so I had to find our raincoats and then fit the rain cover over the stroller, which Paula didn't like as it restricted her vision; she kept trying to kick it off. As a result we left the house later than we should have done and had to walk quickly. Not the best way to start the new school year!

Although we weren't late – the Klaxon hadn't sounded – we were one of the last to arrive in the playground. It was full of chattering parents and children sheltering under their umbrellas, which was probably why I didn't spot them straight away. Then I heard two female voices call, 'Hi, Cathy!' and 'Over here!' I looked over to see Fran and her daughter and, to my surprise, Laura, with the pram and Kim, waving to me.

I began towards them but the Klaxon sounded, so I made a detour to the entrance. Because it was raining the children didn't have to line up in their classes; they could go straight in. As I said goodbye to Adrian a friend joined him in the queue to go in and Adrian immediately brightened as they began talking. 'Have a good day,' I said to the both of them. Adrian smiled and gave a little wave, which was a relief.

Paula now began agitating and kicking the inside of the rain cover, wanting to get out. 'No, you have to stay there. It's raining. Baby Liam's over there.'

I crossed the playground to Fran and Laura. Their children had now gone into school and they were standing under Fran's umbrella waiting for me. Laura, like me, didn't have an umbrella but had her hood up, as it's virtually impossible to manoeuvre a pram or stroller while holding an umbrella.

'How are you? Good to see you,' Fran said, tilting her umbrella to one side so we could cheek kiss.

'I'm fine. Lovely to see you both.' Then to Laura I added, 'What a nice surprise.'

'I surprised myself!' Laura joked, and laughed easily.

'Did you have a good summer?' Fran asked me.

'Yes, very relaxing. And you?'

'We went camping in France. Three weeks. Bliss. I wish I was there now.' She pulled a face and looked up at the sky.

'Rather than stand here getting wet, why don't you both come back to my place for coffee?' Laura suggested. 'We can talk there.'

'I'd love to,' Fran said. 'But I've got the plumber coming in half an hour to quote for a new boiler. Another time.'

'I'm free,' I said.

'Good,' Laura said. 'And you're in luck – Mum was with us at the weekend and made one of her cakes.'

'Even better,' I said.

'I'm jealous,' Fran joked.

We left the playground together and then Fran said goodbye and went on her way.

'How is Liam?' I asked, glancing into the pram. I couldn't see much of him because of the rain cover.

'He's doing very well. Putting on weight. You'll notice a difference; he's grown so much.'

'Baby Liam!' Paula cried from under the rain cover and gave it another kick. The rain had eased now to a light drizzle, so I stopped and drew back the top part of the cover so she could see out.

'Baby Liam!' she cried, much happier now. Pushing herself up in the stroller, she tried to peer into the pram, but it was too high.

'You can see Liam when we go to my house,' Laura said to her.

'We're going to Liam's house,' I confirmed to Paula.

Now she was free of the cover and had the promise of seeing Liam, she was happy to stay in the stroller rather than walk. Laura and I made polite conversation as we walked.

'Is your husband home now?' she asked. I must have mentioned a while back that he was due home at the end of August.

'No, unfortunately not, he's been delayed. A technical hitch with the project he's working on.'

'Oh dear. What a disappointment.'

'It was, but he's hoping to be home in a couple of weeks. The time will soon pass.'

'It will. I can't believe Liam is over six months old already.'

We continued making polite conversation, small talk on safe, general, non-probing subjects: the weather, the children, and the new classes they were in. I asked her how Gina and Geraldine were. I didn't ask how she was feeling – I couldn't think of a way of phrasing it that didn't make it sound blunt or intrusive. Laura looked well, but then she had done the last time I'd seen her, before her setback. That's the problem with mental health; it's often hidden, not like a broken arm, which is obvious. But of course ignoring Laura's health or that she'd had issues with her social worker was like ignoring the elephant in the room. She must have felt it too, for once we were in her hall and she'd closed the front door and was removing the waterproof from Liam's pram she said, 'You know, Cathy, it's OK to ask me how things are. I won't go to pieces and embarrass you.'

'I'm sorry,' I said.

'Don't be. I know it's difficult. Let's settle the children. I'll make us a drink and tell you what's been happening.'

Fifteen minutes later we were all in her living room, with Liam in his bouncing cradle being kept amused by Paula, who was showing him a selection of toys from a box Laura had brought in. She had a bottle ready for Liam when he needed it and on the coffee table was a beaker of water and a biscuit Paula had wanted. Laura and I were sipping coffee and tucking into Gina's delicious walnut and butter-icing sponge cake – another recipe I'd be asking for. Paula had tried a little of mine but hadn't liked the ground nuts.

'Thank you for telephoning the social services,' Laura began, setting her cup in its saucer. 'It was a great help. Andy was going to phone you to thank you, but I told him I'd be seeing you in the playground.'

'That's OK. I'm pleased it helped,' I said.

'It did, a lot. I've been given a new social worker, but what really helped me was when the one I had telephoned and apologized. She admitted that once it had been pointed out to her she could see that the way she'd approached some aspects of my case could have been handled differently. You see, Cathy, she kept giving me advice and referring to meetings she'd had with other professionals involved in my case, so I felt they were taking over and running my life. It was like when I was really ill and Geraldine took over. My confidence went and I felt useless. I began overthinking everything again, questioning everything I was doing. There's this internal dialogue going on in your head, telling you you're a waste of space and you'll never cope. Everything the social worker said seemed to make it worse, and then I started to have the distant, far-away feeling I'd had before when I was ill, like I was not fully there and was watching myself in a movie. If that makes sense.'

'It sounds dreadful,' I said. I'd stopped eating my cake and was concentrating fully on Laura. It was the first time she'd talked candidly about what she'd actually experienced, and I began to have an insight into just how frightening it must have been for her.

'I was nowhere near as bad this time as I was when I was very ill,' she continued. 'But there were enough reminders to make me scared. I knew where it could go if I didn't say something and get help. I felt I was being dragged towards the edge of that cliff again. It's a very scary place, Cathy, a dark and dangerous place, and I knew I mustn't ever go there again. Before, when I was really ill, I used to sit in here huddled up at one end of the sofa and cry silently for hours and hours.' She shuddered. 'I kept the curtains closed so the room was always dark. It seemed safer, but I began to feel as though the walls were closing in and crushing me and I couldn't breathe. I felt I was being crushed to death.

'And poor little Liam,' she said, glancing towards him. 'I thought he hated me – when I was really bad, psychotic, before I went into hospital. It seems ridiculous now, but the way he looked at me and wouldn't cooperate seemed to confirm it. When I tried to feed him he'd turn his head away sometimes, and would scream if I changed his nappy or bathed him. I know all babies do that, but when I was in that dark place I thought it was because of me. At night he wouldn't settle for me, but he would for Geraldine and Andy, so I thought he'd be better off without me. Now, of course, I realize he was probably picking up on my anxiety. But at the time I thought I was such a bad and wicked mother that I'd been punished by giving birth to the devil's child.'

'Oh, Laura,' I said. 'You poor thing.'

'Thankfully he was unaware of it,' she said stoically. 'But when I started having issues with that social worker and began to slide again I knew I needed help. Geraldine and

Andy saw me in tears and I was able to tell them how I was feeling. As soon as I'd told them, and we had a plan of action to try and change social workers, I started to feel a bit better. I felt I was taking control again. Then after Andy spoke to the manager and the social worker phoned and apologized, I felt vindicated. It wasn't all my fault, and a huge weight lifted from my shoulders. Even if I hadn't been given a new social worker, I think I would have got by – once she'd acknowledged there was a problem and it wasn't just me. I haven't met the new social worker yet, but she sounded nice when she phoned. I think you know her.' She gave the name of Shelley's social worker.

'Yes,' I said, smiling. 'You're in safe hands there.'

'I feel I am,' Laura said, finally picking up her cake again. 'I know I'm going to be just fine, thanks to you.'

'Thanks to you,' I said firmly. 'You're a great mum. Your children are very lucky to have you, Laura.' And I felt my eyes fill.

I stayed for a second cup of coffee and a slice of cake and then left with a copy of the recipe and a big hug from Laura, in the happy knowledge that she and her family were going to be all right. They had come through a very difficult time but were now looking forward to a brighter future, their family stronger from the experience they'd shared. Sadly, this wasn't true for Samson, who at present was blissfully unaware that very soon he would be packing more than a backpack and going away for a lot longer than a few days' respite, possibly for good. I felt for him having to leave his family and endure all the changes that lay in store, but at least now that I knew it was almost certain he would be arriving on Friday I could plan ahead, unlike with an emergency placement when there is very little notice.

That afternoon I changed the duvet cover and matching pillowcase again in what would shortly be Samson's room, putting on one suitable for a six-year-old boy. It was light grey with images of action heroes – Spiderman, Superman and so on. I took down the posters of cute, cuddly animals and then gave the room a good dust and hoover, as it had been standing empty for a while. That evening after dinner I told Adrian that it was very likely Samson would be coming to live with us on Friday and I asked him how he felt about it.

'OK,' he said. 'But he won't be allowed to bring Bruno, will he?'

'No, although he's going to miss him.'

'Perhaps he could have a photo of him,' Adrian suggested. 'Like the children have of their parents.'

'Good idea.' I always encouraged the children I fostered to bring some photographs of their family with them, and Bruno was part of Samson's family.

Although Adrian seemed OK about having Samson come to live with us, I would be keeping a close eye on them, especially in the early weeks while Samson was settling in, as well as making sure all the children received their fair share of attention. While Samson's behaviour on respite hadn't been too bad, I knew it could be very different when a child came to live long term with a carer. Angry, hurting and confused at having to leave their family and wanting to test their carer's commitment, their behaviour can deteriorate rapidly and become very challenging. Then they adjust to being in care and their anger begins to leave them. They decide you've passed their test and have proven that no matter what they throw at you, you will still care about them, and they turn the corner and settle down. Well, that's the theory, at least.

On Tuesday, after taking Adrian to school, I drove into town and bought some new posters for Samson's bedroom: of the moon, a robot, a shark leaping from the water, a large male lion roaring, and one showing the times tables, which I knew he was struggling to learn at school. I also bought a poster each for Adrian's and Paula's bedrooms so they didn't feel left out. On returning home, Paula came with me to Samson's room and 'helped' me decide where the posters should hang. There was already a clock on the wall and a child's calendar, which were useful for a child of any age. Satisfied that the room was welcoming and ready for Samson, I came out and closed the door.

I knew I'd have to establish a routine for Samson that would include time for learning as well as play. We couldn't hold sports days and pretend birthday parties every evening and weekend, although I would of course give him a proper party when it was his birthday, which was some months away yet. I would also need to put in place guidelines for when and how long he watched television and played on his PlayStation, which I assumed he would want to bring with him. He would still be allowed these, of course, but as a recreation, something to do in his spare time, not as a tool for babysitting or keeping him quiet. I'd have to check the PlayStation games for their suitability. If they weren't age appropriate, which, from what he'd told me, I assumed many of them weren't, then I'd put them away until he was older and inform his social worker I'd done so. I could foresee Samson kicking off big time if I did have to put away some of the PlayStation games, but it would be irresponsible of me as a foster carer and a parent to allow him to view inappropriate material in any form, on the PlayStation, on television or in magazines.

I knew Samson's school work was a long way behind what it should be, especially his literacy skills, and I would be helping him to catch up, a little at a time. Adrian was learning to read and he was in the routine of reading to me for a while every evening, as well as doing any homework set by the school, before he played or watched television. But of course it's easier to establish a routine when you've had your child since birth, whereas Samson would have to relinquish some of what he was used to before accepting my guidelines. It was for his own long-term good, although I doubted he'd see it that way. But I'd take it gently, one step at a time. You can't make too many changes all at once or the child can withdraw or rebel. I was also mindful that Adrian, a year younger, was well ahead of Samson academically, and I'd need to make sure Samson didn't feel this, as it could undermine his confidence. As far as I knew, Samson didn't have learning difficulties and his lack of progress was due to neglect at home, so he should be able to catch up. I'd know more about his abilities and his background when his social worker gave me the placement information on Friday.

On Wednesday morning as I showered and dressed my thoughts went to Samson's gran, who at this moment was rising and getting ready for three days in court. I didn't know if anyone else from the family would be going, but my heart went out to her. She wasn't in good health and going to court is an anxious and gruelling ordeal for anyone, even more so for someone of her age, and of course she was fighting to keep her only grandchild. What must she be feeling!

I walked back from school that morning with Laura and I mentioned that I was expecting a new child on Friday, although I didn't give any details. I saw her face grow serious and she went very quiet. 'You know, Cathy,' she said after some moments, concentrating on the pram, 'that really scares me, hearing you say that. The poor family, having their child taken away. That moment when you have to say goodbye and hand your child to another person ... I don't know how they cope.'

'Neither do I,' I said quietly.

CHAPTER TWENTY-TWO

A REPRIEVE

On Thursday morning my thoughts turned again to Samson's gran and how she was coping as she faced her second day in court. The adversarial nature of our court system in care proceedings meant that his gran and any other family members responsible for Samson would be in court, represented by a solicitor and barrister who would argue their case for Samson not going into foster care. If the child's parents are not living together then they are likely to have a solicitor and barrister each, the child often has their own legal representation, and the social services has a legal team. In addition to the judge there is a court recorder, an usher and other court staff, although journalists and the public are not allowed in, which is why these proceedings are sometimes referred to as taking place behind closed doors. But like any court there is a correct procedure, which must be strictly adhered to, as statements are scrutinized and witnesses called to give evidence. While solicitors do their best to explain procedures to their clients, it can still be daunting, confusing and complex, especially for someone like Samson's gran, who presumably had never been involved in care proceedings before. It's also very nerve-racking to have to stand in front of a court, swear an oath, give evidence and then be cross-examined by a barrister.

I wasn't expecting to hear from Samson's social worker until Friday when the judge had made his or her ruling. I'd planned to take Paula to the mother-and-toddler group on Thursday afternoon as I had been doing the previous term. She enjoyed the contact with the other children and I enjoyed the company of the other mothers and one father. However, mid-morning on Thursday I received a telephone call – or rather an SOS – from Chris, another foster carer I knew.

'Cathy, could you do me a big favour and look after Elspeth for an hour or so this afternoon? I've been up all night with raging toothache and I've made an emergency appointment at the dentist for one-thirty.'

'Yes, of course,' I said. 'You poor thing.' We arranged for her to bring Elspeth to me just after one o'clock.

Fosters carers often network in the area in which they live, for company, emotional support and to help each other out. It's difficult as it is to attend appointments with a small child, but it's even more so for a foster carer when babysitters have to be identified to the social services in advance. You can't, for example, simply ask a random friend to help out in an emergency as you would with your own child.

Elspeth was the two-year-old girl Chris had been fostering for over a year, and after lunch I explained to Paula that she was coming to play for a while. She tried to say 'Elspeth' and was still practising when they arrived. It had been a couple of months since I'd last seen Elspeth, and in that time she'd grown and was now more adorable than ever. With her mop of loose black curls, large dark eyes and chubby little cheeks she looked like a life-size doll. 'This is Elspeth,' I said to Paula.

'Elf,' she said, smiling at her.

Chris didn't have time to come in so I wished her good luck and she kissed Elspeth goodbye.

'Bye,' Elspeth said, waving.

'Bye,' Paula repeated, also waving.

Two little cuties. Chris smiled as she left, despite the pain she was in.

Six months older than Paula, Elspeth (or rather Elf) chatted away to Paula and kept her amused, when she wasn't chasing the cat. Elspeth didn't have any pets at her house, so Toscha was a novelty. She was fascinated by the way she cleaned herself with her paw and purred when stroked. Chris was only gone for an hour and returned with a prescription for antibiotics and another appointment in ten days' time, when I said I'd look after Elspeth again if necessary. She thanked me and stayed for a quick cup of tea before we both had to leave and go our separate ways to collect our children from their schools. I knew the care plan for Elspeth was originally for her to return to her mother, but that was looking increasingly less likely as the poor woman kept dropping out of the methadone programme she was in and returning to heroin. I knew that before long the social services would have to decide if going home was feasible and, if not, they would place Elspeth for adoption. Sad though this would be, it's unfair to leave a child in care indefinitely and deny them a chance of a permanent family of their own.

On Friday morning my thoughts turned again to Samson's gran and they continued to do so as the day wore on. By early afternoon I knew the judge would have probably heard all the evidence and would be delivering his or her judgment. I thought Samson's gran (and other family members) were probably resigned to their fate by now and would just want to get the inevitable over and done with – to hear the decision and prepare to say goodbye to Samson.

I collected Adrian from school, gave Samson's room a final check and then made dinner. I was expecting his social worker to telephone at any time, but by 5.30 when she still hadn't phoned I assumed she'd been too busy and would simply arrive with Samson after contact, which finished at six o'clock. I knew how hectic it was for social workers after a court hearing when they had to bring a child into care. I'd no idea what personal possessions Samson would be bringing with him, but if necessary he could use the spare clothes I kept until he had some of his own, either from home or bought by me. Hopefully his gran would pack his favourite toys, which would help him settle in.

When the phone rang at 5.45 I was relieved to hear Samson's social worker. 'Sorry I haven't been in touch sooner,' she said. 'This is the first opportunity. It's been non-stop.'

'I can imagine,' I said.

'I doubt it. We didn't get the order. Samson's not coming into care. Not now, at least.'

'Oh,' I said. I didn't know whether to feel relieved or disappointed – I felt a bit of both.

'The judge wants more support put into the family, with a review in three months' time. I'm not sure what else we can do, but we have to accept and abide by the ruling. The hearing had its moments, though. The first day was a fiasco. The whole family turned up: aunts, uncles, cousins I'd never heard of, his gran, his father – no sign of the mum. They brought the dog with them too, which they tied up outside the court.'

'Oh no!'

'You could hear it barking from inside the courtroom. The judge wasn't impressed and said it was cruel to leave it tied up all day, and also it was terrorizing those coming into and leaving the building. He told them not to bring it back the next day.'

I had to smile; having met Bruno, I fully appreciated the scene.

'But Gran's barrister made a good case for Samson staying at home, with more support. So that's what we're going to do, starting with fumigating the flat.'

'Pardon?' I said, thinking I'd misheard.

'They've got bed bugs. Gran told the judge she'd been asking the council for weeks to fumigate the flat, but nothing had been done. She pulled up her top and showed him her bite marks. The family laughed, but they were bad, and the judge criticized us for not doing anything about it sooner. I've just contacted pest control now; they're fumigating the flat next week. I hope Samson didn't bring any bugs with him when he stayed with you.'

'So do I!' I said, grimacing and involuntarily scratching my arm.

'Check the room he slept in. Especially the bedding and curtains. They are easily transported on clothes and in luggage and can reproduce very quickly. Do you know what they look like?'

'Yes, I think so. I've seen pictures.'

'So, Cathy, that's it really. Samson will continue to have supervised contact with his father once a week, and we'll look at what other support we can put into the family. I expect you'll be asked to have Samson again on respite.'

'That's fine if I haven't got another child,' I said.

'I've put your name back on the board again. I'm going home now. I'm exhausted. Have a good weekend.'

'And you.' We said goodbye.

I could tell she was disappointed at the ruling, as indeed to some extent I was. All that planning and organizing had come to nothing. Clearly the social services had believed that bringing Samson into care full time was the right course of action or they wouldn't have applied for an order, but now they had to comply with the judge's decision, whether they agreed with it or not. What would happen in three months' time would depend on the progress the family had made in meeting Samson's needs, but for now he could stay at home and I had to readjust to that, as would his social worker. I went into the living room where Adrian and Paula were playing with Lego and I told them that Samson wouldn't be coming to live with us after all.

'Oh,' Adrian said, surprised. 'Why not?'

'The judge has decided he should stay with his gran, although he may come to us again on respite.'

'That's good for him and his gran then,' Adrian said perceptively.

'Yes, it is. Very good,' I said. 'Can you watch Paula for a few minutes? I need to check Samson's room – I mean, the spare room.'

Adrian nodded. He was responsible enough that I could leave him with Paula while I went upstairs for a while. It still seemed to me to be Samson's room with the bedding and posters I'd chosen with him in mind. I went in and began searching for any uninvited guests: little brown bugs that turned red after feeding on human blood and caused their host a lot of itching and painful swelling. I checked the walls first, especially the corners, for while bed bugs feed on their hosts at night in bed they can live anywhere in a room. Although the bedding was freshly laundered I carefully pulled back the duvet, watching for any signs of life, and removed the cover and thoroughly checked it inside and out. Then the pillowcase, sheet and mattress protector. I turned the mattress and examined it on both sides but it was clear. I'd have been surprised if I had found bugs, as I regularly change the bedding, vacuum and thoroughly clean the room, so even if Samson had brought any with him they should have been disposed of in the cleaning. Lastly, I checked behind the curtains, the drawers and wardrobe, and they were clear too, but just to be perfectly sure I'd vacuum the room again tomorrow when I had time. As I refolded the bedding I looked around the room. I'd invested so much time in preparing and customizing it for Samson's arrival. It seemed a sad place now, lonely and empty, as though in losing its purpose it had lost its soul. But even well-laid plans can and do change abruptly, and accepting this, adjusting and moving on is all part of fostering.

My name was on the whiteboard again at the social services as being free to foster, so it was possible I could have a child placed with me over the weekend as an emergency. The following morning, as soon as Adrian and Paula were up, I thoroughly cleaned the spare room again. I didn't know the age or sex of the child I might be asked to foster, so for the time being I left up all the posters and remade the bed with the superhero duvet cover I'd put on fresh for Samson.

As it turned out my preparations didn't go to waste this time. Although I didn't receive a call to take a child as an emergency over the weekend, on Monday morning I was surprised to receive a phone call from Samson's social worker.

'Hello again,' she said, sounding more upbeat than she had on Friday. 'Did you have a good weekend?'

'Yes, thank you. Did you?'

'Wonderful. I slept for most of it.' She gave a small laugh. 'The reason I'm phoning is that Samson's flat is being fumigated tomorrow, Tuesday, and while it's OK for them to go back into the flat once the chemical has dried, Gran has asked if Samson can be looked after for the night, just to be safe.'

'Yes, sure,' I said. 'His room is still ready from Friday.'

'That's great. Thank you. I'll tell Gran to pack an overnight bag for him to take to school with him tomorrow morning. Then you can collect him from after-school club at five o'clock and take him straight home with you.'

'Yes, that's fine.'

'On Wednesday morning take him to breakfast club with his bag, and he'll go home at the end of the day as normal.'

'That works well for me,' I said.

'Good.' She gave me the name and address of the school, which I wrote down. 'Thanks, Cathy.'

I was pleased to be looking after Samson again, even if it was only for one night, although I'd be checking his bag to make sure he hadn't brought any bed bugs with him. I knew from an article I'd read previously just how quickly an infestation can occur and how difficult it was to get rid of.

When I saw Laura in the playground that afternoon she asked why I hadn't got another child with me, as I'd told her I was expecting a child to arrive on Friday. I said only that the judge hadn't granted the social services the Care Order, and she was surprised. 'So they don't get it automatically?' she asked.

'No. They have to prove their case.' She looked puzzled. 'If there are concerns about a child,' I explained, 'and the parents don't agree to placing the child in care voluntarily, the social services have to apply to court for a Care Order. They can't just take a child away.'

'I see,' she said. 'Well, that is reassuring. I assumed the social services had complete authority. I didn't realize a judge could overrule them.'

'I think a lot of people believe that,' I said. 'I've heard similar said before, but the social services have to prove to the judge that there are sufficient grounds to remove a child. If there aren't then the child remains at home and the social services usually continue to monitor the family.'

'I see,' she said again. Then as we walked home together Laura said, 'I think that child's family will try harder in the future, now they've had the shock of nearly losing him.'

'It does happen,' I said. 'A wake-up call. Although you have to remember that not everyone has the support of a loving family, as you and I do. It can be very difficult for some families to get their lives back on track. You'd be shocked at just how alone some people are. And some people haven't had good role models when they were growing up, or were treated badly. These factors can have a huge impact on the way a person treats their own children.'

Laura nodded. I didn't know how much of this was relevant to Samson's situation, but it was true generally. Although there were a lot of members in Samson's extended family, they appeared to let his gran get on with raising Samson without helping or supporting her. And Gran herself sometimes seemed cold and uncaring.

'Well, I hope that child's family can change,' Laura said. 'I know I would do anything to keep my kids.'

That evening I explained to Adrian (and Paula) that Samson would be coming to stay for one night and outlined the arrangements for collecting him from school the following day and returning him on Wednesday morning.

'Why don't I go to breakfast club?' Adrian asked.

'There is no need. I don't have to leave the house early to go out to work.'

'Does Samson's gran work?' he asked. He knew something of Samson's family from what Samson had told him and from what he'd picked up by going to his flat.

'No, she doesn't,' I said. 'But it helps her if he has breakfast at school, and I think he likes it.'

'Is that why he has to stay for after-school club as well?' Adrian asked. 'To help her?'

'Yes,' I said.

'Samson said it was to get him out from under her feet.'

'I guess that is helping her then,' I said with a smile.

The following day the arrangements worked perfectly. With Samson staying late at after-school club, I had plenty of time to collect Adrian and then drive to Samson's school where I parked in a side road and we waited until it was time to go in and collect him. A noticeboard outside the school gate said that the after-school club was held in the main hall, so we followed the other parents in. The children were ready with their jackets on, waiting to be collected.

'That's her!' Samson yelled as we entered the hall, making

everyone turn to look. He ran over with his school bag on one shoulder and a large holdall on the other.

'Hi, Samson, good to see you again,' I said. He high-fived Adrian and then Paula. I showed the person in charge my foster-carer ID and we left.

'We've got bed bugs,' Samson announced proudly.

'Really?' Adrian said, impressed, not knowing what these were.

Samson told him. 'They live in your bed and while you're asleep they crawl all over you and suck your blood.'

'Not *your* blood,' I reassured Adrian, who was looking worried. 'We haven't got bed bugs.'

'We have!' Samson declared, as though it was an achievement. 'Gran told the judge and showed him where they'd eaten her alive and sucked out all her blood like a vampire.' I thought Samson had been watching too many horror films again, but it was interesting that his gran had told him she'd been to court. I wondered what else she'd told him.

'Bed bugs are only very small,' I reassured Adrian. 'They take a tiny bit of blood, like a mosquito. But they're nasty and make you itch. They have to be got rid of.'

'We're having them exterminated,' Samson said as we walked to the car. 'Like the daleks. Exterminate! Exterminate!' Raising his arm, he fired at us in a dalek-like extermination and Adrian and then Paula fired back. It was good to see him again, and in a way I felt sad that he wouldn't be staying for long.

Once home, I settled the children with some toys in the living room while I took Samson's holdall outside, onto the patio. I opened it and, one item at a time, shook out his clothes, watching for any sign of wildlife. I was impressed by the amount he'd brought with him this time. It was far in excess of the contents of the backpacks he usually brought. Now he'd remembered pyjamas, a dressing gown, wash bag containing a face flannel, toothbrush and paste, a towel, clean underwear, a set of casual clothes and a change of school uniform for the morning, all neatly folded and packed. Having shaken out all the contents of the holdall, I turned the bag over and gave that a good shake too. Relieved that nothing ran out, I quickly repacked the bag and returned indoors, placing it at the foot of the stairs ready to be taken up on my next trip. I returned to the living room where the children were still playing nicely. I thought Samson seemed a lot calmer tonight.

'Who packed your bag?' I asked him casually.

'Gran,' he said. 'She said she had to do it to make sure I had everything I needed.'

'Excellent,' I said. So perhaps Laura was right and the shock of nearly losing him had given her a wake-up call.

When we were having dinner and his behaviour continued to impress me I praised him. 'Good boy. You're doing very well,' I said.

'Thanks,' he said with his impish smile. 'Gran says I have to behave or the social worker will come and take me away forever. I'm not allowed out on the estate at night any more since I got in trouble with the police. And I've got to stop cheeking the teachers at school, but that ain't easy. It gives me a headache trying to be good all the time, but I don't want to be taken away.'

While I wasn't sure I agreed with threatening a child with being taken away if they didn't behave, if it worked for his gran, who was I to criticize?

After dinner I heard both boys read from their school books and then I left them playing while I took Paula up to bed. I couldn't have done that when Samson had first come to us on respite; I'd had to watch him the whole time. Once Paula was settled I returned downstairs to the living room where the boys were now sitting side by side on the sofa. Was it my imagination or were they looking a little guilty, as though they had a secret?

'What's going on?' I asked lightly.

They giggled, nudged each other and then Adrian said, 'Samson's got a pet. Can you guess what it is?'

'That's easy,' I said. 'I've met Bruno. He's a big dog.'

Both boys laughed raucously. 'No!' Adrian said. 'He's got another pet. A new one. Guess what it is.'

I thought the last thing Gran needed was another mouth to feed, for even small pets need a lot of care and looking after.

'Is it a cat?' I asked.

'Noooo!' they chorused together and laughed conspiratorially.

'A rabbit?'

'Noooo!'

'A gerbil?' I suggested.

'Noooo!'

'A snake, spider, alligator, elephant, giraffe?' I said in a rush, also laughing.

'Noooo!' they yelled.

Then Adrian turned to Samson. 'Go on, show her. She won't mind.'

I felt a stab of anxiety and misgiving as Samson dug his hand into his trouser pocket, took out a matchbox and began to open it.

'No, just a minute!' I cried, going over. 'Don't open it yet. What's in there?'

'It's his pet bug,' Adrian said, grinning.

'What sort of bug?'

'A bed bug,' Samson declared. 'Don't tell Gran. I've saved him from being exterminated. He's called Bruce.'

'Bruce Lee, martial arts fighter,' Adrian qualified.

My first impulse was to grab the matchbox and throw Bruce as far as I could down the garden, or stamp on it, but that would have upset Samson. I needed a more subtle approach.

'Samson,' I said, eyeing the closed box carefully. 'It was kind of you to save the bug.'

'Bruce,' he corrected.

'It was kind of you to save Bruce, but do you know what would happen if he escaped into the house? Very soon there would be hundreds and thousands of bed bugs sucking our blood and making us itch, just like they do at your home.'

Having heard this, Adrian lost some of his enthusiasm and shifted away from Samson.

'But Bruce is my friend,' Samson said.

'In that case, the kindest thing to do would be to let him go in the garden.'

'What if I make sure he doesn't escape?' he asked, unwilling to give him up.

'It's not fair to keep him in that tiny box,' I said. 'He'll die without air or water. I think we should find a new home for him in the garden. I know just the spot! Come with me and I'll show you. It's a special place only a few of us know about.'

My enthusiasm combined with the hint of secrecy captured Samson's interest, as I thought it would. Clutching the box carefully in one hand he slid off the sofa. 'Come on then, where is this place?' he asked.

'We'll need to put on our shoes first – it's at the very end of the garden,' I said, lowering my voice to maintain the air of mystery. The boys followed me down the hall to where our shoes were paired and we carried them to the back door and put them on. Paula was asleep upstairs, but we wouldn't be long.

It was still light outside and I led the way across the patio, down the lawn and to the shed at the bottom of the garden, like an explorer on an adventure. Just behind the shed, standing on a brick, was an upside-down plant pot, under which I kept the key to the shed. Not for security but so I could find it. 'This is the secret place,' I said, crouching down. They crouched down too, and I carefully lifted up the pot. A few ants scurried away.

'This will be his new home,' I said. 'He'll be safe here, and he's got the whole garden to play in rather than that little box.'

'I'll leave the box under the pot,' Samson said. 'That can be his bed.'

'Excellent,' I said. I moved the key to one side to make room for the matchbox and Samson carefully placed it beside the key and then slid it open to reveal Bruce, a large bed bug, reddish-brown from previously gorging on someone's blood. I resisted the urge to shudder. 'He'll be safe here,' I said, and carefully lowered the pot.

'Night, Bruce,' Samson said.

'Night,' Adrian and I chorused, and we returned indoors. Crisis averted, although I would check Samson's school bag and jacket to make sure he didn't have any other 'pets' concealed in matchboxes.

CHAPTER TWENTY-THREE

GOING HOME

The following morning Samson wanted to check on Bruce, so I said that after breakfast, once everyone was ready for school, we could have a look. I guessed the bug would be long gone, so I told Samson I thought he would be playing in the garden.

'Bugs don't play,' he scoffed. 'They suck people's blood.'

But of course when we looked the matchbox was empty.

'Mum was right,' Adrian said, impressed. 'Bruce is playing in the garden.'

And just for a moment Samson looked as though he might believe him, and perhaps he did.

The talk from Samson that morning in the car as I drove him to school was about exterminating, and not just bed bugs. Samson had watched far too many gruesome films about people being exterminated – by axe-wielding psychopaths, out-of-control robots, flesh-eating aliens and an array of other evil forces. I hoped that while Samson's gran was upping the level of care she provided for him she would also begin censoring what he was allowed to watch. His head was full of macabre nonsense and scenes of violence, so much so that he was becoming desensitized to horrors that would normally shock or deeply affect a child (or adult), which would be no good for his psychological or emotional development, now or in the future.

I took Adrian and Paula with me into Samson's school to see him to breakfast club. He gave his overnight bag to a member of staff for safe keeping and we said goodbye and that we hoped to see him again.

'Look after Bruce!' he called as he went to collect his breakfast.

'We will!' Adrian and I replied.

We returned to the car and I took Adrian to his school. By the time I returned home I'd been out of the house on the school run for an hour and a half. It was a sample of what it would be like if Samson came to live with us, although I knew other carers who spent even longer in their cars doing the school run. It's generally considered better for a child when they go into care, less unsettling, if they stay at the school they are familiar with and where their friends are, but it can mean long journeys.

That morning Samson's social worker telephoned to see how his overnight stay had gone and I was able to tell her lots of positives. She was pleased and made some notes, but laughed when I told her about Bruce the bug. I didn't know if or when we'd see Samson again, as it would depend on when he needed respite and if I was looking after another child and had room to take him.

As it was a pleasant September day I was planning on making the most of the last of the good weather before autumn set in and taking Paula to the park that afternoon. However, all that changed when the telephone rang again. It was a different social worker and she needed an emergency placement for a small child.

'Hayley is three,' she said hurriedly. 'She's at the police station. Her mother was arrested this morning at the shopping centre, drunk. Can you collect Hayley as soon as possible? The police are holding the mother and will release her when she is sober.' It's an offence to be drunk while in charge of a small child.

'Yes,' I said. 'I'll leave straight away. Will she be staying with me overnight?'

'Not sure yet. It will depend when the police think the mother is fit to go.'

'Do we know anything about the child?' I asked. 'Does she have any allergies?'

'I don't know. The family has never come to the attention of the social services before. I'll ask the police to ask the mother about allergies. They can tell you when you arrive.'

'Thank you.' This was important information that would have been included on the placement forms, along with other essential information, if the move had been planned.

As soon as I'd replaced the handset I began helping Paula into her jacket and shoes, and then put on mine. 'We're going in the car to the police station,' I told her as we left the house. 'To collect a little girl.'

'Baby?' she asked.

'No, she's three. She's coming to play with you for a while.'

The police station was about a ten-minute drive from my house. I parked in a side road close to the main entrance. Holding Paula's hand, I walked with her round to the front of the building and up the steps where I pressed the bell to be admitted. My pulse had stepped up a beat with anxiety and concern for the child. Inside I showed the duty officer behind the desk my ID and I said I was a foster carer. I didn't have to say any more.

'Yes. The social worker said you were on your way,' he said. 'Hayley is being looked after by one of our WPCs [woman police officer]. I'll take you through.'

We followed him down a short corridor and into an office where the WPC was sitting with Hayley on her lap, drawing pictures to keep her amused.

'This is Cathy, the foster carer,' the officer said, introducing us before returning to the front desk.

'Time for you to go now, poppet,' the WPC said gently to Hayley, lifting her from her lap. 'I have to do some work. Cathy's going to look after you.'

'Where's Mummy?' the poor child asked, looking very frightened.

'She's staying with us for a while,' the WPC said kindly. 'We'll look after her until she can come and collect you.'

'Do we know when that will be?' I asked.

'Once she's sober,' the WPC replied a little brusquely, clearly not impressed by the mother's behaviour. Then looking at me, 'I asked her mum if Hayley had any allergies and she said she didn't.'

'Good.'

She brought Hayley over to me and I took her hand. She was a pretty child with long fair hair, petite features and blue eyes – which were now wide with fear. 'This is Paula,' I said, hoping this would help put her at ease.

'I want my mummy,' she said, rubbing her eyes and close to tears.

'I know, love. You'll see her later,' I reassured her.

I felt her hand clench mine and hold it very tightly as though she feared I, too, might leave her. With Hayley on one side of me and Paula on the other, I followed the WPC into reception where she saw us out.

'We're going in the car to my house,' I told Hayley as we began towards my car. 'You'll be able to play with Paula.'

'Where's Mummy?' she asked again, her little brow creasing.

'You'll see her later.'

'I want Mummy.'

'I know you do, love.'

I opened the rear door of the car and strapped Paula into her seat and then Hayley into Adrian's, adjusting the straps so that they fitted her correctly.

'All right, love, try not to worry,' I said, seeing the fear in her eyes. But clearly that was asking a lot of a small child who'd gone shopping with her mother, had been taken away by the police and was now having to come home with a stranger. 'You'll see Mummy again soon,' I said, hoping I was right, and I closed the car door.

Hayley didn't say a word on the way home but stared wide-eyed through her side window, mute with fear. I kept glancing at her in the mirror and offering her words of reassurance, but without success. Paula was looking at her anxiously too. Once home, I parked on the drive and helped both girls out of the car. 'Is Mummy here?' Hayley asked as we approached the front door.

'No, love. You'll see her later. This is my house.' It was all I could say.

Indoors, I asked her if she wanted to go to the toilet and she shook her head. I told her that when she did she should tell me and I would take her. I showed the girls into the living room and got out plenty of toys that I thought would interest Hayley, but she put her thumb in her mouth and just sat on the floor looking at them, despite my encouragement to play. Ten minutes later she wet herself – not surprising given the stress she must have been under. I reassured her, changed her into dry clothes from my spares and put her own clothes in the washing machine. I tried again to engage her in play, as did Paula, but she had no interest in any toy or activity we showed her, and she didn't want a hug. It was pitiful to see her so unhappy, and when it was time for me to make lunch I took both girls with me into the kitchen. Hayley managed two mouthfuls of lunch and then wet herself again. I reassured her and changed her into more spares. The only words she spoke all afternoon were 'Mummy?' 'Where's Mummy?' or 'I want my mummy.' It was heartbreaking.

I finally gave up trying to engage her in play and sat both girls on the sofa where, with an arm around each of them, I read stories until it was time to collect Adrian from school. I explained to Hayley where we were going. 'Mummy?' she asked again hopefully.

'Not yet, love.' I wondered if her mother had any idea of the distress her irresponsible behaviour was causing her daughter.

We walked to school and Adrian wasn't completely surprised to see me in the playground with another child, as it had happened before with an emergency placement. I introduced Hayley, but despite Adrian saying a very friendly, 'Hi, how are you?' she just looked at him, lost and bewildered.

Laura saw us and waved, but stayed behind in the playground talking to Fran.

Hayley held my hand very tightly all the way home, and once there she wouldn't let me out of her sight. She came with me into the kitchen while I made dinner and then wet herself again. I changed her into her own clothes, which were now dry. I think she was toilet trained, for she was old enough and hadn't come in a nappy, but acute stress can cause loss of bladder and bowel control. It was an indication of just how traumatized she was by the day's events. If she had to stay overnight I knew I would be up most of the night settling her. With no idea what time her mother would be released from police custody, or indeed if she would be released that evening, I continued with our usual routine as much as possible while looking after Hayley. At 5.30, just as I was about to serve dinner, the telephone rang and I answered it in the kitchen. I don't think I've ever been so pleased to hear from a social worker in my life.

'Cathy, the police are going to release the mother in an hour,' she said. 'Is it all right if I give her your address so she can come straight to you and collect Hayley?'

'Yes, of course,' I said.

'I'll let them know now, thank you. The mother is called Catherine.'

It wasn't for me to ask what had led to the mother's heavy drinking, but the social services must have been satisfied that Hayley wouldn't be in danger if she returned home or they would have asked me to keep her longer while they investigated.

'Mummy coming?' Hayley asked hopefully as I replaced the handset.

'Yes, love.'

'Mummy coming?' she asked again, unable to believe that her nightmare was finally coming to an end.

'Yes. She's coming here to collect you after we've had dinner.' I settled her at the table, called Adrian and Paula, and served dinner, of which Hayley ate a very small amount.

It's always difficult meeting a foster child's parent(s) for the first time, as I'm sure it is for the parents to meet the foster carer. I try not to form preconceptions, but I'll admit they can creep in. However, any idea I had about Hayley's mother vanished at seven o'clock when I opened the front door. Slightly built, late thirties, quietly spoken and well dressed, she was close to tears.

'Cathy?' she asked, her face creasing just as Hayley's had.

'Yes. Catherine?' She nodded. 'Come in. Hayley will be so pleased to see you. She's with my son and daughter in the living room.'

I didn't have to show her through, as Hayley, having heard her mother's voice, had run into the hall. 'Mummy! Mummy!' she cried. With a mixture of absolute relief and excitement, she rushed to her mother.

Catherine dropped to her knees so that she was at her daughter's height and, encircling her in her arms, held her close. The tears she'd been holding back fell. 'Oh, love, my precious, I'm so sorry. I've been so stupid. How can you ever forgive me?'

They clung to each other and cried openly. Adrian and Paula, worried by what they could hear, came into the hall. 'It's OK,' I reassured them. 'You go and play. Hayley will be all right soon.' Adrian took hold of Paula's hand and led her back into the living room.

I gently touched Catherine's shoulder. 'Would you like to come and sit down and I'll get you a drink.'

'Thank you.' I helped her to her feet. Hayley still had her arms wrapped around her mother's neck and her legs tightly around her waist.

I took them through to the kitchen-cum-diner and drew out a chair at the table for Catherine to sit down. Hayley was on her lap. I placed a box of tissues within reach. 'What would you like to drink?'

'Water, please.'

I poured a glass of water and placed it on the table, then pulling out a chair I sat beside them. Hayley was still clinging to her mother for all she was worth. 'Has she had a drink?' Catherine asked, taking a tissue from the box.

'Yes, and a little bit of lunch and dinner. But not much.'

'Thank you for looking after her,' she said, wiping her eyes. 'I feel so ashamed. Now I'm sober I can't believe what I've done.' Fresh tears fell.

'We all make mistakes,' I said, touching her arm.

She shook her head in despair and couldn't speak for emotion, but now Hayley was with her mother she was starting to look a bit better and her confidence was returning. 'Don't cry, Mummy,' she said, wiping the tears from her mother's cheeks. Which of course made Catherine cry even more.

I waited until she was able to speak. 'Thank goodness I didn't have to stay at the police station overnight,' she said.

'I would have looked after Hayley,' I reassured her.

'I know, that's what the police lady said. Thank you.' She wiped her eyes again and looked at me. 'I want you to know I don't normally behave like that. It was completely out of character. I can't justify what I did, but I did have a good reason.' I looked at her and waited while she composed herself again. 'Last night my husband left me,' she said. 'Just like that. After ten years of marriage, he told me he'd fallen in love with his secretary. I mean, what a cliché! He said they couldn't help it, but it had just happened, like it wasn't his fault and he wasn't responsible. He said it was best for everyone if he left. Best for him, more like it!' Catherine's voice had risen and I could see that Hayley was looking at her anxiously.

'Perhaps Hayley would like to go and play with Adrian and Paula while we talk,' I suggested. But she snuggled closer to her mother, not wanting to be parted from her.

'It's all right. I won't go into all the details,' Catherine said. 'I just want you to know I'm not a bad mother. I love my daughter more than anything and would never harm her. But what he said was such a shock. I was up all night and I began drinking. I don't know how but I got through nearly two bottles of wine and by this morning I'd hatched a plan to shame him and his secretary. I went down to the shopping mall with Hayley. He's the manager of the department store there. He wouldn't see me, so I started shouting and causing a fuss, telling everyone what he'd done. The store security called the police, and the rest you know.' I nodded sympathetically as she held Hayley close and kissed the top of her head. 'This is going to take a lot of getting over,' she said more calmly. 'But at least we've got each other.'

'Yes,' I agreed. 'You have.'

'Can we go home now, Mummy?' Hayley asked in a small voice.

'Yes, of course, we'll go now.'

I offered to take them home in the car – they lived about two miles away – but Catherine said they would be all right on the bus, so I saw them to the door. Catherine thanked me again for looking after Hayley, and then said that if ever I saw them in the town would I please not mention what had happened, as she was so embarrassed. I reassured her I wouldn't and I wished them well for the future. I knew that if Catherine and her husband were divorcing then she'd have a lot of sorting out and adjusting to do, but I also knew she wouldn't make the same mistake again. Having the police involved, and her daughter taken into care, even though it was only for a day, had obviously shocked her deeply. Hopefully some good would come out of it, for sometimes we need a jolt to allow us to re-evaluate our lives and see what really matters.

I stood for a few moments at the front door after they'd gone, aware of the fresh, slightly autumnal air. The sun had set, the birds had gone to bed and the night was still. Most people were home now and only the occasional car passed. A lone dog barked in the distance. For tonight, at least, it seemed that my spare room would remain empty, although I knew it wouldn't be long before another child arrived. Somewhere out there, maybe not far away, was another family in crisis, with a child or children who would shortly need foster care. Perhaps it would be the child of someone like Laura, who was ill but didn't have a family network to help her through. Or maybe someone like Shelley, who had no parents, or someone like Catherine, whose error of judgement had unintentionally placed her child at risk of harm. Or possibly the next child I fostered could be someone like Samson, who would be part of my family long term and would need firm and consistent boundaries as well as love, care and attention. Or maybe, and most upsettingly, it would be a badly abused or neglected child, when I would put on a brave face as I bathed their bruises and reassured them they were safe, and then later in the solitude of my bedroom I would cry myself to sleep. I didn't know who my next child would be, but for tonight at least I felt satisfied that I'd done my best for the children I'd looked after – Darrel, Samson, Hayley and even little Elspeth. They were all home now with their families, and Laura was with hers. And for a foster carer there's no better ending than that.

EPILOGUE

Laura continued to make good progress, and Kim and baby Liam flourished. I saw them regularly on the way to and from school and sometimes we got together with other mums for a coffee. Laura didn't have any more setbacks and at the end of twelve months the social services ended their monitoring, although Laura still attended a support group where she'd made friends. I saw Gina a couple of times when she visited and we always had a good chat. I also saw Geraldine if she was helping out and collecting Kim from school. She just about managed a small nod in my direction, but then that's Geraldine. Her heart is in the right place, and it wouldn't do if we were all the same.

Adrian, Paula and I went to see Shelley sing with her choir at their Christmas concert, and it was beautiful. The hall was gaily decorated for Christmas with garlands and a tall tree that glittered with silver lights. The singing was perfect, ethereal, a choir from heaven. The songs were a mixture of traditional Christmas carols and popular children's Christmas songs, some of which the audience were invited to join in with. During the concert we saw Darrel sitting with another family and I rather guessed it might be

Carol. After the concert the audience could mingle while enjoying a drink and a mince pie, which gave Shelley the chance to introduce us to Carol and her adult children. I immediately warmed to them and Carol said they were all looking forward to having Shelley and Darrel at Christmas. Shelley also introduced us to her young man, Michael, and his parents, although I'd already guessed who he might be from the way he kept looking at Shelley while they were singing. He came across as a charming, sincere person who clearly thought the world of her, as did his parents. He also appeared caring of and committed to Darrel, which was so important. I didn't ask if I could expect to hear wedding bells soon, but I wouldn't be surprised, and Shelley deserved happiness and security after her unsettled early life. Adrian and I were still humming Brahms's 'Lullaby' at night sometimes and Paula was picking up the tune too.

The next time Samson needed respite care I was already fostering another child and didn't have the room, so he had to stay with a different carer. It was a pity, and it cemented the plans John and I had previously discussed in respect of extending the back of the house to create more room downstairs and another bedroom upstairs. The matchbox Samson had so carefully placed under the plant pot by the shed stayed there all winter, as I didn't have the heart to throw it away – the little reminder of Samson and his pet bed bug Bruce!

John's homecoming was delayed again and he finally arrived home in the middle of October, in time to attend my degree award ceremony. Unfortunately, a week later he had to work away again, but that's another story. So, too, is the story of the child I'm looking after now, who like all the other children I've fostered is being so brave and trying not to cry.

A true little hero. But then they all are, and I admire them greatly.

For the latest updates on these children and those in my other fostering memoirs, please visit www.cathyglass.co.uk.

SUGGESTED TOPICS FOR READING-GROUP DISCUSSION

What were the reasons for Geraldine and Andy not consulting a doctor earlier when it became clear Laura was unwell?

Can there ever be any justification for not consulting a doctor about a mental-health issue?

Is there still a stigma attached to mental illness? If so, why do you think this is? What could be done to change this?

Cathy is very careful when dealing with Laura's family not to cross the boundary between being friendly and neighbourly and being intrusive and nosey. Does she get it right or should she have intervened earlier and alerted the social services?

Do you think Cathy, as a foster carer, reacts differently to Laura's situation than perhaps the average person might?

Shelley tells Cathy that she is not introducing her boyfriend, Michael, to her son Darrel until she is 'completely sure of him'. What do you think she means by this, and what might her reasons be?

Based on what you know, was the social worker's decision to apply to court for a Care Order for Samson the correct one? Why? If you had been the judge would you have refused or granted the Care Order? What extra support could have been given to the family?

The update on Cathy's website, www.cathyglass.co.uk, shows that Samson became his gran's carer until she died. Does knowing this change your view as to whether or not Samson should have been returned home as a child?

It could be said that Catherine, who was drunk in charge of a child, was treated harshly by the law. Do you think arresting her was the correct action? Were there any alternatives?

The ending of the book gives satisfactory resolutions for all those involved. Is there any other information you would have liked to see included?

Cathy Glass

One remarkable woman, more than **150** foster children cared for.

Cathy Glass has been a foster carer for twenty-five years, during which time she has looked after more than 150 children, as well as raising three children of her own. She was awarded a degree in education and psychology as a mature student, and writes under a pseudonym. To find out more about Cathy and her story visit www.cathyglass.co.uk.

Nobody's Son

Born in a prison to a drug-dependent mother and brought up in care, seven-year-old Alex has only ever known rejection

He is longing for a family of his own but again the system fails him.

Can I Let You Go?

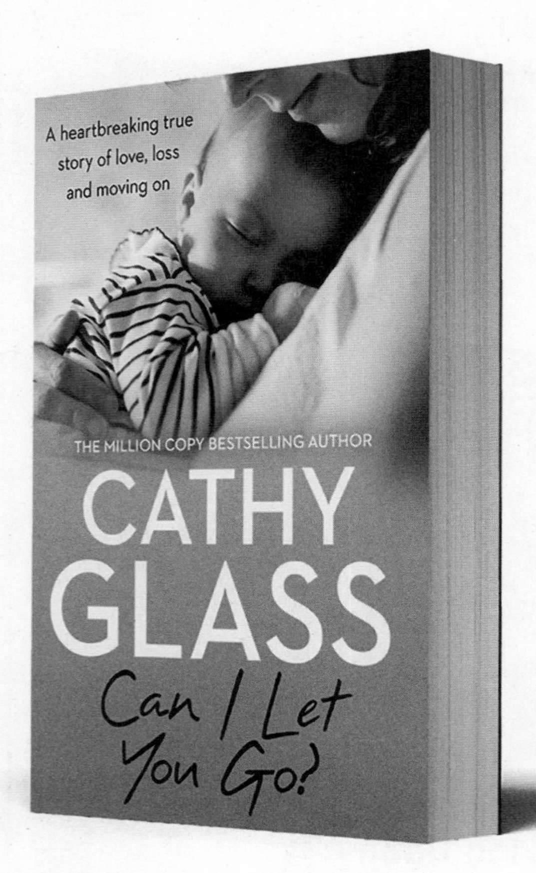

Faye is 24 and pregnant, and has learning difficulties as a result of her mother's alcoholism

Can Cathy help Faye learn enough to parent her child?

The Silent Cry

A mother battling depression. A family in denial

Cathy is desperate to help before something terrible happens.

Girl Alone

An angry, traumatized young girl on a path to self-destruction

Can Cathy discover the truth behind Joss's dangerous behaviour before it's too late?

Saving Danny

Danny's parents can no longer cope with his challenging behaviour

Calling on all her expertise, Cathy discovers a frightened little boy who just wants to be loved.

The Child Bride

A girl blamed and abused for dishonouring her community

Cathy discovers the devastating truth.

Daddy's Little Princess

A sweet-natured girl with a complicated past

Cathy picks up the pieces after events take a dramatic turn.

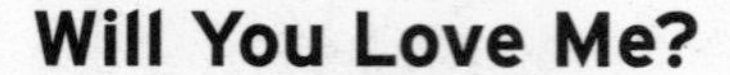

Will You Love Me?

A broken child desperate for a loving home

The true story of Cathy's adopted daughter Lucy.

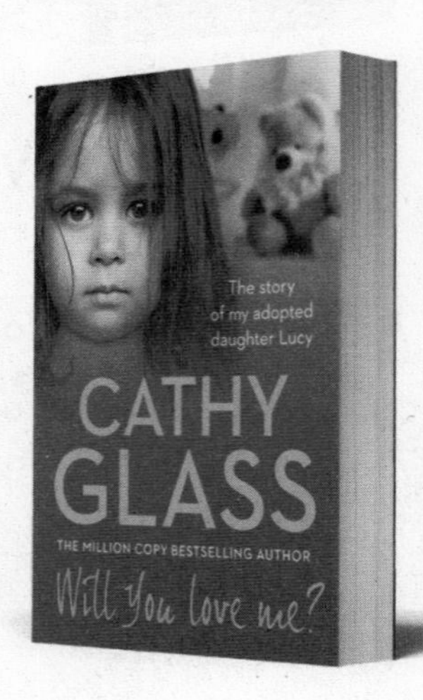

Please Don't Take My Baby

Seventeen-year-old Jade is pregnant, homeless and alone

Cathy has room in her heart for two.

Another Forgotten Child

Eight-year-old Aimee was on the child-protection register at birth

Cathy is determined to give her the happy home she deserves.

A Baby's Cry

A newborn, only hours old, taken into care

Cathy protects tiny Harrison from the potentially fatal secrets that surround his existence.

The Night the Angels Came

A little boy on the brink of bereavement

Cathy and her family make sure Michael is never alone.

Mummy Told Me Not to Tell

A troubled boy sworn to secrecy

After his dark past has been revealed, Cathy helps Reece to rebuild his life.

I Miss Mummy

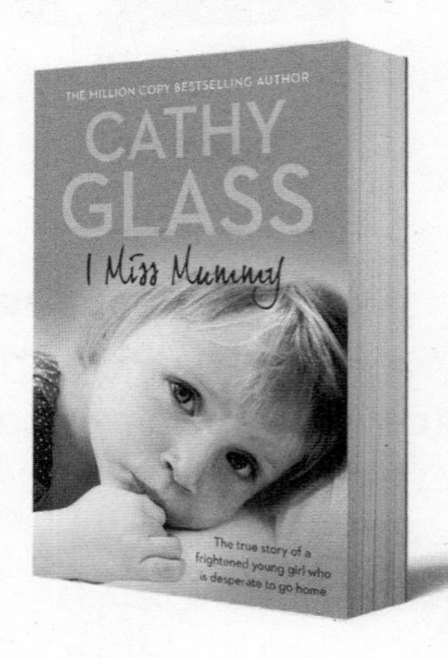

Four-year-old Alice doesn't understand why she's in care

Cathy fights for her to have the happy home she deserves.

The Saddest Girl in the World

A haunted child who refuses to speak

Do Donna's scars run too deep for Cathy to help?

Cut

Dawn is desperate to be loved

Abused and abandoned, this vulnerable child pushes Cathy and her family to their limits.

Hidden

The boy with no past

Can Cathy help Tayo to feel like he belongs again?

Damaged

A forgotten child

Cathy is Jodie's last hope. For the first time, this abused young girl has found someone she can trust.

Inspired by Cathy's own experiences...

Run, Mummy, Run

The gripping story of a woman caught in a horrific cycle of abuse, and the desperate measures she must take to escape.

My Dad's a Policeman

The dramatic short story about a young boy's desperate bid to keep his family together.

The Girl in the Mirror

Trying to piece together her past, Mandy uncovers a dreadful family secret that has been blanked from her memory for years.

Sharing her expertise...

About Writing and How to Publish

A clear and concise, practical guide on writing and the best ways to get published.

Happy Mealtimes for Kids

A guide to healthy eating with simple recipes that children love.